America

National

Security

D0196549

Ch. 9

191 – 207

American National Security

Sixth Edition

AMOS A. JORDAN

WILLIAM J. TAYLOR, JR.

MICHAEL J. MEESE

SUZANNE C. NIELSEN

The Johns Hopkins University Press
Baltimore

© 1981, 1984, 1989, 1993, 1999, 2009 The Johns Hopkins University Press
All rights reserved. First edition in 1981. Sixth edition in 2009
Printed in the United States of America on acid-free paper
2 4 6 8 9 7 5 3 1

The Johns Hopkins University Press
2715 North Charles Street
Baltimore, Maryland 21218-4363
www.press.jhu.edu

Library of Congress Cataloging-in-Publication Data

American national security / Amos A. Jordan . . . [et al.]. — 6th ed.
   p. cm.
Rev. ed. of: American national security / Amos A. Jordan. 5th ed. 1999.
Includes bibliographical references and index.
ISBN-13: 978-0-8018-9153-3 (hbk. : alk. paper)
ISBN-10: 0-8018-9153-1 (hbk. : alk. paper)
ISBN-13: 978-0-8018-9154-0 (pbk. : alk. paper)
ISBN-10: 0-8018-9154-X (pbk. : alk. paper)
   1. National security—United States.   2. United States—Military policy.
I. Jordan, Amos A.   II. Jordan, Amos A.   American national security.
   UA23.J66 2008
   355'.033073—dc22   2008027262

A catalog record for this book is available from the British Library.

Special discounts are available for bulk purchases of this book. For more information, please contact Special Sales at 410-516-6936 or specialsales@press.jhu.edu.

The Johns Hopkins University Press uses environmentally friendly book materials, including recycled text paper that is composed of at least 30 percent post-consumer waste, whenever possible. All of our book papers are acid-free, and our jackets and covers are printed on paper with recycled content.

Contents

IV   International and Regional Security Issues

V   National Security Policy: Current and Future Issues in American National Security Policy

Foreword

That we now have the publication of the sixth edition of *American National Security* is testimony not merely to its continuing value as a primer but also to the permanency of the role of the United States as the leading world power. Yet, the permanency of that role should not be taken to suggest the permanency of the challenges that faces the United States. To the contrary, the challenge of National Security is *always changing*, as over the decades, the world changes. In this connection, it is important to note that the new edition of *American National Security* has been substantially revised.

Twenty years ago, the collapse of the Soviet Empire and the subsequent disintegration of the Soviet Union itself radically altered the external challenge that had preoccupied the United States over the 40 years of the Cold War. The Cold War had fostered something of an illusion of permanence in that our preeminent concern remained unchanged over many decades, though, nonetheless, the specific political and military challenges themselves did undergo continued adjustment.

The Soviet collapse, however, implied much more fundamental change. Not only did it mean that the threat to the security of Western Europe—our focus for so many decades—was removed, but it also meant the end of a possible conventional offensive by the Warsaw Pact against Western Europe, which implied that reliance on the nuclear deterrent and on the role of nuclear weapons could be significantly reduced and that the critical position of Europe itself would recede. It also meant that, geostrategically, Europe, if not exactly a backwater, had now become a secondary theater, which implied a major task of making something out of NATO—that was more than an exercise in Alliance nostalgia.

It also meant a growing focus on Asia, particularly the rising power of China, as its economic growth and its economic potential rapidly grew. The rise of China and India reflect a substantial and continuing shift that is increasing the prospective power of these rising entities at the general expense of the West.

Perhaps even more important is the increasing challenge of the Middle East. Starting with the Iranian Revolution, the United States was suddenly transformed in the view of the Iranian government from a friendly power, if not an ally, into the role of the Great Satan.

The defeat of the Soviet Union in Afghanistan meant that the jihadists, initially encouraged by the United States to battle the Soviet Union, refocused the direction of their enmity. The position taken by Osama Bin Laden and others was that their mujaheddin had defeated one superpower in Afghanistan and should now appropriately turn to defeating the other superpower, the United States. This represented a crucial change in our external environment, which we in this country did not fully understand until 9/11. Needless to say, these changes are compounded by the dependence of the United States and, indeed, the outside world on energy supplies from the highly volatile Middle East.

A high degree of political instability in the Middle East carries with it a major issue with respect to the formulation of strategy. Such instability is both internal and external. Internally, we may observe shifts in power among various groups— far more significant than any adjustments of party positions in Western democracies. The rise of Hezbollah in Lebanon alters Lebanon's internal stability as well as creates a more threatening relationship with Israel. In the Palestinian territories, we have witnessed the rise of Hamas in Gaza, which has undermined the previous dominance of the PLO. Both Hezbollah and Hamas are regarded as terrorist groups by the United States government. And, of course, the relative position of various internal groups has undergone continued change with in Iraq, especially since the start of the Surge.

Such changes steadily contribute to changing tensions among the states of the region. This continual kaleidoscopic change may make things rather fascinating for the student and the geopolitician, but it makes it quite hard for the strategist. Efforts have been underway in Washington to map out a comprehensive strategy for the Middle East. But, given the ever-changing landscape, such efforts are futile. One cannot develop a comprehensive strategy for the Middle East, because today's vision is likely to be obsolete tomorrow. Strategy in the Middle East must both assess and adjust to the ongoing changes. In short, like the states of the region themselves, correct strategy must take into account the ever-present probability of significant change and be prepared to adjust both strategy and policy to the ever-changing scene, which appears to be unavoidable.

In short, what had appeared to be a reasonably stable, but potentially highly dangerous, international scene had gradually become far more complicated, though much less dangerous than in the era of a potential major nuclear exchange. It meant that the greater complexity and the more rapid change in the external challenges to national security required a much greater degree of nimbleness than had been needed during the Cold War. But nimbleness in the face of change and of more rapid adjustments in the formation of national security policy does not come easily to governments, perhaps particularly democratic governments and also to the large institutions that provide the framework for the American democracy.

As external conditions and the challenges to national security change with time, adjustments to our strategy and posture must be embraced and articulated by the head of the executive branch, the president. An incoming president may choose to formulate changes in strategy at the outset of his administration. President Eisenhower, for example, did so with the so-called Solarium exercise, carried on entirely in secret, to define our strategy toward the Soviet Union during his long tenure. President Nixon, perhaps inspired by his service under Eisenhower, did the same when he authorized NSSM-1 (National Security Study Memorandum #1). In both cases, because it was the height of the Cold War, those exercises tended to be dominated by the calibration of our strategy and force posture with respect to the Soviet Union.

A president must embrace the overall structure for national security, or the departments will likely drift. A president may choose to delegate initial responsibility to senior officials, as President Truman did with respect to Europe to Secretaries Marshall and Acheson. He notably did not follow that course of action with respect to the emerging Palestinian crisis in 1948.

It is crucial to distinguish real strategy—*how* best to employ national capabilities to achieve the nation's political objectives—from useful though contentless rubrics. For example, we frequently and properly observe that strategy should employ all of the instruments of national power—military, diplomatic, economic, etc. This is a useful formula, but it is only a formula. Strategy to be useful must be based on realities. Too frequently, so-called national strategy is not a strategy at all, but simply a listing of national objectives, which turns out to be an expression of hope or of exhortation. Again, real strategy must embrace the difficult task of defining *how* those instruments of national power will be employed to achieve the nation's political objectives.

Finally, one must acknowledge and accept the constraints imposed by our democratic political system. One needs to acknowledge these constraints because steadiness in our political system is difficult to sustain. Steadiness in our political system may be altered by the vicissitudes of public opinion—and by the fact of regular elections. Governance in our system has been uncharitably described as undergoing a frontal lobotomy every four or eight years. Alexis de Toqueville in his great study of *Democracy in America* stated that the great weakness of democracies in foreign policy was, among other things, their inability to sustain steadiness of purpose or consistency in strategy. Throughout forty years of the Cold War, the United States steadily maintained its purpose, most notably our Watch on the Elbe. Since the end of the Cold War, as domestic concerns have once again come to dominate policy formation, the jury remains out on whether de Toqueville's concerns may have become more relevant again.

Some analysts of national purpose and national strategy tend to deal with an idealized world and to ignore the constraints that our system imposes on long-term national policy. They tend to chafe at the restraints imposed by the American political system. In the back of their minds, they imagine that there is a Cardinal Richelieu, who for so long determined French policy during the Thirty Years War, mapping out our long-term strategy on some kind of international chessboard. The Richelieus and the Bismarcks are very rare phenomena in human history and even rarer in democracies. In the American democracy, one cannot count on the long-term sustainability of any strategy. One can only do one's best and hope that that strategy will be sustained over time by the public and by one's successors.

Nevertheless, the necessity of continually reappraising strategy in shifting international and domestic environments makes it essential that policy makers and the attentive public alike have a clear understanding of the fundamental policy and process challenges that confront the nation. The authors of this sixth edition have provided a timely and valuable contribution toward gaining that understanding.

James Schlesinger

Preface

The sixth edition of *American National Security* has been almost entirely rewritten to reflect the significant changes in national security policy formulation in the last decade. This edition also brings the book full circle, back to its origins in the United States Military Academy's Department of Social Sciences. The genesis of the first edition was an idea of the late Dr. Frank N. Trager, who observed in 1972 that there was a crying need for a textbook on U.S. national security. His forecast was that, after the trauma of Vietnam was behind the country, the nation's faculties and youth would share a renewed interest in the study of national and international security. He was, of course, proven correct. He suggested to two of his friends on the West Point faculty, Amos A. Jordan and William J. Taylor, Jr., that they undertake the task of writing a textbook that could meet the needs of students at most colleges, universities, and professional military schools to gain a basic understanding of the policies and processes involved in American national security.

In 1972, Jordan and Taylor completed a detailed outline of one hundred sixty pages and drafted the first few chapters. Thereafter, major changes in assignments and responsibilities denied these two the long periods of consistent research and careful attention that a sound textbook requires. Finally, in 1980, the principal authors carved out the major block of time needed for a complete rewrite and update of the manuscript. This effort was assisted by several people in the Department of Social Sciences, U.S. Military Academy, who read, critiqued, and worked in last-minute research. Their contributions are acknowledged in that first edition. The penultimate draft was critiqued carefully and most helpfully by one of America's leading soldier-statesman, the late General Maxwell D. Taylor, to whom we are deeply indebted for writing the foreword to the first and second editions. Various chapters were reviewed and critiqued by several distinguished scholars and practitioners—George Carver; Chester Crocker; William T. R. Fox; Lieutenant General Robert G. Gard, Jr.; Alexander Haig; James Schlesinger; Lieutenant General DeWitt C. Smith; and Admiral Stansfield Turner, among others.

The first edition was very well received. Feedback to the authors and to the Johns Hopkins University Press was most positive, as were the published reviews of the book. As Jordan and Taylor approached the second edition (and each subsequent edition), they solicited comments from professors who had used the book in the classroom as well as from their own students in the national security courses they taught at the Georgetown University School of Foreign Service. They asked for appraisals of strengths and weaknesses and sought guidance on additions or deletions. Responses indicated that the book should retain its basic approach, with the authors adding updates as necessary. That advice was followed. The second edition met with the same success as the first. *American National Security* became the standard national security text in the United States and was widely translated for use abroad. Lawrence J. Korb of the Brookings Institution became a coauthor for the third and fourth editions, which were similarly successful. By the time of the writing of the fifth edition, both Jordan and Taylor were working in Washington with the Center for Strategic and International Studies (CSIS). They were joined by CSIS colleague Michael J. Mazaar, who coauthored the fifth edition in 1999, which addressed many of the changes in national security that occurred in the United States and the world soon after the end of the Cold War.

Since the publishing of the fifth edition, significant changes have once again taken place in all aspects of American national security policy and practice. Johns Hopkins University Press had numerous requests for an updated version of the textbook to meet the needs of today's national security studies educators and students. To partner with them in this edition, Jordan and Taylor again turned to the United States Military Academy and enlisted the support of coauthors Michael J. Meese and Suzanne C. Nielsen. Interestingly, Meese and Nielsen now hold the same positions in the Department of Social Sciences that Jordan and Taylor held more than a quarter century ago when the first edition was conceived. Together, the four coauthors represent an unbroken lineage of service in the U.S. Army from 1946 until today, more than one hundred years of combined service in the Army, and more than fifty combined years of teaching national security subjects to cadets at the U.S. Military Academy.

We have long believed in the utility of political cartoons to convey fundamental ideas and have used cartoons in all previous editions. We were very much impressed by the ability of one political cartoonist in particular, Ranan Lurie, to understand trends and forecast events in a unique way. He has been a contributor to all previous editions; for this sixth edition, our respected friend granted us permission to select from a wide variety of his cartoons for inclusion in the text.

We four coauthors are also indebted to our colleagues at the United States Military Academy who worked with us on this latest edition. Several faculty members from the Department of Social Sciences provided significant revisions to many of the chapters, in some cases basically redrafting them to adapt to the new national security environment. We would like to especially acknowledge the work of Matt

Abbruzzese ("Intelligence"), Ruth Beitler ("Middle East"), Eric Bjorklund ("Evolution of Policy"), Meena Bose ("President and Executive"), Brad Bowman ("Looking Ahead"), Tania Chacho ("Europe"), Roland De Marcellus ("Economics"), Brian Dietzman ("Intelligence"), Jon Dunn ("Conventional War"), Rozlyn Engel ("Economics"), Brian Fishman ("Asymmetric Conflict"), James Forest ("Sub-Saharan Africa"), John Gallagher ("Middle East"), Mike George ("Homeland Security"), Amanda Gookins ("Intelligence"), Thomas Greco ("Role of the Military" and "Planning, Budgeting, and Management"), Chris Hornbarger ("Putting the Pieces Together"), Cindy Jebb ("Globalization and Human Security"), Lianne Kennedy-Boudali ("Globalization and Human Security"), Paul Kucik ("Diplomacy, Information, and Military Posture"), Jin Pak ("East Asia"), Rebecca Patterson ("Traditional Approaches"), Ken Robbins ("Congress"), Thom Sherlock ("Russia"), Scott Silverstone ("Looking Ahead"), Bill Skimmyhorn ("Shaping the International Environment"), Don Snider ("Role of the Military"), Thomas Stocking ("Latin America"), Scott Taylor ("Nuclear Policy"), Rick Waddell ("Latin America"), Blair Williams ("Congress"), Ike Wilson ("Irregular Challenges, Military Intervention, and Counterinsurgency"), and Blaise Zandoli ("South and Southeast Asia").

Additionally, Michael Hendricks from the Department of Geography and Environmental Engineering, U.S. Military Academy, provided significant cartographic design assistance to this project, which is reflected in the maps in section four. Caitlin Conley provided valuable research assistance and editorial expertise as the final draft of the book was being completed. Henry Tom was a gracious and helpful executive editor at the Johns Hopkins University Press, and the book was improved in the editing process by the copy editors, Jeri Litteral, Elizabeth McKendry, and Heather Wilcox. Of course, any errors or omissions remain the responsibility of the authors.

We hope that this book provides the foundation of understanding for teachers, students, and practitioners of national security policy. It is one of the most important and least understood topics in public policy today. The more that individuals from all backgrounds learn about American national security, the more they will be able to contribute to improving policy development and implementation.

Abbreviations and Acronyms

ABM	antiballistic missile
ACDA	Arms Control and Disarmament Agency
AFRICOM	U.S. Africa Command
AIPAC	American-Israel Political Action Committee
ANZUS	Australia, New Zealand, and United States Treaty
ARF	ASEAN Region Forum
ASEAN	Association of Southeast Asian Nations
AU	African Union
BCPs	Budget Change Proposals
BMDS	Ballistic Missile Defense System
BRAC	Base Realignment and Closure Commission
C^3I	command, control, communications, and intelligence systems
C^4I	command, control, communications, computers, and intelligence systems
C^4ISR	command, control, communications, computers, intelligence, surveillance, and reconnaissance capabilities
CAFTA-DR	Central America–Dominican Republic Free Trade Agreement
CBO	Congressional Budget Office
CBRN	chemical, biological, radiological, or nuclear weapons
CCP	Chinese Communist Party
CENTO	Central Treaty Organization
CFE	Conventional Forces in Europe Treaty
CIA	Central Intelligence Agency
COMINT	communications intelligence
CPA	Coalition Provisional Authority

CSIS	Center for Strategic and International Studies
CTR	Cooperative Threat Reduction
DC	Deputies Committee
DCI	Director of Central Intelligence
DEA	Drug Enforcement Agency
DHS	Department of Homeland Security
DMZ	demilitarized zone
DNI	Director of National Intelligence
DoD	Department of Defense
ELINT	electronic intelligence
ESDP	European Security and Defense Program
EU	European Union
FARC	Colombian Armed Revolutionary Forces
FBI	Federal Bureau of Investigation
FEMA	Federal Emergency Management Agency
FIRE	Firefighter Investment and Response Enactment
FISA	Foreign Intelligence Surveillance Act
FISINT	Foreign Instrumentation Signals Intelligence
FMLN	Farabundo Marti National Liberation Front
FSB	Federal Security Service
FTAA	Free Trade Area of the Americas
FY	fiscal year
G7	Group of Seven
G8	Global Eight Forum
GDP	gross domestic product
GEOINT	geospatial intelligence
GNP	gross national product
GPRA	Government Performance and Results Act of 1993
GPS	global positioning system
HASC	House Armed Services Committee
HEU	highly enriched uranium
HPSCI	House Permanent Select Committee on Intelligence
HSC	Homeland Security Council
HUMINT	human intelligence
IADB	Inter-American Defense Board
IAEA	International Atomic Energy Agency
ICBM	intercontinental ballistic missile
ICC	International Criminal Court
IGOs	intergovernmental organizations
IMF	International Monetary Fund
IMI	international military information
IMINT	imagery intelligence
INF	Intermediate-Range and Short-Range Nuclear Forces Treaty
JCS	Joint Chiefs of Staff
KGB	Committee for State Security

KMT	Nationalist Kuomintang Party
MAD	mutually assured destruction
MASINT	measurement and signature intelligence
MERCOSUR	Common Market of the South (Spanish)
MINUSTAH	United Nations Stabilization Mission to Haiti
MIPT	Memorial Institute for the Prevention of Terrorism
MIRVs	multiple, independently targetable re-entry vehicles
MNCs	multinational corporations
MWe	megawatt
NAFTA	North American Free Trade Agreement
NATO	North Atlantic Treaty Organization
NCTC	National Counterterrorism Center
NEC	National Economic Council
NEO	noncombatant evacuation operations
NGA	National Geospatial-Intelligence Agency
NGOs	nongovernmental organizations
NIE	National Intelligence Estimates
NORAD	North American Aerospace Defense Command
NORTHCOM	U.S. Northern Command
NPR	Nuclear Posture Review
NPT	Nuclear Non-Proliferation Treaty
NRO	National Reconnaissance Office
NSA	National Security Agency
NSC	National Security Council
NSC 68	National Security Council Report 68
NSC 162	National Security Council Report 162
NSG	Nuclear Suppliers Group
NSS	National Security Strategy
OAS	Organization of American States
ODA	Official Development Assistance
OMB	Office of Management and Budget
ORHA	Office of Reconstruction and Humanitarian Assistance
OSCE	Organization for Security and Cooperation in Europe
OSD	Office of the Secretary of Defense
OSINT	open-source intelligence
PA	Palestinian Authority
PC	Principals Committee
PCC	Policy Coordination Committee
PCPs	Program Change Proposals
PEO	peace enforcement operations
PFIAB	President's Foreign Intelligence Advisory Board
PfP	Partnership for Peace
PIOB	President's Intelligence Oversight Board
PKO	peacekeeping operations
PLA	People's Liberation Army (ground forces)

PLAAF	People's Liberation Army (air forces)
PLAN	People's Liberation Army (naval forces)
PLO	Palestinian Liberation Organization
PMA	Presidential Management Agenda
PNSDD	Presidential National Security Decision Directive
POM	Program Objective Memorandum
PPBES	Planning, Programming, Budgeting, and Execution System
PPBS	Planning, Programming, and Budgeting System
PRC	People's Republic of China
PRI	Institutional Revolutionary Party (Mexico)
PSI	Proliferation Security Initiative
QDR	Quadrennial Defense Review
R&D	research and development
RMA	revolution in military affairs
ROC	Republic of China
RRW	Reliable Replacement Warhead Program
S/CRS	Office of the Coordinator for Reconstruction and Stabilization
SALT	Strategic Arms Limitation Talks
SALT I	Strategic Arms Limitation Talks I (1972)
SASC	Senate Armed Services Committee
SCO	Shanghai Cooperation Organization
SDI	Strategic Defense Initiative
SEATO	Southeast Asian Treaty Organization
SIGINT	signals intelligence
SORT	Strategic Offensive Reductions Treaty
SSCI	Senate Select Committee on Intelligence
START	Strategic Arms Reduction Treaty
TPFDL	Time-Phased Force Deployment List
UAE	United Arab Emirates
UN	United Nations
UNRG	Guatemalan National Revolutionary Unity
USAID	United States Agency for International Development
USA PATRIOT	Uniting and Strengthening America by Providing Appropriate Tools Required to Intercept and Obstruct Terrorism
USIA	United States Information Agency
US-VISIT	U.S. Visitor and Immigrant Status Indicator Technology
WHO	World Health Organization
WMDs	weapons of mass destruction
WTO	World Trade Organization

I

National Security Policy: What It Is, and How Americans Have Approached It

1

The International Setting

Every day, newspapers, television news channels, and Internet sites cover a wide variety of political, economic, and military developments around the world. Given this vast volume and variety of information, it can be difficult to determine which events and trends are most likely to affect the national security of the United States. Although the derivation of a constant set of generic criteria may be impossible, theories and concepts from the discipline of political science can help concerned observers analyze and assess a complex international system.

Unfortunately, there is no "silver bullet" or simple answer that holds the key to understanding international politics and their setting. However, reliable conclusions are more likely when an analyst explicitly acknowledges assumptions, is unambiguous about the meaning of key concepts, and can clearly state the logic of his or her cause-and-effect arguments. This approach best prepares the analyst to analyze the evidence and test assessments in light of competing views and explanations. Of course, all analyses of important issues are likely to be accompanied by uncertainty. A sensible approach for both analysts and policy makers would include an estimate of the degree of uncertainty associated with a particular assessment, an exploration of potential implications, and a provision for hedging against key uncertainties wherever possible. Although a sound understanding of the international environment is not sufficient to ensure good national security decisions, it is an essential starting point.

National Security

The term *national security* refers to the safeguarding of a people, territory, and way of life. It includes protection from physical assault and in that sense is similar to

3

the term *defense*. However, national security also implies protection, through a variety of means, of a broad array of interests and values. In one definition the phrase is commonly asserted to mean "physical security, defined as the protection against attack on the territory and the people of the United States in order to ensure survival with fundamental values and institutions intact; promotion of values; and economic prosperity."[1] Preserving the national security of the United States requires safeguarding individual freedoms and other U.S. values, as well as the laws and institutions established to protect them. The specific definitions used by different analysts may vary, and the prioritization of national interests may be difficult and controversial. Nevertheless, in essence, national security encompasses the protection of the fundamental values and core interests necessary to the continued existence and vitality of the state.[2]

This traditional conception of national security, which focuses on preserving the state from threats, is being challenged from several directions. One set of questions has been raised by those who believe that traditional notions of national security have focused too much on threats from other states and have paid inadequate heed to a variety of transnational phenomena. Some of these transnational forces, such as migration, narcotics, transnational crime, and terrorism, have human beings as the main actors. However, other phenomena, such as environmental degradation, critical resource shortages, and infectious diseases, might not be the specific product of human intention, yet they still pose critical challenges to states. Advocates for a focus on this broader security agenda—an agenda that has received greater emphasis since the end of the Cold War—believe that these issues deserve a place next to traditional military and economic issues as national security priorities.[3]

A second challenge, related but even more fundamental, is raised by scholars and policy advocates working in a field known as *human security*. They question the adequacy of the concept of national security itself by challenging the presumption that the state rather than the individual is the key unit of value. Particularly in predatory, failing, or failed states, security from external threats may not be the most meaningful concern. As one recent study states, "during the last 100 years far more people have been killed by their own governments than by foreign armies." The study goes on to note that violent conflicts within states "now make up more than 95% of armed conflicts."[4] Scholars vary in the definition of human security that they use, with some focusing on the full range of threats to personal well-being and dignity and others focusing more narrowly on political violence. However, they agree on putting the welfare of individuals at the center of their analyses. Though this volume focuses primarily on traditional national security issues, the new security agenda and human security are discussed in greater depth in Chapter 25.

A third challenge to traditional concepts of national security is one of emphasis rather than content. One could argue that protection of the home territory has always been a priority, even if in certain periods of U.S. history it could be taken somewhat for granted. However, after the September 11, 2001, terrorist attacks that killed almost three thousand people on U.S. territory, homeland security has received new emphasis. The terrorist attacks highlighted limitations in the understanding of important threats; inadequacies in the United States' ability to prevent attacks; the need for organizational reforms in federal bureaucracies; and the imperative to enhance cooperation across federal, state, and local levels of government. When President George W. Bush signed legislation creating the Department of Homeland Security (DHS) in November 2002, he created an organization intended to "prevent terrorist attacks within the United States; reduce America's vulnerability to terrorism; and minimize the damage and recover from attacks that do occur." To accomplish this, the new DHS "would mobilize and focus the resources of the federal government, state and local governments, the private sector, and the American people."[5]

Though properly considered to be a component of national security, a new focus on homeland security has highlighted problems not previously emphasized due to the historical tendency of national security analysts to focus on external threats. The increased salience of homeland security concerns will be particularly evident in Part II of this volume, on national security actors and processes, and is the specific focus of Chapter 6.

The term *national security* is an elastic one; its meaning and implications have expanded, contracted, and shifted over time. Reminiscent of Dr. Samuel Johnson's definition of patriotism as "the last refuge of scoundrels," protection of national security has sometimes even been invoked to justify or conceal illegal acts. Because national security issues can involve high stakes, it is especially important to critically analyze arguments invoking national security as a justification for a position or action. It is also useful to remember that national security policy in the U.S. context serves both material interests and nonmaterial values and to return occasionally to first principles. Does a particular policy further U.S. security or economic interests while preserving the U.S. Constitution and the framework it establishes for the American way of life? If the answer to that question is uncertain, then so may be the grounds on which a particular policy rests.

Perspectives on International Politics

Among scholars of international relations, three of the most important intellectual perspectives are realism, liberalism, and constructivism.[6] These worldviews affect such basic assumptions as which phenomena are truly important and how the world is expected to operate. These perspectives have practical relevance because, just as scholars may accept core assumptions of a particular worldview, so may policy makers. It is useful for both scholars and policy makers to be self-conscious about their perspectives so they understand the likely strengths and weaknesses of their approaches. Clarity about core assumptions may also help policy makers anticipate circumstances under which their various initiatives may be mutually reinforcing or internally contradictory.

Realism.   The oldest and perhaps most dominant tradition with regard to the nature of international politics is *realism*. With intellectual roots dating back to Thucydides and Machiavelli, realists see international politics as a dangerous, conflict-prone realm in which security is far from guaranteed. States are the primary actors and can be analyzed as if they were unitary and rational actors whose core national interest can be defined as power. Given the presence of anarchy—defined as the lack of a single authority with sovereign power over states in the international system—realists assert that states must pursue self-help strategies in order to survive. Though some states may seek only to maintain their own survival, others may seek universal domination. To preserve independence and prevent destruction, states seek to balance the power of other states either through alliances or through internal means of increasing their relative power, such as arms build-ups or economic mobilization. Although alliances may be useful forms of cooperation, they should be expected to last only as long as the common threat that initially brought the allies together.

An important contribution of the realist school of thought is its emphasis on the central concept of power. Though it can be tempting to define power as influence or as the ability to get one's way, this approach can easily become misleading. For example, Canada's victory in a trade dispute with the United States does not make it reasonable to conclude that Canada is more powerful. Political theorist Kenneth Waltz sought to give the term a more scientific and measurable formulation, arguing that power was a combination of seven components: size of population, territory, resource endowment, economic capability, military strength, political stability, and competence.[7] All these elements must be considered in any assessment, though the weighting of the different elements varies in different contexts. Waltz's central prediction is that states can be expected to react to the power of other states by engaging in balancing behavior. He argues that if "there is any distinctively political theory of international politics, balance of power theory is it."[8]

In an effort to refine Waltz's approach, Stephen Walt argues that power is important but not fully adequate to explain what motivates state behavior. States respond not just to power, but to *threat*, with threat defined as encompassing power as well as geographic proximity, offensive power, and aggressive intentions.[9] Though Waltz and Walt differ slightly on the key motivator for balancing behavior, they have in common the majority of assumptions that characterize the realist school of thought: The world is a dangerous place in which each state must ensure its own survival by obtaining and competently applying power.

Although realism has proven itself an enduring and valued paradigm, it has weaknesses as well as strengths. Realists have traditionally emphasized the primacy of the state and the relative importance of relations among the great powers.[10] In an era marked by the decreasing relevance of state boundaries and by weak and failed states as the source of critical transnational threats, the primacy that realists give to great power competition is challenged. A second issue is the priority that realists give to power and security—especially military security. Realists may be right about the centrality of these state concerns, but this may simultaneously make realism a less valuable approach to explaining state policies in other issue areas. For example, although a realist perspective may help to explain international trade issues in some cases, convincing scholarship has argued for the frequent significance of other variables, such as domestic interests, domestic and international institutions, the structure of the international economy, and the interactions of state and nonstate actors.[11]

Finally, realism does not contain within itself an adequate explanation of change. To a great extent, realists have taken pains to point out continuity in international politics. For example, realists might argue that the same fear that Sparta had of an increasingly powerful Athens—which Thucydides argues contributed to war between those powers more than two thousand years ago—could just as easily serve as a powerful explanation for war today.[12] This emphasis on the balance of power between states and states as key actors makes realists less likely to explore such potential system-transforming phenomena as the rising importance of transnational actors and the impact of the processes of globalization on the international system.

Liberalism.   A second major international relations tradition has its roots in the political writings of Immanuel Kant and other Enlightenment thinkers. Whereas the core value for realists is state security, the core values for liberals are individual liberty and moral autonomy. Though states may still be seen as the key actors in international politics, their status rests on whether or not they can reasonably be seen as the legitimate guarantors of the rights and aspirations of their populations. This perspective underpins the right to rebel that exists within the political theory of important liberal thinkers, such as John Locke.[13] Where a realist may be content to assume that a state is unitary and not carefully analyze domestic institutions or politics, a liberal sees societal actors as having central importance.[14] According to the liberal tradition, democratic institutions, as well as liberal democratic values within a population, will have an important impact on foreign policy behavior.

With regard to U.S. national security, perhaps the single most important international relations insight stemming from the liberal tradition is *democratic peace theory*. This theory seeks to explain the empirical reality that liberal democracies have rarely gone to war with one another. Though the exact mechanisms through which this result has been achieved are the focus of ongoing research, explanations generally focus on the nature of democratic institutions and norms. Democratic institutions require consensus and therefore create time for debate, as well as preclude wars for unpopular purposes (presumably war with another liberal democracy would be unpopular). Democratic norms emphasize peaceful conflict resolution and compromise—especially with another democratic government, which is seen as the legitimate custodian of the interests of its people.[15]

In addition to focusing greater attention on the domestic characteristics of states, liberalism also differs from realism in the mechanisms it suggests for the maintenance of international peace and stability. Though realists would likely dismiss any suggestions that a permanent peace between states is possible, they would hold that periods of relative peace and stability can be achieved if states prudently look to their interests (defined as power) and pay adequate attention to ensuring a balance of power in the international system.[16] Liberals, on the other hand, would be more likely to look to the mechanisms identified by Kant in his political essays "Perpetual Peace: A Philosophical Sketch" and "Idea for a Universal History with a Cosmopolitan Purpose."[17]

In the first of these essays, Kant hypothesizes that a permanent peace would have three characteristics: All states would have representative, elected governments; these governments would form a federation among themselves to resolve differences and to ensure an overwhelming response to any state's aggression; and individuals would enjoy the basic right of not automatically being treated as an enemy when arriving in a foreign land. This last provision, a minimal human right that opens the door to commerce, identifies a mechanism for the development of peaceful relations, which is further developed in the second of Kant's essays. According to this essay, trade will increase the interconnectedness between societies, which will in turn increase the benefits of peaceful relations and heighten the costs of increasingly destructive wars.

Although scholars working within the liberal tradition have refined these basic arguments and developed more specific propositions since Kant's time, his central ideas still underpin much of the liberal approach. Democratic peace theorists explore the possible benefits of democracy in terms of peace and security. Kant's notion of a federation of states is an early articulation of the focus of modern liberal theorists on the roles that international institutions and international law can play in furthering common interests among states. Finally, the idea that increased trade can promote peace continues to inform liberal thinking. For example, Robert Keohane and Joseph Nye developed an approach called *complex interdependence* that sees the mutual dependence between states created by economic interconnectedness as making conflict less likely.[18]

For most liberals, these ideas are underpinned by some concept of universal rights and the view that the freedom and moral autonomy of the individual are central values. A classic statement of this viewpoint can be found in the U.S. Declaration of Independence: "We hold these truths to be self-evident, that all men are created equal, that they are endowed by their Creator with certain unalienable Rights, that among these are Life, Liberty and the pursuit of Happiness. That to secure these rights, Governments are instituted among Men, deriving their just powers from the consent of the governed."[19] The liberal desire to protect the individual is embodied in international law, such as the "Universal Declaration of Human Rights" adopted by the United Nations (UN) in 1948, as well as in the Law of War.[20]

Like realism, liberalism has both strengths and weaknesses. It is a historical fact that liberal democracies have rarely if ever fought one another, though the process of democratization can itself be quite dangerous to international peace and security.[21] International law can be useful in defining standards, in establishing a mechanism to punish individuals when domestic systems cannot, and in providing legitimacy, but its most significant shortcoming is the lack of guaranteed enforcement. Similarly, international institutions have been significant mechanisms in helping states to achieve mutually beneficial outcomes—think of the contribution of the General Agreement on Tariffs and Trade (later the World Trade Organization) in facilitating free trade—but are also limited by uncertain enforcement. Finally, increased international commerce has improved individual welfare around the world—if unevenly—and the mechanism of mutual dependence has been used to make war less likely between states. As an example, Germany and France established the European Coal and Steel Community (which has now evolved into the European Union [EU]) in the early post–World War II years with the intent of making war between them less likely. But, even in the area of trade there have been disappointments. In 1910, Sir Norman Angell published *The Great Illusion*, arguing that economic interconnectedness made war obsolete and conquest counterproductive. Of course, World War I broke out only four years later. Overall, the world wars in the middle of the twentieth century were great setbacks to the liberal vision. Enlightenment did not necessarily mean progress, and economic interdependence, democracy, and international institutions were not adequate to preserve the peace.

Neoconservativism.   Although it is not an enduring tradition of international relations, such as those discussed above, an American school of thought that achieved prominence and influence in U.S. foreign and security policy in the late twentieth and early twenty-first centuries is *neoconservativism*—a perspective that actually blends propositions from the realist and liberal traditions. Neoconservatives have much in common with the realist view, seeing the international environment as dangerous and as more characterized by conflict than by cooperation. Like the realists, they put power at the center of their analyses and see it as the responsibility of the great powers—or, more precisely, the United States, as the world's only remaining superpower—to manage world affairs and to provide what peace and stability can be attained.[22] They are skeptical of the notion of an international community and of the idea that consensus among states that uphold different values confers meaningful legitimacy. They also question the value of international law and international institutions, especially the UN, which has proven itself, in their view, to be the "guarantor of nothing."[23]

Despite these commonalities with a realist perspective, neoconservativism also incorporates strands of liberal thought, viewing realism as ultimately inadequate for its lack of moral vision. The use of U.S. power should always be guided by moral values and should be used to promote "democracy, free markets, [and] respect for liberty."[24] As have many liberal-tradition thinkers, neoconservatives have argued that doing the morally right thing—such as supporting the development of liberal, democratic governments abroad—would also be the best way to promote U.S. interests. Neoconservatives share with at least some liberals the notion that the condition of international affairs is improvable, though by using U.S. power rather than by strengthening mechanisms of global governance. International institutions and international law, in the neoconservative worldview, often merely mask efforts of weak or undesirable actors to restrict U.S. freedom of action.

The reader can evaluate the degree to which the neoconservative outlook reflects traditional American approaches to national security by consulting Chapter 2. Here, it is sufficient to note that both realists and liberals challenge the neoconservative outlook for different reasons. Neoconservatives have argued that "America must be guided by its independent judgment, both about its own interest and the global interest."[25] Realists would deride the notion of a "global interest," as well as the claims of any state to possess and to be acting in accordance with universal moral values. Liberals would question the legitimacy of U.S. claims to this decision-making authority and question the ability of the United States to exercise it well. A second issue stems from the neoconservative claim that the United States is a uniquely benign global hegemon, which validates and enables its world leadership.[26] Realists might question the importance of a benign status but be even more skeptical of the notion that the United States is capable of remaking the world in its own image. Liberals question whether the unilateral use of U.S. power, particularly the U.S. military, can succeed at democracy promotion and whether such an approach would preserve global perceptions that the United States is benign. Whatever its future, neoconservatism has been charged with being excessively realist for its focus on material power and U.S. national interests, as well as excessively idealist in its agenda of democracy promotion abroad.[27] It has also been widely criticized as the rationale for increased unilateralism and the decision to invade Iraq in 2003.

Constructivism.   In addition to realism and liberalism, a third worldview is offered by scholars working within a paradigm known as *constructivism* who examine the potential importance of nonmaterial as well as material factors in shaping situations and affecting outcomes. For example, Alexander Wendt rejects the centrality that a realist might give to the distribution of material capabilities, arguing instead that relative material capabilities only affect behavior in the context of amity or enmity between the actors involved. As an example, the imbalance of power between the United States and Canada does not foster the same sense of insecurity that is created by the imbalance between India and Pakistan (see Chapter 19). Shared knowledge and the practices of the actors involved are also important in understanding how states will behave in any given situation.[28]

Besides illuminating the potential importance of nonmaterial factors in shaping the relations among states, an additional constructivist contribution is to provide an explanation for change. The constructivist asserts that identity not only shapes but is also shaped by social interaction over time. Because change may occur at a level of values and fundamental interests rather than just at the level of behavior, the fundamental character of international politics could change over time as the interactions among states affect the identity of the actors involved.

The constructivist view of international relations aids in the examination of a number of issues of potential significance to national security. For example, constructivism provides an approach that facilitates an understanding of aspects of identity, such as strategic or organizational culture, that may help to explain a state's behavior.[29] As a second example, constructivists have looked at the role of international norms, such as those that govern state intervention into other states, to evaluate how they may shape behavior as well as how they have evolved over time.[30] As a final example, constructivists examine socialization processes—such as the interaction of states in international institutions—for their potential explanatory power.[31] Constructivists offer an alternative worldview that adds to the manner in which scholars and policy makers can seek to understand the behavior of key actors in international politics.

Key Concepts

This section introduces four concepts that are essential tools to critical and analytical thinking about international politics: anarchy, sovereignty, levels of analysis, and power.

Anarchy.   As used in international relations, the term *anarchy* refers not to mere disorder, but instead to a lack of formal and authoritative government. It is the existence of anarchy that distinguishes international politics from the domestic realm. Although there may be such mechanisms as international institutions intended to provide some degree of governance within particular issue areas, in the world as it exists today, there is no single authority to which one can turn that can arbitrate disagreements and enforce the decisions that result from such arbitration.

The traditions of international relations discussed above agree on the existence of anarchy; they merely disagree on its implications. For such realists as Hobbes, where there is no overarching authority, there is no law and no peace because individuals must constantly compete with one another merely to survive.[32] Among states in a condition of anarchy, one should expect constant suspicion and the ever-present possibility of war. For such liberals as Locke, on the other hand, society is possible in the absence of a common authority. Instead of constant war, the state of nature is one of inconvenience because enforcement is uncertain. An implication of this view is that states could form some type of rudimentary society in which, even in the absence of world government, they could cooperate to achieve mutual gains. For constructivists, either the realist or the liberal outcome could be possible, depending on the identities of the states involved and the social context of their interactions.

Sovereignty.   The modern conception of sovereignty dates to the Peace of Westphalia in 1648, which many mark as the origin of the modern state system. Intended to bring a bloody period of religious conflict to a close, the Peace of Westphalia also reflected a desire to limit future wars by establishing the principle of sovereignty. In essence, sovereignty means that each state has total authority over its own population within its own territory. Modern recognition of sovereignty can be found in the UN Charter. This document recognizes the "sovereign equality" of all of the member states of the UN and affirms that "nothing contained in the present Charter shall authorize the United Nations to intervene in matters which are essentially within the domestic jurisdiction of any state."[33]

Many important national security issues involve the concept of sovereignty. A first instance is the concept of the formal legal equality of all states. Though this is recognized in the UN General Assembly, where each state gets one vote, the limits to this idea are also recognized in the UN Security Council, where five permanent, great-power members get a veto. States may be legally equal, but relative power also shapes how they interact. A second issue is the contrast between the ideal of sovereignty and the fact that many of the world's more than 190 states lack sufficient capacity to exercise full control over their populations and territories. This shortcoming in governance helps to create, and makes it more difficult to resolve, a variety of transnational security concerns. A third issue relates to limits to sovereignty. In 1951, for example, the Convention on the Prevention and Punishment of the Crime of Genocide went into force, which commits the contracting states to "undertake to prevent and to punish" acts of genocide.[34] This international agreement makes clear that genocide, perhaps the most egregious form of human rights violation, justifies the intervention of states into each other's affairs. As states decide when to intervene in response to either human rights or security concerns, the value of preserving the ideal of sovereignty as a limiting force in international conflict is a value that must be carefully weighed.

Levels of Analysis.   As an organizing framework, levels of analysis can be of great utility in aiding clear and critical thinking about international affairs. Introduced by Waltz in *The Man, the State, and War* in 1959 as the three "images" of international relations, the concept of levels of analysis has become a common organizing framework for thinking about the causes of outcomes in international politics.[35] As a useful simplification, the causes of international developments can be thought of as stemming from the nature of individuals, domestic factors, or the international system as a whole. Though one or another may have greater explanatory power in a given instance, all may well bear on a given case.

Individual Level of Analysis.   One place to look for causes of events is at the individual level of analysis. As an example, some argue that war will always be a part of the human experience, because the tendency toward competition and violence is intrinsic to human nature. This view that war is embedded in human nature has been held by a number of leading realist thinkers, including Thucydides and Hans Morgenthau. Though perhaps plausible, this perspective cannot provide a complete account, because an unchanging human nature cannot explain variations in war and peace over time. There are other explanations that also reside at the individual level of analysis that are more helpful in accounting for variation. These explanations may draw upon the role of psychological factors or even specific personalities. As a case in point, analysts argue that Saddam Hussein's personal characteristics played a role in the defeat of his regime at the hands of U.S.-led coalition forces in 2003.[36] Caution is called for here as well. Although the characteristics of individuals may often be important, a focus upon them must be accompanied by an explanation as to the process through which individual motivations and dispositions are able to affect state action.

Domestic Level of Analysis.   A second approach suggests that actions in international affairs are best understood as the product of the internal character of states.

Vladimir Lenin's view of the imperialistic activities of capitalist states is an example.[37] He believed that the capitalistic states' struggle for markets, resources, and profits would inevitably lead them to dominate and exploit the underdeveloped areas of the world. As the potential colonial territory of the world diminished, Lenin foresaw increased competition that would ultimately result in violent conflict among the imperial states and the end of the capitalist system.

Other possible characteristics of states that have been hypothesized to affect international behavior include their political institutions, culture, ideology, and bureaucratic and organizational politics. Democratic peace theory provides an example of the first two. In explaining why liberal democratic states do not war with one another, some analysts emphasize the characteristics of democratic institutions, while others highlight shared cultural beliefs and values that conduce to the peaceful resolution of differences. The third characteristic mentioned above, ideology, is of course not always peaceful. Defined as a set "of beliefs that give meaning to life" and "an explicit or implicit program of action," the program-of-action component can constitute a threat to states of differing ideologies.[38] As exemplified in the German Third Reich, Nazism was a threat to every other ideology. Finally, numerous scholars have examined the manner in which bureaucratic politics within a government and the characteristics of large government organizations can influence state behavior.[39]

International Level of Analysis.   A final place to focus when seeking to understand actions or outcomes in international politics is the international system as a whole. Accepting anarchy as a starting point, those who look to the international system generally focus on one of two categories—process or structure.

Those who look to *process* examine the interactions of states or even the transnational forces that are not clearly motivated by or confined within particular states. An example of the focus on states is provided by theorists who focus on the weight of international institutions in shaping state behavior. Given the existence of self-interested states in an anarchic system, it may nevertheless be possible to structure their interactions through institutions so that cooperation is more likely.[40] An example of the focus on transnational forces is provided by scholars and policy makers who argue for the importance of globalization. Although there is not one single agreed-upon definition, *globalization* is generally seen as an ongoing process that is decreasing the significance of state borders.[41] Enabled by reductions in transport and communication costs, new technologies, and the policy choices of many of the world's political leaders, international trade is increasing, international flows of capital are on the rise, the nature of international business activity is changing, and there is a tremendous diffusion of cultural forms. Although it may be difficult to point to globalization as the specific cause of any one event or outcome, its processes are arguably changing the character of international politics by altering the relative economic power of states, raising the salience of certain transnational concerns, increasing the challenges of global governance, and empowering new actors (see Chapter 25).

In addition to process, the *structure* of the international system can also be useful for understanding international politics. Perhaps the clearest formulation of this is in Waltz's *Theory of International Politics*. He argues that as long as anarchy exists and two or more actors seek to survive, it is possible to understand a lot about the nature of international politics merely by knowing the number of great powers in the international system.[42] For instance, a world with one great power which outstrips all others, or *unipole* (as is arguably the case with the United States today), will see other powers seeking to balance against that dominant state. At the same time, the unipole will be tempted into an overactive role in the world, because its power is unchecked.[43] Waltz's argument helpfully illuminates general tendencies, but it is unlikely to yield the specific, context-sensitive prescriptions needed by policy makers.

National Power.   Despite the central importance of the concept of power, there is no universally accepted definition. This lack of agreement partially stems from four aspects of power that make it difficult to settle on a single formulation. The first of these is that power is *dynamic*. New instruments of power have appeared continuously over the centuries, and new applications for old forms are always being found. Even a seemingly backward society can achieve surprising results under strong political leadership that is willing and able to engender sacrifice and a sense of purpose among its people. The defeat of the French in Vietnam and the subsequent failure of the U.S. intervention to support South Vietnam are classic cases. The collapse of the Soviet Union in the early 1990s provides an example of the manner in which a particular state's power can change dramatically over time.

In addition to being dynamic, power is also *relative*, *situational*, and at least partially *subjective*. Power is relative because its utility depends in part on comparing it with whatever opposes it, and it is situational because what may generate power in a particular set of circumstances may not in another. Finally, it is subjective in that a reputation for being powerful may be sufficient to achieve results without power actually having to be applied.

Despite these difficulties, it is nevertheless possible to say something useful about power by focusing on its relatively objective characteristics—measurements of capabilities. One of the classic definitions is Morgenthau's from *Politics Among Nations*. He defines power as consisting of: geography, natural resources, industrial capacity, military preparedness, technology and innovations, leadership, quantity and quality of armed forces, population, national character, national morale, quality of diplomacy, and quality of government.[44] Morgenthau argues that these aspects must be evaluated for the both the present and the future, and that an assessment requires analyzing each factor, associated trends, and how these trends are likely to interact over time.[45] Waltz, in his later definition already introduced above, emphasizes only seven elements. Though simpler, Waltz's formulation is similar to Morgenthau's in that they both cannot fully resolve difficulties in assessment stemming from imperfect information, weighting, and aggregation. Because of these difficulties, even careful efforts to assess and measure relative power will always be accompanied with a degree of uncertainty.

In the parlance of some observers of international relations, the definition of power as capabilities is also known as *hard power*. This is to distinguish it from a competing concept, *soft power*. Originally coined by Nye, soft power refers to "the ability to achieve desired outcomes in international affairs through attraction rather than coercion." He explains:

> It works by convincing others to follow, or getting them to agree to, norms and institutions that produce the desired behavior. . . . If a state can make its power legitimate in the perception of others and establish international institutions that encourage them to channel or limit their activities, it may not need to expend many of its costly traditional economic or military resources.[46]

If power is not thought of as an end in itself, but rather as a means to further U.S. interests and values, Nye argues that the power of attraction and legitimacy can help the United States to secure these interests and values at lesser cost. Skeptics, on the other hand, argue that soft power will tend to have little or no force in shaping the behavior of other states when they have important interests at stake.

Assessing national power is an art, not a science; any specific assessment will be open to a variety of challenges. National security analysts in and out of public office are inescapably faced with the task of identifying a moving and ill-defined target and of counting that which has often yet to be adequately measured. Still, policy makers in Washington and the rest of the world must act, however scant and unreliable their information may be. National power, in one sense or another, is generally a central feature of the analyses behind their actions.

Practical Assessments of Power.   When decision makers actually assess power, they invariably do so in specific contexts; that is, they engage not in some general, theoretical exercise but in a specific, situational analysis: *Who* is involved, over *what issue, where,* and *when*? Taking each of these questions in turn, the *who* element is crucial. Not only are all states not equal in quantity of resources, but the quality also differs. Health, education, motivation, and other factors confound attempts to establish reliable equivalency ratios. As an example, Israel manages to more than hold its own against adversaries many times its size. Though no government can make something from nothing, clearly some can and do have the organizational, managerial, technical, scientific, and leadership skills that enable them to make much more with equal or lesser amounts of similar resources.

This leads to the second element of situational analysis—namely, the *issue*. Its significance lies largely in the support or lack thereof given to national leaders over a particular matter. All governments depend on at least the passive support of their citizens in order to function, and none can expect to endure once it has lost that minimum loyalty embodied in the term *legitimacy*. As long as a government satisfies the minimum expectations of the politically active or potentially active members of its society, there is little chance of internal upheaval.[47] Mobilizing resources to apply to national security tasks requires more than passive support, however; it invariably necessitates some degree of sacrifice and active involvement. For some issues, such support may be difficult to muster; others have an almost electrifying effect upon a nation's consciousness, eliciting enormous willingness to sacrifice. The attack on Pearl Harbor in 1941 had such an effect on the American people; the terrorist attacks on 9/11 arguably had the same potential—at least initially. The morass of Vietnam had little such support even at the outset and, like the war in Iraq begun in 2003, gradually generated quite the opposite. Between extremes of support and dissent lie most national security issues. In these cases, leaders must build support for those tasks they believe important or resign themselves to impotence.

The third situational feature of power is geographic—*where* events take place. All states are capable of making some sort of splash somewhere in the pool of world politics, normally in their own immediate areas. No matter how large a splash may be, its effects tend to dissipate with distance from the source. The ability to apply resources at a distance sufficient to overcome resistance generated by those closer to the conflict has always characterized great powers; it continues to provide a useful test by which to appraise claimants to that status.

This introduces the final situational feature of power, *time*. The interplay of leaders' ambitions and creativity, changes in resources, technological developments, and the public response to challenges all work to effect a continual redistribution of global power. Empires acquired to the great satisfaction of their builders have overtaxed the abilities of their successors to maintain them, resulting not only in the loss of domain but in the collapse of the founding unit as well. The Soviet Union's demise makes this point dramatically. Similarly, the piecemeal application of resources may ultimately produce a long-term drain that adversely affects areas of national life not originally thought vulnerable. This insight in part motivates those concerned about U.S. activism abroad during the 1990s and into the early twenty-first century.

Application of Power.   Power for its own sake can be likened to money in the hands of a miser; it may delight its owner, but it is of little consequence to the world because it is applied to no useful purpose. The American experience between the two world wars in many ways resembles such a situation. In profound isolation, the United States forfeited its initiative in world affairs to other states, principally to the traditional European powers and Japan. The reputation of the United States as a significant military power, established in the Spanish-American War and World War I, plus its geographic advantage of being separated from other great powers by oceans served to protect the nation and its interests during this period. But reputation is a fleeting thing, especially for great powers that are identified in their own time with the existing world order. Steamship and bomber technology partially overcame the barrier of the oceans, while a foreign policy of isolationism eroded the American military reputation. Pearl Harbor and four very expensive years of war were the result of ignoring the relevance and uses of power.

The purpose of power is to overcome resistance in order to bring about or secure a preferred order of things. When the resistance is generated by other human beings, the purpose of power is to persuade those others to accept the designs or preferences in question or to destroy their ability to offer continued resistance.

LURIE'S WORLD

"Now, if you'll just put it down carefully....."

Copyright 1985 CARTOONEWS INTERNATIONAL Syndicate, N.Y.C., USA.
Reprinted with permission of Ranan Lurie.

Depending upon the importance attached to the goal, the capabilities available to the respective protagonists, the skills they possess in applying those capabilities, the vulnerabilities each has in other areas upon which the opposition may capitalize, and the history of conflict between them, the techniques of persuasion can take either of two principal forms: rewards or punishments.

Rewards themselves are of two types: the presentation of some benefit in exchange for the desired reaction or the willingness to forgo negative behavior in exchange for compliance. Threats in this context are considered part of the reward approach to persuasion, because unless and until the threatening actor delivers on its threat, no actual harm has occurred. Either type of reward will work as long as all parties concerned feel they are getting something worthy of the exchange or are minimizing their losses in a situation where all the alternatives appear worse.

Since the early 1990s, U.S. negotiations with North Korea over the status of its nuclear weapons program provide examples of each. The United States has proven willing to offer North Korea aid and other incentives for verifiable disarmament. At the same time, the United States has threatened economic embargo and even harsher measures in the absence of compliance. (For more on the North Korean nuclear situation, see Chapter 18.)

When nations in a dispute decide to carry out a threat or initiate negative action without prior threat, they are seeking to persuade through *punishment* or coercion. Clearly, such persuasion works only if the actor being punished can avert its predicament by compliance. Therefore the threatened punishment, its timing, and its application must be chosen carefully in order to achieve the desired effect. To punish indiscriminately not only squanders resources, driving up costs, but also may be counterproductive in that it antagonizes and sharpens resistance by forcing a change in the perception of stakes.

International Relations Theory and National Security Policy

International relations theories can often be associated with such international relations traditions as realism, liberalism, and constructivism, but theories are more carefully specified. A *theory* consists of assumptions, key concepts, propositions about causal relationships, and an articulation of the conditions under which it can be expected to hold. These elements should be sufficiently clear so that the theory can be subjected to testing and possible falsification. Two examples from the realist perspective include *balance of power theory*, which looks at expectations of state behavior given different relative power situations, and the *theory of hegemonic stability*, which examines the manner in which a single, dominant power in the international system can foster an open system of international trade.[48] Two liberal tradition examples are *neoliberal institutionalism*, which examines the role of international institutions in fostering cooperation, and *democratic peace theory*, which seeks to explain peaceful relations among democracies. A theory is useful to the extent that it contributes to describing, explaining, and predicting international events and has implications for policy prescription.

When approaching a particular national security problem or situation, every policy maker has a theory. It may be held more or less self-consciously or be more or less carefully specified, but it nonetheless exists. As international relations scholar Walt states, "theory is an essential tool of statecraft. Many policy debates ultimately rest on competing theoretical visions, and relying on a false or flawed theory can lead to major foreign policy disasters."[49] As an example, Walt gives the "infamous 'risk theory'" of German Admiral Alfred von Tirpitz before World War I. His theory held that Germany's ability to threaten British naval supremacy would cause Great Britain to accept Germany's preeminence on the continent; the opposite proved to be true. As a more recent example, advocates of the U.S. war in Iraq in 2003 "believed war would lead to a rapid victory, encourage neighboring regimes to 'bandwagon' with the United States, hasten the spread of democracy in the region, and ultimately undermine support for Islamic terrorism. Their opponents argued that the war would have exactly the opposite effects."[50] As Walt goes on to explain, at stake here are propositions about the fundamental dynamics of international relations that theories can help to illuminate.

An example that shows the significant policy implications of theoretical differences is the rise of China. A realist, balance of power theorist would expect an increasingly powerful China to become increasingly assertive and a possible threat to its neighbors. As a counter, the United States should shore up regional alliance arrangements and potentially increase various facets of its own power. A neoliberal institutionalist, on the other hand, might focus on China's increasingly extensive engagement in regional and international institutions and recommend policies to encourage and reward this engagement as a way of fostering common interests and the value that China places on peaceful relations. A constructivist might argue that China's future behavior will be decisively governed by the dominant Chinese "national ideas about how to achieve foreign policy goals" and the extent to which these ideas are achieving success.[51] If China's current policies meet setbacks, and alternative national ideas are present within important Chinese domestic constituencies (emphasizing, for example, separation from or the revision of the international system), China's policy approach could be expected to change in potentially dangerous or disruptive ways. (For more on China, see Chapters 18 and 26.)

Though it might be frustrating for a policy maker to be given such contrasting visions of important policy problems, the preservation of multiple perspectives is valuable. These competing explanations and prescriptions suggest a continuing need to engage with available evidence and test reality when making critical policy choices.

Characteristics of the Current International System

One way of examining the nature of the international system today focuses on globalization and its effects. As introduced above, the economic, cultural, and political processes associated with globalization will lessen the significance of state borders over time, change the relative power among states, increase the importance of nonstate actors, and contribute to the challenges associated with global governance. Although a state can still decide to close itself as much as possible to the outside world—North Korea is the most dramatic example—the costs of doing so are only increasing over time (see Chapter 18).

The forces of globalization do not have purely positive or purely negative effects. In economic terms, although technological diffusion, increased trade, and increasingly international capital flows have improved the welfare of millions of people around the world, all countries and individuals are not able to benefit equally. Even within countries, the benefits from an increasingly open international trading system are not evenly spread. In addition to economic issues, the forces of globalization can be disruptive or even unwelcome to traditional societies in which rapid change may be difficult to assimilate and can empower violent nonstate actors.[52] (For more on globalization and human security, see Chapter 25.)

Despite the importance of globalization, states will remain the key actors in international politics for the foreseeable future. For one thing, both independently and through their actions in such international institutions as the World Trade Organization, the decisions made by states will affect the pace and nature of globalization. In addition, until or unless more effective institutions of global governance are constructed, states will remain the actors with the most capability to solve problems.[53] Even individuals or groups with a transnational agenda will need to work with or through states in order to realize their goals. Any who are tempted to take a determinist view of the impact of globalization would be wise to keep in mind the capabilities and political choices of states.

In addition to the ongoing processes of globalization, international relations scholar Robert Jervis argues that from the perspective of international security there are three remarkable aspects of the international system in the early twenty-first century. The first is the existence of a security community among the great powers: "war among the leading powers—the most developed states of the United States, Western Europe, and Japan—will not occur in the future, and is indeed no longer a source of concern for them."[54] Jervis goes on to argue that though war may be possible between Russia or China, or between one of these countries and one of the members of the security community, the diminished prospects of war between the leading powers (which are also the most economically developed and democratic) is a remarkable historical development. There is no guarantee as to duration, and possible tensions with Russia or China retain significance, but the existence of the security community is an important aspect of the current international environment that can all too easily be taken for granted.

A second important characteristic of the current international system, noted by Jervis as well as many others, is the extraordinary concentration of political, economic, and military power in one state—the United States. The status of the United States as a single, dominant power is likely to have a significant impact on international relations for the foreseeable future, though interpretations of its implications vary widely. The realist expectation is that other states will seek to balance against the power of the United States; as this expectation has not been fully met in the early twenty-first century, analysts have looked for forms of "soft balancing" as evidence that states are still seeking ways to resist and restrain U.S. power.[55] Others argue that the U.S. position of dominance enables it to play the role of global hegemon, serving as a key provider of the collective goods that sustain the international economy. The extent to which this is sustainable depends on the will of the American population as well as the extent to which other major powers in the system also see the United States as acting in their interest.[56] Finally, analysts from the liberal tradition might argue that U.S. unipolarity is an opportunity to reinforce the rule-governed international system, which it played such an important role in founding after World War II, through a multilateral approach to international affairs and an embrace of international institutions.[57] Though the above interpretations have limitations as well as strengths, they have in common the insight that U.S. national security policy decisions are likely to have uniquely significant force in a world in which it holds such disproportionate power.

The third characteristic of the international system identified by Jervis is the rise of terrorism and the U.S. response to the attacks on its own soil on 9/11. This characteristic is related to the second issue above, as "the American response is clearly conditioned by the nation's great capabilities and the lack of challenges from peers."[58] The unique position of the United States in the world means that actions that the United States takes in this area may have broad repercussions for international politics for years to come.

Despite important changes in the international strategic environment of the United States over time, there are also constants. One of the most important of these is that the United States will always face the need to balance the limited means it is willing to devote to national security policy with the ends it seeks to pursue. The traditional American approaches likely to shape this balance are the subject of Chapter 2; the manner in which the United States has managed or not managed to strike this balance over time is the subject of Chapter 3. Whether one assesses the current and future international environment to be extremely threatening or relatively benign, the challenges faced by U.S. policy makers in balancing U.S. national security needs with other interests and domestic priorities remain great.

Discussion Questions

1. Define the terms *national security* and *human security*. Are there any tensions between these two concepts?

2. What is the realist worldview? What are strengths and weakness of the realist perspective on international politics?

3. What does balance of power theory predict? Can you provide examples of balance of power theory in action?

4. What are the main mechanisms through which adherents of the liberal tradition believe that peace can be furthered in international politics? What are their strengths and weaknesses?

5. What is the constructivist critique of the idea that anarchy causes security competition among states?

6. What is *national power*? Can you quantify national power? How?

7. What is *soft power*? Is soft power important in explaining the U.S. role in the world? Why or why not?

8. How important are theories of international relations to policy makers? Should they be? Why or why not?

9. What are the most important characteristics of the international strategic environment of the United States today?

Recommended Reading

Allison, Graham T., and Philip Zelikow. *Essence of Decision: Explaining the Cuban Missile Crisis.* 2nd ed. New York: Longman, 1999.

Art, Robert J., and Robert Jervis. *International Politics: Enduring Concepts and Contemporary Issues.* 8th ed. New York: Longman, 2006.

Bhagwati, Jagdish. *In Defense of Globalization.* New York: Oxford University Press, 2004.

Doyle, Michael W. *Ways of War and Peace: Realism, Liberalism, and Socialism.* New York: W. W. Norton, 1997.

Friedman, Thomas L. *The World Is Flat: A Brief History of the Twenty-First Century.* New York: Farrar, Straus, and Giroux, 2005.

Fukuyama, Francis. *The End of History and the Last Man.* New York: The Free Press, 1992.

———. *America at the Crossroads: Democracy, Power, and the Neoconservative Legacy.* New Haven: Yale University Press, 2006.

George, Alexander. *Bridging the Gap: Theory and Practice in Foreign Policy.* Washington, DC: U.S. Inst. Peace Press, 1993.

Huntington, Samuel P. *The Clash of Civilizations and the Remaking of World Order.* New York: Simon & Schuster, 1996.

Jervis, Robert. *Perception and Misperception in International Politics*. Princeton, NJ: Princeton University Press, 1976.

Kaplan, Robert. *The Coming Anarchy: Shattering the Dreams of the Post Cold War*. New York: Vintage, 2001.

Keohane, Robert O. *After Hegemony: Cooperation and Discord in the World Political Economy*. 1st Princeton classic ed. with a new preface by the author. Princeton, NJ: Princeton University Press, 1984, 2005.

Keohane, Robert O., and Joseph S. Nye. *Power and Interdependence*. 3rd ed. New York: Pearson Education, 2001.

Kissinger, Henry. *Diplomacy*. New York: Simon & Schuster, 1994.

Mearsheimer, John J. *The Tragedy of Great Power Politics*. New York: W. W. Norton, 2001.

Morgenthau, Hans. *Politics Among Nations: The Struggle for Power and Peace*. 2nd ed., rev. and enlarged. New York: Knopf, 1954.

Russett, Bruce M. *Grasping the Democratic Peace: Principles for a Post-Cold War World*. Princeton, NJ: Princeton University Press, 1995.

Thucydides. *History of the Peloponnesian War*. Translated by Rex Warner. New York: Penguin Books, 1972.

Walt, Stephen M. *Origins of Alliances*. Ithaca: Cornell University Press, 1987.

———. *Taming American Power: The Global Response to U.S. Primacy*. New York: W. W. Norton & Company, 2005.

Waltz, Kenneth N. *Man, the State, and War: A Theoretical Analysis*. New York: Columbia University Press, 1959.

———. *Theory of International Politics*. New York: McGraw-Hill, 1979.

Wendt, Alexander. *Social Theory of International Politics*. New York: Cambridge University Press, 1999.

Internet Resources

The United Nations, www.un.org

U.S. Central Intelligence Agency *World Factbook*, www.cia.gov/library/publications/the-world-factbook/index.html

U.S. Department of State, www.state.gov

The White House, www.whitehouse.gov

World Trade Organization, www.wto.org

2

Traditional American Approaches to
National Security

Generalizations about distinctly American approaches to national security matters should be advanced with the same caution warranted by all large generalizations. Americans are a heterogeneous group and tend to differ on policy
issues along lines that may include age group, sex, party affiliation, region, socioeconomic status, education levels, religion, and ethnicity. Americans are
likely to vary in their opinions, for example, on defense spending. At times of
low defense budgets, some citizens have argued for greater armament; high
defense budgets always have their antagonists. Even when the United States
has been committed to war, a portion of society has been dedicated to pacifism.
Invariably, some segment of the population has felt that the United States
has committed to war at the wrong time, for the wrong cause, or in the wrong
place.

Despite wide divergence in individual opinions, some central trends in the
American approach to national security recur. Short of war, for instance, Americans have traditionally focused much of their energy on the pursuit of private interests and consequently have viewed national security as a secondary matter. On
the other hand, once conscious of a threat, U.S. attitudes have tended to shift
quickly and dramatically. American attitudes are affected by both "changes in the
domestic and foreign political-economic situation involving the presence or absence of threat in varying degrees" and "the character and predisposition of the
population."[1] This chapter focuses on the latter variable, briefly examining certain
tendencies of thought and action arising from the American experience and its historic context. The first variable will be examined in Chapter 3, as well as in other
chapters of this text.

Public Involvement and National Security Policy

What role should public opinion play in the national security policy process? Some view the involvement of the public in national security policy as detrimental. The realist position, for example, typically argues that foreign policy making should be reserved for the elites in society who are capable of making decisions secretly, effectively, and coherently.[2] Elites should either lead the public to support their chosen policies or ignore the public's preferences altogether.[3] The reasons for this are twofold. First, national security policy is so important that it must be controlled by the most knowledgeable, who will make decisions based on rational calculations of the national interest. Public opinion is all too often uninformed and based on emotion. Second, decisions in the areas of foreign policy and national security are sometimes urgent and at other times require policy makers to take a long-term perspective. Public opinion will lack utility as a guide to action in both of these cases. It will be too slow to crystallize to be of use in a crisis and too mercurial to be of benefit in long-term strategic planning.

Of course, there are always two sides to important issues, and there are those who argue that public involvement not only is essential to democracy but also can improve policy formulation and sustainability. Although realists emphasize rational calculation, the starting point for the liberal argument is the normative view that policy should reflect the views and values of the people. A process that is open to democratic participation and accountability will not only be best for a particular society but may also produce more mutually beneficial interactions with other states. It is a core proposition of the liberal tradition in international affairs, for example, that liberal democracies tend to be more peaceful than nondemocracies— at least, in their interactions with one another. This is in part because the public plays a constructive role in constraining policy makers.[4] A second way in which the involvement of the population can be beneficial is that public debate can help to clarify major issues. Some scholars have argued that public opinion is more stable and rational than the realist perspective allows.[5]

In addition to aiding policy formulation, public involvement may also be an asset in policy execution and sustainability. Public involvement is more likely to create harmony between popular opinion and government policy, which will tend to enhance legitimacy.[6] In addition, involvement of the public can help sustain support for the sacrifices for which foreign and national security policies may call.

The Importance of Values.　Whatever the position taken on the desirable degree of public involvement, it is clear that any U.S. security policy requiring sustained national sacrifices must be founded, in large part, upon basic public values. Although values are often imprecise, diverse, and apt to change, policy makers have a responsibility to clarify, interpret, synthesize, and articulate them, as they bear upon particular foreign and national security issues. Policy makers must reconcile diverse perspectives and competing values in relation to a particular aspect of national security, and a degree of compromise is often necessary. However, the values at stake in policy formulation cannot be avoided.[7]

One time-tested means of generating consensus, especially for the executive branch, is to couch policy in terms that command broad support within American society. Political leaders may seek to articulate their initiatives in terms of values so cherished by the polity that it would appear "un-American" to challenge them. This practice is generally recognized by policy makers as desirable and, on occasion, politically necessary. Examples include President Woodrow Wilson's call for moral action in foreign affairs, President Jimmy Carter's stress on human rights in American foreign policy, and President George W. Bush's declaration in 2002 that the United States would "actively work to bring the hope of democracy, development, free markets, and free trade to every corner of the world."[8]

The Sources of Public Opinion and Its Impact on National Security Policy. Public opinion in the United States is informed by basic values, as well as numerous information sources that are mostly in private hands. From within the government, however, it is traditionally the executive branch that wields the greatest influence. This corresponds to the leadership role of the president in national security affairs and reflects the information advantages held by the president as well as his or her ability to speak with a single voice. At any given time, the relative influence of the president may also be affected by the tendency to increase executive prerogative in times of war or crisis. During the Cold War, for example, the decades-long threat of the Soviet Union and its satellites demanded focused leadership in Washington. This dynamic strengthened the presidency in its legislative and policy battles with Congress.[9] Immediately after the terrorist attacks of September 11, 2001, on U.S. soil, Congress again tended to defer to presidential leadership. (For more on executive prerogative, see Chapter 4.)

The role that public opinion plays can vary even when circumstances are similar. For example, after the bombing of the U.S. barracks in Lebanon killed 241 marines on October 23, 1983, it took the full efforts of administration officials and congressional Republicans to convince President Ronald Reagan to redeploy U.S. forces in spite of strong public sentiment opposing continued U.S. involvement. Conversely, when eighteen American soldiers were killed and seventy-eight wounded in Somalia on October 3, 1993, President Bill Clinton quickly reversed his policy in the face of a similar negative public reaction by announcing the withdrawal of American troops by March 31, 1994.[10]

In historical terms, public opinion has played a relatively limited role in the national security policy process—with a few notable exceptions. One of these exceptions is that, during periods not characterized by a single overriding security concern, public opinion can make the formulation of clear priorities and a coherent agenda problematic. Some have argued that this was characteristic of the 1990s.[11] Public opinion can also become powerful when particular national security policy issues become significant due to their perceived cost. The public's role and interest in American national security policy, for example, took a dramatic turn in spring 1968, when the casualties of the Vietnam War received significant publicity after the Tet offensive.[12] As a more recent example, public opinion may prove to be influential in shaping continued U.S. involvement in Iraq, which began with the U.S.-led invasion in 2003. Polls taken in April 2007 show that 64% of Americans disapproved of the president's handling of the war, 59% of Americans believed that the United States had made a mistake in going to war in Iraq, and 50% believed that the war had become hopeless.[13] Such public opinion data as these make it more difficult for the president to exercise leadership.

An influential study of past U.S. popular support for war policy "demonstrates the importance of leadership and objective events and conditions in the level of the public's commitment to an ongoing military operation."[14] This study suggests that the most important sources of influence on U.S. public opinion during a war will be the actual progress of events and prospects for overall success, as well as the extent to which national leaders are united or divided on war policy. In turn, public opinion will affect the future actions of elected leaders. The government both affects and is affected by many different voices over time.[15]

When the public becomes engaged in national security issues, Congress tends to respond with increased involvement in the national security policy process. For example, as the political salience of the Vietnam War grew in the late 1960s and early 1970s, many members of Congress became concerned with the erosion of congressional authority relating to the initiation and execution of the war. In response, Congress passed legislation specifically prohibiting the funding of U.S. efforts in portions of Southeast Asia, as well as the War Powers Act.[16] As the legislation prohibiting funding demonstrates, Congress can shape ongoing military operations through its power of the purse. However, a prohibition on funding is a blunt instrument and a difficult one to wield when U.S. armed forces are already in combat. As for the War Powers Act, though its original purpose was to ensure that Congress and the president would share in making decisions that could get the United States involved in armed hostilities, assessments of its actual impact are mixed at best.[17] (For more on the issue of Congress and the War Powers Act, see Chapter 5.)

Public interest in U.S. military operations has varied widely, particularly in the last thirty years. Some interventions, such as Panama in 1989 and Desert Storm in 1991, attracted sustained public scrutiny, while others, such as Bosnia in the mid- to late 1990s, attracted only moderate and fleeting public interest. Despite these variations, the potential importance of public opinion in national security policy is something U.S. policy makers cannot afford to neglect.

Primacy of Domestic Affairs

Throughout U.S. history, domestic affairs have generally taken priority over foreign and security policy. To some extent, this has been a product of good fortune and circumstance. For much of the nation's history, great distances and ocean barriers made physical security a matter that could largely be taken for granted. The fact that British sea power was committed to preserving the status quo in North America for most of the nineteenth century was further reason for complacency. In addition, much of early American history took place during the century of unprecedented world peace from the Congress of Vienna in 1815 to the outbreak of World War I in 1914. For Americans, of course, there was the bloody domestic experience of the Civil War midway through that period, and there were also several great power wars abroad. Relatively speaking, however, the world was generally peaceful, and there was no general war among the great powers. Though few Americans gave much thought to the exceptional nature of this era, the extended period of peace allowed Americans to focus almost exclusively on things close to home—continental expansion and consolidation of hemispheric interests.

Although domestic affairs have traditionally taken precedence, there have been sporadic reversals of this sentiment. The Spanish-American War began a period of expansion into the Caribbean and the Pacific and marked a shift in the foreign involvement of the United States. The size of the U.S. army almost doubled from 1898 to 1901, as the United States emerged from the "Splendid Little War" as a great power with limited imperial possessions in both the Pacific and the Caribbean. These holdings were unrelated, however, to the impulse to that drew the United States into World War I. Violation of American rights as a neutral power, especially the sinking of the *Lusitania* by German submarines in 1915 and revelation of German plots in Mexico, finally ended a great debate over America's involvement in a European war. The United States entered World War I in 1917 as an "associated power" of the Allies.

Following World War I, America tried again to turn its back on the world outside the Western Hemisphere, rejecting Wilson's hope for the League of Nations, pushing for rapid disarmament, and renouncing war "as an instrument of national policy" in the Kellogg-Briand Pact of 1928. Americans focused on a return to "normalcy"—that is, getting on with domestic concerns. The Great Depression in late 1929 and the 1930s ensured that public attention would remain riveted on internal problems. Meanwhile, the United States sought to legislate itself out of foreign political entanglements through the Neutrality Acts of 1935, 1936, and 1937, which barred sales or shipments of munitions to belligerent nations. A popular "lesson" derived from World War I was that the United States had been unwittingly dragged into war by the deceit and trickery of European diplomats. The response: "Never again!"

Dissociation and Depreciation of Power and Diplomacy

To Americans, not only does normalcy refer to the primacy of domestic affairs, but it also reflects a belief that tranquility is the normal condition of the world order. This is not surprising when one recalls that, until the twentieth century, most of the American experience had been peaceful. In addition to history, the political philosophy that informed the founding of the United States also encouraged a belief that order is the norm. American political heritage has been strongly influenced by the age of Enlightenment and particularly by John Locke, whose basic precepts were well known to the Founding Fathers of the United States and were important in both the American Revolution and in the framing of the Constitution.[18] Locke conceived of the state of nature as a condition of peace, mutual assistance, and preservation.[19] He posited the ability of people to arrive at a conception of "the right" through their innate humanity, reflecting a degree of trust in the rationality and even goodness of human beings. Rational people would not want war. Therefore, states that adequately represent the will of their peoples could and should resolve their differences through discussion and compromise.

Americans have tended to ignore the contrary views of an earlier English philosopher, Thomas Hobbes, who wrote in *Leviathan* that, in the state of nature, a person's life is "solitary, poor, nasty, brutish, and short."[20] Without a central controlling power, there would exist a war "of every man against every man," a war in which there would be no industry, no culture, and no real society.[21] Also lacking a common power over them, states interact much like individuals in the state of nature:

> In all times, kings and persons of sovereign authority, because of their independence are in continued jealousies, and in the state and posture of gladiators; having their weapons pointing, and their eyes fixed on one another; that is, their forts, garrisons, guns upon the frontiers of their kingdoms; and continual spies upon their neighbors; which is a posture of war.[22]

States must constantly seek power to secure themselves, and therefore the normal state of affairs among them is actual war or an ever-present possibility that war will break out.

Embracing Locke and rejecting Hobbes, the traditional American view is that diplomacy should represent a process of ironing out differences through discussion, with eventual agreement based on rational accommodation of reasonable interests.[23] In this view, power in relation to diplomacy is at best largely irrelevant and at worst immoral. Further, diplomacy became depreciated in many American minds because of diplomats' longstanding reputation in the Western world for deviousness, duplicity, and secrecy.

As noted above, both during and after World War I, the opinion was widely held that secret dealings of diplomats were largely responsible for that war.[24] Committed to this view, Wilson was largely instrumental in the development of a new diplomatic procedure for "registering" and publishing treaties. "Open covenants, openly arrived at" became his credo. But the principles of open methods "almost wrecked diplomacy on the shoals of impotence."[25] With public negotiations often proving non-productive, little wonder that politicians have often laced formal instruments of agreement and their public statements with platitudes and left important details to secret exchanges. President Jimmy Carter relearned this lesson in the 1970s; his promises to return to open diplomacy proved short lived as he encountered the realities of power politics.

Idealism

The Judeo-Christian ideals and the philosophy of the Enlightenment embedded in the Western political heritage have affected not only American values and goals but also the means Americans typically embrace for attaining national goals. Humanity's presumed innate goodness and natural preferences for peace have tended to condition the American approach to issues of national security.

The standards by which Americans judge the world have been constructed quite organically out of their own experience. By the early twentieth century, the United States had become not only a great power but also a relatively satiated power enjoying phenomenal economic growth and social harmony. The United States had become a status quo country, its people essentially satisfied with life as they knew it, holding their condition of peace and harmony at home as the ideal for rational people everywhere. They believed in the virtues of democracy and took it for granted that democracy should be viewed as beneficial and a meaningful goal by all people throughout the world.[26]

Given this experience and the important role of religion in the origins of the republic, it was only natural that the American people early on developed a sense of mission that was idealistic, messianic, and hopeful of divine favor for national aspirations.[27] From the time of the Puritan theologian Cotton Mather (1663–1728) forward, Americans have tended to borrow biblical metaphor and to view their country as a "city on a hill," a beacon for all to see and emulate. In the 1840s, in an article on the Mexican War, Albert Gallatin provided a classic statement of the prevailing sense of mission:

> Your mission is to improve the state of the world, to be the "model republic" to show that men are capable of governing themselves, and that the simple and natural form of government is that which also confers most happiness on all, is productive of the greatest development of the intellectual faculties, above all, that which is attended by the highest standard of private and political virtue and morality.[28]

This sense of mission arose again in the 1880s, this time to check the baser rationales of American imperialism. It held back outright imperialist designs in Hawaii and in the Caribbean until 1898, when its defenders were overcome by the patriotic fervor of the Spanish-American War. This messianic drive reappeared in 1917 as a national sense of responsibility to save democracy in Europe. Wilson became its champion, taking the lead after the war to form the League of Nations. It gave short-lived impetus to the "Good Neighbor Policy" in Latin America in the 1930s and helped give birth to the concept and realization of the United Nations and the Marshall Plan after World War II. Even during times when the sense of mission was undercut by the forces of realism or imperialism, the leaders of such forces clothed their designs in terms of American ideals. They knew that the American self-image was a powerful block to any program expressed purely in terms of power or narrow material gain.

For much of the twentieth century, many Americans have been preoccupied with a long series of projects for shaping a better international system and for returning the world to the natural order of peace and harmony. These Americans have often rested their hopes on various formal legal codes and international institutions. In addition, a common perception of the proper American role has often been one of leadership by example rather than by major participation in cooperative international projects. Many people continued to think that the sheer weight of American example would exert a decisive influence upon the rest of the world.[29] But, as will be pointed out later, this traditional idealism has increasingly given way in recent decades to the realization that, while they are still vital, ideals and examples by themselves are not enough.

Aversion to Violence and Implications for Military Policy

The Judeo-Christian gospel, which has been central in forming American values, teaches "Thou shalt not kill," and the liberal culture of Western civilization has applied that ideal to people in collective entities called nations. The Enlightenment philosophy of secular perfectionism further strengthened this belief, emphasizing that violence is not only morally wrong but irrational and unnatural. Despite counterexamples, such as immoral actions against Native American populations during continental expansion, Americans have generally been unwilling to consider war as anything other than a scourge. It kills, maims, and separates family and friends. War and preparedness for war also interrupt the routine cycle of self-directed materialism and prosperity.[30]

In the traditional American view, war and peace are viewed as polar opposites. The resort to war or threats of violence between nations are seen as aberrations within the normal, peaceful course of international affairs. With such a set of perceptions, many Americans have difficulty processing military theorist Carl von Clausewitz's statement that "war is merely the continuation of policy by other means."[31] War cannot be an instrument, in a typical American view, for it is a pathological aberration.

As a related point, peace has been viewed as the responsibility of civilian policy makers, and war is the province of the military. This dichotomy leads to the further notion that the military should have no peacetime function in policy making, and that civilian policy makers should not have detailed involvement in the execution of military operations.[32] As a consequence, until U.S. intervention in World War II, military policies were often formulated largely without knowledge of relevant political objectives or consequences, and political decisions were reached without professional military advice about military capabilities.[33] (For more on the role of the military in national security policy, see Chapter 8.)

Traditionally, the American approach to war has leaned on one main proposition. The United States should participate only in a *just war*—a "war fought either in self-defense or in collective defense against an armed attack."[34] Fighting in any other type of war is considered "unjust." Among other things, this proposition has historically ruled out preventive (striking an adversary who may become a future threat) or pre-emptive war (striking an opponent first who is clearly making preparations to attack you).[35] President Harry Truman made the point explicit: "We do not believe in aggressive or preventive war. Such war is the weapon of dictators, not of free democratic societies."[36]

Tied to the traditional devotion to the status quo in the international order, as noted previously, the American aversion to violence has also tended to deny the legitimacy of violent revolution against sitting governments. Somehow, Americans have been inclined to forget that their own founders were steeped in the Lockean philosophy, which recognized the legitimacy of "the right to rebel," and that the United States was itself born of revolution.

Unwisdom of Standing Military Forces

Given the traditional view, which sees no necessary connection between diplomacy and armed might and abhors violence, it is not surprising that until recently Americans have only in exceptional periods accorded much importance to the military. In fact, one could go even further and argue that American liberalism is fundamentally hostile to the military and its functions.[37] The distrust of large standing military forces within the United States dates back to the colonial era and the Revolutionary War. This distrust is partially related to fear of militarism, manifested in either the displacement of civilian government by the military or the imposition of military values, perspectives, and ideals on the rest of society. Unbridled militarism could become a threat to freedom and democracy.

In addition to concerns over militarism, Americans have also believed strongly that a military force of *citizen-soldiers*—citizens called to arms in times of crisis—would be sufficient to defend the nation, and in their hands freedom would be most secure. Problems in the employment of militia forces date back to the Revolutionary War, as emphasized by George Washington in his call for a "moderate, compact force, on a permanent basis," instead of militia forces.[38] Yet an almost unquestioning faith in these forces persisted. Indeed, it acquired reinforcement in the ability of the United States to call its militia to arms to fight victorious wars against foreign foes in 1812, 1846, 1898, 1917, and 1941.

Because America's wars were to be fought by citizen-soldiers, *conscription*, or a draft, in peacetime has generally been viewed as "un-American." This belief has also had the effect of limiting standing military forces over time. In wartime, conscription was used late in the Civil War and again in World Wars I and II. However, the first peacetime conscription law was not passed until September 1940. Even with substantial threats looming over the horizon, this legislation barely passed over substantial congressional opposition. Following World War II, in August 1945, Truman asked Congress for a peacetime draft for an indefinite period to replace overseas veterans. A two-year conscription bill was finally passed in June 1948 and was renewed thereafter each year until 1972.[39] This historical survey reveals that the United States has conscripted standing forces in the absence of a declared war during only about 10% of its existence.

Except in crisis, Americans traditionally have wished that the minimum essential military establishment would do whatever it had to do, but with the smallest possible diversion of public attention and funds. Once a crisis has passed, as indicated earlier, Americans have traditionally sought to demobilize as soon as possible. A dramatic first illustration was the hasty deactivation of the Continental Army in 1784. The Continental Congress directed the commanding officer:

> to discharge the troops now in the service of the United States, except twenty-five privates to guard the stores at Fort Pitt, and fifty-five privates to guard the stores at West Point and other magazines, with a proportionate number of officers; no officer to remain in service above the rank of captain.[40]

The rush to "bring the boys back home" after World War II was another dramatic example of this same phenomenon. In less than two years, the United States demobilized almost 11 million soldiers, sailors, and airmen, leaving a scattered residual force of about 10% of its wartime strength to safeguard the victories in Europe and Asia.

The Crusading Spirit

Because the United States rejects the notion of war as an extension of politics, it cannot logically use the military instrument to restore a balance of power, to protect economic interests abroad, or to fulfill any other mundane purpose. Instead, America goes to war as a last resort and in the name of moral principles—"to make the world safe for democracy" or "to end all wars." In the twenty-first century, this trend continues. The 2006 National Security Strategy argues, for example, that the country is at war not just to protect the security of the American people but also to address the "inseparable" priority of "promoting freedom as the alternative to tyranny and despair."[41] The United States gives its sons, daughters, and treasure only in righteous indignation or outrage and usually while claiming to serve purposes broader than its own national interest.

Although aversion to violence may be one of America's best characteristics, it also has the potential to spark moral outrage in response to the actions of others, which unleashes the crusading spirit. Because the crusading spirit can itself be a catalyst for violence, it is evident that America's worst characteristic (the crusading spirit) has sometimes been the other face of its best (aversion to violence). Yet Americans do not have a tradition of glorifying violence, per se. The problem has always been the relationship of ends to means: A cause that is noble enough justifies violent means. In retrospect, the sufficiency of some causes has been a matter of considerable debate among American historians and philosophers.

Consistent with American idealism, the crusading spirit considers war essentially in terms of good versus evil. To engender public support for war—to get the public to sustain the dangers and privation—policy makers often couch their causes in black-and-white terms. Atrocious behavior of U.S. enemies has often made it easy to explain and justify the outbreak of war in terms of the criminal conduct of an inhuman and perhaps degenerate foe.[42] This has obvious benefits for the war effort, but it is also very hard to turn off the public's emotions once they have been aroused. If the president mobilizes support for specific military interventions abroad, he or she may find later that options become restricted or foreclosed by the emotional stakes and simplified expectations of the public. It becomes difficult to fight a war for limited objectives when the process of limitation involves negotiating with ultimate evil, represented by the enemy. Once policy makers have advocated total victory, it tends to become a driving goal, and progress toward such a goal must be demonstrated. Protracted war with limited objectives tends to obscure victory. Highly competitive by nature, Americans do not relish tie games.[43] They want to win big, early, and quickly.

LURIE'S WORLD   P/39 Feb 28 '95

Copyright 1995 CARTOONEWS INTERNATIONAL Syndicate, N.Y.C., USA.
Reprinted with permission of Ranan Lurie.

Impatience

As just noted, the crusading spirit is marked by impatience and irritation with time-consuming complexity. Americans believe that with a little common sense and know-how, things can be done in a hurry.[44] Neither protracted, limited war nor costly, sustained military preparedness fit this temper. These traits are likely to produce public outcry for cessation of American involvement in a prolonged conflict demanding self-sacrifice that is inadequately related to any clear vision of overriding national interest. Such was the case in the Vietnam War, as well as the more modern example of Somalia in the early 1990s.

Impatience may mix with the American proclivity for retreat into domestic affairs to yield boredom with or aversion to national security affairs. As an example, although many would agree that the greatest direct military threat to the security of the United States is in the nuclear realm, Americans tend to ignore this danger. Despite occasional peaks of public attention to specific events, such as Libya's agreement to dismantle all components of its nonconventional weapons program in 2003, it is difficult to get public resolution behind longer term policies related to such issues as control over fissile materials in Russia.[45] Policy makers can expect to find it challenging to sustain public support for nonmilitary, nondramatic actions to counter efforts by rogue states to develop nuclear, chemical, and biological programs.[46]

Old Traditions and New Realities

The American experience since World War II has transformed some important aspects of the traditional American approach to national security. Driven by factors that have included relative U.S. power, the Cold War threat of the Soviet Union, the seemingly accelerating processes of globalization after the end of the Cold

War, and the rising importance of such transnational concerns as international terrorism, the sustained engagement of the United States abroad reflects a realization that Americans can no longer seek security by focusing on hemispheric concerns and otherwise pursuing isolation. A second area of transformation in the traditional American approach to national security relates to the salience given to military affairs. Important aspects of traditional attitudes toward the military that seem to have been transformed in the latter half of the twentieth and early part of the twenty-first centuries include higher public levels of trust in the military, the increased involvement of uniformed personnel in national security policy making, a willingness to devote continuing substantial resources to defense even in the absence of a declared war, an increased reliance on professional soldiers, and an expansion of the circumstances under which Americans are willing to use force abroad. A third area of transformation is an enhanced appreciation of the role of power in diplomacy and the increased salience of a multilateral approach to managing international affairs.

Although there has been change, there have also been important elements of continuity in American approaches to foreign policy and national security. Arguably, as briefly mentioned above, American tendencies toward idealism and the crusading spirit persist. The United States continues to explain its overseas military actions and foreign policies in terms that reflect moral concerns and purposes that are broader than merely American self-interest. Importantly, though the United States has remained engaged in global affairs for over sixty years, for many Americans the primacy of domestic concerns still persists.

Despite the continuing pull of old traditions, after World War II, Americans reluctantly and gradually came to accept the new role of the United States as a world power with global responsibilities. The specter of communism as a global challenge and the advent of Soviet nuclear capability destroyed Americans' traditional sense of continental security. Past reliance on geographical location and the U.S. military's capacity to protect the physical integrity of the North American homeland gave way to an assumption that the security of the United States depended upon the balance of power and the role played by actors operating beyond the Western Hemisphere. This belief that events and developments around the world are relevant to U.S. security and prosperity has remained a basic underpinning for American foreign and national security policy during the more than six decades since World War II.[47]

Changes in the American Approach to Military Affairs. The series of post–World War II changes in the nation's approach to military affairs, mentioned in the previous section, deserve further examination. First, although distrust of the military was an important part of early American experience, U.S. confidence in the American military as an institution is now quite strong. In fact, a 2008 poll showed the military to be the institution in the United States in which the public had its greatest confidence. Survey data reveals that 71% of Americans had confidence in the military as an institution, while the next highest institution was small business, at 60%. The presidency and Congress were at 26% and 12%, respectively.[48] The military has topped this poll since 1987, and during the decade prior to that was either at the top or displaced only by "the church or organized religion."[49] In fact, the position of the military in American society today has even caused some to write with concern about the phenomenon of a "new American militarism."[50] As a smaller and far from representative portion of U.S. society serves in uniform, Americans have come to have increasing respect for an institution that they generally know less and less about.

A second change relates to the traditional American tendency to isolate the military from decisions about war and peace. The systematization of the role of the U.S. military in the national security process, which began during World War II, continued to grow after victory in 1945. The National Security Act of 1947 signaled an enduring conceptual overhaul, because, through its provisions, military views became an inherent part of overall defense and policy planning. A new organization, the National Security Council, was established to determine at the highest level of government the relationships between national objectives and military policy in peacetime and in war—and in the gray area in between. In the decades following, the national security policymaking process has been continuously adjusted by executive order and by legislation, including the highly significant Goldwater-Nichols Department of Defense Reorganization Act of 1986. Among its many important provisions is one that mandated that the president develop and set forth a national security strategy to guide the entire national security system according to a set of shared priorities. (For more on the organization of the national security policymaking system over time, see Chapters 3 and 10.)

A third change has been to the traditional American aversion to devoting significant resources to national security. From the 1950s through the 1980s, the Soviet threat drove Americans to allocate a substantial share of the nation's wealth to defense. Although the armed forces faced significant budget stringency in the years following the Vietnam War, the last few years of the Carter administration again saw budget growth. The budget then grew significantly during the Reagan years, from $359 billion in fiscal year (FY) 1980, before Reagan took office, to $486 billion in FY 1988. With the subsequent demise of the Soviet threat worldwide, Americans began to expect a peace dividend. President George H. W. Bush began downsizing the military as well as cutting the budget during his administration, and these cuts were accelerated during the early years of the Clinton administration. However, the end of the second Clinton administration again saw defense authorizations on the rise. During FY 2000, the second of two years in a row of budget increases, defense spending was $290 billion. After the terrorist attacks of 9/11, George W. Bush dramatically increased defense spending. The annual defense budget in FY 2007 reached $603 billion.[51] Though this amount does not represent a high proportion of U.S. gross domestic product in historical terms—the number is approximately 4%—it does reflect the largest single category of discretionary spending in the U.S. federal budget. By some necessarily imprecise calculations, it is also close to the military expenditures of the rest of the world combined.[52] Although, there have been important fluctuations in defense spending since the end of World War II, when the first century and half of the country's existence is compared with the last six decades, it is clear that Americans have become consistently willing to make significant investments in standing military forces even during times of ostensible peace.

A fourth change has been to U.S. military manpower policy, which shifted significantly during the Nixon administration and has remained essentially constant since. In 1968, during his first presidential campaign, Richard Nixon announced his intention to end the draft and to create an all-volunteer force. The debate in American society and in Congress on this was wide ranging and reflected views on the Vietnam War, the duties of citizens, and conceptions of fairness as they related to conscription. Nevertheless, appropriate legislation was ultimately passed, and the last conscript left the force in November 1974. Since that date, the United States has relied on professional, often long-serving volunteers to constitute its standing military forces. Though by the early twenty-first century the all-volunteer force has become widely accepted, there are still recurring concerns about the separation of the military from the society it serves and the relative merits of compulsory military service.[53]

A final change in traditional American attitudes toward military policy relates to the conditions under which the United States is willing to use force abroad. There are three important trends here. First, as mentioned above in relation to the crusading spirit, the United States has tended to articulate its reasons for war in terms of moral principles and to have therefore sought total victory over unjust enemies. But the period after World War II saw the country repeatedly engaged in limited wars for limited purposes in such places as Korea in the 1950s and Vietnam in the 1960s and early 1970s. To some extent, the idea of limited war in these conflicts reflected limited U.S. interests, which, accordingly, limited the means that the United States was willing to bring to bear. However, the limitations also reflected recognition of the importance of preventing a broader conflagration that could bring the United States into direct armed conflict with the Soviet Union.

The motivations for armed intervention have also evolved. In the past, war has been seen as only justified in the event of an attack upon the United States or in support of collective defense in response to an act of aggression. This latter justification can, in part, explain U.S. leadership in the Gulf War in 1991, which was in response to Iraq's invasion of Kuwait. However, new justifications for the use of force have arisen since the end of the Cold War. Internal conflict involving massive humanitarian disasters (Somalia, Haiti, and Bosnia in the 1990s) and state sponsorship of terrorist attacks (Afghanistan in 2001) have been seen as justifying armed intervention.[54] Importantly, the U.S. aversion to preventive war may also be evolving.[55] The 9/11 terrorist attacks appear to have altered perceptions of acceptable risk among key national security policy makers; waiting for an attack to occur prior to responding was no longer seen to be acceptable. As stated in the 2002 National Security Strategy:

> We must be prepared to stop rogue states and their terrorist clients before they are able to threaten or use weapons of mass destruction against the United States and our allies and friends. . . . in an age where the enemies of civilization openly and actively seek the world's most destructive technologies, the United States cannot remain idle when dangers gather.[56]

This statement constitutes a portion of the intellectual justification for what many observers characterize as a U.S. preventive war against Iraq in 2003. A second portion of the justification was the conviction that the regime of Saddam Hussein simply could not be trusted and that the key to lasting peace was total regime change from dictatorship to democracy. Whether the options of preventive or preemptive war have become an enduring component of the American approach to national security remains to be seen.

Changing U.S. Approaches to Diplomacy and Engagement.   Several facets of the U.S. approach to diplomacy and international engagement were also transformed in the post–World War II era. A first is that the historical American depreciation of the relationship between power—to include military force—and diplomacy has receded. Secretary of State Henry Kissinger during the Nixon administration and Secretary George Shultz during the Reagan administration, among others, sought to use this relationship to further U.S. interests. In a 1984 speech, Shultz argued that "power and diplomacy are not alternatives. They must go together, or we will accomplish very little in this world." Shultz acknowledged an American tendency to believe that diplomacy and military options were "distinct alternatives" but saw this viewpoint as expressing a flawed understanding of international politics.[57]

A second important change relates to a historical tendency toward unilateralism and wariness of foreign commitments, which was sometimes accompanied by the idealistic belief that the force of American example would be enough to bring about desired changes in the nature of world affairs. Speaking broadly, the approach of the United States to international affairs after World War II has been explicitly multilateral; that is, the United States has explicitly sought to address challenges in international affairs in cooperation with other states. On issues of security, the United States participated in the formation of the United Nations (UN) in 1945, the foundation of the North Atlantic Treaty Organization (NATO) in 1949, and an expanding set of bilateral and regional security relationships throughout the next several decades. On issues associated with the international economy, the United States was a key player in the Bretton Woods Agreement in 1944, which planted the seeds for the formation of international institutions of economic governance in the areas of postconflict reconstruction, economic development, finance, and trade. As it fostered these agreements and participated in the resulting international institutions, the United States was agreeing to be bound by international commitments while also laying the groundwork for exercising leadership—at least among a significant number of the countries of the world—through consent.[58]

Though U.S. multilateralism has varied in degree and specific manifestation in the more than six decades since World War II, it nevertheless marks a significant departure from early American history. In the latter half of the twentieth century, there was an enduring consensus among national security policy makers that it would be easiest to secure American liberty and security within a rule-governed system, even if freedom of action were to be somewhat constrained. In the early years of the twenty-first century, many have seen the administration of George W. Bush as straying from the multilateralism that has characterized much of U.S.

foreign policy since World War II. High-profile examples included U.S. decisions to reject the Kyoto Protocol on global warning, the International Criminal Court, and a new protocol to enhance enforcement of a biological weapons convention.[59] Despite these examples, many forms of U.S. multilateralism persist. The extent to which multilateralism will remain central to the U.S. approach to international affairs in the future remains to be seen. (For more on the role of multilateralism in U.S. foreign and national security policy, see Chapter 26.)

The Persistence of Idealism as an Influence on U.S. Policy Abroad.   Although there have been significant departures from traditional American approaches to national security in some areas, there are other trends that persist. For example, traditional faith in the rationality of people was expressed in U.S. efforts to create the UN in 1945. Yet other agreements—military alliances formed during the next several decades—hedged the bet on rationality as far as communists were concerned. In part, too, American idealism was revived in the rebuilding of a shattered Europe through the Marshall Plan and in the impulse to foster economic development through foreign assistance. However, although these initiatives were partially rooted in idealism, they were also integral to the U.S. policy of containing global communism through military and economic measures.

This mixture of idealism and pragmatic concern for U.S. national security remains characteristic of the U.S. approach to the world in the twenty-first century. For example, the traditional American desire for moral clarity may help to partially explain the approach of the administration of George W. Bush to diplomacy. This administration at times avoided rewarding "bad" actors, such as North Korea, Syria, and Iran, by refusing to accept bilateral talks.[60] A mixture of idealism and pragmatism is also evident in the National Security Strategy of 2006:

> The goal of our statecraft is to help create a world of democratic, well-governed states that can meet the needs of their citizens and conduct themselves responsibly in the international system. This is the best way to provide enduring security for the American people.[61]

In other words, what is beneficial for the world is also in accordance with both American values and American security interests.

In addition to idealism, a second American tendency that still persists to some extent relates to the primacy of domestic affairs. This point should not be overstated and is in fact challenged by some of the points made above: the perception of many Americans that the United States must be globally engaged to preserve its prosperity and security, the willingness of Americans to devote significant national treasure to defense even in the absence of declared war, and perhaps also U.S. willingness to use force abroad for primarily humanitarian purposes. However, as is the case with many countries, domestic politics will remain important and often play a primary role.[62]

One example of the primacy of domestic affairs may be the fate of George H. W. Bush in his presidential re-election bid in 1992. Although the 1991 Gulf War led to a quick and decisive victory, and the president's consequent poll numbers soared, he still lost office. Clinton's winning 1992 campaign slogan, "It's the economy, stupid," illustrates that, although national security is important, domestic affairs often take priority. Similarly, in the 2000 election, George W. Bush ran and won on a platform of modest foreign policy, including decreasing American involvement in nation building. Even after the terrorist attacks of 2001 and during ongoing military operations in Afghanistan and Iraq, a 2006 survey on U.S. foreign policy attitudes found that 55% of Americans felt that the government should be paying more attention to domestic issues.[63] Of course, much depends on exactly how questions are asked. Another poll in 2007 found that most Americans (66%) thought that the war in Iraq should be one of the top issues dealt with by the president and Congress, followed by the health care (20%) and the economy (14%).[64] Still, given the volatility of public opinion, the tendency to give primacy to domestic affairs seems to be a natural one to which Americans will return whenever circumstances permit.

Discussion Questions

1. How would you describe the traditional dispositions of Americans with regard to national security policy?

2. What is *public opinion*? How important is it today in national security policy formulation?

3. How could public opinion both enhance and inhibit an effective national security policy?

4. How have the ideas of Locke and Hobbes been reflected in American national security policy? Which school of thought seems more prevalent in today's security environment?

5. If Americans are traditionally averse to war, how can you explain the fact that the United States has been involved in numerous wars and maintains a large military establishment?

6. How would you describe the historical role of the military in peacetime national security policy? How has it changed?

7. What has been the traditional American approach to diplomacy? How has it changed?

8. Do you believe that the traditional American perspective that places primacy on domestic affairs is still relevant today?

9. Does *preventive* or *pre-emptive* describe the U.S. attack on Iraq?

Recommended Reading

Bacevich, Andrew J. *The New American Militarism: How Americans Are Seduced by War.* New York: Oxford University Press, 2005.

Baum, Matthew A. *Soft News Goes to War: Public Opinion and American Foreign Policy in the New Media Age.* Princeton, NJ: Princeton University Press, 2003.

Boot, Max. *The Savage Wars of Peace: Small Wars and the Rise of American Power.* New York: Basic Books, 2003.

Elshtain, Jean Bethke. *Just War Against Terror: The Burden of American Power in a Violent World.* New York: Basic Books, 2003.

Finnemore, Martha. *The Purpose of Intervention: Changing Beliefs About the Use of Force.* Ithaca: Cornell University Press, 2003.

Fukuyama, Francis. *America at the Crossroads.* New Haven: Yale University Press, 2006.

Gaddis, John Lewis. *Strategies of Containment.* New York, Oxford University Press, 1981.

———. *The United States and the End of the Cold War.* New York: Oxford University Press, 1992.

———. *Surprise, Security, and the American Experience.* Cambridge, MA: Harvard University Press, 2004.

Haass, Richard N. *The Reluctant Sheriff: The United States After the Cold War.* New York: The Council on Foreign Relations, 1997.

Hobbes, Thomas. *Leviathan.* New York: Collier Books, 1962.

Huntington, Samuel P. *The Soldier and the State.* Cambridge, MA: Harvard University Press, 1957.

McDougall, Walter. *Promised Land, Crusader State: America's Encounter with the World Since 1776.* Boston: Houghton Mifflin, 1997.

Mead, Walter Russell. *Special Providence: American Foreign Policy and How It Changed the World.* New York: Routledge, 2002.

National Commission on Terrorist Attacks. *The 9/11 Commission Report: Final Report of the National Commission on Terrorist Attacks upon the United States.* New York: W. W. Norton, 2004.

Rosenthal, Joel H. *Ethics and International Affairs: A Reader.* Georgetown: Georgetown University Press, 1999.

Russett, Bruce M. *Controlling the Sword: The Democratic Governance of National Security.* Cambridge, MA: Harvard University Press, 1990.

Shy, John W. *A People Numerous and Armed: Reflections on the Military Struggle for American Independence.* Ann Arbor: University of Michigan Press, 1990.

Silverstone, Scott A. *Preventive War and American Democracy.* London: Routledge, 2007.

Walzer, Michael. *Just and Unjust Wars.* 4th ed. New York: Basic Books, 2006.

Weigley, Russell F. *The American Way of War.* New York: Macmillan, 1973.

Internet Resources

Center for Strategic and Budgetary Assessments (CSBA), Defense Budget Studies, www.csbaonline.org

The Gallup Poll, www.gallup.com

PollingReport.com, www.pollingreport.com

Public Agenda, *Confidence in U.S. Foreign Policy Index*, www.publicagenda.org/foreignpolicy/index.cfm

3

The Evolution of American National Security Policy

National security strategy and military structure are shaped by the interactions of a number of influences, many of which defy precise identification. However, there are three principal categories of variables through which the evolution of strategy and military structure can largely be traced. They are international political and military developments, domestic priorities, and technological advancements. This chapter follows these variables through the evolution of national security policy since World War II, helping to reveal patterns of continuity and change. A sound appreciation of today's prospects and challenges must take into account this history, as it goes far in explaining today's national security policy process and the capabilities and limitations of current U.S. military structure.

Before proceeding, a brief clarification of terms is necessary. As used here, the term *strategy* refers to an "idea or set of ideas for employing the instruments of national power in a synchronized and integrated fashion to achieve theater, national, and/or multinational objectives."[1] A national security strategy provides the conceptual framework within which a state pursues its security. *Military structure*, in contrast, refers to the size, composition, disposition, and capabilities of the armed forces. In an ideal situation, military structure would provide national policy makers with capabilities optimized to support the achievement of their strategic vision. The term *national policy* is used to refer to "a broad course of action or statements of guidance adopted by the government at the national level in pursuit of national objectives."[2] Policy can therefore relate to either matters of strategy or matters of structure, depending on the issues at hand.

The National Security Environment

International Political and Military Developments.   The international environment is an important and constantly changing influence on U.S. policy. U.S. strategy is largely a response to perceived threats to American interests and objectives that exist in the international arena. The United States is secure to the extent that it is not in danger of having to sacrifice core values, such as national independence or territorial integrity, if it wishes to avoid war and to the extent that it is able to protect those values if war breaks out.[3] The perception of international threats to U.S. core values and interests is the basis for the formulation and execution of national security strategy.

One important characteristic of the international environment is the presence or absence of alliances. The defense efforts of friendly and allied states help to define U.S. security problems and the type and size of the U.S. effort required. The capability of the United States to pursue national security objectives is also conditioned by the impact of nonaligned states or nonstate actors. (For more on the role of nonstate actors in the international system, see Chapter 25.)

Domestic Politics.   A nation's security policy is also heavily influenced by domestic politics. At a minimum, the internal environment determines the amount of effort that a society will devote to foreign and defense policy.[4] Domestic goals have a great impact on the development of a state's security policy and its allocation of resources. In the United States, the impact of domestic politics is seen most directly in the budgetary process, but it is also felt in such related areas as military manpower policy. Defense budgets and programs may not determine strategy, but national security options are heavily conditioned by the nature and extent of the resources available.

Domestic (and international) media organizations also play important roles in shaping U.S. national security policy. The tremendously varied media sources currently available to Americans provide continuous access to information and images from throughout the world. Although members of the media do not make national security policy, they can influence the agenda and frame issues for debate.

Technological Change.   The impact of technological advance upon security concerns and calculations is enormous. One need only look at the carnage of World War I to see the results of policy not keeping pace with technology. A century of relative peace in Europe had left military strategy and tactics largely as they were at the time of the Congress of Vienna, yet there had been a century of unparalleled technological advancement between 1815 and 1914. The military plans of 1914 simply were not adequate for the proper employment of existing technological capabilities, and the bloody stalemate that developed on the Western front was due in large part to an inability to adapt military strategy and tactics to the new realities of war.

What is possible in American national security is in considerable part determined by the technological capabilities of both the United States and its adversaries. For much of the era following World War II, the security of the United States and its allies relied in large part upon the strength and invulnerability of

U.S. strategic nuclear weapons.[5] Perceptions abroad of U.S. capability and willingness to employ its vast nuclear arsenal are still relevant to deterring potential threats from other states today. However, the rise of nonstate armed groups that seek these or other weapons of mass destruction (WMD) and yet are not easily deterred by threats of U.S. nuclear retaliation has changed the nature of the challenge that they pose to national security. Nonnuclear technological advances, such as "smart weapons" and revolutionary improvements in information technology, can also have great effects on national security. One need look no further than the impressive coalition victory in the 1991 Gulf War or the rapid defeat of Iraq's armed forces in 2003 to see the tremendous advantages advanced technology can provide.

Strategy and Structure

National security strategies are largely implemented by military force structures. Because international relations and domestic politics are intertwined, national security policy (which comprises both strategic and structural policies) exists in two worlds. Decisions about strategy are made largely in response to perceived threats in the international environment; they deal primarily with commitments, deployment and employment of military forces, and the readiness and development of military capabilities. Structural decisions are more strongly influenced by domestic politics and deal primarily with the budget and decisions on defense personnel, materiel, and organization.[6] The two types of decisions interact at all levels. Strategic decisions determine required force structures, yet the resources made available through structural decisions limit strategic options. Moreover, ongoing programs created through structural decisions can have a dynamic of their own in shaping future strategy.

The closely intertwined yet ever-changing relationship between strategy and structure aptly describes the dominant theme in the evolution of American national security policy. This chapter begins with the period immediately following World War II and progresses through each subsequent presidential administration, focusing on the relationship between strategy and structure and how international political and military developments, domestic priorities, and technological advances have affected this relationship for more than six decades.

President Harry S. Truman and the Origins of Containment

The Return to Normalcy, 1945–1946.   The end of World War II saw the United States emerge as the most powerful nation on earth. Its homeland was untouched by war, and its enormous industrial potential had served as the "arsenal of democracy" for itself and its allies. The collapse of Germany and Japan led to visions of a prolonged peace implemented through the collective security machinery of the new United Nations (UN). Technologically, the United States was also in an unchallengeable position. The U.S. creation and use of the atomic bomb was probably the single most important development affecting postwar international relations.[7]

With victory came enormous public and congressional pressure for the United States to demobilize its armies and bring the troops home. This domestic political pressure led to one of the most rapid demobilizations in history. On V-J Day, the Army had more than 8 million soldiers, but less than a year after the end of the war, it was down to less than 2 million.[8] From 1945 to 1947, the United States allowed its overall armed forces to decline from a wartime peak of 12 million soldiers, sailors, and airmen to a low of 1.4 million.[9]

This massive disarmament occurred even though the wartime alliance between the United States and the Soviet Union was being replaced by rapidly increasing tension. American policy makers, confronted with what they perceived to be aggressive Soviet intentions in Eastern Europe, Greece, Turkey, Iran, and the Far East, came to agree on the need for a tougher line. In 1947, U.S. diplomat George Kennan expressed this emerging consensus when he advocated a policy of *containment*: "The main element of any United States policy toward the Soviet Union must be that of a long-term, patient but firm and vigilant containment of Russian expansive tendencies."[10]

Containment became the theoretical framework that structured American strategic policy for the next four decades. Opposition to communist expansion became the fundamental principle of American foreign policy. Despite disagreements over the means to achieve this policy, there was little disagreement on the goal itself. The policy of containment led in turn to the development of the strategy of *deterrence*.

The New Strategy and the Old Military Structure.   Successful implementation of the policy of containment required ready forces sufficient to deny the Soviets the ability to expand their empire. For this purpose, mobilization potential was clearly less useful than having existing forces already at hand and ready to meet immediate needs. In December 1947, Secretary of Defense James Forrestal listed the "four outstanding military facts of the world" as (1) the predominance of Russian land power in Europe and Asia, (2) the predominance of American sea power, (3) U.S. exclusive possession of the atomic bomb, and (4) American superior production capacity.[11] The ground and air units of the United States and its allies were inadequate to contain the Soviet Union's conventional force capabilities, and the United States lacked adequate doctrine for countering this Soviet superiority with its tiny atomic arsenal. The United States could threaten the Soviet homeland with atomic attack if Soviet armies marched into Western Europe, but the atom bomb was of little help in other defense tasks, such as preserving the integrity of Iran, deterring attack on Korea, or suppressing guerrillas in Greece.[12] Conventional ground and air power seemed essential for these latter tasks, yet the U.S. force structure was weakest in precisely those respects.

Continued Reliance on Mobilization.   Implementing the policy of containment raised the difficult problem of how to deal with domestic political constraints on the size of the military effort. Overriding a presidential veto, Congress passed a general income tax reduction bill in early 1948, thereby limiting the revenue available for domestic and military expenditures. Despite the president's requests, no substantial tax increases were approved until after the outbreak of the Korean War. Furthermore, because President Harry Truman was determined to balance the budget, the administration imposed a ceiling on military expenditures consonant with the reduced resources available. Domestic political priorities ensured that there would be inadequate monies for the forces-in-being that were assessed as needed to contain Soviet power. Thus, by default, reliance on mobilization continued.

A second constraint on the successful implementation of the policy of containment was the doctrinal orientation of the military. American military thinking was still preoccupied with preparations to mobilize forces to win a major war if one should occur.[13] The Army continued to insist that World War III would be similar to the war it had just prosecuted so successfully.[14] Although the Air Force and the Navy believed the weapons of World War II were obsolete and began to push for new strategic systems, in the immediate postwar years the concept of deterrence by forces-in-being had little place in their military planning.[15] The goals of each of the armed services had been set prior to the end of World War II, and because there was no unified force design or budgetary process, each service became locked into its own vision of its future role and mission. As political scientist Samuel Huntington observed, "The two great constraints of effective military planning, the doctrinal heritage from the past and the pressure of domestic needs, combined to produce a serious gap between military policy and foreign policy."[16]

In response to these challenges, the Truman administration secured passage of the National Security Act of 1947. Among other things, the act separated the Air Force from the Army and consolidated the military services under the Department of Defense (DoD). In addition, the act empowered the new secretary of defense to, in theory, be able to neutralize service biases by crafting an overall strategic vision that the services would be required to support. However, despite a revision to the act in 1949 to give the secretary of defense more power, the service chiefs remained focused on their own agendas. Another key feature of the 1947 legislation was the creation of the National Security Council (NSC), which provided a potentially powerful tool for presidents to formulate and shape national security priorities.

The Truman Doctrine.   On March 12, 1947, Truman appeared before a joint session of Congress and outlined what he believed was the necessary U.S. response to communist pressure in Greece and Turkey. In what came to be known as the *Truman Doctrine*, the president argued that the United States must help other nations to maintain their political institutions and national integrity when threatened by aggressive attempts to overthrow them and institute totalitarian regimes. This was no more than a frank recognition, Truman declared, that totalitarian systems imposed their will on free people, by direct or indirect aggression, and undermined the foundations of international peace and hence the security of the United States.[17]

The Truman Doctrine represented a marked departure from the U.S. tradition of minimal peacetime involvement in international affairs. The doctrine set forth themes justifying American foreign involvements and initiated military and economic aid programs to nations resisting communist aggression. The justification it contained for American intervention in foreign lands was used repeatedly by subsequent administrations.[18]

The Marshall Plan.   *The Marshall Plan*, a massive U.S. economic aid program launched in 1948, was designed to help restore the war-shattered economies of Europe. American leaders believed that the ability of Europe to resist communist aggression was dependent on its rapid economic recovery.[19] The Marshall Plan, taken in conjunction with the Truman Doctrine, marked the emergence of the United States as a world power bent on promoting stability in international affairs. This heralded a new U.S. willingness to expend major resources and adopt an activist role in seeing that U.S. interests abroad were protected.

Events in 1948 and 1949 solidified the U.S. view of the communist threat. The forced communization of Czechoslovakia and the blockade of surface access routes to West Berlin, both occurring in 1948, intensified Western perceptions of the Soviet Union as an overtly hostile state. In 1949, two even more dramatic events affected the formulation of U.S. security strategy. In August, the Soviet Union exploded its first nuclear device. The U.S. monopoly on atomic weapons had been broken much sooner than anticipated by U.S. planners. In late 1949, the Communist Chinese completed the conquest of the mainland, creating the appearance of a monolithic communist adversary stretching from Central Europe across the length of the Asian continent.

NSC 68 and Its Implications.   The disturbing events of 1948–1949 highlighted inadequacies in U.S. military posture. Awareness of these shortcomings led to the first serious attempt to reconcile strategy with structure—that is, to balance the strategy of containment with a force designed to implement the tenets of the strategy. A joint committee of the State and Defense departments was instructed "to make an over-all review and reassessment of American foreign and defense policy."[20] The report, labeled NSC 68 and delivered to the NSC on April 1, 1950, advocated "an immediate and large scale build up in our military and general strength and that of our allies with the intention of righting the power balance and in hope that through means other than all out war we could induce a change in the nature of the Soviet system."[21] NSC 68 called for a substantial increase in defense expenditures, warning that the United States must be capable of dealing with both limited and all-out war. The problem was how to sell a substantial increase in the defense budget to an administration committed to a policy of economy and balanced budgets. The problem was solved on June 25, 1950, when North Korea invaded South Korea and overran the UN observers on the border between them.

War and Rearmament.   The invasion of South Korea provided the immediate crisis that generated public support for vastly increased defense spending. Expenditures for national security programs rose from $13 billion for FY 1950 to $50.4 billion in FY 1953.[22] Nevertheless, important differences of opinion remained within informed American circles concerning Soviet intentions in South Korea and elsewhere. Some felt the North Korean attack was part of a general Soviet plan for worldwide expansion, while others saw it as a feint designed to divert resources from Europe.[23] Despite these differences, Communist China's entry into the war in late 1950 solidified U.S. perceptions of an aggressive, monolithic communist threat to the Free World.

The outbreak of the war found the United States with an extremely limited conventional capability. The rearmament effort was characterized by three competing, but complementary purposes: (1) immediate prosecution of the Korean War, (2) creation of a mobilization base for the long term, and (3) development of active forces to balance Soviet strength and to deter further Soviet aggression.[24] In short, the war in Korea made rearmament possible, but rearmament was not directed solely at the problem of fighting the war. Forces were also developed for worldwide deterrence purposes.[25]

NATO: The Institutionalization of Containment.   Soviet political pressure on its neighbors, and the Soviet Union's very large conventional forces, caused widespread and increasing concern about the security of Western Europe. As a consequence, the United States deemed it necessary to enter into a peacetime alliance with foreign states and for the first time to deploy forces on the territory of allies in the absence of armed conflict. The North Atlantic Treaty was signed in April 1949, and the twelve signatories from Europe and North America agreed that an attack on one would be considered an attack on all. Europe became America's first line of defense; the North Atlantic Treaty Organization (NATO) was the expression of the U.S. effort to contain communism by military means.

Despite an initial goal of ninety NATO divisions (half active, half reserve) by 1954, deemed by experts and agreed upon by political leaders as necessary for conventional defense of Europe, it quickly became obvious that the goal would not be met. By 1952, European members of NATO, less fearful of Soviet aggression in Europe, began to reduce military budgets, cut terms of service for draftees, and stretch out arms procurements. NATO members subsequently approved a drastic reduction in force goals and came to rely heavily on the tactical and strategic nuclear weapons of the United States to deter Soviet aggression.

Conflicting Priorities.   With continuing casualties and costs, as well as a stalemated military situation, the American public became increasingly sour on the war in Korea. It also became evident that the war had not marked the beginning of a general Soviet assault on the West. Public resentment over military spending levels rose, and by 1952, the Truman administration made a marked shift toward domestic priorities. At the same time, however, it was accepted by U.S. policy makers and the public that the international communist threat to U.S. and European security was real and immediate. Acceptance of the strategy of containment and the necessity for forces-in-being to implement it reflected an acknowledgement of the realities of international and technological affairs. The challenge for President Dwight

Eisenhower, as he took office in 1953, was to reconcile these conflicting demands for increased spending for both domestic needs and enhanced defense.

The Eisenhower Administration, 1953–1960: Massive Retaliation and the New Look

From the outset, Eisenhower regarded the threat to U.S. security as dual—military and economic. The military threat posed by the communist powers was obvious, but Eisenhower also believed that continued high levels of defense spending threatened the stability of the U.S. economy and were, therefore, also significant long-term threats. Because the dual threat was a continuing one, domestic and military expenditures would have to be properly balanced for an extended period.

Domestic Priorities and Strategic Reassessment.   To preserve U.S. economic vitality, Eisenhower was determined to reduce military expenditures and balance the federal budget. An impasse developed between the administration and the military Joint Chiefs of Staff (JCS), who were committed to a substantial military buildup in line with NSC 68. The old JCS were replaced, and in May 1953 the new JCS assumed the task (even before they took office) of wrestling with difficult problems of strategic reassessment at which their predecessors had balked.

The NSC Planning Board, in a study labeled NSC 162, made an effort to define future national security policy in the broadest sense. The paper recommended the continuation of the policy of containment but with greater reliance on nuclear weapons and strategic air power and an expansion of capabilities to defend the continental United States from air attack. The JCS concluded its reassessment, which was called the Sequoia Study (named after the secretary of the Navy's yacht, upon which the final discussions had been held) and recommended further development of air defenses and strategic retaliatory forces, withdrawal of some U.S. forces overseas, creation of a mobile strategic reserve, reliance upon allies for their own defense buttressed by U.S. air and sea power, and strengthening of U.S. reserve forces.[26]

The Strategic Impact of Technology and the New Look.   In essence, technology provided the means by which Eisenhower escaped from the strategy versus structure box. American technological and numerical superiority in nuclear weapons systems provided strategic options that conceivably made possible the achievement of domestic goals. Technology, in the form of strategic nuclear air power and tactical nuclear weapons, would make worldwide containment affordable.

The Eisenhower *New Look* defense program made a number of assumptions about the international environment. It assumed that there would be no significant increase in international tensions and no significant change in the relationship between U.S. and Soviet power. The key aspect of the New Look was the decision to place very high reliance upon nuclear weapons and to threaten massive retaliation in response to aggression.[27] Strategic air power became the mainstay of the U.S. deterrent posture, and tactical nuclear weapons were to be used to replace the reduced levels of conventional forces in forward defense areas.

The critical strategic change was expressed by Secretary of State John Foster Dulles on January 12, 1954: "There is no local defense which alone will contain the mighty land power of the Communist world. Local defenses must be reinforced by the further deterrent of massive retaliation power."[28] Therefore, Dulles stated, the president had made the basic decision "to depend primarily upon a great capacity to retaliate instantly and by means and at places of our own choosing."[29] In sum, America would rely on nuclear weapons to meet even those military contingencies threatening less than general war. NATO members subsequently agreed to deploy tactical nuclear weapons in Western Europe and to authorize military planners to assume that nuclear weapons would be used in the event of hostilities.

Extending Containment. Extending the American military alliance system beyond NATO (and the earlier Organization of American States) became an integral part of containment strategy. Prior to the adoption of an explicit strategy of massive retaliation announced in 1954, the United States had already begun a process of expanding defense commitments worldwide with the goal of containing communism. One principal lesson of the Korean War, as perceived by U.S. policy makers in the 1950s, was that American disengagement and equivocation had tempted the communists to invade Korea. America's commitment to defend important friendly territories adjacent to communist countries must be made specific; the most obvious way to do so was through military alliances.

The network of alliances began to form soon after the outbreak of hostilities in Korea. In 1951, the United States negotiated a security treaty with Japan that guaranteed the defense of Japan and granted the United States military the right to maintain military bases in Japan. A similar mutual defense treaty was signed with the Philippines. Also in 1951, the United States signed the ANZUS Treaty with Australia and New Zealand, pledging U.S. support for the security of those two states. In 1953, following the armistice, Korea and the United States signed a security pact pledging consultation in the event of armed attack and establishing the disposition of land, sea, and air forces in and around the Republic of Korea. In 1954, the United States signed a treaty with Taiwan that called for joint consultation in the event of danger of armed attack and specified the disposition of U.S. forces on Taiwan and the Pescadores.

In 1954, the United States established the Southeast Asian Treaty Organization (SEATO) with Australia, France, New Zealand, Pakistan, the Philippines, Thailand, and the United Kingdom. Each of these members committed to "act to meet the common danger" in the event of hostilities in the treaty area. In addition to joining SEATO, the United States also sent millions of dollars in military aid to Indochina to help finance the French war with the Viet Minh. In 1954, as the French position in Vietnam became tenuous, the French government requested the commitment of American troops but was refused by Eisenhower.

In 1959, the Central Treaty Organization (CENTO), which the United States expressly supported but did not formally join, was also launched. The alliance, intended to prevent Soviet expansion southward, linked the UK, Turkey, Iran, and Pakistan. Additionally, the United States signed bilateral defense agreements with

Pakistan and Iran. Given the widespread concern in the United States about communist aggression, the presumption that American nuclear weapons could and would serve to deter both large and small aggressions, and the policy of a balanced budget, it appeared to make sense in the 1950s to strengthen governments on the periphery of the communist bloc by doing the following:

- Pledge U.S. support to prevent or stop communist-inspired aggression
- Provide military assistance to strengthen the defenses of governments bordering the communist bloc
- Provide economic or military assistance to preserve or to help create political and economic stability for governments that were allies in the anticommunist cause
- Train and support foreign troops in their own country because it was less expensive than maintaining American troops abroad
- Establish basing rights as the quid pro quo of assistance

In short, the United States included Asia in its ring of containment and, attempting to prevent another Korea, sought to knit the states of the region into a network of military alliances under U.S. leadership.

The New New Look, 1956.   In 1954, when the policy of massive retaliation was formally established, the United States possessed the ability to destroy the military forces of the Soviet Union with little likelihood of serious retaliatory damage in return. By 1956, however, this was no longer clearly the case. Major Soviet catch-up efforts and technological innovations had led to an arms spiral; in an astonishingly short time, mutual vulnerability to nuclear devastation had apparently become a fact.[30] The rapid growth of Soviet strategic nuclear power had undermined the New Look's two key assumptions: that the earlier ratio of Soviet-to-American nuclear power would not be radically altered and that U.S. nuclear retaliatory forces would deter both large and small aggressions. Even at the outset, the doctrine of massive retaliation had been criticized by analysts who argued that the threat of massive nuclear retaliation would not be effective in deterring local, ambiguous wars because it was not believable. Only conventional forces, they held, could deal effectively with such relatively low-level conflicts.

The administration began to look for a strategy that permitted greater flexibility. The resulting *New New Look* adjusted existing programs without increasing military expenditures. The dominant characteristics of the New New Look included (1) continuing efforts to stabilize military spending; (2) downgrading of mobilization, readiness, and reserve forces; (3) accepting that U.S. strategic retaliatory capability was sufficient, but only sufficient, to deter a direct attack on U.S. territory or equally vital interests; and (4) recognizing, if only grudgingly, the need to build and maintain capabilities for limited war.[31]

It should be noted that the New New Look continued to emphasize that tactical nuclear weapons were a credible means of waging limited war. Indeed, one of the major distinctions of the new approach was the direct mating of tactical nuclear weapons with the strategy of limited war.[32] Writing in the October 1957 issue of *Foreign Affairs*, Dulles explained that "in the future it may . . . be feasible to place less reliance upon deterrence of vast retaliatory power" because the "nations which are around the Sino-Soviet perimeter can possess an effective defense [through tactical nuclear warfare] against full-scale conventional attack."[33]

Eisenhower's programs were shaped by the twin pressures of Soviet and American technological achievement and an American economy that was plagued by both continuing recession and inflation. Largely as a result of inflation, defense costs were rising. Confronted with a choice between increasing the national debt and reducing military spending, the Eisenhower administration chose the latter. In constant dollar terms, military spending was less in 1960 than it had been in any year since 1951.[34]

The final years of the Eisenhower presidency saw a number of international and technological pressures brought to bear on U.S. national security policy. In August 1957, the Soviets announced the successful test of an intercontinental ballistic missile (ICBM). In October of that year, the Soviets launched the first artificial satellite, Sputnik, causing an intense reexamination of U.S. strategic programs. The Gaither Committee, appointed early in 1957 by Eisenhower to study a fallout shelter program for the United States, presented its report shortly after the launching of Sputnik. Defining its mandate very broadly, the committee recommended a substantial increase in the defense budget, aimed primarily at improving U.S. strategic posture.[35] Though the committee's recommendations were largely rejected, the discussion of strategic capabilities that it evoked helped provoke the "missile-gap" controversy that became an issue in the 1960 presidential campaign.

The Kennedy-Johnson Years, 1961–1968: Flexible Response

As the new decade began, changes in both the external environment and technology dictated a serious reappraisal of military strategy. The growth of Soviet nuclear capabilities cast increasing doubt upon the wisdom and credibility of U.S. retaliatory threats, and the missile-gap controversy raised questions about the adequacy of U.S. nuclear force levels. Western awareness of the increasingly bitter dispute between China and the Soviet Union aggravated the problem of deterrence as China came to be viewed as a potential power center and threat in its own right.

Changes in weapons technology and force structure also made a reexamination of U.S. policy imperative. Reliance on tactical nuclear weapons, particularly in Europe, was increasingly viewed as dangerous for two main reasons. First, in view of the relatively weakened U.S. strategic position, deterrence could fail. If it did, escalation to all-out nuclear war would be hard to check because there is no discernible firebreak between tactical and strategic nuclear weapons. Second, should a crisis arise, shortages of conventional forces created the ultimate dilemma of choosing between nuclear retaliation and inaction. Turbulence in the developing countries of the world also demonstrated the shortcomings of U.S. retaliatory strategy. The Soviet Union and China were giving military and economic assistance to "wars of national liberation" in Asia, Africa, and Latin America. Massive retaliation was inadequate to deal with these complexities. Just a few years earlier, technology was seen as a panacea capable of ensuring containment while limiting military spending. Now, however, the domestic political debate focused on the potential dangers of reliance on nuclear technology.

Military Structure and the McNamara Pentagon.   When Robert McNamara became President John Kennedy's secretary of defense in 1961, despite the goals of the National Security Act of 1947 and subsequent reforms, the missions of the country's armed services were still largely determined independently. Monies were allocated on a "fair share" basis, and each armed service developed programs within its budget constraints with little regard for what the others were doing. National strategies and priorities were supposedly set forth in an agreed NSC document called the Basic National Security Policy. However, this document was a vague compromise that provided little real guidance. General Maxwell Taylor summarized the document's weaknesses: "The sharp issues in national defense . . . have been blurred . . . the Basic National Security Policy document means all things to all people and settles nothing."[36] Given vague guidance, the armed services had a great deal of latitude to continue to develop their own programs.

McNamara, when he came into office, was appalled: "The Army planning, for example, was based, largely, on a long war of attrition, while the Air Force planning was based, largely, on a short war of nuclear bombardment."[37] Strategic nuclear programs were also developed independently by each service. For example, Navy briefings to McNamara in 1961 on the number of Polaris missile submarines it required never mentioned the existence of the U.S. Air Force or any of its strategic retaliatory forces. When the Air Force analyzed how many Minutemen missiles were required, it simply assumed that the number of Polaris submarines would remain constant.[38] McNamara was determined to control and rationalize the development of U.S. military forces. He received two instructions from the president: "Develop the force structure necessary to our military requirements without regard to arbitrary or predetermined budget ceilings. And secondly . . . procure it at the lowest possible cost."[39]

Before the formal elaboration of a new strategy, McNamara applied a number of "quick fixes" to the U.S. force structure. He accelerated the procurement schedule for the submarine-launched ballistic missile (the Polaris), doubled the production capacity for Minutemen ICBMs, and placed one-half of the bombers of the Strategic Air Command on a quick-reaction alert.[40] Improvements began immediately in airlift and sealift capabilities, and the Army, Marine Corps, and the tactical Air Forces were expanded.[41] McNamara's purpose was to increase U.S. combat strength measurably and quickly while developing a new military strategy.

Flexible Response.   The strategy of flexible response was developed to give the president the capability to respond effectively to any challenge with the appropriate level of force. Flexible response within the strategic nuclear posture provided policy makers the options of massive retaliation, limited nuclear countervalue (i.e., city) attacks, and counterforce strikes. The Kennedy and Johnson administrations greatly increased the strategic inventory dramatically, developing the capability to inflict "unacceptable damage" on the Soviet Union even after absorbing a surprise first strike.[42] At the other end of the force spectrum, it also focused on increased attention to counterinsurgency.

Though these changes were significant, it was in the area of conventional forces that the doctrine of flexible response differed most drastically from that of massive retaliation. To provide adequate options, conventional force capabilities had to be improved and modernized. The Army was increased from twelve to sixteen divisions, the Navy surface fleet was enlarged, and the reserves and National Guard were revitalized. Special operations forces were also enhanced. In general, the United States sought a "two-and-a-half" war posture—that is, the United States sought to be capable of fighting simultaneously a large-scale war in Europe, another sizable war somewhere else in the world, and a third, smaller-scale conflict.

American efforts to introduce flexible response doctrine into NATO initially encountered Allied resistance. Early reliance on conventional forces caused uneasiness among Europeans, who feared erosion of the nuclear deterrent. Whereas the Eisenhower administration had asserted that nuclear weapons might well be used, by the end of the Johnson administration, the United States was reluctant to contemplate the use of nuclear weapons in limited wars.

Conventional Forces and Intervention.   Improvements in conventional capabilities were not matched by the development of clear doctrine governing intervention and the application of force. In his inaugural address, Kennedy had made his famous pledge: "Let every nation know, whether it wishes us well or ill, we shall pay any price, bear any burden, meet any hardship, support any friend, or oppose any foe to assure the survival and the success of liberty."[43] Such an open-ended commitment was, of course, unrealistic, for it did not provide any useful guidance for deciding when the use of force was in the national interest and when it was not. In 1965, the United States deployed ground combat troops to the Republic of Vietnam and also intervened in a civil upheaval in the Dominican Republic. As the Vietnam involvement lengthened and deepened, popular dissatisfaction grew, and domestic dissent and economic pressure began to play a significant role in the formulation of U.S. strategy. By FY 1968, defense spending had climbed to $78 billion, $20 billion of which represented the direct cost of the war in Vietnam.[44] The incoming Nixon administration was faced with the prospects of stalemate on the nuclear level and an unpopular, costly war on the conventional level.

The Nixon and Ford Administrations, 1969–1976: Strategy of Realistic Deterrence

By 1969, the national consensus on U.S. national security policy had seriously weakened. The prolonged and seemingly unsuccessful U.S. intervention in Vietnam called into question the ability of the United States to deal with insurgencies around the world, and the nature of the strategic balance dictated a reassessment of American defense policy. The policy of containment, practically unchallenged for several decades, came under increasingly critical scrutiny. It no longer seemed to reflect a realistic appraisal of the international situation.

Reassessment of the Strategic Environment.   By 1968, the Soviet Union had achieved rough nuclear parity with the United States. Both sides could inflict unacceptable damage on one another even after absorbing an enemy's first strike. Under these conditions, the United States and the Soviet Union seemed to realize that it was in their best interest to limit the possibilities of confrontation. From such reasoning, at least on the U.S. side, came the concept of *détente* and the associated Strategic Arms Limitation Talks (SALT).

At least two other important factors informed thinking about U.S. military policy. First, public and congressional disenchantment with the war in Vietnam dictated a reevaluation of where and how U.S. conventional forces might be used. Second, economic constraints also had an impact. The position of the dollar in the world economy deteriorated as wartime inflation proceeded, and domestic social and economic problems seemed to demand greater investment. Yet, in FY 1964, the last pre–Vietnam War budget, defense spending represented 41.8% of the federal budget; roughly a decade later, in FY 1975, defense expenditures accounted for just 27.1% of federal outlays.[45] This defense-spending decline was not just relative but also absolute when measured in constant dollars.

Strategic Sufficiency.   Given the Soviet Union's nuclear arsenal and its demonstrated ability and willingness to respond to improvements in American strategic forces, the Nixon administration concluded that nuclear superiority would be impossible to maintain.[46] Any attempt to do so would only escalate the arms race without increasing security for either side. However, President Richard Nixon was also unwilling to allow the Soviet Union to achieve a position of nuclear dominance. Planning for U.S. forces thus focused on "strategic sufficiency." Reflecting an acceptance of nuclear parity, this doctrine included a number of precepts:

- *Assured destruction:* The United States would maintain three separate and independent offensive systems—ICBMs, submarine-launched ballistic missiles (SLBM)s, and manned bombers—which would ensure that the United States would be able to inflict unacceptable levels of damage on the enemy through destruction of its population and economy even in the event that the United States had been struck first.[47]

- *Flexible nuclear options:* Flexibility of forces and targets would allow the president to tailor any U.S. strategic response to the nature of the provocation.

- *Crisis stability:* Enhanced and flexible response capabilities would reduce Soviet willingness to stage a less than all-out attack and eliminate a Soviet incentive to strike first.[48]

- *Perceived equality:* A rough balance of strategic capabilities would prevent coercion or intimidation of the United States or its allies.

Conventional Force Policy.   In 1974, the Nixon administration's appraisal of conventional war policy reaffirmed one traditional commitment and modified another. The U.S. commitment to NATO was reaffirmed and strengthened following the U.S. withdrawal from Vietnam. Although the overall size of the U.S. Army was reduced by 50%, U.S. NATO forces—which had been stripped of personnel and equipment during the Vietnam War—were strengthened and re-equipped. Additionally, the United States abandoned the so-called two-and-a-half war strategy and began to maintain forces based on a one-and-a-half war strategy. (In reality, the change was not that dramatic, for the United States had never approached the level of forces needed for two-and-a-half wars.) The NATO commitment became the primary planning contingency for structuring U.S. conventional forces.

A major reappraisal of U.S. policy was also made concerning the feasibility of deterring or fighting local conflicts and insurgencies in developing countries. The resulting policy, known as the Nixon Doctrine, concluded that the United States would no longer automatically intervene against externally supported insurgencies. The Nixon Doctrine could be expressed as three essential principles: self-help, primary regional responsibility, and residual U.S. responsibility.[49] The principle of *self-help* dictated that the country being threatened must take responsibility for its own security. Further, in the case of insurgency, the United States would expect the local government to initiate vigorous programs of economic and political development.[50] Experience had taught that military action alone could not defeat an insurgency; it must be accompanied by political and social programs. The second principle, *regional responsibility*, meant that the United States expected neighboring countries to work together to eliminate or deal with causes of instability in their areas. If military operations were required, the neighbors of the country under attack would provide at least some of the forces.[51] Finally, the principle of *residual U.S. responsibility* indicated that the United States might provide military assistance but would intervene directly only if vital American interests were threatened. President Gerald Ford and later President Jimmy Carter endorsed this policy of strictly limited U.S. involvement as the basis for U.S. action in dealing with insurgencies in developing nations.

The Carter Administration, 1977–1981: Strategic Reassessment

As customarily occurs with the advent of a new administration, Carter initiated a reappraisal of U.S. national security policy when he took office in January 1977. Such reappraisal was clearly warranted, for much had changed. Turning first to the international environment, the steady strengthening of Soviet nuclear forces had underscored the momentum of the strategic arms race and the importance of moving forward with arms control. A second important dynamic involved the People's Republic of China. Nixon's reestablishment of the U.S.-China dialogue in 1972 had reversed a longstanding policy of treating that country as a prime danger. A final trend related to the proliferation of newly independent countries since World War II and the increasing demands made by these countries for a more just international order.

Another important cause for reassessment concerned past U.S. policy. A central theme of the Nixon administration's approach to foreign affairs, détente, had been discredited. The original goal of détente had been to lessen tension and hostility between the superpowers. By the beginning of the Carter administration, however, it appeared that the Soviet Union had interpreted détente as mere acknowledgment of the new power balance and a license to expand its influence. Although the earlier SALT negotiations (SALT I) institutionalized the policy of détente at one level, they seemed only to encourage Soviet expansionism at other levels. Americans were unhappy with a policy that seemed incapable of checking the adventurism of the Soviet Union and its allies in the noncommunist world.

Domestically, the United States had also changed dramatically. The wars in Korea and Vietnam seemed to illustrate the reduced utility of military force, feeding renewed skepticism about defense spending and worldwide military deployments. The recession of 1974–1975 reemphasized domestic priorities and raised further questions about the extent to which resources should be channeled into expensive defense programs. Then presidential candidate Carter emphasized his intent to reduce military spending in favor of domestic priorities. Despite evidence of a continuing, massive Soviet military buildup, there was sufficient uncertainty to permit both presidential candidates in 1976 to downplay the specter of future Soviet adventurism.

Technology also had, to some extent, restructured the security environment. Continued technological advancements—such as multiple, independently targetable reentry vehicles (MIRVs) for nuclear weapons; cruise missiles; and anti-satellite capabilities—threatened to upset perceptions of nuclear stability. Improvements in such conventional weapons as TV-guided bombs and laser-guided artillery shells had enhanced military capabilities with less than fully understood consequences for the stability of conventional force balances.[52]

As a consequence of the factors discussed above, and in light of its own comprehensive assessment of the comparative strengths of the United States and the Soviet Union, the Carter administration set forth the main lines of its strategy in a series of announcements and policy initiatives during the course of 1977. It reaffirmed the importance of maintaining a balance in strategic nuclear forces, choosing the label of *essential equivalence*. It continued to rely upon the doctrine of "mutually assured destruction" but appeared to back away from any concept of even limited counterforce capabilities or any plans for the so-called limited nuclear options with which the Nixon administration had tinkered. Also, in the context of essential equivalence, the Carter administration picked up the lagging SALT II talks and pressed them vigorously. The subsequent treaty signed by Carter and General Secretary Leonid Brezhnev in Vienna in 1979, though never ratified by the U.S. Senate, continued to define the upper limits of essential equivalence into the 1980s.

With regard to Europe, the Carter administration underscored the key role of NATO and reaffirmed the existing forward strategy. The overall concept of having forces sufficient to simultaneously fight a major war in Europe and a smaller war elsewhere—the one-and-a-half war strategy of the Nixon administration—was endorsed as the guiding principle behind the size and character of the defense forces. Special attention was focused on the Persian Gulf as the possible site of the one-half war. Although measures to create the kind of force projection capability required for such an area as the Persian Gulf were slow to get under way, the administration at least staked out a declaratory policy that accorded the region higher and more explicit priority than it had earlier received.

In a bid to stabilize the power balance in Asia and to create a more satisfactory framework for U.S.-Soviet relations, the administration proceeded with the normalization of American relations with the People's Republic of China. Formal recognition was accomplished in early 1979, immediately preceding the visit to the United States by Vice-Premier Deng Xiaoping. Also, in fulfillment of the president's campaign promises, the administration began preparations to withdraw American ground forces from the Republic of Korea. Congressional opposition, however, forced the administration to reverse its course in the matter.

In terms of overall national security policy, the decade of the 1970s ended on a somewhat surprising note. The Soviet Union's impressive and continuing defense buildup, its invasion of Afghanistan in 1979, and its gains in a number of other regions—generally propelled by Soviet arms and advisers and sometimes by Cuban proxies—had so alarmed large sectors of the public and Congress that a stronger defense policy and increased spending were pressed on a reluctant president. This was further exacerbated by the Islamic revolution in Iran earlier in 1979 that saw an American hostage crisis as well as the loss of a U.S. ally in a strategic region. President Carter's final defense budget and five-year defense plan were marked by substantial increases.

The Reagan Administration, 1981–1988: Redressing the Military Balance and Reform

America entered the 1980s with a new administration committed to strengthening U.S. power, to resisting further Soviet-supported communist expansion, and to leaving Marxism-Leninism on "the ash heap of history." From 1981 to 1988, the U.S. defense budget almost doubled—the largest peacetime military buildup in American history. The United States moved rapidly to deploy a new-generation triad of strategic nuclear systems, to expand the U.S. naval fleet toward 600 ships, and to modernize U.S. conventional land and air forces. One of the more dramatic developments in U.S. national security policy during this period came in March 1983 when the president called for the development of a system to defend the United States against ballistic missile attack. Such a system could radically alter the forms of future military confrontation.[53]

In the developing world, the Reagan administration turned to a more activist policy of American support for noncommunist insurgencies against Soviet-supported communist regimes. This policy, generally known as the Reagan Doctrine, enjoyed several successes. It probably contributed to the Soviet Union's decision to withdraw its support for the Marxist government in Angola and, in part, to the Soviet decision to withdraw from Afghanistan in 1989. In Central America, support for the anticommunist contras led to free elections and the demise of the Sandinista government in Nicaragua, setting the stage for the eventual settlement of the communist-backed insurgency in El Salvador. U.S. military intervention in 1983 also stopped the threat of a communist-supported takeover in Grenada.

The emergence of Mikhail Gorbachev as the leader of the Soviet Union in 1985 presented the opportunity for beginning a new dialogue with the Soviets in the midst of confrontation. The Reagan administration's strategy of deferring major efforts at arms control until it was in a position to negotiate from strength began to pay off in a series of Soviet concessions that eventually led to the Intermediate Nuclear Forces Treaty of 1987. With subsequent dramatic changes in Eastern Europe and the breakup of the Warsaw Pact, other negotiations yielded the Conventional Forces in Europe Treaty of 1990 and the Strategic Arms Reduction Treaty of 1991.

Gorbachev's policies of *glasnost* (openness) and *perestroika* (restructuring) and the sheer force of his personality, combined with deep domestic economic problems and erosion of the Soviet empire, led to the end of the Cold War by 1989 and, ultimately, to the demise of the Soviet Union. The United States and its allies had effectively contained the Soviet Union for forty years. After an aborted putsch in Moscow in August 1991 aimed at overthrowing Gorbachev and his reforms, the old Soviet Union was finished, although the future of its fifteen former republics remained to be settled.

Goldwater-Nichols.   Although the preceding decades had seen numerous shifts in national security policy as the threat evolved, many in Congress and the executive branch believed the formulation and communication of national security strategy were flawed. Also, past national security policies had generally failed to provide adequate focus in pursuing national values, interests, and goals. Moreover, these strategies still did not provide the integration that the 1947 National Security Act was meant to foster. In response, Congress passed the most significant legislation on national security since the 1947 law. The Goldwater-Nichols Department of Defense Reorganization Act of 1986 required the president to report the administration's national security strategy to Congress on an annual basis. In this document, the president would codify the values, national interests, and key objectives that would drive security and defense policies. The report would also allow Congress to evaluate the coherence and feasibility of the administration's reconciliation of ends, ways, and means.

In addition to providing focus, Goldwater-Nichols also sought to better integrate the different service components of the DoD. Despite the intent of the 1947 legislation and McNamara's reforms, interservice rivalry still dominated discussions on budget allocation, weapons programs, and the planning and execution of military operations. In response, the 1986 act strengthened mechanisms for integrating service-specific budget programs and streamlined the operational chain of command from the president through the secretary of defense to theater commanders. The chairman of the Joint Chiefs of Staff became the principal adviser to the president, and the respective service chiefs were no longer in the operational chain of command.[54] Instead, theater combatant commanders gained unified control over all service elements within their areas of operations. The Goldwater-Nichols legislation also addressed weaknesses in joint war-fighting capabilities, revealed in a failed attempt to rescue U.S. hostages in Iran in 1980 and during 1983 military operations in Grenada, by mandating improved service interoperability. (For more on the role played by Congress in U.S. national security affairs, see Chapter 5.)

The George H. W. Bush Administration, 1989–1992: Toward a New World Order

The NSC staff under President George H. W. Bush began a national security strategy review right after he took office in 1989, but events in the Soviet Union and Eastern Europe were moving so fast that publication of the administration's national security strategies was delayed in 1990 and 1991. Both reports received considerable criticism for their lack of precise guidance. Yet, the 1991 report did point to fundamental changes:

> More than preceding reports, this one attempted to broaden the definition of national security. In purely military terms, it proclaimed regional conflict as the organizing principle for American military forces, and suggested that new terms of reference for nuclear deterrence would shortly be needed. Politically, it attempted to turn the compass on arms control from east-west to north-south for a much expanded discussion of policy to retard proliferation. Even more than the previous reports, the document attempted to communicate the idea that American economic well-being was included in the definition of national security, even though discussions of specific programs to improve competitiveness or to combat trade and budget deficits were generally lacking.[55]

Reflecting new realities and anxious to satisfy domestic cravings for a "peace dividend" in the wake of the Cold War, Secretary of Defense Richard Cheney and Chairman of the Joint Chiefs of Staff Colin Powell appeared before the Senate budget committee in January 1991, during the Gulf War, to propose a multi-year 25% reduction in American forces from 1990 levels. By 1995, those cuts would reduce active-duty Army divisions from eighteen to twelve, the Air Force from thirty-six fighter wing equivalents to twenty-six, the Navy from 546 ships to 451, and reserve forces and DoD civilian employees by over 200,000 each. In addition, Cheney and Powell announced plans to cancel one hundred weapons programs and to close or realign over two hundred bases and facilities worldwide. In the words of Secretary Cheney, "The cuts would reduce the U.S. military to its lowest end strength since before the Korean War; they would cut our share of the Federal budget, once as high as 57%, to 18%, the lowest level in forty years. The defense budget would fall by 1997 to 3.4% of GNP, by far the lowest level since before Pearl Harbor."[56]

The new military strategy guiding this "defense build-down" reflected the shift from containing the spread of communism and deterring Soviet aggression to a more variegated, flexible strategy. The major elements were:

- Strategic deterrence and defense, requiring a reliable warning system, modern nuclear forces, the capability and flexibility to support a spectrum of response options, and a defensive system for protection against limited strikes.

Copyright 1991 CARTOONEWS Inc., N.Y.C., USA. Reprinted with permission of Ranan Lurie.

- Forward but reduced presence of U.S. conventional land, sea, and air forces at a high level of readiness in regions vital to U.S. national interests; in this context, strengthened alliances as well.

- The ability to respond to regional crises that could arise on very short notice involving U.S. forces unilaterally or as part of a multilateral effort.

- A force reconstitution capability against major military threats based on longer warning time and involving the formation, training, and fielding of new fighting units, mobilization of previously trained manpower, and activation of the U.S. defense industrial base, which would maintain the capability for technological superiority.[57]

Some of the impetus for reorienting defense posture was created by the 1991 Persian Gulf War. Although Iraq's invasion of Kuwait in August 1990 was a surprise to the Bush administration, it responded with firm diplomatic and military action. With the support of a UN Security Council resolution, the U.S. led a coalition of over thirty states that included over 500,000 American troops to a swift and decisive defeat of the Iraqi Army and liberation of Kuwait. In the aftermath of this operation, the Bush administration felt confident that its words and deeds against armed aggression would prove to be an effective deterrent. Also during this time, George H. W. Bush interpreted international humanitarian crises as creating a potential threat to the national interest, as evidenced by the U.S. deployment of forces to Somalia in the waning months of the administration. In 1992, as the FY 1993 defense budget was being debated on Capitol Hill, it appeared that Congress largely agreed with the administration—for the time being—that U.S. military capabilities would not be allowed to plummet as had occurred after earlier wars.

The Clinton Years, 1993–2000: Cautious Change

President Bill Clinton's first secretary of defense, William Perry, sought to respond to the complexities of a post–Cold War World with a defense strategy organized along three basic lines. First, the United States would prevent threats from emerging; second, the United States would deter threats that did emerge; and third, if the first two lines of defense failed, the United States would have the capability to defeat threats using military force. In the first category, threat prevention, Perry emphasized a range of confidence-building measures and the strengthening of democratic societies, as well as the maintenance of strong alliances, efforts to counter the spread of WMD, the forging of a pragmatic partnership with Russia, engagement in multilateral security dialogues, and the pursuit of comprehensive engagement with China.

On the second line of defense, deterrence, Perry asserted that only the United States could deter threats worldwide. To do so, the United States required a reduced but effective nuclear force; strong, ready, forward-deployed conventional forces with a clear power projection capability; and the demonstrated will to use those forces when vital interests were threatened. Third, on the final line of defense, Secretary Perry stressed the need for U.S. dominance built on readiness, high technology weapons, and superior information systems to ensure victory.[58]

Military Structure.   To implement this strategy, the Clinton administration did not make any dramatic changes to military force guidance or structure. Beginning in 1993, the defense drawdown begun by the preceding administration continued as defense spending remained relatively stable. The Clinton administration's two major reviews of defense policy, the Bottom-Up Review of 1993–1994 and the Quadrennial Defense Review (QDR) of 1996–1997, basically enshrined the status quo. The core planning guide in both reviews was the need to be able to fight two nearly simultaneous major theater wars, such as a second Persian Gulf War as well as a war on the Korean peninsula, without major allied assistance. Force structure and budgetary requirements flowed from this concept. The DoD proposed to fight these wars along conventional lines, funding each military service in fairly traditional percentages and avoiding major doctrinal changes.

Critics found much to dislike in this thoroughly customary approach to defense planning. Initially, some worried about a major mismatch between forces and budgets. Projected budgets could not provide sufficient new tanks, planes, ships, and other hardware to keep the overall force in fighting trim. These observers began to worry about the "coming defense train wreck" that would occur when the current generation of military hardware reached its maximum service life and there was no new generation to take its place.[59] Other critics pointed to a so-called revolution in military affairs underway in defense technology and strategy—a revolution based on real-time, battlefield intelligence; precision sensors and strike systems; information warfare; new weapons, such as unmanned aerial vehicles and nearly automated stealth ships; and other elements—and claimed that the Clinton administration was doing nothing to make it a reality for the U.S. military. Some worried the United States was doing what all leading powers had done through history—assuming that the next war would be like the last. Finally, a host of critics from across the political spectrum argued that the Clinton administration was not doing enough to reverse the Cold War nuclear arms race that had left each side with thousands of nuclear weapons. They called for faster action before the continuing U.S.-Russian nuclear standoff served to undermine East-West relations once again.

Clinton administration officials had ready answers to these criticisms. Beginning in the mid-1990s, they added money to defense budgets to help redress the force structure-budget imbalance and argued that it made little sense to embark on a new round of equipment modernization before the new, revolutionary generation of hardware was fully ready. They suggested that they were experimenting with radical new equipment and tactics, but that integrating them into the military in a stable and effective way would naturally take some years. Finally, they pointed out that the United States and Russia could only destroy so many nuclear warheads in any given year, and that their nuclear reductions were proceeding as fast as technology allowed. In a retrospective defense of the Clinton administration's stewardship of the armed forces, defense analyst Michael O'Hanlon argues, "The Clinton Pentagon oversaw the most successful defense drawdown in U.S. history—cutting military personnel by 15% more than the previous administration had planned while retaining a high state of readiness and a strong global deterrence posture. It enacted a prescient modernization program. And the military it helped produce achieved impressive successes in Bosnia and Kosovo."[60]

Military Intervention.   Although the Clinton administration took a cautious approach to structural change of the armed forces, it was more activist in its willingness to use force abroad. Though Clinton inherited the Somalia intervention from his predecessor, he later intervened with U.S. armed forces in humanitarian crises and postconflict situations in Haiti (1994), Bosnia (1995), and Kosovo (1999). Many critics questioned whether these interventions represented a wise use of U.S. military power given the questionable relationship between developments in these situations and vital U.S. national interests. Others were concerned about the legitimacy of these endeavors given the norm of state sovereignty, which militates against intervention in another state's domestic affairs. Finally, from a U.S. domestic perspective, there were concerns over cost and the impact of a greatly increased pace of operations on a smaller, all-volunteer military that was still structured largely along Cold War lines. This debate became louder during the 2000 presidential election season.[61]

As the twentieth century came to a close, U.S. defense policy was clearly in transition. Debates on the significance of international political developments, the ensuing tension between competing forces within domestic politics, and the impact of technology all continued to play significant roles in national security policy. However, without a clearly defined threat or a unifying crisis, these debates were not subject to easy resolution.

The George W. Bush Administration, 2001–2008: Crisis and Transformation

Much like those of the preceding two presidents, the incoming Bush administration struggled to articulate U.S. national security policy goals in the post–Cold War environment. As a presidential candidate, Governor George W. Bush formulated a modest agenda and sought to scale back the foreign policy activism of the Clinton years. Key advisors to his campaign criticized the Clinton administration for failing to prioritize international affairs, for overusing the military to the point that "thinly stretched armed forces came close to a breaking point," and for embracing multilateralism at the expense of the U.S. national interest.[62] In an April 2000 debate, George W. Bush promised to pursue a "humble" foreign policy.[63] However, the terrorist attacks of September 11, 2001, suddenly presented the United States with a genuine crisis and a concrete threat. This event galvanized the American people and spurred the U.S. government to take a new approach to national security.

New Threats and a New Strategy.   Surprise attacks on U.S. territory are rare in American history. As historian John Lewis Gaddis points out, the only other examples are "the British burning of the White House and Capitol in 1814 and the Japanese attack on Pearl Harbor in 1941." Gaddis also argues that such attacks can set the stage for radically new national security strategies by seeming to show that previous policies had failed.[64] Throughout the Cold War and into the 1990s, the policy of containment and the strategy of deterrence informed U.S. national security policy. In the aftermath of devastating terrorist attacks on U.S. soil, and given challenges from nonstate armed groups and the risk of WMD proliferation, these traditional approaches appeared obsolete. In his May 2002 graduation speech at West Point, President Bush was explicit: "New threats also require new thinking." He went on to assert, "deterrence . . . means nothing against shadowy terrorist networks with no nation or citizens to defend. Containment is not possible when unbalanced dictators with weapons of mass destruction can deliver those weapons on missiles or secretly provide them to terrorist allies."[65] Responding to these concerns, *The National Security Strategy of the United States of America* issued in September 2002 represented a shift in U.S. national security policy. Bush summarized his approach by saying, "We will defend the peace by fighting terrorists and tyrants. We will preserve the peace by building good relations among the great powers. We will extend the peace by encouraging free and open societies on every continent."[66]

An important element of this new approach was an effort on the part of the Bush administration to redefine the doctrine of *preemption*. Preemption has traditionally been seen as justified under international law, reflecting the right of a state to defend itself by acting first in the face of an imminent danger. In effect, the Bush administration argued that the standard of imminence should be relaxed when the threat of concern related to WMD: "In an age where the enemies of civilization openly and actively seek the world's most destructive technologies, the United States cannot remain idle while dangers gather."[67] Critics responded by arguing that the Bush administration was really just talking about classic preventive war: acting now to prevent a potential future threat. An American embrace of preventive war would challenge American traditions and set a bad precedent for countries around the world. In the eyes of these critics, the U.S.-led invasion of Iraq in 2003 showed the risks of preventive war, as WMD were not found and the invasion's aftermath proved more dangerous and complex than U.S. planners had apparently expected. (For more on American traditional approaches to national security, see Chapter 2.)

The debate on this element of the Bush national security strategy continues. Robert Jervis identifies three challenges to the Bush approach. First, it is inherently difficult to predict future threats. Second, important and relevant intelligence on past behavior and capabilities can be both scarce and difficult to interpret. Third, it may be difficult to sustain both domestic support and international legitimacy when using force based on problematic information.[68] Gaddis, however, argues that, although this doctrine is controversial, it may have been successful in thwarting subsequent terrorist attacks on U.S. soil. Gaddis also supports the Bush administration's view that the traditional definitions of preemption and prevention are no longer relevant in the face of new threats.[69]

In addition to fighting terrorists and tyrants, the other two elements of the Bush national security strategy related to building positive relationships with great powers and fostering democracy. In practice, these aspects of the national security strategy proved difficult to implement consistently. Though the United States sought good relations with other great powers, it also resisted the inevitable constraints associated with seeking international consensus or support for its actions. And despite a desire to foster democratic development, the United States found itself working with many nondemocratic regimes in its struggle against international terrorists. The tensions have been classic ones. With regard to cooperation with other great powers, the freedom of unilateralism must be weighed against the advantages in capability and legitimacy provided by multilateralism. With regard to democracy promotion, U.S. values must at times be weighed against material national security interests. These challenges are likely to prove enduring.

The Wars in Afghanistan and Iraq.   Over the long term, a strategy is likely to be judged by its perceived consequences. Evaluations of the national security policy of the Bush administration are likely to be most strongly defined by the wars in Afghanistan and Iraq. For this reason, even as these wars continue, a brief review of their origins and conduct is useful here.

Afghanistan.   Within one month of the attacks of 9/11, U.S. forces, with substantial assistance from CIA paramilitary operators, launched combat operations to invade Afghanistan. The purpose of the operation was to target the al-Qa'ida central leadership, including Osama bin Laden, and the Taliban regime in Afghanistan that had supported al-Qa'ida's operations. After several months of fighting, in which U.S. conventional and Special Operations forces worked closely with the indigenous Northern Alliance militias, the Taliban were defeated.[70] The UN sponsored a series of meetings in Bonn, Germany, which eventually led to an interim government led by a Pashtun leader, Hamid Karzai. Karzai was appointed as the interim President of Afghanistan and became the first democratically elected President of Afghanistan on October 9, 2004.

Since the initial defeat of the Taliban, military operations to support the newly formed Afghan government and to impede al-Qa'ida operations in the region have continued. Consolidating national power in Afghanistan has been difficult and al-Qa'ida operatives, reportedly including Osama bin Laden, continue to operate in remote areas of Afghanistan and the Federally Administered Tribal Areas (FATA) of neighboring Pakistan. Beginning in August, 2003, NATO initiated its first operation outside the Euro-Atlantic area and created the International Security Assistance Force (ISAF) to "assist the government of Afghanistan and the international community in maintaining security."[71] U.S. forces have worked with the ISAF, but the amount of U.S. military power that can be committed to Afghanistan has been constrained by the total amount of forces available, especially after operations began in Iraq. (See also Chapter 19 for more on the war in Afghanistan.)

Iraq.   In response to Iraqi President Saddam Hussein's evasiveness regarding the enforcement of UN Security Council Resolutions relating to suspected WMD programs, and in line with the emphasis the Bush administration placed on the danger from "unbalanced dictators" with WMD in a world plagued by transnational terrorists, U.S. forces led an invasion of Iraq in March 2003. In three weeks, the U.S.-led coalition toppled the regime of Saddam Hussein in a series of synchronized military operations that demonstrated American military dominance over the Iraqi Army. Most Iraqi leaders fled and were eventually captured or killed, with Saddam Hussein being captured in December 2003, eight months after the invasion.

The political challenge of establishing a new representative government in place of an authoritarian regime proved to be much more difficult than the military operation required to defeat that regime. For the first fourteen months, until July 2004, the United States established a Coalition Provisional Authority, led by Ambassador L. Paul Bremer that administered Iraq and worked toward the creation of democratically-based government structures in a state where little tradition of democratic governance had ever existed.[72] Some initial decisions, such as limiting the number of U.S. forces deployed for stabilization operations, disbanding the Iraqi Army, and excluding senior members of Saddam Hussein's Ba'ath Party from government, were criticized as contributing to the post-war disorder and lawlessness that developed in many parts of Iraq. Despite the U.S. transfer of sovereignty back to Iraqi leaders on July 1, 2004, the situation did not improve. In fact, as the U.S. military attempted to develop the Iraqi army and police forces, insurgents that opposed the government and U.S. forces increased their attacks and violence spread in many of Iraq's provinces. This violence received additional fuel from external forces, including al-Qa'ida and Iran, both of which saw Iraq as an opportunity to embroil the U.S. in a long-term conflict. After the bombing of the Golden Dome Mosque in Samarra in February 2006, the situation evolved into a sectarian civil war with over 3000 Iraqis killed per month in November-December 2006. In response to these developments, Congress appointed a bipartisan Iraqi Study Group to attempt to chart a new way forward.[73] By December 2006, the U.S. Ambassador to Iraq, Zalmay Khalilzad, and the U.S. Commander, General George Casey, concluded that the current strategy was not working and that "the coalition was failing to achieve its objectives."[74]

In January 2007, the President Bush announced a new strategy, which included a "surge" of five brigades of the U.S. Army and two Marine battalions, a concomitant surge of Iraqi forces (Iraqi military and policy forces increased by more than 100,000 in 2007), a focus on the Baghdad area, and additional diplomatic, political, and economic pressure. The surge was implemented by a new commander, General David Petraeus, who employed a counterinsurgency strategy that emphasized partnerships with Iraqi Security Forces and focused on protecting the Iraqi population. At the same time, political overtures toward moderate tribes, initially in Anbar and then throughout Iraq, took advantage of the extent to which al-Qaida in Iraq and other violent extremist groups had overplayed their hand and alienated themselves from local populations. This "awakening" of the tribes led over 100,000 former insurgents to join organizations called "Sons of Iraq," which worked with the coalition and Iraqi forces to provide local security. This movement also had the potential to serve as a step toward political reconciliation to the extent that it served as a means for integrating the former insurgent groups into a peaceful political process. (See also Chapter 20 for more on the war in Iraq.)

Though as of late 2008, the ultimate outcomes of the wars in Afghanistan and Iraq are uncertain; already the cost and difficulty of these wars have exceeded initial estimates. The development of these conflicts reinforces several themes that will be identified later in this book: the importance of diplomatic, information, and economic power—beyond just the military instrument—are discussed in

Chapters 11 and 12. The inherent uncertainty and challenges of using military power and the criteria that should be considered before using it are discussed in Chapter 13. The specific principles of and challenges with counterinsurgency warfare are discussed in Chapter 16. These two major military operations of the Bush administration reinforce the importance of carefully understanding, developing, and implementing national security policy in way takes into consideration the long-term interests of the United States and the inherent difficulty in implementing policy. As discussed later in the section on defense transformation, the Afghanistan and Iraq wars also once again widened the gap between an administration's strategy and the less flexible structure available to support that strategy.

Nuclear Weapons and Space Policy.   Although it identified the limits of deterrence in the face of new threats, the Bush national security policy acknowledged the continued relevance of nuclear weapons for strategic deterrence against potential state adversaries. Its *New Triad* of nuclear deterrence consisted of conventional and nuclear offensive strike systems, active and passive defenses that emphasized ballistic missile defense, and a responsive nuclear infrastructure.[75] Each of these elements relies heavily on the technological advantages the United States continues to hold over its competitors. Despite the absence of a Soviet threat during the years since the end of the Cold War, the United States has largely maintained its nuclear weapons capability. In terms of weapons available, some analysts even posit the United States will soon have a degree of nuclear superiority it has not enjoyed since the end of World War II and are concerned with the potentially destabilizing effects of future arms races motivated by a desire to counter U.S. capabilities in this area.[76] On the other hand, recent problems involving the surety of nuclear weapons indicated that U.S. nuclear competence has eroded. A 2008 Task Force appointed by the Secretary of Defense concluded that "there has been an unambiguous, dramatic, and unacceptable decline in the Air Force's commitment to perform the nuclear mission and, until very recently, little has been done to reverse it."[77] Unless it is corrected, the U.S. may face a significant security dilemma—other nations developing technology to counter U.S. nuclear superiority and a loss of the means and tradecraft required to safely maintain that superiority.

The Bush administration also undertook a more activist policy toward space. Acknowledging the importance of using space for security and economic purposes, the national space policy asserts "freedom of action in space is as important to the United States as air power and sea power."[78] The administration saw U.S. national security as being dependent upon space capabilities, believed that this dependence would only grow, and hoped to retain U.S. space primacy. Thus, much to the chagrin of such states as China and Russia, the U.S. showed reluctance to support international agreements that could in any way threaten American preeminence beyond the Earth's atmosphere.

Defense Transformation.   As the Bush administration sought to think beyond the traditional parameters of containment and deterrence in its national security policy, it focused heavily on transforming the military to respond to new threats. Even before the terrorist attacks of 9/11, Secretary of Defense Donald Rumsfeld returned to lead the Pentagon after a twenty-five year absence with transformation as his mandate. Creating a special Office of Force Transformation, Rumsfeld sought to focus not only on high-technology, precision weapons but also on new ways of fighting enemies who would attempt to challenge American hegemony asymmetrically. In the 2001 QDR, the Pentagon shifted away from the previous "two major theater war" force design construct. Rumsfeld also sought to eliminate many military bases in Europe and East Asia that were established during the Cold War. His goal was the creation of a lean, effective, joint force that could deploy rapidly anywhere in the world on short notice.[79]

Many of these elements of transformation were showcased effectively during the U.S. campaign in Afghanistan in 2001–2002. Small land forces worked closely with coalition partners, utilizing unmanned aircraft. This joint collaboration with U.S. air assets from temporary bases in neighboring Uzbekistan and Kyrgyzstan seemed to epitomize the efficacy of transformation as well as the administration's success in rapidly changing the culture of a huge governmental institution. The strengths of transformation were again highlighted in the buildup and execution of the U.S. overthrow of Saddam Hussein in Iraq. Nevertheless, as postconflict operations in Iraq and Afghanistan relied less on advanced technology and more on sustaining large, expensive ground forces, the focus of transformation initiatives seemed increasingly distant from current national security needs. Once again, strategy and structure began to appear out of alignment. Although the 2006 QDR still highlighted transforming the military into a more agile and expeditionary force, it readily admitted it was not a programmatic or budget document.[80] Instead, the 2007 defense budget of $439 billion (up 7% from 2006 and 48% from 2001) highlighted more traditional goals of maintaining soldier readiness and procuring conventional and nuclear weapons systems.[81]

A final issue of national security structure that became more salient during the Bush administration relates to the interagency processes of the U.S. government. Since the Goldwater-Nichols reforms of 1986, the DoD has made significant strides in integrating the military services in order to improve their capabilities and effectiveness in joint military operations. However, these efforts focused solely on the DoD. As the landscape changed in the early twenty-first century, it became clear that the United States would require more than effective armed forces to meet its national security needs. It would need to combine the expertise of various agencies and departments in the U.S. government to deal effectively with new challenges, such as a catastrophic terrorist attack on the U.S. homeland, or postconflict reconstruction abroad. Despite increasing calls for another such landmark reform as Goldwater-Nichols or the National Security Act of 1947, it seems unlikely that the challenges associated with making the interagency process work more effectively will be resolved in the near term.[82] (For more on this topic, see Chapter 10.)

Looking to the future, it is likely that many of the characteristics of the strategic environment to which the Bush administration responded will endure. The proliferation of WMD and activities of transnational terrorist groups are likely to be of growing serious concern. Whether future administrations will adopt key tenets of the Bush administration's national security policy as an appropriate response to these challenges remains to be seen.

Discussion Questions

1. What international and technological developments caused the United States to abandon its longstanding reliance on a policy of mobilization? How does a strategy based on deterrence differ from one based on mobilization?

2. The policy of containment was based on the perception of an aggressive, monolithic communist bloc of nations. What events of the late 1940s and early 1950s caused the United States to take this view of the communist threat? What impact did such an assessment have on established U.S. political and military policies?

3. How do domestic considerations make foreign and security policies different than they would be on the basis of international and strategic considerations alone?

4. How have technological innovations affected the evolution of U.S. security policy since the end of World War II? To what extent can it be said that technology determines strategy?

5. Should the United States maintain its current high level of investment in nuclear capabilities? What are the potential advantages and disadvantages of such a policy?

6. Given changes in technology as well as the rising importance of security threats posed by nonstate actors, is there a meaningful distinction between *preemption* and *prevention* in the current strategic landscape? What are the national security implications of attacking threats before they are fully formed?

7. The 1986 Goldwater-Nichols Department of Defense Reorganization Act was a watershed reform effort that greatly influenced American national security policy. Given the increased complexity of today's challenges, does the United States need another major reform of the national security bureaucracy?

8. One of the enduring themes in the evolution of U.S. national security policy is the tension between strategy and structure. Does current policy achieve a successful reconciliation between these two?

9. Since 9/11, the United States has identified the spread of Islamic fundamentalism to be a threat to U.S. national interests and global prosperity. Is this a long-term threat? How can the United States deal effectively with this problem?

Recommended Reading

Dougherty, James E., and Pfaltzgraff, Robert L., Jr. *American Foreign Policy: FDR to Reagan.* New York: Harper & Row, 1986.

Fukuyama, Francis. *The End of History and the Last Man.* New York: Free Press, 1992.

———. *America at the Crossroads: Democracy, Power, and the Neoconservative Legacy.* New Haven: Yale University Press, 2006.

Gaddis, John Lewis. *Strategies of Containment: A Critical Appraisal of Postwar American National Security Policy.* New York: Oxford University Press, 1982.

———. *Surprise, Security, and the American Experience.* Cambridge, MA: Harvard University Press, 2004.

George, Alexander, and Smoke, Richard. *Deterrence in American Foreign Policy: Theory and Practice.* New York: Columbia University Press, 1974.

Huntington, Samuel P. *The Common Defense.* New York: Columbia University Press, 1961.

Jervis, Robert. *American Foreign Policy in a New Era.* New York: Routledge, 2005.

Kennan, George. *American Diplomacy.* Chicago: University of Chicago Press, 1963.

Kissinger, Henry A. *American Foreign Policy.* 3rd ed. New York: W. W. Norton, 1977.

Leffler, Melvyn. *A Preponderance of Power: National Security, the Truman Administration, and the Cold War.* Palo Alto, CA: Stanford University Press, 1992.

Lippmann, Walter. *U.S. Foreign Policy: Shield of the Republic.* Boston: Little, Brown, 1943.

Osgood, Robert. *Ideals and Self-Interest in America's Foreign Relations.* Chicago: University of Chicago Press, 1953.

Reagan, Ronald. President Reagan: Speech to the House of June 8, 1982. Available at: http://www.fordham.edu/halsall/mod/1982reagan1.html.

Tucker, Robert. *The Purposes of American Power.* New York: Praeger, 1981.

Internet Resources

The Avalon Project at Yale Law School, Documents in Law, History and Diplomacy, www.yale.edu/lawweb/avalon/avalon.htm

National Security Council, www.whitehouse.gov/nsc

NSC Historical List of Policy Documents, http://clinton4.nara.gov/textonly/WH/EOP/NSC/html/historical

U.S. Department of Defense, www.defenselink.mil

II

National Security Policy:
Actors and Processes

4

Presidential Leadership
and the Executive Branch

"The direction of war implies the direction of the common strength; and the power of directing and employing the common strength forms a usual and essential part in the definition of the executive authority."[1] With these words, Alexander Hamilton described the crucial role of the president in national security affairs. An appreciation of this vital role was shared by all the founders of the United States, but it was counterbalanced by their determination to avoid investing in the president the "sole prerogative of making war and peace" exercised by the British monarch.[2] As a result, the Founding Fathers documented in the Constitution a system in which the president and Congress were given complementary, and at times naturally conflicting, roles in the national security process. To successfully implement initiatives in the national security arena, presidents need to make maximum use of their sources of authority while carefully managing constraints.

The Presidency and the Constitution

The Executive and Congress, Sharing Power. Under the Constitution, the president is the commander in chief of the Army and Navy, but the president has nothing to command unless Congress uses the power it possesses to raise and support armies and to support and maintain a navy. In addition, Congress is empowered to make rules for the governance and regulation of those forces. The president has the authority to make treaties and to appoint ambassadors and other public ministers, as well as members of his national security team, such as the secretaries of state and defense, the director of national intelligence, and the chairman of the Joint Chiefs of Staff (JCS). Each of these actions, however, is subject to the "advice and consent" of the Senate.

The president is responsible to ensure that the laws are faithfully executed, and he or she has been vested with the "executive power" to this end. It is Congress, however, that is responsible to "make all laws which shall be necessary and proper for carrying into execution the foregoing powers vested by this Constitution in the Government of the United States."[3] The Constitution gives the president substantial authority and initiative in foreign affairs. However, having given the president important powers to make and execute national security policy, the Founding Fathers were deliberate in granting Congress the power to declare war. As a consequence of these built-in dynamic tensions, the Constitution has presented to each president and Congress an "invitation to struggle for the privilege of directing American foreign policy."[4]

A History of Increasing Presidential Prerogative.   The outline of the national security process provided by the Constitution was quickly elaborated upon by the actual conduct of public affairs. In 1793, George Washington asserted the prerogative of the president to act unilaterally in time of foreign crisis by issuing, without congressional consultation, a neutrality proclamation in the renewed Franco-British war. Succeeding administrations continued to struggle with questions of presidential versus congressional prerogative. In 1812, President James Madison was unsuccessful in restraining congressional "war hawks" who helped precipitate war with England. On the other hand, in 1846, it was President James Polk who presented Congress with a fait accompli by placing American troops along the Rio Grande. The resulting clash of arms between U.S. and Mexican soldiers quickly led to a declaration of war.

Presidential prerogative in foreign affairs, claimed first by Washington and embellished by his successors, was a generally established concept at the time of the Lincoln administration. Abraham Lincoln greatly expanded the potential range of presidential action by invoking the notion of a *war power* as a derivative of the commander-in-chief clause of the Constitution. The growth of presidential power in the Civil War foreshadowed the relationship between national emergency and executive power. Time and again, the law of national self-preservation was used to justify placing extraordinary power in the hands of the president.[5]

Prior to World War II, President Franklin Roosevelt's carefully orchestrated policy of aiding Great Britain and its allies once again revealed the power of the president to set national security policy unilaterally. Using executive agreements of dubious constitutionality to avoid confronting an uncertain and isolationist Congress, FDR increasingly bound the United States to the Allied cause. With the attack on Pearl Harbor, the power of the executive further expanded to confront the crisis of global war.

With the termination of World War II, the anticipated climate of peace under the aegis of a powerful international organization did not materialize; instead, the postwar years ushered in a period of continuing confrontation—the Cold War. An ideological conflict permeated the international environment and created a war of nerves stretched particularly taut by the specter of nuclear war. In these circumstances, too, crisis spurred the growth of executive prerogatives.

President Harry Truman led the United States into the Korean conflict in 1950 under the auspices of the United Nations (UN) without seeking a congressional declaration of war. Similarly, President John Kennedy escalated the small (less than one thousand personnel) military advisory effort in Vietnam, begun under President Dwight Eisenhower, into a sixteen-thousand-man effort that included not only advisers but helicopter transportation companies and other logistical elements.

Vietnam.   In the mid-1960s, presidential initiative in foreign affairs brought the United States into an extended conflict in Vietnam. As the war dragged on, presidential prerogative in foreign affairs came under vigorous attack. The "imperial president" became the subject of congressional and popular opposition. Congressional opposition culminated in the passage of the War Powers Resolution, over President Richard Nixon's veto, in July 1973. This measure set a sixty-day limit on the president's power to wage war without Congressional authorization.[6]

The War Powers Resolution, however, has thus far not proved an important constraint on the president's power to take the country to war. Presidents have repeatedly refused to embrace this legislation, and each of Nixon's successors has called the act unconstitutional. Congress essentially played no role in President Ronald Reagan's decisions to invade Grenada and place Marines in Lebanon in 1983, put mines in Nicaraguan harbors in 1984, bomb Libya in 1986, or escort reflagged Kuwaiti ships in the Persian Gulf and engage in several battles with the Iranian Navy from mid-1987 through mid-1988. Nor did Congress play a meaningful part in the decisions of the country's forty-first president, George H. W. Bush, to invade Panama in 1989.

The Gulf War in 1991.   The inability of Congress to restrict the president's war-making powers was amply demonstrated during the 1991 war in the Persian Gulf. After Iraq overran Kuwait in August 1990, George H. W. Bush decided to send American troops to Saudi Arabia to prevent Iraq from conquering that oil-rich desert kingdom. Nearly six months later, on January 8, 1991, Bush finally requested legislative approval to undertake military actions. However, by that time, the UN had already authorized military action, and the United States had over five hundred thousand troops in the area, about the same number as it deployed to Vietnam. Bush's unilateral actions had brought the nation to a point where turning back was not a realistic option. Even a Congress controlled by an opposition party could not reject the president's request without severely damaging U.S. credibility and image. After Congress approved his request, Bush said in a rare moment of candor, "I don't think I need it."[7] Although many members of Congress were upset about Bush's lack of consultation with them all during the fall and winter 1990, the success of Operation Desert Storm muted any public criticisms about a possible violation of the War Powers Resolution.

The lesson is clear: If the president is determined to use military force, the Congress may find it difficult to stop him. If the military operation is successful, as was Desert Storm, there will be few public complaints about abuse of executive power. However, if the military conflict turns out poorly, like Vietnam or Lebanon, there will be outcries over the presidential abuse of power.

The World After the Terrorist Attacks of September 11, 2001.　　The preeminence of the presidency in foreign affairs became even more evident after the 2001 terrorist attacks in the United States. In the immediate aftermath, Congress swiftly passed a joint resolution authorizing the president "to use all necessary and appropriate force against those nations, organizations, or persons he determined planned, authorized, committed, or aided the terrorist attacks that occurred on September 11, 2001, or harbored such organizations or persons."[8] Just weeks later, Congress passed the USA PATRIOT Act, which expanded the government's ability to conduct surveillance on terrorist suspects. When the country's forty-third president, George W. Bush, announced in October 2001 that the United States would use military force against Afghanistan to strike down al-Qa'ida terrorist camps supported by the ruling Taliban regime, he had strong congressional and public support for his actions.[9] After the United States had been attacked, the need for strong executive leadership to guide the country in its fight against terrorism seemed self-evident.

This consensus on presidential primacy in foreign policy began to dissipate with the U.S. invasion of Iraq in 2003. George W. Bush quickly secured congressional support for military action. Internationally, the United States secured a UN Security Council resolution calling for "serious consequences" if Iraq did not comply with weapons inspections.[10] But the Security Council could not reach agreement on a second resolution explicitly authorizing military force, and the United States waged war against Iraq in spring 2003 without official UN backing. Domestically, although Congress and the public initially supported the president, critics became more vocal as the difficulty of constructing a new regime in Iraq became evident.[11]

Furthermore, five years after 9/11, resistance to some of the president's policies in the broader struggle against international terrorist groups had developed in both the legislative and judicial branches. In 2005, Congress passed legislation—popularly known as the Detainee Treatment Act—that set guidelines for interrogating detainees and explicitly prohibited torture. In 2006, the Supreme Court ruled five to three (one justice abstained) in the landmark case *Hamdan v. Rumsfeld* that the president did not have the independent authority to establish military tribunals for detainees in the war on terror and declared that Congress must establish guidelines for these trials. Members of Congress, including senior leaders in George W. Bush's own party, called for strict guidelines that would comply with international treaties signed after World War II. Congress ultimately passed legislation that appeared on the surface to comply with international law while also garnering White House approval, spurring critics to insist that the guidelines would be challenged in court. These conflicts raised many questions about whether the United States was witnessing a "new imperial presidency," with presidential power exceeding constitutional boundaries to a degree unprecedented since the abuses of power in the Nixon era. An alternative interpretation held that the expansion of presidential power was due less to executive usurpation and more to congressional reluctance to challenge the president during times of crisis in foreign affairs.[12]

The President and National Security

The Roles of the President.   The president plays multiple roles in the execution of the office. Not only is he or she chief of state, commander in chief of the armed forces, chief diplomat, principal initiator of legislation, and chief executor of laws, but the president also acts as party leader, national spokesperson, peacekeeper, manager of prosperity, and world leader.[13] These roles tend to place the president at the center of national security policy making. The president as chief of state personifies the United States in its dealings with the world, and, through constitutional powers to appoint and receive ambassadors, the president is placed at the focal point of diplomatic activity. As commander in chief, he or she is positioned at the apex of a large and elaborate security apparatus. None of these roles can neatly be isolated from the other, and the president must satisfy the particular demands of each when confronting problems of national security. Moreover, in these various roles, the president must deal with a variety of entities, each with its own interests and viewpoints; these are shown in Figure 4.1.

Various trends have increased the prerogatives associated with the president's national security roles. These trends include: the increasing involvement of the United States in world affairs and an accompanying atmosphere of constant danger; the development of a national contingency system around the president to enable effective response to threats; enhancements in weapons technology that have increased the stakes in crisis management; and enhancements in communications technology that have accelerated the tempo of communication and response and have also made it easier for a president to intervene more deeply into operational matters. The national security process has become saturated with information, and it is the executive who largely controls the organizations capable of assimilating large volumes of data and the communication channels through which decisions

FIG. 4.1   Relationships between the President and the External Environment

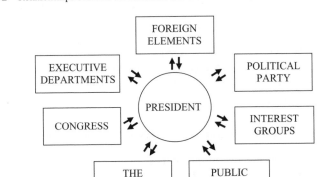

based on that information can be relayed. Although vigorous presidents have always reached out to grasp the levers of government, recent trends have encouraged modern presidents to be especially activist.

Presidential National Security Functions.   Despite the complexity of the president's roles, three major functions in the conduct of national security can be identified: resource allocation, policy planning, and the coordination and monitoring of operations.[14] These are discussed below.

Resource Allocation.   The maintenance of national security is expensive and requires a major commitment of resources each year in the president's budget. The budget is the main vehicle through which presidential priorities relating to resource use are communicated. The Office of Management and Budget (OMB), discussed briefly in subsequent pages, is the principal instrument that the president uses in this allocation function.

Policy Planning.   Policy planning involves the development of long-range designs, such as the Marshall Plan for the reconstruction of Europe after World War II, or ongoing efforts, such as the enlargement and evolution of the North Atlantic Treaty Organization (NATO). It also includes less sweeping and shorter-term plans to advance U.S. interests and cope with emerging problems. The efforts of the George W. Bush administration to cope with Iran's nuclear capabilities and development may be an example of this type of plan. Generally, those engaged in policy planning seek to shape future events as well as prepare for contingencies. Historically, the focus of such planning has shifted among (or been shared by) the Department of State, the Department of Defense (DoD), and the president's national security assistant, who heads the National Security Council (NSC) staff. Unfortunately, this function, which is inherently hard conceptually and difficult to accomplish bureaucratically, has not often been done well.

Coordination and Monitoring of Operations.   Coordination of operations requires overseeing the countless day-to-day foreign and defense policy actions of government organizations and officials so they remain consistent with and advance American policy. The associated monitoring function is designed to provide feedback to the executive branch to ensure that appropriate actions are being taken in light of policy guidance and to ensure awareness of new data or changing conditions or assumptions. In practice, the president has leaned on the Department of State or the national security assistant for the coordination and monitoring task.

The Institutionalized Presidency and National Security Affairs

The complexity, scope, and magnitude of these functions have given rise to the institutionalized presidency. The president, as an individual, has been augmented by staffs acting in the president's name. This institutionalized presidency, together with certain executive departments, forms the principal means of developing, directing, and coordinating national security. The key elements of this collective executive are the White House Office, the NSC and staff, the DoS, the DoD, the Central Intelligence Agency (CIA), and the OMB (see Figure 4.2). Since 2001, the Homeland Security Council and staff have also become key elements of the national security policy process (see Chapters 6 and 10 for a more detailed discussion of these new entities and their roles).

The White House Office.   According to George Reedy, former press secretary to President Lyndon Johnson, "the life of the White House is the life of a court."[15] Extending the analogy, the White House staff members can be seen as the president's courtiers. They are the personal and political assistants to the president. Without outside constituencies, they owe their status and position wholly to the person of the president. Accordingly, the organization and use of the White House staff is the function of a president's personal style.

In recent history, FDR operated probably the most chaotic of staffs, but the chaos was purposeful: " FDR intended his administrative assistants to be eyes and ears and manpower for him, with no fixed contacts, clients, or involvements of their own to interfere when he had to redeploy them."[16] There was overlapping of assignments, lack of coordination, and often frustration on the part of the staff, but these factors served FDR well by presenting him competing sources of information and analysis that enabled him to develop and maintain his personal options. This freewheeling approach was somewhat curtailed by the advent of World War II, as sources of information became channeled through secrecy and censorship systems, and the focus of efforts turned to the operational concerns of global war.[17]

Eisenhower was at the opposite extreme. His staff was organized tightly around its chief of staff, initially Sherman Adams. With some exceptions, access to the president was through Adams, who was not hesitant to ask if a meeting was really necessary. Responsibilities were clearly defined, and there was a military aura of hierarchy, neatness, and order. In the 1960s, the Kennedy and Johnson administrations utilized a less formal staffing system, allowing a small staff concerned with national security more direct and frequent access to the president.

Under Nixon (1969) and Gerald Ford (1974), the White House staff was again organized along more structured lines. Jimmy Carter (1977) endeavored to establish a more informal advisory system, initially operating without a chief of staff, but he soon found that the increased demands upon the Oval Office necessitated some formal staffing procedures. Reagan (1981) employed a hierarchical staffing system in which he empowered cabinet secretaries and relied heavily on delegating authority to a close handful of aides who understood his intent. Though George H. W. Bush (1989) largely continued this model, he engaged more directly with his advisers in policy making, particularly in foreign affairs. Clinton (1993) faced some organizational difficulties in his first year in office, stemming largely from his reluctance to delegate authority to his chief of staff and other advisers, but he ultimately did develop more structured White House operations, albeit with more informality than seen in his immediate predecessors. The only chief executive

FIG. 4.2 The Government of the United States

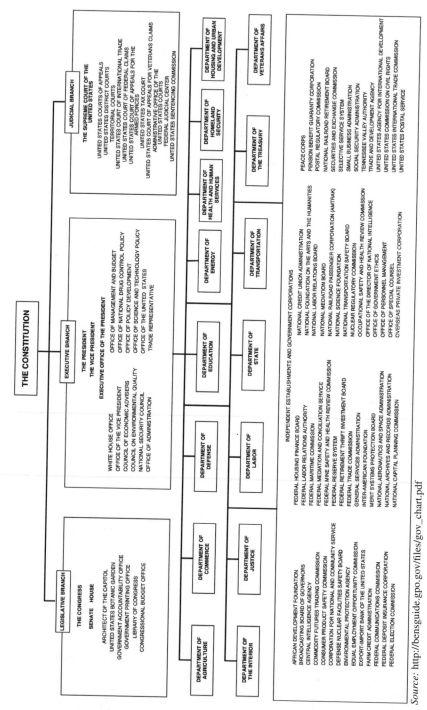

Source: http://bensguide.gpo.gov/files/gov_chart.pdf

to hold a master of business administration, George W. Bush (2001) not surprisingly adopted a structured and hierarchical White House staffing system, consistent with a corporate management style.

The position of assistant to the president for National Security Affairs, popularly known today as the "national security advisor," was created by Eisenhower in 1953.[18] Eisenhower employed his special assistant primarily as a policy coordinator, but since the 1960s, the position has also assumed an advocacy role, serving as a significant post in the White House for foreign policy making. In each administration—as is typical of relationships in the White House—the role of the assistant to the president for national security affairs has been largely a function of the assistant's personal relationship with the president and how the president wishes the office to be discharged. The role also has developed in conjunction with the evolution of the NSC staff, which the assistant heads.

Despite the similarities and differences in the functioning of the White House staff under different presidents, there have been some pronounced trends. The most obvious is growth. The entire Herbert Hoover presidency was staffed by three secretaries, a military and a naval aide, and twenty clerks. In contrast, approximately four hundred people work in the George W. Bush White House, plus another one hundred to one hundred fifty sent from other agencies on special assignments.[19] The growth in numbers is a symptom, and some would argue a cause, of a centralization of decision making. In this regard, one should be mindful that centralization can cause a serious cleavage between policy makers and the instruments of policy. Another aspect of White House staff growth is the tendency for it to shield the president from the outside world. The life of the court can easily become one clouded by perceptions divorced from reality. Finally, as the NSC system has evolved and the position of the assistant directing its staff has strengthened, other White House office staffs have played ever-diminishing roles in national security matters.

National Security Council.   The formalized coordination and policy-planning functions of the presidency in national security matters are located in the NSC, created by the National Security Act of 1947. The NSC inherited many of the functions that previously had been exercised by cabinet members in the State-War-Navy Coordinating Committee, itself an ad hoc product of World War II operations. As constituted in 1947, the NSC comprises the president, the vice president, the secretary of state, the secretary of defense, and the director of the Office of Civil and Defense Mobilization.[20] Because the latter office has long since been abolished, there are now only four statutory members. Additionally, the secretary of the treasury and the national security advisor regularly attend NSC meetings; the chief of staff to the president, counsel to the president, and assistant to the president for economic policy usually are invited to attend as well. The director of national intelligence and the chairman of the JCS serve as statutory advisors.[21] (Since the term "NSC" tends to be used loosely to mean the NSC staff, rather than the Council itself, there is often public confusion about the NSC's composition.)

Truman was instrumental in shaping the NSC to respond directly to the needs of the president rather than merely extending the interagency arrangements of the

State-War-Navy Coordinating Committee. One scholar notes that Truman's "adroit maneuvers scotched the scheme of those who wanted to assure defense domination of the National Security Council by housing it in the Pentagon . . . and by designating the Secretary of Defense as Chairman in the president's absence."[22] In addition, the legislation that the Truman administration shepherded through the Congress to become the 1947 National Security Act provided for a separate staff to support the NSC and did not rely, as was previously done, on staff contributed from involved agencies. In this manner, Truman established the NSC as responsive to the president rather than to competing executive departments.

With the advent of the Eisenhower administration, the NSC system was restructured to reflect both the new president's style as well as his view of the world situation.[23] In keeping with his view of the importance of economic health to security, Eisenhower regularly invited his treasury secretary and budget director to attend NSC meetings. He attempted to systematize the decision-making process in line with his experience with military models of decision making and coordination. He used the NSC apparatus regularly in the belief that, as he later wrote:

> the secret of a sound, satisfactory decision made on an emergency basis has always been that the responsible official has been "living with the problem" before it becomes acute. Failure to use, on a continuing basis, the NSC, or some similar advisory body, entails losing the capacity to make emergency decisions based on depth of understanding and perspective.[24]

The passing of the torch from the Eisenhower to the Kennedy administration involved a distinct change in presidential outlook and operating style.[25] In regard to the NSC, this was reflected in a move to a more ad hoc system. At the heart of criticism of the Eisenhower system was the view that it impeded initiative and flexibility by subjecting proposals to overly formalized bureaucratic argument. Regarding the world as inherently dynamic, Kennedy hoped to shape a national security system capable of coping with rapid change. In lieu of the previous interagency focus, Kennedy built a strong staff in the White House, under his special assistant for national security affairs, to assist him in drawing advice from and coordinating operations of the various agencies involved with national security.

Further, Kennedy chose to immerse himself in the details of selected aspects of policy much more than his predecessor. Shortly after Kennedy took office, the CIA supported an invasion of Cuba at a location on the island known as the Bay of Pigs. The invasion failed after only a few days and was a lesson for Kennedy which he did not soon forget. He had relied on the experts and judgments of the preceding administration, and he remarked a year and a half later, "The advice of every member of the Executive Branch brought in to advise was unanimous—and the advice was wrong."[26] (Of course, his critics also point out that his last-minute intervention in canceling air support for the invasion force contributed to the fiasco.) Partly as a result of the Bay of Pigs, the president relied increasingly on his national security assistant to provide policy options. The full NSC met less frequently and tended to consider long-term questions that had already been extensively explored by ad hoc task forces. These interagency task forces dealt with such specific problems of the early 1960s as Laos, Berlin, and the Nuclear Test Ban Treaty.

Although established to provide a coherent means of coping with the urgency of the atomic age, the formal NSC in practice was not the locus of crisis management. As demonstrated in the Cuban Missile Crisis, Kennedy relied instead on a specially selected "Executive Committee" to bear the burden of deliberation and policy development. Consisting of the president's most trusted advisers and unfettered by the statutory membership requirements of the NSC (though many of those advisers did participate), it represented a continuation of Kennedy's more individualized approach to national security policy making.

With the assassination of Kennedy in November 1963, Johnson was thrust into the presidency. Although he was a master of congressional politics, he had limited experience in international affairs. This lack of background, as well as his desire to bring a sense of continuity to his administration, resulted in few immediate changes to the Kennedy NSC system. Central coordination and direction continued to be provided by the special assistant for national security affairs.[27]

The emergence of the Vietnam conflict in the mid-1960s became the central drama and tragedy of Johnson's foreign policy legacy. Accepting the existing national security apparatus and—unlike Kennedy—lacking the inclination to go beyond his advisers to key points in the bureaucracy, Johnson narrowed the process of deliberation and decision to a few people. In July 1965, the decision to expand America's hitherto-limited commitment reportedly rested on the advice of a handful of people. The NSC and Congress were consulted only after the decision was made.[28] Other important national security decisions were made at the informal, largely unstructured discussions at the president's periodic "Tuesday lunches," which generally included only the NSC members and a few invited guests.

In March 1966, the Johnson administration decided to provide more structure to the NSC system. National Security Memorandum 341 established a permanent interdepartmental committee called the Senior Interdepartmental Group, headed by the undersecretary of state. Subordinate to this group, Interdepartmental Region Groups for each region of the world were created and chaired by regional assistant secretaries of state. In theory, policy planning and coordination of policy decisions would flow through these organizations and up to the NSC. In practice, Vietnam dominated presidential considerations, and Johnson was unwilling to employ his new system in dealing with Vietnam. As a consequence, the interdepartmental groups found themselves working largely on peripheral issues, while crucial decisions concerning Vietnam continued to be resolved by the president and a few advisers.

The Nixon administration departed from the largely ad hoc arrangements of the Kennedy-Johnson years and returned in 1969 to a centralized system more akin to Eisenhower's. Nixon placed the national security machinery firmly in the White House under the control of the president's security assistant, Dr. Henry Kissinger. The focus of the new NSC staff effort was to develop rigorously a set of carefully considered options for presidential choice without engaging the president in the sometimes tumultuous deliberations leading up to those options.

Kissinger adapted the interagency arrangements of the Johnson administration by assigning issues to interdepartmental groups chaired by assistant secretaries of state. These groups were responsible for studying problems, formulating policy choices, and assessing various alternatives. A Senior Review Group was constituted at the undersecretary level, chaired by Kissinger, to deal with interdepartmental group recommendations. By this process, less important or uncontentious issues were decided at subordinate levels rather than being forwarded to the NSC. Although this approach allowed for the inclusion of the views of operating agencies, it lodged control squarely in the White House, where Nixon clearly wanted it.

The Nixon-Kissinger NSC structure was further complicated or "systematized" by the creation of various special groups subordinate to the NSC. For example, major issues centered on the Vietnam War were handled by a Vietnam Special Studies Group, while crisis planning was done by the Washington Special Actions Group. This evolution represented a further strengthening of the hand of the assistant for national security affairs and the dominance of the NSC staff over the Department of State. It is noteworthy that, since leaving office, Kissinger has decried this trend, recommending that a president should make the secretary of state "his principal adviser and 'use' the national security adviser primarily as a senior administrator and coordinator to make certain that each significant point of view is heard."[29]

In broad outlines Carter's initial approach was to "streamline" his NSC staff but to entrust it with the same basic functions and powers as the Nixon-Ford staff. A number of NSC committees of the earlier era (which were really separate entities in name only) were collapsed into three basic committees: the Policy Review Committee, the Special Coordination Committee, and the familiar, assistant-secretary-level interdepartmental groups.

The organizational arrangements of the NSC system in the Carter administration initially led to an increase in the secretary of state's power at the expense of the NSC adviser. Through his chairmanship of many of the substantive Policy Review Committees, Secretary of State Cyrus Vance at first was able to shape many of the fundamental policies of the Carter administration in such areas as human rights policy and arms transfers. As the focus shifted from policy making to implementation, the power of NSC adviser Zbigniew Brzezinski increased. Under Brzezinski's direction, the Special Coordination Committee dealt with issues concerning arms control, covert actions, and crisis management. Management of the Iranian hostage crisis, which consumed much of the last year of the Carter presidency, was handled by Brzezinski and the NSC staff.

Reagan came to office determined to downgrade the role of the NSC and the assistant to the president for national security affairs. His first adviser for NSC affairs, Richard Allen, did not even report directly to him, and NSC management receded in visibility. Although reporting relationships were changed for Allen's five successors (William Clark, Robert McFarlane, John Poindexter, Frank Carlucci, and Colin Powell), who reported directly to Reagan, up to the time of the misconceived, mismanaged Iran-Contra affair neither the NSC nor the assistant played a dominant role in formulation of national security policy.[30] The secretaries of state and defense largely reigned supreme in their own areas of responsibility, with less direct involvement from the White House.[31]

Under George H. W. Bush, Reagan's successor, the assistant and the NSC once again became centers of policymaking power. Brent Scowcroft, Bush's NSC assistant who had held the post briefly under Ford, made himself chairman of a Principals Committee at the cabinet level. His own deputy, first Robert Gates and then Jonathan Howe, was placed in charge of the senior subcabinet interagency forum, the Deputies Committee, which reviewed and monitored the work of the NSC interagency process and made recommendations on the development and implementation of policy.

George H. W. Bush held few formal NSC meetings, preferring to rely on the Principals and Deputies Committees to formulate and implement long-range strategy. For example, in April 1989, it was the Deputies Committee that drafted the document that spelled out the Bush administration's policy toward Iraq. Bush preferred to handle crisis situations in selected ad hoc groups or in one-on-one meetings. For example, the August 4, 1990, meeting at Camp David to review military options after the Iraqi invasion of Kuwait was attended by twelve people—the president, the vice president, the secretaries of state and defense (the NSC members), the NSC assistant, the chairman of the JCS and the director of central intelligence (the NSC advisers), the White House chief of staff and spokesman, the military commanders, an undersecretary of defense, and an NSC staff director. But in early October 1990, when Bush was trying to decide whether to let sanctions work or to adopt an offensive strategy, he met in the Oval Office with the secretary of defense, the chairman of the JCS, and the NSC assistant. His NSC committee system resembled that of the Nixon era in formality, while his own personal decision-making style resembled the informality of Kennedy. General Powell, the chairman of the JCS, has described Bush's NSC process as too relaxed and convivial, with no beginning, middle, or end.[32]

When he took office in 1993, Clinton enlarged the membership of the NSC and included a much greater emphasis on economic issues in the formulation of national security policy. This was illustrated by the incorporation into the NSC of the secretary of the treasury and the assistant to the president for economic policy.[33] Still, the NSC retained emphasis on traditional national security issues as well. Clinton's first national security advisor, W. Anthony Lake, played a primarily behind-the-scenes role until the need to better explain Clinton's foreign policy led him to begin to accept more speaking engagements. Lake's successor in 1997, Samuel R. Berger (known as "Sandy" Berger), had been Lake's deputy since 1993.[34] As the national security advisor, Berger took a more active role in communicating the president's foreign policy, as well as developing support for the president's policies in Congress.[35]

Clinton retained both the structure and functions of the Principals and Deputies Committees. The Deputies Committee consisted of cabinet deputies, as well as the vice chairman of the JCS and deputy director of the CIA. The interdepartmental groups, which had been called the Policy Coordinating Committees by his predecessor, were renamed Interagency Working Groups by Clinton in 1993. Under this structure, there were seven regional and six functional interagency working groups composed of assistant-secretary-level representatives from the appropriate agencies. One criticism of the Clinton administration's national security system was that it produced an ad hoc approach to national security policy by focusing on crisis management and proving to be ineffective at overall planning.[36]

At the start of his first term in 2001, George W. Bush selected Dr. Condoleezza Rice to be his national security adviser. Rice was one of the president's closest foreign-policy advisers and family friends, which raised the visibility of her position tremendously. She was responsible for coordinating NSC meetings, but she faced competition for controlling foreign policy from several sources, including Vice President Richard B. Cheney and Secretary of Defense Donald Rumsfeld.[37] When Rice became secretary of state in Bush's second term, her successor as national security adviser, Stephen J. Hadley (previously Rice's deputy) maintained a less public face for his office and the NSC. The structure of Bush's NSC system did not change significantly from that of Clinton; most of the regional and functional bureaus remained essentially the same, with the names of some changed a bit. Bush did hold more formal NSC meetings than his recent predecessors, holding them daily for a period after the events of 9/11, and weekly thereafter.

The Department of State.   Since its creation in 1789 under its first secretary, Thomas Jefferson, the Department of State has been the customary operational arm of the U.S. government in the conduct of foreign affairs. The department performs two basic functions: It represents the interests of the United States and its citizens in relations with foreign countries, and it serves as a principal source of advice to the president on all aspects of foreign affairs—including national security policy (see Figure 4.3).[38]

A member of the cabinet, the secretary of state is traditionally the president's principal adviser on foreign policy, although this tradition has waned somewhat since the 1960s with the emergence of a succession of powerful presidential assistants for national security affairs. In all cases, the secretary's role is the result of his or her own talents, the personal relationship between him or her and the president, and the president's propensity to become directly involved in foreign policy. The more a president desires to become involved in foreign policy, the more difficult it is for the secretary of state to take initiatives and conduct his or her office. Because presidents normally anticipate their own policymaking tendencies in selecting secretaries, much of the criticism of a "weak" secretary of state should be directed at activist presidents. Nixon's choice in 1969 of William Rogers as secretary of state and his systematic bypassing, even humiliation, of the secretary is an eloquent case in point.[39] On the other hand, such presidents as Reagan, who wished to delegate day-to-day activities of the foreign-policy process and downgrade the NSC's management role, appointed strong secretaries of state, such as Alexander Haig, former White House chief of staff and NATO commander, and George Shultz, who had served in earlier administrations as secretary of labor, secretary of the treasury, and director of OMB before accepting the state post in 1983.

FIG. 4.3 United States Department of State

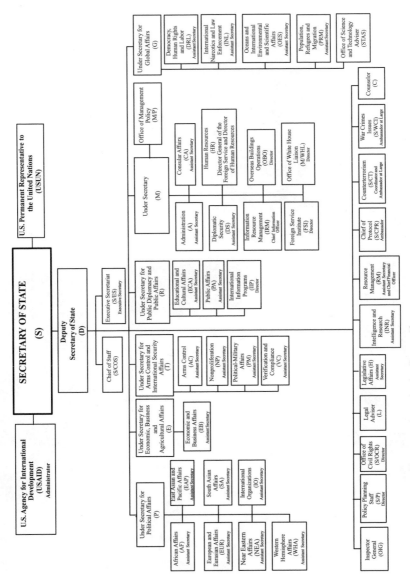

Source: www.state.gov/documents/organization/8792.pdf

Copyright 1992 CARTOONEWS Inc., N.Y.C., USA. Reprinted with permission of Ranan Lurie.

88

By contrast with Reagan's approach, his successor, George H. W. Bush, wanted to focus heavily on certain areas of foreign policy. He therefore appointed a close friend and confidant, James Baker, to handle the areas where he did not focus. Thus, the president personally managed the Gulf War deployment and execution, while Baker followed up the victory by arranging a Mideast peace conference in Madrid in 1991. In some ways, Bush was his own secretary of state, while Baker functioned as his close and powerful deputy.[40]

The combination of a "weak" secretary of state and a president who prefers to focus on the domestic agenda—such as Warren Christopher in Clinton's first term—can produce a foreign policy whose notable successes become associated with key subordinates. From Richard Holbrooke and the negotiation of the Dayton Peace Awards to the predominant role of Special Envoy Dennis Ross in the Middle East peace process, the first Clinton administration will likely be remembered for several distinct foreign policy personalities.

Under Clinton's successor, George W. Bush, the position of secretary of state varied in authority from his first to second terms in office. Bush's first secretary of state, Powell, came to the office with a distinguished military record capped by service as the chairman of the JCS. Powell had also received special permission from Congress to serve during his military career as Reagan's national security adviser and thus had built expertise in the political realm as well. Yet Powell as secretary of state was continually stymied by the president's more powerful allies, notably Cheney and Rumsfeld. Powell was reportedly also regularly at odds with his White House counterpart, national security adviser Rice. For example, Powell was unable to persuade the president to give more time for arms inspections before waging war against Iraq in 2003.[41] When Rice became secretary of state in Bush's second term, she appeared to have a more prominent role than Powell in foreign policy, thereby demonstrating once again the importance of individual relationships with the president.

Presidential-secretarial dynamics aside, the secretary of state faces a complex task in managing the internal workings of his or her bureaucracy. The Department of State is broadly organized along two lines: geographic-regional responsibilities and functional responsibilities. Special "desks" within the regional bureaus monitor the more detailed actions and interactions of specific countries within the purview of a regional assistant secretary. An alternative view of international dynamics is provided by the functional organizations, such as the Bureau of Military Affairs. These functional bureaus present analysis that cuts across strictly geographic lines and sometimes across analyses arising out of the regional desks as well.

The nature and structure of the department presents any secretary of state with a complex managerial and coordination problem. The desk system of organization in the department, in which deeply grounded experts on each country or functional problem funnel their analyses and recommendations to the various assistant secretaries, provides the needed expertise, but it can also generate parochial responses to policy problems. This in turn can lead to striking contrasts in the nature of advice received by the secretary (a good example might be the advice provided by Arabists versus experts on Israel). As a consequence, the secretary of state is often forced to sort out contradictory recommendations while shepherding a fragmented organization through the policy process. For those observers of public affairs who long for quick and efficient solutions to difficult problems (and who often think that the world is more malleable than it is), the Department of State is a source of constant frustration. Owing in part to the department's lack of a natural constituency within the United States and in part to the public's belief that American interests and policies can and should always prevail, this frustration is often translated into vigorous and often mistaken widespread criticism of its role.[42]

Presidential displeasure with the Department of State seems to be a recurring and nonpartisan reaction. In general, presidential complaints about the State Department have centered around six issues: (1) quality of staff work in terms of analysis; (2) slowness with which the State Department responds to requests and problems; (3) resistance to change and new approaches; (4) inadequacy in carrying out presidential decisions; (5) failure to lead in foreign affairs; and (6) the feeling that leadership at the State Department does not have control of its own department.[43] These misgivings about the State Department—though in many cases exaggerated—have often led activist presidents and activist secretaries to bypass the institution and pursue largely individual initiatives in foreign affairs.

For example, Baker—who had served as the undersecretary of commerce, White House chief of staff, and secretary of the treasury before becoming George H. W. Bush's secretary of state in 1989—brought in a group of outsiders with relatively little foreign policy experience to most key positions and often ignored career foreign service officers.

The appropriate employment of the Department of State in the national security process has long been a problem for presidents and secretaries. Periodic attempts have been made to harness the expertise in the context of policy planning, such as Secretary of State George Marshall's creation in 1947 of the Policy Planning Staff, with Ambassador George Kennan as its head.[44] The Policy Planning Staff was designed to focus planning on current issues and to anticipate future contingencies. Yet that staff and its successor organization, the Policy Planning Council, have invariably fallen short of expectations. Mid- and long-range planning for a complex and untidy world is intrinsically difficult, and it requires exceptionally talented people who are sensitive to the purposes and limits of policy and who can draw clear linkages among policy realms and between policies and programs. Such talents, however, are always in short supply. If the people who possess them are kept sufficiently close to genuine issues so their planning is relevant to the real world, then they are constantly drawn into short-range, operational planning and policy advice. In short, if the planners are talented and their subject timely, they tend to be diverted; if they are not, they tend to be ignored. Operational demands ("putting out fires") and the inherent tension between useful specificity and diplomatic generality have made the exercise of policy planning in the Department of State a perennial problem. This situation has tended to shift much of the weight of policy planning to the NSC staff and the DoD.

There is one area in which the Department of State has largely maintained its hegemony: namely, the daily conduct of American policy in foreign countries. The department's mandate to coordinate all American activities in foreign lands was strongly reaffirmed by Eisenhower in his (and subsequent presidents') endorsement of the "country team" concept. This approach places the American ambassador in charge of all American programs within the country to which he or she is accredited. (The mandate does not extend to American military forces in the field, though it does apply to military assistance teams and defense attachés.) The country team represents an important attempt to unify the implementation of American national security policy within each foreign country under the direction of the ambassador.[45] Succeeding administrations have continued to endorse this concept, but there is a continual tendency by departments other than the State Department to fight it.

The Department of Defense.   The DoD is the president's principal arm in the execution of national defense policy. Composed of the three military departments (Army, Navy, and Air Force), the JCS and the associated joint staff, ten regional and functional commands (e.g., European Command and Special Operations Command), and numerous defense agencies with responsibility to provide services across the entire department (e.g., the Defense Intelligence Agency), the department provides the military instrument essential to credible policies (see Figure 4.4).

As originally created in 1947, the position of the secretary of defense was that of a weak coordinator. In the course of a series of defense reorganization acts, the latest of which was enacted in 1986, the secretary's role has been greatly strengthened and the department centralized to improve the efficiency and responsiveness of the military instrument. The essentials of the secretary's role, as they have evolved, have been described as follows:

> Foreign policy, military strategy, defense budgets and the choice of major weapons and forces are all closely related matters of basic national security policy and the principal task of the Secretary of Defense is personally to grasp the strategic issues and provide active leadership to develop a defense program that sensibly relates all these factors. In short, his main job is to shape the defense program in the national interest. In particular, it is his job to decide what forces are needed.[46]

During Robert McNamara's tenure as secretary (1961–1968), secretarial control was extended throughout the DoD by the application of systems analysis techniques to generate and justify military programs. The thrust of McNamara's approach was to steer the nature of debate in the DoD on strategy and forces away from the intangibles of military judgment toward quantitative, management-oriented analyses in which civilian officials could dominate. Although the effects of the McNamara revolution have endured in considerable measure, subsequent secretaries have tended to turn more to military professionals in the department for expertise and advice. Indeed, during the tenure of Caspar Weinberger (1981–1987), the military professionals largely regained a position of preeminence in the department.

FIG. 4.4 The Department of Defense.

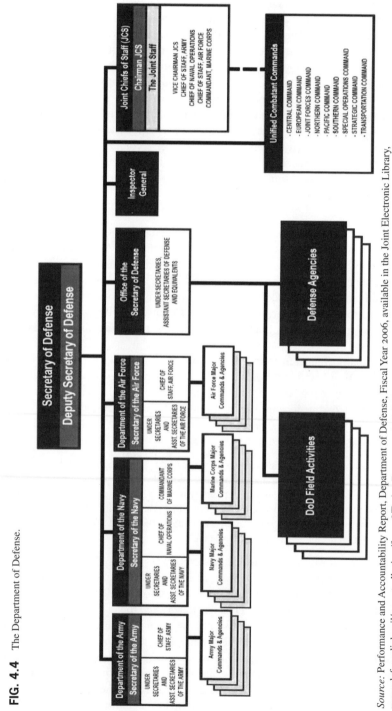

Source: Performance and Accountability Report, Department of Defense, Fiscal Year 2006, available in the Joint Electronic Library, www.defenselink.mil/comptroller/par/fy2006/Entire_Document_(7.8_MB).pdf.

Note: The addition of Africa Command in 2007 has increased the number of unified combatant commands.

Though the formal hierarchy is clear, the relative influence of the civilian leadership of the Pentagon vis-à-vis its most senior uniformed leaders has varied over time. During the 1990s, some observers were concerned about what they saw as the inappropriate assertiveness of uniformed members of the military on policy issues. By contrast, George W. Bush's first defense secretary, Rumsfeld, was dominant in shaping the president's defense policies and was known for having a directive and demanding leadership style toward military subordinates. Though the relationship varies, a key challenge—ensuring democratically appropriate and strategically effective civil-military relationships in which professional military leaders provide senior civilian policy makers with the best possible expert advice—will remain.

The president exercises his or her constitutional authority as commander in chief of the armed forces directly through the secretary of defense to the commanders of the ten unified combatant commands. In strict legal terms, the chairman of the JCS and the JCS as a body are not in the chain of command; in practice, defense secretaries generally involve the chiefs, drawing on their professional advice on policy and operational means to implement presidential directives. Although the normal flow of advice from the chiefs goes up through the chairman and the secretary of defense, the 1986 Goldwater-Nichols Act explicitly gives the individual members of the JCS a statutory right to provide advice directly to the president. This provision was designed to assuage opponents to reorganization who feared that independent military opinion would be stifled by a partisan secretary of defense or a dominant chairman.[47]

As the "hinge" between the highest civilian authorities and the uniformed military, the members of the JCS have two distinct roles in the DoD. In one, corporately, they are advisers to the president, the NSC, and the secretary of defense with the chairman designated as the principal military advisor. In the other, individually, they are the leaders of their respective services. As a corporate body, the JCS includes not only the Army and Air Force chiefs of staff, the chief of Naval operations, and the commandant of the Marine Corps, but also the chairman and vice chairman of the JCS. The chairman or the vice chairman represents the JCS at meetings of the NSC and in other interagency forums. Although the president leans on the chiefs for military advice, the president also depends on them for supporting opinions when undertaking politically controversial national security policy initiatives. Such support has often been crucial. A further discussion of the role of the uniformed military in the national security process is in Chapter 8.

The Central Intelligence Agency.   The CIA was established under the National Security Act of 1947, with responsibility for the overall coordination and integration of the intelligence efforts of various governmental groups engaged in national security matters. Its director was named an adviser to the NSC. The CIA inherited many functions of the wartime Office of Strategic Services, including gathering and analyzing information and conducting covert operations.

Prior to America's entry into World War II, the gathering of intelligence was not institutionalized in any one agency but was incidental to the activities of several agencies, notably the State Department and the Army and Navy attachés. The climate of opinion was such that intelligence activities were looked down upon. Henry Stimson, as secretary of state in the Hoover administration, dismissed the "spying" business with the maxim that "gentlemen do not read other gentlemen's mail."[48] However, the ravages of global war and the threat of communism obscured the gentlemanly distinctions of an earlier age. Beginning in 1947, the CIA became a powerful force in the twilight battles of the Cold War.

Through the 1950s and 1960s, the CIA played a major role and amassed considerable power within the government. As the dimensions and stakes of the Cold War expanded, so did the CIA. Moreover, the agency enjoyed unusual autonomy. From 1947 until 1977, the CIA was the only federal agency exempt from openly defending its budget and subjecting its activities to congressional oversight. Funds for the CIA were disguised in the defense budget, rendering outside assessment of program effectiveness impossible. The CIA was also strengthened by its primacy in intelligence gathering and analysis. Information is power, in government as elsewhere. As a result of long-term assignments to specific areas, the CIA's agents in the field, as well as its analysts at home, produced relatively high-quality work.[49]

Since its inception, the CIA has also been involved in covert operations. In Iran in 1953 and in Guatemala in 1954, for example, the CIA sponsored coups that overthrew existing regimes. In the Bay of Pigs in 1961, the CIA was the agent of an unsuccessful attempt to remove Castro from power. Such episodes of clandestine warfare, combined with CIA activity in Chile during the overthrow of Salvador Allende and a few instances of improper actions by its personnel at home, convinced a number of critics that the CIA's scope and power should be curtailed. Some members of Congress and the public were prepared to sacrifice operational effectiveness to whittle down the CIA's power. The fact that the Cold War was presumably replaced by détente and intervention by retrenchment in the early 1970s reinforced this tendency to downgrade the CIA.

In due course it became apparent to many that the downgrading of the CIA in the early 1970s went too far. When the Carter administration found itself caught off guard in 1979 by the seizure of the American embassy in Teheran and the Soviet invasion of Afghanistan, it began the process of revitalizing the CIA. Subsequently, during the Reagan administration, the CIA played a major role in American efforts to destabilize the Sandinista government in Nicaragua. These activities, plus the agency's role in the Iran-Contra affair, again led to congressional and public criticism and a drop in public trust in the latter 1980s. By the early 1990s, the imposition of strict internal controls did much to restore public confidence and agency morale.

The end of the Cold War and the collapse of the Soviet Union undermined one principal purpose of the CIA. In response, the agency has attempted to deal with the new environment by adjusting its mission. For example, in the early 1990s, the CIA began to intensify its economic intelligence activities, to coordinate U.S. and foreign intelligence on global terrorism, and to integrate intelligence and law enforcement activities against narcotics producers and traffickers. However, its inability to predict major events, such as the collapse of the Soviet Union, the Iraqi invasion of Kuwait, and the terrorist attacks of 9/11, again damaged its credibility.

The role of the CIA is further complicated by the creation of the Office of the Director of National Intelligence. Based on recommendations from the 9/11 Commission, Congress and George W. Bush approved the Intelligence Reform and Terrorism Prevention Act of 2004. This law authorized the creation of a Director of National Intelligence (DNI) to coordinate the efforts of more than a dozen independent federal intelligence agencies, such as the CIA, the National Security Agency, and the Defense Intelligence Agency. The role of this official and his or her relationships with existing intelligence agencies continue to evolve.[50] More detailed attention is given to the role of intelligence in Chapter 7.

Office of Management and Budget.   Questions of strategy and national security have their dollars-and-cents counterparts. With his defense budget, the president structures the priorities of national defense. In the creation of this budget and in the daily oversight of executive operations, the OMB plays a crucial role. As Theodore Sorensen remarks, "Any president, in short, must always be setting priorities and measuring costs. The official most often likely to loom largest in his thinking when he makes a key decision is not the Secretary of State or the Secretary of Defense but the Director of the Budget."[51]

As presidents have sought to extend their control over an expanding bureaucracy, OMB has become an effective instrument of influence. OMB personnel establish, under presidential guidance, departmental budget obligations and spending ceilings within which departments must plan. Budgets from the departments, including the DoD, are routinely subjected to OMB review prior to presidential approval and submission to Congress to ensure that they are in accordance with the president's priorities. This process helps restrain the special relationships that tend to proliferate between executive bureaus and congressional committees. In addition, as part of its management responsibilities, the OMB exercises a continuing oversight role over ongoing federal programs. This, too, enhances its position within the executive branch.[52]

Still, the ability of the OMB (and of the executive branch in general) to manage spending has long been at odds with congressional control of the purse strings and the penchant of members of Congress to add items to spending bills designed to satisfy lobbyists or constituents in their home districts. These incentives shape the perennial conflict between OMB and Congress over defense spending.

The Nature of Presidential Power

Central to the Constitution's design was the concept that no institution should hold an unchallenged position of dominance in all aspects of the conduct of public affairs. This constitutional precept and the consequent governmental framework fundamentally shape the president's ability to influence the behavior of institutions, people, and the overall environment of governmental activity. Richard Neustadt has succinctly and insightfully described this system as one "not of separation of power but of separated institutions sharing powers."[53] The president, as a result, sits in a position where many actors require his help in achieving their objectives. By the same token, the president is also dependent on other actors to accomplish his own purposes. As discussed in the opening paragraphs of this chapter, this interactive process is clearly illustrated by the dynamic and historic tension between the president and Congress.

In the context of our system of government, presidential power is generally the power of persuasion. Teddy Roosevelt called the presidency a "bully pulpit"; FDR said it was a "place of moral leadership."[54] More prosaically, Neustadt noted that presidential power rests in the ability to induce others to "believe that what he [the president] wants of them is what their own appraisal of their own responsibilities requires them to do in their own interests, not his." At the heart of the process of persuasion is bargaining. As Neustadt emphasizes, "power is persuasion and persuasion becomes bargaining."[55]

All too often, the give and take of the bargaining system is obscured by the symbols of power and authority that surround the presidency. The president commands attention in the media by virtue of his office. He enjoys the prestige of being chief of state, as well as the head of government. He has at his disposal a wide spectrum of rewards and a significant number of penalties. These potential points of advantage in the bargaining process should not, however, be confused with presidential power, which actually rests on the ability to wield these instruments in a manner that persuades other people that cooperation advances their own interests.

The bargaining advantages accrued by a president come not only from political acumen and public relations and persuasive skills but also from an ability to do the following: (1) develop and articulate an overall policy framework and strategy that give coherence to his actions; (2) choose able subordinates and weld them into an effective team; and (3) establish a pattern of successful leadership in important matters that will encourage those who are neutral to cooperate and those who would oppose to await a more favorable time. Establishing a pattern of success is partly a matter of good fortune (but, as Machiavelli observed, a successful leader grasps good fortune and uses it), but it is also a matter of readiness to sort out priorities and make hard decisions.

One example of a president who was highly successful in foreign policy was George H. W. Bush. This success so frustrated his opponents that they criticized him not for failing in foreign policy, but for paying too much attention to it. His success was due largely to his foreign-policy background (ambassador to the UN, envoy to China, and director of central intelligence), his personal contacts with world leaders (developed during his eight years as vice president), and the ability and loyalty of his foreign-policy team. During 1990 and 1991, Bush successfully led a thirty-state coalition (and obtained UN approval) in imposing sanctions and then winning a decisive war to evict Iraq from Kuwait. Bush also had success presiding over the end of the Cold War, facilitating the peace process in the Middle

East, preserving most favored nation trading status for China, and receiving trade concessions from the Japanese.

The only person who truly can view an issue from a presidential perspective is the president; all others' views are colored by their own responsibilities. To protect and advance presidential power, the president cannot squander time and influence. He or she must carefully weigh choices so they contribute to presidential influence on issues deemed critical to the administration and to the nation. The president must anticipate major issues early and seek out their crucial elements. When the matter is an important one, the president cannot hesitate to invest reputation and prestige, for they are important elements in the equation of power. As evidenced by Nixon's inability to lead the nation after the Watergate scandal, even the soundest policies and most adroit bargaining can be doomed if the president is suffering from a negative image.

On the other hand, reputation and prestige have acted as a buffer for many presidents in the face of controversy. Weinberger's 1987 departure as secretary of defense was widely viewed as a protest against Reagan's softening of his attitude toward the threat of Soviet Communist expansionism. The political impact of Weinberger's action, even among the right wing of the Republican Party, was muted by Reagan's longstanding reputation as a virulent anticommunist, and Reagan was able to get the Senate to ratify the Intermediate Nuclear Forces Agreement in the spring of 1988.

Constraints on Presidential Power

Although the president sits astride important action channels, presidential power is constantly challenged and tempered. The dynamic tension between the president and Congress is only the most dramatic of the checks on presidential action. (This tension is further discussed in Chapter 5 on the role of Congress.) Among the other important countervailing forces are public opinion, interest groups, the impact of past policies and programs, the responsiveness of the executive bureaucracy, and the views, interests, and expected reactions of other nations.

Yet even with constitutional and political checks on executive power, presidents still wield greater influence in foreign and national security affairs than in domestic policy. In 1966, political scientist Aaron Wildavsky declared that the United States had "two presidencies," one with limited constraints in national security and foreign affairs and one with more active checks and balances from Congress, public opinion, and other actors in domestic policy.[56] Wildavsky's thesis prompted many critiques, particularly in the post–Cold War era, about the difficulty of measuring checks on presidential power, as well as the challenge of separating foreign from domestic policy. Nevertheless, the expansion of presidential power in the aftermath of the 9/11 terrorist attacks suggests the continuing relevance of Wildavsky's analysis.

Public Opinion.   As introduced above, the president can use the "bully pulpit" to advantage. However, public opinion can still be a constraint. Effective presidential leadership can tolerate short-term reverses in public acceptance, but over time a president must have a favorable popular consensus behind his policies. The demise of Johnson's "Great Society" under the burden of the Vietnam War's unpopularity, the resignation of Nixon in the wake of Watergate, and the weakened ability of Reagan to set budget priorities and establish trade policies after the Iran-Contra scandal offer three striking examples of this phenomenon.

Because public opinion is a vital factor in maintaining and projecting presidential influence, it is also a subject for focused presidential attention. In discussing his approach to press relations, Johnson revealed his view of the nature of the process:

> There's only one sure way of getting favorable stories from reporters and that is to keep their daily bread—the information, the stories, the plans, and the details they need for their work—in your own hands, so that you can give it out when and to whom you want. Even then nothing's guaranteed, but at least you've got a chance to bargain.[57]

In addition to underscoring the motif of bargaining as a means of presidential leadership, Johnson's remarks are suggestive of the complex nature of public opinion formation. Public opinion is seldom a spontaneous expression of the people's will. It is a reaction to selective information provided by institutions and individuals, often with contradictory purposes. Moreover, the public is frequently highly differentiated. The views of opinion leaders or the "attentive public" are often at variance with those of the mass public. Which "public's" opinion counts will differ with circumstances, but the president cannot long ignore the ability of the media to raise and to frame issues.

In the realm of national security affairs, the president has a substantial initial advantage in the formation of public opinion. External crises tend to have a cohesive effect on opinion. In addition, the executive frequently dominates the channels of information. This was vividly demonstrated during the Persian Gulf War in January and February 1991. The president and his key advisers decided to manage the flow of information in such a way that the president and the military appeared flawless in their execution of Operation Desert Storm. Unlike Vietnam, where reporters were allowed to roam freely, reporters were confined to escorted pools, and the Pentagon placed sharp restrictions on when and how they could talk to the troops. Two results were that George H. W. Bush's popularity and public support for the war climbed dramatically. In the fall of 1990, less than half the population supported the war, and the president's approval rating was below 50%. On the eve of the war, support had risen to 62%; once hostilities began, support for the war and the president climbed above 90%. This support remained high even after subsequent analysis showed that Bush's policies and the military execution were not entirely flawless. The initial impression about the president's decisiveness and the military's success remained the predominant factor in shaping public opinion about the Persian Gulf War.[58]

Adverse opinion becomes crucial when it is expressed in the electoral process. In spite of growing dissension within the nation, Johnson "survived" the Vietnam debate until Eugene McCarthy's near victory in the 1968 New Hampshire primary translated opinion into adverse votes. Similarly, Carter's perceived weaknesses in dealing with the Soviet invasion of Afghanistan and the taking of American hostages at the Iranian embassy, coupled with his delay in rebuilding America's military strength, proved to be fatal to his reelection effort. To political leaders, including the president, the electoral process is the most forceful and attention-getting expression of popular opinion.

Public opinion provides a barometer of popular feeling. For a beleaguered president, however, the need is more often for a compass than a barometer. Public opinion polls report general reactions but seldom provide a president with clear policy direction. Moreover, public opinion generally lags behind the problem. FDR's struggle to awaken an indifferent or negative America to the dangers prior to World War II is a case in point. The ability to both interpret public opinion and to influence it has proven to be a difficult yet essential presidential art.

Interest Groups.   Another form of public opinion, expressed in a more concerted and organized manner, is the pressure exerted by interest groups. Since the end of the Cold War, the dissolution of the Soviet Union, and the resulting drop in public interest in foreign affairs, domestic interest groups have become even more powerful and effective. This has been especially true for ethnic interest groups, such as those representing Jewish, Greek, Armenian, Irish, Cuban-American, and East European communities.[59] All have influenced U.S. foreign and security policy to varying degrees. Examples include the Irish-American influence on U.S. policies and actions with respect to Northern Ireland (and the adverse effects to U.S.–United Kingdom relations during the first Clinton administration) and Greek opposition to the sale of U.S. military equipment to Turkey.

Other types of interest groups also affect U.S. national security policy and decision making by the president and Congress. The business community played a significant role throughout the 1990s in keeping the U.S. "engaged" with China by lobbying for permanent normal trade relations. Business interests were also very vocal in their support of expanding trade opportunities around the world. By contrast, an alliance among labor unions, environmentalists, and other interest groups was the deciding factor in the congressional failure to approve "fast track" trade negotiating authority for the president in the fall of 1997, despite the intense interest of the business groups that had rallied on its behalf.

Past Policies and Programs.   As each president assumes office, the rhetoric of autumn campaigning takes on a different perspective. The responsibilities of the presidency, including the continuing programs and initiatives of a previous chief executive, now belong to the new officeholder. An example of this situation is the Bay of Pigs invasion in 1961. Kennedy inherited from Eisenhower a small army of Cubans poised in Guatemala for a strike against the Castro regime. With planning in its final stages and with Eisenhower's previous endorsement, Kennedy pondered the decision to proceed with the assault. Some would have interpreted cancellation as an admission that Castro was too powerful and too popular to be overthrown; others would see cancellation as a sign of presidential weakness and a disavowal of the "free" Cubans.[60] On a practical level, Kennedy was confronted with the problem of disarming and disbanding a sizable and fanatical military force should he opt for cancellation. He chose to let the Cubans strike but resisted recommendations that crucially needed, planned air support be provided. The results were disastrous. The invaders were routed, Fidel Castro's prestige was enhanced, and the image of the United States was tarnished. Kennedy's mishandling of his dubious inheritance was a serious blow to his young administration.

As the foregoing indicates, policy is not created in a vacuum; rather, each new decision must be made within the context of already existing decisions and commitments. Powerful among these legacies are the budget decisions of previous administrations. This is especially true with regard to the development of weapons, for the military procurement process is characterized by long lead times. A new president is often unable to influence the types and amounts of weapons available to conduct military operations—availability that may shape overall strategy during his term of office.

Lack of Bureaucratic Responsiveness.   Presidents often find their ability to execute or even influence national security policy diminished by their inevitable reliance on the bureaucracy for the implementation of policy decisions. The expansion of the executive bureaucracy has been in many respects a two-edged sword. Presidents derive from this expanded bureaucracy greater access to and control over information, as well as the ability to develop and analyze a broader range of policy options. However, executive decisions are necessarily implemented through the bureaucracy, and its growth serves to widen the gap between policy making at the top and implementation at the grassroots level. Within that gap, the occasion often arises for presidential decisions to be delayed, amended, or even nullified.

Though senior agency officials are generally appointed by the president, the federal bureaucracy is largely staffed at middle and lower levels by career civil servants who may not fully share the president's perspectives on national security affairs. Experienced bureaucrats often learn to influence the policymaking process by manipulating the number and range of policy options developed for consideration, by drafting implementation instructions that blunt the impact of a particular policy, or by delaying the implementation of a policy to the point that it becomes "overtaken by events." Oftentimes, bureaucratic "leaks" develop that alert the media, and thereby the public, to particularly controversial policies under consideration before they can be implemented.

One need not always invoke mischievous motives, however, to explain how the executive bureaucracy can act as a constraint on presidential power. To receive the careful analysis and consideration that they deserve, major policy initiatives are circulated, or "staffed," among the various agencies of the bureaucracy with an interest in the ultimate policy outcome. Again, due to the increased size of the bureaucracy, this staff coordination can be a time-consuming process. Although clearly possessing the means to bypass much of this process, presidents who attempt to short-circuit the full consideration of policy initiatives do so at the risk of an incomplete or inaccurate understanding of the implications of their actions. In short, presidents are often constrained in implementing major policies by the time required to study and analyze, as well as implement, such initiatives.

In many respects, the president's role in national security policy making is the most fluid and least predictable of all the major actors' in the decision-making process. In both a constitutional and an institutional sense, the president is the focal point of the national security policy process. But more than most participants in that process, the president has wide latitude in defining his or her role. Patterns of presidential involvement have varied according to the style and experience of various presidents. Always subject to important constraints, some presidents have chosen to become personally enmeshed in the details of policy making and implementation. Others have chosen a more passive role, while delegating broad responsibilities to their cabinet and other senior officials. Given the nature of presidential authority and power, however, even the most passive chief executives of recent decades have occupied pivotal positions in the national security process.

Interests of Other Nations. Both in traditional foreign policy matters and also in what might initially appear to be domestic matters—such as environmental issues—the president must take into account the views of other nations' leaders. As interdependence deepens in the years to come, this constraint on presidential freedom of action will clearly grow in importance. Examples of this factor can be deduced or found in Chapters 18 to 25, which deal with regional and transnational issues.

Discussion Questions

1. How does the Constitution divide responsibility between the president and Congress in foreign affairs?

2. How has the War Powers Resolution of 1973 shaped presidential decision making on the employment of U.S. military forces?

3. How have changes in technology influenced the scope of presidential prerogative in national security policy?

4. The evolution of the national security policymaking process reflects a generally expanding role for the assistant to the president for national security affairs (popularly known as the national security adviser). What factors have contributed to this trend? Is this trend irreversible?

5. What factors have tended to hinder the role of the Department of State in the formation of national security policy?

6. How have the agencies created by the National Security Act of 1947—including the CIA, the DoD, the JCS, and the NSC—evolved from their inception into the twenty-first century?

7. What is the function of the OMB in national security?

8. Has the expansion of presidential power in the twenty-first century resulted in an imperial presidency? Why or why not?

9. How have the 9/11 terrorist attacks on U.S. soil affected presidential power in national security affairs?

Recommended Reading

Allison, Graham, and Philip Zelikow. *Essence of Decision: Explaining the Cuban Missile Crisis.* 2nd ed. New York: Longman, 1999.

Crabb, Cecil V., and Kevin V. Mulcahy. *Presidents and Foreign Policy Making: From FDR to Reagan.* Baton Rouge: Louisiana State University Press, 1986.

Destler, I. M. *Presidents, Bureaucrats, and Foreign Policy.* Princeton, NJ: Princeton University Press, 1972.

Fisher, Louis. *Presidential War Power.* 2nd rev. ed. Lawrence: University Press of Kansas, 2004.

———. *Military Tribunals and Presidential Power: American Revolution to the War on Terrorism.* Lawrence: University Press of Kansas, 2005.

Hilsman, Roger. *The Politics of Policy Making in Defense and Foreign Affairs.* New York: Harper & Row, 1971.

Inderfurth, Karl F., and Loch K. Johnson. *Fateful Decisions: Inside the National Security Council.* New York: Oxford University Press, 2004.

Kissinger, Henry A. *The White House Years.* Boston: Little, Brown, 1979.

———. *Years of Upheaval.* Boston: Little, Brown, 1982.

Lowenthal, Mark. *The National Security Council: Organizational History.* Washington, DC: Congressional Research Service, 1978.

Lowi, Theodore J. *The Personal President: Power Invested, Promise Unfulfilled.* Ithaca, NY: Cornell University Press, 1985.

May, Ernest R., and Zelikow, Philip D. *The Kennedy Tapes: Inside the White House During the Cuban Missile Crisis.* Cambridge, MA: The Belknap Press of Harvard University Press, 1997.

Neustadt, Richard E. *Presidential Power.* New York: John Wiley & Sons, 1960.

Report of the President's Special Review Board (Tower Commission). Washington, DC: U.S. Government Printing Office, 1987.

Prados, John. *Keepers of the Keys: A History of the National Security Council from Truman to Bush.* New York: William Morrow, 1991.

Rossiter, Clinton. *The American Presidency.* New York: New American Library, 1960.

Rudalevige, Andrew. *The New Imperial Presidency: Renewing Presidential Power After Watergate.* Ann Arbor: University of Michigan Press, 2005.

Tucker, Robert, and Hendrickson, David. *The Imperial Temptation: New World Order and America's Purpose.* New York: Council on Foreign Relations, 1992.

Yoo, John. *The Powers of War and Peace: The Constitution and Foreign Affairs After 9/11.* Chicago: University of Chicago Press, 2005.

Internet Sources

The Center for the Study of the Presidency, www.thepresidency.org

The National Security Council, www.whitehouse.gov/nsc

The Office of Management and Budget, www.whitehouse.gov/omb

The Peter S. Kalikow Center for the Study of the American Presidency, Hofstra University, www.hofstra.edu/academics/colleges/hclas/prssty

The U.S. Department of Defense, www.defenselink.mil

The U.S. Department of State, www.state.gov

The White House National Security Policy, www.whitehouse.gov/infocus/nationalsecurity

5

Congress

Over two hundred years ago, Alexander Hamilton laid out the constitutional framers' rationale for the distinct roles of Congress and the president with these words: "The essence of the legislative authority is to enact laws, or, in other words, to prescribe rules for the regulation of the society; while the execution of the laws, and the employment of the common strength, either for this purpose or for the common defense, seem to comprise all the functions of the executive magistrate."[1] Their experience during the Revolutionary War convinced the framers that the lack of a strong executive sharing power with an equally strong legislature had nearly cost them victory. In a letter to William Gordon, George Washington wrote, "to suppose that the general concern of this Country can be directed by thirteen heads, or one head without competent powers, is a solecism, the bad effects of which every Man who has had the practical knowledge to judge from, that I have, is fully convinced of; tho' none perhaps has felt them in so forcible, and distressing a degree."[2] Reflecting this concern, the Constitution authorized extensive power to the federal government. The distribution of this centralized power among the branches of government was to prevent any of them from wielding power arbitrarily.

Congress and the Constitution

Congressional Powers. The Constitution provides Congress with a formidable array of tools that authorize it to participate in national security matters. It has the power to declare war, to raise and support armies, to provide and maintain a navy, to determine the rules and regulations governing the military, and to call forth the militia in times of crisis. Additionally, presidents must seek the "advice and

103

consent" of the Senate for treaty ratification and the appointment of senior governmental officials, including military officers. Ultimately, Congress influences the executive via the power of the purse. With the ability "to lay and collect Taxes, Duties, Imposts and Excises, to pay the Debts and provide for the common Defense and general Welfare of the United States," Congress determines the appropriations levels for the entire executive branch, including the national security apparatus. The Constitution specifies that the Army should not receive operational and pay appropriations for longer than a two-year term, so technically each Congress must reestablish the army or it must demobilize.[3] This provision reflects the Founding Fathers' fear of standing armies under the control of a despotic leader (in their case, the king of England during the Revolutionary War).

Mindful of its institutional power, Congress carefully protects its ability to use the power of the purse to shape foreign policy. In the debate over the 1994 defense appropriations bill, which occurred shortly after the death of eighteen American soldiers during the U.S. intervention in Somalia, Senator Robert Byrd (D-WV) stated:

> This is the appropriate bill on which to debate our policy in Somalia, because it highlights the importance of the power of the purse—the ultimate arrow in Congress' quiver—to effect the policy of the Nation in such weighty matters as war and deployments of American Forces. The Framers of the Constitution were well aware that the power of the purse was the key to the power of this institution, and we cannot guard the American people and it too closely.[4]

Despite the intent to assert congressional prerogative, it is evident in these comments that Congress is reacting to national security policies already set in motion by the president. Presidential initiatives create a momentum that even a united Congress can find difficult to overcome, and the 535 members of Congress have perhaps never held uniform views or priorities.

Richard Fenno suggests that legislators have three key motivations: reelection, good public policy, and advancement to higher office.[5] On the campaign trail, members of Congress rarely focus on foreign and national security policy. These are not the characteristic bread-and-butter issues that bring federal largesse to home districts and states. Characterizing this paucity of attention to this aspect of national policy, Senate Foreign Relations Committee Chairman Richard Lugar (R-IN) observed, "There's almost no political sex appeal. . . . For those who get involved it's strictly a pro bono service."[6] In fact, public opinion generally lags behind the course of international events; consequently, Congress ends up legislating for future events against the errors of the past. Recent examples of this include the clarification of interrogation techniques by Congress after the prisoner abuses by U.S. personnel at the Iraqi Abu Ghraib prison in 2003 and the 2006 sanctioning of military tribunals for unlawful combatants already detained at a U.S. military facility at Guantanamo Bay. In effect, in the national security arena, the president often acts and then asks Congress for retroactive permission.

Executive Branch Advantages.   When it comes to dealing with foreign powers, the executive enjoys the inherent advantage of unity of command. Hamilton writes, "That unity is conducive to energy will not be disputed. Decision, activity, secrecy, and dispatch will generally characterize the proceedings of one man in a much more eminent degree than the proceeding of any greater number."[7] The Constitution not only vests the president as the commander in chief of the armed forces, but it also makes him or her both head of state and head of government. In periods of crisis, particularly during armed conflict, presidential powers reach their pinnacle. Centralized authority is required for swift and effective action. Responding to emergencies, presidents have claimed implicit prerogatives not specifically mentioned in the Constitution. President Abraham Lincoln famously suspended the writ of habeas corpus during the Civil War without congressional approval. Under a "doctrine of necessity," Lincoln claimed he had to break the Constitution in order to save it.[8] President George W. Bush similarly claimed powers as commander in chief in authorizing warrantless wiretapping and in establishing military commissions to try unlawful combatants during the Iraq and Afghanistan wars. In responding to these extraordinary assertions of authority, Congress faces a difficult choice: It can actively counterbalance presidential declarations of power and assume greater responsibility for the resulting outcomes, or it can accept executive hegemony in national security affairs.

The executive branch also has an informational advantage over Congress. John Lehman writes, "In terms of expertise, the disparity is enormous. In the executive departments, the richness and sophistication in scientific, technological, military, diplomatic, statistical, medical, educational, geological, fiscal, legal, and sociological skills are truly awesome. Congressional staffs have a smattering of knowledge in all of these areas, but only a smattering."[9]

Congressional Branch Passivity and Activism.   Due to its relative lack of knowledge, fractious nature, torpid decision-making pace, and inability to maintain confidentiality, Congress has often been the minor partner in the national security process. Traditional periods of congressional passivity in foreign affairs include President Thomas Jefferson's Louisiana Purchase, President Theodore Roosevelt's initiation of the Panama Canal project, President Franklin Roosevelt's launching of the Lend-Lease Program, President Lyndon Johnson's stimulation of the Gulf of Tonkin Resolution, and the first five years immediately following the September 11, 2001, terrorist attacks on United States soil.

Despite these examples of executive preeminence, there are occasions where Fenno's three incentives align uniformly across Congress to impel institutional action. Cecil V. Crabb and his colleagues classify three conditions necessary for congressional activism in national security and foreign policy: (1) a clear public opinion groundswell regarding America's international role, (2) tentative or weak presidential leadership, and (3) urgent domestic affairs overpowering foreign policy.[10] Historical events that meet these conditions include congressional activity during and after the American Revolution; President James Madison's dealings with congressional hawks prior to the War of 1812; the Reconstruction Period following the Civil War; the Senate's refusal to ratify the Treaty of Versailles, which denied President Woodrow Wilson's desire to join the League of Nations; the isolationist movement in Congress prior to World War II; and congressional activism in the decade following the Vietnam War and the power abuses of the Nixon administration.

Aside from periods of passivity and activism, Congress has also acted in concert with the president as a full partner in setting national security policy and processes. However, these occurrences are rare. The primary example of bipartisan and equal partnership occurred during the early Cold War years, when both the executive and legislative branches saw the Soviet Union as a dire threat to the United States.

Congressional National Security Institutions

When considering the establishment of national security policy, Lehman writes, "it is the executive that proposes but the Congress that disposes."[11] Yet how Congress disposes is a complicated process whereby members must placate varied constituencies, moneyed interests, personal ideological considerations, and, most importantly, each other. To bring their policy ideas to fruition, legislators must line up support across the institution. They must generate legislative momentum through cosponsorship, the logrolling of votes, and compromise. Power bases in Congress are broad and diverse. Members must forge coalitions with other members in various committees and subcommittees. Roger Davidson and Walter Oleszek report that, between the House and Senate, there are twenty-three committees with jurisdiction over national security and foreign policy.[12] (During the energy crisis of the late 1970s, there were eighty-three committees and subcommittees of the House of Representatives alone with some claim to jurisdiction in energy matters, and 421 of the 435 House members belonged to one or more of these!)[13]

Armed Services.   The Senate and House Armed Services Committees (SASC and HASC, respectively) are the authorizing committees for the Department of Defense (DoD; including the Departments of the Army, Navy, and Air Force); military research and development; the national security aspects of nuclear energy; the pay, promotion, benefits, and retirement system for members of the armed services; and the strategic natural resources related to national security. These committees make substantive policy through the introduction and passage of bills that authorize the terms and conditions of programs and activities related to defense. They also recommend appropriation levels for spending. Although some members join these committees out of an intense public policy interest, other legislators are members for the traditional purpose of safeguarding constituency interests, with the aim of being reelected. As evidence, during the 109th Congress (2005–2007), the average House member had approximately 3,627 defense-related employees in his or her district, while HASC members had three times that amount, at 10,031. Furthermore, HASC member district economies relied twice as much on defense spending (5.18%) as their noncommittee member peers (2.66%).[14]

As a result of member incentives, geographical and economic constituencies surrounding military bases have disproportionate influence on these committees' policy decisions. Key issues recently considered by these committees include the 2005 Defense Base Realignment and Closure (BRAC) Commission's recommendations, the authorization of funding to refit and replace equipment damaged or destroyed in the Iraq War, and the question of whether the military is taking all the necessary measures required for the procurement and issue of adequate body and vehicle armor to deployed troops. As these examples suggest, the focus of committee activity is frequently on the resource allocation of defense-related personnel and materiel.

Appropriations.   Once defense authorization bills are reconciled and passed, the Senate and House Defense Appropriations Subcommittees provide the funding. No money is transferred in this process, but rather Congress grants budgetary authority to the authorized agencies, activities, and programs. With budgetary authority, a federal entity can make obligations requiring immediate or future expenditures, or *outlays*. Of the thirteen annual appropriations bills, most national security spending comes primarily from three—defense, energy and water development, and military construction. The normal appropriations process supplies two thirds of defense-related funding. The other one third is provided through continuing resolutions and supplemental appropriations measures.[15] As is the case with the HASC, membership in the House Defense Appropriations Subcommittee is affected by constituency concerns. During the 109th Congress, the percentage of their district economy that was defense related was 5.41% for House Defense Appropriations Subcommittee members, while only 2.81% for nonmembers. The districts of House Defense Appropriations Subcommittee members had an average of 8,525 active-duty military and civilian employees, compared to 4,077 defense-related personnel in nonmember districts.[16]

Foreign Affairs.   The Senate Foreign Relations Committee and House International Relations Committee are two other important national security players in Congress. The Senate Foreign Relations Committee assesses treaties with foreign governments and approves diplomatic nominations. Due to their "advise and consent" mandate, members see themselves as equal partners of the president in setting national security and foreign policy. Senator Jacob Javits (R-NY) wrote that the committee must "be a source of independent judgment and a potential check upon the actions of the executive branch on such fundamental matters as the use of military force, the conclusion of international commitments, the appointment of principal policy-makers, and the financing of military and diplomatic programs."[17] Extensive television and media coverage of the Senate Foreign Relations Committee make its members among the most well-known politicians in Washington. As for the House International Relations Committee, its membership primarily relies on the House's power of the purse to shape foreign policy.[18]

Other Committees with National Security Jurisdictions.   There are a number of other committees that impact national security policy. Both the House and the Senate have Energy Committees, for instance. The House and Senate Select

Committees on Intelligence deal with the intelligence community, including the Central Intelligence Agency, the National Security Agency, and others. The functions of these committees are limited to policy and procedural oversight; the authorization and appropriation functions for the majority of the intelligence community are handled elsewhere in Congress. Both the House and the Senate have recently empowered committees with specific jurisdiction over the function of homeland security. Relatively new, the impact of these committees has not yet materialized. Their prestige and power will rest on their ability to exert jurisdiction over a broad governmental responsibility that was previously shared across many committees. Their nascent position and jurisdictional claims highlight a key aspect of congressional policy making—diffuse power bases. Jurisdiction for national security policy is not cleanly divided among committees. Divergent constituency interests, opposing ideological considerations, and old-fashioned political power plays characterize the disjointed nature of congressional policy formulation and national security institutions.

National Security Policy

Analytically, national security policy can be separated into three varieties: structural, strategic, and war powers. *Structural policy* relates to the allocation of resources. *Strategic policy* concerns these actions as well as the military, economic, and political posture of the U.S. government toward the accomplishment of nationally identified goals and objectives. Finally, *war powers policy* guards the nation from imminent danger both at home and abroad.

Structural Policy.   Structural policy involves the resource allocation of defense-related personnel and material. This includes weapons procurement, military base infrastructure, foreign arms sales, private contractor deals, and defense personnel policies. These activities provide legislators with the opportunity to steer important projects to their districts, thus enhancing their reelection chances. As a result, structural policy formulation receives the greatest congressional attention of the three policy areas.

Military Base Infrastructure.   Due to the economic dependence of local communities on neighboring military bases, the topic of military base infrastructure is a hot-button political issue. As far back as the early 1900s, when obsolete frontier bases faced closure, members of Congress fought ferociously to keep them open. When faced with the closure of the cavalry station in Brownsville, Texas, a young congressman named James Nance Garner (later vice president of the United States under FDR) marched into Secretary of War William Taft's office to demand that the station remain open for economic reasons. Taft retorted, "What's the cavalry to do with economics?" Garner responded, "Mr. Secretary, it's this way. We raise a lot of hay in my district. We've got a lot of stores, and we have the prettiest girls in the United States. The cavalry buys the hay for its horses, spends its pay in the stores, marries our girls, gets out of the army, and helps us develop the country, and then more replacements come and do the same thing. It *is* economics. It *is* economics."[19]

From the viewpoint of a member of Congress, Garner's rationale is still very salient. The Constitution grants Congress the authority to "dispose of and make all needful rules and regulations respecting the territory or other property [of the federal government]."[20] This includes the "erection of forts, magazines, arsenals, dockyards, and other needful buildings."[21] As with many other enumerated powers, Congress has delegated restrictive authority to the executive branch with respect to the management of military property. Yet, when it comes to the closure of military bases, Congress faces a collective dilemma. To achieve the general national goal of eliminating obsolete military bases, it must impose particular pain on those states and districts where the bases are closed.

Unfortunately in the past, the parochial reelection interests of a number of members have generally trumped the diffuse national benefit that would be realized from the elimination of outdated installations. Prior to the late 1980s, the military had been unable to close a number of major bases for thirty years.[22] The Pentagon estimated that it had a 30% overage in military infrastructure capacity. To overcome parochial interests, Congress had to devise an extraorganizational procedure that protected targeted members from constituency fury over a base closure, while at the same time providing the appearance of congressional oversight. Thus the Defense Base Closure and Realignment Commission (BRAC) process was born.

With four closely spaced BRAC rounds (1988, 1991, 1993, and 1995) and a later, recent round (2005), Congress successfully overcame the collective dilemma of base closures. The process begins with the formation of an independent bipartisan BRAC commission nominated by the president and approved by Congress. The Pentagon submits a list of proposed closures and realignments to the commission, which travels to various military bases and holds hearings on the proposed list. Threatened members of Congress publicly fall on their swords defending their local bases while highlighting the fact they are powerless as individual members to stop or change the process. The commission can modify the list or leave it unaltered, submitting their final recommendation to the president. After the president approves it, Congress has forty-five days to disapprove the list in its entirety or it becomes law. The BRAC process limits congressional tampering while achieving the general political goal of eliminating bases. Furthermore, the process insulates members from adverse political repercussions. Such a unique process is not required for other types of structural policy formulation.

Weapons Procurement.   Unlike the BRAC process, Congressional action toward defense procurement follows the more traditional bipartisan distributive process of bringing federal dollars to constituents. Congress routinely spreads defense largesse as widely as possible so that many constituencies benefit. It is not unusual for a weapons system to involve multiple subcontractors spread across virtually the entire United States. It is also not uncommon for members of Congress to supersede the Pentagon's program priorities with their own. For example, in 2006 the Navy planned to reduce its attack submarine force to forty, but House members voted to require the Navy to maintain a fleet of forty-eight submarines. In addition to approving the president's proposed $2.5 billion for a Virginia-class attack submarine, legislators also added an extra $400 million to begin construction of another unrequested submarine to be completed in the next two years.[23] Furthermore, the benefit of building the Virginia-class submarine is stretched across numerous constituencies, with one half of the hull being produced by one defense contractor while a second contractor builds the other half.[24]

Predictably, Congress reacts caustically to the proposed shutdown of expensive weapons systems. In 2006, for example, the Pentagon requested $390 million to cease production of the C-17 Globemaster transport aircraft. Not only did Congress vote to shift the requested funds toward the production of three more airplanes, but it also forced the Air Force to maintain a fleet of 299 long-range transport aircraft—all but necessitating the production of more C-17s.[25] It is also not uncommon to find legislators playing one military service against another or against the Office of the Secretary of Defense.

Another defense procurement phenomenon is that lengthy development times cause legislators to develop parochial attachments to weapons systems. As a result, projects suffer ballooning costs and have dubious strategic and tactical value when ultimately completed. For example, when describing the F/A-22 Raptor fighter jet, former Assistant Secretary of Defense Lawrence Korb writes:

> This plane, which is arguably the most unnecessary weapons system currently being built by the Pentagon, was originally designed to achieve superiority over Soviet fighter jets that were never built. Back in 1985 the Air Force claimed it could build 750 of these stealth fighter jets for $35 million each or at a total cost of $26 billion. . . . At the current time [2006], the Pentagon says its can buy 181 planes for $61 billion.[26]

At this figure, the F/A-22 increased in cost per plane from $35 million to $337 million—an increase of 963%. Legislators are loath to relinquish such projects as the F/A-22, for which over one thousand manufacturing contractors are spread across forty-three states.[27] In fact, Congress nearly doubled the Pentagon's request for F/A-22s in Fiscal Year (FY) 2007 to twenty aircraft, funded at $2.7 billion, and provided a further $687-million advance for another twenty aircraft in FY 2008.[28]

Foreign Arms Sales.   For Congress, foreign arms sales policy is a natural extension of the distributive politics of domestic military procurement. From 2000 to 2003, U.S. arms sales to developing countries were $35.8 billion.[29] With the end of the Cold War in the early 1990s and the contraction of the U.S. defense budget, the arms industry went through a series of consolidations and mergers to survive. To maintain profit margins and sell off excess inventory, the industry sought revenues earned in the international arms export market. Citing the need to make American manufacturers more competitive in the crowded international market and to protect endangered defense industry jobs in their states and districts, Congress cooperated by relaxing a number of provisions of the Arms Export Control Act and the Foreign Assistance Act. These are the two major components of the International Traffic in Arms Regulations.[30]

In 1996, Congress enacted the Defense Export Loan Guarantee program. This law essentially created risk-free subsidies for the U.S. armament industry. Under this program, the Pentagon can guarantee up to $15 billion in private sector loans to foreign nations for the purchase of U.S. weapons. If the importing country defaults on the sale or lease payment, then the U.S. government covers 100% of the principal and interest of the loans. In the same year, Congress amended the Arms Export Control Act to allow the president to waive "re-coupment fees" that foreign purchasers had previously paid to cover the American's taxpayers' investment in weapons system research and development. The government could waive fees if it appeared that a sale would be lost with their inclusion in the final cost. These are two of many instances over the last decade where Congress has used its power to help the defense industry. In fact, a CATO Institute study found that between 1991 and 1999, the U.S. taxpayer actually paid $10 billion to finance arms exports between private American firms and foreign countries (this does not include the $2 billion provided to Saddam Hussein for the purchase of weapons technology prior to his 1990 invasion of Iraq).[31] Examinations of the underlying causes of these export policy decisions repeatedly reveal that members of Congress follow the familiar distributive logic of protecting constituency interests to enhance their reelection prospects.

Personnel Policy.   Military personnel policy is the last major structural policy area that receives substantial congressional attention. Active-duty, guard, and reserve service members, their families, and military retirees make a formidable coalition of well-educated, organized citizens who vote in large numbers. Backed by powerful lobbying organizations, this vocal group has considerable sway on Capitol Hill.[32] In fact, the average congressional district has 4,022 military retirees who annually contribute $73 million to the local economy. HASC-member district averages are much higher, with 7,318 retirees who contribute $144 million.[33]

These military interest groups and their respective patrons annually lobby Congress for increased pay and benefits. In the FY 2007 National Defense Authorization Act, Congress considered a broad range of personnel policies, such as percentage of annual pay increase for active-duty members, time-in-grade requirements for military officer promotion, targeted shaping of the manpower distribution of the military, increase in manpower end strength of the U.S. Army and Marine Corps, treatment of posttraumatic stress disorder, and minor changes to military health care and retiree benefits.[34] In recent years, Congress has even exceeded the Pentagon's "comparability-with-civilian-pay" target for increased military pay and benefits. Legislators always seek to cultivate with their constituents a reputation for taking care of the troops.

Military personnel policies that receive substantial national attention provide legislators the opportunity to take substantive policy stances that play to wider domestic and cultural audiences. These actions can be seen as a form of position taking for the benefit of constituents. David Mayhew defines *position taking* as a "public enunciation of a judgment statement on anything likely to be of interest to political actors . . . the electoral requirement is not that [members] make pleasing things happen but that [they] make pleasing judgmental statements. The position itself is the political commodity."[35] As examples, the recurring coverage of the "Don't Ask, Don't Tell" policy that bans homosexual conduct in the military is routinely debated in every Congress; recently, Congress has publicly investigated allegations of sexual and religious harassment at the U.S. Air Force Academy. Legislators have also scrutinized the procedures for dealing with friendly-fire incidents in Afghanistan and Iraq (such as the 2004 incident in which former professional football player Pat Tillman was killed in Afghanistan). These public hearings have provided legislators the opportunity to voice their positions on larger political and cultural issues that are important to constituents back home, but actual congressional changes to personnel policy have been relatively minor. Most changes come from recommendations of the Pentagon. In the last thirty years, Congress has effectively asserted itself in a large way only once—with the landmark passage of the Goldwater-Nichols Department of Defense Reorganization Act in 1986.

Goldwater-Nichols and Congress as an Agent of Reform.   Glaring deficiencies in joint military service cooperation were contributing factors to a number of national security disasters in the late 1970s and early 1980s. These included the failed Desert One operation to rescue Americans held hostage by Iran in 1980, the suicide bombing of the Marine barracks in Beirut in 1983, and the poorly coordinated invasion of the island of Grenada in 1983. For a number of influential legislators and key general officers, these incidents solidified the notion that reform of the DoD was required. These influential members of Congress included the chairman of the SASC, Barry Goldwater (R-AZ), as well as Bill Nichols (D-AL), Sam Nunn (D-GA), and Les Aspin (D-WI), while the senior military leaders included chairman of the Joint Chiefs of Staff (JCS), General David Jones, and Army chief of staff, General Edward "Shy" Meyer. This group faced the daunting task of affecting significant structural reform of the DoD and its individual services. Complicating this task, the average member of Congress benefited from the status quo, for legislators habitually exploited the decentralized nature of the Pentagon in order to distribute federal dollars back to their home districts and states. As Amy Zegart writes, "military duplication and inefficiency filled the trough of pork barrel politics."[36]

Despite an uphill battle, Goldwater-Nichols passed Congress because a number of key political factors aligned. First, the primary architect of the legislation, Goldwater, was retiring. Freed from electoral concerns, as a staunch military advocate he was uniquely qualified to carry the bill forward. Second, President Ronald Reagan stayed on the sidelines of the debate. Possibly distracted by other political issues, Reagan's lack of involvement weakened the strident resistance within the Pentagon to the proposed reforms. Due to weak presidential opposition and with Goldwater's name as political cover, the congressional reformers fashioned a coalition of legislators to vote for the bill. It passed, and on October 1, 1986, Reagan signed Goldwater-Nichols into law.[37]

Goldwater-Nichols affected three fundamental DoD reforms. First, the chairman of the JCS replaced the corporate body of the JCS as the "principal military advisor to the President." Second, as a requirement for promotion to general officer, the law required officers to serve in positions outside their service branch. (These positions are known as "joint" assignments in the military.) And crucially, the law clarified the chain of command for regional combatant commanders. These commanders now responded directly to the secretary of defense and, ultimately, the president for their orders and authority. This minimized service chief interference in operational combatant commands and reduced individual service parochialism.

Many observers believe that Goldwater-Nichols was an important factor in the success of the American military in the Persian Gulf War. They also cite the numerous successes of the military in the post—Cold War era and the initial victories of the military in Afghanistan and Iraq. Because of the gains in effectiveness, as well as the efficiencies wrought by Goldwater-Nichols, many have called for similar reforms within or across other executive branch agencies.

Strategic Policy. Strategic policy concerns the accomplishment of nationally identified political, economic, and military goals. These goals enhance the power of the United States and heighten national security. As the head of both the government and the state, the president sets these goals with advice from his or her cabinet and other senior executive branch decision makers. These goals orient the work of vast executive agencies, such as the Departments of Defense, State, Treasury, Homeland Security, and Commerce. Many strategic goals continue through multiple presidential administrations, such as the goal of communist containment during the Cold War. To support its strategic goals, the U.S. government also relies upon agreements with other governments, its membership in numerous international organizations (such as the North Atlantic Treaty Organization [NATO], the World Trade Organization, and the United Nations [UN]), and its support of international treaties.

Budgetary Power. Congress's primary power to shape strategic policy lies in its ability to fund all functions of the government. The Constitutional power of the purse allows Congress to appropriate money across federal agencies to support its vision of the important aspects of strategic policy. The president sends a budgetary request to Capitol Hill on the first Monday in February every year. This request asks for the funds to support all government operations, including the president's national security strategy. Though Congress is not bound to the president's budget, this request serves as an initial point in negotiations between the executive and legislative branches over priorities. Due to the president's veto power, Congress cannot ignore presidential preferences.

Following the president's submission, Congress sets forth its own unified provision with the passage of the annual Concurrent Budget Resolution on April 15.

This resolution regulates the remainder of the budget process until its final passage. Within the bounds of the budget resolution, Congress passes thirteen different appropriations bills. Approximately one third of the FY 2008 federal budget comes from the allocation of discretionary funds. (Nondiscretionary funds, which account for the other two thirds, include such items as interest on the national debt, social security, and Medicare.) National security spending makes up 60% of discretionary funding, at $554 billion.[38] Although this is a large amount, military spending as a proportion of gross domestic product (GDP) is at low levels in historical terms. Over the last six decades, the defense proportions of GDP are as follows: World War II, 1944 (38%); Korean War, 1953 (14%); Vietnam, 1968 (9.5%); the Reagan era buildup, 1986 (6.2%); and Iraq-Afghanistan, 2005 (3.9%). Even during the 1970s, when many were seeking a peace dividend after the Vietnam War, the proportion never fell below 4.5%.[39]

To guide strategic policy with respect to national security funding, Congress mandated in 1997 that the DoD undertake a Quadrennial Defense Review (QDR).[40] The QDR required that the secretary of defense do the following:

> conduct a comprehensive examination of the national defense strategy, force structure, force modernization plans, infrastructure, budget plan, and other elements of defense programs and policies of the United States with a view toward determining and expressing the defense strategy of the United States and establishing a defense program for the next 20 years.[41]

Congress intended the 1997 QDR to be a top-to-bottom review of the Clinton administration's national security strategy. An independent committee of outside experts, the National Defense Panel, was created to provide Congress with a critique of administration policy. Legislators wanted to link long-term policies, programs, and procurement to the budget. The 1997 QDR was a disappointment to members of Congress. Legislators desired the QDR "to drive the defense debate to a strategy-based assessment of our future military requirements and capabilities," yet instead it became "a budget-driven incremental massage of the status quo."[42]

In 1999, Congress made the QDR mandatory every four years. The second QDR occurred in 2001, prior to the terrorist attacks of 9/11; therefore, its recommendations did not reflect the changed nature of the threat facing the United States. The third QDR was prepared in 2005 and released in early 2006. This QDR was more congruent with the original intent of Congress, but reviews were still mixed. Those who praised the QDR pointed out its focus on national capability to meet emerging threats; critics emphasized a lack of consistency between statements of the strategic challenge and the DoD's own program submission. According to critics, the statement of the problem was fairly sound, but the corresponding adjustments to the structure of the armed forces appeared to be lacking.[43]

Despite weaknesses in the QDR process, it retains some utility for Congress. Using this document as a source, members of Congress can seek to influence an administration's strategic policies via the use of public hearings. Furthermore, legislators now have a further guide enabling them to link budgetary funding to policy goals. In conjunction with the power of the purse, Congress can be expected to continue to use the QDR or similar reviews to influence the president's near-dominant ability to set strategic policy.

Treaty Ratification. Relationships with foreign states also shape the strategic policy of the United States. These relationships are codified by formal treaty agreements between the United States and other members of the international community. As head of state, the president negotiates the terms of these treaties, yet the Constitution gives the Senate the power of treaty ratification. Two thirds of the Senate must be present and vote its approval for a treaty to go into effect.[44] As a result of the Senate's power, the president normally keeps key legislators privy to treaty discussions to facilitate ratification. In some rare cases, presidents have even requested that senior senators serve as active treaty negotiators with foreign powers. In terms of Senate history, only twenty-one treaties have suffered outright rejection, while another forty-three never went into effect because the Senate's modifications to the initial agreements were either (1) too onerous for the foreign parties to agree to or (2) unacceptable to the president.[45] Given that the Senate has considered over fifteen hundred treaties, these occurrences are relatively rare.

When it comes to treaty termination, the Constitution is silent. However, historical precedent is that the president is the sole authority who can cease American participation in a treaty. As a recent example, in 2001 George W. Bush withdrew the United States from the 1972 Anti-Ballistic Missile Treaty with Russia. It was originally negotiated with the former Soviet Union at the height of the Cold War to bring stability to the nuclear standoff between the United States and the Soviet Union. The Bush administration withdrew from the treaty so the United States could legally develop a limited antiballistic missile defense shield to protect against attacks by rogue states.

Recent treaty consideration by the Senate highlights some of the ways it can affect strategic policy. In December 2000, President Bill Clinton signed a treaty making the United States party to the International Criminal Court (ICC) but did not submit it to the Senate for ratification. In May 2001, George W. Bush renounced any American involvement with the treaty. The primary concern of the Bush administration was that the ICC could assert legal jurisdiction over American soldiers and policy makers through trumped-up charges of war crimes for legitimate uses of force during armed conflict and peacekeeping.[46] There was also concern that the court would assert jurisdiction over nonsignatory nations, including the United States. As a result, Congress went further than the president and passed the American Service-members' Protection Act in 2002. This law severed military assistance to any country that would not vow to not extradite U.S. citizens to the custody of the ICC if they were indicted. Two years later, in 2004, Congress acted to extend the aid cuts to all economic assistance.[47] Aside from Bush's renouncement, these congressional actions disconcerted many of America's European allies, who were steadfast proponents of the new court. Many observers believed these congressional actions undercut the moral authority of the United States and its credibility in authoring future international law, bolstered the impression of U.S. unilateralism, and hampered the ability of the United States to build coalitions in Iraq and Afghanistan.[48]

This concern can be generalized to Congress as an institution. It does not generally act with an international audience in mind; instead, it focuses on a domestic constituency with an eye to reelection. Although in the ICC situation George W. Bush was generally supportive of congressional action, future presidents may not concur with the stance taken by Congress in international affairs. Congress may not have the ability to set strategic policy, but it can certainly complicate matters for the president.

War Powers Policy.   When it comes to the ultimate strategic decision, the commitment of U.S. forces to combat, Congress has struggled with the president over who is the definitive arbiter of policy. In July 1993, Army General Raoul Cedras deposed Haiti's democratically elected president, Jean-Bertrand Aristide. Cedras pledged to return power to Aristide in October. However, after Cedras failed to return power as promised, the UN Security Council voted to impose sanctions on Haiti. Clinton sent U.S. ships to enforce the UN embargo and reported that the action was "consistent with the War Powers Resolution." The president also used the War Powers Resolution as justification to send fifteen hundred U.S. troops to Haiti as part of a UN mission. Senate Minority Leader Robert Dole (R-KS) and other members of Congress disagreed with the president's action. The disagreement sparked a year-long battle over the president's continued support to the UN mission despite several nonbinding votes by Congress to the contrary. It was not until October 1994 that Congress officially authorized the intervention and set a timetable for withdrawal a year later.[49] The example of Haiti is one of many in the long historical struggle between Congress and the president over war powers.

The Origins of War Powers.   War powers are a shared responsibility between the president and Congress. As noted earlier, the power to declare war was given to Congress in the Constitution.[50] Along with the ability to raise and maintain both an Army and Navy, this power gives Congress an unambiguous role. The president's power stems from the role of commander in chief of the armed forces.[51] This is far more than a symbolic appointment, reflecting a general consensus among the framers of the Constitution that unity of command was necessary for effective military action.

Despite numerous historical military engagements, Congress has only declared war five times in over two hundred years. In fact, on four of these occasions, a state of war existed prior to the formal declaration. On over three hundred separate occasions, U.S. forces have been deployed abroad without a formal declaration of war.[52] These cases range from short engagements that lasted for a matter of weeks, such as Grenada (1983) and Panama (1989), to longer wars, such as Vietnam (1964–1975) and Iraq (2003–2009 and beyond).

What is consistent in most of these cases is that the decision to enter the conflict was made by the president, often with little or no prior consultation with

Congress. Additionally, Congress is unlikely to assert its authority in an attempt to block the president from acting. There is a great deal of deference given to the president in protecting vital U.S. interests abroad. Once the nation is committed, Congress finds it equally difficult to stop the president from acting for fear of being open to political attacks for not supporting the armed forces in conflict. For instance, during the 2008 presidential campaign, Iraq War critic Senator Hillary Rodham Clinton (D-NY) said, "At this point, I am not ready to cut off funding for American troops. I am not going to do that."[53]

The War Powers Resolution: The Vietnam Era.   The Vietnam War brought the issue of executive power to the forefront of political debate in the United States. Concerned that future presidents would overstep their constitutional authority as commander in chief by committing the United States to future military actions, Congress passed the War Powers Resolution of 1973. In doing so, Congress attempted to strike a balance between the two competing branches of government. It recognized that the president must have the ability to make decisions providing for the immediate defense of the nation in a time of crisis; equally important, the president must be prevented from having a "blank check." Congress thought it necessary to compel presidential consultation once an immediate crisis had subsided. Failing to compel congressional authorization would give the president the unfettered ability to continue war actions indefinitely under the guise of the original crisis conditions.[54]

The War Powers Resolution outlines a set of rules regarding the use of the military by the president. It requires:

> The President to submit a report to Congress within 48 hours after introducing U.S. armed forces in the absence of a declaration of war into hostilities or into areas of imminent involvement in hostilities. In the absence of congressional authorization of such activities, forces must be withdrawn within 60 days, with a possible extension of 30 days in cases of pending danger to forces during withdrawal.[55]

In addition to its being vague, the law spurned a vigorous debate as to its constitutionality. At its time of passage, many political scientists regarded the War Powers Resolution as evidence that Congress was once again willing to assert its constitutional role in the foreign policy process.[56] However, rather than weaken executive power, it is possible that the War Powers Resolution actually strengthened it by codifying executive powers that until 1973 were debatable. The War Powers Resolution can be interpreted as saying that the president can unilaterally send a military force into conflict for sixty days. It is unlikely the framers would have ever so allowed.[57]

Between 1973 and 2003, 111 reports were submitted by presidents to Congress about U.S. troop deployments abroad.[58] In some circumstances, the action was so brief that no report was filed. Additionally, some presidents argued that certain actions did not invoke war powers, as there were no imminent hostilities. Such was the case with Reagan sending military advisors to El Salvador in 1981.[59]

Neither Congress nor the president was inclined to pursue military adventures in the late 1970s, with the memory of Vietnam still so vivid in the national consciousness. Thus, congressional attention turned from the issue of war powers to other aspects of national security. In 1974, Congress, through a series of joint resolutions, was able to force the Ford administration to stop arms sales to Turkey after its invasion of Cyprus, despite repeated threats of a presidential veto. This type of involvement in national security continued during the Carter administration when a threat of congressional disapproval forced the president to modify plans to sell Airborne Warning and Control System aircraft to Iran in 1978.[60]

Persian Gulf War.   The fall of the Iron Curtain and the collapse of the Soviet Union occurred rapidly from late 1989 to 1991. In quick succession, the Warsaw Pact and greater Soviet empire disintegrated into a number of smaller countries with serious economic problems stemming from years of neglect. The U.S. Cold War military structure seemed antiquated for a post-Soviet world. However, in August 1990, Hussein dispatched Iraqi forces into Kuwait. The ease with which Iraqi forces took Kuwait alarmed many, creating fears that Saudi Arabia and its rich oil fields might be the next target. President George H. W. Bush launched an aggressive diplomatic campaign to build an international consensus in opposition to Hussein. In addition to pushing for several UN resolutions condemning Iraq's actions, the administration secured pledges of financial and military support for a combined operation to drive Hussein's forces out of Kuwait.[61]

Despite the almost universal condemnation of Hussein's actions, many in the United States expressed significant concern over the potential outcome of such a military operation. Although initially rejecting a constitutional need for congressional support, George H. W. Bush did eventually ask for an authorization resolution. A vigorous debate in early 1991 ended with a one-hundred-vote margin in the House and a five-vote margin in the Senate in favor of the resolution. However, the close vote in the Senate did not reveal the true political situation. By the time of the vote, there were over five hundred thousand U.S. troops already in the region preparing for combat operations. Under these circumstances, anything besides authorization was unlikely.[62]

Challenges of the Post–Cold War Era.   The fall of the Soviet Union presented many opportunities and challenges regarding foreign policy and national security. While removing the one large threat the United States had faced for nearly fifty years, the end of the Cold War destabilized many countries that no longer had superpower financial support. One result was small regional and ethnic conflicts that sometimes turned to civil war. Once again, the president and Congress struggled over how to respond to crises.

One of the most demanding challenges of the early to mid-1990s was the disintegration of Yugoslavia and the resulting brutal ethnic conflict within Bosnia-Herzegovina. When the various warring groups agreed to end the conflict in 1995, it became clear that a large military force would be necessary to sustain the peace; the Clinton administration struggled to convince a Republican-controlled Congress of the necessity of committing U.S. forces to this endeavor. Many legislators saw this as a European problem that should be resolved by Europeans.

Copyright 1995 CARTOONEWS INTERNATIONAL Syndicate, N.Y.C., USA.
Reprinted with permission of Ranan Lurie.

In pushing for NATO and U.S. commitment to the mission, Clinton essentially involved the U.S. military by default. Only the U.S. Army was large and powerful enough to maintain the fragile Dayton Peace Accords. In the end, believing that the public would be unwilling to support a more substantial commitment, Congress and the president agreed to a one-year deployment.[63] After the U.S. military was committed to peacekeeping in the Balkans, Congress begrudgingly extended American involvement beyond the initial one-year mandate. Ultimately, American forces remained in Bosnia for more than a decade. This highlights that once Congress gives authorization to commit U.S. forces, the president largely controls their employment and mission timeline. The president is the one who declares "mission accomplished" and brings the troops home.

Congress and National Security in the Aftermath of the Terrorist Attacks of September 11, 2001.   The U.S. government's response to the 9/11 terrorist attacks again demonstrates the inherent tension between the branches on national security and foreign policy. The attacks could be interpreted as sufficient cause for allowing the president to take immediate action without prior authorization by Congress. However, even in this situation, according to the War Powers Resolution, the president would need authorization to continue hostilities beyond the sixty-day limit. The negotiation that followed with Congress, though brief, underscores the issue. George W. Bush desired a resolution that gave him broad authority not only to act against those deemed responsible for the attacks but also to allow him to actively deter and preempt future attacks. Congress ultimately gave Bush only the authority for the first for fear the second portion would be construed too broadly. The final resolution was passed on September 14, 2001, by a vote of 98 to 0 in the Senate and 420 to 1 in the House.[64] The president clearly had the advantage in these negotiations, knowing that ultimately Congress would need to act in some manner to demonstrate to the public that it understood the seriousness of the situation and intended to support the president's efforts.

Although it overwhelmingly supported the president and the invasion of Afghanistan to defeat the ruling Taliban regime and elements of al-Qa'ida, Congress was more assertive when it came to overhauling the domestic security apparatus in the United States. George W. Bush initially appointed a homeland security advisor and envisioned the position to have a similar function and role to that of the national security advisor. This appointment would remain within the White House and thus not be subject to congressional oversight. Congress opposed this approach and advocated a separate agency responsible for securing the homeland. By elevating the position to cabinet level, Congress would gain budgetary, oversight, and confirmation power over homeland security functions and personnel. Although the president initially rejected this approach, he ultimately acquiesced, and the Department of Homeland Security was created. With the creation of this federal bureaucracy, Congress could inhibit future presidents from acting unilaterally on homeland security issues. This issue area also created a new distributive political opportunity in that legislators could dispense new lucrative federal contracts in their states and districts. (For more on homeland security, see Chapter 6.)

A third important national security action taken after the 9/11 attacks was the U.S. decision to use force against Iraq. Shortly after the success in Afghanistan, George W. Bush and many of his advisors suggested that such states as Iraq were actively supporting terrorists and could supply them with weapons of mass destruction (WMDs). A terrorist attack using WMDs would be so catastrophic that it could be necessary to launch preventive wars to keep this technology from falling into the wrong hands. Citing intelligence reports about Iraqi WMDs, Congress authorized the use of force against Iraq in 2002, and the U.S.-led invasion of Iraq began in March 2003. Although the U.S. military rapidly overthrew Hussein's government, no WMDs were found. The consequent insurgency, sectarian strife, and significant loss of both Iraqi and American lives led many members of Congress to question their initial support. Riding a wave of public disenchantment with the war, Democrats recaptured Congress in 2006 after twelve years of Republican hegemony. Newly in charge, key Democratic leaders, such as Speaker of the House Nancy Pelosi, argued that the people of the United States had "lost faith in the President's conduct of this war" and that Congress had a responsibility to act.[65]

War Powers and the Future.   Presidents continue to claim that the War Powers Resolution is unconstitutional, yet they are not eager to test its provisions in court for fear of restricting their power. Congress, faced with the unenviable position of denying a president freedom of action in a time of a crisis, has generally given the president the authority sought. However, Congress has also sought to reassert its prerogatives when it has perceived executive overreach. The executive and legislative branches are likely to continue to struggle over war powers policy.

Conclusion

The Framers gave Congress a distinct role in setting national security strategy, yet inherited institutional weaknesses have at times hampered Congress's ability to counter or condition presidential initiatives. Due to diffuse power bases, divergent member preferences, and slow decision-making processes, Congress has often been a sideline player in setting national security policy. However, this generalization admits important exceptions; Congress has on occasion successfully altered executive branch initiatives and checked presidential power. When considering the three varieties of national security policy, Congress tends to be dominant in structural policy, where its members have the most at stake due to the distributive nature of relevant policies. Due to uncoordinated and conflicting member preferences, Congress is weakest when attempting to set strategic policy. Finally, when considering war powers policy, Congress and the president actively wrestle for control, with the president historically holding the advantage.

Having examined Congress's impact on past national security policy, it is useful to recognize that new dynamics may shape the future somewhat differently. It is unlikely the Framers foresaw that the United States would become the sole global superpower or imagined that the U.S. president would become one of the most influential political leaders in the world. These developments, which have been accompanied by significant new challenges to U.S. security, have tended to strengthen the position of the president. Nevertheless, the view of the Founding Fathers that Congress provided the closest and most direct link to the American people remains valid. For this reason, the role of Congress in formulating and executing national security and foreign policy will remain important. The extent to which Congress aggressively plays this role will continue to be affected by both institutional capacity and the character of external challenges.

Discussion Questions

1. What are the constitutional powers of Congress in the national security arena?

2. What are the advantages of the president in the making of foreign and security policy? What explains periods of relative congressional activism in national security affairs?

3. What are the institutions within Congress with the greatest role in national security affairs?

4. What are the varieties of national security policy? In which policy area does Congress play the greatest role? Why?

5. Is Congress well suited to playing the role of reformer within and among executive branch agencies? Why or why not?

6. What is the War Powers Resolution? Has it enhanced the role of Congress in national security affairs?

7. In the aftermath of the 9/11 terrorist attacks against the United States on its own soil, is Congress likely to play a greater or lesser role in national security policy vis-à-vis the president? Why?

Recommended Reading

Blechman, Barry M., and Ellis W. Phillip. *The Politics of National Security: Congress and U.S. Defense Policy.* New York: Oxford University Press, 1995.

Crabb, Cecil V., Glenn J. Antizzo, and Leila E. Sarieddine. *Congress and the Foreign Policy Process.* Baton Rouge: Louisiana State University Press, 2000.

Davidson, Roger H., and Walter J. Oleszek. *Congress and Its Members.* Washington, DC: CQ Press, 2006.

Dodd, Lawrence C., and Bruce I. Oppenheimer, eds. *Congress Reconsidered.* Washington, DC: CQ Press, 2004.

Fenno, Richard F. *Congressmen in Committees.* Boston: Little, Brown, 1973.

Fisher, Louis. *Presidential War Power.* 2nd rev. ed. Lawrence: University Press of Kansas, 2004.

Hamilton, Lee H., *How Congress Works and Why You Should Care.* Bloomington: Indiana University Press, 2004.

King, David C. *Turf Wars: How Congressional Committees Claim Jurisdiction.* Chicago: University of Chicago Press, 1997.

Lehman, John. *Making War: The 200-Year-Old Battle Between the President and Congress Over How America Goes to War.* New York: Charles Scribner's Sons, 1992.

Locher, James R. *Victory on the Potomac.* College Station: Texas A&M Press, 2002.

Mann, Thomas E., and Norman J. Ornstein. *The Broken Branch: How Congress Is Failing America and How to Get It Back on Track.* New York: Oxford University Press, 2006.

Mayhew, David R. *Congress: The Electoral Connection.* New Haven: Yale University Press, 1975.

Smith, Steven S., Jason M. Roberts, and Ryan J. Vander Wielen. *The American Congress.* Cambridge: Cambridge University Press, 2005.

Zegart, Amy B. *Flawed by Design: The Evolution of the CIA, JCS, and NSC.* Stanford: Stanford University Press, 1999.

Internet Resources

Library of Congress THOMAS federal legislative information site, www.thomas.gov

National Archives, www.archives.gov

U.S. House of Representatives, www.house.gov

U.S. Senate, www.senate.gov

6

Homeland Security

Protecting the U.S. homeland and its citizens against all manner of threats has been one of the foremost duties of government throughout the country's history; to this end, the Constitution empowers Congress to "raise and support Armies . . . provide and maintain a Navy," and "provide for calling forth the Militia to execute the Laws of the Union, suppress Insurrections and repel Invasions."[1] The terrorist attacks of September 11, 2001, focused the nation on a dimension of the security challenge that had been receiving scant attention. The result was the most significant reorganization of the U.S. government since 1947, a reorganization that included the creation of a new Department of Homeland Security (DHS). In addition, the Department of Defense (DoD) formed a new combatant command to plan and implement the U.S. military's actions in securing the homeland, and Congress passed significant legislation designed to facilitate the prevention of future attacks.

These efforts have brought to light fundamental questions associated with providing homeland security in a liberal democracy with a federal system of government. Defining their respective roles and forging effective cooperation among the many organizations and federal, state, and local jurisdictions with a stake in some aspect of homeland security are predictably difficult. The process of making resource allocation choices on what to protect and how to protect it is fraught with political consequences. Important judgments on the desired balance between liberty and security underpin most major homeland security decisions, as demonstrated in debates over the limits of law enforcement authority and the proper role of the military in the homeland. This chapter outlines the development of U.S. homeland security efforts and explores many of these issues.[2]

Growth of the Homeland Security Bureaucracy

Prior to the terrorist attacks of 9/11, the term *homeland security* was rarely used. Protection of the U.S. homeland was accomplished by a variety of organizations at the federal, state, and local levels that performed law enforcement, national defense, counterespionage, border protection, health, and emergency management functions.[3] During most of the country's history, homeland security actions largely centered on defense of borders and coastlines against external attack. This theme continued through the Cold War, with emphasis on civil defense activities and preparation for the possibility of a nuclear strike.

During the 1990s, concern over terrorist attacks began to dominate the U.S. homeland security agenda. The 1993 bombing of the World Trade Center, which killed six and injured over one thousand, focused attention on the emerging threat posed by transnational Islamist terrorist groups, as did a string of attacks against the United States on foreign soil: the 1996 Khobar Towers bombing in Saudi Arabia, the 1998 bombings of the American embassies in Kenya and Tanzania, and the 2000 attack on the USS *Cole* in Yemen. In addition, the 1995 bombing of the Murrah Federal Building in Oklahoma City and the 1995 sarin gas attack on the Tokyo subway by Aum Shinrikyo provided deadly examples of domestic terrorism. Several natural disasters—most notably Hurricane Andrew in 1992—demonstrated potential problems in the nation's capability to respond to catastrophic events.

Against this backdrop and the growing realization that transnational terrorist networks and the proliferation of nuclear, biological, radiological, and chemical weapons technology posed a major threat to the U.S. homeland, various government and academic groups began to take a harder look at the country's ability to prevent and, if unsuccessful, mitigate the impact of terrorist attacks. Well before 9/11, reports by the U.S. Commission on National Security/21st Century (The Hart-Rudman Commission) and the Advisory Panel to Assess Domestic Response Capabilities for Terrorism Involving Weapons of Mass Destruction (the Gilmore Commission) recommended improvements in information sharing on terrorist threats, increased efforts on national preparedness for attacks, clarification of national priorities and objectives through strategic planning, and significant organizational changes in the executive branch.[4]

The events of 9/11 crystallized much of this thinking, and the government quickly embarked on an enormous reorganization designed to deal more effectively with the threat of future attacks. The key elements of this effort included the creation of the DHS, an extensive reorganization of the intelligence community, and passage of legislation including the Uniting and Strengthening America by Providing Appropriate Tools Required to Intercept and Obstruct Terrorism (USA PATRIOT) Act of 2001, commonly referred to as the *Patriot Act*. The U.S. Northern Command, a new military combatant command focused on homeland security issues, was also established.

The Department of Homeland Security. President George W. Bush announced the creation of the Office of Homeland Security on September 20, 2001, launching a whirlwind of action to put responsibility for most homeland security tasks under a single organizational umbrella. On November 25, 2002, the DHS was formally established by the Homeland Security Act. This new department subsumed the Office of Homeland Security and brought together all or part of twenty-two organizations, including the Transportation Security Administration, U.S. Customs and Border Protection, the Federal Emergency Management Agency (FEMA), the U.S. Secret Service, and the U.S. Coast Guard, with wide-ranging duties and charters. With over one hundred eighty thousand employees, the department became the third-largest in the U.S. government. The organization of DHS is depicted in Figure 6.1.

The department was assigned the broad mission to "prevent terrorist attacks within the United States, to reduce America's vulnerability to terrorism, and to minimize the damage and recover from attacks that may occur."[5] The Homeland Security Act also formally established the Homeland Security Council (HSC), an organization similar to the National Security Council (NSC), to advise the president on homeland security matters and to coordinate interagency policy development and implementation (for more on the HSC, see Chapter 10). Many states and local communities instituted similar organizational changes, with the same goal of improving unity of effort in securing the homeland.

Despite general consensus on the need for change, criticism of the Homeland Security Act reflected basic American tensions regarding the role and efficiency of federal government. Some argued that, in at least two key ways, the government may not have gone far enough in centralizing power. First, the Federal Bureau of Investigation (FBI), which leads law enforcement counterterrorism activities, was left in the Department of Justice, and other critical homeland security functions, such as intelligence gathering and analysis, also remained outside DHS control.[6] Second, the department's primary focus on terrorism, rather than an all-hazards approach to homeland security, could result in missed opportunities to create a more seamless system.

Others felt that the reorganization stretched too far, claiming that the wide variety of organizations brought together under the department created the potential for abuse of power and produced too big a management challenge. As an example of the latter, some critics of FEMA's poor response to the devastation caused by Hurricane Katrina in 2005 argued that the agency had not received adequate funding and attention since its inclusion in the department. In any case, the initial years of the DHS's operations were marked by the type of bureaucratic infighting, budget debates, and inefficiencies that would be expected to accompany any governmental reorganization this extensive. The ultimate effectiveness of the department remains to be seen.

Other Organizational and Policy Changes.   Reform of the intelligence community, geared toward enhancing information sharing and effectiveness in identifying and countering threats to the homeland, also took place as a result of 9/11. Signed in December 2004, the Intelligence Reform and Terrorism Prevention Act established the position of the Director of National Intelligence (DNI) to serve as

FIG. 6.1 Department of Homeland Security

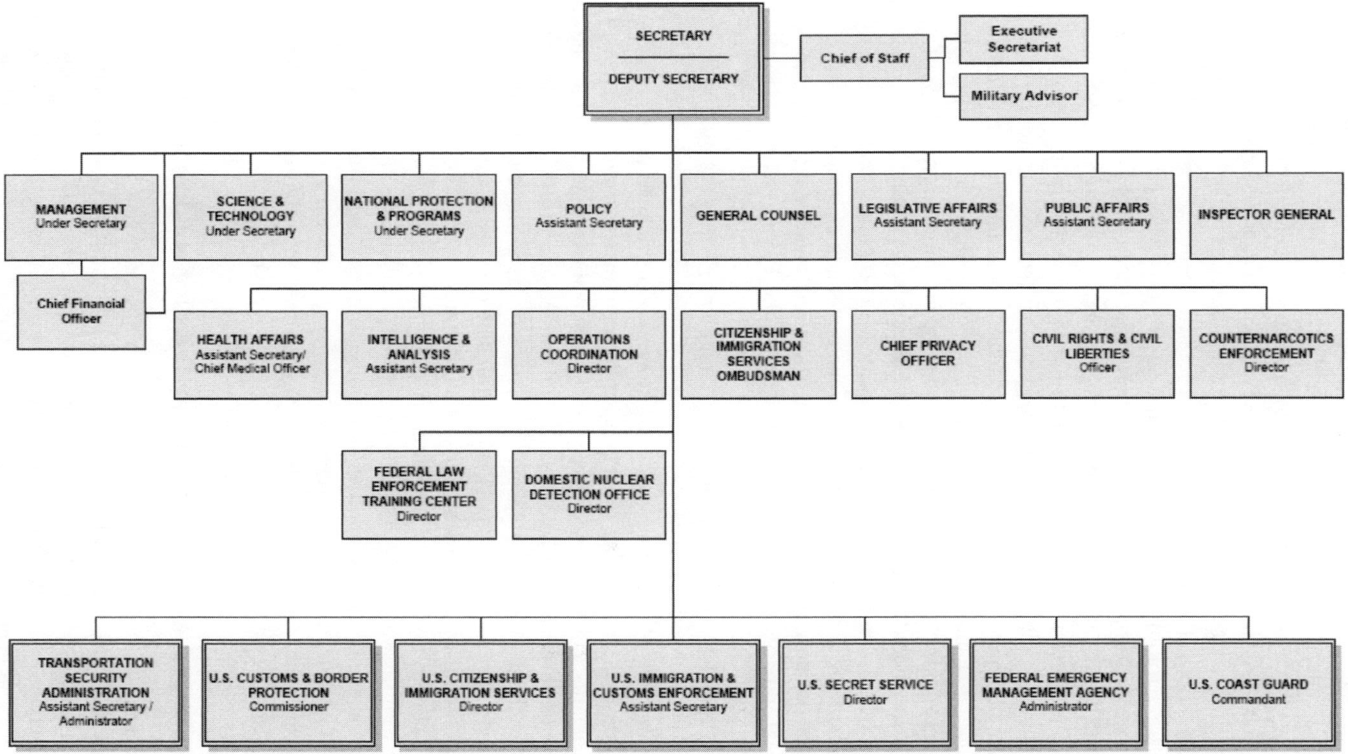

Source: www.dhs.gov/xlibrary/assets/DHS_OrgChart.pdf

the president's principal advisor on intelligence matters and as the head of the U.S. intelligence community. Previously, the director of central intelligence had served in this capacity; the act essentially established an additional bureaucratic layer at the top of the intelligence structure to provide stronger centralized direction.

The Office of the DNI includes the National Counter-Terrorism Center, formally launched in December 2004 and chartered to serve as a focal point for integrating, analyzing, and disseminating terrorist-related intelligence from all U.S. sources. This integrating and information-sharing function is seen as particularly critical for counterterrorism intelligence, which may hinge on finding links between disparate bits of information from an array of sources, such as local law enforcement officers, electronic surveillance, and military forces operating abroad. Critics of intelligence reform have generally argued that the DNI has not been given adequate authority to force a truly integrated national intelligence effort; most notably, DoD intelligence organizations, which include the Defense Intelligence Agency and National Security Agency and spend approximately 80% of the country's intelligence budget, continue to operate largely outside the control of the DNI. A further discussion of the intelligence community and the role of intelligence in the national security process can be found in Chapter 7.

Passed during the same post-9/11 timeframe as several other major congressional initiatives and reauthorized in 2006, the Patriot Act quickly became the most publicized and debated piece of homeland security legislation. The Patriot Act expanded government authority to fight terrorism by easing some restrictions on foreign intelligence gathering in the United States, facilitating information sharing between the intelligence and law enforcement communities, defining new crimes, and streamlining processes for prosecuting terror-related crimes. Despite safeguards and the requirement for congressional oversight built into the act, opponents have charged that it does not do enough to protect individual privacy and leaves the door open for abuse.[7] Provisions of the act have been challenged with varying success in the courts, and the debate over the optimal limits of government authority in combating terrorism continues.

Taken as a whole, the enormous post-9/11 organizational, policy, and legislative reforms were designed with one purpose: facilitating rational action to protect the homeland. As discussed in the next section, however, *rational* action is difficult to define or achieve—decisions on what specific actions to take and where to allocate scarce resources to maximize homeland security must weigh many factors, and they are made in a complex political environment.

Challenges in Homeland Security Planning and Execution

Securing the homeland is fundamentally a matter of risk management, in which limited resources are applied to an essentially unlimited list of potential tasks. An open society, individual liberty, and a vibrant free market economy result in tremendous vulnerability. All levels of government must therefore make difficult choices on what to protect and how to protect it, allocating limited financial and personnel resources to deter or prevent attacks and mitigate the effects of attacks

FIG. 6.2 Daily U.S. Security Challenges

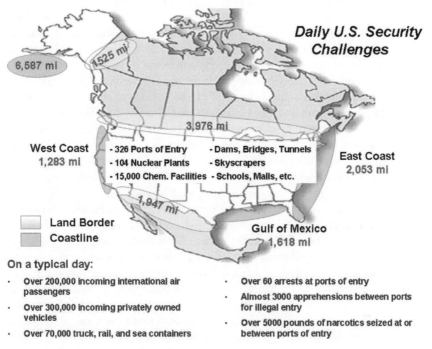

Daily U.S. Security Challenges

6,587 mi

1,525 mi

3,976 mi

West Coast
1,283 mi

- 326 Ports of Entry
- 104 Nuclear Plants
- 15,000 Chem. Facilities

- Dams, Bridges, Tunnels
- Skyscrapers
- Schools, Malls, etc.

East Coast
2,053 mi

1,947 mi

☐ **Land Border**
☐ **Coastline**

Gulf of Mexico
1,618 mi

On a typical day:

- Over 200,000 incoming international air passengers
- Over 300,000 incoming privately owned vehicles
- Over 70,000 truck, rail, and sea containers

- Over 60 arrests at ports of entry
- Almost 3000 apprehensions between ports for illegal entry
- Over 5000 pounds of narcotics seized at or between ports of entry

Source: Northern Command Briefing Materials, 2005

or disasters when they occur. Decisions at the federal level impact subsequent risk calculations at the state and local levels, and vice versa. And there are myriad security challenges, as reflected in Figure 6.2.

The Risk Management Process. Theoretically, the risk management process is straightforward, if complex. In deciding what to protect, homeland security risk can be conceptualized as the product of three factors:

1. *Threat:* the probability that a specific type of attack or disaster will occur, as determined by intelligence or other indicators

2. *Vulnerability:* the probability that an attack or disaster will result in damage

3. *Consequences:* the costs of an attack or disaster[8]

For example, the threat of damage from hurricanes may be highest in major cities along the Gulf Coast or Atlantic seaboard. The threat of terrorist attacks is probably higher in major metropolitan areas, such as New York City, or such cities as Washington, D.C., with higher concentrations of important symbolic targets than in less densely populated rural locations. Vulnerability is a function of variables, such as how physically hardened potential targets are, the likelihood that a threat against an area will be discovered before an attack or disaster occurs, and the anticipated response times and effectiveness of people and organizations that could prevent or defeat an attack. Consequences may include the predicted injuries or loss of life from an attack, direct and indirect financial losses, and psychological impacts.[9] An absence of redundancy in key systems, such as electrical grids, could result in higher costs if a single critical node were destroyed.

Given the observed tendency of such terrorist organizations as al-Qa'ida to seek high-profile strikes against targets of symbolic value or mass transit systems in densely populated areas, a shopping mall in suburban middle America could be characterized as having a low threat of terrorist attack using small arms and explosives (absent intelligence to the contrary). However, a lack of sizeable, well-trained security organizations and intrusive inspection procedures could make the same mall highly vulnerable—that is, an attack, if launched, would have a good chance of succeeding. The consequences of such an attack, in terms of potential loss of life and general panic, could be moderate to high. On the other hand, the threat to the Empire State Building may be high (as it fits the profile of desired terrorist targets), and the consequences of an effective attack would certainly be high, but it may be less vulnerable as a target due to existing security measures. In practice, of course, it is difficult to assign values to threat, vulnerability, and consequences and rank-order possible targets; risk management often involves as much art as science. However, such initiatives as the DHS's effort to identify and manage risk to critical U.S. infrastructure demonstrate that a reasonable assessment can be accomplished, given considerable time and attention.[10]

Once a risk assessment is complete and a rough priority of what ought to be protected is decided upon, the next logical step, which adds a significant layer of complexity, is to determine how to protect it. In other words, policy makers must then determine the most efficient and effective risk-reduction measures. For example, policy makers must decide how to apportion resources among the following tasks:

- *Reduce threat:* Deter attacks, disrupt terrorist networks that may plan attacks at a future time, or attempt to alter conditions that may increase the susceptibility of populations to radicalization and terrorist recruitment.

- *Reduce vulnerability:* Prevent or defeat attacks once they are planned or attempted, through such measures as improved airport baggage-screening procedures or enhanced intelligence sharing.

- *Reduce costs:* Mitigate the effects of attacks, for example by improving the capability of local first responders to assess damage and save lives.

George W. Bush's arguments justifying preemptive attacks to prevent states or terrorist networks from acquiring weapons of mass destruction (WMDs) were in part based on the belief that such a course would be more effective and efficient than other possible risk-reduction measures. The claim that "the greater the threat, the greater is the risk of inaction—and the more compelling the case for taking anticipatory action to defend ourselves, even if uncertainty remains as to the time

FIG.6.3   Homeland Security Risk Management

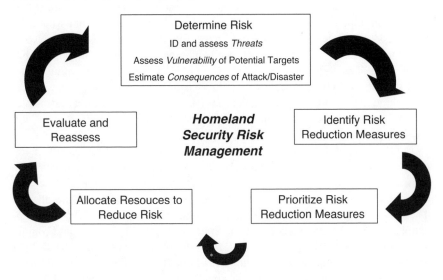

and place of the enemy's attack" is inherently a judgment about risk-management strategy.[11]

Once potential risk-reduction measures are determined and prioritized, finite resources may be dedicated accordingly. Risk is reduced in some areas and, inevitably, accepted in others. Evaluation of the effectiveness of risk reduction measures and continuous monitoring of any changes to previous assessments of threat, vulnerability, and consequences then are used to inform future decisions. In summary, risk management for homeland security is conceptually a continuous, rational process, conducted by governments at the federal, state, and local levels, which includes the general steps outlined in Figure 6.3.

Challenges in Practice.   Despite the analytical clarity of this model, in practice it is extraordinarily difficult to apply in an orderly way. Part of the reason is that, as mentioned, estimating risk and gauging the likely efficiency and effectiveness of risk-reduction measures is not a scientific process. Witness the intense debate over preemption as an integral part of homeland security strategy. Although some maintain that striking threats before attacks take place is preferable to defending at home, others claim operations abroad could breed anti-American resentment and increase the pool of potential terrorists while draining attention and resources from more productive efforts to reduce vulnerability in the homeland.[12]

Another intractable problem is that politically, homeland security presents a classic collective action dilemma.[13] As decisions are made regarding allocation of scarce resources, if political leaders at all levels attempt to secure resources for their jurisdictions (of which there are some eighty-seven thousand in the United States) rather than support a "national interest" in homeland security (especially because this "national interest" is a difficult-to-define product of many subjective assessments and therefore easy to dispute), the result is likely to be political bargaining and a pattern of resource allocation that differs greatly from what a rational risk-management process would prescribe. Emergency responders across the nation will all want the most advanced equipment, regardless of the probability they will have to use it. Members of Congress will lobby for awarding homeland-security-related contracts to firms in their districts. Mayors will attempt to ensure that key facilities in their towns are included in lists of critical infrastructure, if inclusion means additional funding or security. The combined result will inevitably be suboptimal from a national perspective.

In fact, this predicted dynamic has been observed repeatedly in the allocation of homeland security grants. In the wake of 9/11, Congress took several actions to provide money through states to local jurisdictions to reduce vulnerabilities and enhance the ability to prevent and mitigate the effects of disasters and attacks. These included doubling funding for the Firefighter Investment and Response Enactment (FIRE) Act and authorizing the State Homeland Security Grant Program and the Urban Area Security Initiative. For each of these programs, risk did not appear to be the foremost determinant of fund distribution. For example, Montana received $9.33 per capita in FIRE grants made through February 2004, while California (a far more likely terrorist target) received $0.86 per capita; additionally, Republican (majority party) districts on balance received more FIRE funding than Democratic districts. State Homeland Security Grant Program funding included a "floor" (mandated by the Patriot Act) that ensured rural states benefited disproportionately. Even the Urban Area Security Initiative, intended to provide funding for America's fifty most vulnerable cities without any minimum distribution requirement, resulted in many grant results that seemed out of proportion to risk. For example, New Haven, Connecticut, received $77.00 per capita compared to New York City's $5.84 per capita in fiscal year 2004.[14]

Making decisions about government allocation of resources for homeland security is crucial, but homeland security action is by no means limited to government. Public and private companies, nongovernmental organizations, and individual citizens are also involved. For example, an estimated 85% of critical infrastructure in the United States is owned by the private sector. An issue area of critical importance to both security and economic prosperity is information technology and communications networks. Each nongovernmental entity must also make decisions about identifying and reducing risk, and preparedness efforts vary widely, just as they do among various state and local jurisdictions. To summarize, leaders at all levels apply a risk management process, explicitly or implicitly, in a politically charged environment that includes many public and private players and interests. The overall result is a highly complex, loosely integrated system for protecting the homeland.

Homeland Security and Civil Liberties

In addition to the factual and theoretical considerations discussed above, there is a significant normative aspect to homeland security choices. As demonstrated by the debate over provisions of the Patriot Act, the United States maintains a dynamic balance between two fundamental and sometimes conflicting imperatives: protecting the homeland and safeguarding the freedoms upon which the country was founded. In short, the organizations, policies, and actions that may be most effective in preventing attacks on the homeland may threaten civil liberties and run counter to basic American values; however, American citizens may be willing to accept some reduction of liberty to increase their security. The result of this interplay tends to be a somewhat cyclical process in which institutions and policies to increase security are strengthened during times of perceived danger, weakened (often through enhanced congressional oversight) when liberty is unduly restricted or abuses take place, and then strengthened again if the institutions appear to be ineffective at accomplishing their missions.[15]

Taking a wide view of recent history, this cycle appears to be in evidence. In 1975 and 1976, the U.S. Senate Select Committee to Study Governmental Operations with Respect to Intelligence Activities (the Church Committee) conducted an investigation that led to several significant recommendations to limit the power of intelligence agencies and draw a clearer line between intelligence and law enforcement. This use of congressional oversight was a response to FBI actions, including unauthorized searches and electronic surveillance, used to monitor and disrupt domestic dissident groups. It also resulted from the conclusion that the Central Intelligence Agency (CIA) had engaged in unauthorized domestic activities and gone too far in conducting covert operations abroad. The Church Committee's recommendations helped produce the Foreign Intelligence and Surveillance Act of 1978, which established procedures and restrictions on gathering foreign intelligence information. (This act was modified by the Patriot Act in 2001.)

During the early years of the Reagan administration (1981–1985), CIA covert operations, especially in Central America and Afghanistan, again grew in frequency and significance. In 1986, revelations that the NSC staff had coordinated a program to provide aid to the Contra rebels in Nicaragua using profits from arms sales to Iran (in clear violation of congressional intent) led to a new wave of congressional oversight regarding covert operations and intelligence activities.

Many have charged that, during the 1990s, the CIA's human intelligence capability was overly curtailed in favor of technological means of collection, policies on recruiting foreign agents were too restrictive, and the line between intelligence and law enforcement became a barrier to reasonable information sharing. The country's inability to discover and stop the 9/11 attacks has been attributed in part to these shortcomings. The perception of increased danger following 9/11 then provided an environment conducive to passage of the Patriot Act.

Much of the "liberty versus security" discussion also hinges on expectations. What is an acceptable level of violence for the United States, and what financial and nonmonetary costs are the public willing to pay to achieve this standard? The United States suffers over forty thousand fatalities due to automobile accidents and over fifteen thousand murders each year; absent major efforts to reduce them, these numbers appear acceptable from a macro perspective. If the expectation is that the country should never again experience a fatal terrorist attack, deterrence and prevention activities would logically demand great sacrifice in terms of resources and limitations on personal freedom. If the country is willing to live with low levels of terrorist violence and infrequent major attacks, the calculus changes significantly. Leaders thus face the difficult task of gauging the public's demand for security (and willingness to bear the costs to achieve it), developing policies and allocating resources in accordance with this demand, and attempting to ensure that public expectations are aligned with the realities of risk management. The dissonance of messages along the lines of "a future attack is inevitable, but we don't need to make radical changes to our daily lives" is understandable in this context. The unsteady American equilibrium between maintaining civil liberties and protecting the homeland will be a permanent aspect of the political environment in which homeland security decisions are made.

Homeland Security Issue Areas

Is the United States safer now than it was before 9/11? In addition to making the major organizational changes discussed above, the U.S. government has focused on increasing its capability to reduce homeland security risk through programs and plans in several specific areas. Assessments of progress have been mixed, with many critics arguing that many important homeland security initiatives have still not received adequate resources or attention.[16] This section outlines efforts to counter two of the more significant threats: terrorist attacks using nuclear devices and an outbreak of pandemic influenza. These examples illustrate many of the challenges of securing the homeland covered throughout this chapter.

Nuclear Terrorism.   In July 2004, the HSC, in partnership with the DHS, published a list of fifteen all-hazards scenarios for use in federal, state, and local homeland security preparedness planning and other activities.[17] Scenario 1 is "Nuclear Detonation—10-Kiloton Improvised Nuclear Device" in a large city. Estimates of fatalities from such an attack range into six figures; treating hundreds of thousands of injuries and decontaminating up to thousands of square miles would make for a very difficult, costly recovery period. These enormous costs, in light of the threat posed by transnational terrorist organizations that have attempted or stated their intent to acquire nuclear material, make preventing this scenario a clear priority in any homeland security risk-management system.

The U.S. approach to countering the possibility of nuclear terrorism includes a mix of interrelated actions to reduce the threat, vulnerability, and consequences of an attack. In terms of reducing threat, operations to kill or capture terrorists abroad, combined with international efforts to disrupt terrorist financing and enhanced domestic surveillance and information sharing, are designed to reduce the ability of transnational terrorist networks to plan and execute operations against the United States. These actions are, in theory, integrated into a broader diplomatic, informational, military, and economic strategy to lower motivation for anti-American terrorism, especially among radical Islamist groups.

With regard to the specific threat of nuclear terrorism, most major U.S. policies and programs have been designed to reduce vulnerability. Conceptually, a terrorist group attempting to execute this type of attack must perform several general functions, not necessarily in this exact order: acquiring nuclear material, building a workable device, delivering it (and, if necessary, operatives) to the United States, planning and organizing for the attack, and carrying it out. The likelihood that a potential attack will succeed can be reduced by making any of these functions more difficult.

Preventing terrorist acquisition of nuclear material or nuclear weapons requires close international cooperation, and the United States has developed several major programs to this end. The Cooperative Threat Reduction (CTR) Program, established in its original form in 1991, is designed to provide funding and expertise to prevent the spread of WMDs and related materials, technologies, and expertise from former Soviet states. The Global Threat Reduction Initiative, launched in 2004, is a similar effort to secure vulnerable nuclear and radiological materials worldwide. Related bilateral and multilateral agreements, such as the 2006 Global Initiative to Combat Nuclear Terrorism and the 2005 U.S.-Russian Bratislava Nuclear Security Cooperation Initiative, also seek fundamentally the same objective—keeping nuclear material out of terrorist hands.

Should these international efforts fail, the next objective is preventing delivery of nuclear weapons or materials to the United States; this could be accomplished at the point of embarkation, in transit, or at the U.S. border. The Container Security Initiative, in place at over forty major international seaports, allows for but does not ensure prescreening of most cargo containers bound for the United States. The Department of Energy's Second Line of Defense Program provides radiation-detection equipment to key foreign airports, seaports, and borders. The Domestic Nuclear Detection Office, established within the DHS in 2005, is responsible for developing and planning for employment of radiological-detection technology in the United States. The amount of cargo scanned at U.S. ports of entry has been increased dramatically but is still, as of 2007, far from sufficient.

As a complement to programs targeted at finding nuclear materials, enhanced border security measures and immigration policies may prevent the movement of terrorists to the United States. Under the U.S. Visitor and Immigrant Status Indicator Technology (US-VISIT) program, almost all visitors to the country provide digital finger scans and digital photographs, which are checked against terrorist-related watch lists. All applicants for U.S. visas are similarly screened. Especially along the U.S.-Mexican border, improved—but still inadequate—security infrastructure, such as fencing and detection capability, seeks to make illegal entry more difficult. Operation Jump Start in 2006 saw the deployment of approximately six thousand National Guard troops to the four southwest border states to assist the growing border patrol by providing surveillance, infrastructure development, and logistical support.

If terrorists nevertheless manage to bring nuclear material to the United States, the onus for preventing an attack shifts to law enforcement organizations at the federal, state, and local levels. There are approximately eight hundred thousand full-time sworn law enforcement officers in the country; the major challenge facing them is sharing intelligence and connecting disparate bits of information that may reveal a planned attack. The FBI's National Joint Terrorism Task Force and a system of smaller Joint Terrorism Task Forces in one hundred major cities (including over thirty-five hundred members, over four times the pre-9/11 number) are designed to perform part of this role.

Should a nuclear or radiological attack succeed, as for other major attacks or disasters, the DHS would have overall responsibility for coordinating the national response to mitigate its effects. The National Response Plan, discussed in more detail below, includes a Nuclear/Radiological Incident Annex outlining responsibilities for major actions. Recent years have seen a growth in national, state, and local capability for nuclear incident response, with funding provided through such sources as the DHS Homeland Security Grant Program. In addition, the National Guard is fielding WMD Civil Support Teams in each state and territory to support initial consequence management operations if required.

Overall, this diverse array of U.S. actions to counter the threat of nuclear terrorism provides an instructive example of the sort of layered, interconnected planning required in many homeland security areas. The strategy involves a complicated system of responsibilities and activities at the international, federal, state, and local levels. Given limited resources, prioritizing is an essential task, especially because each agency and jurisdiction is likely to argue for the criticality of its role. Many critics of the U.S. effort against nuclear threats maintain that international initiatives, such as the CTR Program, have been underemphasized relative to their importance, because stopping terrorists from acquiring nuclear materials in the first place may be the most effective way to prevent an attack.[18]

As with all homeland security choices, measures to prevent nuclear terrorism come at a price: Intrusive or time-consuming inspection procedures hinder the flow of commerce; overly restrictive immigration policies run counter to America's political culture as a country of immigrants; and effective domestic surveillance measures risk violating individual liberties. Weighing these factors against the catastrophic cost of failure calls for delicate judgment.

Pandemic Influenza.   Although the thrust of U.S. efforts regarding nuclear terrorism has largely been on prevention through international cooperation, enhanced detection capability, and border control measures, countering an outbreak of pandemic influenza is primarily a problem of mitigation. Many analysts fear that a type-A strain of influenza virus capable of efficient and sustained human-to-human transmission will develop. If this occurs, completely preventing its spread would not be possible.

The human and economic consequences of an influenza pandemic could be catastrophic. The Spanish Flu pandemic of 1918 caused over five hundred thousand deaths in the United States (including over forty-three thousand U.S. military service members) and over 50 million fatalities worldwide. Estimates of possible U.S. fatalities if an outbreak of avian influenza occurs in the near future, likely through multiple waves of infection, range well into the hundreds of thousands.

Many more people would become ill, and work absenteeism would severely hamper economic productivity. As opposed to most sudden attacks and natural disasters, an avian influenza pandemic would cause a sustained public health emergency requiring a well-coordinated response over the course of several months.[19]

The U.S. approach to pandemic influenza centers on dampening these effects by limiting the spread of the disease to and within the United States and taking action to minimize its health, social, and economic impacts. In November 2005, George W. Bush published the *National Strategy for Pandemic Influenza*, which was augmented by a more detailed implementation plan in May 2006. The strategy calls for a massive cooperative effort among a complex and diverse group of international, federal, state, local, and private-sector organizations.

Internationally, the World Health Organization (with considerable financial and planning support from the United States) is the United Nations agency responsible for coordinating the global response to human cases of avian influenza. Major responsibilities include providing early diagnosis and warning of an outbreak, containing an outbreak if and when it occurs, and coordinating research and planning efforts to increase worldwide capacity to cope with a pandemic.

Within the United States, under the overall lead of the DHS, the Department of Health and Human Services is assigned responsibility for coordinating the U.S. public health response. Its major tasks include providing assessments and guidance to state and local agencies and the public and managing the national effort to create and distribute vaccines. Other key federal players include the Department of State, responsible for coordinating U.S. involvement in the international response; the Department of Agriculture, responsible for veterinary response and food safety; the Department of Transportation, responsible for managing the country's transportation system to limit the spread of disease while preserving economically essential movement; and the DoD, responsible for providing assistance as required to maintain public order, distribute vaccines, and continue essential government services. The 2006 implementation plan includes over three hundred specific tasks for federal agencies; monitoring performance and ensuring all agency efforts are complementary is an enormous management challenge.

Federal plans and programs notwithstanding, effective response to limit the impact of pandemic influenza will hinge on state, local, and private-sector efforts. Prioritizing recipients of vaccines, planning for the continued delivery of such essential government services as law enforcement, and maintaining key infrastructure and systems remain largely state responsibilities. As with natural disasters and other emergencies, however, state autonomy often leads to considerable variation in the approach and quality of plans. Specifically, state plans for detection and monitoring, vaccination, and containment in case of a pandemic influenza outbreak are, in many cases, inconsistent.[20] Similar dynamics also occur with local and private-sector efforts, adding to the coordination challenge.[21] Homeland security decision makers must weigh the requirement for coherent national action against the benefits of allowing lower jurisdictions to shape a strategy that addresses their unique circumstances.

The challenge of ensuring unity of effort is compounded by the fact that there are many unknowns involved in pandemic influenza planning. The time and place of outbreaks, the virulence of the disease, the effectiveness of vaccines, and the reaction of the public cannot be determined in advance; disagreements over planning assumptions are inevitable. In addition to these factual issues, an outbreak of pandemic influenza would present difficult normative choices. Questions of who should receive limited vaccines and what restrictions on travel and other personal liberty would be acceptable in trying to limit the spread of disease will have great political consequences.

The Utility of Homeland Security Planning.   The threats of pandemic influenza and nuclear terrorism are representative of the breadth and complexity of most major homeland security issues. Thinking in detail about these scenarios, actions, and systems designed to reduce the risks of nuclear terrorism or pandemic influenza may also be helpful in addressing other threats; most homeland security functions are not threat specific. For example, border control measures that make it more difficult for terrorists to bring nuclear material into the country may also reduce vulnerability to other types of terrorist attacks or slow the influx of illegal drugs. Systems for providing medical care to victims of an influenza outbreak may be equally useful following natural disasters or other mass-casualty events, especially bioterrorist attacks. In addition, planning, coordination, and exercises among the many agencies and jurisdictions with a stake in preventing nuclear terrorism or limiting the impact of pandemic influenza may facilitate cooperation on other homeland security issues.

One agency with critical responsibilities and interests in almost all homeland security scenarios is the DoD. The next section will explore its involvement in protecting the homeland in greater depth.

The Military's Role

Since the days of colonial militias, American military forces have played a prominent, continuous role in securing the homeland against state and nonstate threats and in providing internal order when required. In addition to more traditional roles, such as fighting in the War of 1812 and the Civil War, conquering American Indian tribes, and providing coastal defense, military forces have been employed in the homeland to suppress rebellions and riots, explore the American West, put down strikes, enforce school desegregation, and respond to the full gamut of natural and man-made disasters. Despite American unease with using military forces (especially regular forces) in domestic roles, their manpower, resources, planning capability, and surge capacity ensure that they will always be considered as an option when nonmilitary security and relief organizations appear inadequate.[22]

The Creation of NORTHCOM.   As with homeland security in general, the national reaction to the 9/11 attacks involved a more focused debate on the desired role of the military and led to rapid organizational change. The major development was the creation in October 2002 of U.S. Northern Command (NORTH-COM), a combatant command with responsibility for a geographic area including the United States, Canada, Mexico, the Gulf of Mexico, and portions of the Atlantic and Pacific oceans. NORTHCOM is charged with deterring, preventing, and defeating threats to U.S. territories and interests within this area and providing assistance to U.S. civil authorities as directed. The former role is known as *homeland defense*, the latter as *civil support*.[23]

In its brief history, NORTHCOM has further defined and planned for its homeland defense responsibilities while executing multiple civil support operations. Many missions are conducted in close coordination with North American Aerospace Defense Command (NORAD), the U.S.-Canadian organization responsible for aerospace warning and aerospace control for North America. NORTHCOM's civil support tasks have included supporting the National Interagency Fire Center in fighting wildland fires, providing security for such high-profile national events as presidential inaugurations and national political conventions, and offering detection and monitoring assistance to federal agencies interdicting drugs and other illicit traffic across U.S. borders. Major actions related to homeland defense have included the designation of quick-reaction land forces to respond to threats, enhancement of the awareness of potential maritime threats through better information sharing, preparation to fire ground-based interceptors as part of the emerging ballistic missile defense system, and deployment of an integrated air defense system for the Washington, D.C., area. Forces that may be necessary for NORTHCOM operations, both those permanently assigned as well as those assigned for specific missions, are kept at various stages of alert based on intelligence about potential threats.

Considerations for Domestic Use of the Armed Forces. Refining the capability to conduct effective military operations in and near the homeland is part of a broader strategy of creating a layered, in-depth defense for the United States. Given the choice, it would normally be more desirable to engage threats abroad, before they reach the homeland. Of course, it may not be possible to detect or defeat all threats outside U.S. territory, and some threats may not be apparent until an attack is imminent. In these cases, an appropriate response may require action by law enforcement organizations, the DHS, the military, or a combination. When the employment of military forces is necessary, operating in the U.S. homeland presents at least three unique challenges.

Legal and Policy Restrictions. The first challenge is that, resulting from traditional American concerns, there are significant legal and policy restrictions on the domestic use of military forces. One commonly cited example is the Posse Comitatus Act of 1878, as amended[24]:

> Whoever, except in cases and under circumstances expressly authorized by the Constitution or Act of Congress, willfully uses any part of the Army or Air Force as a posse comitatus or otherwise to execute the laws shall be fined under this title or imprisoned not more than two years, or both.

Originally intended to prevent local sheriffs and U.S. marshals from using federal troops to enforce the law in the South, the Posse Comitatus Act in effect restricts the ability of active-duty forces to act in a law-enforcement capacity. There are important exceptions, however. Most notably, Congress has long authorized the president, through the Insurrection Act of 1807 (broadened in 2006 and renamed the Enforcement of the Laws to Restore Public Order Act), to use federal troops to restore public order under a variety of circumstances, and federal troops have been authorized in law to assist civil authorities in some counterdrug operations and disasters involving WMDs.[25]

There are also legal and policy restrictions on the use of military assets for domestic intelligence collection and storing of information on U.S. persons. In general, domestic military intelligence activities are limited to analysis of information gathered by other sources to anticipate potential homeland defense threats. Even for actions unrelated to intelligence, government policy limits the ability of military commanders to employ forces domestically. Although they vary with the level of threat, systems for authorizing movement of forces and engagement of threats in the U.S. homeland generally require approval at high civilian levels. For civil support operations, such as disaster relief, authorization by the president or secretary of defense is required for federal forces to act.

Interagency Cooperation.   The second challenge for military operations in the homeland is that, to a much greater degree than for actions abroad, federal forces are unlikely to ever operate alone; domestic missions will inevitably involve a large group of other federal, state, and local organizations, and the federal military does not have lead responsibility in most cases. The DHS and multiple law enforcement agencies are frequent partners, and the National Guard is likely to be involved in any major domestic operation. In responding to emergencies or providing security for designated events, the National Guard generally acts under the control of state governors, which is referred to as State Active Duty or Title 32 status (Title 32 refers to the title of the U.S. Code that pertains to the National Guard. It is in contrast to Title 10 of the U.S. Code, which pertains to federal armed forces). The advantage of this arrangement is that National Guard forces retain law enforcement authority when they are not federalized—Posse Comitatus Act restrictions only apply to federal (Title 10) forces. However, coordination challenges may result when separate chains of command for state and federal forces are in place, making unity of effort harder to ensure. The following chart provides a basic comparison of command and control, funding, and law-enforcement capability for troops in a Title 10, Title 32, and State Active Duty status (see Table 6.1).

Table 6.1   Military Forces: Duty Status Comparison

	Command and Control	Funding	Law Enforcement Authority
Title 10 (Active Duty and Federalized Forces)	President and secretary of defense	Federal	No (Posse Comitatus Act applies)
Title 32	State governor	Federal	Yes
State Active Duty	State governor	State	Yes

The fundamentally interagency nature of homeland defense and civil support operations places a special premium on effective interagency cooperation, which is often difficult to achieve. Government organizations are frequently concerned with guarding their autonomy and minimizing uncertainty; therefore, they are often reluctant to enter into interdependent relationships or cede control over their activities to others.[26] Realistic homeland security and homeland defense exercises involving all major players, the extensive use of liaisons, and frequent communications between military and civilian organizations are needed to strengthen cooperation in deterring, preventing, defeating, or mitigating the effects of attacks and disasters.

The Need for Unique Capabilities. The third challenge is that the probable types of military operations in the homeland call for a somewhat different set of capabilities than combat operations abroad. If detected in time, the most likely terrorist threats could be defeated without placing a large strain on military capabilities, but any use of military force for homeland defense would have to take significant political sensitivities into account. A great degree of precision and limitation of collateral effects, rather than application of a blunt instrument, would generally be required. For example, if military forces were directed to shoot down a hijacked civilian airliner or defend a base against attack, limiting damage in the area would be critical. Troops deployed to restore order in an area with widespread rioting would face the challenge of minimizing casualties and avoiding the use of lethal force when possible.

In addition, homeland defense operations are likely to be extremely time sensitive. If threats are not detected until an attack is ongoing or imminent, an effective response would demand having trained and ready forces on short alert. Finally, military forces must be prepared and equipped to assist with a variety of consequence management scenarios in the homeland. If an attack with a WMD succeeds, elements of the U.S. Armed Forces would undoubtedly be called on to help mitigate its effects. Development of the types of military capabilities that may be required in the homeland—precision engagement; rapid response capacity; enhanced detection and tracking systems; and the ability to respond to chemical, biological, radiological, and nuclear attacks or disasters—requires the dedication of financial resources and training time.

Case Study: Hurricane Katrina Relief and the National Response Plan

The response to Hurricane Katrina reveals many of the issues that will likely face the United States in any scenario involving preparedness for and response to major natural or man-made disasters. A brief overview of the case provides a useful illustration of the challenges of homeland security planning and execution described in this chapter.

Katrina, which ravaged the city of New Orleans as well as large swaths of the Mississippi and Alabama coast on August 29, 2005, was the costliest natural disaster in U.S. history. It resulted in over $80 billion in property damage, including approximately three hundred thousand destroyed or severely damaged homes. The hurricane caused over eighteen hundred deaths and displaced approximately seven hundred seventy thousand people. The disaster occurred *after* many relevant reforms had recently been made: The DHS had been created, the National Incident Management System and National Response Plan were published in 2004 (together, these provide a framework for managing disaster preparation and response activities across all levels of government), and NORTHCOM had been created to plan and execute military civil support operations. Nevertheless, the government response to Katrina was widely and rightly criticized.

Reflecting the U.S. federal system of government, the National Response Plan essentially establishes a *bottom up* or *pull* model for disaster response. By design, local and state leaders request federal assistance when their resources are exhausted or overwhelmed. Federal assistance is provided through emergency support functions, such as transportation, communications, and urban search and rescue, each led by the appropriate federal agency and coordinated by interagency centers at the local through national level. Agencies request support from other federal organizations, including the DoD, as required to implement their emergency support functions.

In the case of Katrina, the magnitude of the initial damage and especially the flooding resulting from levee breaks in New Orleans prevented a rapid, comprehensive assessment of needs. Local, state, and federal organizations could not accurately describe the assistance they required. This problem was exacerbated by the breakdown in communication infrastructure and power supply during the critical days after Katrina's landfall. As a result, there were well-publicized delays in relief reaching the affected areas, which led to additional suffering and increased civil disorder. There was a three- or four-day gap between the presidential disaster declaration for Louisiana on August 29 and specific formal requests for federal assistance from the state. Significant relief for the approximately nineteen thousand people at the Morial Convention Center did not begin until September 2.

Another explanation for the delays was that FEMA, the DHS organization primarily responsible for the coordination of the federal response to disasters, was overwhelmed by the massive scale of Katrina and unable to deploy adequate command and control capability and basic supplies (such as food, water, and ice) in a timely manner. According to most assessments, whether through lack of staffing, planning, or leadership, FEMA was simply not up to the task of quickly coordinating the enormous relief effort. This effort involved many government organizations and civilian relief organizations, such as the American Red Cross and Salvation Army, that also bring response and recovery resources to devastated areas.

As is normal for any large disaster, the military was called upon to bring its comparative advantage in deployable manpower and large-scale logistical capability to bear following Katrina. More than twenty thousand active troops and fifty thousand National Guard troops from all fifty-four states and territories were involved in the operation, primarily in Louisiana and Mississippi. Among other tasks, they performed search-and-rescue missions in coordination with the U.S.

Coast Guard, provided medical care, established air traffic control for the area, and moved and distributed humanitarian relief supplies. Despite the magnitude of this effort, the speed and coordination of the military response also received criticism. Joint Task Force Katrina, built around the First U.S. Army, was activated on August 31, and military leaders acted on guidance to "lean forward" as much as possible by positioning supplies and equipment in the area without specific requests. However, significant numbers of active-duty ground troops did not reach New Orleans until September 6. Just as some of the FEMA delay was due to the lack of clear requests from the affected states, a large part of the delay in employing military assets can be attributed to the absence of clear requests for assistance from FEMA. A response system that relies on requests from local, state, and federal organizations will not work optimally if those requests are not timely and accurate.

The military response was also marked by inadequate coordination between active-duty forces and the National Guard, which operated under control of the state governors in a State Active Duty and then a Title 32 status. There was only a relationship of coordination between commanders of active forces and the State Adjutants General that commanded National Guard troops, and nothing mandated that these distinct chains of command exchange information. Especially given the complexity and time sensitivity of the initial response, it is unsurprising that the efforts of active and National Guard troops were not always complementary. For example, there were anecdotes of search-and-rescue teams from both components going to the same locations while other citizens waited for rescue, and lower-level leaders often did not have a clear picture of what units were near them and what missions they were performing. Maintaining separate chains of command has advantages. National Guardsmen in a Title 32 status retain some law enforcement authority, and the governor retains the ability to direct his or her state's troops, which may be politically important. However, the disadvantage is that separate chains of command will always create a coordination challenge, especially in a crisis situation. Coordination challenges are exacerbated if the ultimate commanders of the components—the president for Title 10 forces and the governors for Title 32 forces—do not agree on priorities for military action.

Although there is certainly much to criticize in the local, state, and federal preparation and response to Katrina, many of the difficulties resulted from the bottom-up National Response Plan model being overwhelmed by the historically rare scale of the disaster. For the vast majority of incidents, however, this model is effective, and it is a logical fit for a federal system of government. Reversing it and guaranteeing immediate federal assistance for all disasters could run the risk of reducing the incentive for local and state jurisdictions to plan and prepare for disaster response.

Much of the analysis of Katrina has centered on recommendations to anticipate and improve plans for circumstances in which a disaster is so catastrophic that federal assistance, including military aid, is immediately pushed to affected areas.[27] These plans may be especially important in the case of a no-notice terrorist attack, such as a nuclear detonation in a populated area, or a natural disaster, such as a major earthquake. For hurricanes, though precise damage cannot always be estimated, there is at least some warning and a preparation period when evacuations can be ordered and supplies pre-positioned.

The debate on the homeland security issues raised by Katrina will certainly continue. In the end, decisions about assigning responsibility for disaster preparedness and response in a federal system, allocating resources, and defining the desired role of active-duty and state military forces will always be subject to the same types of risk-management and political considerations that influence all homeland security efforts.

Enduring Considerations

The specific issues and threats at the top of the U.S. homeland security agenda will vary over time; however, the fundamental factors that make protecting the homeland such a difficult task will persist. These considerations define the environment in which homeland security choices are made.

Vulnerabilities will always exceed homeland security capability in a free society. The number of potential targets in the United States and the amount of traffic entering the country by land, sea, and air make it impossible to defend everywhere against any potential threat.

Even in a political vacuum, risk-management processes are hard to apply in making homeland security choices. If threats, vulnerabilities, and consequences can be agreed upon, which is no easy task, resources can still be applied in very different ways in terms of function (deter, prevent, defeat, or mitigate the effects of attacks and disasters), location (the homeland, approaches to the homeland, or abroad), and jurisdiction (local, state, federal, or international). There is considerable room for reasonable people to disagree on risk-mitigation strategies.

Political leaders making homeland security choices will often favor their constituencies rather than a national perspective. Decisions regarding homeland security grants and other homeland security actions are subject to the same considerations of distributional politics that accompany all federal, state, and local governmental-spending decisions.

Homeland security requires action by a huge number of public and private organizations, each of which has its own organizational interests. The country's federal system of government ensures that preparation for and response to attacks and disasters inevitably involves many players at the local, state, and federal levels. Even if they agree in general terms on a common goal, effective cooperation among large bureaucratic organizations is difficult to achieve. Concerns over guarding autonomy, reducing uncertainty, and increasing resources play a powerful role in shaping organizational behavior.

The military will always have a role in the homeland, and the country is likely to remain uneasy with it. Unless resources spent on homeland security are radically increased, some problems (such as major natural disasters or attacks with nuclear, biological, chemical, or radiological weapons) will require capabilities that only the U.S. Armed Forces can bring to bear. Especially in the case of federal forces operating in the homeland, traditional U.S. unease will persist, and any major action is likely to renew debates about the military's proper role.

The optimal balance between securing the homeland and safeguarding civil liberties will remain a contentious issue. Shifts in either direction will continue to occur, in large part based on the level of threat the American public perceives and the amount of security it demands. Each shift will also be hotly debated. In a democratic state, founded upon individual freedoms and confronted by new threats and challenges, this dynamic is both inevitable and appropriate.

Discussion Questions

1. What is the acceptable level of loss to terrorist attacks for the American people, and how does it vary over time?

2. How is the acceptable level of risk shaped by U.S. willingness to pay associated financial and nonmonetary costs?

3. What principles should guide decisions about allocation of scarce resources for homeland security? Which functions (deter, prevent, defeat, mitigate), types of threat, and locations (local, state, federal, abroad) should be favored?

4. What are the most significant barriers to application of a rational risk-management process to homeland security choices, and how can they best be mitigated?

5. What lessons from the post-9/11 reorganization of government should guide similar actions in the future?

6. Do law enforcement and intelligence agencies have adequate tools to counter threats to the homeland? How should their powers be limited to protect civil liberties?

7. Is the National Response Plan model for disaster response appropriate, and what (if any) changes should be made to it?

8. What role should the U.S. military—both active and Reserve Component forces, including the National Guard—play in homeland security? Should the military be given a more significant role following catastrophic incidents?

Recommended Reading

Brinkerhoff, John R. "The Posse Comitatus Act and Homeland Security." *Journal of Homeland Security* (Feb 2002). www.homelandsecurity.org/newjournal/articles/brin kerhoffposse comitatus.htm.

Eisinger, Peter. "Imperfect Federalism: The Intergovernmental Partnership for Homeland Security." *Public Administration Review* 66, no. 4 (July/Aug 2006): 537–545.

Flynn, Stephen. *America the Vulnerable: How Our Government Is Failing to Protect Us from Terrorism.* New York: Harper Collins, 2004.

Howard, Russell D., James J. Forest, and Joanne C. Moore. *Homeland Security and Terrorism: Readings and Interpretations.* New York: McGraw-Hill, 2006.

Huntington, Samuel P. "American Ideals Versus American Institutions." In *American Foreign Policy: Theoretical Essays*, 2nd ed., edited by G. John Ikenberry, 251–283. New York: HarperCollins College Publishers, 1996.

Kohn, Richard H. "Using the Military at Home: Yesterday, Today, and Tomorrow." *Chicago Journal of International Law* 4, no. 1 (Spring 2003): 165–192.

Maxwell, Bruce. *Homeland Security: A Documentary History.* Washington, DC: CQ Press, 2004.

National Commission on Terrorist Attacks upon the United States. *The 9/11 Commission Report.* Washington, DC: U.S. Government Printing Office, 2004.

Nicholson, William C., ed. *Homeland Security Law and Policy.* Springfield, IL: Charles C. Thomas, 2005.

Olson, Mancur. *The Logic of Collective Action: Public Goods and the Theory of Groups.* Cambridge, MA: Harvard University Press, 1965.

Sauter, Mark A., and James J. Carafano. *Homeland Security: A Complete Guide to Understanding, Preventing, and Surviving Terrorism.* New York: McGraw-Hill, 2005.

White, Jonathan R. *Defending the Homeland.* Belmont, CA: Wadsworth, 2004.

The White House. *The Federal Response to Hurricane Katrina: Lessons Learned.* Washington, DC: The White House, February 2006.

Willis, Henry H., Andrew R. Morral, Terrence K. Kelly, and Jamison Jo Medby. *Estimating Terrorism Risk.* Santa Monica, CA: RAND Corporation, 2005.

Wilson, James Q. *Bureaucracy: What Government Agencies Do and Why They Do It.* New York: Basic Books, 1989.

Internet Resources

Homeland Security Council, www.whitehouse.gov/hsc
Homeland Security Institute, www.homelandsecurity.org
U.S. Department of Homeland Security, www.dhs.gov
U.S. Government Accountability Office, Homeland Security Reports, www.gao.gov/docsearch/featured/homelandsecurity.html
U.S. Northern Command, www.northcom.mil

7

Intelligence and National Security

The Framers of the Constitution foresaw, in Alexander Hamilton's words, that "accurate and comprehensive knowledge of foreign politics" would inevitably be required in the management of America's external relations.[1] Intelligence, managed prudently, would be a useful and indeed necessary capability for the infant republic.[2] More than two hundred years later, national security policy makers in the more mature American republic still recognize their reliance on, and indebtedness to, accurate information about the external world. When intelligence fails, as it did on the issue of whether Saddam Hussein's regime had weapons of mass destruction (WMDs) prior to the U.S.-led invasion of Iraq in 2003, the consequences for U.S. policy can be significant.

What Is Intelligence?

The concept of intelligence is often confused with information.[3] Although information is anything that can be known, *intelligence* is a subset that includes information selected or tailored to respond to policy requirements or needs: "Intelligence refers to information relevant to a government's formulation and implementation of policy to further its national security interests and to deal with threats from actual or potential adversaries."[4] Although many associate the term strictly with military information, intelligence for national security is more than a description and analysis of armed capabilities. It also can include political, economic, social, cultural, and technological aspects of an adversary.[5] One way of categorizing intelligence is to refer to the time horizon in which intelligence is expected to be used.[6] Strategic intelligence examines issues with long-term implications, such as political and economic trends over time. Tactical intelligence, on the other hand, responds to immediate, pressing concerns and is intended to inform near-term decisions.[7] Some of the threats now present in the external environment, such as new nuclear weapons states or terrorist networks, have resulted in increased concern over effectiveness at gathering and using extremely time-sensitive intelligence. As a recent study summarizes, "the first priority should always be to get there before the bomb goes off."[8]

Intelligence professionals exist to support decision makers. The role that members of the intelligence community play in policy making is ideally that of "seasoned and experienced advisors," who add expert analysis to collected information.[9] Intelligence professionals attempt to envision possible or likely futures by analyzing and synthesizing current data and provide decision makers with background projections against which to measure policy alternatives. They may also develop policy options for policy makers and provide an analytical basis for choice among the options. An example of this direct policy use is furnished by Secretary of State Henry Kissinger's specific request to the CIA, shortly after the 1973 Middle East War, "to examine all aspects of possible Sinai withdrawal lines on the basis of political, military, geographic, and ethnic considerations. Eight alternative lines were prepared for the Sinai, a number of which Secretary Kissinger used in mediating the negotiations between Egypt and Israel."[10] Although the best intelligence cannot guarantee sound policy, policy made with inadequate intelligence support can succeed only by accident.

The Intelligence Production Process

Intelligence is divided into a five-part cycle: planning and direction; collection; processing and exploitation; analysis and production; and dissemination. As with all theoretical constructs, the intelligence cycle model is not perfect in describing reality.[11] Although an actual intelligence process may involve more complex and dynamic interactions, the conceptual clarity of the intelligence cycle is of great utility in structuring thinking about core intelligence functions. The five stages of the intelligence cycle are depicted in Figure 7.1 and will be discussed in turn below.

FIG. 7.1   The Intelligence Cycle

Source: Adapted from www.intelligence.gov/2-business.shtml

Planning and Direction. Consumers (policy makers and their advisers) take an active role in the *planning and direction* phase, which in turn influences the entire intelligence process.[12] The planning stage of the cycle begins with the determination of the consumers' specific information needs or a reaffirmation of continuing interests. Intelligence managers review consumer requests, and, if ongoing efforts or existing databases are unable to satisfy them, these requests are approved as new intelligence requirements. These requirements are then tasked to agencies with the requisite operational capabilities. Requirements developed through this process may be long term and require continuous attention, or they may generate a discrete project.

Problems in the planning stage stem from two areas: first, the development of national security policy; and second, the management of the intelligence community to inform that policy.[13] On the first issue, national security policy may not be sufficiently clear or specific with regard to content or priorities to provide adequate guidance to intelligence planners. On the second issue, inadequate management can cause agencies within the intelligence community to work at cross purposes with one another, making it difficult to create a timely, consolidated intelligence picture.[14]

Collection. Once requirements have been established, the second stage of the intelligence cycle is *collection*. There are six basic methods of intelligence collection: open-source intelligence, human intelligence, signals intelligence, imagery intelligence, measurement and signature intelligence, and geospatial intelligence.[15] Taken together, they can be complementary in facilitating the cross-checking of data. Each has unique capabilities that can offset limitations of the others.

Open-Source Intelligence. Open-source intelligence (OSINT) is derived from print and broadcast news; academic studies; popular literature; the Internet; and other freely available, "open-source" media. With advances in information technology, the Internet and other resources create easy access to an "explosion of information," shifting the challenge away from being one of information scarcity to that of distilling relevant material from information overabundance.[16] The major collectors of OSINT in the intelligence community are the Foreign Broadcast Information Service and the National Air and Space Intelligence Center.[17]

A very large part of the intelligence on most issues comes from open sources. Due to the threat of attack from international terrorist networks, open-source information is especially important. The Internet and public media are often used by terrorists to pass private messages or incite mass politics.[18] Open-source information can be essential in understanding the ideology and strategic plans of terrorist groups, such as al-Qa'ida.[19]

Human Intelligence. Human intelligence (HUMINT) is information collected from a human source via overt or covert means. Examples of government collectors include attachés and intelligence agents.[20] Sources originating from the adversary's side can come in two forms: friendly (walk-in or refugee) or hostile (detainees or prisoners of war). Though crucial, human intelligence receives only a small fraction of all the resources devoted to intelligence collection. Technological collection systems (such as imagery satellites) are more expensive and also extremely capable against certain types of intelligence problems. However, human intelligence may be the best—and, on occasion, the only—method for gaining reliable information on the intentions of an adversary's leaders. As the intelligence community increasingly focuses on nonstate actors, HUMINT will become even more important in gaining understanding of aspects of the threat.[21]

The production of quality HUMINT is accompanied by many challenges. First, running HUMINT operations can be difficult. Obstacles range from language barriers to the difficulties associated with persuading people to do things that may be against their own best interests. Second, information garnered from human beings will only be as reliable and insightful as the sources themselves. Objectivity and accuracy may be hard to judge. Third, great patience—sometimes over the course of years—may be required for the cultivation of important sources. Finally, HUMINT operations cannot be done remotely. Those involved may face danger and are also susceptible to adversary counterintelligence efforts.[22] The importance of human intelligence against such national security challenges as terrorism increases the potential benefits that can be derived from effective collaboration with foreign intelligence services.

Signals Intelligence.   Signals intelligence (SIGINT) is subdivided into three areas: communications intelligence (COMINT); electronic intelligence (ELINT), which is primarily the interception of radar signals; and foreign instrumentation signals intelligence (FISINT), which is the interception of instrumentation signals, such as radio command signals.[23] Depending on the target's characteristics, a communications intercept analyst may gain access to only the *externals* (such data as activity time, frequency, location, or similar characteristics). In some cases, however, the analyst will also gain access to the *internals* (the content) of intercepted communications. The interception of noncommunications emitters can also provide analysts with critical information about threat activity or intentions.[24]

Although SIGINT is a tremendously productive collection method, it is also expensive in terms of money and human resources. The sheer volume of information gathered is staggering. In addition, with the advance of information technology, new denial and deception techniques to avoid interception are constantly being created and used. Problems also stem from access and legality issues. A final concern is that, as with all collection methods, the use of actionable intelligence from SIGINT may result in a compromise of the collection method and source.[25]

Imagery Intelligence.   Imagery intelligence (IMINT) includes representations of objects reproduced electronically or by optical means on film, electronic display devices, or other media. Imagery collection efforts use photography and related imagery-producing techniques from *nonair breathers* (space-based satellites with surveillance equipment) and *air breathers* (manned or unmanned aircraft with surveillance equipment). Types of IMINT products include electro-optical, multispectral, infrared, and radar imagery.[26]

Imagery intelligence often enables the study of areas that would otherwise be inaccessible. Although expensive, unmanned aerial collection platforms give real-time intelligence while reducing the risk to human life. Imagery is also graphic and compelling intelligence; with the right interpretation, it is easy to understand. Downsides to IMINT include the fact that satellite orbits are predictable, thus allowing adversaries to avoid detection. Air breathers are less predictable and can be diverted instantly to a target, but they may have limited dwell-time capabilities.[27] Despite remarkable advances in technology, it is important to keep in mind that reconnaissance and surveillance systems cannot see everything. The United States was reminded of this as it sought to find Iraqi SCUD missiles in the desert during the 1991 war in the Persian Gulf, and again a decade later as it looked for WMDs in Iraq before and after the 2003 U.S.-led invasion.

Measurement and Signature Intelligence. Professionals producing measurement and signature intelligence (MASINT) employ a broad group of techniques relating to optical, radio frequency, thermal, acoustic, seismic, and material characteristics of targets. Examples of MASINT include intelligence garnered from the noise of passing vehicles or the chemical composition of air and water samples.[28]

Geospatial Intelligence. A newer method, geospatial intelligence (GEOINT), is the analysis and visual representation of security-related activities on the earth. It is produced through an integration of imagery, imagery intelligence, and geospatial information.[29]

Processing and Exploitation. The third phase of the intelligence cycle takes collected information and makes it relevant. Considerable resources are devoted to *processing and exploitation*, or the "synthesis of raw data into a form usable by the intelligence analyst or other consumers," and also to the secure telecommunications networks used to store it.[30] Without this stage, data collected is just information without significance. For example, reels of intercepted communications are of no utility until exploited by trained analysts: "No one has any use for intelligence that is gathered and not processed—that is, teased out for the most relevant and timely pieces of information."[31] Intelligence processing can involve "exploiting imagery; decoding messages and translating broadcasts; reducing telemetry to meaningful measures; preparing information for computer processing; storage and retrieval; [and] placing human-source reports into a form and context to make them more comprehensible."[32] These processes are carried out across the entire intelligence community.[33]

Analysis and Production. In the fourth stage of the intelligence cycle, collected intelligence that has been exploited and processed is further collated, assessed, related, integrated, and made understandable. Intelligence analysts are ideally experts in all aspects of their targets—including the language and culture—and also adept at integrating volumes of data produced by a variety of collection methods into a comprehensive, coherent, and succinct portrayal.[34] For even the best analysts, fragmentary and uncertain information makes prediction problematic. Instead of predicting the future, the analyst spots and highlights trends, assigns probabilities to various outcomes, and illuminates choices available to policy makers. This stage is critical to the effectiveness of the overall intelligence effort. Because a policy maker can only read a portion of available intelligence, the analytical quality and brevity of intelligence reports clearly affect the quality of national security decision making.

One of the more intractable problems of the intelligence process is bias. The analyst must act as a funnel, condensing and interpreting large amounts of raw information to create a succinct intelligence report or briefing. During this process, the analyst's personal knowledge and experience will affect the final product. The problem of bias can manifest itself in several ways. A first problem is that of *projection* or *mirror-imaging*, in which an analyst attributes personal value systems and thought processes to his or her analytical subject. This can result in flawed analyses, because the subject may not operate according to the analyst's standard of logic or rationality. Bias may also stem from the conscious or unconscious incorporation of personal or organizational interests into one's assessments. An example of the latter could be the inflation of military threat estimates by an analyst to support budget interests. Intelligence analysts could also become reluctant to challenge their agency's view or party line.

In addition to problems with mirror-imaging or parochial behavior, three additional sources of bias are status quo bias, wishful thinking, and premature closure. The *status quo bias* causes an analyst to expect continuity in a target. *Wishful thinking* relates to a tendency of an analyst to avoid uncomfortable conclusions. Finally, *premature closure* relates to a situation in which an analyst makes an early judgment and then is resistant to future contradictory information.[35] Although efficiency is a legitimate concern, some competition and duplication within the intelligence community can provide a healthy cross-check against blind spots and biases.

When dealing with vast amounts of raw data, analysts risk oversimplifying reality and failing to alert the consumer to the dangers within ambiguities. As mentioned in the context of OSINT, an excess of information can sometimes be as much of a challenge as a lack of information: "Technological advances have . . . produced a 'paradox of plenty.' Plenty of information leads to scarcity—of attention."[36] Constraints in this phase stem from both funding and time. Intelligence managers must accept risk by deciding where to focus their limited resources and do their best to ensure that uncertainties are accurately conveyed.[37]

Dissemination and Feedback. In the final stage, intelligence products—usually written reports or briefings—are disseminated to other interested agencies and to consumers, such as law enforcement agencies, the military, or policy makers, who can act on them. As with all the stages in the intelligence cycle, dissemination is also marked with challenges. The product must go to all who need it—at times, foreign as well as domestic consumers—and be timely enough to be helpful. At times, the classification of intelligence can make it unusable by certain consumers.[38] This challenge can be particularly acute for such issues as counterterrorism that require high levels of interagency coordination.

Because of the sensitivity of intelligence sources and methods, as well as the content of intelligence reporting, the traditional intelligence community approach to dissemination has been based on the concept of *need to know*. In other words, only other agencies and policy makers with a specific need for highly classified information would gain access to it. In reaction to the complexity of the current threat environment and the need for extensive cooperation within and among government agencies within the U.S. federal system, there has been a recent shift in emphasis to *responsibility to provide*—that is, finding a way to disseminate intelligence to all who may have a need for it.[39] Though this philosophy may improve dissemination, some constraints relating to procedures and levels of classification will persist.

If the original information needs are not satisfied, or if new questions emerge, consumers may restart the intelligence cycle by generating additional intelligence requirements. This feedback loop drives future intelligence operations. The process is a continuous one, with many requirements in various phases of the cycle at all times. However, the production of intelligence does not always follow this model. Consumers seldom take the time to articulate even their major continuing interests with a precision sufficient to drive the cycle. As a result, intelligence managers frequently generate information needs and requirements, providing consumers with intelligence they need but cannot or do not specifically request.

The Importance of the Policy Maker in the Intelligence Production Process

As noted earlier in this chapter, the reason for the intelligence community's existence is to meet the needs of the makers and implementers of national security policy. Accordingly, an effective relationship between intelligence professionals and policy makers is important. However, in practice, the role of the intelligence community can fluctuate with each new administration and sometimes even by issue area.[40]

Policy makers can increase the quality and relevance of intelligence by clearly stating priorities and initiating requests. Nevertheless, experienced intelligence officials agree that one of the most striking and persistent deficiencies affecting intelligence production is the "inadequacy of guidance by policy-makers as to their needs."[41] When the prioritization of threats is not clear, the intelligence community is left to "play daily triage" in response to pressing national security issues.[42] Unfortunately, "this is too often a hit-or-miss proposition, because it depends on the inclination of analysts who are dealing with other pressing problems."[43]

Policy makers may also be more effective consumers of intelligence if they are aware of its limitations as well as its capabilities. For a variety of reasons, including limited collection resources, time, limited expertise, and adversary efforts at deception and denial, there is no way to know everything. As one intelligence official states, "The point to keep in mind is that perfection in intelligence is not achievable. By its very nature it is an imperfect process."[44] Intelligence can "identify current developments and trends that will shape the future and affect U.S. interests" and give policy makers "a much better understanding of the situation they face."[45] However, at the time of decision, there will still be room for judgment, and even good intelligence and accurate predictions cannot prevent bad policy choices.

A key challenge for analysts is to meet policymaker needs while still adequately conveying uncertainties.[46] Policy makers can become dismissive of intelligence that is either too imprecise or too uncertain. For example, General Norman Schwarzkopf noted in his report to Congress after the 1991 Persian Gulf War that intelligence reports were so "caveated, footnoted, and watered down that we [the forces] would still be sitting over there if we were dependent on that analysis."[47] Though analyses that are more forceful and unqualified are more likely to be influential, intelligence professionals must remain accurate and not overstate their cases.

In addition to playing positive roles in the intelligence process, policy makers can also play negative roles if their involvement results in the politicization of intelligence. Described as "an act of intellectual corruption," politicization can stem from both the consumer and the producer.[48] *Downward politicization* occurs when the policy maker influences analytical conclusions by incentivizing desired conclusions or, more subtly, by being intolerant of unwanted information or analyses.[49] Analysts who carve out or shape information to please a superior or to fit a specific desired outcome engage in *upward politicization*. Many critics, in and out of government, have charged that senior civilians in the Department of Defense (DoD) were guilty of politicizing intelligence leading up to the 2003 U.S.-led invasion of Iraq. Politicization inevitably reduces the quality of the intelligence product.

A critical issue in the environment following the terrorist attacks of September 11, 2001, has been the need for *actionable* intelligence, particularly relating to future terrorist threats. Information is evaluated according to a number of criteria: (1) specificity as to time, location, manner, perpetrator; (2) credibility of sources; (3) corroboration of information by multiple sources; and (4) potential severity of consequences. Analysts use these criteria in evaluating whether information needs to go to key decision makers, and policy makers use them to decide whether they have sufficient basis to take action.

The Policy Implementation or Covert Action Role of Intelligence

In addition to producing intelligence, portions of the intelligence community also have the capability to act more directly as instruments of foreign policy through covert action. *Covert action* is activity performed by the U.S. government to influence political, economic, or military conditions abroad, where it is intended that the role of the U.S. government not be apparent or acknowledged publicly.[50] Especially during the Cold War era, American leaders conceived of and used the intelligence agencies as means of affecting or influencing events abroad in accordance with U.S. foreign policy goals. Among these implementing actions have been such activities as subsidizing foreign newspapers and political parties, arming guerrilla forces, and supporting foreign military organizations or operations logistically or paramilitarily.

Covert action has been the subject of much controversy both within and without the intelligence community. It has been a significant foreign policy tool and can continue to provide national policy makers with a regulated alternative for carrying out selected policy decisions by means not within the purview or capability of other agencies. For example, in 1991, President George H. W. Bush reportedly authorized the Central Intelligence Agency (CIA) to develop plans, including covert action, to block the proliferation of WMDs to the Third World.[51] More recently, the CIA played an important role in the U.S. invasion of Afghanistan to overthrow the Taliban regime in 2001.[52]

Despite its potential utility, there is a danger that unduly focusing on the covert action aspect of the broader intelligence scene can generate control mechanisms and create a climate, at home and abroad, of opinion prejudicial to the overall intelligence mission. Another danger lies in the fact that *covert action* is a very imprecise, elastic term. It covers everything from having lunch with a foreign journalist to encourage her to write an editorial that may well have been written anyway to running elaborate, large-scale paramilitary operations over time spans measured in years. It is therefore hard to discuss this concept in a rational, meaningful way—especially in a public forum.

Though clandestine activities have long been part of statecraft, only since the late 1970s have the mechanisms by which they are conducted and controlled come under close public scrutiny in the United States. When Congress created the CIA in 1947 to perform certain intelligence coordination functions, it directed the agency to also undertake "such other functions and duties related to intelligence affecting the national security as the President or the National Security Council may from time to time direct."[53] Since then, National Security Council (NSC) directives have given the CIA authority to conduct covert operations abroad consistent with American foreign and military policies.[54] Over time, Congress began to assert its oversight in this realm. An important step was the 1974 Hughes-Ryan Amendment, which required the CIA to report any planned action to the appropriate committees of Congress "in a timely manner."

By the early 1980s, following general public dissatisfaction over the inability to extricate American hostages from Iran during the Carter administration, the covert action function had regained a sense of vitality. This new trend toward a more fully developed covert action capability was short lived, however, as the consensus that had been building in support of covert action was severely weakened by the highly publicized 1985–1986 Iran-Contra affair. As a result of this episode, new legislation was enacted and signed by George H. W. Bush in the summer of 1991 that required the president to give written approval for any covert action undertaken by any component of the U.S. government and to notify Congress in a timely fashion. In addition, the president must notify Congress when third countries or private citizens are to be used or take part in covert activity in any significant way.[55]

Although covert operations survive in theory as an important vehicle for foreign policy implementation in special cases, there is a real question about their future practicality. In addition to the challenge of preserving the secrecy necessary to their success, these operations are often risky in terms of lives as well as the costs their revelation can impose on the achievement of broader national security policy goals. As a twenty-first century example, questions about the existence and operations of a secret CIA prison system stirred up great controversy during the administration of President George W. Bush. Critics sought explanations as to why a clandestine detention system was superior to existing legal and open detention and interrogation practices.[56] In the process of responding to public and congressional inquiries, an administration may find it necessary to reveal information that made a secret program attractive in the first place. Controversies such as these may also negatively affect both domestic public support and the image of the United States abroad.

Counterintelligence

Counterintelligence efforts attempt to deny real or potential adversaries the ability to collect information that can be used against the United States. Counterintelligence is one of the least understood and appreciated functions of the intelligence community. It has been defined as:

> the national effort to prevent foreign intelligence services and foreign-controlled political movements (which are often supported by intelligence services) from infiltrating our institutions and establishing the potential to engage in espionage, subversion, terrorism and sabotage. Counterintelligence involves investigations and surveillance activities to detect and neutralize the foreign intelligence presence, the collation of information about foreign intelligence services and the initiation of operations to penetrate, disrupt, deceive, and manipulate these services . . . to our advantage.[57]

In the current era, with foreign intelligence agencies in many cases focused on acquiring classified technological data and business and economic secrets, the definition of counterintelligence needs to be broadened to include frustration of foreign efforts to acquire sensitive information of all kinds.

Like covert action, counterintelligence operations often lead to controversy. There is general distrust of intelligence activities within the United States, yet this is precisely where counterintelligence officers must operate. This distrust is only heightened in the face of occasional revelations of agency misconduct. For example, in 2007, Robert Mueller, the director of the Federal Bureau of Investigation (FBI), was called before the Senate Judiciary Committee to explain failures on the part of the FBI to appropriately manage "national security letters"—instruments that enable the FBI to obtain communications and financial records without initial court oversight.[58] Even when counterintelligence activities are flawlessly managed, they still raise sensitive issues relating to potential infringement on the liberties of U.S. citizens.

Direction and Leadership of the Intelligence Community

The intelligence community is a collection of executive branch agencies and organizations that work both separately and together to conduct intelligence activities necessary for foreign relations and the protection of the national security of the United States.[59] Some knowledgeable observers, however, contend that the term *intelligence community* overstates the degree of cohesiveness in the American intelligence establishment. The community concept expresses the intent to get disparate entities to work together in sufficient harmony to develop the best possible intelligence products while avoiding excessive duplication of effort. The practical challenges associated with realizing that intent are formidable.

Direction of the Intelligence Community. The NSC is the highest executive branch entity (other than the president) providing direction to the national intelligence effort. The NSC announces the National Security Strategy and the national foreign intelligence objectives and priorities, which are then translated into specific guidance for the intelligence community. The NSC also reviews all proposals for special activities (i.e., covert actions), making recommendations on each to the president. In addition, it assesses proposals for sensitive intelligence collection operations and is aware of counterintelligence activities. Theoretically, the NSC evaluates the quality of the intelligence product as well. It is important to note that most of these missions are, in fact, accomplished by the national security staff acting under the direction of the assistant to the president for national security affairs or by a lower-level interdepartmental group. The NSC itself seldom provides specific direction to the intelligence effort.

Leadership of the Intelligence Community. The National Security Act of 1947 established the position of director of central intelligence (DCI) to lead the intelligence community in responding to executive direction and mandated that the head of the CIA would play that role. Although the DCI's position was progressively strengthened in the decades following 1947, management and coordination of the community as a whole remained problematic. The DCI had supervisory responsibility but did not have the authority to truly command the community and did not control the majority of the resources dedicated to the intelligence function.

The most significant change to the leadership of the intelligence community came after the 9/11 terrorist attacks on U.S. soil. One of the recommendations of the 9/11 Commission that investigated these attacks was to replace the DCI with a "National Intelligence Director" with two main responsibilities: "(1) to oversee national intelligence centers on specific subjects of interest across the U.S. government and (2) to manage the national intelligence program and oversee the agencies that contribute to it."[60] This recommendation led to the Intelligence Reform and Terrorism Prevention Act of 2004—the most significant legislative reform since the intelligence community's inception—which created the position of the Director of National Intelligence (DNI). As explained by George W. Bush when he signed the legislation into law in December 2004, the DNI:

> will serve as the principal advisor to the President on intelligence matters. The DNI will have the authority to order the collection of new intelligence, to ensure the sharing of information among agencies and to establish common standards for the intelligence community's personnel. It will be the DNI's responsibility to determine the annual budgets for all national agencies and offices and to direct how these funds are spent.[61]

The DNI now serves as the head of the intelligence community and acts as the principal advisor to the president, the NSC, and the Homeland Security Council for intelligence matters related to national security. The Office of the DNI also has within it the National Intelligence Council. This council provides the entire intelligence community with an independent analytical and estimative capability and also prepares national intelligence estimates using all the community's resources as well as nongovernmental experts.

Although the creation of the DNI was a significant reform, the new position has weaknesses as well as strengths. Perhaps the two most significant strengths relate to resources and personnel. The DNI directs and oversees the creation of the National Intelligence Program—a role that gives the DNI control over the budgets for the national missions of the intelligence agencies. In terms of personnel, the DNI also has authority over community-wide personnel programs. This authority may enable the DNI to affect the career patterns and incentive structures of career intelligence officials to become supportive of community-wide goals.[62] However, the position of the DNI also contains major weaknesses. These concerns were summed up by Senator John Rockefeller in confirmation hearings for a new DNI in February 2007:

> We did not pull the technological collection agencies out of the Defense Department and we did not give the DNI direct authority over the main collection or analytical components of the community. We gave the DNI the authority to build the national intelligence budget, but we left the execution of the budget with the agencies. We gave the DNI tremendous responsibilities. The question is, did we give the position enough authority for him to exercise those responsibilities?[63]

Congress is likely to continue to assess this question for some time to come.

In addition to creating a stronger head of the intelligence community, another major reform directed by the Intelligence Reform and Terrorism Prevention Act of 2004 was the codification in law of the National Counter-Terrorism Center (NCTC). Established in 2003 by the president as the Terrorist Threat Integration Center, the president subsequently renamed it the NCTC in an August 2004 presidential executive order. Congress codified it in its 2004 legislation and placed it within the Office of the DNI (see Figure 7.2). The key purpose of this center is to ensure unity of effort within the intelligence community on an issue of critical

FIG. 7.2 Structure of the Office of the Director of National Intelligence

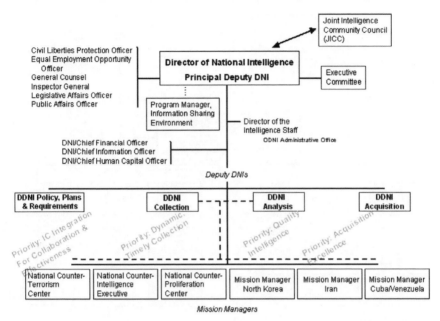

Source: www.odni.gov/org_chart

importance to national security. As with the role and effectiveness of the DNI, this organization and its functions are likely to continue to evolve. The 2004 act also provides for and seems to envision the creation of additional, similar centers focused on other key national security concerns. One, the National Counter-Proliferation Center, has already been established.

Members of the Intelligence Community

The intelligence community within the United States currently has sixteen components that all fall under the oversight of the DNI. Of these entities, the CIA is the only one that is independent. All the others fall under executive departments within the government: eight within defense, two within homeland security, two within the Department of Justice, and three within other executive departments. These are listed in Figure 7.3 and will be discussed in turn below.

Central Intelligence Agency.　The CIA collects information abroad and serves as the national manager for human source collection. It is the only agency within the community authorized to conduct covert activities, although the president can direct other agencies to be involved. Though its operations are conducted almost entirely outside the United States, it can participate in counterintelligence activities at home in support of the FBI, as well as in certain limited domestic activities that support overseas collection operations.

FIG. 7.3 The Intelligence Community

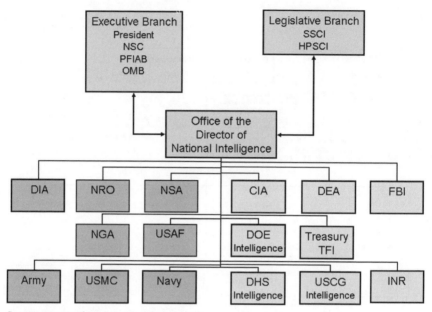

Source: www.wmd.gov/report/wmd_report.pdf

Department of Defense. The importance of defense-related concerns to the intelligence community is reflected in the fact that half of its components reside within the DoD. Whereas the CIA serves primarily national consumers, these DoD components also serve military commanders at all levels. The importance of the intelligence entities within the DoD was reflected in Secretary of Defense Donald Rumsfeld's creation of the Office of the Undersecretary of Defense for Intelligence in 2003. (Earlier, intelligence was at the assistant secretary level.) The third-highest-ranking official in the Pentagon, the undersecretary of defense for intelligence is responsible for coordinating efforts within the defense intelligence community and serving as the focal point for interaction with the DNI and the rest of the intelligence community.[64]

Defense Intelligence Agency. Headquartered in the Pentagon, the DIA produces military and military-related intelligence for the DoD. The director of the DIA serves as the principal advisor on substantive military matters to the secretary of defense and the Joint Chiefs of Staff. The DIA also provides military input for national intelligence products and supervises the work of all military attachés abroad. Within DIA is also the Central MASINT Organization, the focus for all national and DoD MASINT matters.

National Security Agency. The National Security Agency (NSA), headquartered at Fort Meade, Maryland, has two main strategic missions. The first of these is to conduct signals intelligence (explained above), and the second is information assurance. In this latter capacity, NSA "prevents America's adversaries from exploiting sensitive U.S. government communications by giving policy-makers and warfighters a secure means of communicating."[65] Because of the nature of its responsibilities, the NSA operates in the dynamic realm of information technology and must constantly adapt to be effective at its core missions.

National Reconnaissance Office. The National Reconnaissance Office (NRO) "develops and operates unique and innovative overhead reconnaissance systems and conducts intelligence related activities essential for U.S. national security."[66] Due to the sensitivity of its responsibilities, the existence and functions of the NRO were only declassified in September 1992. The NRO is jointly managed by the secretary of defense and the DNI, though it is the latter who establishes its requirements and collection priorities.[67]

National Geospatial-Intelligence Agency. The new National Geospatial-Intelligence Agency (NGA) replaced the National Intelligence Mapping Agency. The national manager for both classified and unclassified imagery products, it is also responsible for providing timely, relevant, and accurate GEOINT in support of military forces and national requirements.

Army, Air Force, Navy, and Marine Corps Intelligence. In addition to the above agencies, each of the armed services has intelligence and counterintelligence capabilities. These service component entities provide support to decision makers at tactical, operational, and strategic levels.

Department of Homeland Security. Two components of the intelligence community reside within the Department of Homeland Security (DHS). The first of these is the Office of Intelligence and Analysis, which is responsible for overseeing and integrating all the intelligence elements of the department (see Chapter 6 for the organizational structure of the DHS). The Office of Intelligence Analysis is also responsible for coordination between the DHS and state and local governments, the rest of the intelligence community, and Congress. The second component of the intelligence community within the DHS is Coast Guard Intelligence, which was transferred with the rest of the Coast Guard from the Department of Transportation when the DHS was created.

Department of Justice. Two components of the intelligence community are agencies within the Department of Justice. The first of these is the FBI. Although primarily a domestic investigative and law enforcement agency, the FBI has extensive domestic counterintelligence and security responsibilities. After the 9/11 terrorist attacks, the "overriding priority" of the FBI became "protecting America by preventing future attacks."[68] In 2005, George W. Bush directed the creation of a National Security Service in the FBI, and the agency responded by creating the

National Security Branch. Within this organization, FBI counterterrorism, counterintelligence, and intelligence functions all reside. The director of this branch also coordinates FBI national security efforts with the rest of the intelligence community. In addition to the National Security Branch, the FBI also fulfills its national security responsibilities through fifty-six field offices in major U.S. cities, over four hundred resident offices in smaller communities, and fifty offices located in embassies worldwide.[69]

The second component of the intelligence community within the Department of Justice is the Drug Enforcement Agency (DEA). The DEA's Office of National Security Intelligence "is responsible for providing drug-related information responsive to intelligence community requirements."[70] The DEA is experienced with operating in foreign environments and—with eighty-six offices in sixty-three countries—has the largest the U.S. law-enforcement agency presence abroad.[71]

Department of State.   Diplomatic reporting is a valuable information-gathering resource. Representatives of the State Department stationed overseas regularly report to Washington regarding developments relevant to U.S. foreign policy, including information about foreign political, sociological, economic, and scientific trends or events. For the rest of the community as well as for the secretary of state, the department's Intelligence and Research Bureau generates intelligence products pertinent to U.S. foreign policy. The secretary of state works closely with the DNI, and the State Department with the CIA, to ensure that intelligence activities are both useful to and cognizant of American foreign policy.

Department of the Treasury.   Treasury's Office of Intelligence Analysis, established in 2004, is a member of the intelligence community. Run by an assistant secretary and residing within the Office of Terrorism and Financial Intelligence, this office coordinates with the rest of the intelligence community and investigates such issues as nuclear proliferation financing and terrorism financing.[72]

Department of Energy.   The Department of Energy participates with the State Department in overt collection of information on foreign energy matters, particularly nuclear energy, and also produces such intelligence as the secretary of energy may need to discharge the duties of the office. A particular value added of the Office of Intelligence and Counterintelligence within the Department of Energy is its ability to provide technical expertise when evaluating and helping to counter such threats as nuclear proliferation.

Intelligence Oversight

Because there is no explicit provision in the Constitution for the control of intelligence, authority for it must be inferred from provisions for the national defense and foreign affairs functions that intelligence serves. As Congress shares power with the president in these functions, its claims to comparable authority in the field of intelligence can be hard for the executive branch to counter. If congressional participation in foreign policy formulation and control is to be significant, Congress must have access to relevant information, providing it an additional incentive to take an active role in intelligence policy.

Congressional Perspective and Actions.   From the enactment of the National Security Act of 1947 until about 1970, there existed a broad consensus on Capitol Hill that acknowledged the president's control of the intelligence community. By the early 1970s, however, that consensus had been eroded by the unfolding Watergate scandal and allegations concerning CIA involvement in Chilean presidential elections. Responding to these developments, Congress in 1974 passed the Hughes-Ryan Amendment to the Foreign Assistance Act. This legislation required that the president, prior to the expenditure of appropriated funds for noncollection intelligence activities in foreign countries, issue a "finding" that declared the activity to be "important to the national security" of the United States and report this finding to appropriate congressional committees. Subsequently, both the House and Senate launched investigations into alleged CIA misconduct.

Although the respective committees operated concurrently, the Senate committee (known as the Church Committee after its chairman, Senator Frank Church) took the lead. Its investigatory charter was broad and open ended, instructing the committee to measure intelligence activities against standards of both legality and propriety. After examining records, listening to witnesses, and deliberating at length, the committee decided that the United States had been implicated in several political assassination plots. Operational authorization procedures within the intelligence community seemed so deliberately compartmented and secretive that a plan to kill a foreign leader could be generated without explicit presidential approval. Much of the public debate on this matter, however, missed an important point. The president had been deliberately insulated from formal involvement in covert actions, not to keep him ignorant of them, but to allow him to take the public line that the chief of state was not involved.

The committee's final report called for adherence to "fair play" ideals. The committee clearly believed that the looseness of operational rules and discretion had sometimes led to intelligence operations resembling those of the country's totalitarian competitors. Remedies suggested by the committee included clear legislative delineation of the scope of permissible activities (via a statutory charter for the intelligence community) and better procedures for supervising intelligence agency operations (including more and better congressional oversight).

After the completion of these investigations, Congress had before it two self-imposed tasks: to put its oversight machinery in order and to pass legislative charters setting forth authorizations and restrictions for the intelligence community. The Senate Select Committee on Intelligence (SSCI) was created in 1976, and the House Permanent Select Committee on Intelligence (HPSCI) followed in 1977. In a 1977 report, the SSCI stated its intent to serve congressional and constitutional interests in the following ways:

1. *Obtain information relevant to foreign policy decisions.* The select committee was instructed by the Senate to "provide informed and timely intelligence necessary for the executive and legislative branches to make sound decisions affecting the security and vital interests of the nation." Access to intelligence products became a matter of institutional right.

2. *Use the budget process as a control mechanism.* During the committee's first year, it helped prepare legislation specifically authorizing appropriations for all aspects of intelligence, including a project-by-project review of covert action. This review procedure was a major step beyond the past, when intelligence monies were hidden throughout the budget, and opened the way for far more congressional influence than had been felt before in the intelligence arena.

3. *Control by investigation.* In its first year, the Senate committee investigated one hundred allegations of improprieties. The role of Congress as an institutional inquisitor is a well-established one.

4. *Review of covert operations proposals.* An oversight procedure established in conjunction with the executive branch gave the Senate committee what amounted to an approval role in covert action operations. Once the president approves a proposal, the committee is informed. Should the committee feel that pursuit of a covert action would not be in the best interests of the country, its procedures provide for taking the issue to the Senate in closed session. The rules even envisioned disclosure of facts concerning the operation, if confrontation over its advisability persisted.

Work on a statutory charter for the intelligence community proved more difficult than the provision of oversight. After other proposals failed, the Intelligence Oversight Act of 1980 was enacted. This law repealed the Hughes-Ryan Amendment and reduced the number of congressional oversight committees to the two select committees on intelligence. A 1991 amendment to this act defined covert activities and required written approval by the president in advance; it also stipulated that the intelligence committees in Congress be informed as the activities proceeded.[73]

Congressional scrutiny of intelligence operations was strengthened by the 1978 Foreign Intelligence Surveillance Act (FISA). This act required judicial warrants for electronic intelligence surveillance used in intelligence and counterintelligence operations within the United States whenever communications of "United States persons" might be intercepted. This act also created the Foreign Intelligence Surveillance Court, where the judges maintain sufficient clearances to hear the compartmentalized intelligence that supports probable cause warrants for foreign agents.

In the 1980s, there was a lull in legislation despite high-profile actions by members of the intelligence community. The foremost among these were CIA covert actions, such as the mining of Nicaraguan waters and the Iran-Contra scandal. Although the latter incident created a spectacle, it did not lead to any significant restrictions.

In the 1990s, Congress created the bipartisan Commission on Roles and Capabilities of the U.S. Intelligence Community through the Intelligence Authorization

Act of fiscal year 1995. The Commission analyzed the new threats facing the United States after the Cold War and found that improvements were needed in several areas to include community interaction, cost and burden sharing with allies, and public relations.[74]

After the attacks of 9/11, the federal government took another hard look at itself. One result was the creation of the DHS, discussed in Chapter 6. Congress and the president also created the 9/11 Commission and chartered it broadly "to investigate facts and circumstances relating to the terrorist attacks of September 11, 2001," including those that were related to the intelligence community.[75] The 9/11 Commission identified inadequate communication between law enforcement and intelligence agencies, and among members of the intelligence community, to be significant problems.

As discussed above, the Intelligence Reform and Terrorism Prevention Act of 2004 responded to some of these recommendations by establishing the DNI and creating the NCTC to integrate the intelligence effort on high-priority intelligence threats. In addition, the 2004 law created an independent Privacy and Civil Liberties Board. Working as a part of the Executive Office of the president and led by a chair and vice chair, both of whom must be confirmed by the Senate,[76] it ensures the civil liberties of American citizens are not infringed upon by laws, policies, or decisions of the executive branch.[77]

Executive Oversight.   In addition to congressional oversight mechanisms, the executive branch has its own oversight entities and procedures. One entity that presidents have used to exercise oversight over the intelligence community is the President's Foreign Intelligence Advisory Board (PFIAB). Established in 1956 by President Dwight Eisenhower as the President's Board of Consultants, PFIAB has had an on-again, off-again existence since the 1960s. Currently consisting of eleven members, the PFIAB has no line authority, but because it reviews all intelligence activities with a special responsibility for the quality of products and management, and because it reports to the president at least semiannually, it has an important role.

As noted above, allegations of intelligence community abuses—both domestic and abroad—generated considerable concern in the United States in the 1970s. As a result, additional procedures to preclude unauthorized activities were instituted. The President's Intelligence Oversight Board (PIOB), a three-member panel of private citizens appointed by the president, was created by President Jimmy Carter in 1976 to review and report to the president on the intelligence community's internal procedures and operational activities. Within the intelligence community itself, inspectors general and general counsels were specifically made responsible to report to the PIOB on all potential breaches of the law by their agencies. As part of an effort to streamline his office, President Bill Clinton eliminated the PIOB in 1993 and transferred its responsibilities to a committee of the PFIAB. This action eliminated an important safeguard when it erased the direct reporting line to the president.

Executive oversight has varied over time in intensity and effectiveness. Reflecting his concern for reinvigorating the capability of the intelligence community to deal with a wide array of national security threats, President Ronald Reagan, by executive order, provided a strengthened new charter for the community. Unfortunately, the climate created by this executive order, as well as the activities of his influential and strong-minded DCI, William Casey, led to a number of excesses. These included the CIA's mining of Nicaraguan waters without informing Congress and the Iran-Contra scandal. These episodes, in turn, led to congressional investigations, a call for more restrictions on the CIA, and the 1987 appointment of a highly respected, nonpolitical outsider, William Webster, as DCI. (Webster had earlier headed the FBI.)

As is evident from this condensed historical survey, the executive branch not only directs the intelligence community but also seeks independent mechanisms for ensuring oversight. Because administrations take different approaches to the intelligence community, interspersed periods of more and less restrictive executive branch oversight are likely to continue. Given this factor, as well as the nature of the intelligence function and the continuously changing national security environment, both branches of government are likely to continue to reassess and readjust their mechanisms for exercising intelligence oversight.

Judicial Oversight.   Judicial oversight of the intelligence community has been historically minor, primarily because most intelligence activities take place overseas and are directed against foreign nationals or nations. Arguably, the initial interaction of the judiciary and the intelligence community was the use of wiretaps by law enforcement agencies and the Supreme Court's 1967 decision in *Katz v. United States*. In this case, the Court held that Katz had a reasonable expectation of privacy that society was prepared to recognize in his phone-booth conversations.[78] This case overruled an earlier (the Olmstead) case that stated if there was not a physical invasion into a constitutionally protected space, there was no need for a warrant.

The aftermath of the Watergate scandal and revelations of the recording of personal communications without warrants fueled the public's desire to see all warrants governed by a legal process. The 1978 FISA legislation authorized the Chief Justice of the United States to designate seven federal district court judges to review applications for warrants related to national security investigations within a Foreign Intelligence Surveillance Court.[79] FISA also requires that a court order or warrant be obtained from this court for all electronic surveillance for intelligence purposes within the United States.[80] Warrant applications under FISA are drafted by attorneys in the General Counsel's Office at the NSA at the request of an officer of one of the federal intelligence agencies. Each application must contain the attorney general's certification that the target of the proposed surveillance is either a "foreign power" or "the agent of a foreign power" and, in the case of a U.S. citizen or resident alien, that the target may be involved in the commission of a crime.[81]

The first change to FISA came as a result of the Patriot Act. Perhaps the most significant provisions of the Patriot Act were those intended to lower the barriers blocking cooperation between intelligence and law enforcement by lowering the threshold for getting a surveillance warrant, expanding the ability of the FBI to gather information without a warrant, and expanding surveillance on the Internet. In addition, it expanded the time periods for which the Foreign Intelligence Surveillance Court can authorize surveillance and increased the number of judges serving the court from seven to eleven.[82] George W. Bush's controversial authorization of warrantless wiretaps by the NSA on international calls in 2001, avoiding FISA procedures as too cumbersome and lengthy, constitutes another arena in which judicial oversight and presidential prerogative clash.

Though judicial oversight is not unimportant, the judiciary is limited to the realm of legal interpretation. This is in sharp contrast to Congress, which has the ability to subpoena, address policy issues, and control the funding for elements of the intelligence community.[83]

Looking Ahead

As is evident in this chapter, today's intelligence community operates in a challenging and dynamic environment. In addition to the complexity of the international security environment and the dynamism of modern technology, many elements within the intelligence community have experienced at least some degree of organizational change in response to the lessons of 9/11. Due to the recent nature of some of these changes, such as the creation of the DNI and the NCTC, the significance of these reforms and their impact on the quality of the U.S. intelligence effort remains to be seen.

In the midst of these developments, the intelligence community suffered a significant blow to its reputation with the failure to discover its predicted WMDs in Iraq after the 2003 U.S.-led invasion. In the words of the "Weapons of Mass Destruction Commission" report:

> On the brink of war, and in front of the whole world, the United States asserted that Saddam Hussein had reconstituted his nuclear weapons program, had biological weapons and mobile biological weapons production facilities, and had stockpiled and was producing chemical weapons. All of this was based on the assessments of the U.S. Intelligence Community. And not one bit of it could be confirmed when the war was over.[84]

The commission acknowledged the difficulty of the intelligence problem that WMDs pose but nevertheless found that this major intelligence failure was also the product of shortcomings in collection, analysis, and the manner in which available intelligence was made available to policy makers. The related question of how policy makers used assessments that were provided to them by the intelligence community has yet to be similarly investigated.[85]

As the intelligence community continues to evolve, one thing is clear: It will continue to be held accountable to both the president and Congress. Without cooperation with and from both branches, the community will not be able to acquire the resources or authorizations it needs to operate effectively. In addition, given the importance of counterterrorism and concern about homeland security, the role played by judicial oversight of the intelligence process is likely to increase. The way ahead is challenging.

Discussion Questions

1. What is intelligence, and what contribution does the intelligence community make to the national security decision-making process?

2. How is the intelligence community structured? Who leads the intelligence community?

3. How did the events of 9/11 help shape the current structure?

4. What resources are used in OSINT? How important is OSINT to the U.S. intelligence effort?

5. In what ways can bias impact analysis? How can policy makers and the intelligence community guard against the effects of bias?

6. How has oversight over the intelligence community changed over the years? Which branches of the government maintain oversight today?

7. With an increased focus on nonstate actors in the current international security environment, what types of intelligence collection will become most important?

8. Should covert action remain an important instrument of U.S. national security policy? What are the strengths and weaknesses of this policy tool?

Recommended Reading

Andrew, Christopher. *For the President's Eyes Only: Secret Intelligence and the American Presidency from Washington to Bush.* New York: Harper Perennial, 1996.

Cilluffo, Frank J., Ronald A. Marks, and George C. Salmoiraghi. "The Use and Limits of U.S. Intelligence." *Washington Quarterly* 25, no. 1 (2002): 61–74.

Clark, Robert M. *Intelligence Analysis: A Target-Centric Approach.* 2nd ed. Washington, DC: CQ Press, 2007.

Dupont, Alan. "Intelligence for the Twenty-first Century." *Intelligence and National Security* 18, no. 4 (Winter 2003): 15–39.

George, Roger Z., and Robert D. Kline. *Intelligence and the National Security Strategist: Enduring Issues and Challenges.* Washington, DC: NDU Press, 2004.

Lowenthal, Mark M. *Intelligence: From Secrets to Policy.* 3rd ed. Washington, DC: CQ Press, 2006.

National Commission on Terrorist Attacks. *The 9/11 Commission Report.* New York: W. W. Norton & Company, 2004.

Odom, William E. *Fixing Intelligence: For a More Secure America.* New Haven, CT: Yale University Press, 2003.

Scott, Len, and Peter Jackson. "The Study of Intelligence in Theory and Practice." *Intelligence and National Security* 19, no. 2 (June 2004): 139–169.

Shulsky, Abram N., and Gary L. Schmitt. *Silent Warfare: Understanding the World of Intelligence.* 3rd ed. Washington, DC: Brassey's, 2002.

Stiefler, Todd. "CIA's Leadership and Major Covert Operations: Rogue Elephants or Risk-Averse Bureaucrats?" *Intelligence and National Security* 19, no. 4 (Dec 2004): 632–654.

Taylor, Stan, and David Goldman. "Intelligence Reform: Will More Agencies, Money, and Personnel Help?" *Intelligence and National Security* 19, no. 3 (Sept 2004): 416–435.

Treverton, Gregory F. *The Next Steps in Reshaping Intelligence.* Santa Monica, CA: RAND Corporation, 2005.

Internet Sources

Central Intelligence Agency Center for the Study of Intelligence,
　www.cia.gov/library/center-for-the-study-of-intelligence/index.html
Office of the Director of National Intelligence, www.odni.gov
President's Intelligence Advisory Board, www.whitehouse.gov/pfiab
U.S. House of Representatives Permanent Select Committee on Intelligence,
　http://intelligence.house.gov
U.S. Intelligence Community, www.intelligence.gov/index.shtml
U.S. Senate Select Committee on Intelligence, http://intelligence.senate.gov

8

The Role of the Military in
the Policy Process

The military plays a unique and crucial role in U.S. national security policy for a number of reasons. First, the military's coercive capabilities make democratic political control a matter of central importance. This concern shaped the drafting of the U.S. Constitution and, therefore, the legal framework that continues to govern military affairs to this day. Second, since the Korean War in the 1950s, the U.S. military has made a consistently large claim on national resources. The Department of Defense (DoD), with a budget of over $400 billion in fiscal year (FY) 2006 and over 3 million employees who work in more than 163 countries, is "America's largest company."[1] Military spending constitutes the single largest category of discretionary spending in the U.S. federal budget (see Chapter 9). Finally, the importance of the military instrument of power to U.S. national security policy makes the effectiveness of America's military institutions a matter of great consequence (see Chapters 13 through 17).

The American Historical Experience

Early American History and the U.S. Constitution. As discussed in Chapter 2, America's wariness of standing armies is rooted in the colonial experience. Not only did the Founding Fathers experience the negative effects of a powerful and often oppressive British army, they also recognized the unfortunate consequences of militarism within the countries of Europe.

At the conclusion of the Revolution, the American army was essentially disbanded, and the national government was left with the task of governing under the Articles of Confederation. Under the Articles, the national government had very little power to maintain an army or even to raise one for national emergencies.

After several violent domestic incidents (most notably an uprising of farmers in 1786 and 1787 against crushing debt and higher taxes known as Shays' Rebellion), and in the presence of increasing border threats, the Founding Fathers went to great lengths to fix a government that was decidedly weak in many facets of national security.

The "fix" was ultimately the U.S. Constitution. As they debated its final content, the Framers found it challenging to agree on wording that would provide for physical security from foreign and domestic threats while simultaneously protecting the state and society from a potentially dangerous standing army.[2] Douglas Johnson and Steven Metz write:

> Amid intense debate and calls to ban a standing army altogether, the Framers of the Constitution crafted a compromise between military effectiveness and political control. They trusted balance, the diffusion of power, and shared responsibility—all basic elements of the new political system—to control the military.[3]

These elements were codified in the final document through several provisions designed to "provide for the common defense":[4]

- Article 2, section 8, of the Constitution gives power over the military to the legislative branch by listing such specific powers as "To declare War," "To raise and support Armies," and "To provide and maintain a Navy." Moreover, the Constitution provides the states with the authority to maintain militias. These provisions were intended to preclude the executive branch from making war without the consent of the legislature and to balance state and federal power.

- Article 2, section 2, of the Constitution gives the roles of chief executive and commander in chief to the president. This ensures civilian supremacy by placing the chief executive at the top of the military chain of command and also aids military effectiveness by providing for unity of command in the employment of military forces.

- The Second Amendment emphasizes the role of the citizen-soldier by providing for "the right of the people to keep and bear Arms." Like the militia clause, this provision also limits the federal government's monopoly on the means of war.

- The Third Amendment protects U.S. citizens from the pre-Revolutionary custom of quartering soldiers in private homes "without the consent of the Owner."

This intricate system of checks and balances was meant to enable the establishment and employment of an effective military while ensuring it could never become a danger to the society it was created to protect. This formulation also ensured the involvement of both the president and Congress in the creation of military policy (see Chapters 4 and 5).

Historic Noninfluence.   Prior to World War II, it was only in exceptional cases—those directly linked to wartime circumstances—that the military significantly influenced the formulation of national policy. General Winfield Scott, commander in Mexico in 1846, established occupation policies as he conquered.

Again during the Civil War, the influence of the commanding general of the army upon the secretary of war, the president, and Congress was great, especially in the latter years of Ulysses S. Grant's ascendancy. Perhaps the most direct instance of military policy making in that conflict occurred with the reestablishment of state and local governments in the South; the programs instituted by military commanders for such governance were underwritten as national policy by President Abraham Lincoln in 1863.

Military influence in policy formulation was also evident during the occupation of the Philippines immediately after the Spanish-American War. During World War I, General John J. Pershing was given wide discretion in dealing directly with Allies and in establishing requirements on the national government at home. Shortly after World War I, both General Peyton C. March and Pershing proposed plans to Congress for maintaining an army substantially stronger than the pre–World War I establishment. These plans were at least seriously considered before being rejected.[5]

The examples above typify the generally accepted rule prior to World War II: that the military should play a role in the formulation of national security policy only when the duress of war made the armed forces responsible for executing such policy. The general absence of any major threats to the nation's existence, apart from the Civil War, left the military services with only the routine problems of continental defense, suppression of Indians, internal development (especially of rivers and railroads), protection of trade, contingency planning, and passive support of a largely isolationist foreign policy. Neither the structure of government nor the necessity of military missions compelled sustained involvement of the military in national policy.

World War II and the National Security Act of 1947.   World War II and the immediate postwar years marked a total break with the past. The clear wartime need for interdepartmental coordination of political-military affairs led to the establishment of the State-War-Navy Coordinating Committee in late 1944. Consisting of ranking civilian officials from each department and supported by a system of interdepartmental subcommittees, including senior military participants, the State-War-Navy Coordinating Committee marked the beginning of institutionalized military influence at the highest levels of the national security policy formulation apparatus.

The demands of World War II also led to other important changes in the role of the military in the national security policymaking process. First, the uniformed chiefs of the services began to meet regularly as the Joint Chiefs of Staff (JCS) and to maintain direct liaison with the president.[6] Second, due to factors that included the relative detachment of the State Department from military operations and the goal of "total victory," the services played the leading role in developing war termination and postwar occupation policies. For example, the key political decision of whether Berlin was to be taken by the U.S. Army was not decided in Washington but left to the discretion of the military commander in the field.[7] In occupied areas, including Berlin, officials of the military government made the critical decisions. The question of the number and ideological composition of the political parties permitted to develop in postwar, allied-occupied Germany, for instance, was determined by senior War Department officials.[8] General Douglas MacArthur ruled over the occupation in Japan with virtual independence. Third, superior organization and resources enabled the military to play an expanded role in all areas of national security policy formulation. Especially effective was the Operations Division of the War Department's general staff, which formed the core of wartime and immediate postwar political military planning for the U.S. effort.[9]

In the immediate postwar years, civilian elements gradually began to reassert their traditional roles in foreign policy.[10] State Department leadership in postwar European recovery, symbolized by the Marshall Plan, and the central role of the State Department in the structure that conducted postwar political and economic planning shifted the initiative in policy making away from the military establishment. Not only did the military's advantage in organizational terms shrink, but so did its vast resources. Military appropriations dropped sharply, and Army strength contracted from over 8 million personnel on V-J Day to less than 2 million a year later.[11] At the same time, rapid changes in military technology meant that vehicles and aircraft accumulated during the war were already obsolete.

Despite these trends, the lessons of political-military coordination learned during World War II were retained. The many joint and interdepartmental committees and advisory groups formed during the war were first brought into a formalized plan for civil-military coordination in the National Security Act of 1947.[12] In addition to establishing the National Security Council (NSC) and a secretary of defense (see Chapters 4 and 10), the act created a "national security establishment" consisting of the three service departments (Army, Navy, and Air Force) linked together by a series of joint committees and coordinated by the three services' chiefs sitting collectively as the JCS. The members of the JCS were authorized staffs and became the principal military advisors to the president and secretary of defense. The act also provided the legal basis for the creation of U.S. military unified and specified commands worldwide.

In the Key West Agreement of 1948, the JCS was designated to be the executive agent for unified and specified commands. This meant that the JCS would be responsible for day-to-day communications and supervision of operational forces, as well as coordination among the services to define the roles and missions of each. Legislation in 1949 strengthened the role of the secretary of defense by creating a unified DoD with authority over the services. It also removed the service secretaries from the president's cabinet and from the NSC, increased the size of the joint staff, and added a chairman to preside over the JCS.

The slow unification of the national military establishment during and after World War II, first codified in the 1947 National Security Act, dramatically changed the power relationships between and among the services, Congress, and other executive branch departments. With America irreversibly involved in global affairs after its overwhelming victory, how each institution or organization influenced national security policy in relation to the others became a dynamic issue that continues to challenge policy makers to this day.

The Cold War and the Goldwater-Nichols Act of 1986.   By 1949, the Communist Party's victory in China's civil war; Soviet initiatives in Greece, the Middle East, Berlin, and Eastern Europe; and the Soviet acquisition of nuclear weapons had prompted a series of Western countermeasures, which together constituted the policy of *containment* discussed in Chapter 3. In turn, recognition of the urgent necessity for Allied cooperation led to the provision of large amounts of U.S. military assistance to friendly states.[13] Military expertise was also drawn on in constructing the North Atlantic Treaty Organization (NATO) alliance and in securing Allied agreement to the rearmament and participation of Germany in the buildup of NATO.[14] Military proconsuls, such as MacArthur in Japan and Lucius Clay in Germany, as well as distinguished World War II leaders, such as George Marshall, Dwight Eisenhower, and Omar Bradley, continued to serve in positions of great responsibility and influence.

With the beginning of the Korean War in 1950, a major shift in resources again took place, and this time the change was more permanent. In a period of four years (1950–1954), the share of gross national product devoted to national defense rose from 5.2% to 13.5%, and military expenditures increased from \$13 billion in FY 1950 to \$50.4 billion in FY 1953.[15] As the hostilities in Korea once again expanded the military's role in the formulation and execution of policy, they also complicated it. One of the first messages of the Korean War was that the World War II concept of autonomy for the theater commander in the prosecution of the war was to be curtailed significantly. MacArthur's relief from command in the Far East by President Harry Truman was the result of a long series of attempts by MacArthur to shape U.S. policy in his theater independent of events in Europe or of general national policy.[16] At a time when expectation of war with the Soviets in Europe was high, the view of a local commander could no longer be followed without regard for worldwide ramifications of local actions. The JCS and their civilian superiors feared that the communist attack in Korea was a feint and prelude to a full-scale assault in Europe. As the United States moved through the uncharted waters of limited war, military leaders were forced to examine political and military objectives in strikingly different ways from the unconditional surrender and total victory formulations of World War II. They also had to adjust to fighting a war unsupported by a total national mobilization.

Despite the enlarged military establishment after the Korean War and the increased projection of military influence abroad, strong interservice rivalries weakened the military's voice within the national security establishment. Such rivalry was not without certain advantages. The conflict of ideas and doctrines protected against unanimous error. Moreover, potential conflict between civil and military institutions was deflected into competition among military groups. Because the resolution of these basic conflicts required civilian judgment, civilian control was enhanced. Not only were civilian political leaders able to find military support for almost any plausible strategy they might propose, but they also were given a convenient political cover: Interservice rivalry provided "a whipping boy upon whom to blame deficiencies in the military establishment for which (just possibly) they (political leaders) conceivably might be held responsible."[17]

Yet the deficiencies of these rivalries were obvious. Cost-effective management of the DoD proved inordinately difficult, with the uniformed services sometimes appealing departmental—or even presidential—decisions to congressional allies and winning support. The JCS was seldom able to agree upon an overall defense program within budgetary ceilings. In turn, confidence in the efficacy of military judgment, so high in the early years after World War II, tended to be eroded by the spectacle of public disagreement and dissension. More serious were fears that the defense organization was simply ineffective, relying on logrolling and compromise without effective planning or real control by anyone.[18]

In the years that followed the National Security Act of 1947, subsequent efforts at DoD reorganization repeatedly sought to increase civilian control over the military while reducing the harmful tendency to allocate resources and to develop policies on a bargaining-for-shares-of-the-pie basis. Controversies over weapons systems procurement and service missions also prompted efforts toward centralization of control. In 1958, the National Security Act was again amended to give the secretary of defense greater authority, more influence in strategic planning, and greater control over the JCS. The military departments were further downgraded administratively, and the functions of the military services were revised to exclude control over unified and specified commands. Under the new provisions, these commands were controlled directly by the secretary of defense.

The reforms of the 1950s empowered the secretary of defense to exercise greater control of the department and the services. The tools of cost accounting and systems analysis developed under Secretary Robert McNamara in the 1960s made this control a reality. Supported by a host of young, talented "whiz kids," McNamara used the new techniques to preempt military influence in both procurement and strategy.[19] In part, this greater centralization was a logical outcome of the development of new budgetary and analytical techniques. More fundamentally, however, it grew out of persistent service disagreements, extension of civilian staff, and increased demand for civilian control over the military (see Chapter 9 for a more thorough discussion of the McNamara revolution).

Although necessary for both strategic and economic reasons, centralization posed a severe dilemma for the military, especially for the JCS. Unanimous agreements among the chiefs could usually be obtained by compromises, which were often unsupported by systems analysis. Split decisions, however, were even worse from the perspective of the military—they placed the locus of final decisions on military matters squarely in civilian hands. The personal loyalties of the individual chiefs to their services were, of course, sometimes a factor in disagreements, but continued rivalry also reflected fundamental differences over strategy and the relative capabilities of the various military staffs. As noted earlier, the JCS as a whole was provided with only a small staff to assist in the joint area. Each service chief also had a larger, more prestigious staff; not surprisingly, the advice of these service staffs was often colored by individual service perspectives and interests.

To overcome service parochialism and provide unified staff work, the 1958 DoD reorganization directed the joint chiefs to concentrate on their joint responsibilities and to delegate running the services to their vice chiefs. Furthermore, control of the joint staff was transferred from the JCS as a whole to the chairman of the JCS. The joint staff was increased in size to four hundred positions and split evenly among the services. In practice, however, this did not solve the problems mentioned thus far in this chapter—it took nearly three more decades and several poor performances by the military (including the failed hostage rescue attempt in Iran in 1980 and an uncoordinated invasion of Grenada in 1983) for Congress to once again address military effectiveness and civilian control. That legislation was the Department of Defense Reorganization Act of 1986. *Goldwater-Nichols*, as the act is commonly known, is the most far-reaching legislation to address these issues since the National Security Act of 1947 (see also Chapter 5).

The act had several key features that were intended to promote "jointness" among the services. First, the authority of the chairman of the JCS was strengthened. The chairman was designated the principal military advisor to the president, the NSC, and the secretary of defense and was no longer required to report only JCS positions but was provided the latitude to offer advice that the chairman deemed appropriate. Second, the new position of JCS vice chairman was created with the expectation that this officer would act in the interest of the military establishment as a whole, with a focus on integrating the separate research, development, and procurement activities of the services. Third, the authority of commanders of unified and specified commands was also strengthened through the establishment of a chain of command that ran directly from the president to the secretary of defense to these commanders. Finally, legislation created a joint specialty within service personnel systems and required the services to send a fair share of their most outstanding officers to both the joint staff (in Washington) and the unified commands (in the field). Services were then required to ensure that officers who had joint backgrounds received their fair share of promotions. In sum, this push for "jointness" and interservice cooperation was the underlying purpose of the 1986 act.

The above discussion illuminates a number of trends that converged to shape the evolution of the role of the military in the national security process during the Cold War. First, military power remained a central means through which the United States pursued its security. Although defense spending declined again under Eisenhower from its Korean War levels, during the Cold War it never subsided to its demobilization nadir of the late 1940s (see Chapter 3). This commitment to larger military forces and, after 1961, to forward defense and some form of the doctrine of *flexible response* inevitably gave rise to an important role for military advice and to increased emphasis on professionalism in the officer corps. During international crises, presidents generally sought the counsel of experienced commanders who understood political objectives as well as military realities.

Second, the period of the Cold War saw the further institutionalization of the role of the military in the national security policy process. As discussed in Chapter 10, the formal decision-making structure supporting the president and the NSC evolved and grew to meet the policy coordination needs of a superpower that had assumed a global role. As military officers participated in interdepartmental coordinating committees, they were often influential in shaping policy in Washington as well as in the field. In fact, during the 1960s, there was concern in some quarters that the military had too much influence with regard to U.S. policies in Southeast Asia. That the military significantly influenced national policy during the Vietnam War is incontrovertible, but it is equally clear that military voices were subordinated to civilian perspectives.[20] Rather than view the Vietnam War as a period of military influence, the lesson that many in the professional military drew from that conflict is that senior military officers—and particularly the JCS—were not forceful enough in providing their professional military advice to senior civilian decision makers.[21]

Third, continuing and expanding overseas defense commitments increased military involvement in policy making and also ensured that such involvement was not always limited to purely military issues. When Eisenhower, first supreme commander in Europe, reported to Congress on his mission in 1951, he stated clearly the nature of civil-military relations with regard to NATO:

> I spoke in every country to the Prime Minister and foreign minister at their request, and then I talked to the defense ministers and their chiefs of staff. There is no escaping the fact that when you take an area such as involved in all Western Europe and talk about its defense, you are right in the midst of political questions, economic, industrial, as well as strictly military, and you couldn't possibly divorce your commander from contact with them.[22]

In addition to senior levels of leadership, increasing numbers of officers served overseas in military advisory missions. Working with partners from other U.S. government agencies, military personnel often were advantaged by the comparatively large resources that the DoD wielded. Not only did military personnel frequently outnumber State Department personnel assigned to a given overseas mission, but many of the competing bureaucracies, such as the Agency for International Development, were relatively weak in the field and in the levels of Washington staffing necessary to support field operations.[23]

Fourth, individual members of the military were periodically selected to serve in important advisory roles at senior levels. For most of the Eisenhower Administration (from 1954–1961), General Andrew J. Goodpaster was the White House Staff Secretary and Defense Liaison. During the Kennedy years, senior officers and especially General Maxwell Taylor—who served for a time as the military representative to the president and, after retiring from the military, as ambassador to Vietnam—gained influence. During the Nixon Administration, General Alexander Haig served as the Deputy to National Security Advisor Henry Kissinger and later as White House Chief of Staff. The role of military officers in senior national policy positions was critically questioned in 1987, when Marine Lieutenant Colonel Oliver North was alleged to have conducted illegal covert operations as an NSC staff member with the approval of Vice Admiral John Poindexter, then assistant to the president for national security affairs. Ultimately, the North-Poindexter episode came to be seen as an isolated incident that did not preclude then Lieutenant General Colin Powell from being appointed the president's national security advisor within a year and serving with distinction in that position, which is normally occupied by a civilian.

Fifth, the Cold War saw both the intensification of interservice rivalry and repeated attempts to resolve it. As mentioned above, the system under Truman and Eisenhower, who first set a budget ceiling and encouraged services to compete for their share, led to intense interservice competition. To a marked extent, the McNamara era in the Pentagon fundamentally changed this dynamic. At least officially, budgets were to be determined by how much was needed for national defense rather than arbitrary ceilings. Rather than competing with one another for shares of a set budget, the policy under McNamara put the services in the position of pitting their professional views against the judgments and methods of analysis of their civilian superiors. The positions of the services gradually improved as they responded to the need to develop their own experts in systems analysis to better communicate (and compete) with the civilians in the Office of the Secretary of Defense (OSD). The services also had an incentive to compromise and to support one another as the locus of competition changed from among the services to between the services and the secretary of defense and civilians in the OSD.[24]

A sixth trend, partly the result of those previously discussed, is that military officers during the Cold War became increasingly capable of operating at higher levels of the U.S. government and also influential in national security policy matters. This was partially a product of staff with greater experience working in more senior positions in the interagency arena. Goldwater-Nichols contributed to this trend. The legislation created additional billets in which officers would serve at the political-military nexus, and the career incentives it created encouraged some of the most promising military officers to pursue joint opportunities that broadened their perspectives early in their careers.[25] Greater experience was complemented by a military education system that began to produce large numbers of officers with advanced civilian university degrees. These advanced degrees became increasingly important to military promotions. In 1965, no members of the JCS had advanced degrees; by 1981, they all did.[26] In addition, senior professional schools (such as the service's war colleges where colonels spend one year of study prior to being eligible for promotion to general or admiral) added study of the nonmilitary aspects of national security to their programs.[27] During the 1990s, a recognition that the national security credentials of the military partners in the civil-military nexus were substantial and growing relative to their civilian counterparts in the executive branch and Congress led some observers to fear a lack of balance in national security decision making.[28]

Post–Cold War Issues in American Civil-Military Relations.   As the tensions that had marked the more-than-fifty years of armed standoff between the United States and the Soviet Union receded, the U.S. armed forces once again entered into combat during the Persian Gulf crisis of 1990 and 1991. In those military operations, President George H. W. Bush gave JCS Chairman Powell the forces he requested and allowed him and the theater commander to conduct the campaign with little detailed political oversight. As an example of his influence, Powell was reportedly instrumental in getting George H. W. Bush to stop the ground war after one hundred hours.[29] The war resulted in a lopsided military victory for the U.S.-led coalition: "In less than six weeks, 795,000 Coalition troops destroyed a defending army of hundreds of thousands, losing only 240 attackers."[30] Despite a tremendous military success, however, analysts quickly began to point out failures in planning for war termination and shortcomings in U.S. political achievements as a result of military victory.[31] Consequently, the lessons for U.S. civil-military relations were mixed. Some praised the high degree of military professional autonomy evident in the design and conduct of the military campaign, while others argued that greater political involvement—especially in planning for war termination—would have led to a better political outcome for the United States.[32]

As the 1990s progressed, the U.S. military experienced a post–Cold War drawdown as well as increased use of the armed forces for operations other than war. The number of service members on active duty went from 2.1 million in 1990 to 1.4 million in 2000, and this smaller military was operationally deployed to crises that included Somalia, Haiti, Bosnia, and Kosovo (see Chapter 3).[33] A further important dynamic was created by the election of Bill Clinton, who served as president from 1993 through the end of the decade. In general, Clinton and senior members of his administration had little or no military experience, and the president himself had a reputation for a general lack of interest in military affairs as well as a personal lack of regard for the military.[34]

Civil-Military Relations in the 1990s.   Two main issues dominated discussions of U.S. civil-military relations in the 1990s. The first centered on the idea, primarily among some academics and journalists, that there was a "crisis" of civilian control. Concern stemmed from the continued size and influence of the U.S. military, as well as anecdotal evidence, including incidents that indicated that the professional military lacked appropriate respect for Clinton as commander in chief; increased partisan identification among military officers; and increased influence by powerful JCS chairmen, particularly Powell.[35]

Some observers attributed perceptions of a crisis to timing; an administration that suffered from a lack of credibility in military affairs came into office at the same time that the JCS had a particularly popular and activist chairman in the person of Powell. Others emphasized structural factors, to include a concern that Goldwater-Nichols had centralized too much power in the chairman and the JCS.[36] A third potential source of friction was the nature of the missions assigned to the military in the 1990s, missions that the services did not necessarily view as core tasks and in which decisive victory could not be the goal.[37] However, consensus about the seriousness of the problem was never reached, with most analysts agreeing that claims of a crisis were exaggerated.[38] Even during the Clinton administration, at least one observer saw the balance being restored during the tenures of successive chairmen of the JCS.[39]

Copyright 1995 CARTOONEWS INTERNATIONAL Syndicate, N.Y.C., USA.
Reprinted with permission of Ranan Lurie.

One enduring issue that stems from the 1990s crisis debate relates to political behavior by serving or retired members of the military. For example, despite the fact that he had approval from his civilian superiors at the time, analysts debate the appropriateness of Powell's publication of his views on intervention in the Balkans in the *New York Times* and his views on the use of military power in *Foreign Affairs.*[40] As a practical matter, the first of these articles in particular had the potential to constrain the next president's freedom of action on an important foreign policy issue. Other forms of political behavior included the increasingly public and occasionally political roles played by retired generals or admirals. One example is retired admiral and former chairman of the JCS William Crowe's endorsement of candidate Clinton in the 1992 presidential campaign. After Clinton was elected, he appointed Crowe to the position of ambassador to the United Kingdom. This politicization issue resurfaced in 2006, as a number of retired flag officers called for the resignation of Secretary of Defense Donald Rumsfeld.[41] Although some believe that such statements by retired flag officers serve an important function in better informing Congress and the American public, who have limited access or knowledge of such views, others argue that the continued association of these senior officers with the active military makes their public critiques of policy and civilian policy makers dangerous to civil-military relations.[42] Taken as a whole, the political activities discussed here raise concerns about an erosion of the tradition of military neutrality and abstention from politics.[43]

The second and more serious major issue in U.S. civil-military relations that surfaced during the 1990s was the possibility of a growing gap between the all-volunteer, professional military and the rest of American society. Scholars examining this issue posed their research question this way: "Has a 'gap' in values between the armed forces and civilian society widened to the point of threatening the effectiveness of the military and impeding civil-military cooperation?"[44] Research confirmed that, over the preceding generation, the proportion of officers that self-identified as Republican had increased from 33% to 64% and that other important differences between officers as a group and civilians existed: Officers were more conservative than civilian elites but not than the general American public, officers were somewhat more religious than civilian elites, officers expressed skepticism about the quality of political leadership and were hostile to the media but expressed more trust in government institutions than their civilian counterparts, and officers were much more hostile than civilians to the notion of homosexuals serving openly in the U.S. military.[45] A particular source of concern was that a sample of successful midgrade officers believed that they should "insist" (rather than merely advise) on "'setting rules of engagement' (50 percent), developing an 'exit strategy' (52 percent), and 'deciding what kinds of military units (air vs. naval, heavy vs. light) will be used to accomplish all tasks' (63 percent)."[46] Those who ascribed salience to a growing civil-military gap in general did not argue that it rose to the level of a crisis, but rather that indicators of a gap were worthy of more attention by senior civilian and military leaders responsible for the relationship.

Civil-Military Relations During the Administration of President George W. Bush.   In contrast to the civil-military relations of the 1990s that generated concerns about outsized military influence, U.S. civil-military relations in the first decade of the twenty-first century generated concerns about lack of balance in the opposite direction.[47] When Rumsfeld, who had served a previous tour as secretary of defense under President Gerald Ford, reassumed that office in January 2001, he had a definite agenda: Two of his priorities were transformation of the military and the assertion (or reassertion) of stronger control of the OSD over the services in the Pentagon, as well as stronger civilian control over the military. Rumsfeld's transformation agenda drew upon considerable military thinking about an ongoing "Revolution in Military Affairs" based on high-technology, precision, standoff weapons systems and information dominance (see Chapter 3 and Chapter 15). The priority on reestablishing civilian control seemed to draw on a belief that the defense establishment "had become too independent and risk-averse during eight years under President Bill Clinton."[48] Rumsfeld pursued his definite agenda with a high degree of personal self-confidence and aggressiveness—a personality sometimes described as domineering or arrogant. Though praised by JCS Chairman Richard Myers as having healthy relationships with senior officers and the joint staff, Rumsfeld was described by many others as "frequently abusive and indecisive, trusting only a tiny circle of close advisers, seemingly eager to slap down officers with decades of distinguished service."[49]

One of Rumsfeld's first tasks at the Pentagon was the Quadrennial Defense Review of 2001. This process generated such tension between Rumsfeld and the services, as well as between Rumsfeld and Congress, that there was speculation that Rumsfeld could be the first member of George W. Bush's cabinet to depart.[50] However, this dynamic was completely altered by the terrorist attacks on September 11, 2001, and the apparent success of the subsequent invasion of Afghanistan. This U.S. and coalition campaign appeared to validate Rumsfeld's intensely hands-on management style because he had influenced the campaign plan significantly, and his transformation agenda focused on the conduct of a more high-tech form of warfare.[51]

Despite vast budget increases in the wake of 9/11, relations between Rumsfeld and senior military leaders continued to deteriorate during the planning stages of the war in Iraq and after the invasion in 2003. A public incident related to testimony given by Army Chief of Staff Eric Shinseki before the Senate Armed Services Committee in February 2003, when he was asked for his estimate of the forces that would be required to stabilize Iraq after an invasion. His ultimate advice of "several hundred thousand" drew official and public repudiations from Deputy Secretary of Defense Paul Wolfowitz, Rumsfeld, and Vice President Dick Cheney.[52] The reaction of these senior civilian leaders to Shinseki's testimony implied a war-planning process for Iraq that did not include broad and open consultations with senior military leaders. Although Shinseki was not in the operational chain of command, as the Army's chief of staff he would be responsible for supporting the combatant commander's force requirements and sustainment needs. The fact that this incident was followed by an early leak of Shinseki's intended replacement indicated an effort by civilian leaders to further diminish his status and to signal an expectation of silence to other senior military figures.[53]

One notable characteristic of the planning stages of the Iraq invasion was Rumsfeld's active intervention in operational and logistical details.[54] The most striking was his decision to remove specific units from the Time-Phased Force Deployment List (TPFDL), a technical document that governs the flow of forces and necessary logistical support as they deploy into a theater of operations. Even a defender of Rumsfeld's role in the process, Mackubin Owens, argues that, in retrospect, Rumsfeld's decision to remove a cavalry division from the TPFDL was a mistake. His explanation, however, is even more interesting from the perspective of civil-military relations: "Rumsfeld was inclined to interpret the Army's call for a larger force to invade Iraq as just one more example of what he perceived as foot dragging. . . . he had come to believe that the TPFDL . . . had become little more than a bureaucratic tool that the services used to protect their shares of the defense budget."[55] If this assessment is correct, it suggests that use-of-force decision making was severely inhibited by the lack of a constructive civil-military partnership characterized by trust and mutual respect.

The failures in planning and adaptability, which led to serious U.S. difficulties in post-invasion Iraq, were undoubtedly complex and occurred at many levels. Current histories are too plentiful to adequately survey here, and the evidence supporting such assessments will probably improve as time provides additional perspective.[56] However, the view that at least a portion of the problems in post-invasion Iraq can be attributed to unhealthy civil-military relations has been supported by the 2006 Iraq Study Group, which found:

> The U.S. military has a long tradition of strong partnership between the civilian leadership of the Department of Defense and the uniformed services. Both have long benefited from a relationship in which the civilian leadership exercises control with the advantage of fully candid professional advice, and the military serves loyally with the understanding that its advice has been heard and valued. That tradition has been frayed, and civil-military relations need to be repaired.[57]

The report went on to recommend that "the new Secretary of Defense should make every effort to build healthy civil-military relations, by creating an environment in which the senior military feel free to offer independent military advice not only to the civilian leadership in the Pentagon but also to the President and the National Security Council, as envisioned in the Goldwater-Nichols legislation."[58]

Perhaps contrary to expectations, the role of the military in the national security process has continued to grow—and to grow increasingly complex—in the post–Cold War world. A debate over whether the military has exercised an appropriate level of influence in the appropriate venues of national security policy continues, and a stable equilibrium remains elusive.

The Current Structure of the National Military Establishment

Although Goldwater-Nichols has been less than fully successful in breaking service dominance in the development and funding of military programs, the legislation is generally viewed as having been very successful in improving "the areas that the original sponsors of the Goldwater-Nichols Act considered most pressing—military advice, the unified commanders, contingency planning, joint officer management, and military operations."[59] Such success is due in part to an organizational structure that places a premium on military effectiveness through efficient planning and coordination. (For the structure of DoD, see Figure 4.4 in Chapter 4.)

With the establishment of U.S. Africa Command in 2007 (see Figure 8.1), six combatant commands now have responsibility for specified regions of the globe while four other combatant commands are assigned worldwide functional responsibilities not bounded by geography. The regional combatant commanders seek to address a wide variety of security-related needs depending on the region of concern. Meeting these demands requires extensive coordination within the U.S. government as well as the maintenance of a direct line of communication with their chains of command, which include the secretary of defense and the president (with communications generally flowing through the JCS).

FIG. 8.1 Area of Responsibility of Africa Command

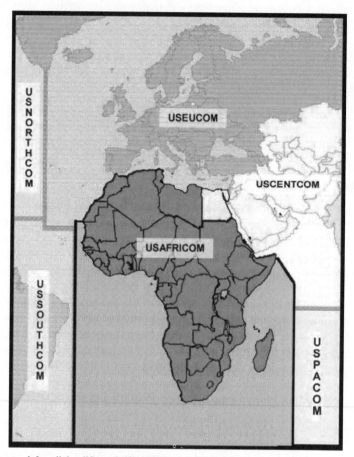

Source: www.defenselink.mil/home/pdf/AFRICOM_PublicBrief02022007.pdf

Although the combatant commanders are given wide areas of responsibility, their success hinges upon close interaction and coordination with the individual services. The services themselves (Army, Navy, Air Force, and Marine Corps) are responsible for training, equipping, maintaining, and providing the forces that are, or may be, assigned to the combatant commands and then supporting them for the duration of their deployments; however, they have little direct influence in the conduct of operations, except through their service chiefs as part of the JCS.

The JCS, consisting of the chairman, vice chairman, and service chiefs, play a preeminent role in coordinating actions among the individual services and the unified combatant commands. Because the service chiefs also sit as members of the JCS and have the statutory authority to provide expert advice, they are the natural links between the services and the combatant commands. The JCS is also a critical nexus of interaction between civilian policy makers and the uniformed military.

Within the DoD, the OSD plays a prominent role in defining and overseeing national security and military policy. Internal DoD directives mandate that "in providing immediate staff assistance and advice to the Secretary of Defense, the OSD and the JCS, though separately identified and organized, function in full coordination and cooperation."[60] This requirement is intended to enhance civilian control as well as to ensure that the secretary of defense receives the best possible staff products and advice. Normally, the OSD has a number of exceptionally qualified military officers aboard, as well as talented civilians.

Locating the Military's Role in National Security

There is fundamental agreement on at least one point: In the United States, civilian control—or, perhaps more precisely, democratic political control—is accepted as the central, guiding principle. The U.S. military is subordinate to the president and to certain designated officials in the executive branch, as well as to elected political leaders in Congress. According to the U.S. Constitution, the executive and the legislative branches of the federal government share authority and responsibility for military affairs.

Despite a broad consensus on this issue, there is nevertheless plenty of room for disagreement on more subtle points. Issues that are still under debate include whether there are any appropriate prudential limits to civilian involvement in the formulation and execution of military policy, strategy, and operations; the appropriate role and relative influence of Congress in military policy and strategy; and the appropriate extent and exercise of military influence during the formulation and execution of national security policy. Although there is no serious concern over a military coup or military revolt in the United States, not all important issues in American civil-military relations are settled. The optimal pattern of U.S. civil-military relations would ensure democratic political control while also facilitating sound strategic decision making and the creation of effective military institutions.[61]

The "Purist" Vs. "Fusionist" Schools of Thought.   As has often been observed, the American military is far from monolithic in character or in outlook. One of the recurring differences since World War II has been over the military's appropriate role in the formulation and execution of national security policy. General Matthew Ridgway, Army chief of staff in 1955, expressed the traditional, *military purist* point of view:

> The military advisor should give his competent professional advice based on the military aspects of the programs referred to him, based on his fearless, honest, objective estimate of the national interest, and regardless of administration policy at any particular time. He should confine his advice to the essential military aspects.[62]

The purist case does not necessarily deny the complexity of national security issues; they are recognized to be a blend of economic, political, and military components, but they are determined by civilian policy makers. The professional officer is only an expert in the military component. In providing advice to policy makers, therefore, professional officers should confine themselves to purely military considerations. In this view, officers are not competent, nor should they be asked, to provide economic or political judgments or assumptions in offering advice.

The alternate view, the *fusionist* approach, maintains that in the changed environment of national security policy in the post–World War II environment, purely military considerations do not exist.[63] In a world of global terrorism and proliferating weapons of mass destruction, in which the military consumes significant economic resources and in which the use of force may have tremendous political implications, military decisions inevitably have considerable economic and political consequences and vice versa. Therefore, in giving their advice, professional officers should incorporate political and economic considerations along with military factors.

Many civilian and military leaders have tended to be fusionists. President John Kennedy explicitly espoused the fusionist thesis in a speech to graduating West Point cadets when, after stressing future military command responsibilities, he added:

> The non-military problems which you will face will also be the most demanding— diplomatic, political, economic. You will need to know and understand not only the foreign policy of the United States, but the foreign policy of all countries scattered around the world. You will need to understand the importance of military power and also the limits of military power. You will have an obligation to deter war as well as to fight it.[64]

Taylor, former chairman of the JCS and military representative to the president, was clear: "Nothing is so likely to repel the civilian decision-makers as a military argument which omits obvious considerations which the president cannot omit . . . if they (the Joint Chiefs) want to persuade the President, they had better look at the totality of his problem and try to give maximum help."[65]

This debate was held among scholars as well as practitioners. Perhaps the foremost critic of fusionism was Samuel P. Huntington, who warns in *The Soldier and the State* (1957) that if the military "broadened" its professional worldview to incorporate civilian-defined "political realities," it might gain access to supreme levels of the policy process, but it would no longer speak on strategic matters from an adequately military perspective. The country and the national security process would be better served by a military that cultivated its autonomous ethic in a politically neutral, professional institution. In return, the state would gain a "politically sterile and neutral" professional officer corps "ready to carry out the wishes of any civilian group which secures legitimate authority within the state."[66] Huntington's analysis is a variation of the purist view, reinforced by a dose of cultural isolation.

A leading advocate of fusionism was Morris Janowitz, who lays out his perspective in *The Professional Soldier* (1960).[67] In contrast to Huntington's view on professional autonomy and a degree of separation, Janowitz believed it would be unrealistic to rely on an apolitical and relatively detached military to ensure political control: "In the United States, where political leadership is diffuse, civilian politicians have come to assume that the military will be an active ingredient in decision-making about national security."[68] To be effective during the Cold War, the U.S. military would have to be aware of the international political conse-quences of military action and understand the primacy of political objectives and the occasional need for limited applications of force.[69]

In practice, both the purist and the fusionist perspectives have shortcomings. The purist perspective tends to posit a degree of separation between political and military affairs that simply does not and cannot exist. As military theorist Carl von Clausewitz argues in his *On War*, at the highest level of decision making, the idea of a "purely military" opinion makes no sense, because "no major proposal for war can be worked out in ignorance of political factors." He goes on to argue, "To bring a war, or one of its campaigns, to a successful close requires a thorough grasp of national policy. On that level strategy and policy coalesce."[70] It is un-helpful for officers to expect that there will bright lines between political and mil-itary issues. A second challenge is that a purist perspective may tend to foster a conception of military expertise that is inadequately narrow. For example, an Army that focuses primarily on fighting and winning major conventional wars may well have difficulty achieving military and political objectives in other envi-ronments that demand a broader array of skills.[71]

The fusionist perspective may lead to the opposite challenge—a vanishing pro-fessional ethos and loss of clarity with regard to core military tasks. The military's functional expertise as prioritized by the purists, and the military's political so-phistication and responsiveness as emphasized by the fusionists, are complemen-tary values, yet ones that are always in tension. Within that tension, a circum-scribed sphere of professional autonomy within which the military can develop its ethos and practical expertise will be necessary to ensure the military's functional effectiveness as an instrument of national security policy.

Guiding the Partners' Behavior in Civil-Military Relations.   In the United States, the military's leaders are not asked by their political superiors when and where to wage war. Rather, they are asked how the military instrument can be used most effectively at a particular time for a given strategic purpose. In 1983, the JCS was not asked whether the United States should take up peacekeeping duties in Lebanon or evict the communists from Grenada but rather how to accomplish those missions. Similarly, in 2001, George W. Bush and Rumsfeld did not ask the JCS or the combatant commander whether the United States should invade Afghanistan but only for proposals as to how.

An understanding of the military's role in the national security policy process must be grounded with this fact clearly in mind: The American military lacks the charter, the inclination, and the opportunity to play the *primary* role in the estab-lishment of strategic ends. Nevertheless, the military can be influential, albeit largely indirectly, at the most senior levels: "The potential impact of the chiefs' views on the public and the Congress can never be ignored by a president or a secretary of defense. . . . The chiefs no doubt retain power to influence national decisions to some degree on some security issues, and to add legitimacy to one view or another."[72]

Although the Goldwater-Nichols legislation is credited with strengthening civilian control of the military, the preceding discussion underscores the challenges still associated with having a professional officer corps deeply involved in the planning and execution of national security policy. As a result, a fundamental question arises: "How can trusting relationships between the civil and military authorities that result in effective policy be cultivated?"[73] One answer is a guiding set of principles, or norms, that govern the behavior of both military and civilian leaders in the formulation and execution of national security policy.

According to one analyst, "The military profession's first obligation is to do no harm to the states' democratic institutions and the democratic policymaking processes they establish. The civilian political leadership sets political objectives that the military supports in good faith. The military leadership should apply its expertise without 'shirking' or taking actions that, in effect, have a self-interested effect on policy outcomes."[74] This means that there are three primary functions in which the military should participate:

- Military leaders should always represent the uniquely military perspective in all policy deliberations and discussions, both public and private.
- When asked for their professional opinions and advice, military leaders must render such advice forthrightly and apolitically.
- Once national level policy has been formulated and announced, whether it be a budget, a strategy, or an operational concept, it is the responsibility of military leaders to execute all legal orders from competent authority to execute such policy successfully.

Establishing and gaining adherence to norms that ought to govern civilian behavior presents different challenges. Competitively selected military officers stay on continuous active duty for up to thirty-five years, practicing their military arts daily whether in peace or war, advancing through several levels of professional military education, and constantly adapting new professional knowledge to their experiences. On the civilian side, however, leaders are elected or appointed only episodically. Few, if any, serve a full career in the national security arena, and often the senior civilian leadership changes entirely with changes in presidential administrations. Although this is by design under the U.S. constitutional system, it also has immense drawbacks.

One such drawback is the general lack of familiarity among civilian leaders with national security affairs at the beginning of each new presidential administration.[75] Civilian political leaders come into the policymaking arena essentially cold on the issues and without the extensive personal networks necessary to create effective security policy on a global scale. Although this is normally largely overcome within a year or so, during this period, military advisors are far more knowledgeable. Such situations require personal relationships to be developed at each level of civil-military interface in which trust and comity are sought, in which mutual exploration of policy and learning can occur, and in which sound policy can be constructed and vetted appropriately.

Although the civil-military dialogue will always be "unequal" in that civilians have the last word, it is possible to conceive of norms to govern civilian behavior in the civil-military relationship in the interest of facilitating effective policy making. One scholar has wisely articulated the principal norm for civilian leaders to follow as "equal dialogue, unequal authority."[76] Civilian leaders ultimately responsible for critical national security decisions are more likely to be successful if they are aware of the full range of military views on a particular issue. An "equal dialogue" should be employed to support the civilian decision makers' "unequal authority." Clearly, this norm has too often been ignored, most recently during Rumsfeld's tenure.[77] The adoption of such a norm would be facilitated by the intentional preparation of civilians for leadership within the national military establishment. One modest proposal would be to open the military war colleges to large numbers of civilians from the intelligence, diplomatic, and congressional staff communities.[78]

Looking Ahead

The role of the uniformed military in the national security process will undoubtedly continue to evolve and fluctuate with changes in civilian leadership and changes in the use of the military as an instrument of foreign policy. Because the United States is likely to remain a world power deeply involved in the international political system, it is highly unlikely that the impact of the military will ever again be as insignificant as it was prior to Pearl Harbor. Ensuring that the future military role in the national security process is both effective and appropriate will be a continuing challenge.

Discussion Questions

1. How and why did the extent of military influence increase significantly immediately prior to and through World War II?

2. How did changes in U.S. foreign policy following World War II influence the restructuring of the national security establishment?

3. How does organizational structure and statutory guidance influence the military's participation in the policy process?

4. How did the Goldwater-Nichols Act of 1986 alter the role of the military in the policy process?

5. What are the responsibilities of the military departments and the combatant commands? What is the role of the chairman of the JCS and the collective JCS in the relationships among these entities?

6. What have been the consequences of an increased centralization of decision making in the DoD?

7. Do you believe that U.S. civil-military relations are healthy? Why or why not?

8. What is the *proper* role of the military in the policy process?

Recommended Reading

Betts, Richard K. *Soldiers, Statesmen, and Cold War Crises.* Cambridge, MA: Harvard University Press, 1977.

Cohen, Eliot A. *Supreme Command: Soldiers, Statesmen, and Leadership in Wartime.* New York: Free Press, 2002.

Desch, Michael C. *Civilian Control of the Military: The Changing Security Environment.* Baltimore: Johns Hopkins University Press, 1999.

Feaver, Peter D., and Christopher Gelpi. *Choosing Your Battles: American Civil-Military Relations and the Use of Force.* Princeton: Princeton University Press, 2004.

Feaver, Peter D., and Richard H. Kohn, eds. *Soldiers and Civilians: The Civil-Military Gap and American National Security.* Cambridge, MA: MIT Press, 2001.

Herspring, Dale R. *The Pentagon and the Presidency: Civil-Military Relations from FDR to George W. Bush.* Lawrence: University Press of Kansas, 2005.

Huntington, Samuel P. *The Common Defense: Strategic Problems in National Politics.* New York: Columbia University Press, 1961.

———. *The Soldier and the State.* Cambridge, MA: Belknap Press of Harvard University Press, 1957.

Janowitz, Morris. *The Professional Soldier.* London: Collier-Macmillan Limited, 1960.

Kohn, Richard H., ed. *The United States Military Under the Constitution of the United States, 1789–1989.* New York: New York University Press, 1991.

McMaster, H. R. *Dereliction of Duty: Lyndon Johnson, Robert McNamara, the Joint Chiefs of Staff, and the Lies That Led to Vietnam.* New York: HarperCollins, 1997.

Snider, Don, and Miranda Carlton-Carew. *U.S. Civil-Military Relations: In Crisis or Transition?* Washington, DC: Center for Strategic and International Studies, 1995.

Stevenson, Charles A. *Warriors and Politicians: U.S. Civil-Military Relations Under Stress.* New York: Routledge, 2006.

Taylor, Maxwell D. *Swords and Plowshares.* New York: W. W. Norton, 1972.

Internet Sources

Joint Chiefs of Staff, www.jcs.mil

National Security, www.whitehouse.gov/infocus/nationalsecurity

The National Security Council, www.whitehouse.gov/nsc

Unified Command Plan, www.defenselink.mil/specials/unifiedcommand

U.S. Department of Defense, www.defenselink.mil

9

Planning, Budgeting, and Management

A central problem of national security strategy is the limitation on the resources that can be allocated to meet security objectives. A nation's available resources—traditionally categorized by economists as land, labor, and capital—are valued by society, because they can be used to produce a variety of outputs of goods and services that the society desires. When some of those resources are transferred to the government to meet national security objectives, an *opportunity cost* is imposed on society, defined as the lost opportunity of producing other goods and services with those resources to meet private consumption or other social goals. The opportunity cost of defense is not new. It was best described by President Dwight Eisenhower in 1953:

> The cost of one modern heavy bomber is this: a modern brick school in more than 30 cities. It is two electric power plants, each serving a town of 60,000 population. It is two, fine, fully equipped hospitals. It is some 50 miles of concrete highway. We pay for a single fighter plane with a half million bushels of wheat. We pay for a single destroyer with new homes that could have housed more than 8,000 people.[1]

Even with a president whose background and personal experience would suggest that he would favor military expenditures, the contentious issue of "how much is enough," and precisely what national security capabilities the nation should develop, was a major concern.

The ultimate fiscal constraint on security expenditures is most directly related to the potential *gross domestic product*, the dollar value of all final goods and services that could be produced in the nation in a given year if all its resources were fully employed. Invariably, unemployment or excess productive capacity will cause actual output to fall below its potential level, but the potential level is useful in national security analysis because, within the constraints of time and transitional costs, considerably more resources could be pressed to maximum use in an emergency.

Competing claims on the nation's total output are made by individuals for consumption; by firms for investment; and by local, state, and federal governments for a host of public programs, including national security. Even when resources already allocated to the federal government are examined, expenditures are constrained by interdepartmental competition. How should the proportion of total resources directed to national security objectives be determined? In theory, advocates of national security expenditures should demonstrate that the societal benefits of those expenditures exceed the benefits society would derive from equal expenditures on other government programs or private consumption and investment. Of course, the values at stake are not easily weighed against one another, and the resulting choices are never likely to be entirely free of controversy.

Given competing demand for scarce resources, one objective of national security policy must be to obtain the most security possible for each dollar of expenditure. But even if a system could be designed to achieve the greatest possible efficiency in one sector of national security—say, defense—it would be impossible to meet all the ideal national security goals in other sectors. Resource constraints translate ideal goals into less than ideal objectives. National security objectives are therefore not absolutes but are defined by the process of evaluating the available options. The realistic options facing society are not bankruptcy with perfect security on the one hand or prosperity while risking national security disaster on the other. Rather, society must confront the far more difficult questions of how much expenditure for national security is required, and how much risk it is willing to accept so that adequate resources are available for other government programs, private consumption, or investment.

The Challenge for Strategic Planners

The preceding discussion suggests that the first questions that national security planners must answer are the following: What are the nation's national security objectives, and how can national resources and the instruments of national security be leveraged to effectively meet these objectives? The central challenge in answering these questions arises out of the fact that there is not a unified national security apparatus (an agency or department) that has jurisdictional control over the many aspects of security. Moreover, not only must national security policy makers agree on objectives and the instruments that will be used to pursue them, but they must also grapple with how much of each instrument should be used. In a broad sense, this means agreeing on the right approach—the use of force, diplomacy, or a combination—to national security; it also means agreeing on how to allocate scarce resources to create the required capabilities.

The National Security Council (NSC) is responsible for coordinating national security policies among many agencies, but it possesses no statutory power to control the actions of these agencies. Moreover, law makers do not annually debate and deliberate on a single national security budget proposal but are compelled to analyze the proposed achievement of security objectives in a piecemeal manner. Multiple agencies compete for their shares of national security dollars and for important roles in shaping and executing national security policy.

In previous chapters, a wide range of actors has been identified as playing key roles in the national security process. Although many actors participate in shaping strategy, a more distinct subgroup of entities actually plays a role in executing it with federal monies. Broadly speaking, current treatment of national security planning, budgeting, and management is limited to three distinct government entities: defense, homeland security, and international affairs (diplomacy). Nested within these three broad areas of security are other security-related areas, such as intelligence, law enforcement, and economic instruments of power.

In terms of resources allocated and expended, defense clearly dominates the various components of national security. This is not surprising, nor is it anomalous historically or when compared to security planning and budgeting in many other countries. The resources required to sustain defense are typically tremendous; in the United States, defense spending constitutes the single largest discretionary government expenditure. Because of its significant role and tremendous weight within the security policy process, the Department of Defense (DoD) is the primary focus of this chapter. However, an evaluation of the DoD's role in national security planning and budgeting offers insight to the problems and tensions that exist in the entire community.

The Federal Budget

The crafting of the federal budget is a highly charged political process, but one that works quite well, given the high stakes and the amount of money involved. It is a process characterized by both conflict and resolution. Conflict stems from the fact that the budget process is not only a matter of allocating huge sums of dollars but also one of setting national priorities. The political nature of such an endeavor naturally lends itself to conflict among a wide range of potentially powerful actors— Congress, its individual members, the president, his or her staff, a huge federal bureaucracy, the military services, states, lobbyists, citizens, and sometimes even international actors. The stakes are clearly high because resources are limited, and any pursuit of one's specific objectives will likely be challenged by another's pursuits. Despite this intense conflict, budgets "must be resolved." Budgetary procedures regulate conflict by parceling out tasks and roles, establishing expectations and deadlines for action, and limiting the scope of issues that are considered. Conflict is dampened by these repetitive tasks that are completed with little or no change, year after year, and by the patterned behavior of individuals involved.[2]

Process.   The executive and legislative branches play the preeminent roles in the budgetary process. The actors within these branches of government include, but are by no means limited to: the president, the Office of Management and Budget (OMB), federal departments and agencies, congressional tax and budget committees, the Congressional Budget Office (CBO), congressional authorization committees (the committees with jurisdiction over certain governmental programs, such as the Senate Armed Services Committee), the congressional appropriations committees and their subcommittees, and the Government Accountability Office. Budgeting involves thousands of participants, but very often their roles in the process are prescribed by the repetitive and sequential budget process.

By law, the president must submit a budget to Congress by the first Monday in February each year. Although this officially begins the annual budget cycle, federal agencies have to begin this process much sooner. During the spring a year prior to the budget submission, budget policy is developed. The OMB first presents the president with an analysis of the economy, and they discuss the budgetary outlook and policies. The OMB then issues guidelines to agencies, which in turn review current programs and submit budgetary projections for the upcoming year. The OMB then reviews these projections and prepares recommendations to the president on final policy, programs, and budget levels. The president then establishes guidelines and targets. During the summer, agencies submit their budget estimates and future year projections to the OMB, which then prepares a budget recommendation for the president. The president reviews these recommendations and decides on the agencies' budgets and overall budgetary policy. Once agencies revise their estimates in conformance with the president's decisions, the OMB again reviews the budget, drafts the president's budget message, and prepares the budget document. Finally, the president revises and approves the budget message and transmits the budget document to Congress.[3]

According to the Constitution, Congress must authorize all federal appropriations. As a result of the Congressional Budget and Impoundment Control Act of 1974, this process has become highly standardized. Table 9.1 shows the congressional budget process, which includes several key steps. First is the adoption of a *budget resolution*. The resolution is an agreement between the House and Senate

Table 9.1   Budget Process

Date	Action to be Completed
First Monday in February	President submits budget to Congress.
February 15	CBO submits report on economic and budget outlook to budget committees.
Six weeks after president's budget is submitted	Committees submit reports on views and estimates to respective budget committees.
April 1	Senate Budget Committee reports budget resolution.
April 15	Congress completes action on budget resolution.
June 10	House Appropriations Committee reports last regular appropriations bill.
June 30	House completes action on regular appropriations bills and any required reconciliation legislation.
July 15	President submits mid-session review of budget to Congress.
October 1	Fiscal year begins.

Source: Robert Keith and Allen Schick, *Introduction to the Federal Budget Process, CRS Report for Congress* (Washington DC: GPO, 2004), 13.

on the overall size of the budget and the general composition of the budget in terms of functional categories (e.g., national defense, international affairs, and so forth). The amounts in these functional categories are then translated into allocations to each congressional committee with jurisdiction over spending; subsequent legislation considered in the House and Senate must be consistent with these allocations as well as the aggregate levels of spending and revenues. In some years, the budget resolution may also contain *reconciliation instructions*. These instructions identify committees that must recommend changes in laws affecting revenues or direct spending programs within their jurisdiction in order to implement the priorities agreed to in the budget resolution. All committees receiving such instructions must submit recommended legislative proposals to the Budget committee in their respective chamber. Reconciliation bills are then considered, and possibly amended, by the full House and Senate.

Congressional approval of each year's spending is divided into thirteen separate appropriations bills that cover broad categories of spending. Appropriations bills are drawn up by the House and Senate Appropriations Committees and their subcommittees. These committees and subcommittees review the requests of particular agencies or groups of related functions. During committee and subcommittee hearings, agency representatives are required to answer questions and defend their requests for the fiscal year (FY). In addition to government officials, lobbyists and other witnesses may testify. Although the appropriations committees have broad discretion in allocating funds, they must stay within the totals set forth in the budget resolution.

When examining the interaction between the federal bureaucracy and Congress, it is important to note the difference between authorization and appropriation legislation. *Authorization legislation* is an act of Congress that establishes a government program and defines the amount of money it can spend. For defense, this is normally done by the House and Senate Armed Services Committees. An authorization bill, however, does not provide money. Only an *appropriations act* can do this. These appropriations acts originate in the Appropriations Committees; for security issues, they originate in their subcommittees on defense. The process for developing a defense budget, within the overall federal budget, is discussed separately in a later section of this chapter.

Spending for National Security

The DoD holds an exceedingly large share of the national security budget. However, national security spending is not only for military forces but also for homeland security, plus diplomacy and foreign affairs under the national security umbrella. Of course, the vast and disparate bureaucracies involved—in terms of personnel, funds, and missions—create an ongoing puzzle for national security planning. How do these individual organizations overcome bureaucratic barriers to develop an effective, unified approach to achieving national security objectives? How can scarce resources be effectively allocated among multiple agencies and departments, given that these separate entities are typically in competition with one another?

FIG. 9.1   Fiscal Year 2008 Federal Budget Outlays

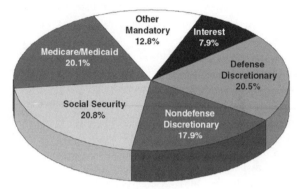

Source: Mid-Session Review, Budget of the U.S. Government, Fiscal Year 2009, Office of Management and Budget, p. 4, www.whitehouse.gov/omb/budget/fy2009/pdf/09msr.pdf

Figure 9.1 illustrates spending for FY 2008. The pie chart represents the entire federal budget, including mandatory, interest, and discretionary spending. *Mandatory* spending usually comes in the form of entitlements, such as Medicare, Medicaid, and Social Security, but may also be found in other programs. Entitlements "give eligible recipients a legal right to payments from the government and as such, the government is obligated to make such payments even if the budget and appropriation acts do not provide sufficient funds."[4] Although Congress may set an amount of funds aside for a particular entitlement program, any shortfalls incurred during budget execution must be covered with additional appropriations. Mandatory spending programs have often caused the most political tension in Washington because funding such programs is a foregone conclusion. Politicians and the public are typically unwilling to cut mandatory spending because of the role of these programs in society. These programs have the "combined effect of cushioning households against the cyclical shocks of recession and temporary disability, and against the secular shocks of old age and infirmity."[5] The only way to reduce mandatory spending is to change the timing or eligibility for benefits, which is extremely difficult for political leaders to do. In short, these programs provide the "social safety net" that most Americans are not willing to forego despite the clear trade-offs—including national security spending—that inevitably arise.

The *discretionary* portion of the federal budget (a combination of the "Defense Discretionary" and "Nondefense Discretionary" categories in Figure 9.1) provides the most room for conflict and debate over the proper allocation of scarce resources. Discretionary funding proposals must not only be renewed by departments and the president each year, but they must also survive both the authorization and appropriation processes in Congress. The ability to "kill" a discretionary program throughout this process is greatly enhanced because of the several decision points it must pass. As one can imagine, this type of process lends itself to a great deal of jockeying and compromise.

FIG. 9.2   Growth in Mandatory Spending

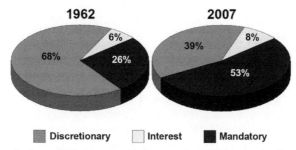

Source: Mid-Session Review 2008 Charts, www.whitehouse.gov/omb/pubpress/msr/2008_msr_charts.pdf

During the latter half of the twentieth century, mandatory spending increased so that it came to dominate the federal budget. In 1940, the share of the budget consumed by mandatory spending was only approximately 18%. By 1962, it stood at approximately 26%, and since the turn of the century has reached approximately 53% (see Figure 9.2). Spending growth stems from a variety of sources, most importantly the creation of many new mandatory spending programs in the twentieth century (such as Social Security in 1935 and Medicare in 1965). Another important source is changing demographics. The retiring baby boomer generation, coupled with increased health-care costs and longer life expectancy, is driving up the cost of mandatory spending. As mandatory spending increases, either overall spending must increase, or discretionary spending must decrease to offset it. To pay for any overall increases, the government must either increase taxes or increase debt.

During the first half of the twentieth century, the president had a tremendous amount of power over federal budgeting. In the 1960s, however, a variety of factors motivated Congress to reassert its institutional prerogatives. This trend came to a head in the early 1970s, when Congress and President Richard Nixon fought over budget priorities and procedures. The result was the Congressional Budget and Impoundment Control Act of 1974. Although this act did not alter the formal role of the president in the budget process, it did give Congress a considerably larger role in making informed fiscal decisions. The act provided for Congress "to adopt an annual budget resolution that sets revenue, spending, the surplus or deficit, and debt totals, and [allocates] spending among 20 functional categories."[6] Congress began to develop its own budget projections and was in a stronger position institutionally to evaluate and counter the president's proposals.[7] The result was a system that furthered conflict between the executive and legislative branches. Discretionary funding proposals in particular became the primary battleground on which each branch fought for its vision of national priorities. As the discretionary funding proportion decreased, these battles became more decisive and divisive.

As depicted graphically in Figure 9.1, discretionary spending constituted only 38.6% of FY 2007 budget outlays. As a share of discretionary spending only, defense dominated with approximately 51.6%. The other components of security spending—homeland security (at 3.0%) and international affairs (at 3.1%)—combined equate to approximately 6.1% of discretionary spending.[8] What stands out most in this analysis is the disproportionate share of funds allocated to the military when compared to other instruments of national security policy. One reason for this imbalance is simply that large, high-quality, standing armed forces are expensive. It is noteworthy that, as a share of the budget, defense spending has risen and fallen throughout the past century based on a variety of factors, while spending on international affairs has remained essentially unchanged.

Developing a balanced national security program and translating it into budgets acceptable to Congress, the public, and other executive agencies is a major, extraordinarily demanding effort of public policy. Accomplishing it requires establishment of national security goals and objectives, identification of departmental and agency strategies and specific capabilities required to meet the defined objectives, and setting of priorities that apportion risks given that no amount of spending will address all the possible security concerns that strategists and planners identify. What follows addresses these challenges specifically as they relate to the DoD, and how the DoD seeks to overcome them through the Planning, Programming, Budgeting, and Execution System (PPBES).

Evolution of Defense Budgeting

Prior to World War II and the creation of the DoD, the Department of the Navy and the Department of War (which included the Army and the Army Air Corps) would submit their budgets proposals separately. These budget proposals would be approved by the president and then addressed by two separate authorizing committees in each House of Congress. After the National Security Act of 1947 and its amendments in 1949, 1953, and 1958, the DoD submitted a consolidated, centralized budget. This centralization provided the Office of the Secretary of Defense (OSD) with additional authorities to make tradeoffs among defense programs and better shape national security policy.

Though the successive defense reorganizations brought the secretary of defense increasing authority, reform of the budgetary process proceeded more slowly. Ideally, a budgetary process assists an organization in performing three essential functions: planning, management, and control. The planning process, which translates the goals of an organization into specific objectives, must provide some mechanism for adjusting objectives and resource allocations to total levels of expenditure. The management function involves the establishment and execution of projects or activities to meet the approved objectives. Finally, the control process monitors the results of various activities measured against the objectives and ensures that expenditures fall within specified limits. The issue that faced the DoD was how to enable the secretary of defense to exert his or her statutory authority to plan, manage, and control defense resources.

The person who is most famous for bringing enhanced budgetary tools to address this need was Secretary of Defense Robert McNamara, who took office with the Kennedy administration in 1961. Unlike most of his predecessors, McNamara viewed his role as being a leader in shaping defense policy rather than as a reviewer of plans and budgets prepared by the services. Moreover, he had a strong presidential mandate to shift the nation's defense posture from one of massive retaliation, relying primarily on Air Force and Navy nuclear weapons, to one of flexible response. Although strategic nuclear delivery systems were still necessary, the shift required new emphasis on mobile general purpose forces. The mandate was to be able to fight simultaneously major wars in Asia and Europe and a "brush-fire" war anywhere in the world—the so-called "two-and-a-half war" strategy. To accomplish these more ambitious objectives, President John Kennedy freed McNamara from specific budgetary ceilings and eliminated any review of the defense budget in the executive branch outside the DoD.

In his approach to the problem, McNamara heeded the advice of the numerous critics of defense budgeting practices in the 1950s. These critics had observed that sound national planning required an evaluation of alternative methods of accomplishing security objectives on the basis of comparative outputs and the costs of each alternative.[9] For example, several strategic nuclear weapons systems, such as Minuteman missiles, strategic bombers, and Polaris missile submarines, contributed to the same objective of deterring nuclear attack. In deciding how much of the defense budget to allocate to each of these strategic systems, the cost and effectiveness of each system should be considered simultaneously. This was virtually impossible in the budgeting system that McNamara inherited, because it was arrayed in terms of service inputs—personnel, operations, maintenance, and military construction—which were accounting categories used by the services and Congress. Budgeting was not done in terms of end products or missions. While forces and weapons were normally considered "horizontally" across services in the planning process, expenditures were portrayed "vertically" within each service by accounting category. The integration of military planning (the domain of the Joint Chiefs of Staff [JCS]) with budgeting (the domain of the civilian secretaries and comptroller organization) required a link between mission objectives and expenditures.[10]

The solution McNamara adopted was *program budgeting*, under which all military forces and weapons systems were grouped into mission-oriented defense programs according to their principal military purpose, even though these missions cut across traditional service boundaries. Programs were then subdivided into program elements (e.g., the General Purpose Forces Program included both Marine and Army forces, such as brigades and divisions, as program elements). With expenditure data arrayed in the program format, a decision maker could readily observe how funds were distributed over mission-related outputs and how those funds were allocated over different forces and weapons systems within each program.

McNamara used the potential of program budgeting to establish the preeminence of the OSD in the national security budgeting process. The Planning, Programming, and Budgeting System (PPBS) that he instituted made it possible to link expenditures more closely to the national security objectives to which they were directed, to compare the relative value of various expenditures, and to enforce the resultant decisions on force structure and weapons procurement. The PPBS improved the ability of the DoD to analyze defense decisions and coordinate interrelated activities. In practice, it also centralized power in McNamara's and the OSD's hands, providing a systematic methodology for identifying key issues, focusing the attention of the senior leadership on them, organizing the sequence of and participation in the decision process, recording decisions, and shaping the defense program and budget to reflect them. As it was applied during 1961–1968 under McNamara, with emphasis on quantitative analysis of alternatives, the PPBS became a powerful centralizing tool that was resisted by the armed services. McNamara held strong cards, though, in the form of firm presidential backing. His personal style, as well as management approach, and his willingness to discount or ignore military expertise led to continuing tension within the Pentagon during his tenure.

Although the PPBS has been criticized continuously since its inception, it has been retained as the basic structure for defense strategy, program, and budget development through successive presidential administrations.[11] In fact, as a result of numerous government-wide management initiatives over the last two decades, other departments and agencies have essentially adopted the PPBS model. In 2003, the DoD made significant changes to the PPBS, now calling it the PPBES. The sections below outline this process and explain the rationale for this change.

The Planning, Programming, Budgeting, and Execution System

The purpose of the PPBES is to allocate resources effectively within the DoD. It is important for program managers and their staffs to be aware of the nature and timing of each of the events in the PPBES, because they may be called upon to provide critical information that could be important to program funding and success. In the PPBES, the secretary of defense establishes policies, strategy, and prioritized goals for the department. These are subsequently used to guide resource allocation decisions that balance the guidance with fiscal constraints. As indicated by the acronym, the PPBES consists of four distinct but overlapping phases: planning, programming, budgeting, and execution.

Planning.   The *planning* phase of the PPBES, which is a collaborative effort by the OSD and the joint staff, begins with an articulation of national defense policies and military strategy known as the Strategic Planning Guidance. The Strategic Planning Guidance is used to lead the planning process, now known as the Enhanced Planning Process. This process results in fiscally constrained guidance and priorities—for military forces, modernization, readiness and sustainability, and supporting business processes and infrastructure activities—for program development. The results of this planning effort are then articulated in a document known as the Joint Programming Guidance. The Joint Programming Guidance is the link between planning and programming, and it provides guidance to each DoD component (military department and defense agency) for the development of a program proposal known as the Program Objective Memorandum (POM).

Programming.   The *programming* phase begins with the development of a POM by each DoD component that responds to the guidance and priorities of the Joint

Programming Guidance within fiscal constraints. When completed, the POM provides a fairly detailed and comprehensive description of the proposed programs, including a time-phased allocation of resources (forces, funding, and manpower) by program projected six years into the future. In addition, each DoD component may describe important programs not fully funded (or not funded at all) in the POM and assess the risks associated with the shortfalls. The senior leadership in the OSD and the joint staff review each POM to help integrate the various DoD component POMs into an overall coherent defense program. In addition, the OSD staff and the joint staff can raise issues with selected portions of any POM, or any funding shortfalls in the POM, and propose alternatives with marginal adjustments to resources. Issues not resolved at lower levels are forwarded to the secretary of defense for decisions, and the resulting decisions are documented in a Program Decision Memorandum.

Budgeting.   The *budgeting* phase of the PPBES occurs concurrently with the programming phase; each DoD component submits its proposed budget estimate simultaneously with its POM. The budget converts the programmatic view into the format of the congressional appropriations structure, along with associated budget justification documents. The budget projects resources only two years into the future but with considerably more financial detail than the POM. Upon submission, each budget estimate is reviewed by analysts from the Office of the Undersecretary of Defense (Comptroller) and the OMB. The purpose of their reviews is to ensure that programs are funded in accordance with current financial policies and are properly and reasonably priced. The review also ensures that the budget documentation is adequate to justify the programs presented to Congress. Typically, the analysts provide the DoD components with written questions in advance of formal hearings where the analysts review and discuss the budget details. After the hearings, each component prepares a decision document (known as a Program Budget Decision [PBD]) for the programs or appropriations under its area of responsibility. The PBD proposes financial adjustments to address any issues or problems identified during the associated budget hearing. The PBDs are circulated among other components for their comments and forwarded to the deputy secretary of defense for decisions. These decisions are then reflected in an updated budget submission provided to the OMB. After that, the overall DoD budget is provided as part of the president's budget request to Congress.

Execution.   The *execution* review occurs simultaneously with the program and budget reviews. The purpose of the execution review is to provide feedback to senior leadership concerning the effectiveness of current and prior resource allocations. To the extent performance goals of an existing program are not being met, the execution review may lead to recommendations to adjust resources or restructure programs to achieve desired performance goals.[12]

The Rationale for the PPBES.   In May 2003, the DoD adopted the PPBES as an improvement to the decades-old PPBS to make the process more effective and to provide a greater emphasis on execution. The result was not only a change in name: One of the key changes was to move from annual to biennial budgeting. As discussed above, the new system supports two-year budget cycles that result in two-year budgets. The basic concepts behind the new system are consistent with the submission of a biennial DoD budget that is part of the president's budget request to Congress for even-numbered fiscal years. These even-numbered years are referred to as *on-years*, while the odd-numbered years are referred to as *off-years* (see Figure 9.3).

It should be noted that Congress does not actually provide the DoD with biennial appropriations. An amended budget justification must be submitted for the second year of the original budget request so Congress will appropriate funds for that second year. The department uses a restricted process in the off-year to develop an amended budget that allows for only modest program or budget adjustments.[13] In the off-year, assuming no major threat changes, there are no significant changes to policy, strategy, or fiscal guidance. In fact, there may be no issuance of revised Joint Programming Guidance. If revised Joint Programming Guidance is provided, it would only contain minor revisions (although it could direct studies to support major decisions on strategy or program choices for the following year's Strategic Planning Guidance or Joint Programming Guidance). In addition, in the off-year, the DoD components do not provide revised POMs or budget estimates. Instead, the DoD components are allowed to submit Program Change Proposals (PCPs) or Budget Change Proposals (BCPs) to account for fact-of-life changes (e.g., program cost increases or schedule delays). BCPs and PCPs are limited to a single issue and must identify resource reductions to offset any program or budget cost growth. PCPs address issues over a multiyear period, whereas BCPs address issues focused on the upcoming budget year. PCPs are reviewed in a manner similar to on-year program issues, and BCPs are resolved through the issuance and staffing of PBDs.

Although the budget process is built upon a biennial structure, the PPBES in its entirety is a four-year process that coincides with presidential terms. Figure 9.4 identifies key events in the process by year. In the first year of the administration, the president approves a new National Security Strategy (NSS), which establishes (1) the worldwide interests, goals, and objectives that are vital to national security; and (2) the foreign policy, worldwide commitments, and national defense capabilities necessary to implement national security goals and objectives. Once the new administration's NSS is established, the secretary of defense, in consultation with the chairman of the JCS, leads the Quadrennial Defense Review (QDR). The QDR is a comprehensive review of all elements of defense policy and strategy needed to support the national security strategy. The defense strategy is then used to establish the plans for military force structure, force modernization, business processes and supporting infrastructure, and required resources (funding and manpower). The QDR final report is provided to Congress in the second year of the administration.

In the PPBES, the QDR final report serves as the foundation document for defense strategy and business policy. Because this document is not available until the second year, the first year of the administration is treated as an off-year,

FIG. 9.3 PPBE Cycles

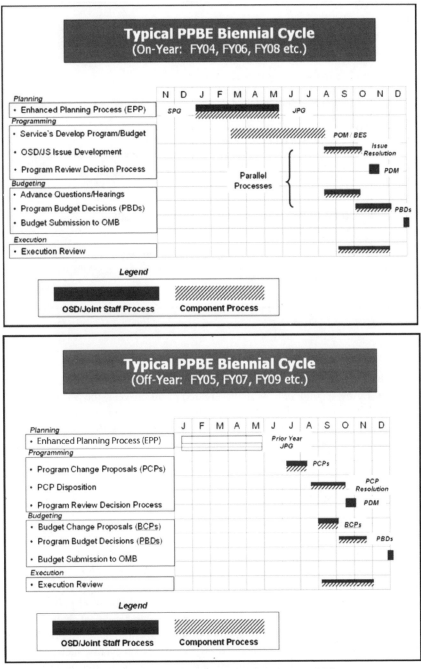

Source: Defense Acquisition Guidebook, https://akss.dau.mil/dag/Guidebook/IG_c1.2.asp

FIG. 9.4   PPBE Process and Presidential Terms

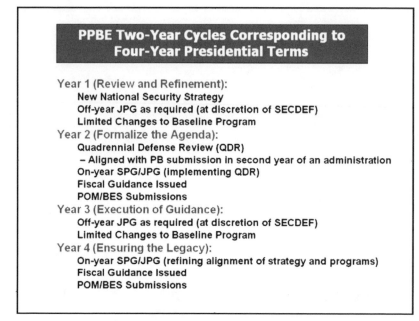

Source: *Defense Acquisition Guidebook*, https://akss.dau.mil/dag/Guidebook/IG_c1.2.asp

using the president's budget inherited from the previous administration as a baseline. In the second year, which is treated as an on-year, the Strategic Planning Guidance and Joint Programming Guidance are rewritten to implement the QDR of the new administration.[14] (For further discussion of the role of the QDR in defense policy and the extent to which it has met the intent of congressional reformers, see Chapter 5.)

Supplemental Appropriations

In recent years, total discretionary spending has risen significantly. According to the CBO, "[i]n 1990, both funding and outlays stood at about $500 billion. By 2000, they exceeded $600 billion and grew rapidly from there, reaching about $1 trillion in 2005."[15] A major source of this significant increase is a growth in supplemental appropriations. Between September 11, 2001, and December 2005, eleven separate supplemental appropriations totaling in excess of $300 billion were passed. These appropriations have presented a wide array of practical and political challenges.

One of the most important advantages of supplemental appropriations is that they allow the government to react quickly to unforeseen events, such as natural disasters, or unforeseen military operations. Although the regular appropriation process lasts up to nine months, on average supplementals pass within a four-month period.[16] During the 1990s, supplemental appropriations were used first for the 1991 Persian Gulf War and later for numerous peacekeeping missions from Somalia to the Balkans. They were also used for hurricane relief, flooding, and other domestic issues. In the twenty-first century, supplementals have been used in much the same manner, for military operations and disaster relief.

Though supplemental appropriations bring with them the advantage of responsiveness, their use is also a source of controversy. Prior to the Congressional Budget and Impoundment Control Act of 1974, there were relatively few controls on supplementals. After this act, however, the use of supplementals was limited to "unanticipated expenses." An additional constraint was created with the passage of the Budget Enforcement Act of 1990. That legislation imposed spending caps; if a supplemental exceeded such caps, it would have to be offset with a corresponding reduction in spending somewhere else or with a revenue increase. Of course, if the supplemental were deemed necessary for a "dire emergency," it would be funded out of deficit spending.[17]

Since 2001, the use of supplementals by the administration of President George W. Bush has received a great deal of criticism. Though supplementals had been used to support past U.S. military operations, they were often requested and expended early. They served their emergency function of supplying funds for clearly unforeseen needs.[18] By contrast, law makers have accused George W. Bush of building a "shadow budget" by continuing to fund overseas military operations through supplemental requests to escape the scrutiny, oversight, and debate that accompany regular appropriations. In addition, because of the "dire emergency" status attached to these bills, they are not subject to traditional spending caps. The short-term result has been increased deficit spending. Over the longer term, policy makers will be forced to adjust to new spending-level realities and manage the consequences of deficit spending.

Looking Ahead

Ideally, the distribution of scarce government resources to security expenditures would perfectly reflect the government's foreign and security policies and explicit trade-offs between investment in security and other social values. In practice, this is impossible to accomplish, in large part because of the fragmented nature of the U.S. national security apparatus.

Under the PPBS and later the PPBES, the DoD has made important progress in relating the internal allocation of its budget expenditures to security objectives. The highly centralized process of the McNamara era has evolved into a somewhat more decentralized system of participatory management that places increased weight on the military services' measures of effectiveness. Nevertheless, the essential elements of the system remain.

Unfortunately, the ability of the government as a whole to decide how much to spend on national security and to evaluate defense versus other types of expenditures has lagged far behind. Throughout the 1970s and 1980s, efforts to introduce program budgeting to the remainder of the federal bureaucracy were largely unsuccessful. With a series of reforms in the 1990s, most notably the Government Performance and Results Act of 1993 (GPRA), the federal bureaucracy began to move closer to successful program budgeting in various departments. The Presidential Management Agenda (PMA) announced in 2001 by George W. Bush was aimed at expanding upon or improving many aspects of the GPRA. Although the value of these initiatives is still being evaluated, it is widely agreed that performance management leads to more efficient practices. Yet, despite the success individual agencies may experience in linking budget requests to performance results, there still remains the important question of whether or not the United States government as a whole has properly allocated its resources to meet national security objectives, not just within each agency but also among them.

Given the fact that national security goals are essentially unlimited, but national resources to achieve them are scarce, how does one effectively manage the national security process? The answer is elusive, for though the president can use the NSC to coordinate the actions of several agencies, there is no unified national security apparatus with the capability to plan, manage, and control all national-security-related spending. In addition, the checks and balances built into the U.S. system of government inevitably lead to tension and cross purposes in the process. It is difficult for the president and Congress to agree on national security priorities; even when there is general agreement on objectives, there will still be disagreements over what instruments of power to use and the relative emphasis appropriate to each. The structure and processes currently in place, although better than those of the past, do not lend themselves to efficient unified decisions.

Discussion Questions

1. Is it inherently impossible to achieve all our ideal national security goals? Why or why not?

2. Should the United States seek to create a more unified national security apparatus? If so, what should it look like? What political factors would make the formation of such an organization difficult?

3. What agencies and organizations play a central role in the federal budget process? Are some agencies more powerful than others? Why?

4. What factors limit the ability of the president and Congress to radically reshape the federal budget?

5. What is the difference between *mandatory* and *discretionary* spending? Why are these categories significant to national security?

6. Why has discretionary spending decreased steadily as a proportion of the federal budget in recent decades? What factors affect discretionary spending priorities?

7. What is *program budgeting*, and how is it different from previous budgeting practices?

8. Describe the overall PPBES cycle. What is the role of the president, the DoD, and Congress in this process?

9. How do supplemental appropriations impact the budget cycle? From the standpoint of the various actors in the budget cycle, what are the advantages and disadvantages associated with the use of supplemental appropriations?

Recommended Reading

Allison, Graham T., and Gregory Treverton. *Rethinking America's Security.* New York: W. W. Norton, 1992.

Davis, Thomas M. *Managing Defense After the Cold War.* Washington, DC: Center for Strategic and Budgetary Assessments, 1997.

Enthoven, Alain C., and K. Wayne Smith. *How Much Is Enough?* New York: Harper & Row, 1971.

Fallows, James. *National Defense.* New York: Random House, 1981.

Korb, Lawrence J. *The Joint Chiefs of Staff: The First Twenty-Five Years.* Bloomington, IN: University Press, 1976.

Lewis, Kevin. "The Discipline Gap and Other Reasons for Humility and Realism in Defense Planning." In *New Challenges for Defense Planning: Rethinking How Much Is Enough,* 101–132, edited by Paul K. Davis. Santa Monica: RAND Corporation, 1994.

McCaffery, Jerry L., and L. R. Jones. *Budgeting and Financial Management for National Defense.* Greenwich, CT: Information Age Publishing, 2004.

McNaugher, Thomas. *New Weapons, Old Politics: America's Military Procurement Muddle.* Washington, DC: Brookings Institution, 1989.

O'Hanlon, Michael E. *Defense Strategy for the Post-Saddam Era.* Washington, DC: Brookings Institution, 2005.

Pfaltzgraff, Robert. *New Directions in U.S. Defense Policy.* Newbury Park, CA: Sage, 1991.

Schick, Allen. *The Federal Budget: Politics, Policy, Process.* Washington, DC: Brookings Institution, 2000.

Snider, Don M., et al. "The Coming Defense Train Wreck . . . And What to Do About It." *Washington Quarterly* 19, no. 1 (Winter 1996): 87–124.

Taylor, Maxwell D. *The Uncertain Trumpet.* New York: Harper, 1959.

Widalvsky, Aaron. *The Politics of the Budgetary Process.* Boston: Little, Brown, 1964.

Wilson, George C. *This War Really Matters: Inside the Fight for Defense Dollars.* Washington, DC: CQ Press, 2000.

Internet Sources

Center for Strategic and Budgetary Assessments, www.csbaonline.org

Office of Management and Budget, www.whitehouse.gov/omb

Office of the Under Secretary of Defense (Comptroller), www.defenselink.mil/comptroller

RAND Corporation, www.rand.org

10

Putting the Pieces Together: National Security Decision Making

National security decision making is complex and fascinating because of the two worlds it involves. As Samuel Huntington explains: "One [world] is international politics, the world of balance of power, wars and alliances, the subtle and brutal uses of force and diplomacy to influence the behavior of other states. The other world is domestic politics, the world of interest groups, political parties, social classes with their conflicting interests and goals."[1] National security affairs have an impact on and are influenced by both worlds, for national security often involves the application of national resources to the international arena in an attempt to make the domestic society more secure.

The institutional arrangements that have evolved to advise and assist the president in security matters are often referred to as the *national security decision-making process*, or the *interagency process* (after the agencies that participate). When trying to understand American foreign and national security policy and actions, such factors as the global environment or domestic politics will tell only part of the story. How decisions are made can be at least as important, so understanding the national security decision-making process is essential.

The national security decision-making process is a system of formal and informal coordination within the executive branch intended to ensure that issues requiring presidential attention are identified and raised in a timely manner; national interests and objectives are clearly defined; viable options are thoroughly considered; costs, benefits, and risks are deliberately evaluated; and overall coherence of policy is maintained. The process encompasses the full breadth of national security decisions, from developing national strategy to determining the content of particular presidential speeches. The national security decision-making process doubles as a management system that helps the president carry out his or her responsibilities as head of the executive branch by enabling the president's staff to adjudicate and coordinate issues that straddle department and agency seams.

The president's staff—specifically, the National Security Council (NSC) and Homeland Security Council (HSC) staffs in concert with others in the Executive Office of the President—actively administers the process. The backbone of the formal process is a constant churn of interagency meetings, commonly referred to as the *NSC system* (and, since 2001, the *HSC system*), supported by formally prepared and staffed memoranda, intelligence estimates, and other papers. At the top, the meetings include the president, the president's senior advisors, and the heads of departments and agencies, known as the *principals*. Below this level, all presidents have been served by some structure of subordinate councils and working groups (see Chapter 4). The majority of activity occurs in these subordinate meetings, without the president's or the principals' direct participation. Around this formal apparatus, a set of informal arrangements invariably evolves in response to the needs of the president.

The cousin of the national security decision-making process is the annual president's budget process. These processes are fed by many diverse and important systems internal to departments and agencies. These internal systems are augmented by a growing number of lateral agency-to-agency coordination mechanisms and an increasing number of interagency centers, such as the National Counter-Terrorism Center (NCTC) discussed in Chapter 7, that integrate elements of various agencies into a single organization with a specific mission. The national security decision-making process is actually a system of processes that extends from the White House deeply into a variety of executive branch entities.

It is tempting to assume that the interagency process operates in a regularized way according to rules and timelines. Sometimes it does; more often, it does not. For every rule governing how the interagency process is supposed to function (e.g., "this committee handles that issue"), there are exceptions. Indeed, there is no real rule book, though documents that purport to be such abound.[2] The processes used to support major decisions have differed significantly across administrations and even within the same administration on different issues.

Factors That Shape the Formal Process

A key component of the national security decision-making system is the formal process. This section surveys the important factors that shape its nature.

The Presidency.   The president's job is unique. In the words of Richard Neustadt: "No one else sits where he sits or sees quite as he sees; no one else feels the full weight of his obligations."[3] The president, unlike most of his foreign counterparts, is both head of state (the country's symbolic leader) and head of government (the chief executive of the unitary executive branch). Executive power is broadly vested in the president directly by the Constitution, not granted by Congress. The president's national security powers are formidable and, as discussed in Chapter 4, have continued to expand over time. As a result, the president is stretched thin.[4] Moreover, domestic and international publics place high expectations on the most powerful leader in the world. In addition to these demands, foreign and national security policies also present the president's best opportunity for a legacy. The national security decision-making process belongs to the president, enabling him or her to respond to these imperatives.

Separation of Powers, Pluralism, and Federalism.   The national security decision-making process reflects the basic characteristics of the U.S. political system.[5] For the purposes of this chapter, two features stand out. The first, the subject of Chapters 4 and 5, is the U.S. system of *separated powers* or, more accurately, separate institutions sharing power.[6] The second is *political and social pluralism.* The more pluralist the society—that is, the more there are distinct ethnic, cultural, religious, or other disparate groups within it—the greater the number of entities that interact with the decision process and structure, and the more difficult it becomes to develop coherent national strategy and policy.[7]

While pluralism is the defining characteristic of the American domestic policy realm, the foreign policy realm is different. There are far fewer interest groups, and most do not pack the political clout of domestic policy groups. In *Fortune* magazine's 2001 list of the twenty-five most powerful interest groups, only one— the American Israel Public Affairs Committee—had a foreign policy or national security focus.[8] Excepting the media, whose influence in both spheres is comparable, the most influential voices in foreign policy debates emanate from a small population of national security elites, from a few public policy think tanks, and from America's top academic institutions. While the number of lobbies is on the rise, the foreign policy arena is less crowded than the domestic policy arena.

Political scientist Aaron Wildavsky asserted in 1966 that there are, in fact, two presidencies: one for domestic affairs and one for foreign affairs. Wildavsky's thesis has lost traction in some areas (for example, on international trade), but it remains useful in the national security realm. Says Wildavsky: "The President's normal problem with domestic policy is to get congressional support for the programs he prefers. In foreign affairs, in contrast, he can almost always get support for policies that he believes will protect the nation—but his problem is to find a viable policy."[9]

Until relatively recently, the two presidencies thesis meant good news for the president in national security affairs. Presidents have been able to act without the express approval of Congress far more often in foreign affairs than in domestic ones. However, the political reality of two presidencies now cuts both ways. Since the first World Trade Center attack in 1993; the Oklahoma City bombing in 1995; and, most dramatically, the terrorist attacks of September 11, 2001, the president's national security responsibilities have expanded decisively in the domestic realm (see Chapter 6). Protecting the country now requires, in the words of the 9/11 Commission, "unity of effort across the foreign-domestic divide."[10]

From the average American's perspective, the conceptual distinction between national security and homeland security may be largely meaningless. However, the distinction has practical significance. First, the domestic implications of homeland security policy mean that the president cedes power to Congress. Wildavsky says, "It takes great crises . . . for Presidents to succeed in controlling domestic policy," and a president's domestic policy proposals are more than twice as likely to fail as his national security proposals.[11] The events of 9/11 triggered such a crisis, but the president's ability to get his way at home eroded far more quickly than his ability to get his way abroad. For example, President George W. Bush's proposal to give first responders smallpox inoculations died, but three months later he was able to lead the country into war with Iraq. Second, the president's power in homeland security matters is eroded by the vigorous engagement of interest groups with Congress and the bureaucracy. Because homeland security policies touch the daily lives of Americans and frequently collide with competing domestic priorities, interest groups become involved. Third, the president shares power with the states, and governors are frequently not compliant: The president has his interests, and they have theirs. For all these reasons, since 9/11, the president's national security prerogative simply does not exist for an enormously important range of security policy.[12]

The impact on national security decision making is three-fold. First, as post-9/11 expectations that the president will protect the country have risen, the heightened relevance of domestic issues to security has meant that the president's power has diminished. Second, developing and implementing coherent national security policy has become more challenging due to the involvement of domestic agencies (e.g., the Department of the Interior) and policy instruments (e.g., regulation) traditionally far outside the realm of national security policy. *Iron triangles*—the durable relationships among interest groups, relevant executive branch agencies, and corresponding congressional committees—mean policy making takes longer, involves more compromise, and is incremental. Third, the center of gravity for many security issues has shifted from the Senate to the House of Representatives, whose members' votes more often reflect how policy affects their districts as opposed to the nation as a whole (immigration policy and port security provide examples).

Domestic Politics.   Senator Arthur H. Vandenberg may have rightly claimed that "politics stops at the water's edge," but this perspective is currently misleading.[13] Domestic politics do not necessarily preclude desirable courses of action, but they do mean that some presidential decisions will be tougher to make or more costly. Domestic politics can narrow or color options (President John Kennedy's talking tough on Cuba in the 1960 presidential election surely influenced his decision to approve the Bay of Pigs operation), put new options on the table (President Richard Nixon, the ardent anticommunist, could open up relations with Communist China), or simply roil the waters (the 1995 budget showdown between President Bill Clinton and congressional Republicans complicated the final negotiations of the Dayton Accords).[14] Once in a rare while, domestic politics can remove some presidential options completely, usually through a showdown between the formal powers of the president and Congress (for example, the congressionally mandated halt to bombing in Cambodia toward the end of the Nixon administration).[15]

Perhaps the most important domestic political factor affecting many of the president's power calculations is the electoral cycle. The president's prospects for reelection constrain choices. In the second term, more freedom to act is likely to be accompanied by less influence with Congress. In both cases, options may be significantly affected by foreign leaders whose understanding of the U.S. political system rivals that of Americans.[16]

The impact of domestic politics is not always felt at the margins, nor is it new. Ernest May argues that the Monroe Doctrine, the bedrock of American strategy toward Latin America for nearly a century, can also be explained in terms of domestic politics.[17] The geopolitical situation mattered to President James Monroe, but Monroe also believed that boldly trumpeting American primacy in Latin American would enhance the political prospects of his party. In fact, John Quincy Adams, who helped formulate the Monroe Doctrine as Monroe's Secretary of State, was elected to succeed President Monroe at least in part because of the domestic popularity of this international policy. Domestic politics is a critical variable—sometimes the most important variable—in the national security decision-making process. This need not be cause for cynicism; in a democracy, good policy is policy that gets done (and politics is how it gets done), and good security strategy is strategy that can be maintained. The effective policy maker must be a pragmatist, not a perfectionist.

Ever-Increasing Complexity in National Security Affairs.   No realm of affairs has grown more complex more quickly than national security, which must integrate political, diplomatic, military, economic, technological, cultural, and psychological dimensions.[18] Each new challenge creates a policy demand. Government adds a function, agencies specialize, and jurisdictions overlap. Integrating national security policy simultaneously gets more important and more difficult. The burden on the president rises.

As complexity rises, so does the interrelatedness of issues. The most familiar example is the connection between security and international economic policy, but interrelatedness is growing in many specific policy areas (e.g., counterterrorism intelligence) and individual programs. Fewer problems fall solely within the purview of a specific agency, and it is increasingly unlikely that individual departments and agencies are sensitive to all the ways in which their policies and programs relate and interact.[19] At a minimum, agencies differ in their priorities.

For most of the last sixty years, this phenomenon affected domestic and economic policy more than national security policy—the Department of State, the Department of Defense (DoD), and the Central Intelligence Agency (CIA) enjoyed distinct, even exclusive statutory authorities for most of what they do. This has changed. The 9/11 Commission report observes that, even given national security professionals committed to collaboration, it has become harder to get agencies to act in concert. The NSC and HSC systems must untangle these interconnections to forge coherent policy.

With respect to each new challenge of interrelatedness, the president has three choices: (1) assume a new coordination burden, (2) decide that a particular issue is not a sufficiently high priority to warrant presidential attention, or (3) provide guidance or impose requirements on the agencies to effect lateral coordination on their own. Option 1 has the cost of increasing the size and diffusing the focus of the president's staff. Option 2 runs the risk of miscalculation, as a seemingly low

Table 10.1 Senate-Confirmed Positions

	1940	1960	1998	2004
Secretaries	10	10	14	15
Deputy secretaries	0	6	23	24
Under secretaries	3	15	41	46
Total	13	31	78	85

Source: Paul C. Light, *Fact Sheet on the Continued Thickening of Government* (Washington, DC: Brookings Institution, 2004).

Note: Positions without a title of "secretary"—such as Director, FBI; Director, CIA; Administrator, Environmental Protection Agency—are not included.

priority issue may surface as a major problem later. Option 3 is problematic at best. Presidential commands are "but a method of persuasion . . . and not a method suitable for everyday employment."[20]

Growth of the Federal Government.   As policy needs expand, so does government. The number of agencies with national security missions is growing—including cabinet departments, such as Agriculture; independent agencies, such as the Environmental Protection Agency; quasi-independent agencies, such as the Coast Guard; and unique entities, such as the Office of the Director of National Intelligence (DNI). Congress adds new committees and subcommittees. Not only do agencies proliferate, but they sprout new specialized bureaus, offices, and centers to address new demands.[21]

The number of political appointees grows apace, as does the White House staff. For the most part, each of these officials has an important job, and the departments they administer are responsible for key functions. For example, the undersecretary of defense for intelligence is one of five new undersecretaries added between 1998 and 2004 (see Table 10.1). The political appointee in charge of all intelligence functions of the DoD has an important role to play but simultaneously adds to the number of players involved in the interagency process.

Departmentalism, Parochialism, and Turf.   As articulated by Elliot Richardson (who has held four cabinet positions), "Cabinet members are forced by the very nature of their institutional responsibilities to be advocates of their departmental programs."[22] Career civil servants almost always stay in one department and have the power to passively stymie political leaders.[23] To get things done, agency executives need the support of their bureaucracy.[24]

Inevitably, the views of agencies and, over time, of their politically appointed leaders are more parochial than the president's. Cabinet secretaries become defenders of their departments' functions and constituencies—they seek to stake out and to defend their turf.[25] Because cabinet members respond to more than just the president's agenda, the president has an incentive to centralize decision making in the White House and to use the national security decision-making process to assert control.

What Executive Officialdom Needs.   Not only the president but also the involved agencies need the national security decision-making process. As interrelatedness increases and the president's coordination burden rises, so does theirs—the result is more conflict that only the president can adjudicate. Writing about Kennedy's cabinet during the Cuban Missile Crisis, Graham Allison and Neustadt state: "What top officials needed from the President [was] . . . a forum for discussion, a referee for arguments, assurance of a hearing, and a judgment on disputes. Their jurisdictions were at once divided and entangled. . . . None could act alone."[26] As reported by the Tower Commission, "The NSC system will not work unless the president makes it work."[27]

The Foundation: The National Security Act of 1947 and the National Security Council

The bedrock institutional architecture for the formal national security decision-making process was established by the National Security Act of 1947. When World War II ended, the wartime structure of ad hoc relationships and temporary committees dissolved, but the nation's security interests could not be pursued effectively by agencies acting independently. With an appreciation for this challenge, President Harry Truman gave a speech in December 1945 that called for a unified defense establishment.[28] Supporting his call for unification were the Army and War Departments. Opposing it was the Navy, which favored decentralization—a stance that persisted through various centralizing reorganizations, including Goldwater-Nichols in 1986.

The National Security Act that emerged in July 1947 was a compromise. The act created a secretary of defense (but no unified department), the Joint Chiefs of Staff (JCS), the Air Force, the CIA, and several other entities. It also created the NSC to "advise the President with respect to the integration of domestic, foreign, and military policies relating to the national security so as to enable the military services and the other departments and agencies of the Government to cooperate more effectively in matters involving the national security."[29] The NSC was authorized a staff managed by an executive secretary. As flaws became apparent, Congress amended the act in 1949, creating a DoD with full authority over the military services, removing the services from the cabinet and NSC, and installing a chairman of the JCS who would serve as the military advisor to the NSC. Additional adjustments occurred in 1958, 1986, and, most recently, in 2004 (see Table 10.2).

The Council in Practice.   By the end of the Truman administration, the basic structure was in place: the statutory NSC with an executive secretary responsible for facilitating meetings, interfacing with the president, and overseeing a supporting staff. The staff was responsible for coordinating interagency committees and managing the preparation of policy papers.[30] The position of national security advisor was created in 1953 (see Chapter 4).

The National Security Act authorized the president to appoint other cabinet secretaries and undersecretaries to the NSC, with Senate approval. No president has sought such approval, though every president has added participants. Table 10.3

compares how Presidents George H. W. Bush, Clinton, and George W. Bush tailored the NSC to their needs. Except for during the Eisenhower administration, when they were more frequent, formal meetings of the NSC have been infrequent—on average, occurring slightly more often than once a month. George W. Bush convened the NSC more frequently: every day for a period following 9/11, and then once or twice a week thereafter, often by secure video teleconference.[31] Whether this remains the practice for his successors remains to be seen. Crises typically generate a flurry of formal NSC meetings; between crises, meetings have been less frequent.[32]

Formal meetings occur relatively infrequently for a number of reasons. First, the president does not need a formal meeting to confer with his national security team. Decisions can be made any time the president gathers the right people or the right advice. Second, much of the value of the NSC system is created by meetings that occur below the principals' level, without the president. These meetings improve the decision process by coordinating policy, crafting distinct options, clarifying differences, and minimizing the issues requiring the president's attention.

The Staff.[33]   The NSC and HSC staffs have three enduring purposes: (1) advise the president; (2) coordinate the development of policy across the executive branch; and (3) monitor the implementation of presidential decisions, policies, and guidance. The most important staff position to fill is the national security advisor, supported by a deputy national security advisor. Clinton added a second deputy for international economic affairs, who also reported to the director of the National Economic Council (NEC). The George W. Bush NSC staff grew to include six deputies for key policy functions (see Figure 10.1). The rationale for additional deputies is to attract a sufficiently senior or high-ranking official to take the job and to ensure that the official has status and clout within the White House and with the departments and agencies. Below the deputies are senior directors responsible for key geographic and functional policy areas, and each senior director typically oversees three to eight directors (the "action officers" of the NSC and HSC staffs). Directors are a mix of policy generalists and expert specialists, each with a specific portfolio. They range from very senior officials with long-time policy experience to talented up-and-comers. A senior director's or director's influence is only partially determined by seniority and is mostly determined by policy acumen, political skill, relationships, and results. The White House is a very entrepreneurial place—results earn relevance—and there is no shortage of strong individuals who are intent on carving out a piece of the action. Tactful and effective directors can earn access to the president, while senior directors and even deputies can be subtly marginalized.[34]

Members of the NSC staff come from a variety of sources: government, academia, the private sector, and think tanks. Many have revolved through several of these categories. Military officers form a special and important category. They have served in every position, from national security advisor to director, and included every rank from four-star general to captain. They have essential military knowledge and experience, and they know how to make staffs function. Perhaps most importantly, officers are bound by their profession to be nonpartisan, so their military advice can be trusted as such, and they offer critical continuity during

FIG. 10.1   National Security Council Staff

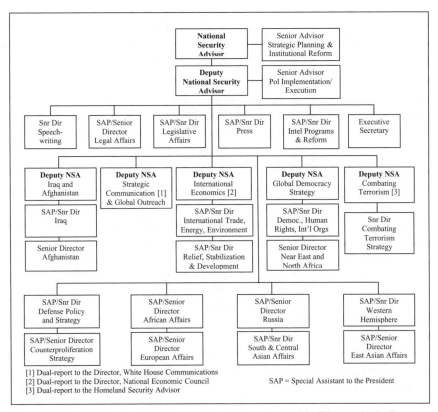

Source: Stephen J. Hadley, "Memorandum: National Security Council Staff Reorganization" (Washington, DC: The White House, 2005).

changes of administration. The challenge for military officers is how to make the transition to the fluidity of the White House and how to walk the line between policy and politics in a place where politics is omnipresent.

The specific policy demands facing an administration shape the staff structure. If the NSC staff and agencies begin to have routine meetings on a particular topic, then it becomes practical to designate an NSC official of appropriate rank, supported by a handful of NSC directors, to manage that portfolio. For example, when hundreds of thousands of veterans of the 1991 Gulf War experienced the mysterious symptoms commonly known as the Gulf War syndrome, Clinton created a Gulf War Illness Affairs directorate, which was later absorbed into the Defense Policy and Arms Control directorate.[35]

The First Post-9/11 Reform: The Homeland Security Council.   During the 1990s, the NSC architecture that had served the country reasonably well throughout the Cold War was forced to adapt. Clinton instituted a variety of

Table 10.4   The Homeland Security Council as Enacted by Congress, November 25, 2002

President	Attorney general
Vice president	Secretary of Defense
Secretary of Homeland Security	Others designated by the president

Source: U.S. Congress, Title IX of *Homeland Security Act of 2002*, Public Law 107-296.

changes, creating a bureau for Transnational Threats, the Counterterrorism Security Group (CSG), and the position of coordinator for Counterterrorism. By the end of his administration, the NSC staff had grown to the largest it had ever been but remained strained. Many current and former government officials recognized that the changes needed were more fundamental than normal institutional evolution would allow.[36]

The events that finally provided the impetus for dramatic change occurred on 9/11. About a month after the attacks, George W. Bush established the Office of Homeland Security (now referred to as the HSC staff), to be headed by a new homeland security advisor, and created the HSC, a cabinet-level committee modeled on the NSC, which was later ensconced in statute (see Table 10.4).[37] The HSC staff was given the task of developing a national strategy for homeland security and for bringing the broad range of domestic agencies with important security responsibilities into the formal system of national security coordination. Given the inexperience of many agencies in the formal interagency process, the HSC staff's coordination task was immense and extended into details of implementation. The staff grew quickly to over one hundred policy people. Much of this staff migrated to the Department of Homeland Security (DHS) after its creation in 2003, and, as the HSC system settled into a more regular pattern of activity, the policy staff was reduced to approximately thirty by 2006.

The coordination challenge is broader than the NSC and HSC staffs. The integration of security and international economic policy was institutionalized when Clinton created the NEC in 1993, with a deputy national security advisor for international economic affairs who is "dual-hatted" as the NEC deputy. However, many homeland security issues also have economic dimensions (e.g., cargo security). In addition, there is a greater need to coordinate national security policy with the White House's domestic policy staff, the Office of Management and Budget (OMB), White House Counsel, and others. Also, Clinton and George W. Bush both gave their vice presidents significant roles in national security affairs, requiring more coordination with the Office of the Vice President than in the past. Figure 10.2 provides an illustration of the basic conceptual overlap between White House coordinating councils.[38]

A Further Post-9/11 Reform: The Director of National Intelligence. The establishment of the DNI was the second major post-9/11 reform to the national security decision-making apparatus. The Intelligence Reform and Terrorism Prevention Act of 2004 established the DNI as the head of the Intelligence Community and the principal intelligence advisor to the president, the NSC, and

FIG. 10.2   Intersection of White House Policy Coordinating Councils

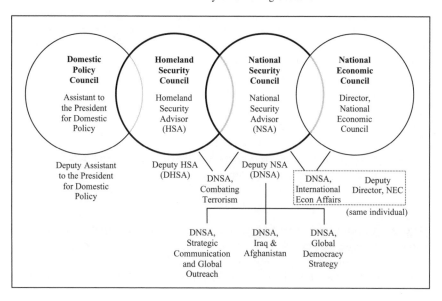

the HSC (see Chapter 7 for a discussion of the DNI and the relationship between policy makers and intelligence).

The DNI is a unique and unprecedented entity in the executive branch structure. The DNI reports directly to the president, but the office is not part of the Executive Office of the President, and the DNI must be confirmed by the Senate. The DNI has statutory authority as head of the Intelligence Community, as did the director of central intelligence (DCI), but unlike the DCI sits formally above the departments and agencies. For the first time, responsibility for coordination of a critical component of the national security decision-making process is lodged outside of the White House but above departments and agencies, and it is subject to congressional oversight.

The DNI is also authorized to create interagency centers, such as the NCTC. These centers, which are not subordinate to a lead department or agency, are new and have significant effects on the national security decision-making process. They add one more entity to the interagency table, and although they improve interagency coordination within their functional area, they complicate the national security decision-making process in the NSC and HSC systems.

The Interagency Process

Though details and titles have varied across administrations, the national security decision-making architecture has been relatively stable since 1989, being comprised of a Principals Committee (PC), a Deputies Committee (DC), and subordinate interagency policy coordination committees (PCCs). It seems likely this structure or one like it will endure.

Principals Committee. A PC meeting is an NSC or HSC meeting without the president (for brevity, the discussion below will use the term NSC, though the process is essentially the same for the HSC). The PC's principal functions are to advise the president and coordinate and resolve interagency policy issues at the national strategic level. The PC historically has met once or twice a week, though in the George W. Bush administration it has met more frequently. The core participants are the council members and advisors (see Tables 10.2 and 10.4) and the national security advisor. Some PC meetings are also attended by the vice president and the president's chief of staff. Others may attend if needed. The national security advisor convenes and chairs the meeting and ensures that the necessary papers (usually three- to six-page memos called *PC papers*) are prepared and disseminated in advance. The PC may meet daily or even twice a day during crises and often handles rapidly unfolding or time-sensitive issues (such as the 2005 London subway bombings).[39]

Deputies Committee. The DC resolves interagency issues that can be handled without engaging the principals, elevates critical or contentious issues that require the attention of the principals or the president, and presents issues to the principals in a manner that sets a foundation for deliberation. The DC, "the engine of policy," has proven particularly useful.[40] While there are few truly strategic decisions, there are many important policy decisions that usually require dissemination and action more than confidentiality. Essential White House and departmental staffers, known as *straphangers*, regularly attend DC meetings, which are less formal than NSC or PC meetings. The DC supervises the work of the subordinate committees, where most policy issues are introduced and some settled. Occasionally, for high-priority initiatives or during crises, important issues are initiated at the DC level and not in the subordinate committees.

The NSC DC typically includes the deputy secretaries of State, Treasury, and Defense; the deputy attorney general; the deputy director of OMB; the deputy DNI (or the director of the NCTC, for counterterrorism issues); the vice chairman of the JCS; the deputy chief of staff to the president for policy; the vice president's national security advisor; and the deputy homeland security advisor.[41] The deputy national security advisor convenes and chairs the meeting (the deputy national security advisor for international economic affairs chairs meetings concerning economic issues with a slightly augmented membership). As with the PC, the NSC staff typically prepares and circulates a DC paper before the meeting. During crises, DC meetings often parallel PC meetings in order to follow up on the principals' decisions and ensure clear communication and coordination. This rhythm can drive an intense cascade of recurring meetings in the agencies to support both policy formulation and implementation.

Policy Coordination Committees. PCCs are interagency committees organized around specific geographic or functional policy areas. PCCs accomplish the bulk of the work of policy integration, adjudicate conflicts, and identify and frame issues for the deputies and principals. Sometimes the PCC elevates an issue to the DC for resolution; sometimes the DC makes a policy decision and sends it to the PCC to work out the details. The number and composition of PCCs vary over time.

The scope, membership, rank of participants, frequency, and authority of a PCC depend on the issues the PCC handles and the level of responsibility afforded it. Members typically include political appointees at the deputy-assistant-secretary or occasionally assistant-secretary level, senior agency officials, senior military officers from the Office of the Secretary of Defense and Joint Staff, and other experts. Membership is a mix of political and career officials. Though attendance is controlled, the roster is relatively flexible. Agencies will send representatives they feel should be involved, and White House staff will attend as circumstances and their portfolios require. An NSC senior director or an assistant secretary from a "lead agency" usually chairs, sometimes with an HSC cochair. Post-9/11, the number of NSC PCCs has expanded significantly, from seventeen PCCs at the start of the George W. Bush administration to thirty in 2005.[42] With HSC PCCs included, the number approaches forty.

A properly led PCC cultivates a sense of teamwork, encouraging collaboration and communication outside of scheduled meetings. Membership and working relationships straddle administrations, so PCCs handle few truly new issues. PCC chairs have no formal authority to override any one agency, making it easy to play defense and prevent consensus on a policy decision. The PCC has three choices: Compromise to achieve consensus, continue to search for common ground, or elevate disputes to the DC. Because PCCs must be selective about what they elevate, there is strong pressure to achieve consensus, which unfortunately can result in watered-down, least-common-denominator policy.[43]

The Counterterrorism Security Group.   The CSG warrants its own discussion, because a group like it will undoubtedly remain part of the decision-making system. The CSG is an NSC-chaired group of high-level counterterrorism and intelligence officials in the departments and agencies. It was established early in the Clinton administration as a midlevel working group that met two or three times per week (see Figure 10.3). After 9/11, George W. Bush created a new deputy national security advisor and director for combating terrorism who reported to both the national security advisor and the homeland security advisor and who assumed responsibility as chair of the CSG. In the years following 9/11, the CSG met every morning, usually by secure video teleconference, prior to the president's daily threat brief to share information and coordinate the U.S. response to evolving threats. During the George W. Bush administration, the CSG included the head of the FBI's Counterterrorism Division, the head of the CIA's Counterterrorism Center, the director of the NCTC, the Department of State coordinator for counterterrorism, the assistant secretary of defense for special operations and low-intensity conflict, and other officials in the Department of Justice, the Joint Staff, and the DHS.

Interagency Working Groups.   PCCs often establish subordinate working groups for high-priority initiatives or to coordinate certain activities. Some of

FIG. 10.3   Intersection "Machinery" of the Formal NSC and HSC Systems
(George H. W. Bush, Bill Clinton, and George W. Bush Administrations)

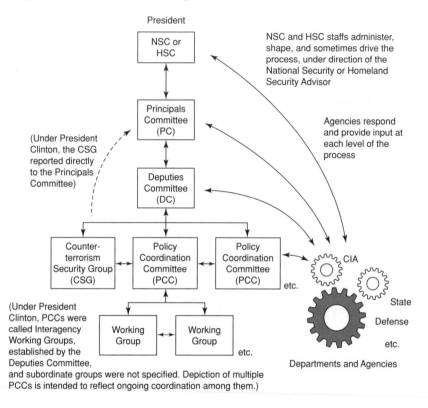

these groups endure as standing bodies, but many dissolve. Occasionally, the DC may establish an ad hoc working group, or the national security advisor may direct a member of the NSC staff to form a focused interagency working group on a policy initiative with the intent of introducing that initiative at the DC or PC level.

Substantive Products.   Many presidential decisions are conveyed orally in confidence to the president's advisors and cabinet secretaries. However, many decisions are communicated in writing, either as overarching statements of policy (e.g., the National Security Strategy [NSS]), guidance to the executive branch (e.g., a presidential directive on human trafficking), essential clarification (e.g., a presidential finding authorizing covert action), or requirements by law. Several such documents are common and important enough to warrant description.

Strategies.   Important articulations of national strategy occur in presidential speeches, which unequivocally reflect the president's thoughts. However, recent presidents have also found value in articulating policy in the form of national strategy documents, some of which are required by law. Since 1986, for example, the president has been required by the Goldwater-Nichols Act to prepare an annual NSS. As of mid-2007, George W. Bush had signed no fewer than fifteen NSSs. Producing such documents can become a major task of PCCs, the NSC and HSC staffs, and the key policy organs of the agencies.

While the Pentagon has a formal system of generating strategic documents, the process within the White House and the interagency system does not follow a similarly cyclical or methodical process. The lack of a rigorous, long-range strategy and planning function within the national security decision-making process has long been a criticism of the NSC staff and interagency system.

Presidential Directives.   Presidential directives are legally binding instruments for communicating presidential decisions about the national security policies of the United States. Most presidential directives include language intended to provide an overarching approach or strategy that must be interpreted, implemented, and reassessed. Because of their broad nature, the degree to which they remain legally binding over time is open to interpretation.

Executive Orders.   In contrast to presidential directives, which are generally broader in nature, executive orders are suitable for issues that can be addressed with specific and unambiguous direction to agencies. Executive orders are legally binding orders issued to federal agencies under the president's constitutional authority to "take care that the Laws be faithfully executed." Most executive orders are issued to carry out laws passed by Congress or rulings by the courts. Some executive orders set new policy.

As of 2006, there were over thirteen thousand consecutively numbered orders, many of which concern national security (and many of those are classified). For example, 97 of the 220 executive orders issued by George W. Bush through the end of 2006 (or about 44%) dealt with foreign policy, military, or homeland security issues (vs. about 33% of Clinton's orders). A modest number of other executive orders issued by both presidents dealt with international economic issues that have some bearing on national security.[44]

Assessing the Value of the Formal Interagency Process.   Sometimes the formal process does exactly as its billing promises: It ensures that the key details of important policy decisions are fully coordinated by agency experts and endorsed by the principals, paving the way for a significant and lasting national security or foreign policy success. The formal process adds value by establishing the setting. The routine machinations of the formal process create an essential foundation of coordination and foster relationships that are needed when nonroutine situations arise.

The formal process is particularly useful for coordinating the details of policy implementation once a presidential decision has been made. It helps ensure that information is not distorted as it moves upward to or downward from the president. It also helps reveal unexamined assumptions; minimizes the chance of overlooking

viable alternatives; and provides an opportunity for the full airing of costs, benefits, and risks. A solid body of scholarly research strongly suggests that such practices improve presidential decision making.[45] The process also provides a foundation for buy-in by the agencies. As former Secretary of State Henry Kissinger
recognized, "a foreign policy achievement to be truly significant must at some
point be institutionalized."[46] Agencies that have had the opportunity to have their
views considered are more likely to support the resulting decision.

Shortcomings of the Formal Process.   The formal process also has flaws and
shortcomings. This section briefly reviews limitations most often cited by presidents and their advisors.

Lack of Presidential Control of the Bureaucracy.   In the words of Senator
"Scoop" Jackson in 1965, the president "has been left in an unenviable position.
He has found it necessary to undertake an endless round of negotiations with his
own department heads."[47] The formal process can help the president rein in the
bureaucracy, but it can also be a hindrance—sometimes the president himself is
the one reined in.

Lack of Accountability.   The formal process, with cumbersome and dense interagency procedures and committees, may produce an overemphasis on coordination and dilute responsibility for policy planning and implementation. Pulling decision making out of the committee process and into the White House helps the
president establish responsibility and accountability among his cabinet and key
advisors for carrying out important decisions.

Inflexibility, Lack of Creativity, and Overcautiousness.   Formal meetings of bureaucrats sitting in their usual seats—with their agendas, position papers, and enu-
meration of second-order effects—do not tend to generate fresh thinking or risky
policy. A powerful example is the formal interagency policy review on the German unification question, National Security Review-5 (NSR-5), which concluded
in early 1989 that "it serves no U.S. interests for us to take the initiative to raise
[German unification]."[48] Frustrated and impatient, George H. W. Bush decided to
"create action-forcing events, including [two] presidential trips [to Europe] and
speeches that would oblige the government . . . to deploy ideas about the direction
of policy."[49] A year-and-a-half after the formal interagency review, a treaty reuni-
fying Germany as a full member of the North Atlantic Treaty Organization was
signed. The formal national security decision-making process did not assist, and
in fact impeded, a major foreign policy success of the last half century.

Inability to Keep Pace.   The world, the White House, and the bureaucracy move
at different speeds. The formal process is hard pressed to keep up with rapid
developments. Opportunities must be seized; nuance must be understood and

accommodated. It is often the march of events, not the methodical deliberation of White House and agency policy makers, that forces the broadest strokes of American policy to emerge.

The president's best chance for a legacy is in the foreign policy arena, and the president must assume that only four years will be available to accomplish it. But the formal process, in particular the PCC-level forums that survive in one form or another for successive administrations, does not mobilize in response to the electoral cycle.

"Death by a Thousand Cuts."   The formal system is geared toward consensus, because the deputies, principals, and the president cannot be called on to settle what a former NSC senior director has described as "extended interagency disputes too small to be seen without the aid of a magnifying glass."[50] Accommodation requires compromise; specific and prescriptive words get replaced with broad, noncommittal language in committee meetings. Presidential advisors have no authority to act as tiebreakers; if they do so without the explicit acquiescence of the group, they corrupt the integrity of the process. Even when a conflict reaches the president, consensus usually rules. "At every meeting," says Kissinger, "to gain the acquiescence of the potential recalcitrant, Nixon would offer so many modifications that the complex plan he was seeking to promote was eventually consumed."[51]

Lack of Confidentiality.   Nixon's explanation to his staff about the close-hold process that led to U.S. rapprochement with China effectively illustrates the problem of confidentiality: "Without secrecy, there would have been no invitation or acceptance to visit China."[52] Nixon argued that his bold stroke would have been impossible if he had received his advice through the formal national security decision-making process.

Lack of Strategic Coherence.   A major criticism of the NSC system and the NSC staff is its inability to do long-range planning. The NSC staff is uniquely positioned to administer such a function but tends to be drawn into the short-term world of deadlines and immediate political needs. President Dwight Eisenhower established a formal planning board to conduct strategic (if not grand strategic) planning, but that architecture was dismantled by Kennedy, and nothing similar has been resurrected.[53]

Role of the National Security Advisor

One person sits at the crossroads of the formal process and the unique needs of the president. It is often said that power in the executive branch is determined by proximity to the president, and few are more proximate than the national security advisor. Debate about the proper role of the national security advisor revolves around the degree to which he or she should be a policy-neutral honest broker, a policy advocate, or some combination of the two. This is largely determined by the president. Within the boundaries of the law, the national security advisor serves the president's needs.

Honest Broker.   There is broad consensus that the national security advisor and NSC staff must be the custodians of the formal interagency process. This involves: exercising quality control, conveying (and by necessity filtering) information, ensuring that relevant information and intelligence is available, conveying the president's views when authorized and appropriate, ensuring that a full range of options has been considered and prepared, ensuring that agency heads have an opportunity to express their views, accurately presenting those views to the president, guaranteeing the confidentiality of advice, accurately communicating decisions, and monitoring implementation of presidential decisions and policies.[54]

Policy Advocate.   Because national security advisors who act as advocates risk alienating the principals, policy advocacy is often seen as undermining effective brokerage. However, even effective brokers may have an obligation to express their views to the president within appropriate boundaries. For example, the president may need to hear an underrepresented point of view.[55] Sometimes, national security advisors faced with intransigent agencies and an unresponsive process have resorted to advocacy to move policy forward.[56]

Other Roles of the National Security Advisor.   Other controversial roles of the national security advisor, depicted in Figure 10.4, can be seen as extensions of the policy advocacy role. The roles of policy design, public communication, diplomacy, and certainly implementation all associate the advisor with specific policies. These additional roles may also serve as a source of tension with principals. For example, if the national security advisor represents the president's policies in the media, this

FIG. 10.4   Roles of the National Security Advisor and NSC Staff

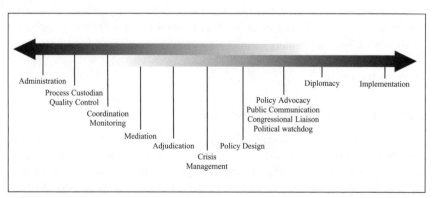

Modified and adapted from Christopher C. Shoemaker, *The NSC Staff: Counseling the Council* (San Francisco: Westview Press, 1991), 23.

may compete with the secretary of state's traditional role as the sole voice on foreign affairs. For reasons such as this, presidents are wise to ensure that their national security advisors can work collegially with the secretaries of state and defense.

What the President Needs: The Importance of Informal Process

Every president must balance the need for high-quality decisions with the need for consensus and the prudent use of time and other policymaking resources. The president also has limited windows of opportunity when circumstances and political forces align to make certain choices possible. Presidents need to be able to make decisions at different speeds and with different levels of effort.[57] For these reasons, every president has stepped outside the formal process to get advice.

Smaller, informal meetings foster essential collegiality and are more confidential, candid, and productive. Principals devote their energy and time for such meetings in a way that they do not for formal committees.[58] Principals bargain with one another, breaking the logjams produced by the formal process. Informal and one-on-one consultations also allow the president to draw on input from others without yielding any power in the process.[59] Because they have greater freedom to brainstorm and backtrack, informal groups can be more conducive to creativity.

Small, informal groups become particularly important to presidents during crises. All the factors impinging on presidential decision making become more acute, and the constraints become more formidable. The most famous example is Kennedy and the Cuban Missile Crisis. His ad hoc, advisory Executive Committee arrived at a course of action (a naval "quarantine") that can be interpreted as a successful result of informal process. Neustadt and Allison argue that the improvised procedures of this group gave Kennedy's advisors "the very things they needed, under circumstances bound to minimize parochialism, strengthening their sense of common service to the top."[60]

However, small informal groups are prone to a variety of flaws common to faulty decision processes. There is the possibility of groupthink, which can lead to excessive optimism and risk taking, discounting warnings, ignoring ethical and moral consequences, stereotyping adversaries, pressuring group members who express strong dissenting arguments, self-censoring of doubts and counterarguments, sharing the illusion of unanimity concerning judgments, and self-appointed "mind guards" who shelter the group from adverse information that challenges the group's thinking.[61] Another problem with small groups is that they shut out of the process officials in the departments and agencies who need access and guidance. Moreover, there is reason to be concerned that small groups might have difficulty managing multiple crises at once.

Improving the Prospects for Good Decisions

Presidents choose management models that fit their personality, their management style, and their needs. Richard Tanner Johnson has categorized presidential management models into three types: formalistic (president at the top, orderly policy procedure, hierarchical; example: Eisenhower), collegial (president at the center, informal procedures, decision-making team led by the president; example: Kennedy), and competitive (president at the top, organizational ambiguity, multiple channels of communication to the president, encouragement of debate; example: Franklin D. Roosevelt).[62] One can group the descriptions of presidential management and leadership in Chapter 4 into these categories, which each have advantages and disadvantages. A formal decision-making process is less prone to erroneous assumptions but restricts the information flow to the president and obscures covert bargaining among advisors.[63] A collegial approach gives the president greater control of the process but is extremely demanding of the president's time and energy.[64] A competitive approach ensures that the president retains control over the majority of decisions but breeds dysfunction and mistrust in the staff and cabinet.

Looking Ahead

The president's job is unique and uniquely demanding, with impossibly broad responsibility, high expectations, and a relatively weak management hand in practice. Domestic politics frame every choice, even if the president chooses to disregard or minimize their significance. The challenges are multiplying as the problem of homeland security has blurred distinctions between the traditional national security and domestic policy realms. The complexity of national security policy has increased, resulting in more specialized functions, greater interrelatedness among issues, and a larger bureaucracy, while congressional committees remain as dispersed and distinct as ever. New entities, such as the DNI and interagency centers, promise to improve coordination in key functional areas, but they also complicate decision making.

As a result, the incentive for future presidents to pull national security policy further into the White House is growing. Their use of informal processes and confidential advice is likely to rise, and the trend that national security advisors perform roles other than that of the broadly accepted honest broker is likely to continue. Large White House national security policy staffs are more likely to exist than not, and a hierarchical, multilayered interagency committee architecture is likely to endure. While the formal national security decision-making process becomes more important as a means to effect interagency coordination, its value as an advisory system may decline.

Can the institutional presidency realistically handle the full burden of national security policy development and coordination across the executive branch? Constitutionally, of course, the president alone bears the responsibility. Practically, someone with a manageable scope of responsibility is needed to sit above the departments and agencies with the legal authority to herd their efforts. Earlier in this chapter, it is noted that the president has three options with any coordination challenge: (1) coordinate it, (2) leave it alone, or (3) tell the agencies to coordinate with each other. There is a fourth option: Delegate to someone else with sufficient legal authority. The DNI is the first such entity and may become a model for further reforms in the national security decision-making process in the coming years.

Post-9/11 changes to the national security decision-making process have been largely structural, as this chapter emphasizes. However, future adjustments may well involve changes in how national security personnel are managed. A growing chorus is calling for legislation to require national security personnel to receive some form of interagency education or serve in agencies other than their "home agency" in order to advance in their careers. As discussed in Chapter 5, the Goldwater-Nichols Act of 1986 created similar requirements among the military services. Whether the Goldwater-Nichols Act can serve as a useful precedent for the broader national security community remains to be seen.

Discussion Questions

1. If you were just hired to the policy staff of the NSC, what issues from Chapters 4 through 10 of this book would you most keep in mind?
2. How does the nature of the U.S. political system affect the national security decision-making process? How has this changed over time?
3. What factors have contributed to the growth of government over the last decade? What positive or negative effects might this have on policy and decision making?
4. Given the importance of career civil servants, should the Congress require that national security professionals rotate through various agencies throughout their careers?
5. How have the coordination challenges facing the NSC and HSC and their staffs grown more complex since 9/11?
6. Is it possible to move some of the growing interagency coordination burden outside of the presidency? How? What would the president gain or lose as a result?
7. Can the formal interagency process be improved? What changes might be appropriate, and what would be their advantages and disadvantages?
8. What are the appropriate roles for the national security advisor, and why? How might those roles evolve? What will happen to decision making as a result?
9. If you were the president-elect of the United States, what management style—formalist, collegial, competitive—would you adopt, and why?
10. If you were president, what informal advisory arrangements would you institute? What would you look for in the first six months of your term to determine whether your advisory structures were serving you well?

Recommended Reading

Allison, Graham T., and Philip Zelikow. *Essence of Decision: Explaining the Cuban Missile Crisis.* 2nd ed. New York: Longman, 1999.

Burke, John P. "The Neutral/Honest Broker Role in Foreign-Policy Decision Making: A Reassessment." *Presidential Studies Quarterly* 35, no. 2 (2005): 229–258.

Burke, John P., and Fred I. Greenstein. *How Presidents Test Reality: Decisions on Vietnam, 1954 and 1967.* New York: Russell Sage Foundation, 1989.

Destler, I. M. "National Security Advice to U.S. Presidents: Some Lessons from Thirty Years." *World Politics* 29, no. 2 (1977): 143–176.

George, Alexander L. "The Case for Multiple Advocacy in Making Foreign Policy." *American Political Science Review* 66, no. 3 (1972): 751–785.

———. *Presidential Decisionmaking in Foreign Policy: The Effective Use of Information and Advice.* Boulder, CO: Westview Press, 1980.

Haney, Patrick J. *Organizing for Foreign Policy Crises: Presidents, Advisors, and the Management of Decision Making.* Ann Arbor: University of Michigan Press, 1997.

Heclo, Hugh, and Lester M. Salamon, ed. *The Illusion of Presidential Government.* Boulder, CO: Westview Press, 1981.

Janis, Irving Lester. *Groupthink: Psychological Studies of Policy Decisions and Fiascoes.* Boston: Houghton Mifflin, 1982.

Johnson, Richard Tanner. *Managing the White House: An Intimate Study of the Presidency.* New York: Harper & Row, 1974.

Neustadt, Richard E. *Presidential Power and the Modern Presidents.* 3rd ed. New York: Free Press, 1990.

Porter, Roger B. *Presidential Decision Making: The Economic Policy Board.* New York: Cambridge University Press, 1980.

Rothkopf, David J. *Running the World: The Inside Story of the National Security Council and the Architects of American Power.* New York: Public Affairs, 2005.

Wilson, James Q. *Bureaucracy: What Government Agencies Do and Why They Do It.* New York: Basic Books, Inc., 1989.

Internet Sources

Homeland Security Council, www.whitehouse.gov/hsc

National Security Council, www.whitehouse.gov/nsc

The 9/11 Commission Report, www.9-11commission.gov/report/911Report.pdf

Office of the Director of National Intelligence, www.dni.gov

U.S. Department of Defense, www.defenselink.mil

U.S. Department of Homeland Security, www.dhs.gov

U.S. Department of State, www.state.gov

III

National Security Policy: Ways and Means of National Strategy

11

Shaping the International Environment

Dean Acheson, one of America's wisest and most successful secretaries of state once said, "The purpose for which we carry on relations with foreign states is to preserve and foster an environment in which free societies may exist and flourish. Our policies and actions must be tested by whether they contribute to or detract from achievement of this end."[1] Shaping the environment in a far from malleable world is a continuing major challenge requiring all the instruments of national power, including diplomatic, information, military, economic, and a range of other tools.[2]

In addition to being able to induce other nations to act in ways that it desires through its capacity to wield carrots and sticks, the United States has historically been a powerful magnet that has attracted other nations to align with U.S. policy. This capacity to attract—to get others to identify with its objectives and to cooperate with its policies—is sometimes referred to as *soft power*, in contrast to the *hard power* of military force. Among the various soft power instruments are diplomacy, foreign aid, trade assistance or denial, partnerships, alliances, leadership of international organizations, humanitarian activities, international public health operations, cultural and educational exchanges, public diplomacy, military posture, and international mediation. Several of these are discussed in this chapter, with economic instruments discussed in the next chapter. Of course, one of the principle sources of America's soft power is the example it provides by the success of its values and institutions, reflected in the attraction it holds for immigrants across the globe.

Many of the soft power tools of the United States are not wielded by the government, but by the private sector. Private foundations, religious entities, nongovernmental organizations, and other civic institutions have enormous capacities

233

to serve the public good abroad as well as at home. In some cases, such as in the field of public health, cooperative public-private efforts are highly effective. Enlisting these private sector assets and activities in a common effort to shape the international environment in ways that foster and protect free societies requires a measure of trust on all sides, which has not always been the case.

Diplomacy

Diplomacy is the first-resort instrument in the nation's policy tool kit. It can be defined as "the management of international relations by negotiation; the method by which these relations are adjusted and managed by ambassadors and envoys; the business or art of the diplomatists."[3] The goal of American diplomacy is to advance and secure national interests to the greatest degree possible without generating conflict or inspiring resentment. Although, as noted in Chapter 2, diplomacy has traditionally been devalued or distrusted by many Americans, it is an essential tool in the nation's array of instruments of power.

Diplomacy is rarely used in isolation; it often serves as a precursor or a complement to other foreign policy tools. Given the complexity of the challenges and threats that the United States faces, America pursues diplomacy through many methods. Among the most significant are: exchanging envoys, creating or adapting international institutions, participating in international meetings, establishing alliances, and signing treaties. These methods are pursued in different arrangements, including bilateral, multilateral, and regional relationships.

Bilateral diplomacy is conducted between two states and is a common form of international diplomacy. Forms of bilateral diplomacy include treaties, military and cultural exchanges, and bilateral agreements. Examples of U.S. bilateral diplomacy include the exchanges of military officers and cadets at foreign military schools; bilateral trade agreements, such as the U.S.-Canada Free Trade Agreement of 1990; and bilateral security arrangements, such as the Anti-Ballistic Missile Treaty of 1972.[4] A main benefit of bilateral diplomacy is flexibility, as the realm of possible agreement between two parties is typically larger than for multiparty groups.

The international system has developed a number of customs for bilateral diplomacy. For example, most states sacrifice a small measure of their own national sovereignty to host embassies and ambassadors from other nations. The embassy property is considered to be the territory of the visiting state rather than the territory of the host country, and ambassadors are granted diplomatic immunity from prosecution. In addition, it is generally understood that governments gather intelligence and provide information on other states following generally accepted norms and practices.

Multilateral diplomacy includes treaties, exchanges, activities, and agreements conducted among three or more countries. Multilateral diplomacy is also practiced through U.S. membership in international institutions and organizations, such as the United Nations (UN) and the World Trade Organization (WTO), Geneva Convention ratification, and Group of Eight (G8) participation. The

United States relies heavily on such organizations and its leadership in them to advance its interests.

Several traditions endure in multilateral diplomacy as well as in bilateral diplomacy. While the international system is without an international government, generally accepted rules provide some order to multilateral activities. For example, UN membership is granted to governments demonstrating sovereign control over historically recognized geographic boundaries, regardless of the popular support such a government enjoys. UN membership obligates members to assume the commitments of previous governments, acknowledge established borders, and commit to noninterference in the domestic affairs of other states.[5]

The relative weight of an individual state's influence in multilateral diplomatic forums depends on the rules of the forum itself. UN rules grant extra influence to members of the Security Council (the five permanent council members—U.S., Great Britain, France, Russia, and China—as well as rotating seats among ten other member states). In contrast, the WTO grants one vote for each member state regardless of size or influence. Other organizations, such as the International Monetary Fund (IMF), grant influence and voting rights based on a country's financial contribution. Because the United States is the IMF's largest financial supporter, it generally has the most influence of any single nation in the IMF.[6]

Multilateral diplomacy is thus more complex but also potentially more powerful. Securing and advancing U.S. interests in large organizations is difficult, but when achieved, it can generally produce more powerful and lasting policies. An additional consideration for the use of multilateral diplomacy is the increasing complexity and interdependence of America's national interests in an era of globalization. As transportation and information technology have increased the interaction among states in tourism and commerce, for example, multilateral diplomacy has become increasingly important. The threats to U.S. interests have also become increasingly global, because transnational threats, such as environmental destruction, terrorism, and crime, require more than unilateral and bilateral commitments and actions.

Regional diplomacy is one specific and common type of multilateral diplomacy in which relations are conducted by states in a specific geographic region. States in a particular region have a greater stake in the area's economic, security, and environmental issues. As a result, states often choose regional solutions because of their relative simplicity in negotiation and implementation.

Regional diplomacy often takes place through regionally based international organizations. For example, the European Union is an international body affecting the economic policy, security policy, and foreign affairs of its twenty-seven member states. Similarly, the Organization of American States engages the full range of its thirty-five members' interests. Other examples of regional government organizations include the Gulf Cooperation Council and the Association of Southeast Asian Nations. The map in Figure 11.1 depicts some current regional organizations and their memberships.[7]

While regional diplomacy can focus on broad issues of governance, some regional diplomacy is focused on an individual issue area. For example, the North

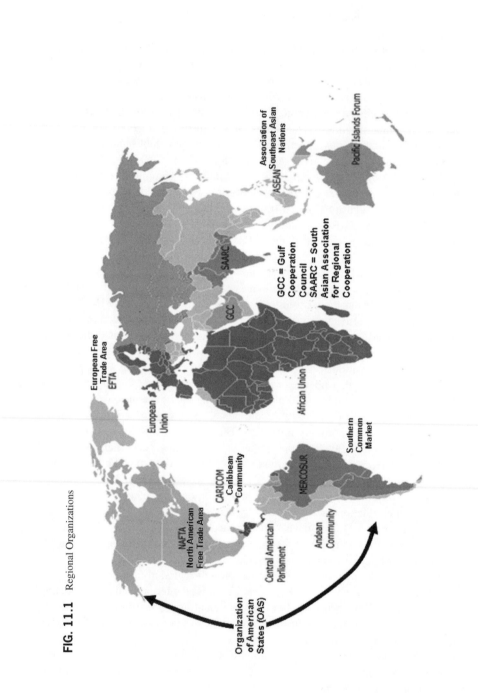

FIG. 11.1 Regional Organizations

European Free Trade Area EFTA

European Union

SAARC

GCC

African Union

Association of Southeast Asian Nations ASEAN

Pacific Islands Forum

GCC = Gulf Cooperation Council
SAARC = South Asian Association for Regional Cooperation

NAFTA North American Free Trade Area

CARICOM Caribbean Community

Central American Parliament

Andean Community

MERCOSUR

Southern Common Market

Organization of American States (OAS)

American Free Trade Agreement (NAFTA) is purely a trade agreement between the United States, Canada, and Mexico designed to reduce barriers to economic exchange among the member states. This agreement institutionalizes free trade practices and helps each state overcome the protectionist motivations of some domestic constituencies. The result has been more trade and greater overall economic welfare for all members of NAFTA.[8]

Given the U.S. position as a superpower, American diplomatic efforts can be highly influential, especially as it simultaneously practices diplomacy in multiple forms. For example, consider the problem of North Korea potentially pursuing nuclear technology with which it could threaten the interests of several other nations.   To face this challenge, the United States has promoted six-party talks, which include South Korea, China, Japan, and Russia, to negotiate solutions with North Korea. The United States has chosen multilateral diplomacy to capitalize on common interests between itself and traditional allies, such as South Korea and Japan, as well as to enlist the relative influence of regionally powerful states, such as China and Russia. Multilateral diplomacy sustains U.S. engagement while leveraging the influence of regional powers with common interests. Deciding whether to engage in multilateral diplomacy involves weighing the potential value of multilateral solutions against the complexity of securing their adoption.

Diplomatic efforts, while potentially powerful, are subject to several limitations. First, compromises are frequently required to achieve diplomatic solutions, as exemplified by the many efforts to gain UN Security Council approval of sanctions on Saddam Hussein's Iraq. Second, significant patience is often required because it takes time for diplomatic solutions to be reached and then implemented, as evidenced frequently in the Arab-Israeli peace process. Third, the relatively small size of the State Department as the chief agency for diplomacy—especially in comparison with U.S. investment in the military instrument of power—limits the institutional capacity of the U.S. government to pursue diplomatic initiatives. For example, the 2008 federal budget allocated only \$35 billion to the State Department. This amount includes foreign aid and provides for only about 30,000 personnel. The same year, the Department of Defense (DoD) budget was \$481 billion (not including the costs of the wars in Iraq and Afghanistan), and the defense workforce included approximately 3 million personnel.[9]

Finally, domestic political conditions can significantly affect a national leader's flexibility in diplomacy. International negotiations, whether they are bilateral, multilateral, or regional, generally reflect a "two-level game."[10] At the international level, policy makers are often constrained in how much they can negotiate based upon their particular domestic political situation. For example, President Woodrow Wilson sought to bring the United States into the League of Nations after the World War I, but his weak domestic position resulted in this proposal's being rejected by the U.S. Senate.[11] On the other hand, domestic political dominance or a particular reputation at home can permit greater flexibility abroad. For instance, President Richard Nixon's reputation as a staunch anticommunist enhanced his flexibility in bringing the relationship between the United States and

LURIE'S WORLD   O/86 Sep 26 '95

"You may now kiss the bride."

Copyright 1995 CARTOONEWS INTERNATIONAL Syndicate, N.Y.C., USA. Reprinted with permission of Ranan Lurie

the People's Republic of China from confrontation to détente in the 1970s. Finally, the need to seek an international agreement can be used by a national leader to advance a particular domestic agenda. For example, international agreements can enable the leaders of developing countries to pursue otherwise unpopular policies of fiscal restraint when these policies are linked to continuing favorable international loans or trade arrangements.

During the past century, the focus of American diplomacy has undergone considerable change. Early in the twentieth century, the United States followed a doctrine termed *dollar diplomacy*, which was designed to advance economic interests abroad. Diplomatic efforts were primarily focused on economic issue areas. From 1914 until the United States entered the war in 1917, World War I shaped U.S. diplomatic efforts as it pursued diplomacy to support the Allied victory in Europe. As discussed in Chapter 2, following World War I, the United States tried again to turn its back on the world outside the Western Hemisphere. To the extent America was engaged abroad, diplomacy was focused on disarmament and conducted largely through international conferences, which attempted, unsuccessfully, to find diplomatic ways to limit the chance and severity of war.[12]

Also discussed in Chapter 2, following World War II, the U.S. approach toward diplomacy was transformed, becoming explicitly activist and multilateral to support the exercise of U.S. global leadership. The United States served as the key player in constructing postwar international institutions designed to support an open international economic order as well as cooperation in the areas of international peace and security. From the late 1940s, U.S. foreign policy was conducted in a bipolar context, focused largely on containment and deterrence of communism and particularly on the threat posed by the Soviet Union. During the 1970s and 1980s, U.S. diplomacy centered on preventing nuclear war through the Nuclear Non-Proliferation Treaty, the Strategic Arms Limitation Treaties, the Anti-Ballistic Missile Treaty, and the Intermediate-Range and Short-Range Nuclear Forces (INF) Treaty. From the fall of the Soviet Union in 1990–1991 to the terrorist attacks of September 11, 2001, U.S. diplomacy focused particularly on the integration into the West and development of the former communist states, nonproliferation and counterproliferation efforts aimed at securing the nuclear weapons and materials of former Soviet States, and securing support for peacekeeping and stability operations in regional and ethnic conflicts. Since 9/11, U.S. diplomatic efforts have centered on building and maintaining support for its efforts to combat international terrorism while continuing to promote regional stability and American economic interests.

The level of U.S. diplomacy has evolved over time as well. Prior to, during, and after World War I, U.S. involvement in world affairs was limited, episodic, and not truly reflective of America's growing relative power. World War II marked a watershed as the United States assumed an activist leadership role it has never since relinquished. During the Cold War, the United States, as one of two superpowers, led in the prevention of nuclear war through the threat of mutually assured destruction and combating the spread of communism worldwide.

Following the Cold War, the United States has become a hegemonic leader, pursuing its interests unilaterally in some cases, through international institutions in others, and through a variety of multilateral and regional diplomatic efforts. While the ability of the United States to effectively conduct diplomacy is an essential dimension of the nation's foreign policy, its successful practice in the context of American values and history is extraordinarily difficult. Former Secretary of State Henry Kissinger has suggested some of the challenges:

> In the twentieth century, no country has influenced international relations as decisively and at the same time as ambivalently as the United States. No society has more firmly insisted on the inadmissibility of intervention in the domestic affairs of other states, or more passionately asserted that its own values were universally applicable. No nation has been more pragmatic in the day-to-day conduct of its diplomacy, or more ideological in the pursuit of its historic moral convictions. No country has been more reluctant to engage itself abroad even while undertaking alliances and commitments of unprecedented reach and scope.[13]

Information Element of Power

The information element of national power can be defined as the use of information resources (including print media, radio, television, and the Internet) to collect, control, and disseminate information that influences the perceptions and behaviors of international audiences. In his book *Soft Power: The Means to Succeed in World Politics*, Joseph Nye notes that governments can exert influence through threats, inducements, or attraction.[14] He asserts that attraction, which relies primarily on others' perceptions, is generally the most cost-effective way to influence others' long-term behavior. The information instrument of national power directly affects perceptions and attitudes, which, in turn, can influence other countries' behavior.

Although the ongoing information revolution has increased the potential significance of the information instrument of national power, it has simultaneously become more difficult to manage and perhaps impossible to control. Information technology enables corporations, individuals, and other nonstate actors to create and rapidly disseminate information for a wide variety of purposes. Of course, movies, television programs, and other entertainment forms also affect perceptions and attitudes at home and abroad. Confronting this complex environment, it is important to understand the various ways in which governments deal with information as it complements diplomatic, military, economic, and other elements of power.

The use of information as an instrument of power is problematic for the U.S. government for at least three important reasons. First, government control of information raises the specter of propaganda that could undermine democratic institutions, impede a free press, and contravene liberties that the American political culture appropriately cherishes. Consequently, facilitating such government control of information is fraught with difficulty. Second, the information provided to an international audience can only be as effective as the policy that it is attempting to promote. If a particular U.S. policy is unfriendly or hostile toward another nation or region, no amount of salesmanship is likely to make that policy palatable.[15] Finally, as a reflection of the American ambivalence toward government control of information, no one agency or department has control of strategic communications. In fact, as noted in the remainder of this section, different government agencies use different terminology, which further complicates understanding.

The term *strategic communications* is sometimes used to describe information as an element of power, because the term implies the use of communication resources to achieve national strategic objectives. A government task force that examined strategic communications divided the topic into four areas of government operations: public diplomacy, public affairs, international broadcasting, and international military information.[16] These concepts are discussed in turn below.

Public diplomacy consists of those efforts by a government to inform or influence the population of a foreign state through direct or indirect communication. Public diplomacy is differentiated from traditional diplomacy (described in the first section of this chapter), because the object of traditional diplomacy is the government of a foreign state, while the target of public diplomacy is the foreign population itself. Direct communication includes government information, media broadcasts, government seminars, meetings with foreign citizens, and other direct contacts between U.S. government individuals or agencies and a foreign population. Indirect forms of public diplomacy include student exchanges, cultural activities, economic engagement, and other events in which foreign populations are exposed to Americans.

Immediately after World War II, the Office of War Information, which had run "the largest propaganda operation in the world," was shut down and was relegated to a small office in the State Department lest the nation be tempted to reinvigorate a large, government-run propaganda operation.[17] As the Cold War progressed, however, the Eisenhower administration created the United States Information Agency (USIA) in 1953, which was designed to counter the Soviet ideological threat with information. Although an independent agency, USIA worked closely with the State Department to operate U.S. Information Services offices throughout the world that provided libraries, books, and publications in hundreds of foreign cities. After the end of the Cold War in 1999, USIA was merged with (and submerged within) the State Department. Public diplomacy has continued to be most directly associated with the State Department, but it is much wider in its sponsorship and activities. Although the George W. Bush administration increased public diplomacy spending and increased its bureaucratic profile somewhat, its status pales in comparison to the emphasis on public diplomacy in the Cold War.

Public affairs, which consist of activities conducted by all government agencies, are intended to provide Americans with accurate information about what their government is doing. Public affairs are distinguished from public diplomacy essentially by target (public affairs focus on domestic audiences, and public diplomacy on foreign audiences). Though this distinction is important, its practical significance has diminished significantly as information technology has advanced and news cycles have compressed. A press conference at the White House or State Department in Washington is instantaneously broadcast around the world and frequently includes content that is designed to influence or "spin" both foreign and domestic audiences. Similarly, a press statement that is made by a U.S. official in Baghdad or Beijing may be intended primarily for the foreign audience but will play to a domestic U.S. audience as well. From an organizational perspective, however, U.S. government agencies maintain the distinction because of the sensitivity of appearing to propagandize domestic audiences.

International broadcasting services funded by the U.S. government transmit news, information, public affairs programs, and entertainment programs to foreign audiences through radio, television, and Web-based systems. During the Cold War, Radio Liberty and Radio Free Europe were part of USIA and extended the mission of public diplomacy onto the air waves. This has continued with Radio Free Asia, Radio and TV Marti directed at Cuba, and the Al Hurra radio and TV stations that broadcast in the Arab world. These serve the same basic purpose as public diplomacy discussed above, are indeed part of public diplomacy, and are only distinguished by the medium—broadcast networks—that conveys the information. These broadcasts compete with other media as they attempt to reach their target audiences. During the Cold War, the challenge was technological: Most information was controlled by the Soviet Union, and USIA broadcasts sought to reach as deeply as possible behind the Iron Curtain. Currently, the challenge is competing with multiple radio, television, and Internet information sources, many of which have approaches that do not favor U.S. policy. To provide any news that is balanced or perspectives that may favor U.S. policy, broadcasters must first attract audiences through entertaining or informative programming.

International military information (IMI) addresses the military's role in strategic communications. Military officials most frequently use the term *information operations* to describe what the DoD conducts in this area. Information operations entail the integrated employment of several types of operations, "in concert with specific supporting and related capabilities, to influence, disrupt, corrupt, or usurp adversarial human and automated decision making while protecting our own."[18] This definition expands beyond merely providing messages to inform and influence target audiences and includes military operations that target the physical and information infrastructure upon which information operations depend. A brief review of the five major components of information operations illuminates this distinction.

Psychological operations seek to influence the perceptions of foreign populations, military organizations, or decision makers in a favorable way. Psychological operations are closely related to public diplomacy and are distinguished by the fact that they are conducted or directed by military organizations in support of a military campaign. They may include the use of broadcast and print media, advertising, or leaflet drops.

The other four capabilities are actually components of military operations, but because of their impact on the control, processing, and dissemination of information, the DoD includes them in the broad definition of information operations. *Military deception* consists of actions taken to deliberately mislead the enemy to help accomplish the military mission. *Operations security* protects information about military operations so that enemy forces can not use that information to their advantage. *Electronic warfare* uses both offensive measures, such as jamming to attack enemy systems, and defensive measures, such as encryption, to protect the friendly military capability to communicate using electronic systems. Finally, *computer network operations* expand electronic warfare to the computer age and include the capability to attack, defend, and exploit computer systems as part of military operations.

While information operations have the potential to significantly aid a military campaign, military wielding of the information element of power can also be problematic because of concerns that a military-controlled propaganda machine could exercise excessive power. For example, the DoD established the Office of Strategic Influence soon after the attacks of 9/11 with the intent of "developing a full spectrum influence strategy that would result in greater foreign support of U.S. goals and repudiation of terrorists and their methods." While a laudable objective, the specter of military officials manipulating information, peddling propaganda, or deliberately providing misleading or incorrect information in foreign media led to a significant backlash among public affairs officials, the media, and others. The Secretary of Defense disestablished the office less than six months after it had been created.[19]

Since then, the U.S. government has continued to struggle to create an organizational structure that could successfully manage information. In 2002, the White House established an Office of Global Communications to coordinate strategic communications with global audiences and to advise on strategic direction and themes for the U.S. government.[20] This office is charged with coordinating the strategic communication activities of various government agencies, such as the Department of State and DoD, but has not assumed an activist, leadership role. The Department of State, which has created a new post of undersecretary for public diplomacy, continues to have organizational primacy in issues of strategic communications. The office of the new undersecretary has secured an increased budget for public diplomacy and has thereby somewhat increased information dissemination, cultural exchanges, speaking engagements, and other related activities. But the worldwide negative public view of America calls for a far more vigorous public diplomacy effort than that mounted thus far. The current public diplomacy budget (about $1.5 billion in 2007) is smaller than the comparable effort by France. Policy, however, is extremely difficult to coordinate within the U.S. government, and even the best public diplomacy efforts can be affected by nongovernmental actors who shape American interaction with the populations of other nations.

Although information is an important component of national power, it will remain one of the most difficult to manage and execute. A renewed emphasis to strengthen it and manage it better is clearly required.

Military Posture

Beyond the actual employment of military force, the United States shapes the international environment through its military force structure and basing during peacetime. Military posture includes the size, equipment, readiness, positioning, and exercising of military units and strategic assets. A strong military posture can reassure allies, deter enemies, and dissuade potential future adversaries from engaging in bellicose behavior or competitive military buildups.

During the Cold War, the United States stationed hundreds of thousands of troops in Europe, as part of the North Atlantic Treaty Organization (NATO), to deter a Soviet attack. They routinely trained with the armed forces of NATO allies, and U.S. commanders assumed primary leadership roles in NATO. After the armistice ended the Korean War in 1953, the U.S. also maintained a large military presence on the Korean peninsula and in Japan. In addition to these significant and sustained commitments, the United States negotiated basing rights with many countries and used Naval forces in joint exercises and port calls to literally "show the flag" in areas of importance to U.S. national security. A forward military presence in strategically critical areas reinforced diplomatic efforts to contain communism and promote U.S. and allied interests in stability and prosperity.

Following the demise of the Soviet Union, it took some time for the United States to adjust its military posture to the post–Cold War environment. However, a reduction in U.S. forces began almost immediately, and some global repositioning was facilitated by the war to liberate Kuwait from Iraqi occupation in 1990–1991. An entire U.S. Army Corps of over one hundred thousand soldiers and their equipment was deployed from Germany to the Persian Gulf and subsequently redeployed to the United States. Though it triggered a degree of withdrawal from Europe, this deployment also demonstrated the continued value of some forward basing. Military officials stressed that Europe was "an ocean closer" to many areas of concern, a fact that was again significant when American forces deployed to the Balkans later in the 1990s.[21]

Following the 9/11 attacks on the United States, the focus of U.S. military and diplomatic efforts became the prevention of terrorist attacks, the destruction of terrorist networks, and the prevention or countering of weapons of mass destruction proliferation. To accomplish these tasks, the United States further shifted its military posture by reducing its forward-deployed presence in Europe and South Korea, increasing its presence in Central Asia, and seeking to develop a more agile and deployable force based within the United States.

The Quadrennial Defense Review of 2005–2006 described five requirements for the U.S. global security posture.[22] First, allied participation in peacekeeping and combating terrorism must be further encouraged, and related efforts to assist allies in modernizing their military capabilities must be increased. Second, assets must be positioned to enable the greatest possible flexibility. Third, forces must be ready and capable of projecting across as well as within regions worldwide. Fourth, international support and transit agreements must support rapid-force projection. Fifth, capabilities, rather than sizes of units or quantities of equipment, must be the basis for planning.

As the United States reduces the number of forward-deployed units, it must consider the political, economic, and strategic realities of the current international environment. Withdrawing forces from Europe and South Korea has a significant impact on local economies and a political impact on U.S. relationships in each region. For example, U.S. and South Korean interests are naturally aligned against the common threat of North Korean aggression. However, if the U.S. priority for forces on the Korean Peninsula evolves to counterproliferation or to regional crisis response, that development has the potential to strain a longstanding alliance. As the U.S. military posture changes, major diplomatic efforts are critical to reassure allies of its commitments while simultaneously securing greater participation and cooperation against international security problems of common concern.

Beyond using its military posture to influence the international security environment through deterrence, dissuasion, and reassurance, the U.S. programs its forces to engage in various peacetime activities, military training exercises, and military exchanges that also enhance U.S. security relationships. As they continue to modify military posture over time, U.S. policy makers would have to consider the diplomatic, political, and economic—as well as purely military—ramifications of their choices.[23]

Other Soft Power Instruments

The use of economic instruments is discussed in Chapter 12 and alliances in Chapter 13. Development assistance is treated in Chapter 12, and in greater detail with regard to Africa in Chapter 21. Here we will focus on only one other major soft power instrument: global health.

Throughout the developing world, there is a severely limited capacity to meet basic health needs. There is an estimated global shortage of more than 4 million health-care workers, and new training centers to train more health care providers are badly needed. Investments in hospitals, clinics, and other infrastructure are similarly required. Clean water supplies are vital to health, yet the World Health Organization estimates that at least 1 billion people do not have access to clean water. Compared with other parts of the challenge, this crippling problem would be relatively inexpensive to correct. American leadership in meeting these needs, which is well within U.S. combined public-private capacity, would send a powerful signal to the international community that the United States is committed to advancing toward this common goal.

A recent report observes, "Health is vital to development. It is also vital for human and national security, for economic growth, and for building stable ties between countries. It is fundamental to every family's livelihood and existence."[24] Given the intrinsic importance of health and the glaring inadequacies of current global health care, there may be no more important means to favorably shape the international environment than by increased American efforts to help improve this situation. Fortunately, the U.S. has substantial assets to deploy. There are already numerous effective private initiatives ready to be strengthened and expanded. The U.S. government has considerable experience in providing development assistance in this field, particularly in Africa. A focused, increased effort to address global health needs is clearly warranted.

Conclusion

Diplomacy, information, and military posture are three significant instruments that the United States can employ to achieve its national security policy ends. These means must be integrated with the economic instrument (discussed in the next chapter) using a holistic approach to shape the international environment. Considering all these instruments of power together can enable policy makers to leverage the strengths and mitigate the weaknesses of each to maximum advantage for the United States.

Discussion Questions

1. What is the purpose of diplomacy, and what elements comprise U.S. diplomatic efforts?

2. Compare and contrast *multilateral diplomacy* with *bilateral diplomacy*. When might each be most useful?

3. Identify some of the limitations of diplomatic efforts. How might these limitations be overcome?

4. Discuss the role of public diplomacy in U.S. foreign policy. Is public diplomacy increasing in importance? Why or why not?

5. What are the ethical considerations associated with the U.S. government's use of the information instrument of power?

6. Many believe that international broadcasting programs, such as Voice of America, present a pro-American view of current events. Would it be better to instead present the full spectrum of views on an issue in an open forum?

7. How has the U.S. military posture changed since World War II? Since the end of the Cold War? Is the current posture appropriate for the threats facing the United States?

8. What diplomacy and information measures are appropriate complements to U.S. changes in military posture?

Recommended Reading

Bartholomees, J. Boone, ed. *U.S. Army War College Guide to National Security Policy and Strategy.* 2nd ed. Carlisle Barracks, PA: U.S. Army War College, 2006.

Carter, Ashton B., and William J. Perry. *Preventive Defense.* Washington, DC: Brookings Institution, 1999.

Department of Defense. *Joint Publication 3–13: Information Operations.* Washington, DC: GPO, 2006.

Hastedt, Glenn. *American Foreign Policy, Past, Present, Future.* 6th ed. New York: Prentice Hall, 2005.

Hogan, Michael J., and Thomas G. Paterson, eds. *Explaining the History of American Foreign Relations.* 2nd ed. Cambridge: Cambridge University Press, 2004.

Ikenberry, G. John. *America Unrivaled: The Future of the Balance of Power.* Ithaca, NY: Cornell University Press, 2002.

Joint Publication 3-13. *Information Operations* (Washington, DC: Government Printing Office, February 2006), GL-7.

Jones, Frank. "Information: The Psychological Instrument." In *U.S. Army War College Guide to National Security Policy and Strategy.* Edited by Bartholomees, J. Boone. Carlisle Barracks, PA: U.S. Army War College, 2006.

Kennan, George. *American Diplomacy.* Chicago: University of Chicago Press, 1963.

Kissinger, Henry. *Diplomacy.* New York: Simon & Schuster, 1994.

Mead, Walter Russell. *Special Providence: American Foreign Policy and How It Changed the World.* New York: Knopf, 2001.

Nye, Joseph S., Jr. *Soft Power: The Means to Succeed in World Politics.* Public Affairs; New York, 2004.

Internet Resources

American Diplomacy, www.unc.edu/depts/diplomat
Central Intelligence Agency, www.cia.gov
United Nations, www.un.org/english
U.S. Department of Defense, www.defenselink.mil/pubs
U.S. Department of State, www.state.gov
University of Southern California Center on Public Diplomacy, http://uscpublicdiplomacy.com

12

Economics

The end of the Cold War gave fresh impetus to the long-held view that economic factors are paramount elements in national security affairs. In the new environment, it is widely asserted that "military capabilities are likely to be less important than they have been in the past. Economic measures will be central."[1] Not only has this view gained adherents, but so has the associated idea that economic strength is an increasingly important dimension of overall national security.

National security has often been characterized as a stool with three legs: military, economic, and political. Such a metaphor does not, however, adequately reflect reality, for the economic and other legs of the stool are intertwined, often integrated in complex ways. There is the simple competitive relationship, epitomized as guns versus butter. There is the instrumental relationship in which economic means can serve a military purpose and vice versa. The 1991 Gulf War offers several examples of this: In large part, the military instrument was used to protect an economic asset, oil; Egypt became a military instrument, as part of the U.S.-led coalition, partly because of a promise of forgiveness of $7 billion of military debt to the United States. There is also sometimes a substitutability relationship: Japan and Germany provided funds rather than forces to the Gulf War coalition.

The intersections of economics and national security, and the relationships between them are countless. Only a few of them can be examined in this chapter—primarily those stemming from interdependence.

Economic power in large measure gives U.S. policy its extraordinary global reach and crucial leverage. In 2008, the annual income of the average American reached $46,999, and gross domestic product (GDP) of the United States totaled more than $14.3 trillion.[2] Americans take such numbers in stride, but they are extraordinary. Before 1973, only the United States had exceeded $1 trillion in annual GDP; by 1998, only six other countries had joined that elite group.[3] Today, the U.S. economy is only slightly smaller than the economies of China, Japan, and Germany combined; it is hundreds of thousands times larger than any of the world's smallest economies, which total in the tens of millions.[4] Indeed, the market capitalization of a single U.S. corporation, Exxon, reached $402 billion in February 2007, roughly equivalent to the annual GDP of Switzerland.[5]

When considering how this situation affects national security, the most obvious connection is that a wealthy country can simply afford to spend more on defense. It can pay for more troops, invest in better technologies and equipment, and train its personnel more intensively. In this sense, the connection between economic power and military power is quite direct: Greater economic capacity can provide greater military capacity. For example, U.S. military spending in 2005 was about $520 billion, more than the total military spending of the next forty-four countries combined. As a fraction of GDP, however, U.S. military spending ranked only twenty-sixth in the world, with less than 4% of national income devoted to the military budget.[6]

The connection between economic power and national power can also be more subtle. Independent of its military hardware and personnel, a nation can use its economic strength to influence the decisions of other states. The United States has frequently imposed economic sanctions on countries that pursue policies antithetical to U.S. values or interests. Two examples are South Africa in the 1980s and Iraq in the 1990s. The United States has also offered economic "rewards" to countries that have supported its policy goals or to encourage policies that the United States would like to see adopted. Examples here include the U.S. role in the quick and successful resolution of Mexico's peso crisis of 1994–1995 and recent free trade agreements with Jordan and Bahrain.[7]

This dual challenge of building and wielding economic power is greatly complicated by the increasingly interdependent nature of international economic relations. The World Trade Organization (WTO) reports that the total value of world trade rose from $95 billion in 1955 to nearly $11 trillion in 2005, a 116-fold increase in fifty years.[8] More than one hundred bilateral and multilateral trade agreements connect the world through a robust web of economic relations. The world's financial flows are even more impressive: Every hour of the day, roughly $200 billion flows through global capital markets, both as payments for international trade and as short-term and long-term investments.

One has only to look at the rapid expansion of U.S.-China economic ties over the past decade to see a striking example of how globalization can make for strange and uneasy bedfellows. The United States has become China's largest single export market. China has grown rapidly, in large part through the strength of its exports, with its economy more than doubling in size over the past decade. The United States has enjoyed a new source of foreign lending in China, which has purchased significant amounts of U.S. government securities in the past five years. China holds foreign exchange reserves worth approximately $1 trillion at its central bank, of which 50% to 60% are U.S. treasury securities. This relationship has allowed China to grow and the United States to keep interest rates relatively low, but it has also raised worries about the future of the U.S. manufacturing base and the level of U.S. indebtedness to China. Economic globalization adds a layer of complexity to the projection of U.S. national power abroad.

Sources of Economic Power

Statesmen have long recognized the importance of economic prosperity to national power and military strength, but their understanding of the sources of economic power has evolved over time. In the seventeenth century, most governments directed international trade with the objective of maximizing balance-of-payments surpluses (that is, of ensuring that exports exceeded imports), which allowed countries to accumulate reserves of gold and precious metals. Under *mercantilism*, as the system was known, a country's natural competitive advantages did not matter much. The system also fomented *beggar-thy-neighbor policies*, as all countries worked to increase exports but restrict imports through tariffs. England, for example, deliberately restricted the development of manufacturing in its colonies in an effort to keep colonial markets dependent on English exports.

Beginning in the mid-eighteenth century, classical economists led by Adam Smith and David Ricardo challenged the mercantilist paradigm, arguing that specialization by individuals, firms, and nations could increase productivity and that unrestricted trade among individuals as well as nations would allocate resources more efficiently for everyone's benefit. Smith argued that if individuals pursued their self-interests, specializing in their relatively most productive tasks, they would maximize economic welfare as if guided by an "invisible hand." Ricardo developed the concept of comparative advantage and demonstrated that all would be better off if states specialized in the production of goods at which they were relatively more successful. Ricardo's model replaced the mercantilist approach with the model of international trade still used today. Both moved economics into the brave new world of free markets and individual autonomy and action.

Modern economic thought has built upon these fundamental insights. Formal models of economic growth now rest on the notion that production is central, because overall welfare and quality of life depends on income and output, rather than the amassing of stores of gold in government vaults. Income is produced as firms employ the various factors of production (raw materials, labor, physical capital, land) and compensate the owners of these factors according to the value that each adds. Growth in income—and thus economic growth—depends upon either increasing the available factors of production or improving the productivity of the existing factors. Short-term variations, such as changes in the money supply, transitory tax breaks, or large government expenditures, will not usually affect the fundamental mechanisms of long-term economic growth.

History, geography, and culture have mixed in complex ways to create a diverse set of economic outcomes around the globe (see Figure 12.1). Because the direct seizure of land, labor, or capital has serious international consequences, and the age of exploration has ended, governments now generally rely on pro-growth

FIG. 12.1 National Size by Size of Economy

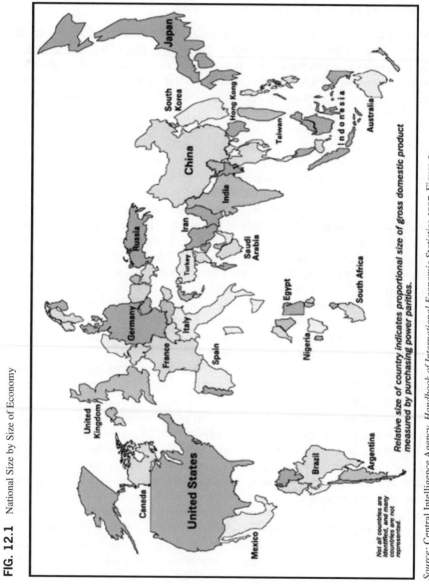

Relative size of country indicates proportional size of gross domestic product measured by purchasing power parities.

Not all countries are identified, and many countries are not represented.

Source: Central Intelligence Agency, *Handbook of International Economic Statistics 1997*, Figure 5.

250

economic policies to increase national output. To raise labor output, for example, a government might seek to increase the number of workers by providing incentives for specific segments of the population (younger workers, elderly, or women) to work, increasing immigration, or expanding the number of hours worked by those already in the labor force. Labor productivity also depends on workers' skills, so government may expand education and training programs to encourage investment in human capital.

Physical capital also contributes significantly to long-term economic growth. No matter how well-trained, healthy, and motivated are a society's workers, their economic output will be highly constrained if the society lacks roads, machinery and equipment, and communications networks. To raise the levels of physical capital, governments can create incentives to increase household and business saving, establish legal regimes that define and enforce property rights, assure adequate infrastructure, and manage public resources in a sustainable manner. They can also pursue responsible fiscal policy, because high levels of government borrowing can lead to higher interest rates, making it harder for private companies to borrow funds for capital projects. This phenomenon is known as the *crowding out* of private capital formation through government expenditures and borrowing.

Finally, advances in technology can increase the total output of an economy. Innovation tends to enable a society to produce more with the same number of workers and capital. Government policies that provide incentives for technological growth—such as strong intellectual property laws, the funding of basic research and development, and reduction of the regulatory burden for opening new businesses—generally enhance economic power. By the same logic, burdensome regulation and weak enforcement of intellectual property law can retard productivity and diminish economic performance.[9]

Although defense policy is not commonly mentioned in discussions of long-run economic growth, it can decisively influence a country's course of development.[10] On the one hand, some level of physical security is a prerequisite for any economic activity. In a war-torn country, just going to work or to market can become an act of faith—one with high potential costs. Such uncertainty and risk reduce the incentive to make longer-term investments. As U.S. efforts at nation-building in Iraq and Afghanistan have shown, basic security has proven to be a prerequisite for successful economic growth and development.

Of course, war itself can be extremely destructive of a country's economic base. War may destroy vital buildings and equipment, disrupt daily routines and supply chains, divert resources from investment, and reduce the skilled labor pool (through death, conscription, or displacement).[11] Even in the absence of open warfare, high levels of military spending can diminish an economy's long-run growth potential by drawing labor and capital away from nondefense industries.[12] Figure 12.2 dramatically illustrates the contrast between two nations with similar resources, labor forces, geography, and history. In contrast to South Korea, North Korea has restricted engagement with much of the world, repressed its labor force, and diverted enormous national resources

FIG. 12.2   Image of Korean Peninsula at Night

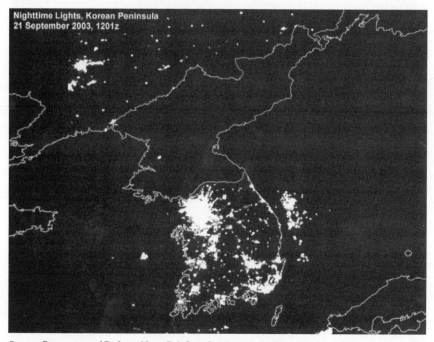

Source: Department of Defense News Briefing, October 11, 2006,
www.globalsecurity.org/military/library/news/2006/10/mil-061011-dod01.htm.

into a massive military buildup. The result is that the average South Korean's
income is $24,200, about fifteen times larger than that of the average North
Korean.[13]

The balancing of these two competing forces—the genuine need for security
and the temptation to overspend—has led to the concept of the *great equation*.
Writing in reference to the Eisenhower administration, Iwan Morgan argues:

> How to balance essential security needs with maximum economic strength was the
> great equation that Eisenhower strove to solve. Along with the pursuit of a safe peace,
> this was his greatest preoccupation as president. . . . He realized that excessive military
> spending might ruin the free economy and result in a garrison state.[14]

During the Cold War, the Soviet Union allocated an estimated 20% to 25% of its
GDP to defense spending in an attempt to match the West in military capabilities.
This massive military commitment drew labor, capital, and technology away from
sectors that might have promised longer-term growth. By contrast, the United
States generally spent between 4% and 6% of its GDP on defense spending dur-
ing the Cold War. Although many factors contributed to the Soviet defeat in the
Cold War, the "imperial overstretch" of the Soviets, as Paul Kennedy puts it, was
certainly a major contributor.[15]

FIG. 12.3 World Merchandise Trade by Major Product Group, 1950–2005

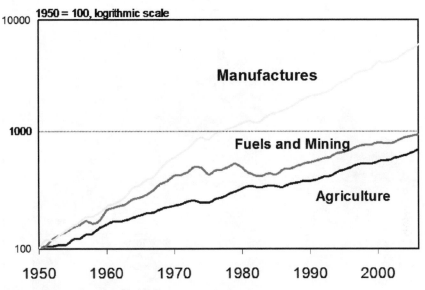

Source: WTO, www.wto.org/english/res_e/statis_e/statis_e/htm.

National Security in an Era of Globalization

It is almost cliché to emphasize how interdependent the world has become. Thomas Friedman, in his popular book *The World Is Flat* (2005), gives many colorful and persuasive examples of the ways in which far-flung regions and peoples now share unexpected connections. Many of these connections are of an economic nature, occurring through markets, and the macroeconomic statistics bear out Friedman's evidence. World trade roughly doubled between 1995 and 2005. Between 1950 and 2005, the volume of world merchandise trade increased exponentially (see Figure 12.3).

Because of the size of its domestic economy, the United States is less dependent on world trade than many other countries. For example, the combined value of U.S. exports and imports in 2003 was less than 20% of the U.S. GDP; by contrast, China's trade represented about 60% of its GDP.[16] However, the vast size of the U.S. economy also means that its trading volumes are still extremely large. According to the WTO, the United States accounted for 16.1% of all world merchandise imports in 2005 (making it the world's leading importer in terms of sheer volume) and accounted for 8.7% in all world merchandise exports (making it the second leading exporter behind Germany).[17] The direction of U.S. trade is also instructive: North America, Asia, and Western Europe are the country's primary trading partners (see Figure 12.4).

Although public attention has focused on the growth of world trade and its implications for U.S. domestic industries and national incomes, the world's largest

FIG. 12.4   Percentage of Total U.S. Trade, by Trading Partner

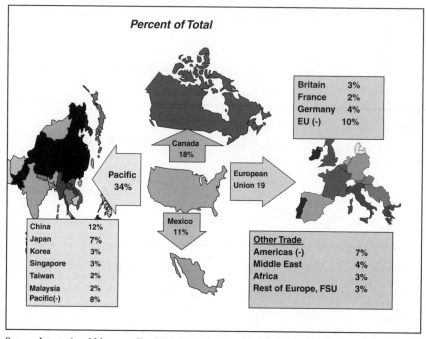

Source: International Monetary Fund, *Direction of Trade Statistics* (Washington, DC: International Monetary Fund, 2007).

single market is not a goods market at all: It is a global market for foreign exchange. Though the WTO now estimates that total world merchandise exports in 2005 exceeded $10 trillion, the Bank for International Settlements reported that *daily* global turnover in foreign exchange reached nearly $1.9 trillion. This means that five days of trading in the foreign exchange market is roughly equivalent to an entire year's worth of merchandise exports. Moreover, this trade has grown rapidly: It rose 36% from 2001 to 2004, for instance, controlling for exchange rate fluctuations.[18]

International portfolio investment—the flow of funds into foreign financial assets, such as stocks, mutual funds, and debt securities—has also grown rapidly. Researchers at the McKinsey Global Institute estimate that $7 trillion in new investments occurred in 2006 and that the total stock of global financial assets reached $140 trillion by the end of that year, approximately three times the level of annual world output. They argue that "this bodes well of the world's economies, since deeper financial markets typically provide better access to capital, improved pricing and efficiency; and better allocation of risk."[19] *Foreign direct investment*—the process by which individuals or companies in one nation own a large part of a foreign company—grew by 34% in 2006 to reach $1.2 trillion, according to the latest estimates from the United Nations (UN) Conference on Trade and Development.[20]

Rewards of Greater Economic Integration. As stated above, economic theorists have long argued that free trade allows for increased specialization by producers and that the patterns of trade follow naturally from each country's comparative advantage. Economic integration, in other words, enhances global productivity. The production of items requiring low-skilled labor will expand in those countries that have a relative abundance of such workers (such as China). Production of items requiring high-skilled labor will expand in those countries that have a relative abundance of these workers (such as Europe and the United States). Although trade will create winners and losers within countries, with attendant political repercussions, the net gains are positive for each country.

Although the debate over the merits and dangers of globalization can reach fever pitch, it is noteworthy that, at the same time that world trade has been rising, the world economy has seen consistently high growth rates. Sala-i-Martin estimates that 235 million people emerged from *poverty* (defined as earning $1 a day or less) between 1976 and 1998.[21] An authoritative study by the U.S. National Intelligence Council forecasts that such trends will continue: "The world economy is projected to be about 80% larger in 2020 than it was in 2000 and average per capita income to be 50% higher."[22] A rising tide lifts many boats. The trend is particularly pronounced in East Asia, a region that was home to more than half the world's poor in the early 1970s but to less than one third by the early 2000s. China, in particular, has grown at an average real growth rate of 8% to 10% annually from 2002 to 2007, implying that the 2007 standard of living for the average Chinese citizen is more than 50% higher than in 2002. Most economists credit the strong performance of the Chinese economy largely to the country's aggressive pursuit of world export markets, indicating an important connection between integration into the global economy and economic growth.[23]

Estimating the U.S. gains from the rise in international trade is difficult, requiring the careful control of the many other economic forces at work in recent years—changes in technology, demographic trends, expanded government spending, and other shifts. Recent research considering the effects of the North American Free Trade Agreement (NAFTA) has shown that the United States enjoyed small positive growth from NAFTA and Mexico enjoyed relatively large effects, much as predicted before NAFTA was implemented.[24] Although there is debate about the size of these estimates, no one really debates that the once-predicted "giant sucking sound" of jobs and livelihoods moving to Mexico never materialized.[25]

Another potential benefit of deepening economic integration is enhanced regional stability. A particularly relevant question for national security policy is whether countries with a greater degree of economic interdependence are less likely to engage in armed conflict with one another. One could argue, for example, that the deepening of U.S.-China economic ties has probably reduced the risk of open military conflict and encouraged cooperation on such issues as North Korea's nuclear ambitions. Similarly, the Western European pursuit of deeper economic integration has mitigated the risk of intra-European conflict.[26]

The same theoretical arguments favoring freer trade in goods and services apply to global capital markets. Although less visible than material goods and services, international financial flows provide much needed capital to households, businesses, and governments around the world. In 2005, for example, the value of foreign-owned assets in the United States increased by more than $1.2 trillion, of which about $1 trillion were private, nonofficial flows.[27]

Risks of Greater Economic Integration.   Although growing interdependence among the world's economies has brought greater prosperity, it also poses economic risks that have implications for managing conflict and for developing national security strategy. In the debate over globalization, even growth itself has been accused of being destabilizing, because it can exacerbate income inequality, accelerate environmental degradation, and generate macroeconomic instability as national economies are whipsawed through large shifts in international financial flows, creating the conditions for a financial crisis.

The Big Four countries within emerging markets (Brazil, Russia, India, and China, collectively called BRIC) provide cases in point. Recent projections suggest that these four rapidly growing economies together could conceivably exceed the economies of the United States, Germany, France, Italy, the United Kingdom, and Japan *combined* by the year 2040. Their rides are likely to be quite bumpy, however; each of the four has numerous problems and vulnerabilities that will surface during this period.

The risks in globalization are not limited to emerging markets, either. The United States has been running large trade deficits in recent years. In 2006, Americans imported and consumed an all-time high of over $800 billion more goods and services than they produced and exported, which reflects 6% of the entire U.S. economy. The United States is borrowing from the rest of the world to finance this appetite for imports. The cumulative effect is increasing levels of debt owed by the United States to its foreign creditors. Between 1994 and 2002, the United States saw its net foreign debt position rise from $311 billion (or 4.4% of its GDP in 1994) to $2.4 trillion (or 23% of its GDP in 2002), and it has remained at this high level through 2008.[28] Increased foreign ownership of U.S. assets or claims to future U.S. payments has significant implications for national security policy. China is now the second-largest creditor of the U.S. government after Japan, holding more than one quarter of U.S. outstanding public debt.[29] On the plus side, Chinese purchase of U.S. government debt has meant that the United States can continue to issue new debt (needed to fund government budget deficits) without increasing the interest rates that it has to pay on the newly issued debt. On the minus side, a cessation of official lending by China— or any major creditor—would mean significantly higher interest rates in the United States, a depreciation of the U.S. dollar, and a very high risk of recession, perhaps a major one. Discerning whether Chinese ownership of huge amounts of U.S. debt is a financial windfall or an impending crisis requires understanding China's reasons for purchasing that debt. For the past decade, China has pursued an export-oriented growth strategy, successfully promoting its exports by keeping its currency (the yuan) artificially low, which makes Chinese goods less expensive compared to those of the rest of the world. To keep the value of the yuan below its true market value, the central bank of China must put upward pressure on the dollar (by buying

U.S.-denominated securities) and downward pressure on the yuan (by selling Chinese-denominated securities to domestic banks). In short, the accumulation of large reserves of U.S. government debt is thus largely a by-product of China's growth policies, not a deliberate attempt to corner the market for U.S. debt to gain power over the United States. If China decides to cease buying U.S. debt or to dump existing debt in some punitive foreign policy action, the dollar would depreciate. The economic repercussions for the Chinese economy would be significant—a reduction in exports (a very large component of Chinese output) and an attendant loss of employment. The depreciation of the dollar would also reduce the value of the Chinese central bank's holdings of all remaining dollar-denominated assets. In short, a strong codependency characterizes the deepening economic relationship between China and the United States. Chinese dumping of U.S. debt, as some observers fear, is still possible but not very likely, as it is a lose-lose proposition.

In addition to risks associated with foreign borrowing and lending, the integration of global financial markets poses additional risks. Chief among those risks are the fallout from a destabilizing financial crisis in an important country and the prospect of a consequent broad *financial contagion*. The Asian financial crisis of 1997–1998—which began in Thailand as a banking crisis and quickly spilled over into global financial markets—illustrates the risks on both counts. On July 2, 1997, in the face of intense speculative pressure from international capital markets, Thailand announced that it could no longer maintain the value of its currency (the baht) at the official "peg." Within a day, the baht lost 25% of its value. Within a year, the baht had depreciated almost 75% (from 25 baht per U.S. dollar to 42 baht per U.S. dollar). Currencies across the region crashed with it, even though they had been relatively sound before the crisis. The Indonesian rupiah, for example, went from roughly 2,500 rupiah per U.S. dollar to nearly 14,000 rupiah per U.S. dollar in the twelve months from June 1997 to June 1998. The economies of many East Asian countries contracted sharply in the economic disorder. In 1998, Thailand suffered a real per capita GDP growth rate of –9.4%; in Indonesia, it was –9.1%; and in South Korea, it was –9.0%.[30] The UN estimated that nearly 13 million people in Asia fell into poverty as a result of the crisis.[31] Countries as far away as Latin America also suffered from the contagion.

It is not difficult to imagine how such crises can raise alarms in national security circles. In the months following the onset of crisis, Thailand revised its constitution and elected a new prime minister. By early 1998, riots erupted in Indonesia, and President Suharto resigned in May 1998, after thirty years in office. A conference on the security risks associated with the Asian financial crisis summarized the concerns:

> The impact of the Asian recession on security has several dimensions, affecting the pace and scope of military modernization, procurement, force structure, military operations and the respective capacity for cooperation, the development of regional institutions, and may be raising a new set of security concerns.[32]

In testimony before the House Committee on Armed Services, Admiral Joseph W. Prueher, then–commander in chief of U.S. Pacific Command, considered the

Asian financial crisis as the most significant new security risk to arise in the Pacific theater during 1998.[33]

The potential risks of an interdependent global economy were also evident in the credit and financial crisis in the United States in September 2008. The proximate cause of the crisis was the fact that several large financial institutions, including investment banking firm Lehman Brothers and insurance conglomerate AIG, had significant investments that were or could have become insolvent. The fear was that the bankruptcy of several financial institutions would not just be bad for those corporations, but would trigger other failures in other institutions throughout the world. As one example, in September 2008, founder and chairman of the World Economic Forum Klaus Schwab expressed concerns that the situation was "probably the first transformational crisis of our globalized age."[34] The complex financial relationships among banks, investment firms, corporations, and governments made it difficult to determine how far beyond Wall Street the financial crisis might spread and the concern for the U.S. and global economy was amplified by the 2008 electoral campaigns. As a result, investors were hesitant to provide short term credit and many economic and political leaders feared a credit crisis that would preclude the normal transactions that are essential to the effective functioning of markets. After several days of deliberation, the House and Senate passed The Emergency Economic Stabilization Act of 2008, which provided up to $700 billion to restore liquidity and stability to the financial system of the United States.[35] While the long term implications of the crisis as well as the government bailout will take years to assess, it was clear from the concerns expressed by foreign leaders that the financial contagion from a specific crisis can have global implications.

Exercising Economic Power in an Interdependent World

Cognizant of the opportunities and risks within the global economic environment, nations must determine how best to wield economic power to accomplish policy goals. As the world's largest producer, largest consumer, and most technologically advanced nation, the United States enjoys substantial and unique leverage within world markets. That power can consist of withholding participation in economic activity to coerce states, of increasing economic engagement with others to reward them, and of promoting economic growth in still other states through foreign aid.

Punitive Trade Policy.   *Punitive trade policy* is a set of tools used by countries to punish an enemy economically. These tools include sanctions, boycotts, embargoes, and tariffs. During wartime, it is general practice to apply a wide variety of punitive trade measures to weaken adversaries. During and even prior to World War II, for example, the United States and its Allies used a range of trade instruments in an orchestrated attack on the viability of the German and Japanese economies. During the Korean War, the United States imposed an embargo on all economic relationships with North Korea and the People's Republic of China. In 1964, the United States imposed a trade embargo on North Vietnam and then extended it to the whole country in 1975, after which it lasted almost twenty years. Recently, the United States has used trade sanctions against several nations, including Myanmar, North Korea, Cuba, Syria, and Iran.

The economics of embargoes and sanctions are relatively complex. The aim of an embargo is to force prices to rise in the target country, lowering standards of living for consumers and raising political pressure on the government. The problem is that these high prices both create incentives for third parties, particularly rival exporters in other countries, to earn profits by selling to the target country and also encourage consumers to switch away from the imported goods toward more readily available substitutes. In many cases, sanctions have enabled the very elites being targeted to profit personally from their ability to circumvent the sanctions. In this way, embargoes—especially those without broad international support and credible enforcement—can be porous and ineffective.

Soon after the Soviet invasion of Afghanistan in December 1979, President Jimmy Carter announced several economic sanctions, including suspension of further grain deliveries (of about 17 million tons, worth $3 billion), halt of all high-technology transfers, sharp constraints on Soviet fishing in U.S. waters, and withdrawal of U.S. participation from the 1980 Moscow Olympics. Although these sanctions had a symbolic effect and had some limited impact on the Soviet economy, they were not effective in their ultimate objective of influencing Soviet policy. They certainly did not prompt the Soviets to withdraw from Afghanistan. Significantly, other nations did not follow suit, and the Soviets were able to adjust their trade patterns to fill the void left by the U.S. embargo.[36] To the delight of midwestern farmers who had suffered much of the impact of the grain embargo, President Ronald Reagan decided to lift it in 1981.

Multilateral sanctions have also generally proven disappointing. The UN unsuccessfully declared an embargo on all economic relationships with Rhodesia after the white-controlled government in that nation declared its "Unilateral Declaration of Independence" from the United Kingdom in 1965. Throughout the 1980s, South Africa became the target of increasingly punitive trade measures in an international effort to protest its policy of apartheid; yet, as late as 1987, South Africa still had 140 trade partners worldwide and did business with forty-six of the fifty-two members of the Organization of African Unity, which had been most strident in its condemnation.[37]

The case of Iraq in the 1990s presented another test, one with nearly ideal initial conditions. After the 1991 Gulf War, sanctions were imposed unanimously by the UN Security Council on a regime that had been defeated by an unprecedented international coalition of nations. Significant intelligence and military resources were in place to enforce the sanctions. Yet, by the late 1990s, Russia, France, and China were already seeking an easing rather than a tightening of sanctions, despite Iraq's open defiance of UN weapons inspectors. The oil-for-food program of the UN, meant to ease the humanitarian costs of the sanctions, relieved the pressure on the Saddam Hussein regime and ultimately undermined the sanctions. The Volker Commission found that the Iraqi government made $1.8 billion in illicit income through manipulation of the program.[38]

Sanctions and embargoes are extreme forms of trade restriction. Tariffs and nontariff barriers, such as quotas or antidumping laws, are more common and less draconian. Although most economists argue against the use of tariffs, there are counterarguments. Tariffs may be warranted, it is claimed (often dubiously), to protect domestic industries deemed essential for national security. Senator Robert Byrd of West Virginia used this argument to defend tariffs on imported steel: "Without steel, we cannot guarantee America's national security. Without steel, we could not have rebuilt after September 11."[39] Similarly, Japan uses the argument of "food security" to protect its rice farmers.

Financial Controls.   Although trade sanctions and embargoes are more visible forms of punitive economic policy because they involve physical goods, financial controls offer a country another set of policies through which to exert economic power to defend its national security and influence the actions of other countries. A country can restrict the flow of financial capital through such policies as capital controls, restrictions on foreign direct investment, the freezing of assets held in its domestic financial system, limitations on its equity markets, and so on. For example, the U.S. Treasury Department, through its Office of Terrorism and Financial Intelligence established in 2004, now tracks and disrupts financial flows to and from organizations suspected of funding terrorist activities.[40] These sanctions appear to have had some effect. After the United States cut off the second-largest state-owned commercial bank in Iran from direct and indirect financial access to the U.S. financial system on the grounds that it had financed terrorist groups, Iran protested to the International Monetary Fund (IMF). The fact that the bank had been unable to issue letters of credit in dollars was affecting deposits. In addition, European and Asian banks with activities in the United States were cutting off the Iranian bank from operations in other currencies.[41]

Open Trade as a Reward and a Catalyst to Democratic Reform.   The limitations of punitive economic policy are clear: A country may hurt itself in the process of punishing its adversary, it may invite retaliation, and it may not succeed. Strategic economic policy can also take the form of open trade as a reward for good relations. Where sanctions and tariffs are the stick, preferential trading arrangements are the carrot.

As international economic integration has grown, so has the number of regional and bilateral trade agreements. Many argue that international trade is an important channel for encouraging democratic reform and political stability in its regional partners. For example, Senator John McCain, in a 2002 debate about the Andean trade pact, stated: "Let there be no doubt: the Andean Trade Preference Expansion Act is important to U.S. national security and to the national security of the democratically elected governments in the Andean region."[42] He made similar arguments during his support of the Central American Free Trade Agreement in 2006.

LURIE'$ BU$INE$$ WORLD   J/3 Sep. 15 '92

©1992 International Copyright by CARTOONEWS Inc., N.Y.C., USA

"I'll open my doors when you open yours."

Copyright 1992 CARTOONEWS Inc., N.Y.C., USA. Reprinted with permission of Ranan Lurie.

Although the general question of whether free trade genuinely spurs democracy remains an open one, the evidence in some specific cases is persuasive. The lure of membership in the European Union—and the reforms required of prospective members—have been credited by some observers with enhancing the political stability of fragile states in Eastern and Central Europe and with hastening their democratization and economic development. Others believe that Mexico's watershed presidential election of 2000, in which the Institutional Revolutionary Party stepped down from power peacefully after seventy-one years of continuous power, followed from the increased political transparency and the diffusion of economic and political power that was facilitated by NAFTA.

The WTO is another channel through which the rewards of open trade exert a liberalizing force upon world economies. To gain membership in the WTO, a country must substantially reduce its trade barriers. The process to gain membership may be long; from the time of Vietnam's application to its formal accession in January 2007 took ten years. With 150 current members, the WTO has become the largest and most influential multilateral framework for international trade negotiations. The WTO has provided a structured environment for negotiating trade agreements and has established international standards and principles to guide those negotiations. In recent years, the WTO has become the target of antiglobalization forces, which blame the organization for promoting free trade at the expense of labor standards, environmental quality, and indigenous cultures. Along with other impediments arising out of protectionist interests, this backlash against globalization has slowed progress on global trade talks in the near term.

Foreign Assistance.   Foreign assistance is also often used to promote a nation's interests and values; in addition, it helps develop new export markets. There will always be difficult choices to make in deciding which countries to aid: those whose populations are in the greatest need, those most likely to best utilize the assistance, or those of strategic interest to the donor. Most governments tend to pursue a blend of these goals. Although U.S. Official Development Assistance (ODA) to sub-Saharan Africa grew 250% between 2000 and 2005, the two largest consistent recipients of U.S. bilateral assistance worldwide remained Israel and Egypt, as has generally been the case since they signed the Camp David Peace Accords in 1978.

The problems of underdevelopment as well as failing and failed states have gained increased prominence as national security issues since the terrorist attacks of September 11, 2001, were perpetrated from the safe haven of destitute Afghanistan. As the September 2002 National Security Strategy states, the United States will use "foreign aid to promote freedom and support those who struggle non-violently for it, ensuring that nations moving toward democracy are rewarded for the steps they take."[43] American ODA increased from $10 billion in 2000 to $27.6 billion in 2005. On one hand, this is a significant absolute dollar value and involves many new initiatives. On the other hand, it represents less than two tenths of 1% of U.S. GDP, about three fourths of 1% of the total U.S. government's expenditure, and only about 5% to 6% of the amount spent on national defense. Although there is room for significant debate about the value of additional foreign aid in achieving U.S. policy goals, in comparing the different tools of national security, the resources expended on foreign aid pale in comparison to the size of the U.S. economy.[44]

The Marshall Plan to rebuild Europe after World War II offers the archetypal example of using foreign assistance to further national interests. Not only did the billions of dollars in assistance alleviate human suffering in Europe, it also blunted the appeal of various local communist parties and rebuilt Allies to defend against potential Soviet expansion. In some instances, the United States has offered assistance in return for the recipient's cooperation on very specific national security goals—with mixed results. Pakistan joined the effort to combat terrorism after the 9/11 attacks and received an increase of U.S. assistance from $91 million in 2001 to $1.15 billion in 2002, supplemented by billions more in subsequent years and through defense reimbursement for Pakistani support to U.S. operations.[45] The Turkish government, however, declined to allow U.S. ground forces to transit Turkey for operations in Iraq in 2003, despite an offer of $6 billion in grant assistance and $20 billion in loan guarantees.

Beyond donor governments, foreign assistance is also carried out by multilateral institutions, such as the IMF, World Bank, and regional development banks. The IMF primarily provides support to currencies under stress as a lender of last resort, while the World Bank and regional development banks primarily provide loans for development projects, such as infrastructure, health, or education. The development banks have increasingly tried to maximize the effectiveness of aid by linking levels of assistance to recipients' economic and governance performance. The banks are working to find the right trade-off, however, in such performance-based allocations. There are many cases of fragile states, such as Afghanistan, where performance has yet to be demonstrated but needs are obvious and critical.

The IMF and World Bank also provide policy guidance to developing countries and technical assistance that shares international "best practices" to promote sound macroeconomic policies, development, and poverty reduction. Both institutions have their critics, including those who charge they are tools of American power. Although the United States as the largest contributor and shareholder has the biggest board vote (about 16%), and both organizations are headquartered in Washington, American control over the institutions is clearly limited. For example, World Bank lending to Iran resumed in 2000 after a seven-year hiatus, despite U.S. opposition.[46] Although it is true that both institutions have shortcomings, they clearly play an important role in the world economy.

The Defense Industrial Base

For decades after World War II, American consideration of economic security focused on the requirements for a defense industrial base sufficient to sustain a major mobilization and large-scale, protracted warfare. Particular attention was given to the needed industrial plants, raw materials, and organizational arrangements and priorities. Stockpiles of scarce minerals, such as aluminum, chromium, cobalt, tungsten, and tin (along with dozens of other materials in potentially short supply), were assembled, and industrial mobilization plans to meet a variety of circumstances were developed.

With the disappearance of the Soviet Union and the end of the Cold War, American policy makers' attention largely shifted to other priorities, although the vitality of the defense industrial base continued to be a consideration, especially in materiel procurement decisions. A greatly diminished stockpile of strategic materials has also been maintained. Mobilization planning, which during the Cold War had been the responsibility of important independent agencies, has been pared down to a modest Defense Priority and Allocation System headed by a fourth-level Department of Defense official, the deputy undersecretary of defense for industrial policy. The Industrial College of the Armed Forces, which once had a considerable focus on defense mobilization, still has a few pertinent courses, but the entire mobilization topic has faded into near obscurity.

With the threat of massive protracted warfare lifted, concerns about the adequacy and reliability of access to scarce raw materials have narrowed down to the single most vital import: namely, petroleum. The United States, with about one twentieth of the world's population, accounts for about one fourth of world oil consumption—60% of it imported. Although the nation maintains a strategic petroleum reserve of about 700 million barrels of crude oil (slated to grow to 1 billion barrels), that amount is clearly insufficient to handle a protracted major interruption of imports, which total about 12 million barrels per day. Policy options, other than a strategic reserve, to assure adequate oil and gasoline supplies for the overall economy as well as essential defense activities clearly need increased attention. Further exploration of this challenge is discussed in Chapter 26.

Looking Ahead

Continued growth of world trade, deepening of world capital markets, increased global diffusion of technology, and overall interdependence among states will remain characteristic trends well into the twenty-first century. Globalization will likely intensify. Like an economic form of global tectonics, these changes will lead to gradual shifts in the patterns of economic and international relations. Those changes have many implications for national security policy. The perennial debate between guns and butter will continue. Tensions will inevitably arise between the security agenda, where the ideals of self-sufficiency and strong fences beckon, and the economic agenda, where arguments favoring interdependence and more open flows of goods, information, and capital tend to dominate. The future will hold a world economy in which the United States is less economically dominant, especially relative to the fast-growing economies in China and India.

Globalization, for all its promise of raising global efficiency, cannot eliminate the problem of making difficult collective choices in the face of limited resources. At the same time, in a more globally competitive world, countries will have to address how to extend the benefits of globalization to countries that will have difficulty competing with Asian exporters, particularly in sub-Saharan Africa, so as to avoid their serving as impoverished exporters of terrorism and disease. Nations will also have to manage the tension between economic policies that promote aggregate economic growth versus those that address income disparities and social welfare. This will be exacerbated by aging populations in most of the industrialized world (particularly in Europe and Japan), which will leave governments facing ever-larger retired populations (and electorates) in need of benefits and ever-smaller pools of workers (and taxpayers) to pay for them. Slower growth in these markets will also affect the world economy and will reduce the ability of these countries to serve as partners in initiatives from foreign assistance to military alliances and coalitions.

The United States will continue to use economic power to further its own economic, security, and political interests, while simultaneously maintaining an economic base sufficient to support its global military capabilities. Success in meeting these challenges will depend on many large and small factors, some of which remain under U.S. control and some of which do not. Foremost, for its own sake and for the health of the international system, the United States must pursue sound economic policies at home: better discipline in its public finances, a tax code that encourages saving and productive investments, and a legal code that promotes innovation and productivity. Simultaneously, it must devote appropriate attention and resources to the defense base so that military forces can be prepared to intervene in a still dangerous world. Even as he emphasized free-market economics, Smith made the essential point succinctly: "Defense is more important than opulence."

Discussion Questions

1. What does the vast economic power of the United States imply for national security policy?

2. Which image better describes the increasingly globalized economy: a house of cards that can collapse with a single failure or a spider web that is resilient in the face of shock or shifts? How does a decision maker's image of the economy affect policy?

3. What are the basic conditions that determine the long-run economic prosperity of a nation? Do the resources of a nation or the policies of a nation matter more in determining prosperity?

4. How can the United States not only accumulate economic power—the possession of which is a necessary condition for military strength—but also exercise such power effectively and intelligently in an increasingly complex world?

5. How does U.S. borrowing from abroad affect national security? To what extent does U.S. foreign debt constrain U.S. leverage within global capital markets or otherwise constrain U.S. foreign policy?

6. How likely is it that China would use its financial leverage over the United States? How credible is the potential economic threat posed by China's significant holdings of U.S. government debt?

7. What might be best practices for applying U.S. economic power to further U.S. foreign policy aims?

8. Why have efforts at economic coercion not been overly successful? Explain the difficulty in coordinating the use of this technique.

9. How effective a tool is foreign aid? Should it be expanded or reduced as a tool of U.S. national security policy?

Recommended Reading

Bhagwati, Jagdish. *In Defense of Globalization.* New York: Oxford University Press, 2004.

Collier, Paul. *Breaking the Conflict Trap: Civil War and Development Policy.* Washington, DC: International Bank for Reconstruction and Development / World Bank, 2003.

De Soto, Hernando. *The Mystery of Capital: Why Capitalism Triumphs in the West and Fails Everywhere Else.* New York: Basic Books, 2000.

Easterly, William. *The Elusive Quest for Growth: Economists' Adventures and Misadventures in the Tropics.* Cambridge, MA: MIT Press, 2001.

Friedman, Thomas L. *The World Is Flat: A Brief History of the Twenty-First Century.* New York: Farrar, Strauss, and Giroux, 2005.

Kennedy, Paul. *The Rise and Fall of the Great Powers.* New York: Random House, 1987.

Maddison, Angus. *The World Economy: A Millennial Perspective.* Paris: Organization for Economic Co-operation and Development, 2001.

O'Rourke, P. J. *On the Wealth of Nations (Books That Changed the World).* New York: Atlantic Monthly Press, 2006.

Sen, Amartya. *Development as Freedom.* New York: Anchor Books, 1999.

Stiglitz, Joseph. *Globalization and Its Discontents.* New York: W. W. Norton & Company, 2002.

U.S. National Intelligence Council. *Mapping the Global Future: Report of the National Intelligence Council 2020 Project.* NIC Report 2004-13. Washington, DC: Government Printing Office, 2004.

Internet Resources

Bureau of Economic Analysis, www.bea.gov
Center for International Comparisons at the University of Pennsylvania,
    http://pwt.econ.upenn.edu
Council of Economic Advisers, www.whitehouse.gov/cea
International Monetary Fund, www.imf.org
UN Economic and Social Development, www.un.org/esa
U.S. Agency for International Development, www.usaid.gov
The World Bank, www.worldbank.org
World Trade Organization, www.wto.org

13

Military Power

Although the diplomatic, information, and economic instruments of national power are important—particularly the economic one, which underpins the others—the military instrument of power has the greatest potential to be decisive. Because the use of military force always brings associated and sometimes significant costs, however, resorting to force should always be a weighty decision considered very carefully by national security policy makers. As many policy makers have learned to their sorrow, going to war is often much easier than disengaging from one on satisfactory terms. Further, it is important to recognize that even when military power is employed, the likelihood of an acceptable outcome will usually be increased through the simultaneous, coordinated application of other U.S. instruments of power.

Strategic Logic: The Use of Force for the Purposes of the State

When one considers the use of force, a number of basic propositions from classic works in military theory hold enduring value. This section draws on two of those classics: Sun Tzu's *The Art of War* and Carl von Clausewitz's *On War*. Because of the enduring nature of their contributions and the power of their insights, it is useful to cite these authors on key points using their own words. Both theorists note that the decision to go to war has significant consequences. From Sun Tzu: "War is a matter of vital importance to the State; the province of life or death; the road to survival or ruin."[1] Similarly, Clausewitz writes that war is "no place for irresponsible enthusiasts" but rather "a serious means to a serious end."[2] These cautionary notes are the best places to start when thinking about employing the military instrument of power.

Clausewitz's famous statement that "war is merely the continuation of policy by other means" has significant implications for those who must make decisions relating to the use of force.[3] It is clear from the context of this passage that Clausewitz is writing against a contemporary view that, when war begins, the role of politics and political leaders recedes and perhaps even vanishes until peace is once again achieved. Clausewitz finds this dichotomous view of peace and war to be "thoroughly mistaken."[4] Politics and diplomacy do not cease when states resort to force; instead, political leaders have just added one more instrument of power to the means that they are applying to achieve their purposes.

Clausewitz argues that war is a unique human activity, inevitably shaped by danger, chance, uncertainty, and such human elements as physical courage, moral courage, and endurance.[5] Its unpredictability also stems from interaction with a living adversary. To Clausewitz, war is neither an art nor a science, but rather a form of human interaction, such as commerce or politics, where the outcome depends on the thinking activities of all participants.[6] Though war takes place in a unique environment, it is also a completely subordinate phenomenon to the political purposes that give it meaning. In Clausewitz's metaphor, war has its own grammar but not its own logic. When those who think about war seek to abstract from its political factors, they are "left with something pointless and devoid of sense."[7]

These insights provide a powerful basis for strategic thinking. First, they clarify that the political end being sought—the politically desired peace that will follow any use of force—must govern all planning. As Clausewitz says, "No one starts a war—or rather, no one in his senses ought to do so—without first being clear in his mind what he intends to achieve by that war and how he intends to conduct it."[8] This way of approaching potential uses of force requires careful consideration and specification of the desired end state. Clarity about the desired end state will make it more likely that appropriate means (military and other instruments of power) and ways (concepts for the application of those means) will be brought to bear: "The political object is the goal, war is the means of reaching it, and means can never be considered in isolation from their purpose."[9]

Sound strategic thinking also reveals that, in some cases, means and ways will have implications for the ends being sought. Although Clausewitz argues that political purposes must govern, they must not "be a tyrant."[10] There may be instances where the strategic planning process reveals costs and risks associated with a particular course of action that political leaders then determine to be unacceptable, or even that the pursuit of a particular political goal is infeasible. One example is President John F. Kennedy's decision not to seek to destroy Soviet missiles in Cuba in 1962 after he was made aware of the scale of the required air strikes and the uncertainty that would characterize their results. Under circumstances such as these, the most rational approach may be to modify the goals themselves. To properly support strategic decision making, senior military leaders must therefore be able to appreciate political purposes while also bringing to bear their expertise in the grammar of war: "On the one hand, he [the general] is aware of the entire political situation; on the other, he knows exactly how much he can achieve with the means at his disposal."[11] The senior general (or admiral) in charge of a theater of operations "is simultaneously a statesman."[12]

According to Clausewitz, the nature of war depends on the characteristics of a particular era, characteristics of involved states and peoples, relations among the belligerents, and the scale of the political purposes at stake. Of course, given the importance of strategic interaction, the political purposes of all involved must be taken into account.[13] Though one side in a conflict may have strictly limited interests at stake and therefore prefer to devote only limited means, an opponent may view the conflict as a struggle for existence:

> The first, the supreme, the most far-reaching act of judgment that the statesman and commander have to make is to establish . . . the kind of war on which they are embarking; neither mistaking it for, nor trying to turn it into, something that is alien to its nature. This is the first of all strategic questions and the most comprehensive.[14]

Recognizing that the history of warfare includes conflicts of all degrees of intensity, Clausewitz posits that the future of conflict will see similarly diverse wars. They will likely vary along a spectrum that ranges all the way from mere armed standoffs to extremely intense struggles for national survival. If a very limited application of force is most in line with a government's limited political purposes in a particular situation, the military commander's "main concern will be to make sure the delicate balance is not suddenly upset in the enemy's favor and the half-hearted war does not become a real war after all."[15]

The emphasis of Clausewitz and Sun Tzu on careful planning and calculation is tempered by their recognition of the uncertainty that pervades war.[16] Sun Tzu emphasizes the fluidity of war and the importance of being able to act with boldness according to the situation. Clausewitz recognizes that political purposes can change during the course of a war due to new diplomatic, political, economic, or military developments. For Clausewitz, this means that close and constant communication between political leaders and generals is required. The influence of policy must be pervasive: "Policy, then, will permeate all military operations, and, in so far as their violent nature will admit, it will have a continuous influence on them."[17]

The uncertainty of war could cause military planners to seek to apply maximum military means, even if the political purposes are strictly limited. However, this approach would ignore costs. Book II of Sun Tzu's classic focuses on the human and material expense of war, arguing for swift rather than prolonged operations to manage costs.[18] Clausewitz describes a somewhat more timeless basis for estimating required resources:

> To discover how much of our resources must be mobilized for war, we must first examine our own political aim and that of the enemy. We must gauge the character and ability of its government and people and do the same with regard to our own. Finally, we must evaluate the political sympathies of other states and the effect the war may have on them. To assess these things in all their ramifications and diversity is plainly a colossal task.[19]

Estimating costs may be difficult, but it is also necessary. To apply unlimited means regardless of these calculations "would often result in strength being wasted, which is contrary to other principles of statecraft," and would also be likely to cause domestic political problems, because the means would be disproportionate to the ends being pursued.[20] A population would be less likely to support an expensive war for a cause not deemed worthy of such sacrifice. The U.S. war in Vietnam may be a case in point.

Given that wars have varying degrees of importance and intensity, Clausewitz recognizes that it may appear that some wars are more political than others. In a relatively unlimited war, such as World War II, where the goal was either national survival or the complete overthrow of the enemy, the political end and military objectives align relatively naturally, and the requirement for detailed political guidance is less. On the other hand, when political leaders seek to use force to achieve specific and also limited purposes, political influence may be more pressing, as the political impact of each military move must be carefully calibrated. For example, U.S. participation in the Korean War became limited to restoring the division of Korea near the 38th parallel because there was no political will to unify Korea, especially as such an expansion of the war would have involved a broader conflict with China and the Soviet Union. In some cases, finding an appropriate military objective to support a particular political goal may be difficult—such as when the United States sought to prevent Serbian President Slobodan Milosevic from continuing the ethnic cleansing of Albanians in Kosovo in 1999—and a proxy must be sought. In these cases, there are times when a chosen "substitute must be a good deal more important" to get an opponent to yield.[21] To return to the Kosovo example, to coerce Milosevic into changing his policy in Kosovo, it was apparently necessary to threaten the survival of his regime. In any event, "while policy is apparently effaced in the one kind of war and yet is strongly evident in the other, both kinds are equally political."[22] Their meaning lies in the political purposes they serve.

Giving a stark warning about the potential consequences associated with the use of force, Sun Tzu says:

> If not in the interests of the state, do not act. If you cannot succeed, do not use troops. If you are not in danger, do not fight. A sovereign cannot raise an army because he is enraged, nor can a general fight because he is resentful. For while an angered man may again be happy, and a resentful man again be pleased, a state that has perished cannot be restored, nor can the dead be brought back to life.[23]

Strategic planners should keep in mind the ends pursued, the significance of strategic interaction, the prevalence of uncertainty, and the costs associated with even limited uses of force.

The military instrument of power is obviously a key tool for U.S. national security policy makers. As discussed in Chapter 8, the U.S. Department of Defense (DoD) not only is America's largest corporation, but as of late 2007 military spending also accounts for more than half of all discretionary spending in the U.S. federal budget (see also Chapter 9). Simply due to its sheer size and claim on national resources, the military instrument of national power is of great significance. Prospects for its successful use would undoubtedly be enhanced if key decision makers engaged in rigorous strategic thinking, carefully reconciling ends, ways, and means, while leveraging all instruments of power relevant to a particular situation.

The military theory discussed in this section also has implications for the patterns of U.S. civil-military relations that are discussed in Chapter 8. In the twentieth century, the U.S. military went from peacetime noninvolvement in national security policy making to extensive and continuous involvement during the Cold War and beyond. The pattern of civil-military interaction in wartime has also changed over time. In World War II, for example, U.S. military leaders often enjoyed tremendous autonomy. The potential difficulties with this degree of autonomy in a more limited conflict were fully revealed as President Harry S. Truman found it necessary to relieve his theater commander, General Douglas MacArthur, during the Korean War for not adhering to his policies. At the other end of the spectrum, the perception of many in the U.S. military was that political leaders granted their military commanders too little autonomy during the Vietnam War—as these leaders engaged in such activities as specific target selection for strategic bombing. More recently, Secretary of Defense Donald Rumsfeld decided to remove specific forces from the "Time-Phased Force Deployment List" for the Iraq campaign before the Iraq War in 2003, which has been widely criticized as inappropriate meddling in the specific expertise of military leaders (see Chapter 8). Neither political leaders' noninvolvement nor their micromanagement is desirable. Prospects for strategic success are generally enhanced when the political leaders of a government retain overall direction and remain involved, but their interactions with their military commanders are characterized by vigorous dialogue and an open, two-way exchange of information regarding relevant diplomatic, political, economic, and military developments.

Military Power

Chapter 1 argues that power is one of the most important concepts in international politics, yet it is also difficult to define precisely for a variety of reasons. To enable measurements and comparison, some scholars, such as international relations theorist Kenneth Waltz, have focused on measurable capabilities. Waltz's definition includes seven elements: size of population, territory, resource endowment, economic capability, military strength, political stability, and competence.[24] Of these, military strength may be the most obvious, yet it is also one of the most difficult to estimate accurately.

As already noted, military strength has as its basic rationale the contribution to a state's national security and the attainment of its political purposes. Practically every major sovereign state has sought such strength. Indeed, until Japan became an exception by minimizing its military forces after World War II, the significance of a country on the world scene had tended to be correlated directly with its armed strength: "No 'great power' in the present or past has failed to maintain a large military establishment, and those states which aspire to great power status allocate a large portion of their resources to developing an impressive military machine."[25]

Despite its intrinsic importance, the link between armed forces and foreign policy objectives is not the only explanation for building military forces. A military establishment has always been one of the trappings of sovereignty, and heads of state may feel compelled to maintain one as a status symbol. For some developing nations, the maintenance of a military establishment to influence external political relations may appear to be an irrational allocation of scarce resources that could otherwise be devoted to internal development. In other less-developed countries, however, the military has been instrumental in preserving internal political order and in fostering economic development.[26] Though interesting and not to be underestimated in an international context, these latter purposes—regional status and influence, internal security, and economic development—are peripheral to the focus here on the role of military force in U.S. national security.

The Nature of Military Power.   It is a fundamental error to characterize military power in the abstract. To observe that the United States is the most militarily powerful state in the world means that, compared to every other country, the United States has the strongest military forces. But that statement is misleading; the United States might be powerless to achieve specific objectives, in certain situations, despite its great military strength. Barry Posen has argued, for example, that the U.S. military in the early twenty-first century enjoys tremendous military advantages in the "global commons"—in space, in the air above thirty thousand feet, and at sea beyond the littoral regions—but does not enjoy comparable advantages in "contested zones," such as littoral and urban areas.[27] It is dangerous to jump from general characterizations of military capabilities to estimates of the prospects of success in any particular application of military power.

The military problem posed by an adversary can be assessed two different ways: by analyzing its *capabilities* or by analyzing its *intentions*. The latter course is often taken by those who believe that potential adversaries have no aggressive intentions or who have strong reasons for wishing to cut defense budgets and forces. Certainly, if there are but a few relatively minor differences of interest with a potential opponent, intentions analysis is an enticing way to proceed. A more cautious (and more expensive) approach is to consider what an opponent is capable of doing. Intentions can change for the worse for a variety of reasons and in a relatively short time, and thus capability analysis is appropriate. Elements of the U.S. government are continually involved in military capability analysis and in providing the supporting data and estimates on the military forces of other states. But a military capability analysis, like a theater ticket, is useful at one time and at one place only. This is so because, as in the case of national power discussed in Chapter 1, the factors involved are *dynamic*—susceptible to constant, and sometimes dramatic, change. Further, factors are *situational*, varying not only with the given time period but also with the particularities of situation and geography. Finally, all factors considered in capability analysis are *relative* to other states' capacities to employ military means directed to the same or related objectives.

A classic example of the dynamic, situational, and relative nature of military capability is the Korean War. At the outbreak of that conflict in the summer of 1950, the United States enjoyed a virtual monopoly of nuclear weapons. One would think that American military capability was almost unlimited. If two atomic bombs dropped on Hiroshima and Nagasaki could end World War II with such finality, why not a repeat performance in Korea?

The reason is that the two cases were drastically different. First, the nature of the threat had changed. By 1945, the United States and its Allies had defeated all other enemies except Japan. In 1950, however, the Soviet Union—an ally of North Korea—was becoming an increasingly threatening Cold War enemy. It maintained powerful conventional forces and had its own fledgling atomic force. In fact, the U.S. Joint Chiefs of Staff (JCS) felt that the Korean War might well be a Soviet diversion and that America needed to save its small arsenal of nuclear weapons for the possibility of a main Soviet attack in Europe. Second, nuclear weapons were not particularly appropriate for the Korean War, where the targets inside North Korea were essentially bridges and troop concentrations rather than cities like Nagasaki. Leveling Chinese cities after China's "volunteers" intervened massively in Korea would have generated all-out war with the People's Republic of China and perhaps with the Soviet Union as well. Third, America's allies, especially the British, and substantial numbers of Americans were strongly opposed to the use of nuclear weapons.[28] Obviously, the United States did not have in 1950 the same freedom to use nuclear weapons that it had in 1945; military capability had changed significantly, because the overall situation had changed fundamentally.

Capability analysis is complex, requiring multivariate analysis. However, the following factors, illustrated at a high level of generalization, must normally be considered:

- *Force size/structure.* How large are the relevant military establishments in terms of forces-in-being and trained reserves? How many people under arms are at the disposal of the various services (e.g., Army, Navy, Air Force, Marines), in how many active and reserve units are they deployed, and how are the units structured and equipped? How well do the branches of each military service operate together, as well as the different land, air, and sea services that make up a country's armed forces?

- *Weapons systems.* How many weapons systems and of what types are at the disposal of the opposing forces? What is the potential of these weapons in terms of range, accuracy, lethality, survivability, and reliability?

- *Mobility.* What are the locations of units and weapons systems? How quickly and by what means could they be moved to strategically and tactically important locations? How much airlift and sealift are available for overseas operations?

- *Logistics (supply).* Because military units can carry only so much equipment with them and must be resupplied if they are to remain in action for more than a few days, how efficient and vulnerable are systems of resupply?

- *Strategic, operational, and tactical doctrines.* What are the nature and the quality of the doctrines of force deployment and military engagement that fundamentally control the employment of military units?

- *Training.* What is the level of training of forces-in-being and reserve units? How proficient are soldiers in employing their weapons under varying conditions? How skilled are forces in combined operations?

- *Military leadership.* How effective are the officers and noncommissioned officers in the chain of command through which orders are issued and carried out?

- *Morale.* A function of many variables and absolutely vital to success in combat, what are the levels of unit morale? Especially important for the armed forces of democratic nations, what would be the level of popular support for the employment of force in various contexts?

- *Industry.* What is the industrial capacity of a given nation to produce military equipment of the types and in the amounts likely to be required for sustained, long-term combat? How quickly can the nation switch from production of civilian goods to war material?

- *Technology.* What is the level of technological capability and integration of existing weapons systems and command, control, communications, and intelligence (C^3I) systems? What is the status of technology of weapons and C^3I at various stages of progress in a nation's military research, development, test, and evaluation processes?

- *Intelligence.* How effective are technical and human intelligence-gathering means? What is the level of competence and speed in analyzing raw intelligence data and producing and disseminating estimates useful to decision makers?

- *Popular will.* How prepared would the population be to sustain the domestic deprivations (conscription, rationing of various types, and so forth) that would result from sustained, large-scale wartime activities or a drawn-out war of attrition?

- *National leadership.* What are the levels of resolve and skill of a nation's leaders? How effective is the leadership in maintaining national unity and at ensuring coordination between military strategy and operations and political purposes? How effective is the national leadership at leveraging national resources toward wartime needs?[29]

- *Alliances and coalitions.* What is the status of alliances and potential coalitions that can change opposing force ratios significantly? What is the quality of alliance and coalition commitments under various conditions, in terms of military units, weapons systems, bases, and supplies likely to be made available?

Taken together, weighed, and blended, these factors can produce a sound judgment of military capability. The judgment process needs to be continuous, for there is insufficient time available in varying crisis situations to gather anew all required data. Ideally, such capability analysis results in a series of cost/risk calculations, which, when coupled with a political assessment of an adversary's intentions, can form the basis for decisions about the preparation and use of the military instrument. Major policy choices confronting decision makers inevitably involve *costs*—material and nonmaterial, domestic and international—arising from the impacts of those choices. *Risk*, in terms of the probabilities of success or failure, is also inherent in virtually all major policy decisions. Military capability analysis aids the policy maker in judging what costs and risks are acceptable relative to the value of the objective sought. The more important the objective, the higher the costs and risks the policy maker is likely to judge acceptable.

The Functions of Force.   Assuming that conflict will continue to mark international life, what are the most suitable means for pursuing or controlling conflict, and how should those means be used? As discussed above, the military instrument is only one such means, albeit the most violent and potentially conclusive one.

Historically, the political purposes served by military force have included aggrandizement and defense, although the distinction between the two has sometimes been blurred. A third purpose has been the resolution of disputes, though such a use must consider the prospect that conflict may be escalated rather than resolved—a particularly dangerous development in an era of weapons of mass destruction (WMDs). In any event, in the international system as it exists today, states retain the ultimate right and capacity to resort to military force: "The legitimacy of force as an instrument of foreign policy, although often denounced by philosophers, historians, and reformers, has rarely been questioned by those responsible for foreign policy decisions of their nations."[30]

In a 1980 article, Robert Art sets forth a valuable framework for thinking about what he labels the four functions of military force. The first of these is the use of military power in a *defensive* role. Defense "is the deployment of military power so as to be able to do two things—to ward off an attack and to minimize damage to oneself if attacked."[31] Art argues that states will choose to develop the capability to defend themselves when possible, because a capacity for self-defense is the most reliable way to ensure one's security. Within defense, Art includes the passive development of military capability as well as active uses of force, such as pre-emptive strikes.

Second, nuclear and conventional military forces can be employed in a *deterrent* role. Again from Art, deterrence "is the deployment of military power so as to be able to prevent an adversary from doing something that one does not want him to do and that he might otherwise be tempted to do by threatening him with unacceptable punishment if he does it."[32] At base, deterrence is a psychological phenomenon; its objective is to master the expectations of one's actual or potential opponent. Yet deterrence must also rest on credible capability—the will and the clear, demonstrable ability to perform the threatened act if the necessity arises. The success of a deterrent approach depends on the deterrer's ability to convince an adversary that an attempt to gain an objective would cost more than it is worth, and that the cost to the deterrer of applying the punishment would be less than conceding the objective.[33]

Deterrence assumes a rational, informed opponent. An irrational (or ill-informed) opponent who will accept destruction or disproportionate loss as a consequence of a selected course of action cannot be deterred. Deterrence must also be considered in relation to the nature of the states, alliances, or groups that are to be deterred and the particular action that is to be deterred. For example, a threat of massive nuclear retaliation could hardly deter a terrorist group from planting bombs on aircraft. In addition to lacking credibility because of its disproportionate nature, deterrence is problematic against an adversary who is difficult to communicate with, to identify, and to locate.

A third function of military force is *compellence*. Compellence is "the deployment of military power so as to be able either to stop an adversary from doing something that he has already undertaken or to get him to do something that he has not yet undertaken."[34] The means of compulsion is the direct application or the threat of application of military force. The objective of compulsion is to cause an adversary to decide that further pursuit of its course of action would incur increasing costs incommensurate with any possible gain. If the application of force is tuned too finely, however, as was the case with the gradual and limited application of U.S. force in Vietnam, then the adversary may be able to take countermeasures that will mitigate the harm and avert compulsion.

Art's final function is *swaggering*, which Art admits is in part "a residual category" in which "force is not aimed directly at dissuading another state from attacking, at repelling attacks, nor at compelling it to do something specific."[35] This category serves as a reminder that military capabilities may not always be developed for purposes rationally connected to a country's national security but instead can at times be pursued in the interest of international or domestic prestige of a particular regime or individual leader.

A fifth function, not clearly subsumed by the above categories, is *acquisitive*. Historically, military force has been an important tool for states seeking to seize the territory or resources of others for exploitation. Although a number of constraints exist for states seeking to employ force for this purpose, perhaps most profoundly demonstrated by the refusal of the United States and other countries to let Hussein retain Kuwait after his successful invasion of that country in 1990, there are conditions under which military conquest has indeed redounded to the material benefit of the conquering state.[36]

Given the security challenges of globalization, transnational threats, and weak and failing states, it is useful to think about a sixth possible function of force: *providing order*. Such a function recognizes that military capabilities—even those developed primarily for other purposes—may help create a secure environment in an area, which is the basic precondition for political stability and economic activity. Such countries as the United States have in the past and will probably continue in the future to turn to the military instrument of power to enable immediate response to human rights catastrophes or other humanitarian disasters that occur either at home or abroad—such as the situation in Somalia in the early 1990s. However, as Art recognizes, "force can easily be used to maim and kill, but only with greater difficulty and with great expenditure of effort, to rule and pacify."[37] Although the employment of military force to fulfill all the functions above may be made more effective when combined or supported by other instruments of national power, in the case of intervention within the territory of another state, military force alone will almost certainly be inadequate to the creation of a sustainable solution (see Chapter 16 for more on military intervention).

Louis XIV called military force "the last argument of kings" and so inscribed his cannons. The situations in which military force remains a final arbiter have been somewhat circumscribed in the nuclear era, at least among nuclear powers and their allies. Accordingly, the employment of "gunboat diplomacy," the diplomatic use of force as a coercive instrument, has dwindled in frequency. Still, the opposing capabilities of military forces do serve to limit and regulate claims among states with competing interests.[38]

Constraints on the Military Instrument.   The use of military force historically has been a "prerogative power," reserved for the decisions of sovereigns. Since the rise of European mass nationalist movements in the Napoleonic era, however, the power bases of heads of state have rested increasingly upon the support of the populace from which the personnel and resources of mass warfare are drawn. Prior to the nineteenth century, battlefields were usually relatively restricted, for the most part touching only the lives of those directly involved in combat. The virtually total wars of the nineteenth and twentieth centuries—that is, the Napoleonic wars, the American Civil War, and the two world wars—changed this situation, bringing the carnage and anguish of war into the lives and homes of entire populations.

The communication and information revolutions have further enhanced the involvement of the general population in warfare, leading to increased scrutiny of the use of military force. World opinion (or, more accurately, the opinion of leading democratic states) has for some time expressed abhorrence of unrestricted warfare, codifying "laws of war" and turning to definitions of "just war," which had long been the province of theologians and philosophers. The League of Nations and United Nations (UN) attempted to frame distinctions between legitimate and illegitimate uses of military force. Although problems of agreed definition as well as uncertain enforcement plague international law, "aggression" is outlawed, and the use of military force for defense against aggression is "just." The just war categories associated with the justice of a war, or *jus ad bellum* (just cause, competent authority, right intention, last resort, reasonable chance of success), and justice within a war, or *jus in bello* (discrimination between combatants and noncombatants, proportionality of each military action), have become important international law criteria in evaluating military action.[39] It should be noted, too, that though the force of international opinion can be a constraint, it can also serve as an impetus for action in cases of egregious human rights abuses or humanitarian disaster.[40]

In addition to international law, constraints on the use of force also flow from advances in technology as well as changes in the distribution of power within the international system. Though nuclear weapons may have deterrent and prestige value, many analysts would argue that they are and should be unusable for any other purposes, including compellence and support to diplomacy.[41] Further, although the United States may enjoy enhanced freedom of action in a world in which it is the only superpower, this distribution of power constrains others. As long as the United States maintains a powerful nuclear arsenal as well as a significant conventional power projection capability, and its national will and alliances remain strong, no other state can make a credible military threat against the United States or one of its allies.

A final international constraint on the use of force lies in the repercussions of such use for a country's other national interests. In day-to-day diplomacy, international consensus against an act of military aggression usually represents more sound than fury. However, the longer-term impact may be quite different. As Princeton political scientist and government advisor Klaus Knorr has pointed out:

> If a state flagrantly flouts an internationally sanctioned restraint on military aggression, it may, in the event of success, gain the object of aggression and in addition perhaps inspire increased respect for its military prowess; but it may also tarnish its nonmilitary reputation and provoke attitudes of suspicion and hostility that, over the longer run if not immediately, will become organized politically, and perhaps militarily as well. This amounts to saying that the respect a nation enjoys—respect for acting properly, with sensitivity to internationally widespread moral standards, and with sobriety and restraint in resorting to military power—is a precious asset in foreign affairs. It is an asset that assists in holding and gaining allies, and generally in promoting a favorable reception for its diplomatic initiatives.[42]

One might argue that the widely respected status of Germany and Japan today disproves the thesis of adverse long-term effects of aggression. Yet Germany and Japan are watched especially carefully by neighboring states, Japan has rejected all but self-defense forces since World War II, and neither state now has—nor is likely to acquire—a military nuclear capability.[43]

In addition to all these international constraints on the use of force, additional domestic constraints exist. Two of the most important of these are *domestic public opinion* and *cost*. In the United States, public opinion is likely to be initially supportive of decisive actions by the president in the area of national security—the "rally around the flag" effect.[44] Nevertheless, over time the degree of public support is likely to be shaped by a variety of factors, including perceptions of the stakes involved, costs in terms of lives and resources, prospects for success or failure, and even international approbation or disapproval. What world opinion cannot accomplish by direct impact upon the leadership of a democratic state, it may over time be able to effect indirectly by influencing public attitudes and national legislatures. Foreign opposition and criticism, for instance, had some impact upon American public attitudes during the U.S. involvement in Vietnam from 1965 to 1975 and even more impact during the U.S. war in Iraq after 2003. Domestic public opposition to the Vietnam conflict resulted in a disastrous congressional cutoff of military supplies to the beleaguered South Vietnamese government. As of 2009, the ultimate impact of domestic opposition to the Iraq War remains to be seen.

A second important domestic constraint on the use of force is cost, particularly for the more industrialized nations with advanced weapons. Technological sophistication has increased the costs of weapons systems enormously. Costs associated with personnel have also skyrocketed in the industrial democracies, particularly in the United States after the introduction of the all-volunteer force in 1973. In the wake of the terrorist attacks of September 11, 2001, the idea of cutting U.S. defense spending has not had political appeal for either of the country's two main political parties. Nevertheless, some politicians and analysts have sought to call attention to what they see as a lack of discipline in U.S. defense spending, with one scholar advocating the rallying cry that "Half a trillion dollars is more than enough."[45]

Though these constraints all have the potential to influence U.S. national security policy, their weight varies over time. For example, President George H. W. Bush seemed highly sensitive to international constraints in advance of the 1991 Desert Storm offensive against the Iraqi invasion of Kuwait and began building a UN consensus to support the action even before taking the case before the U.S. Congress. Other U.S. presidents, including Bill Clinton with regard to Kosovo in 1999 and George W. Bush with regard to Iraq in 2003, made it clear that their actions would not be dependent on obtaining advance approval from the UN. Although the constraints listed here may not necessarily determine outcomes, they are relevant considerations as policy makers decide whether and how to use force.

Alliances and Military Power

The numerous American alliances, treaties of guarantee, and military base agreements around the world constitute a complex alliance structure that is cumulatively a response to the various perceived threats to U.S. foreign policy objectives that have arisen since World War II. In 1947, the United States signed the Rio Pact, breaking a one-hundred-fifty-year tradition of avoiding foreign entanglement. The North Atlantic Treaty Organization (NATO) alliance was concluded in 1949 as a direct result of the growing Soviet threat in Europe. With the outbreak of the Korean War in 1950, the United States began adding Asian allies. In relatively quick order, several alliances were formed: U.S.–Japan (1951), U.S.–Philippines (1951), Australia–New Zealand–U.S. (ANZUS; 1951), U.S.–South Korea (1953), Southeast Asia Treaty Organization (SEATO; 1954), and U.S.–Republic of China (1954), followed by limited participation in the Central Treaty Organization (CENTO; 1956). Further bilateral defense treaties were signed with Iran, Pakistan, and Turkey in 1959. In support of these and subsequent commitments, the United States has dispersed military aid worth many billions of dollars to more than sixty countries around the world and has deployed millions of U.S. service members overseas.

Why Do States Join Alliances?   An *alliance* is a contract that, like all other contracts, bestows rights and advantages but also places obligations and restrictions on the contracting parties. Unlike contracts in domestic law, however, states have no higher authority to which to appeal when there is a breach of contract. The primary consideration of national leaders contemplating an alliance is that the benefits of the prospective alliance outweigh the loss of flexibility incurred in becoming dependent upon acts of omission or commission by other states in the alliance. In this regard, Hans Morgenthau writes, "A nation will shun alliances if it believes that it is strong enough to hold its own unaided or that the burden of commitment resulting from an alliance is likely to outweigh the advantages to be expected."[46]

Faced with an international system best described as "semiorganized anarchy," states seek various forms of cooperative behavior designed to generate strength and reduce risk. They attempt to produce the type and degree of international order that best ensures their own interests. On issues of international peace and security, where power tends to be the common currency, "the question as to whose values or ends will prevail . . . is determined finally by the relative power positions of the [opposing] parties."[47] Stephen Walt has stressed that alliances most often emerge not just in response to imbalances of power but more specifically in response to the perception of a hostile threat from an aggressive power.[48]

Three motives for alliances spring from a focus on power, and all of them relate to a state's attempts to meet its security needs. First, a state may join or create an alliance to aggregate the capabilities necessary to achieve a foreign policy goal (i.e., a state's own means are insufficient for its ends). Second, a state may enter into an alliance to secure favorable treatment in the future; in short, states selectively join alliances to gain calculated advantages in the pursuit of future national goals.[49] Third, a state may join an alliance to reduce costs. This may be true if a state is seeking multiple objectives and does not want to commit all or an undue part of its capabilities to any one specific end. A second variant of this cost-reduction motive relates to defense economy. A good example of this is the establishment of the European Defense Agency as a subordinate organization of the European Union in July 2004. Its specific goals are to enhance Europe's military capabilities and strengthen European defense industries while creating better value for European taxpayers by reducing the redundancy created by separate national defense programs.[50]

In addition to increasing power, Robert Osgood notes that alliances may serve the functions of preserving the internal security of members, restraining allies, or creating a degree of international order.[51] The first of these functions, the preservation of internal security, may prove increasingly important in the future, as states seek to confront the increasing threats of international terrorism, drug trafficking, weapons proliferation, and cross-border refugee flows. The second purpose, restraining allies' behavior, has been historically common; it is practiced by the larger, more powerful actors and the weaker, subordinate actors in an alliance. Finally, alliance structures can create predictable, regulated patterns of interaction that reduce sources of friction and conflict and enhance international order.

Alliances and U.S. National Security Policy.   When thinking about the role of alliances in U.S. national security policy, recognizing the costs is as important as considering the benefits. As discussed in the preceding section, alliances entail commitments that reduce flexibility, and alliance structures can be used to restrain as well as support alliance members. Even when restraint is not the goal, the very existence of an alliance—as well as its decision-making procedures—can have that effect. For example, the existence of the 1991 Gulf War coalition is often cited as having shaped George H. W. Bush's decision not to topple Hussein's regime after expelling Iraq from Kuwait. Whether this was a wise strategic decision could be debated; that it was shaped by incentives created by the existence of a multinational coalition seems certain. Another example can be found in NATO operations against Serbia in 1999. Consensus-oriented procedures generated time-consuming decision-making procedures and a tightly controlled—and therefore less flexible and responsive—strategic bombing campaign.[52]

Within alliances, the power contributions of allies are not simply additive. Even within the well-developed and mature structure of NATO, the pace of technological advance enabled by significant U.S. investment has created interoperability issues between U.S. forces and those of its NATO allies (see Chapter 23). In addition, though operating in the context of an alliance may offer diplomatic and domestic political benefits, "alliance operations pose significant problems at the tactical, operational, and even the strategic level, which often make them less integrated, skillful, and responsive compared to unilateral operations."[53]

In the context of a superpower competition with the Soviet Union, it may have been relatively easy for U.S. policy makers to decide that the benefits associated with membership in formal alliances outweighed the costs. However, since the end of the Cold War, a growing debate has emerged over whether temporary, ad hoc "coalitions of the willing" or even unilateral approaches may be superior. Although many of the benefits of an alliance may be lost, by including burden sharing as well as interoperability, many of the constraints associated with alliances also disappear. Where one comes down on this debate is likely to be shaped by two factors: the importance one ascribes to the legitimacy of U.S. action abroad, and one's perspective on how long the U.S. status as the world's only superpower is likely to last.

An American Perspective on the Use of Force

In what was widely seen as a response to the lessons of the Vietnam War, in 1985, Secretary of Defense Caspar Weinberger presented six major tests to be applied before employing U.S. combat forces:

1. The United States should not commit forces to combat overseas unless the particular engagement or occasion is deemed vital to U.S. national interest or that of U.S. allies.

2. If the United States decides it is necessary to put combat troops into a given situation, it should do so wholeheartedly and with the clear intention of winning. If the country is unwilling to commit the forces or resources necessary to achieve its objectives, it should not commit them at all. Of course, if the particular situation requires only limited force to win its objectives, then it should not hesitate to commit forces sized accordingly.

3. If the United States does decide to commit forces to combat overseas, it should have clearly defined political and military objectives, it should know precisely how U.S. forces can accomplish those clearly defined objectives, it should have and send the forces needed to do just that.

4. The relationship between U.S. objectives and the forces committed—their size, composition, and disposition—must be continually reassessed and adjusted if necessary. Conditions and objectives invariably change during the course of a conflict. When they do change, then U.S. combat requirements must also change.

5. Before the United States commits combat forces abroad, there must be some reasonable assurance it will have the support of the American people and their elected representatives in Congress.[54] This support cannot be achieved unless it is candid in making clear the threats it faces; the support cannot be sustained without continuing and close consultation.

6. The commitment of U.S. forces to combat should be a last resort.[55]

Later, Chairman of the JCS Colin Powell enunciated a briefer, but similar, standard for the employment of U.S. forces. Powell stressed the importance of clear political objectives and adequately sized and decisive means.[56] Like Weinberger's six tests, the Powell Doctrine aimed at keeping U.S. troops out of wars to which the nation was not fully committed.

These propositions have much in common with the strategic logic set forth above. Like Clausewitz, Weinberger emphasizes clear political objectives and the need to carefully and continuously reconcile ends, ways, and means. However, Weinberger also exceeds Clausewitz's logic in his effort to restrict the use of force to instances in which vital interests are at stake, force will be committed "wholeheartedly," public support is assured in advance, and force is used as a last resort. Weinberger's six tests evoked significant debate in Washington, with the most significant opposition coming from Secretary of State George Shultz. Given his repeated view that "force and diplomacy must always go together," Shultz rejected Weinberger's vital interest, last resort, and public support criteria, which he called "the Vietnam syndrome in spades . . . and a complete abdication of the duties of leadership."[57]

Despite its critics, the Weinberger Doctrine has proven to have enduring influence in debates over U.S. national security policy and the use of force. In fact, it is associated in the minds of many with the success of the United States in the Persian Gulf War of 1990–1991 (see Chapter 20), as well as what some see as a beneficial military reluctance to engage in limited military operations in the 1990s, including Somalia, Haiti, Bosnia, and Rwanda (see Chapter 8).[58] The Weinberger and Powell doctrines also appear to have been buttressed by the difficulties faced by the United States in Iraq after the successful 2003 invasion. To some extent, the initial campaign plan was informed by a concept called "Rapid Dominance," which would succeed through creating "Shock and Awe" rather than physically overwhelming an adversary. This concept was initially set out in 1996 in deliberate opposition to what analysts saw as the "Decisive Force" approach then prevailing in the Pentagon.[59] To the extent that this new approach contributed to inadequate U.S. resourcing of the requirements of post-invasion Iraq, the "decisive force" approach of Weinberger and Powell would appear to be validated.

Despite its influence, criticisms of the Weinberger Doctrine by Shultz and others retain merit. As discussed below, political leaders are likely to continue to face an international environment in which they find utility in actual or potential uses of force for less than vital interests, when public support is not guaranteed, and before it is a matter of last resort. Seeking limited purposes, they will seek to employ limited ways and means. Many military leaders, on the other hand, can be expected to continue to adhere to Powell's emphasis on decisive force and to

DESERT STORM

"You were right all along, President Hussein: we'll NEVER leave Kuwait!"

©1991 INTERNATIONAL COPYRIGHT BY CARTOONEWS INC., N.Y.C., USA

Copyright 1991 CARTOONEWS Inc., N.Y.C., USA. Reprinted with permission of Ranan Lurie.

want to use overwhelming means when force is applied.[60] This situation is likely to result in the persistence of tensions between U.S. policy makers regarding the use of force.

American Military Power Today

In the early years of the twenty-first century, the United States faces a complex and uncertain international strategic environment. As discussed in the concluding pages of Chapter 1, the U.S. position is characterized by important strengths. The United States has at its disposal an unrivaled concentration of political, economic, and military power and is able to pursue its national interests in an environment characterized by peace among major world powers. The strongest economic powers in the international system—such countries as the United Kingdom, Germany, and Japan—are also democracies. In relations among these countries and the United States, war has become inconceivable. Although important states, such as Russia and China, remain at least partially outside this group as they continue to pursue their own paths toward economic and political development, the prevalence of peace among the most advanced states is still an unusual situation in the history of international politics.[61]

At the same time, however, the powerful forces of globalization have increased the salience of numerous problems of global governance. Significant challenges include newly empowered nonstate actors as well as other transnational phenomena, such as large-scale immigration and environmental hazards. Increasingly powerful nonstate actors, such as transnational terrorist groups, are able to take advantage of the advances in communication and transportation that have underpinned globalization as well as advances in weapons technology, including WMDs, and therefore have an increased potential to do catastrophic harm to U.S. national interests. In this situation, state weakness or failure in any region of the world has the potential to negatively affect the security of the United States and its allies. Territory that is not under the control of any state can provide hostile groups and actors a safe haven in which they can organize and base their activities. In particular, the JCS have noted the concentration of hostile regimes, problems of state governance, and nonstate actors in an "'arc of instability' stretching from the Western Hemisphere, through Africa and the Middle East and extending to Asia," within which some areas serve as "breeding grounds for threats to [U.S.] interests."[62]

In response to these characteristics of the current international environment, U.S. defense planners have created a framework intended to portray the full range of contemporary threats to U.S. national security. As depicted in Figure 13.1, the four categories of challenges are *traditional, irregular, catastrophic*, and *disruptive*.[63] In its inclusion of traditional challenges, this framework acknowledges the continuing relevance of the potential threats posed by other states with more or less advanced military capabilities (the lower left quadrant of Figure 13.1). However, defense planners also recognize the need to examine challenges emerging— at least to some extent—as a reaction to U.S. relative strengths in traditional areas

FIG. 13.1   Challenges in the U.S. Security Environment

Irregular	**Catastrophic**
Unconventional methods; often used to counter stronger state opponents: terrorism, insurgency, ethnic conflict, civil war, guerrilla warfare	Weapons of mass destruction (WMD) or "WMD-like" attacks on U.S. interests or the U.S. homeland by state or non-state actors
Traditional	**Disruptive**
State-based challenges to U.S. power using uniformed militaries and legacy nuclear forces	Breakthrough, asymmetric counters to U.S. strengths; examples include cyberwar and anti-access strategies

of military competition. To increase prospects of success when seeking to oppose the United States, adversaries can be expected to turn increasingly to activities reflected in the other quadrants in Figure 13.1 (proceeding clockwise beginning in the upper left quadrant): irregular forms of warfare to erode U.S. power; the use of WMDs to paralyze U.S. power; or disruptive capabilities, such as cyber warfare, directed energy weapons, biotechnology, or antispace systems, to marginalize U.S. power.[64]

As recognized by the 2005 National Defense Strategy, these categories of challenges overlap:

> Terrorist groups like al-Qa'ida are *irregular* threats but also actively seek *catastrophic* capabilities. North Korea at once poses *traditional*, *irregular*, and *catastrophic* challenges. Finally, in the future, the most capable opponents may seek to combine truly *disruptive* capacity with *traditional*, *irregular*, or *catastrophic* forms of warfare.[65]

As an example of a "disruptive" challenge to U.S. national security, defense planners look to China as the most likely future peer competitor that is also pursuing ways to counter U.S. strengths through asymmetric anti-access and area-denial strategies (see Chapters 18 and 26). Additionally, China, Russia, and other potential competitors have emphasized cyber-warfare and counter-space operations that can degrade C^4ISR capabilities, which are essential to the effectiveness of both U.S. military forces and economic networks. Notably, in the Russian conflict with Georgia in 2008 (discussed in more detail in chapter 22), there were several reports of a cyber-space offensive that complemented the military offensive in Georgia. These threats, if not effectively countered, has the potential to disrupt internet and other electronic communications, and significantly degrade U.S. capabilities.

FIG. 13.2   U.S. Military Capabilities and QDR Focus Areas

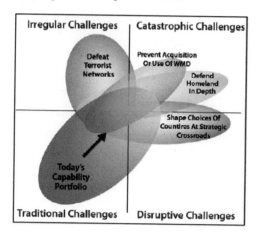

In the 2006 Quadrennial Defense Review (QDR), senior DoD leaders focused on "four priority areas for examination":

- Defeating terrorist networks.
- Defending the homeland in depth.
- Shaping the choices of countries at strategic crossroads.
- Preventing hostile states and nonstate actors from acquiring or using WMDs.[66]

The 2006 QDR argues that the current U.S. portfolio of military capabilities is overoptimized against traditional challenges to U.S. national security as a legacy of the Cold War. While retaining the capability to counter traditional threats, the U.S. military must develop more robust capabilities to counter emerging challenges (see Figure 13.2).[67]

In this text, the role of the U.S. military in homeland security is discussed in Chapter 6. Other applications of U.S. military power are discussed in the four chapters that follow this one. First, Chapter 14 discusses the irregular challenge of terrorism and the catastrophic threat of WMDs in its examination of the role of preemption in U.S. national security policy. Next, Chapter 15 looks at traditional and disruptive state-based challenges to U.S. national security with its examination of conventional warfare and the idea of a revolution in military affairs. Chapter 16 then focuses on forms of irregular warfare other than terrorism and uses of American military power to counter these challenges. Finally, the examination of U.S. nuclear policy in Chapter 17 has implications for traditional, disruptive, and catastrophic challenges to U.S. national security.

Relevant to all the U.S. military instruments of power are three central issues that are likely to be of enduring importance in U.S. defense policy. The first of these is adapting to and implementing change. As discussed above, the 2006 QDR argues that the United States does not have a portfolio of capabilities that is optimized to meet current challenges. This message was reaffirmed when, shortly after the release of the QDR, George W. Bush announced a national change of strategy in Iraq and an initiative to increase the size of U.S. ground forces in January 2007.[68] A look at the historical relationship between strategy and structure in U.S. national security policy, such as that provided in Chapter 3, suggests that a mismatch between the two is not uncommon. Overcoming it will require supportive domestic political developments as well as a concerted effort to change large government bureaucracies, including those in the DoD. Although changing military organizations is always challenging, in this case the problem is further complicated by the broad and diverse range of capabilities being sought.

A second important issue relates to the specific nature of today's security threats and the cooperative approaches necessary to address them. The 2006 QDR notes that common to its four focus areas is

> the imperative to work with other government agencies, allies and partners and, where appropriate, to help them increase their capacities and capabilities and the ability to work together. In all cases, the four focus areas require the application of multiple elements of national power and close cooperation with international allies and partners. The Department [of Defense] cannot solve these problems alone.[69]

As just one example, the irregular challenge of terrorism is not solely—or even primarily—a military problem, and a successful strategy is likely to require diplomatic, informational, economic, financial, intelligence, and law enforcement actions. As noted in Chapter 10, coordination across organizational lines does not come easily to government bureaucracies and can be similarly difficult among different governments. Success in making the already complex U.S. interagency process function more effectively is likely to require determined and sustained effort. Similarly, concentrated effort is needed to enable U.S. departments and agencies to work more effectively with partners abroad.

A final enduring issue relates to planning and budgeting. The United States will never be able to be perfectly secure; defense planners will always face the challenge of apportioning limited means to best manage risks. As discussed in Chapter 9, the challenge is even greater when all the instruments of national power are taken into account. The United States still lacks a national security apparatus with the capability to plan, manage, and control all national security-related spending. This situation is likely to complicate the ability of the United States to create and resource the interagency and international partnerships deemed so important to success against many current and emerging national security challenges.

Discussion Questions

1. What did Clausewitz mean in his famous statement that "War is merely the continuation of policy by other means"?

2. What would Clausewitz argue is the appropriate relationship between a political leader and military commander in decision making about the use of force?

3. How does Clausewitz describe the nature of war? Is this helpful in thinking about the use of force? If so, how?

4. What are the challenges associated with assessing military capability? What factors should be considered when making an assessment?

5. What are the functions of military force? What is *deterrence*, and what factors affect its success or failure?

6. What are important international and domestic constraints on the use of force in the current era? Under what conditions would you expect these constraints to be more or less powerful?

7. Why do states join alliances? In addition to aggregating power, what purposes can alliance membership serve?

8. Is it in the best interest of the United States today to belong to and to act in concert with formal alliances? Why or why not?

9. Is the Weinberger Doctrine a useful guide to U.S. thinking about the use of force? What are its strengths and weaknesses?

10. What challenges in the international security environment do U.S. defense policy makers see as requiring the actual or potential application of U.S. force? If U.S. military capabilities need to evolve in the early twenty-first century, in what areas do they need to become more capable?

Recommended Reading

Art, Robert J., and Kenneth Neal Waltz. *Military Power and International Politics.* 6th ed. Lanham, MD: Rowman & Littlefield, 2004.

Barnett, Thomas P. M. *The Pentagon's New Map: War and Peace in the Twenty-First Century.* New York: G. P. Putnam's Sons, 2004.

Baylis, John, James J. Wirtz, Eliot A. Cohen, and Colin S. Gray, eds. *Strategy in the Contemporary World: An Introduction to Strategic Studies.* 2nd ed. Oxford: Oxford University Press, 2007.

Biddle, Stephen D. *Military Power: Explaining Victory and Defeat in Modern Battle.* Princeton, NJ: Princeton University Press, 2004.

Blechman, Barry M., and Stephen S. Kaplan. *Force without War: U.S. Armed Forces as a Political Instrument.* Washington, DC: Brookings Institution, 1978.

Brooks, Risa A., and Elizabeth A. Stanley. *Creating Military Power: The Sources of Military Effectiveness.* Stanford: Stanford University Press, 2007.

Clausewitz, Carl von. *On War.* Translated and edited by Michael Howard and Peter Paret. Princeton, NJ: Princeton University Press, 1976.

Gacek, Christopher M. *The Logic of Force: The Dilemma of Limited War in American Foreign Policy.* New York: Columbia University Press, 1994.

Handel, Michael I. *Masters of War: Classical Strategic Thought.* London: Frank Cass, 2001.

Hoffmann, Stanley. *The Ethics and Politics of Humanitarian Intervention.* Notre Dame: University of Notre Dame Press, 1996.

Paret, Peter, Gordon A. Craig, and Felix Gilbert. *Makers of Modern Strategy from Machiavelli to the Nuclear Age.* Princeton, NJ: Princeton University Press, 1986.

Posen, Barry R. "Command of the Commons: The Military Foundation of U.S. Hegemony." *International Security* 28, no. 1 (2003): 5–46.

Sun Tzu. *The Art of War.* Translated and edited by Samuel B. Griffith. Oxford: Oxford University Press Paperback, 1971.

Walzer, Michael. *Just and Unjust Wars: A Moral Argument with Historical Illustrations.* 4th ed. New York: Basic Books, 2006.

Weigley, Russell F. *The American Way of War: A History of United States Military Policy and Strategy.* Bloomington: Indiana University Press, 1977.

Internet Resources

Department of Defense, *The National Defense Strategy of the United States of America*, March 2005, www.defenselink.mil/news/Mar2005/d20050318nds.pdf

Department of Defense, *Quadrennial Defense Review Report*, February 6, 2006, www.defenselink.mil/pubs/pdfs/QDR20060203.pdf

The Joint Chiefs of Staff, *The National Military Strategy of the United States of America*, 2004, www.defenselink.mil/news/Mar2005/d20050318nms.pdf

14

Asymmetric Conflict, Terrorism, and Preemption

Perhaps the most significant development in U.S. national security in the past decade has been a broad recognition of the significant way in which terrorism can threaten U.S. national security. Instead of challenging U.S. military strength directly, terrorists and other adversaries can use asymmetric means to exploit U.S. weaknesses and to gain strategic political objectives. While the concepts of asymmetry and terrorism have increased in importance, the basic idea is far from new. Writing more than two thousand years ago, military theorist Sun Tzu argues that "an army may be likened to water, for just as flowing water avoids the heights and hastens to the lowlands, so an army avoids strengths and strikes weaknesses."[1] By focusing on specific vulnerabilities and avoiding strengths, a much weaker enemy can inflict extraordinary damage.

In the modern era, the greatest danger faced by the United States stems from the nexus of two forms of asymmetry: technological and organizational.[2] A *technological* asymmetric threat uses unique technologies in innovative ways either to disrupt conventional military organizations, or to target other specific technological, social, economic, or political vulnerabilities of an adversary. Adversaries that use unorthodox organizational structures and techniques to circumvent the military power of an enemy represent *organizational* asymmetric threats.

After September 11, 2001, President George W. Bush argued that the most dangerous threat to the United States was asymmetric when he said it stemmed from a terrorist organization or rogue state willing and able to strike directly at the U.S. population with weapons of mass destruction (WMDs). Although estimates of the probability of this scenario vary, policy makers deemed the threat dire enough to warrant a complete rethinking of U.S. strategy (see Chapter 3). One of the most significant consequences has been the adoption of preemption as a strategic response to asymmetric threats. In examining the irregular challenge of terrorism and the catastrophic challenge of WMDs, this chapter focuses on the upper left and upper right quadrants of the national security challenges chart used by defense planners and explained near the end of the previous chapter (see Figure 13.2).

Asymmetry

The first official U.S. use of the term *asymmetry* was in the 1997 Quadrennial Defense Review (QDR). This document provides a practical definition of asymmetrical threats and an explanation for why adversaries would seek to develop such capabilities:

> U.S. dominance in the conventional military arena may encourage adversaries to use . . . asymmetric means to attack our forces and interests overseas and Americans at home. That is, they are likely to seek advantage over the United States by using unconventional approaches to circumvent or undermine our strengths while exploiting our vulnerabilities. Strategically, an aggressor may seek to avoid direct military confrontation with the United States, using instead means such as terrorism, NBC [nuclear, biologica, and chemical] threats, information warfare, or environmental sabotage to achieve its goals. If, however, an adversary ultimately faces a conventional war with the United States, it could also employ asymmetric means to delay or deny U.S. access to critical facilities; disrupt our command, control, communications, and intelligence networks; deter allies and potential coalition partners from supporting U.S. intervention; or inflict higher than expected U.S. casualties in an attempt to weaken our national resolve.[3]

One of the critical elements identified by the QDR is that adversaries will resort to asymmetric tools because of American conventional military strength. Despite the fact that potential U.S. competitors, such as China, have made vast improvements in their conventional militaries, the United States retains the most capable conventional military forces. Indeed, George W. Bush made dissuading other states from seeking to challenge the United States in a symmetric fashion part of his 2002 National Security Strategy (NSS).[4] U.S. conventional dominance confers numerous advantages for American national security policy, but it also means that adversaries will seek asymmetric means to challenge U.S. power.

Technological Asymmetry. The Defense Department's 1997 QDR identifies terrorism and WMDs as key asymmetric threats facing the United States, but the U.S. defense community was not immediately reoriented toward these particular threats. Instead, the asymmetric threats that the U.S. defense community focused on before 9/11 were those to American advanced command, control, communications, computers, intelligence, surveillance, and reconnaissance (C^4ISR) capabilities. The QDR report states:

> Areas in which the United States has a significant advantage over potential opponents and increasing capabilities (e.g., space-based assets; command, control, communications, and computers; and intelligence, surveillance, and reconnaissance) could also

involve inherent vulnerabilities that could be exploited by potential opponents (e.g., attacking our reliance on commercial communications) should we fail to account for such challenges. Dealing with such asymmetric challenges must be an important element of U.S. defense strategy, from fielding new capabilities to adapting how U.S. forces will operate in future contingencies.[5]

Increased attention to U.S. technological vulnerability in the realm of information technology was appropriate, even though—in the wake of the 9/11 terrorist attacks—it was clearly overly narrow.

Networked information systems not only are essential to the functioning of today's U.S. armed forces but also are critical infrastructures for the functioning of society and government. Such critical infrastructures include public and private networks that provide telecommunications services, financial services, transportation, water, energy, and even emergency services. These systems have greatly increased economic growth, improved quality of life, and enhanced U.S. national security capabilities, but they have also created important vulnerabilities. These vulnerabilities were recognized by the administration of President Bill Clinton, who began focused U.S. government efforts to redress them with his 1998 Presidential Decision Directive 63 on critical infrastructure protection. Such efforts require the support of government actions at all levels as well as close cooperation between the public and private sectors, because the majority of U.S. critical infrastructure rests in the hands of the private sector.[6] The challenge of information security in many ways reflects other forms of warfare; in *cyber warfare*, there is a daily interaction between attackers and defenders and a constant evolution in tactics, techniques, and procedures.[7]

Technological asymmetry comes in a variety of forms. It might be a unique military technology that confers an overwhelming advantage or even a low-tech method for destroying or disrupting a U.S. technological advantage. Possible strikes against U.S. space-based assets, the ballistic missile threat from North Korea, and China's ability to deny U.S. Naval assets access to the Taiwan Strait with shore-based cruise missiles are all readily conceivable examples. State adversaries almost certainly would attempt to exploit potential vulnerabilities that could substantially degrade U.S. conventional dominance in a future conflict. Iraq's attempt to disrupt U.S. precision-guided bombs—with electronic jammers and smoke from oil fires—during the early stages of the 2003 invasion is an example of a failed asymmetric effort to disrupt U.S. capability.

In the 1990s, U.S. planners became increasingly concerned about the threat posed by WMDs because of three post–Cold War developments. The first was the 1994 nuclear crisis with North Korea (see Chapter 18). The second was the fear that former Soviet states had not kept a close eye on old Soviet weapons stockpiles, technology, and scientists (see Chapter 22). The third was the ongoing, active containment of Iraq and the numerous United Nations missions to discover and dismantle its weapons programs (see Chapter 20). Though the United States has its own vast WMD capabilities, the possession and possible use of such weapons by an adversary can pose an asymmetric threat to the United States, because the various constraints on their potential use by American forces would likely rule out a symmetric response.

In the cases of North Korea and Iraq, U.S. policy makers were particularly concerned that states with weak conventional military capabilities would turn to nuclear weapons as a technological equalizer. That concern was seemingly justified when North Korea claimed to possess nuclear capability as a way of bolstering its position in the world and finally conducted a nuclear test in 2006. Policy makers were also concerned that terrorists would gain access to WMDs, either via transfer from a state or through the acquisition of a weapon or technology on the international black market. A terrorist group with nuclear weapons raised an entirely new set of concerns for U.S. planners because of the uniquely asymmetric characteristics of terrorist organizations.

Varieties of WMDs.   While the term *WMDs* is useful shorthand for describing nonconventional weapons, it also has the unfortunate effect of aggregating numerous weapon types in a single category and obfuscating the actual variability in the nature and impact of these weapons. The term *CBRN*—which delineates Chemical, Biological, Radiological, and Nuclear weapons—is more descriptive and useful than WMDs. In addition to an unusual level of destructiveness, these weapons have in common the fact that they have been rarely used and have unique psychological impacts on the target population.

The effects of CBRN devices can be quite varied. Whereas a full-size nuclear device might kill tens or hundreds of thousands of people immediately, the initial impact of a radiological or chemical device might be comparable to a conventional explosive. The impact of a biological attack could be even more varied; some modes of such attacks—such as the anthrax letters that were sent in the U.S. mail system in late 2001—have very localized effects. However, a different delivery system could have transformed a similar agent into a weapon that could kill hundreds or thousands of people. The common characteristic is that, if effectively employed, CBRN weapons can have a devastating psychological effect that reaches well beyond their immediate destructive power.

Within this chapter, references to WMDs are intended to connote high-impact events: a nuclear detonation or devastating chemical, biological, or radiological attack. Nevertheless, it is worth remembering the ambiguity of the terminology. Not all WMDs are particularly destructive, nor are all technologically asymmetric attacks necessarily deadly.

Terrorists and WMDs.   In addition to how U.S. policy makers view WMDs, it is important to understand the enemy's perspective. While al-Qa'ida is discussed in detail later in this chapter with regard to WMDs, al-Qa'ida leaders recognize that WMDs are different from conventional weapons, and they do not take the decision to use WMDs lightly. Using such weapons would have serious theological and strategic implications. A Saudi cleric, Naser bin Hamad al-Fahd, has issued a *fatwa* (a religious opinion written by a wise man) that justifies the use of WMDs against the West.[8] Al-Fahd justifies the use of WMDs in the right circumstances with the following rationales: The prophet (Muhammad) used catapults in the seventh century (which also killed indiscriminately); destroying an enemy's territory is acceptable "if the fighting requires it"; killing women and children as collateral damage is permissible while striking a legitimate target; only Sharia law applies to Muslims and not international law, which would prohibit such attacks; the United States already has used WMDs against Japan; and everything in Islam should be done to the best of one's ability—including killing. While this fatwa faces some challenges from other Sunni clerics, it does provide an idea of the extent of consideration and justification to use WMDs. Osama bin Laden argues that Muslims have an obligation to develop WMDs as a means of defense against the West.[9] Numerous other al-Qa'ida leaders have since made reference to this fatwa and the use of WMDs, including nuclear weapons, leaving little doubt that they would use them if circumstances permitted.

Organizational Asymmetry.   Despite their recognition of asymmetrical threats, U.S. planners may have historically underappreciated the danger posed by organizational asymmetry. Organizational asymmetric threats are not designed to use or exploit unique technology to defeat the U.S. military. Rather, they are largely focused on circumventing U.S. strength through the creation of organizations that are difficult to detect and disrupt. Organizational asymmetry may also limit the American ability to wage war militarily by degrading the U.S. population's will to fight or denying the U.S. allies. Organizational asymmetry is designed to produce three advantages, listed below.

Surprise.   Organizational asymmetry is invariably designed to allow a weaker enemy to attack a critical target without being interdicted or detected beforehand. Thus, organizational asymmetry creates a difficult intelligence problem. By avoiding detection, asymmetric forces can strike in any number of locations against numerous targets with little or no warning. As the weaker force, surprise is often the only factor that allows tactical success.

Escapability.   Innovative organizational techniques not only allow an adversary to attack without warning, but they make it more difficult to find, track, and punish those responsible for committing violent acts. In traditional guerilla warfare, this often means hit-and-run attacks, ambushes, and the use of remotely detonated weapons.

Deniability.   A quick attack and quick escape also prevent the target force from accurately identifying who organized and implemented an attack. This can be useful for states looking to affect a situation covertly, because they do not want their enemy or a third party to be aware of their involvement. Nonstate actors use the same general principle to limit their enemy's ability to respond to the group with overwhelming force.

Forms of Organizational Asymmetry.   Today, the challenges created by organizational asymmetry are most evident in terrorist groups, but this is not the only place they are found. States also develop asymmetric capabilities, from special forces teams to integrated command structures, such as that employed by the Marines, which tightly links air, sea, and ground forces. The U.S. Navy and the U.S. Air Force have highlighted their asymmetric advantage as a critical strength that they contribute to American defense.[10] Although these techniques are taken for granted in the United States, seen from the outside, they are organizationally and technologically asymmetric capabilities.

Terrorists are different because they elevate organizational asymmetry from an operational innovation to a strategic principle. Unlike Mao Zedong, for example, who conceived of guerilla operations as a means to stalemate an enemy while developing the tools to overcome it conventionally, terrorists often seek to circumvent their enemy's military entirely and attack the civilian population directly.[11] Their plan for victory is inherently political, and their attacks are aimed at achieving strategic political objectives without ever attaining the capability to challenge the U.S. military in direct confrontation. This approach hearkens back to Sun Tzu, who argues that "what is of supreme importance in war is to attack the enemy's strategy."[12]

Terrorists use their limited military means in specific ways to attack the strategies of their enemies. Unable to overcome those enemies directly—or, unlike Mao, unable to conceive of developing the military capacity to do so—they must find ways to subdue their enemy without directly confronting their enemy's army. A terrorist group uses organizational asymmetry to overcome qualitative and quantitative weaknesses. One way they do this is to organize in ways that make them difficult to detect and track, as discussed above. But terrorists also gain an asymmetric advantage by using their disadvantaged position to justify virtually any level of brutality, including massive attacks against civilian targets.

It is important to understand the moral dimension of organizational asymmetry, because it helps frame all sorts of behavior commonly linked to terrorism, from attacks against civilians to the beheadings of captives. The moral aspect of asymmetry is more than just the willing brutality of some terrorist groups; it also stems from limitations that American society puts on its government. From restrictions on torture and demands that prisoners be given trials to the uproar over surveillance programs that incorporate lesser protections for civil liberties, American society sets moral parameters that limit the government's freedom of action. Virtually all states operate within moral parameters of some kind, shaped either by their values or by the need to justify the appropriateness of their cause. Indeed, these basic parameters have become entrenched not only in national life but in the agreements the United States uses to govern its interaction with other states.

Because these restrictions do not operate on terrorists in the same fashion, the moral parameters of a targeted society create seams that terrorists attempt to exploit. These seams are not limited to military affairs; rifts in society, demographics, political culture, and bureaucratic organizations also become exploitable. This dynamic sets up one of the fundamental challenges of counterterrorism for a liberal democracy, such as the United States: It must seek effectiveness against terrorists while preserving the values and institutions that are intrinsic to the American way of life.

Technological and Organizational Asymmetries Combined. While technological and organizational asymmetries can individually be challenging, when combined they can produce a result that is, indeed, catastrophic and pose a significant threat to U.S. policy. As reflected in Figure 14.1, various combinations of technological and organizational asymmetry compose varying levels and types of threats. In some cases, states can achieve technological advances that are disruptive to U.S. defense policy and require technological, political, or diplomatic responses. Alternatively, terrorists can threaten the U.S. by combining their organizational asymmetry with relatively unsophisticated technology. This was exemplified with the skyjacking of various airliners, the seizure of the Achille Lauro cruise ship, and the bombing of relatively soft U.S. military targets in the 1970s and 1980s. These terrorists can be pursued with U.S. technology, intelligence, and law enforcement, much as they had been pursued prior to the 9/11 attacks. If terrorists are able to combine technological asymmetries with their inherent organizational asymmetries, they can have the capacity to inflict devastating harm on the United States or other targets of their aggression. The

FIG. 14.1 Organizational and Technological Asymmetry

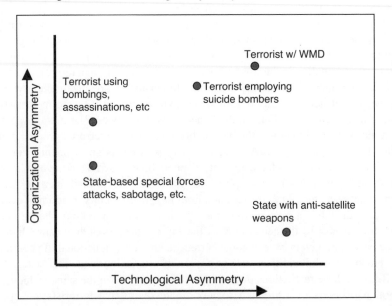

2006 NSS sums up the challenge for policy makers: "We are committed to keeping the world's most dangerous weapons out of the hands of the world's most dangerous people."[13] Countering the potentially devastating effects of terrorism will continue to be an enduring challenge for the United States for the next several decades. Before turning to one potential policy response—preemption—it is important to reflect further upon the nature of the terrorist threat itself.

Terrorism

According to the U.S. government's official definition, *terrorism* is "premeditated, politically motivated violence perpetrated against noncombatant targets by subnational groups or clandestine agents."[14] This definition highlights four important characteristics of terrorism. First, the violence (or, in some other definitions, the threat of violence) is not random or arbitrary but is planned and organized. Second, it is politically motivated, so it excludes criminal activity. Third, it is directed at noncombatants—civilian targets who would normally be protected under international law. Some have used this distinction to explain that, while hijacking and crashing the planes that hit the World Trade Center on 9/11 were acts of terrorism, using American Airlines Flight 77 to hit the Pentagon was an attack against a legitimate military target. The U.S. government, on the other hand, includes the attack against the Pentagon (as well as those against Khobar Towers or the U.S. Marine barracks in Beirut) as terrorism, because it considers military personnel who are off duty or unarmed as not being legitimate military targets. Finally, terrorism is conducted by groups that are subnational or clandestine and not uniformed military organizations. When military organizations conduct violent operations on behalf of a nation, that is not terrorism; it is war. In war, the internationally recognized Laws of Armed Conflict, which define when those operations are legal or illegal (i.e., war crimes), are well established.

What is interesting about the current official definition is that, prior to 2001, it previously included a modifying phrase in which terrorism was "usually intended to influence an audience." Previously, many had believed that "terrorists wanted a lot of people watching and not a lot of people dead."[15] The rationale was that the ability of terrorists to achieve their political aims was a function of the attention and publicity of their acts. If acts could be spectacular, without killing many noncombatants, they would achieve their ends without negative repercussions that could affect recruiting members, raising funds, and promoting other organizational objectives. The deletion of this phrase reflects the recognition that some terrorist organizations today specifically aim to inflict mass casualties in their attacks.

Terrorism is not, of course, a new challenge. It has long been the weapon of the weak against the strong. In the late eighteenth century, during the French Revolution, revolutionaries used terrorism to overthrow the monarchy. In July 1946, in the Holy Land, Irgun, a militant Zionist organization, blew up the King David Hotel, killing ninety-one people, to influence the creation of a Jewish state. From 1970 to 2005, the Irish Republican Army used terrorism, at the cost of hundreds of lives, in an attempt to extend Irish rule in Northern Ireland. Palestinian organizations have used terrorism continually for nearly six decades, again killing hundreds, on behalf of an independent Palestinian homeland. In the 1950s, the Viet Cong, seeking to extend North Vietnam's rule over all of Vietnam, systematically assassinated South Vietnam's village leaders—in front of the villages' people—to paralyze the South Vietnamese government's ability to function. These examples illustrate *revolutionary* or *national liberation* terrorism. While many people were killed in some of these attacks, most of the acts were intended to advance political causes and affect the society well beyond killing individuals in a particular attack.

A second type of terrorism, *state-sponsored* terrorism, has been an important feature of international politics during the past several decades. Adopted as a national policy by a variety of states, such as Libya, North Korea, and Iran, governments of sovereign states have, at different times, funded, explicitly supported, and to some extent influenced the activities of terrorists groups. State-sponsored terrorism has the potential to spread more widely if Islamic extremists succeed in their efforts to take over governments in predominantly Muslim countries.

In just the past few decades, a more deadly variant of terrorism has appeared that might be called *hyperterrorism*, which seeks not to inflect calibrated damage but instead to maximize death and destruction. A prime example is the now disbanded religious cult named Aum Shinrikyo, or "Supreme Truth." Centered in Japan, with numerous branches elsewhere, it burst upon the world's consciousness when its followers released its own manufactured deadly sarin gas in Tokyo's subway system in 1995. Its delivery method was extremely crude, but it nevertheless managed to kill a dozen people and sicken at least one thousand others.

Al-Qa'ida, discussed below, is the current prime example of an organization that deliberately seeks to produce high-casualty attacks.[16] Even if U.S. authorities did not recognize early the intent to cause massive deaths, this goal was clearly indicated in al-Qa'ida's 1993 plot to bomb the World Trade Center and its 1995 plot to bomb twelve airliners over the Pacific Ocean. In December 2004, one of al-Qa'ida's senior strategists, Abu Mus'ab al-Suri (Mustafa Setmariam Nasar), published a letter arguing that if he had been involved in the planning, he would have tried to put WMDs on the planes that crashed into the World Trade Center on 9/11.[17] Had a nuclear or radiation weapon or biological or chemical agents been included in the 9/11 attacks and exploded in downtown Manhattan, tens of thousands (if not hundreds of thousands) of people would have been killed. The economic and psychological damages would have been exponentially worse.

As the example of Aum Shinrikyo suggests, widely varying types of terrorist organizations may develop over the next several years. Given the asymmetric threats that they pose and the pressures of resource constraints, poverty, globalization, and religious extremism, the number of distinct terrorist groups may well increase in the future. Nevertheless, the most significant and most dangerous current group, which will affect U.S. policy for at least a generation, is al-Qa'ida. Just as it was essential during the Cold War for policy makers to understand the ideology, history, background, and thinking of the Soviet Union, it is equally important today for policy makers to fully understand al-Qa'ida. While a complete discussion of al-Qa'ida would take an entire book (the best books on the topic are listed at the end of this chapter), the following brief description provides some of the most important information.

The Nature of the Al-Qa'ida Threat.   The United States and its allies currently confront a global Islamist insurgency that "seeks to overthrow the status quo through subversion, political activity, insurrection, armed conflict, and terrorism."[18] Al-Qa'ida is often viewed as a monolithic terrorist organization. However, due to U.S. successes in Afghanistan as well as continuing sources of radicalization, al-Qa'ida has evolved since 2001 from a relatively cohesive regional organization to a complex, decentralized global movement. According to leading expert Bruce Hoffman:

> Al-Qa'ida thus exists more as an ideology than as an identifiable, unitary terrorist organization. It has become a vast enterprise—an international franchise with likeminded local representatives, loosely connected to a central ideological and motivational base, but advancing the remaining center's goals at once simultaneously and independently of each other.[19]

While most Westerners ambiguously refer to this entire movement as al-Qa'ida, Hoffman argues that it is useful to think of al-Qa'ida in terms of four major dimensions:

- *Al-Qa'ida Central.* This category consists of the remnants of the al-Qa'ida organization that existed prior to 9/11 as well as new players that have risen through the organization to replace leaders that have been killed or captured. Experts believe these individuals reside primarily around the Afghanistan and Pakistan border and continue "to exert actual coordination, if not direct command and control capability, in terms of commissioning attacks, directing surveillance, and collating reconnaissance, planning operations, and approving their execution."[20]

- *Al-Qa'ida Affiliates and Associates.* This category consists of "formally established insurgent or terrorist groups that over the years have benefited from bin Laden's largesse and/or spiritual guidance and/or have received training, arms, money, and other assistance from al-Qa'ida. Bin Laden has attempted to gain support and assistance from these groups by co-opting their local agendas and redirecting their attention and efforts toward the global jihad."[21] Associated groups are operating in places that include Uzbekistan, Indonesia, and the Philippines.

- *Al-Qa'ida Locals.* This category consists of "dispersed cells of al-Qa'ida adherents who have or have had some direct connection with al-Qa'ida—no matter how tenuous or evanescent." These individuals have had some prior experience with terrorism in such places as Algeria, the Balkans, or Chechnya, or they were recruited locally, brought to Pakistan for training, and then returned home with the plans for an attack and the ability to conduct it. Al-Qa'ida locals can be active or dormant, and their targeting choices may be specifically directed or left to the local terrorist cell.[22]

- *Al-Qa'ida Network.* This fourth and final category consists of "home-grown Islamic radicals" around the world who have no direct connection with al-Qa'ida, but who are nonetheless prepared to conduct attacks in support of al-Qa'ida's goals. An example includes the Hofstad Group in the Netherlands.[23]

To understand how the United States and its partners have come to face such a formidable and diverse enemy, it is important to understand the origins of al-Qa'ida and why it began to target the United States.

The Origins of Al-Qa'ida.   It is a great irony that two of the greatest perceived successes of U.S. foreign policy in recent decades—the defeat of the Soviets in Afghanistan in the 1980s and the 1991 eviction of Saddam Hussein from Kuwait—played key roles in the development of al-Qa'ida and the Islamist terrorism that currently threatens the United States.[24] As will be discussed in Chapter 19, when the Soviet Union invaded Afghanistan in December 1979, the United States responded by supporting the local *mujahideen* resistance. Through the provision of money and weapons to the Afghan fighters, the United States sought to weaken the Soviets and reduce Soviet influence on the immediate periphery of the oil-rich Persian Gulf region.

As the Afghan War progressed, a number of Arabs—known as "Afghan Arabs"—came to Afghanistan to assist the Afghan fighters against the Soviets. These fighters came from countries throughout the Arab world, with a significant percentage coming from Saudi Arabia and Egypt in particular. Originally, these Afghan Arabs were scattered among the Afghan fighters, "functioning as morale boosters who could simultaneously teach the Afghans about Islam, aid them with education and medicine, and bring news of the Afghan jihad to wealthy donors in the Middle East."[25] Between 1986 and 1987, however, this changed. Against the advice of many fellow jihadists, bin Laden decided to organize these Afghan Arabs into an independent fighting force. Bin Laden felt his Arab force could serve to motivate Muslims around the world to pursue jihad if his force were able to courageously oppose the Soviets on the field of battle. That the number of Afghan Arabs fighting in Afghanistan probably never exceeded several hundred and that they had little tangible impact on the conduct of the war did not preclude bin Laden and the authors of *Jihad* magazine from lionizing and exaggerating their exploits. By 1988, this core group of Arab Afghans came to represent the nucleus of al-Qa'ida, whose purpose was to "wage jihad around the Muslim world."[26]

The Soviet withdrawal from Afghanistan in 1989 and the subsequent collapse of the Soviet Union in 1991 emboldened bin Laden and his nascent organization. Bin Laden and his followers saw these events as related and directly due to the efforts of the Muslim fighters in Afghanistan.[27] In a March 1997 interview with CNN's Peter Arnett, bin Laden said the victory in Afghanistan destroyed the myth of superpower invincibility in the mind of Muslims and encouraged them to believe they could end foreign influence on their countries.[28] When asked about the significance of the Afghan war for the Islamist movement, bin Laden said, "The influence of the Afghan jihad on the Islamic world was so great; it necessitated that people should rise above many of their differences and unite in their efforts against their enemy."[29] Bin Laden finished his response with a statement that in hindsight makes al-Qa'ida's later decision to target the United States far from surprising. Bin Laden concluded, "any act of aggression against even a hand's span of this land [Islamic world] makes it a duty for Muslims to send a sufficient number of their sons to fight off that aggression."[30]

Why Al-Qa'ida Began to Target the United States.

One reason that bin Laden and al-Qa'ida began to target the United States in the 1990s may be that their efforts to change the status quo by attacking the "near enemy"—regimes viewed as insufficiently Muslim within the Middle East—were not successful. However, the U.S. military presence in Saudi Arabia undoubtedly also significantly influenced this change of approach.

In August 1990, a few months after the Soviet withdrawal from Afghanistan, Hussein invaded Kuwait, threatening Saudi Arabia and its vast oil resources. Emboldened by his success in Afghanistan, bin Laden offered to provide thousands of fighters to oppose Hussein.[31] The Saudi regime rejected bin Laden's offer and instead turned to the United States and the international community for assistance. Within a few months, the U.S. military presence went from fewer than seven hundred military personnel in Bahrain, Kuwait, Oman, Saudi Arabia, and the United Arab Emirates (UAE) combined to five hundred thousand military personnel in Saudi Arabia.[32] This introduction of hundreds of thousands of U.S. troops in the region represented a dramatic turning point. Bin Laden and many others viewed it as a historic development that threatened the most sacred land of Islam.

As early as 1994, bin Laden publicly denounced the U.S. military presence in Saudi Arabia. He followed these initial public condemnations with a message in 1996 entitled "Declaration of Jihad." Bin Laden explained:

> [T]he greatest danger to befall the Muslims since the death of the Prophet Muhammad is the occupation of Saudi Arabia, which is the cornerstone of the Islamic world, place of revelation, source of Prophetic mission, and home of the Noble Ka'ba where Muslims direct their prayers. Despite this, it was occupied by the armies of the Christians, the Americans, and their allies.[33]

Two years later, in February 1998, bin Laden joined Ayman al-Zawahiri and three other Islamist leaders from Egypt, Pakistan, and Bangladesh in issuing a formal declaration regarding the religious duty of Muslims to wage jihad against American military personnel and civilians. After a paragraph of the requisite formalities, the authors immediately give their preeminent reason for the jihad against the Americans:

> Firstly, for over seven years America has occupied the holiest part of the Islamic lands, the Arabian peninsula, plundering its wealth, dictating to its leaders, humiliating its people, terrorizing its neighbors, and turning its bases there into a spearhead with which to fight the neighboring Muslim peoples.[34]

While the Afghan War served as the catalyst for the birth of al-Qa'ida, the deployment of a half million U.S. troops to Saudi Arabia inspired the nascent organization to direct its ire against the United States. The U.S. decision to deploy U.S. forces to Saudi Arabia represented an unprecedented affront to many Muslims that swelled al-Qa'ida's ranks and inspired attacks against the United States and its interests.

This is not to suggest that any U.S. policy maker bears responsibility for the creation of al-Qa'ida or its decision to target the United States. While the United States sent generous aid to the Afghans, there is little to no evidence that the United States directly supported the Arab Afghans or had any connection with bin Laden during the Afghan War.[35] Furthermore, it would have required exceptional foresight to have seen that U.S. support for Afghan fighters might indirectly facilitate the creation of an organization that would later have the capacity and intent to target the United States. Similarly, U.S. interests required the United States to ensure that Hussein did not gain control over Saudi as well as Iraqi and Kuwaiti reserves. Saudi Arabia had to be protected, and Hussein needed to be evicted from Kuwait. It is difficult to imagine a reasonable scenario in which Americans, in deference to popular Islamic sensitivities, would have turned their back on years of informal U.S. security guarantees and refused the Saudi regime's request to deploy U.S. troops to Saudi Arabia. However, as the 1990s progressed and significant numbers of U.S. troops remained in Saudi Arabia, U.S. decision makers are responsible for not responding to the gathering chorus of warning regarding the hostility generated by the U.S. military presence in Saudi Arabia.

Al-Qa'ida Since 9/11.   Several events in recent years have sustained and even strengthened al-Qa'ida. The claims of al-Qa'ida and its associated movements continue to resonate among Muslim populations. Reasons for this include widespread anger and humiliation regarding the U.S.-led invasions of predominantly Muslim Afghanistan and Iraq; the continued suffering of fellow Muslims in Palestine, Chechnya, and Kashmir; and the mistreatment of Muslim detainees at the Abu Ghraib prison, for example.[36]

While a large quantity of evidence exists to indicate that these engines of radicalization continue to supply fresh recruits and supporters for al-Qa'ida, some argue that the resonance of al-Qa'ida's message is better explained by maladies pervasive in the Arab world. The 2006 *National Strategy for Combating Terrorism* largely discounts the role of U.S. policy in Islamist radicalization and instead points to four factors that cause terrorism: "political alienation . . . grievances that can be blamed on others . . . subcultures of conspiracy and misinformation . . . [and] an ideology that justifies murder."[37] This focus on maladies in the Arab and Muslim world allows U.S. policy makers to avoid the uncomfortable necessity of analyzing the potential negative impact of U.S. policies.

The debate between those who point to U.S. policy as a catalyst for Islamist radicalization and those who point to problems within the Arab or Muslim world has raged since 9/11.[38] However, framing the debate in this manner is not necessarily helpful. While terrorism surely does not spring entirely from U.S. policy or from conditions in the Arab or Muslim world, both provide powerful explanations for its continued presence. Efforts to address both are more likely to make U.S. national security policy successful in the years ahead.

Preemption: Arguments For and Against

In response to the events of 9/11 and in recognition of the terrorists and the potential for an asymmetric threat against the United States, the Bush administration made the case for a new American approach to protecting its security interests abroad. The policy—called *preemption*, or the Bush Doctrine—sketched out a proactive American defense posture that would identify and target threats before they had a chance to strike at the United States. Implicit in the Bush Doctrine was the assumption that, in the post-9/11 world, waiting for an enemy to strike before responding was irresponsible and dangerous. Although 9/11 clearly demonstrated that terrorists could cause extraordinary damage while armed only with box cutters, the events of that day also indicated that the U.S. defense and intelligence communities might some day be caught off guard by a terrorist group or rogue state armed with WMDs.

The doctrine of preemption was developed as a practical response to new security conditions and was published in the September 2002 NSS. This occurred just as the public case was being made for the invasion of Iraq, which would take place in March 2003. Not surprisingly, the arguments for and against the new doctrine were wound together tightly with the debate over whether to invade Iraq. It is important to recognize, however, that the two are not necessarily linked. Some adherents of the doctrine of preemption felt it was misapplied to justify the invasion of Iraq. Like any security doctrine, preemption describes sets of conditions when force should be used, but agreement with those principles is not the same as agreeing that the circumstances in Iraq met the standard delineated by the doctrine.

The Argument for Preemption.   Preemption advocates argue that the United States has entered a new, unprecedented era in which the possible linkage of terrorism and WMDs demands an entirely new approach to national security policy. The new approach, preemption, is designed to replace the inadequate security doctrines of the past. The president made this case explicitly when he formally introduced the doctrine of preemption during a graduation speech at the United States Military Academy:

> In defending the peace, we face a threat with no precedent. Enemies in the past needed great armies and great industrial capabilities to endanger the American people and our nation. The attacks of September the 11th required a few hundred thousand dollars in the hands of a few dozen evil and deluded men. The gravest danger to freedom lies at the perilous crossroads of radicalism and technology. When the spread of chemical and biological and nuclear weapons, along with ballistic missile technology—when that occurs, even weak states and small groups could attain a catastrophic power to strike great nations.[39]

George W. Bush's argument stressed the nexus of organizational and technological asymmetry—that in a confusing new era, small groups could possess the ability to bring a superpower to its knees.

The Bush administration articulated and defended the doctrine of preemption around three critical arguments. These arguments, which were made in various arenas during 2002, were used to justify and explain the new doctrine. Several of the arguments were intended to refute and discredit security paradigms used to safeguard the United States during, and immediately following, the Cold War. The purpose of these arguments was to demonstrate that the United States had no alternatives other than taking a proactive, preemptive approach to safeguard the nation. The arguments are:

- Terrorists cannot be deterred, because the United States cannot target what they value.

- WMDs cannot be contained, because individual weapons can be surreptitiously transferred.

- The costs of a reactive defensive policy are prohibitively high, because the impact of a surprise attack can be extraordinary.

Given these conditions, the only means for the United States to ensure its security is to proactively—and preemptively—strike at potential threats. Regardless of whether the United States in future administrations adheres to preemption as a national strategy, a close examination of each point will help illustrate the challenges that confront policy makers.

Terrorists Cannot Be Deterred.   A new strategic doctrine is necessary because the past strategies of deterrence and containment are no longer effective against the current threat. Deterrence requires that, to prevent an attack, a state must be able to disproportionately harm that which the enemy values. During the Cold War, deterrence meant maintaining a nuclear weapons capability that could survive a Soviet first strike to level Soviet cities, as discussed in Chapters 3 and 17. Although the 2002 NSS asserts that many states today are inherently less rational and more volatile than U.S. Cold War enemies, they still may be deterred by threats to vulnerable infrastructure.[40]

Today's terrorist threat does not fit this model. First, al-Qa'ida does not have valuable physical infrastructure or a sense of political responsibility to a distinct population. This situation eliminates the credibility of any deterrent threat, making deterrence impossible. As George W. Bush put it in June 2002, "Deterrence—the promise of massive retaliation against nations—means nothing against shadowy terrorist networks with no nation or citizens to defend."[41]

Second, al-Qa'ida's operatives and leaders share an ideological commitment that values their cause over their own lives. Even if the United States can successfully find and target the perpetrators of an attack, this action may not generate a deterrent effect, because these individuals follow an ideology that values martyrdom.

Third, such terrorists as al-Qa'ida live and operate on territory ostensibly controlled by states and among populations that may not have any affiliation with the terrorist movement. This drastically increases the moral cost of responding to a terrorist attack with annihilating force because of the large chance of collateral civilian casualties. The moral questions reduce the credibility of a threat to respond to provocation with overwhelming force.

WMDs Cannot Be Contained.   Unlike the Cold War, when containment meant limiting the spread of communist governments and Soviet influence, containment today means limiting the spread of a virulent ideology and preventing the proliferation of the world's most dangerous weapons. In spite of great counterproliferation efforts (described in Chapter 17), there is no highly reliable way to prevent states or terrorist organizations from transferring and moving WMDs. George W. Bush argued, "Containment is not possible when unbalanced dictators with weapons of mass destruction can deliver those weapons on missiles or secretly provide them to terrorist allies."[42]

The A. Q. Khan nuclear network that operated from Pakistan illustrates the problems with containment in the modern era (see Chapter 19). As the father of the Pakistani nuclear program, Khan transferred nuclear technology to rogue regimes around the world, including North Korea and Libya. The Khan network demonstrates the inherent difficulty in limiting the spread of information—and potentially weapons themselves—once governments have developed such capabilities. The prospect of a government itself distributing such information is even more dangerous than a rogue element, such as Khan.

The Consequences Are Too Great to Rely Solely on Defense.   The impact of a catastrophic terrorist attack using WMDs would be not only the impact of the weapon itself but the psychological cost of an attack. Once a terrorist organization gained access to a nuclear or biological weapon, preventing that weapon from being moved or used would be virtually impossible. Again, the argument boils down to an issue of intelligence: Once a terrorist organization possesses a nuclear weapon, the group would have the operational initiative, because the United States might not know that the group possesses a nuclear weapon or might be unable to find it. Again, quoting George W. Bush, "We cannot defend America and our friends by hoping for the best. We cannot put our faith in the word of tyrants, who solemnly sign non-proliferation treaties, and then systemically break them. If we wait for threats to fully materialize, we will have waited too long."[43]

Preemption as Necessary and Justifiable.   With no other viable strategic option, the potential nexus of organizational and technical asymmetry demands a much more proactive security posture. George W. Bush said as much during his seminal speech at West Point:

> For much of the last century, America's defense relied on the Cold War doctrines of deterrence and containment. In some cases, those strategies still apply. But new threats

also require new thinking. . . . We must take the battle to the enemy, disrupt his plans, and confront the worst threats before they emerge.[44]

The supposed irrationality of rogue states and the terrorist groups' lack of physical infrastructure mean that deterrence and containment are no longer adequate concepts. Although not nearly so catastrophic as that posed by the Soviet Union during the Cold War, these threats have created a unique danger that makes incidents of massive destruction more likely now. The best way to prevent a massive attack would be to preemptively attack nodes of technological and organizational asymmetry before they could be fully developed and united. This strategy entails taking the fight directly to terrorist organizations around the world while simultaneously preventing so-called rogue states, such as Iran, from developing nuclear weapons.

The Case Against Preemption.   Political and philosophical opponents of the doctrine of preemption began critiquing the new strategy immediately after it was proposed. Interestingly, most preemption opponents do not challenge its proponents' core assumptions about the nature of the world: that the increasing importance of rogue states and terrorist groups coupled with the spread of WMDs demand new approaches to minimize the risk to the U.S. homeland. However, critics argue that the new threats do not warrant a complete reorientation of U.S. strategy, especially when there are legal, moral, practical, and strategic problems with adopting preemption as a strategy. Exploring each of these critiques illustrates the problems facing policy makers.

Legal Arguments.   Just war theory has long distinguished between preemptive and preventive strikes. This distinction is important, because preemptive strikes are often deemed legitimate under international law, while preventive ones are not.[45] In the just war literature, a *preemptive strike* is possible and legally justified against an enemy that poses an imminent threat. A clear example of a preemptive strike was Israel's decision to strike at Egypt and Syria in 1967 after they united their military commands and blockaded Israel's Red Sea ports. An attack on Israel by the Arab countries appeared imminent. Conversely, a *preventive strike* is designed to prevent a growing power from developing the military capacity to threaten another state before there is risk of an imminent attack. An example is Israel's strike on Iraq's Osirak nuclear reactor in 1981. The reactor did not pose an imminent threat; the attack was instead designed to prevent Iraq from eventually developing a nuclear weapon. This attack was widely condemned (including by the United States) as being inconsistent with international law.

Critics argue that the Bush administration adopted preventive war as a principle of national strategy but has sought to disguise this more aggressive strategy by referring to it as preemptive (see Chapter 3). More specifically, critics argue that the U.S.-led invasion of Iraq was an illegal act of preventive war, because Iraq did not pose an imminent threat.

Moral Arguments.   The moral argument is that, as the most powerful democracy in the world, the greatest advantage of the United States over its enemies is its moral authority and the legitimacy of its power. This advantage is lost if the United States adopts a newly aggressive security doctrine based on preemptive military strikes.

Historically, this view has been taken by U.S. national security policy makers themselves. When a surprise attack was considered against the Soviet Union at the outset of the Cold War, it was explicitly rejected in the strategy document of the time (NSC-68) for the same moral reason: "A surprise attack upon the Soviet Union, despite the provocativeness of recent Soviet behavior, would be repugnant to many Americans. . . . Victory in such a war would have brought us little if at all closer to victory in the fundamental ideological conflict."[46] One parallel between the early Cold War and today is that the United States once again faces ideological and material threats. Actions that damage an enemy's current material capabilities may at the same time levy disproportionate costs by making an adversary's ideology more compelling to a broader audience of potential recruits, undercutting the legitimacy of U.S. power among even friendly international publics and governments. It could also legitimate aggressive military actions by other states, which could weaken international norms against using force and thus increase conflict worldwide.

Practical Arguments.   Some critics argue that a preemption strategy requires extraordinarily accurate, reliable, and timely intelligence about a state's or terrorist group's WMD capability and intentions. A realistic understanding of the capabilities and limitations of intelligence suggests that consistent achievement of that level of understanding is unlikely, especially given that the problem of WMDs proliferation is a particularly difficult one. Critics also argue that such high expectations are inconsistent with the recent performance of the U.S. intelligence community (see Chapter 7). If the intelligence community could not provide policy makers with an accurate assessment of Iraq's alleged WMD programs, then that same community is unlikely ever to be able to adequately support a preemption strategy.

The case of North Korea provides an important illustration of this point. Since the United States devastated North Korea, largely through the achievement and exploitation of air superiority during the Korean War in the early 1950s, the North Koreans have focused on the development of an extensive system of underground facilities throughout the entire country. This network makes it very difficult for foreign intelligence services to have high confidence in their assessments of North Korea's military capabilities. In addition, these underground facilities provide significant physical protection. It is unlikely that all highly protected North Korean assets could be destroyed through the use of conventional weapons alone, and, even if this were possible, it would be difficult to confirm success or failure absent forcible occupation of North Korean territory.

Strategic Arguments.　　Strategic critiques of the preemption doctrine seek to synthesize the legal, moral, and practical criticisms to demonstrate that alternative security strategies are superior. In part, these arguments try to salvage some aspects of containment and deterrence and improve those strategies instead of adopting preemption.[47]

Strategically, a preemption doctrine is more likely to be implemented by the United States unilaterally with limited international coordination and support. Critics argue that the United States does not have the intelligence, military, law enforcement capability, or other capacity to implement a proactive strategy without the cooperation of friendly governments. The moral and diplomatic costs of an aggressive security policy carry real strategic consequences because of the consequent lack of international support for U.S. efforts and the overall deterioration of the U.S. image abroad.

Some of these critics concede that there are instances when the United States should preemptively attack states that pose a threat, but they contend that raising this last-resort option into a formal doctrine has had major negative diplomatic consequences. Furthermore, by stating an intention to use preemptive strikes, the United States encourages "potential enemies to hide the very assets we might wish to take preemptive action against."[48] Using a big stick is much more effective if you walk softly beforehand. The inverse problem is that if the United States fails to strike, as in the case of North Korea, the new security doctrine begins to appear hollow.

Conclusion

The invasion of Iraq has brought the debate over the doctrine of preemption squarely into the public's eye. Never since the early days of the Cold War has a president so boldly engaged the public with a clear vision for the strategic direction of the United States and then implemented the strategy. Unfortunately, George W. Bush's doctrine of preemption has been muddied by its fusion with the Iraq War and its failures. Critics argue that these failures demonstrate the fundamental flaws in the strategy, while supporters contend that an implementation failure does not condemn the concept itself.

The preemption doctrine was designed as a response to the modern incarnation of asymmetric warfare and the potentially catastrophic nexus between WMDs and rogue actors. One of the most interesting aspects of the debate over the doctrine is that it often hinges on disagreements over facts rather than strategy. Advocates on either side disagree over critical issues, such as the extent to which the United States has the capability to achieve its security goals unilaterally or whether it can achieve the degree of intelligence reliability needed to make preemption feasible. One issue on which all sides agree is that the problem is not going away. Rogue states and terrorism are here to stay. The technology that enables the creation of WMDs is only proliferating. No strategic doctrine is perfect, but there is more evidence than ever that the United States needs a clear conception of its strategic future, and the debate over preemption will have a critical impact on that conception.

Discussion Questions

1. Is the threat of terrorism today a completely new threat that requires a completely new approach, or can previous defense strategies be adapted to face this threat?

2. To what extent do the organizational structures and technological characteristics of the United States facilitate particular challenges by determined enemies?

3. What policies can the United States adopt to minimize its vulnerability to asymmetric attacks? Should those policies include new material solutions, new methods of operations, new defenses, or other solutions?

4. What are the most relevant characteristics of terrorism to national security policy makers? How have they changed?

5. To what extent does al-Qa'ida's need to provide a theological justification for the use of WMDs provide another possible means of challenging their use of such weapons?

6. Why did al-Qa'ida begin to target the United States? What are the leading sources of radicalization that continue to fuel al-Qa'ida and its associated movements?

7. Can intelligence ever be certain enough to justify preventive war?

8. When the United States decides to use force, how important are national and international perceptions of U.S. legitimacy and moral authority?

9. What are the advantages and disadvantages of enshrining preemption as a core U.S. security doctrine?

10. The war in Iraq is generally considered the first implementation of the preemption doctrine. What are the lessons from this case, and will they apply in all cases?

11. Have the fundamental dynamics of the world changed so much that containment and deterrence are no longer useful security doctrines?

Recommended Reading

Bergen, Peter L. *The Osama bin Laden I Know.* New York: Free Press, 2006.

Brachman, Jarret M., and William F. McCants. *Stealing al-Qa'ida's Playbook.* West Point, NY: Combating Terrorism Center, 2006, www.ctc.usma.edu.

Daalder, Ivo H., and James Lindsay. "Bush's Flawed Revolution." *American Prospect* 14, no. 10 (November 2003): 43–45.

Forest, James F., ed. *Countering Terrorism and Insurgency in the 21st Century.* Westport, CT: Praeger Security International, 2007.

Hoffman, Bruce. *Inside Terrorism.* New York: Columbia University Press, 2006.

Howard, Russell D., and James F. Forest. *Weapons of Mass Destruction.* New York: McGraw-Hill, 2007.

Howard, Russell D., and Reid L. Sawyer. *Terrorism and Counterterrorism.* New York: McGraw-Hill, 2005.

Kastenberg, Joshua. "The Use of Conventional International Law in Combating Terrorism: A Maginot Line for Modern Civilization Employing the Principles of Anticipatory Self-Defense and Preemption." *Air Force Law Review* 55 (Spring 2004): 87–125.

Lambakis, Steven, James Kiras, and Kristin Kolet. *Understanding "Asymmetric" Threats to the United States.* Fairfax, VA: National Institute for Public Policy, 2002.

Laver, Harry S. "Preemption and the Evolution of America's Strategic Defense." *Parameters* 35, no. 2 (Summer 2005): 107–120.

Moghadam, Assaf. *The Roots of Terrorism.* New York: Chelsea House, 2006.

Paz, Reuven. "Global Jihad and WMD: Between Martyrdom and Mass Destruction," in *Current Trends in Islamist Ideology*, Vol. 2, edited by Hillel Fradkin, Husain Haqqani, and Eric Brown, 74–86. Washington, DC: Hudson Institute, Inc., 2005.

Sun Tzu. *The Art of War.* Translated by Roger Ames. New York: Ballantine Books, 1993.

Wester, Franklin Eric. "Preemption and Just War: Considering the Case of Iraq." *Parameters* 34, no. 4 (Winter 2004/2005): 20–39.

Internet Resources

Combating Terrorism Center at West Point, http://ctc.usma.edu

National Counterterrorism Center, www.nctc.gov

15

Conventional War

As the Cold War ended and the "unipolar moment" of U.S. preeminence began, it was reasonable to ask what kind of conventional, state-on-state conflicts Americans might find themselves fighting.[1] With the terrorist attacks of September 11, 2001, and U.S. dominance over any conventional army that it has faced, including the Iraqi Army in 1991 and 2003, some questioned whether the United States would ever fight a conventional opponent and argued that the military should instead shift significant resources toward confronting unconventional and asymmetric threats.[2]

As serious as the threat of terrorism is to the United States today, it is difficult to argue that terrorism is a threat comparable to that posed by the Soviet Union during the Cold War. Even if terrorists used weapons of mass destruction (WMDs) to present a catastrophic challenge to national security, it is unlikely that terrorists would have enough warheads to seriously threaten the continuation of the United States as a nation. States will continue to be the primary actors in the international arena, and any that ignore the potential of military conflict, including conventional war, do so at their own peril.[3]

A discussion of conventional war includes traditional challenges and disruptive challenges—the lower two boxes in the challenges to U.S. national security chart (Figure 13.1 in Chapter 13) considered by defense planners. *Traditional threats* are the force-on-force military operations that occur in a conventional war. To accomplish their political aims, adversaries seek to defeat one another's military forces. *Disruptive threats* include technological or operational advances that enable a potential adversary to challenge or threaten U.S. interests in the future. Both categories of threats have serious implications for U.S. national security policy.

Traditional Threats

Military planning and resource allocation around the world are still heavily focused on the development of armed forces to combat other military forces. How traditional military forces are employed is likely to differ based on the state's degree of commitment to the military operation and the scale of the political purposes at stake.

General War.   *General conventional war* occurs when the resources of a state are mobilized on a massive scale in a war fought for total victory over a clear and defined enemy: either a single state or a coalition. The two world wars in the last century are commonly regarded as general conventional wars in which the resources of opposing coalitions of belligerent states were mobilized on a massive scale in a war fought for victory, requiring unconditional surrender by the vanquished enemy.[4] In both wars, progress toward victory was measured by the geographical movement of battle lines established by mass military formations and by the destruction or capture of enemy units. Victory was achieved by destroying the enemy's economic or military capacity to continue or simply defeating its political will to fight. Such victories are sealed by a formal exchange of signatures on a document of surrender or a treaty that ends the war.

For decades, many theorists have believed that the advent of the nuclear balance of terror has likely precluded another general conventional war along the lines of World War II.[5] Of course, general conventional war is still possible among non-nuclear states fighting for objectives not centrally involving important interests of the nuclear powers; the Iran-Iraq War of 1980–1988 is one example. Theoretically, limited wars could occur even among nuclear states, as long as the states restricted the conflict to the use of conventional forces, with the threat of nuclear retaliation deterring both states from escalating the conflict. The concept of *mutually assured destruction* implies that no rational head of state would invite nuclear self-destruction by the first use of nuclear weapons, and therefore traditional conventional military strategy and tactics remain applicable and possible even among nuclear opponents. Though the logic of these propositions seems sound, they have never been tested in the nuclear era. Indeed, there has not been a general conventional conflict between nuclear powers.[6]

Limited War.   *Limited conventional war* is one in which at least one side fights with only limited resources, in a limited geographic area, or for limited objectives. Limited war "reflects an attempt to *affect* the opponent's will, not *crush* it, to make the conditions to be imposed seem more attractive than continued resistance, to strive for limited specific goals and not for complete annihilation."[7]

Limited war is hardly novel. Historically, few wars have resulted in the utter physical or political demise of a contending state. Rome's total destruction of Carthage occupies a special place in history in large part because it was so unusual an event; the term *Carthaginian Peace* is frequently used to describe the consequences of total war. In contrast, throughout much of Western history, the means, scope, objectives, and consequences of war were sharply curtailed by the limited military power of states and by their limited ability to project that power beyond their own borders. Together, such constraints tended to restrict the objectives for which states went to war and their expectations about what might be achieved thereby.

While familiar to historians and military theorists, the concept of limited war does not fit with traditional American perspectives toward war. As discussed in Chapter 2, Americans historically have approached war in moralistic terms; the United States should only fight "just" wars and not wage war simply for narrow self-interest. Although the Korean conflict (1950–1953) was fought as a limited war, it was not the wellspring of limited war doctrines.[8] The most common reaction to it among Americans was "never again." In fact, Secretary of State John Dulles's formulation of "massive retaliation" with nuclear weapons was designed to deter future limited wars similar to Korea and was still widely viewed as a viable policy into the late 1950s.[9]

Contemporary limited war doctrine is primarily the product of western fears of nuclear war growing out of Cold War hostilities, Soviet development of a thermonuclear capability in the 1950s, Russian sputniks, bomber and missile "gaps," and the balance of terror. Obviously, limited alternatives to massive retaliation had to be found when the impact of nuclear retaliation in response to non-nuclear threats raised the risk of nuclear devastation in one's own country. Moreover, massive retaliation seemed particularly inappropriate to containing the threat of communist subversion in the form of so-called wars of national liberation in the Third World, particularly in the 1950s and 1960s.

American military involvement in Vietnam was influenced in its early years largely by various doctrines of counterinsurgency warfare. After the U.S. troop buildup in 1965, these doctrines were supplemented by limited war and controlled escalation strategies that guided the application of conventional military force. Although they were difficult to achieve, important U.S. objectives—principally, the security of an independent, noncommunist government in South Vietnam—were rather clear and limited at the conflict's outset, in contrast to North Vietnam's unlimited war against South Vietnam. Few could have estimated the effect of the restraints limiting American strategy, tactics, and resources. As limits on U.S. means and actions grew—motivated by mounting casualties, escalating monetary costs, concern about direct Chinese involvement, and international and domestic public sentiment against the war—U.S. objectives became still more limited, settling for the acceptability of any kind of government in South Vietnam as long as it was freely elected and secure from North Vietnamese military aggression. By 1975, the United States was unwilling to dedicate resources even to this limited objective.[10]

The outcome of the American experience with limited war in Southeast Asia has been stated succinctly: "The war is over, the cost enormous, and the side which the United States backed lost."[11] Perhaps few conclusive lessons concerning the general utility of limited war can be drawn from Vietnam, but it was clear that for Americans the utility of the limited approach to warfare was very low indeed throughout the 1970s and 1980s. Indeed, the strategy, tactics, and force superiority that the United States brought to the Gulf War battlefield in 1990 for a quick, decisive victory were in large part a consequence of lessons learned from limitations in Vietnam. Nevertheless, limited war remains an alternative in U.S. national security policy, albeit an approach fraught with various problems.[12]

The Nature of Competitors in Conventional War.   Whether the United States finds itself facing the threat of general conventional war or limited conventional war hinges on the type of potential enemy. Only a viable peer could cause the United States to mobilize its resources on a massive scale for a general conventional war. In the early twenty-first century, no state meets this threshold. However, a peer competitor could arise by attaining strength in one of two ways—internally or externally.[13] *Internal balancing*—a state using its own resources to increase its power—is unlikely to allow any state to achieve peer status vis-à-vis the United States for the foreseeable future in the absence of a technological breakthrough that would close the military capabilities gap with the United States. A major opponent's breakthrough capability to nullify American superiority in command, control, communications and intelligence (C^3I) would be a conceivable example. To the extent that the United States is perceived as a status quo power, it is also unlikely to prompt alliances or coalitions forming against it—that is, by states resorting to *external balancing* that would lead to conventional war.[14] In the absence of a peer competitor, any conventional war that the United States engages in will likely be a limited rather than a general one. However, over the longer term, the possible development of a disruptive threat from future potential peer competitors, such as China, Russia, or India, is something that defense planners must consider and is discussed below.

A more likely scenario, particularly in the near term, is the development of a hostile regional hegemonic power or the escalation of a regional conflict that leads to U.S. intervention. A hostile regional hegemon may decide to use force to advance its own interests because it perceives the United States as being either unwilling or unable to respond. Whether and how the United States would respond would depend on its current level of military commitments, its political will, and the national interest at stake. The U.S. National Security Strategy (NSS) of March 2006 provides some indication of the potential willingness of the U.S. to intervene in limited regional conflicts, even when American national interests do not seem to be directly challenged:

> Regional conflicts do not stay isolated for long and often spread or devolve into humanitarian tragedy or anarchy. Outside parties can exploit them to further other ends, much as al-Qa'ida exploited the civil war in Afghanistan. This means that even if the United States does not have a direct stake in a particular conflict, our interests are likely to be affected over time.[15]

Thus, there are potential regional interests that could warrant U.S. military intervention. Though the statement above is sufficiently ambiguous to invite differing interpretations, a would-be hostile regional hegemon would be ill advised to easily assume U.S. inaction.

Disruptive Threats: Rise of a Peer Competitor

Although the rise of a peer competitor is unlikely in the foreseeable future, its development would present a dangerous strategic situation for the United States, and thus it merits analysis. Although some worry about China, despite its phenomenal economic growth over the last twenty-five years, it is not likely to be able to rival the United States militarily in the near term. Although exact budgetary comparisons are difficult, most estimates of military spending reflect that the United States spends far more than does China on defense. And in *qualitative* terms, the differences are even more profound (see Chapters 18 and 26).

To become a peer competitor and thereby compete militarily, head to head, with the United States, a country would need to achieve a major advance in technology, operational art, or some combination of the two with which it could counter decades of U.S. investment in high-technology weapons. Although technology and the ability to effectively use military systems are important—and often the former is of little usefulness without the latter—the prospect of "leap ahead" technologies preoccupies many defense analysts. Because of the length of time required to procure a new weapons system and the high cost of doing so, after a nation commits to developing a particular system, it is difficult to halt that production cycle in favor of a newer, more potent one. While one country develops the most technologically advanced weapons system (at the time of its decision), another country could "leap ahead" with even more advanced technology. Thus, disruptive threats could emerge.

Research and Development.   Modes of conventional war fighting and war prevention have become inextricably linked to the sophistication and scientific currency of weapons systems. As just noted, it is possible that a seemingly invulnerable superpower could find its interests threatened virtually overnight because of breakthrough technology. It is no longer sufficient to be a World War II–style "arsenal of democracy" and outproduce a potential opponent with average weapons. In the twenty-first century, arms competition has become as much qualitative as it is quantitative.

The establishment and maintenance of a strong technology base and leadership in scientific investigation is a principal determinant of the future technological capability of a state. Military research and development (R&D) capability is an important indicator of the future military power of the state. If the base for future advancement and continuing progress in technological fields is inadequate, the military component of national power will erode as technological advances enable competitors to pass it by. Alternatively, the state will become dependent on imported sophisticated defense systems, which could constrain its policy options. States today appropriately view the technological potential and capabilities of opponents as major factors in capability assessments.[16]

Rapid advances in technology can significantly affect national security in at least three distinct ways. First, a successful technological breakthrough can have a considerable impact on the quality and capability of conventional forces. To highlight one example that worked in favor of the United States, the global positioning system (GPS), which is now commonly used in daily life for such purposes as automobile navigation, was first used in combat in Operation Desert Storm in 1991. Prior to the relatively specific technological breakthrough of GPS, maneuvering several divisions of thousands of vehicles over a desert with few terrain features for orientation and battle space management would have been extraordinarily difficult. But the deployment of and training with GPS only months before the war provided a technology that "revolutionized combat operations on the ground and in the air during Operation Desert Storm and was—as one Allied commander noted—one of two particular pieces of equipment that were potential war winners."[17] If the Chinese military or another conceivable peer competitor could develop a technological breakthrough of similar significance, they would have the potential to disrupt American military predominance in at least one major dimension of combat operations.

A second significant aspect of technology's contribution stems from the uncertainty inherent in newness and change. A sizable R&D program, even if it is unsuccessful in gaining major breakthroughs, contributes the possibility of associated successes or surprise advances. This introduces a degree of uncertainty into a potential adversary's calculations, intensifying its sense of risk over particular policy alternatives. A further fear generated by the unknowable arising out of possible technological breakthroughs is that a breakthrough could make much of a nation's standing military force obsolete. Even if such a breakthrough did not result immediately in military defeat, the cost of rebuilding a security force from the ground up could be prohibitive. At a minimum, a breakthrough could affect the quality of a state's existing military and, subsequently, its calculations of relative power. Quickly changing relative-power and balance-of-power calculations could lead to conventional conflict. Conceivably, the losing state in the R&D competition might, in the absence of other options, feel compelled to initiate conflict with the winner to avoid certain future defeat because of its newfound technological inferiority.[18]

The implications of a true breakthrough pose a dilemma. Given the often lengthy lead time from concept to application and the high rate of technological change in the world, planners of the first state to discover a concept will be reluctant to concede the initiative to the second discoverer, yet they could err by "locking themselves in" to the development, procurement, and deployment of the earliest operational prototype, a *first-generation* system. An opponent, in response, could concentrate instead on the development of more advanced *second-generation* applications and, by skillfully collapsing technological states into each other, could balance the capability with a more advanced system in almost the same time frame. Historically, this case is illustrated by the "missile gap" of 1958–1962. The Soviet Union, by launching Sputnik, demonstrated the technological capability to build an intercontinental ballistic missile (ICBM). Immediately thereafter, Soviet spokesmen began implying that the Soviets were deploying first-generation ICBMs; in fact, they were not.[19] The United States, uncertain about the truth of Soviet statements, rushed missile programs to completion and deployed first-generation ICBMs to counter the supposed threat. The problem of uncertainty and the fear of technological breakthrough contributed to the U.S. reactions. In retrospect, the outcome of this situation was counterproductive for both sides. The Soviet Union suddenly found itself on the inferior side of the strategic balance, faced with a larger U.S. missile force than anticipated. The United States, as a result of its rush to redress, found itself with a costly and obsolete first-generation missile force that had to be phased out and replaced.

Today, to balance the need to adopt advanced technology while attempting to avoid the deleterious impact of locking in a first-generation technology, many military acquisition programs use spiral development. *Spiral development* is a form of evolutionary acquisition in which the end-state technology is not specified when a program starts, but the military requirements are refined incrementally as the technology is developed, depending on feedback from users and technological breakthroughs.[20] As the rate of technological advances increases in the information age, it is critically important for the research, development, and acquisition systems to be able to adapt as well.[21]

The third way that rapid technological change can affect national security is, ironically, the possibility of disproportionate reliance on technological breakthroughs, which appear to provide a significantly advanced capability but, in fact, are less effective or otherwise easily countered when used against a thinking enemy in combat. For example, in conducting the air war against ground units in Kosovo, many military leaders believed that the technological advances and sophistication of the intelligence, aircraft, and precision munitions would and did have a significant effect on the Serbian military in Kosovo. After the war, however, detailed bomb damage assessments indicated that the bombings had at best a "modest effect" on targets, in spite of the advances in technology.[22] In the worst case, fascination with technology can distract national security decision makers from the nature and ultimate purpose of warfare. As Fred Kagan observes:

> The U.S. strategic community in the 1990s was in general so caught up with the minutia of technology that it lost sight of the larger purpose of war, and therefore missed the emergence of a challenge even more important than that of technology—the challenge of designing military operations to achieve particular political objectives.[23]

Although technological breakthroughs can have a significant, even decisive, effect on military competition, overestimating technology's ability to ameliorate the inherent fog and friction of warfare can also lead to failures in national security policy.

The Revolution in Military Affairs and Defense Transformation. Incorporation of the latest technological changes into the military has always been a significant concern for the Department of Defense, and indeed for all military establishments. Changes in equipment, organization, and tactics that the services developed after the Vietnam conflict were so transformative and decisive in the

1990–1991 Gulf War that they were labeled as a "Revolution in Military Affairs" (RMA).[24] With the advent of the George W. Bush administration in 2001, Secretary of Defense Donald Rumsfeld vigorously pursued the RMA, using the term *defense transformation*, created an Office of Force Transformation, and published a Transformation Planning Guidance document to better manage the changes.[25] Regardless of the name given to the adaptation of military capabilities, understanding the characteristics and implications of such changes is an essential component of national security policy.

Information technology and precision weapons played a critical role in shaping the approach to warfare taken by many senior military and civilian leaders in the Pentagon in the 1990s.[26] Many believed that increasingly lethal yet precise weapons, coupled with information dominance, would facilitate decisive military operations without the need for large, mobilized land forces. Thus, defense transformation focused on increasing reconnaissance and intelligence capabilities, standoff munitions, and computers to effectively integrate all components of an increasingly complex and fast-paced battlefield. The defeat of the Taliban in Afghanistan and the overthrow of Saddam Hussein's regime in Iraq seemed initially to validate this approach. As demonstrated by continued operations in Iraq and Afghanistan, however, such dominating conventional capabilities do not necessarily translate to victory when fighting an adversary who purposely avoids such strengths.

Whether described as an RMA or as defense transformation, most analysts agree that there are at least four elements of a potentially significant military adaptation: technological change, systems development, operational innovation, and organizational adaptation.[27] Technological innovation without a concomitant change in the concepts and organization for employing such technology, however, is of limited utility. One such example is the significant time it has taken the U.S. military to adapt organizationally to fully maximize the advantages gained through the use of battlefield-tracking technology.[28] Only with the wars in Iraq and Afghanistan did the Army shift away from its traditional division-centric organization and capitalize on the advances made in precision air power and precision navigation systems.

Changing organizational concepts can lead to the effective exploitation of existing technology. For example, special forces soldiers in Afghanistan integrated centuries-old transportation technology (horses) with sophisticated targeting technology (laser targeting, satellite communications, and precision munitions) to create a capability that Rumsfeld praised as being transformational. As he described it, this integration of sophisticated technology with cavalry skills "shows that a revolution in military affairs is about more than building new high-tech weapons—though that is certainly part of it. It is also about new ways of thinking and new ways of fighting."[29] Organizational and conceptual change may be as important as technological change in creating a new military capability that is effective on the battlefield.

The response by potential peer competitors to the current U.S. defense transformation is particularly interesting.[30] As mentioned above, technology can affect national security planning either because of the technological breakthrough itself or because of the uncertainty associated with newness and change. Traditionally, great powers or those aspiring to be great powers have attempted to keep up technologically by committing themselves to an R&D program within the constraints of the competition for national resources. At the beginning of the twenty-first century, however, states appear to be conceding defeat to U.S. technological superiority. Rather than attempting to match the technological advances of the United States in most or even many areas, such countries as China are focusing more on developing capabilities to exploit potential U.S. weaknesses. During the 1980s, when China focused on responses to possible conflict with the Soviet Union, it concluded that its best defense strategy would be have the capacity to attack "soft targets," such as command posts; electronic weapons control systems; and command, control, communications, and intelligence (C³I) systems.[31] China appears to have decided to take a similar approach to potential confrontations with the United States.

As the United States develops systems of increasing complexity, it will become more vulnerable to attacks against those sophisticated information-based systems. Rather than modifying their strategies to reflect technology, as often happens in the evolution of U.S. strategy, such countries as China may simply employ new technology to fit their existing strategies after the technology has been developed by other, more advanced industrial countries, such as the United States. For example, the idea of the "people's war" remains embedded in Chinese strategic culture. The technological advances of the past twenty years have not fundamentally altered this concept but rather have simply added new meanings.[32]

Other potential responses by those conceding U.S. technological superiority include the acquisition or development of WMDs or the exploitation of asymmetric warfare.[33] Some countries may calculate that their possession of WMDs can deter the United States from using conventional force against them. Based on the U.S. military's record in Iraq and Afghanistan, many countries will likely conclude that asymmetric warfare is the best means of countering U.S. strength in a limited war, because it allows technologically inferior forces to exploit the vulnerabilities of a technology-centric opponent. The most dangerous scenario would be a combination of asymmetric techniques and nuclear capability, as discussed in Chapter 14.[34]

Disruptive Threats and the Escalation of Regional Conflicts

Another possible response to U.S. conventional military superiority is for regional powers to develop a niche military capability that threatens U.S. interests.[35] China's development of the ability to shoot down satellites is an example of this response. Although the rise of a peer competitor to the United States is highly unlikely in the foreseeable future, it is quite possible that states hostile to U.S. strategic interests will develop into regional hegemonic powers and subsequently threaten American national security interests.

The 2006 Quadrennial Defense Review describes potentially disruptive threats as "countries at strategic crossroads" and declares that the United States will use all of its power to "shape these [nations'] choices in ways that foster cooperation and mutual security interests. At the same time, the United States, its allies and partners must also hedge against the possibility that a major or emerging power could choose a hostile path in the future."[36] In other words, the United States seeks the integration of states that represent potential disruptive threats into an international system characterized by peaceful political and economic competition. In the end, that outcome is far more productive for all involved than one of military competition. The United States is most likely to be successful in this aim if it effectively leverages all instruments of national power.

A short list of potential hostile regional hegemonic powers includes China in East Asia, Russia in Central Asia and Eastern Europe, India in South Asia, Iran in the Middle East, and perhaps Venezuela in South America. Whether these rising regional powers are or will become hostile to U.S. strategic interests depends largely on two factors: first, the historical relationship that the country has had with the United States; and second, the extent to which specific foreign policy goals of the two sides diverge or conflict. In the short term, the United States can do little regarding the former, but it has significant control over the latter. Through its positive interaction with potentially hostile regional powers, it is possible that the United States can overcome challenges emanating from a problematic history of relationships.

Although it was not explicitly articulated in this way at the time, the U.S. approach to Japan and Germany since World War II is an example of the productive integration of potentially disruptive powers. Both countries have sophisticated military forces and R&D capacities, and both could develop technologies that could be channeled in ways that would threaten U.S. interests. This has not happened. Instead, American engagement with these states over more than sixty years has helped to make these countries U.S. allies. Though they may compete economically, and sometimes differ diplomatically, it is inconceivable that these countries and the United States would threaten one another militarily.

At first glance, a promising solution to discouraging regional powers from becoming hostile to U.S. interests, or perhaps even reducing existing hostility, appears straightforward. The United States could simply act multilaterally whenever possible and otherwise act in a matter to reduce suspicion about American intentions (see Chapter 26 for a more in-depth discussion of the role of *multilateralism*). Thus, the strategic challenge for the United States is to pursue its fundamental security interests, including its interest in combating terrorism worldwide, without inducing either great power competition or the rise of hostile regional hegemons.[37] But, aggressively combating terror could require the United States to act unilaterally, potentially employing the doctrine of preemption with the unintended effect of provoking hostility or even efforts by other states to strengthen themselves militarily or form alliances to be better postured to oppose—or defend themselves against—the United States.[38]

Whether an aggressive strategy, such as preemption, is likely to do more good than harm is a contentious debate. This topic is further discussed in Chapter 14. One problem with such strategies is that they have adverse, unintended consequences. As Stephen Biddle notes:

> If the chief determinant of balancing is perception of others' intent, then continued erosion of world perception of American intentions can be an important stimulus to great power competition, and energetic American use of force against terror has proven to be an important catalyst for negative perceptions of American intentions.[39]

Though most countries realize that they cannot compete with the United States militarily any time soon, balancing through the formation of hostile regional coalitions remains possible. However, the most probable response by a hostile regional power or coalition is to threaten U.S. national security by attacking U.S. economic or political interests rather than attempting military confrontation. The alignment of France, Germany, and Russia to oppose U.S. intervention in Iraq in 2003, for example, provides a vivid case of an ad hoc coalition undermining U.S. national interests diplomatically. Hugo Chavez and his anti-American efforts in South America demonstrate a hostile regional power attempting to undermine U.S. economic interests. Despite such examples of soft balancing, which can be frustrating diplomatically, the United States is not likely to find itself in a limited or general conventional war against these adversarial regional powers or coalitions over political or economic interests.

Escalation of Regional Conflicts.   Since the terrorist attacks of 9/11, the prospect of regional conflicts has not diminished, and in some cases has perhaps increased. According to the 2006 NSS, "the U.S. strategy for addressing regional conflicts includes three levels of engagement: conflict prevention and resolution; conflict intervention; and post-conflict stabilization and reconstruction."[40] Subsequent chapters provide a more detailed analysis of regional issues confronting the United States and potential state-on-state conflicts and crises that might occur. However, a quick overview of some of the potential contingencies in the international security environment today makes it clear that there are several possibilities for new, limited conventional wars.

The Korean Peninsula will certainly be a major source of friction for the foreseeable future. A great gulf exists between North and South Korea, and, political rhetoric notwithstanding, no major actor in the region supports near-term unification of the peninsula. After its successful testing of a nuclear weapon in 2006, North Korea's nuclear weapons program status is no longer in doubt. Additionally, it maintains a military with more than 1 million service members, potentially armed with chemical, nuclear, and even biological weapons. These forces, most of which are positioned in relatively close proximity to the demilitarized zone separating the two Koreas, pose a constant danger of surprise attack or even unintended military incidents. Those forces would eventually lose a conventional war against the U.S.–South Korean Combined Forces Command of approximately twenty thousand U.S. and six hundred fifty thousand South Korean uniformed personnel. Nevertheless, North Korea's possession of nuclear weapons has dramatically increased the risks. Even absent the use of nuclear weapons, North Korea has the capability to wreak destruction in the greater Seoul metropolitan area, where almost a third of South Koreans and most of the eighty thousand Americans living in South Korea reside.

China continues to undergo a transition from a centrally planned, state-led economy to a more open, market economy. It has experienced tremendous economic expansion over the last twenty-five years.[41] However, the growth has been very uneven—coastal areas have gained disproportionately, while its inland provinces remain comparatively impoverished. Increasing inequality could produce domestic instability within China. Should the leaders of China attempt to shore up domestic support by resorting to hypernationalism and by attempting, by force or dire threat, to regain control of Taiwan, as some feared was the case in 1996 when China tested missiles in the Taiwan Straits, reverberations would be severe. Japan and other Asian powers would be gravely concerned by such Chinese bellicosity, and regional economic relations would be seriously affected. The U.S. relationship with Taiwan, as well as regionally, could result in involvement in any armed conflict between China and Taiwan.

Further, the dispute over Kashmir between India and Pakistan will be a strategic concern for the United States for the foreseeable future. The tense situation in Kashmir has repeatedly led to conventional conflict, and the United States can ill afford to have the tensions result in a full-scale conventional conflict that might escalate into nuclear war. Because both countries are integral players in the U.S. effort to combat terrorism worldwide, it is conceivable—though unlikely—that the United States would directly intervene with conventional forces as part of an international effort to bring any conflict over Kashmir to an early resolution.[42]

The Middle East will likely be the most pressing source of regional instability to preoccupy American strategists for years to come, as described in more detail in Chapter 20. The question of Palestine continues to smolder, while Iraq and Afghanistan continue to struggle, against great odds, in their development of governmental capacity. Iran's regional ambitions could also touch off further conflicts. The United States, dependent on the oil of the region and committed to Israel's security, could become a participant in additional conventional conflicts in the Middle East.

Issues in Conventional War

Responding to these and other various regional instabilities and conflicts will pose challenges that are similar to the limited war concerns that prevailed during the Cold War. At issue will be U.S. interests, objectives, means, and constraints. Each of these four factors will affect the American approach to future conventional wars.

The extent to which future conflicts will be limited will largely be determined by the U.S. interests at stake. The more significant the interests, logically, the more general the war might be. World War II, in which two global powers threatened the United States directly, required a much more complete U.S. response than the localized challenge posed by North Korea. The nature of the U.S. interests involved will also affect limitations in the actual waging of any war. In the 1991 Gulf War, for example, U.S. interests in Saudi Arabian security and the preservation of international access to Gulf oil were deemed by the George H. W. Bush administration to be vital and worth a major, if still limited, effort.

Problems of defining and pursuing interests are more challenging since the end of the Cold War. International politics is not so much a zero-sum game as it was during that era, where every gain for Moscow was perceived as a loss for Washington. In the twenty-first century, it is sometimes difficult to determine what U.S. interests are at risk in the developing world and what level of military action is justified to protect them. The George W. Bush administration decided that the putative possession of WMDs by the Hussein regime posed an unacceptable risk to the United States and that military conflict was necessary to remove the risk. Clearly there was disagreement within the United States and in the international community over this decision.

In terms of objectives, architects of U.S. conventional war strategies face problematic confusion between the concepts of limited and total war. Generally, regional conflicts will threaten only limited U.S. interests and will likely demand only a limited U.S. military effort, but the damage done to a target country could approach that characteristic of a more general or total war. The focus on regional conflicts also lends itself to confusion, if not clashes, between political and military objectives, arising from the tension between a limited war's aims and the highly intense fighting likely to be required.

There is also the possibility that, when decision makers consider responses to a regional "contingency," national security policies—including the military strategy designed to address such events—might encourage them to rely too much on the short-term use of military power to solve what are at heart political, economic, or social problems. This possibility is enhanced by intense media coverage and domestic attitudes that pressure policy makers toward rapid, decisive action. Once a war has begun, however, the opposite presumption—of limited rather than total ends—might emerge in the minds of leaders and the public. In the case of the 1990–1991 war with Iraq, the George H. W. Bush administration from the outset denied that it sought the removal of Hussein from power; at the time, these statements seemed appropriate to a war of limited ends. As it turned out, however, U.S. and coalition interests might have been better served at that time by a more ambitious set of military and political goals *if* allied and public consensus had been possible. Ruling out total victory also complicated war termination. When the key postwar U.S. goal was "getting out quickly," other goals—such as encouraging a transition to a democratic Iraq under different rule or protecting the Kurds and Shiites from Hussein's vengeance—fell by the wayside.

The Iraq War in 2003 presented somewhat different issues in the connection between interests and objectives. In that war, unlike in the 1990–1991 Gulf War, the explicitly stated objective was to remove Hussein from power and to effect a regime change. Not unlike the first Gulf War, however, insufficient attention was given to the problem of transitioning from war to peace after the stated objective had been attained.

It is important to note that military objectives should serve political objectives that are established by political leaders who take into consideration the whole array of U.S. military, political, and economic interests. War is an extension of politics, and political leaders should never begin a war without having a vision for its political end in mind. The 1990–1991 Gulf War and the Iraq War in 2003 demonstrate the difficulty of "winning the peace" when war commences without a clear vision for its political end.

The means used to pursue conventional war also must adjust in an era that includes a persistent conflict with global terrorism. The notion that all international conflicts have important social, economic, and political foundations and cannot be treated merely as military phenomena has gained nearly unanimous acceptance. In the Gulf War, for example, waging a limited regional war involved far more than the purely military tasks of fighting air and ground battles; it entailed the diplomacy needed to assemble an international coalition with the backing of the United Nations, the embargo levied against Iraq, economic incentives offered to certain Arab states (such as Egypt), and response to the environmental hazards posed by Hussein's forces burning Kuwaiti oil fields.

Waging conventional war also required diplomatic negotiation to secure basing rights for ground forces and flyover rights for air forces, assistance from neighboring countries to control cross-border traffic, and the enlistment of nongovernmental organizations to help with countless postconflict reconstruction tasks. In both the Gulf War and the Iraq War, observations that U.S. and coalition military actions were incomplete were frequently based on the fact that important national objectives—even though they may not have been fully articulated at the outset of the campaign—were not achieved.

In the realm of constraints on U.S. action, one of the most powerful will continue to be public opinion. One of the biggest challenges confronting President George H. W. Bush in August 1990, when Iraq attacked its neighbor, was an apparent lack of public support for military action—a lingering "Vietnam syndrome." Polls showed little public enthusiasm for a war to oust Hussein from Kuwait, and Congress balked at the idea of actually declaring war or in some other way authorizing the president to initiate major conflict. President George W. Bush faced a similar challenge as his administration began to make the case for war against Iraq in 2002.

In both cases, of course, public and congressional doubts were overcome, and authorization was given to both presidents. In the Gulf War, this was partly a result of a robust international consensus: Americans were apparently much more willing to accept the use of force in that conflict if it was clear that the world community also accepted it and agreed to stand side-by-side with U.S. forces in the war. Involving friends and allies in any conventional limited war undoubtedly contributes to, and even may be a precondition for, gaining domestic public support.

In the Iraq War, the still-lingering effects of the 9/11 attacks were enough to provide American support for the conflict, despite significant international opposition. The paucity of international support for military action in 2003, which was critical in Gulf War, did not appear to be a binding constraint as the president made the case that removing Hussein from power was a vital national interest that justified military intervention.

One of the clear lessons from both wars therefore relates to the means by which national leaders can create support for a U.S. military intervention. Such support will result from a shared sense of purpose and a perception of a common goal. A significant event, such as a major terrorist attack, would seem to generate a sufficient sense of common purpose and to preclude the need for the support of a significant part of the world community. However, the mostly lone struggle to stabilize Iraq after the removal of Hussein in 2003 will certainly make Americans far more leery of "going it alone" in the future.

The extent of support for conventional operations will depend, of course, on the conduct of the war and how quickly it ends. If it is defined by a specific, powerful moment—the Japanese attack on Pearl Harbor, Iraq's aggression against Kuwait, or the attacks of 9/11—the onset of a war will often serve to galvanize public opinion behind the U.S. military effort. This is consistent with the "rally around the flag" effect discussed in Chapter 2. Often, however, when the war is extended and the casualty lists grow, the citizenry is confronted with the brutal consequences of war and begins to rethink its support. That is certainly what happened in Vietnam. George H. W. Bush never faced this problem in the 1990–1991 Gulf War because of the war's short duration, relatively few casualties, and negligible costs.[43] Many thought that, collectively, Americans had moved beyond the "Vietnam syndrome." The costs in casualties, time, and spending, as well as the outcome in the current conflicts in Iraq and Afghanistan, will significantly affect the constraints on future presidents engaging in conventional wars.

The issues of public opinion and public diplomacy are complicated by the pervasiveness of information technology in today's world, as discussed in Chapter 11. Beginning with the Gulf War, and continuing in the Somalia, Bosnia, Haiti, Kosovo, and Iraq interventions, reporters often broadcast stories in the United States before they are reported through military channels. The requirements of information operations are more demanding than ever as defense leaders may face a media that is occasionally better informed about some aspects of the battlefield situation than they are. If public support is to be maintained, U.S. interventions must be swiftly decisive, and during such operations the government's ability to report accurately must be equal to that of the world's media.

The implementation of the "embedded reporters" plan during operations in Iraq in 2003 was useful as a means of meeting the need for information dissemination, even if some editors and news organizations believed that their reporters had "gone native" and had lost their ability to objectively report on the war. Whether it is through embedded reporters or another program, the media will certainly be a continuous, important element of all future conventional wars.

Looking Ahead

The United States will encounter formidable challenges in the concepts and the conduct of conventional conflicts in the coming decades. Despite the current strategic focus on terrorism and the increasing concern about China's military buildup, limited conventional war will continue to be a distinct possibility for the United States. Policy makers and citizens must understand how to best think about the interests, objectives, means, and constraints involved with conventional war. Perhaps the most useful, succinct guidance—although not necessarily applicable in every case—was furnished by General Colin Powell when he was Chairman of the Joint Chiefs of Staff. A further distillation of Secretary of Defense Caspar Weinberger's tests for employing military force, the so-called "Powell Doctrine" (discussed in Chapter 13) required that any commitment of U.S. military forces must: establish clear objectives, use overwhelming force, ensure public support, and plan an exit strategy for U.S. military forces before entering any direct military conflict.[44]

Discussion Questions

1. How does one define *limited conventional war* versus *general conventional war*?

2. To what extent is the concept of general war relevant to the United States as a policy option? Is it more relevant to other states? Why?

3. During any international crisis, what domestic considerations (if any) might constrain the United States in regard to limited, regional conflicts?

4. Were the Arab-Israeli wars of 1967 and 1973 or the Gulf War of 1990–1991 limited wars? Was the Iran-Iraq War limited or general? The 2003 Gulf War? By what standard? From whose perspective?

5. What effect can a nation's R&D programs have on a potential enemy's perception of its military capability?

6. If the United States had sufficient national interests in a specific region in the world, could a regional conflict escalate into a total conventional war? From whose perspective? Explain.

7. Is there a threat to the United States of a rise of a peer competitor? If so, who might it be, and how should the United States respond?

8. To what extent have technological changes since the end of the Cold War been revolutionary? How have these changes altered the nature of conventional war, if at all?

9. Do the current rapid advances in technology make the prospect of a peer competitor to present a disruptive threat to the United States more likely? How should the United States best respond to such a competitor?

10. How should U.S. interests drive the objectives and affect the means that the United States employs in a conventional war?

11. To what extent should U.S. objectives and means in a conventional war be constrained by U.S. public opinion? By international public opinion? By diplomatic pressure? By other factors?

12. What are the most likely conventional wars that the United States will face in the next ten years? Who will they most likely be with? Why?

Recommended Reading

Brauch, Hans. *Controlling the Development and Spread of Military Technology.* Amsterdam: Vu University Press, 1992.

Gurtov, Mel, and Byong-Moo Hwang. *China's Security: The New Roles of the Military.* Boulder, CO: Lynne Rienner Publishers, 1998.

Haass, Richard N. *Intervention: The Use of American Military Force in the Post-Cold War World.* Washington, DC: Carnegie Endowment for International Peace, 1994.

Kagan, Frederick W. *Finding the Target: The Transformation of American Military Policy.* New York: Encounter Books, 2006.

Metz, Steven, and James Kievet. *The Revolution in Military Affairs and Conflict Short of War.* Carlisle Barracks: U.S. Army War College, Strategic Studies Institute, 1994.

Osgood, Robert E. *Limited War: The Challenge to American Strategy.* Chicago: University of Chicago Press, 1957.

Posen, Barry R. *Inadvertent Escalation: Conventional War and Nuclear Risks.* Ithaca, NY: Cornell University Press, 1991.

Rosen, Stephen Peter. *Winning the Next War: Innovation and the Modern Military.* Ithaca, NY: Cornell University Press, 1991.

Schwartzstein, Stuart J. D., ed. *The Information Revolution and National Security.* Washington, DC: Center for Strategic and International Studies, 1996.

Sullivan, Gordon R., and James M. Dubik. *War in the Information Age.* Carlisle Barracks: U.S. Army War College, Strategic Studies Institute, 1994.

U.S. Department of Defense. *Quadrennial Defense Review Report.* Washington, DC, February 6, 2006.

Walt, Stephen. *Taming American Power: The Global Response to U.S. Primacy.* New York: W. W. Norton and Company, 2005.

Internet Resources

The National Security Strategy of the United States of America, March 2006, www.whitehouse.gov/nsc/nss/2006

The Project on Defense Alternatives (full-text online sources on the Revolution in Military Affairs, information war, and asymmetric warfare), www.comw.org/rma

16

Irregular Challenges, Military Intervention, and Counterinsurgency

In explaining the position and role of the United States in the world, the 2002 U.S. National Security Strategy argues that "America is now threatened less by conquering states than we are by failing ones. We are menaced less by fleets and armies than by catastrophic technologies in the hands of the embittered few."[1] At root, this statement is about the decreasing relative importance of conventional, state-based military-on-military threats to U.S. national security, such as those discussed in the preceding chapter, and the rise of nontraditional challenges, such as the problem of terrorism discussed in Chapter 14. This chapter concentrates on what defense planners have termed *irregular challenges* (see the upper left box in Figure 13.1 in Chapter 13).

The increasing importance of irregular threats to U.S. national security is best seen as the product of broad trends in the international environment and deliberate choices by current or future potential U.S. adversaries. Characteristics of the current strategic environment that have contributed to an increase in the importance of irregular threats include the lack of a rival superpower facing the United States as well as a general condition of peace among the world's most developed, democratic states; the problem of failing and failed states around the world and the resulting lack of governance; evolving norms in the international system that are supportive of state intervention in large-scale human rights catastrophes; the forces of globalization that are increasing the interconnectedness of states and peoples around the world; and the proliferation of weapons of mass destruction (WMDs) that can make the existence of hostile groups and individuals too costly to ignore.

In addition to these broad forces, the rising importance of irregular challenges to U.S. national security interests is also the result of deliberate choices by strategic actors seeking to oppose the United States. As discussed in Chapter 13, U.S. armed forces may be the most capable in the world, but they enjoy this advantage more in some contexts than others. American strengths in conventional warfare and traditional forms of military competition, although still highly valuable, provide incentives for hostile actors to challenge the United States in asymmetric and nontraditional ways.

Of course, these various dynamics are often intimately related. As just one example, the existence of mostly ungoverned territory in the border region between Afghanistan and Pakistan provides hostile groups with a potential sanctuary within which they can organize, train, and plan. These groups can then take advantage of modern communication, transportation, and weapon technologies to strike at U.S. interests around the world.

Defining Irregular Challenges

The 2005 National Defense Strategy describes irregular challenges as coming "from those employing 'unconventional' methods to counter the *traditional* advantages of stronger opponents."[2] These challenges are strategically important:

> Increasingly sophisticated *irregular* methods—e.g., terrorism and insurgency—challenge U.S. security interests. Adversaries employing irregular methods aim to erode U.S. influence, patience, and political will. Irregular opponents often take a long term approach, attempting to impose prohibitive human, material, financial, and political costs on the United States to compel strategic retreat from a key region or course of action.[3]

The dangers posed by irregular challenges have intensified because of the problems of governance in many states around the world, as well as the continued force of "political, religious, and ethnic extremism."[4]

There are several possible ways to distinguish irregular challenges from traditional threats. One is by the legal and political status of the belligerents. In this view, an irregular war is waged between state and nonstate adversaries.[5] Although this distinction has some utility, it is not universally helpful. As the example of state-sponsored terrorism makes clear, states may still be the main players in some irregular challenges to U.S. national security.

A second method to distinguish irregular challenges, and the one favored in the government document cited above, is by the means or methods of conflict. Irregular methods range from piracy to terrorism to insurgency. In theory, the specific form of an irregular challenge could vary greatly as long as it responded asymmetrically to U.S. strengths in conventional forms of combat. In this sense, the possible use of WMDs by nonstate adversaries constitutes an irregular and a catastrophic challenge.

To some extent, the category of irregular challenges is a residual grouping comprised of all uses of force other than traditional state-on-state, relatively symmetric armed conflicts. Although its breadth may limit its analytic utility in some respects, the category is nevertheless useful to defense policy makers and analysts who argue that the U.S. military has yet to adequately transform its Cold War structure—which was optimized toward deterrence and high-intensity combat against a peer adversary—to one that is also capable of meeting U.S. needs in the current strategic environment.

Military Intervention

Irregular challenges also are distinctive, because they lend themselves to military intervention as a possible U.S. preventive measure or response. Richard Haass usefully describes "armed intervention" as entailing "the introduction or deployment of new or additional combat forces to an area for specific purposes that go beyond ordinary training or scheduled expressions of support for national interests."[6] For a variety of reasons, the period immediately following the Cold War saw an increase in the "internationalization" of internal crises and conflicts as states intervened within the territory of other countries in response to these events. Military interventions to meet various irregular challenges are discussed below.

Support to Insurgency and Counterinsurgency.   Political scientists James Fearon and David Laitin define *insurgency* as a conflict between an "incumbent" (a government or occupying power) and its external patrons versus organized, nonstate groups and their patrons who either seek political power within the country or seek to secede.[7] In an important sense, an insurgency is fundamentally the result of a "political legitimacy crisis of some kind."[8] American military doctrine recognizes that "insurgency has taken many forms over time," including "struggles for independence against colonial powers, the rising up of ethnic or religious groups against their rivals, and resistance to foreign invaders."[9]

The United States has played a variety of roles in these conflicts, intervening in some cases in support of insurgents and in others in support of the incumbent. With regard to the former, during the Cold War, the United States sometimes supported insurgent uprisings against communist regimes. A good example is the training and logistical support the United States provided to rebels in Afghanistan during the 1980s against the Afghan government and its Soviet patron. Since the end of the Cold War, U.S. indirect or direct support to insurgents is more likely to stem from a determination that a regime is despotic and a potential threat to international peace and security.[10] An example is U.S. support to separatist insurgents in the conflict between the North Atlantic Treaty Organization (NATO) and Serbia over Kosovo in 1999.

In other cases, U.S. national interests have led policy makers to intervene on behalf of an incumbent government and to support or conduct counterinsurgency operations. According to U.S. military doctrine, *counterinsurgency* consists of "those military, paramilitary, political, economic, psychological, and civic actions taken by a government to defeat insurgency."[11] Examples of U.S. counterinsurgency operations date back to the nineteenth century. The American army fought more than one thousand separate engagements against hostile Native Americans between 1866 and 1890. Perhaps the most broadly known U.S. counterinsurgency campaign occurred in Vietnam beginning in the early 1960s and was the source of much of Chapter 15's discussion of limited war. The intervention in Iraq that began in 2003 may eventually displace the Vietnam experience as the most significant example of counterinsurgency for the American public.[12] Counterinsurgency operations are discussed in greater depth below.

Stability Operations.   The Department of Defense (DoD) *defines stability operations* as "encompassing various military missions, tasks, and activities conducted outside the United States in coordination with other instruments of national power to maintain or reestablish a safe and secure environment, provide essential governmental services, emergency infrastructure reconstruction, and humanitarian relief."[13] In a discussion of major operations and campaigns, the U.S. military's capstone doctrinal manual argues that the re-establishment of conditions favorable to U.S. interests "often requires conducting stability operations in support of broader stability, security, transition, and reconstruction (efforts)." It goes on to argue that stability operations constitute a core U.S. military mission in that they help to:

> establish order that advances U.S. interests and values. The immediate goal often is to provide the local populace with security, restore essential services, and meet humanitarian needs. The long-term goal is to help develop indigenous capacity for securing essential services, a viable market economy, rule of law, democratic institutions, and a robust civil society.[14]

Oft-mentioned examples of U.S. success in postconflict stability operations include the U.S. occupations of Germany and Japan after World War II. As of early 2009, the United States was again involved in stability (as well as counterinsurgency) operations in Afghanistan and Iraq.[15]

Nation Assistance.   A *nation assistance* type of operation involves civil or military assistance provided by U.S. forces to another state while on that foreign state's soil according to an agreement between the U.S. government and the host government. It is distinguished from foreign humanitarian assistance, discussed below, in that its purpose is to promote "sustainable development and responsive institutions" with a long-term goal of fostering regional stability. An example is Operation Promote Liberty—a nation assistance operation to rebuild Panama in 1990—that followed Operation Just Cause, in which U.S. forces toppled the regime of Panamanian dictator Manuel Noriega.[16]

Enforcement of Sanctions and of Exclusion Zones.   *Sanctions and exclusion zones* may be established by the United Nations (UN) or a treaty or armistice, or they may be imposed by a state (with sufficient power) unilaterally. Enforcement of sanctions involves operations "that employ coercive measures to interdict the movement of certain types of designated items into or out of a nation or specified area." A recent example is the multinational effort to enforce UN sanctions after the 1991 Gulf War.[17] The purpose of exclusion zones is to prevent certain types of activities in certain areas (e.g., no-fly or no-drive zones). "Exclusion zones usually are imposed due to breaches of international standards of human rights or flagrant violations of international law by states."[18] After the 1991 Gulf War, the United States also participated in the enforcement of exclusion zones in northern and southern Iraq.

Peace Operations.   U.S. military doctrine defines *peace operations* as encompassing "multiagency and multinational crisis response and limited contingency operations involving all instruments of national power with military missions to contain conflict, redress the peace, and shape the environment to support reconciliation and rebuilding and facilitate the transition to legitimate governance."[19] Two elements of this definition are especially noteworthy. First, just as with the definition of stability operations, it suggests that military forces have a role to play, but alone they will be insufficient. Military operations must complement and support diplomatic and other efforts designed to facilitate a political settlement, looking to the re-establishment of legitimate governance.

Traditionally, there have been two major categories of peace operations:

- Peacekeeping Operations (PKOs). *Peacekeeping operations* are "military operations undertaken with the consent of all major parties to a dispute, and are designed to monitor and facilitate implementation of an agreement and support diplomatic efforts to reach a long term political settlement."[20] Traditional PKO are authorized under Chapter VI of the UN Charter, which covers the "Pacific Settlement of Disputes."

- Peace Enforcement Operations (PEO): Peace enforcement operations "are generally coercive in nature and rely on the threat or use of force . . . PEO may include the enforcement of sanctions and exclusion zones, protection of personnel conducting humanitarian assistance missions, restoration of order, and forcible separation of belligerent parties to a dispute. However, the impartiality with which the [peace operations] force treats all parties and the nature of its objectives separates PEO from major combat operations."[21] PEO may be authorized under Chapter VII of the UN Charter, which authorizes the Security Council to call on member states to respond with force to actions that threaten international peace and security.

In recent revisions to U.S. doctrine, three additional categories of peace operations have been added: *conflict prevention*, *peace making*, and *peace building*. In the first two of these, the military plays a subordinate and supporting role to U.S. diplomatic efforts. Operations in the last category, peace building, begin while PKO or PEO are underway, are expected to be of relatively long duration, and include measures "aimed at strengthening political settlements and legitimate governance and rebuilding governmental infrastructure and institutions."[22] Peace building operations are a special case of stability operations.

The United States could participate in peace operations as part of an international organization, such as the UN, or a regional organization, such as

NATO. The United States could even conduct them unilaterally, though the legitimacy that multilateral action provides may be especially important in the conduct of a peace operation. The United States participated in a few peace operations during the Cold War; one example is the Multinational Force and Observers Mission in the Sinai, which resulted from the 1979 peace treaty between Israel and Egypt. However, U.S. involvement in peace operations accelerated during the 1990s and in that decade included sizeable deployments to Somalia, Haiti, Macedonia, Bosnia, and Kosovo. These missions were the subject of controversy concerning whether the U.S. national interests and values at stake were sufficient to justify the commitment of national resources and whether the wear and tear on the U.S. military overly degraded its readiness to accomplish more critical functions. However, the path of nonintervention was also not without controversy. The most important example of a devastating humanitarian catastrophe to which the United States—as well as the rest of the international community—was slow to respond was the Rwandan genocide in 1994.[23]

In addition to provoking a broad debate relating to national security strategy, the peace operations of the 1990s were met with some ambivalence within the military. U.S. military doctrine in the 1990s, which officially labeled such deployments "operations other than war," reinforced the idea that in conducting peace operations the military services were performing tasks that were peripheral to their core mission of war fighting.[24] In addition, this label may have led many to see an unrealistic distinction between peace operations and combat. In reality, actual fighting—or the ability to prevail if fighting were to break out—may be necessary to create the conditions under which peace can exist. Peace-building operations are then a natural and perhaps inevitable successor to more active hostilities if an enduring solution is sought. Conceptually, then, peace and combat operations may be critical to achieving the political purposes of the United States, even if they demand somewhat different skills.

UN Secretary General Dag Hammarskjold once said, "Peacekeeping is not a soldier's job, but only a soldier can do it."[25] Current U.S. military doctrine differs by acknowledging that peacekeeping is a sometimes soldier's job; military missions are an important component of peace operations.

Foreign Humanitarian Assistance.   U.S. military humanitarian assistance operations abroad are conducted to relieve or reduce the consequences of natural or man-made disasters or to alleviate the effects of endemic conditions, such as disease, hunger, or other forms of privation, in countries outside the United States. Foreign humanitarian assistance operations are generally limited in scope and duration and are intended to supplement or complement efforts of host-nation civil authorities or agencies.[26] Examples include U.S. operations focused on the provision of foodstuffs and shelter to Iraqi Kurds in northern Iraq in 1991 and the initial Somalia intervention of 1992.[27] An example of a foreign humanitarian assistance effort that could also be viewed as a major operation was the U.S. participation in 2005 tsunami relief efforts.[28]

Rescue and Evacuation.   Noncombatant evacuation operations (NEO) are narrowly focused and sharply limited in scale. Their sole purpose is to relocate threatened noncombatants from hostile and threatening environments to environments of relative stability and peace.[29] Most memorable in the U.S. experience is the unfortunate failed rescue attempt of U.S. hostages from captivity in 1980 after they were seized from the U.S. Embassy several months earlier. A second example is the U.S. dispatch of Naval and Marine forces that evacuated 2,690 people, including 330 Americans, from Liberia in 1990 to protect them from threats and violence that accompanied Liberia's civil war.[30]

A Brief History of Insurgency.   Most military historians look to the activities of Spanish irregulars against occupying French forces between 1808 and 1814 as constituting the birth of the modern concept of insurgency. The United States ended the nineteenth century embroiled in a counterinsurgency campaign of its own in the Philippines. In this operation, which began as part of the larger Spanish-American War, U.S. forces fought for fifteen years before the insurrection was finally defeated. As exemplified by these cases, prior to the twentieth century, insurgencies or guerrilla wars were most often efforts by indigenous populations to preserve pre-existing political, social, or cultural arrangements in the face of foreign conquest or intervention.

During the twentieth century, insurgencies began to take on a more revolutionary or ideological character. Prior to World War II, insurgencies were often motivated by a desire to end foreign rule. Even while embracing national self-determination in some contexts, the western imperial powers simultaneously engaged in regular and irregular warfare in the defense of their empires. During the Cold War, and particularly after extensive European decolonization during the 1950s, insurgencies often took on a more ideological character.[31] The United States and the Soviet Union selectively supported either insurgent forces or the incumbent government, depending on the nature of the struggle.

Mao Zedong led a successful communist insurgency against the Chinese Nationalist government during the 1930s and 1940s, culminating in the establishment of the People's Republic of China in 1949. Building on that success, for more than twenty years, Mao sponsored and supported communist insurgencies in a number of Asian nations. These were successful in former French Indochina (Vietnam, Cambodia, Laos) but unsuccessful in a number of others (Malaya, Burma, Indonesia, and the Philippines). In the Philippines, a small communist insurgency sputters on but is overshadowed by a larger, more virulent Islamic insurgency, largely in the southern part of the country.

Insurgencies in the first decade after the Cold War and into the early twenty-first century have much in common with insurgencies in previous periods but also manifest some potentially significant differences. In terms of continuity, as discussed above, insurgencies occur in contexts of contested political legitimacy. They are also more likely to occur in situations in which the perceived relative deprivation of particular groups in society is particularly high.[32] The uneven effects of globalization could aggravate perceptions of relative deprivation, as those facing persistent poverty and underdevelopment are increasingly aware of the living conditions of those who are better off.

Although they share elements of continuity with those of the past, insurgencies in the current era often exhibit new characteristics.[33] A first new characteristic relates to the *underlying circumstances* out of which insurgencies grow. U.S. military doctrine argues that post–Cold War insurgencies "typically emerged from civil wars or the collapse of states no longer propped up by Cold War rivalries. . . . Similar conditions exist when regimes are changed by force or circumstances."[34] When insurgencies flow from conditions of state collapse, state failure, or forcible regime change, a counterinsurgency must build "political order and legitimacy where these conditions may no longer exist."[35]

A second new characteristic relates to the *goals of insurgent forces*. Since the end of the Cold War,

> ideologies based on extremist forms of religious or ethnic identities have replaced ideologies based on secular revolutionary ideals. These new forms of old, strongly held beliefs define the identities of the most dangerous combatants in these new internal wars. These conflicts resemble the wars of religion in Europe before and after the Reformation of the 16th century. People have replaced nonfunctioning national identities with traditional sources of unity and identity.[36]

To the extent that insurgent groups are organized around fundamental aspects of identity and religion, compromise and ultimate political reconciliation will be more difficult.[37]

A third noteworthy characteristic of contemporary insurgencies is their *transnational nature*. As discussed above, during the Cold War the international dimension of insurgencies often consisted of the external involvement of the superpowers or their allies in internal conflicts that had an ideological dimension. These transnational connections have become more complex and extensive over time, enabled by communication technologies and driven by many of the same processes that constitute globalization. For example, through "the internet, insurgents can now link virtually with allied groups throughout a state, a region, and even the entire world."[38] In a prime example, al-Qa'ida draws on local grievances and may either support or participate in internal conflicts as a means of furthering a worldwide, revolutionary agenda. This situation has led some policy makers and analysts to highlight the existence of a new "global insurgency."[39] According to U.S. military doctrine, combating "such enemies requires a global, strategic response—one that addresses the array of linked resources and conflicts that sustain these movements while tactically addressing the local grievances that feed them."[40]

Insurgencies around the world can affect U.S. national security in at least two basic ways. First, as discussed in the opening of this chapter, given modern technology, it is increasingly the case that challenges of governance in any region of the world can have direct implications for the security of the U.S. homeland. Second, as the world's only remaining superpower, the United States has global interests as well as the capability—and some would say responsibility—to play a leading role in fostering peace and stability in the international system. The internal and external instability that flow from insurgency constitute an important challenge to international security.

Counterinsurgency and U.S. National Security

In the first decade of the twenty-first century, counterinsurgency operations are of great significance to U.S. national security in Afghanistan and Iraq. The Iraq War alone has entailed an enormous commitment of U.S. resources, and the outcome has potentially weighty consequences. The bipartisan and independent Iraq Study Group pointed out the potential repercussions of a U.S. failure in Iraq:

> A slide toward chaos could trigger the collapse of Iraq's government and a humanitarian catastrophe. Neighboring countries could intervene. Sunni-Shia clashes could spread. Al-Qa'ida could win a propaganda victory and expand its base of operations. The global standing of the United States could be diminished. Americans could become more polarized.[41]

Developments within Iraq have significance for Afghanistan as well as the region as a whole, because a collapse in Iraq could possibly trigger a broader war or the spread of sectarian strife across state borders. In addition to grave consequences in human terms, increased instability could impinge upon the flow of oil from the region, with serious consequences for the global economy.[42] Arguing that "Iraq is a centerpiece of American foreign policy," the Iraq Study Group found that in Iraq "the United States is facing one of its most difficult and significant international challenges in decades."[43]

In addition to the importance of contemporary counterinsurgency campaigns, it is also useful to look at this type of operation in depth because of what the U.S. experience in Iraq illuminates about general difficulties the United States faces in meeting irregular challenges to American national security. Relevant issues include the appropriateness and the adequacy of the capabilities and capacities of individual U.S. government organizations and agencies; the need for effective, extensive interagency cooperation; the costs of the operations; the requirement for domestic support; and the need for conflict termination planning.

Counterinsurgency Principles.   Every insurgency is likely to have unique characteristics, with their character at least partially "determined by specific historical and cultural circumstances."[44] Nevertheless, U.S. military doctrine argues that basic counterinsurgency principles of general utility can be drawn from historical experience:[45]

- *Legitimacy Is the Main Objective.* What constitutes political legitimacy will vary to some degree according to social, political, and historical context. Nevertheless, the primary purpose of counterinsurgency operations is to buttress the legitimacy of the supported government, and all actions must be informed by this aim.

- *Unity of Effort Is Essential.* As discussed above, a counterinsurgency is not solely a military operation. Where possible, civilian and military counterinsurgency resources should be under a common authority. Military commanders at all levels must coordinate extensively with other government agencies, host-nation forces and agencies, intergovernmental organizations, and even nongovernmental organizations to integrate and synchronize counterinsurgency efforts.

- *Political Factors Are Primary.* Keeping in mind that the main goal of counterinsurgent forces is to establish or buttress the legitimacy of the supported government, political factors must receive foremost consideration in the conduct of operations: "military actions conducted without proper analysis of their political effects will at best be ineffective and at worst aid the enemy."[46]

- *Counterinsurgents Must Understand the Environment.* The goal of counterinsurgency operations and the complex environment in which they take place make it necessary for counterinsurgent forces to have an in-depth understanding of the cultural, social, and political characteristics of their environment, as well as an understanding of important actors and groups and who exercises power and how.

- *Intelligence Drives Operations.* To have the proper effects, the actions of counterinsurgents operating at all levels must be informed by reliable, timely, and detailed intelligence reporting: "With good intelligence, a counterinsurgent is like a surgeon cutting out the cancers while keeping the vital organs intact."[47]

- *Insurgents Must Be Isolated from Their Cause and Support.* Although killing insurgents may be important in a specific situation, to succeed over the long term, counterinsurgent forces must isolate insurgents from material or ideological sources of support from local and international sources. To do this, counterinsurgents may use physical, informational, diplomatic, or legal means.

- *Security under the Rule of Law Is Essential.* The security of the population is essential to the legitimacy of the supported government. Bringing security to the population will require "clear and hold" operations much more frequently than "search and destroy" operations. Counterinsurgent forces should seek to transition from combat operations to police enforcement as rapidly as possible, ensuring that the actions of forces supporting the government are consistent with the rule of law.

- *Counterinsurgents Should Prepare for Long-Term Commitment.* Insurgencies have typically been protracted forms of conflict. Because the population is more likely to give its allegiance to the government when it has a high estimation of the determination and staying power of counterinsurgent forces and their prospects for success, a long-term commitment may be needed.

In addition to these principles, U.S. military doctrine recognizes a number of imperatives for U.S. forces. These include managing information and expectations, using the appropriate level of force, learning and adapting, empowering the lowest levels, and supporting the host nation.[48] These principles and imperatives contain significant lessons for military forces participating in counterinsurgency operations, demanding restraint, intellectual agility, and good judgment at all levels of leadership.

Counterinsurgency Challenges.   Historical as well as contemporary examples of U.S. involvement in counterinsurgency efforts, including those in "Southeast Asia, Latin America, Africa, and now in Southwest Asia and the Middle East," reveal a number of challenges. Many of these are not just characteristic of counterinsurgency operations but are likely to be evident in other forms of military intervention in response to irregular challenges. Because of the intensive ground force requirements of counterinsurgency operations, this section focuses more on the Army and to some extent the Marine Corps than the other military services. However, all the U.S. military services face challenges in reorienting from a Cold War focus toward capabilities needed against irregular challenges.[49]

Military Doctrine and Training.   The preface to the 2006 Army and Marine Corps Counterinsurgency Manual argues, "Counterinsurgency operations have been neglected in broader American military doctrine and national security policies since the end of the Vietnam War over 30 years ago."[50] One reason is that consensus has rarely existed in the United States regarding strategy, doctrine, and operational concepts for effectively dealing with what many have long regarded as low-level conflicts.

At the level of the military services, reasons for neglect may include institutional interest and organizational culture, and the two are intertwined in a complex fashion. Capturing both of these dynamics to some extent, Carl Builder argues that the Army's traditional self-concept as the nation's obedient handyman ready to serve whatever purposes the country's political leaders gave to it was skewed by World War II. Having experienced during that war a form of warfare in which it excelled, the Army ran the risk of overoptimizing against the challenge of high-intensity, conventional combat. This would serve institutional needs and cultural preferences but also entail risk: "[I]f the Army . . . cannot successfully intervene against third-world forces to preserve American interests, many will be surprised and quick to remonstrate with the Army for the inadequacies in its planning, training, doctrine, and equipment."[51] Even during the Vietnam War itself, some see evidence of insufficient adaptation. Andrew Krepinevich argues that an overly strict adherence to the "Army Concept," a belief that the U.S. Army should focus on midintensity, conventional war and rely heavily on firepower to keep casualties down, prevented the Army from adopting appropriate counterinsurgency tactics in Vietnam.[52]

The experience of U.S. ground forces in Iraq after the spectacular initial success of the 2003 invasion suggests that, in addition to being there in adequate numbers, they again faced a situation for which they were not entirely prepared in terms of doctrine or training. Influential critic Nigel Aylwin-Foster, given voice in one of the military's own professional journals, argues that although the U.S. "Army is indisputably the master of conventional warfighting, it is notably less proficient in . . . Operations Other Than War."[53] Recognizing that U.S. challenges immediately following the invasion stemmed from a variety of sources, Aylwin-Foster argues that the actions of U.S. ground forces were also partly to blame for the growth of an Iraqi insurgency in 2004. Citing the statistic that only 6% of U.S. pacification operations in Iraq from May 2003 to May 2005 were focused specifically on providing security to the population, he claims that the U.S. Army was culturally insensitive, overly focused on killing insurgents, and too slow to adapt.[54]

Since that time, as evidenced by the publication of the new counterinsurgency manual, there have been vigorous and broad efforts to respond to the requirements of contemporary insurgency in terms of doctrine and training.[55] However, concerns remain over the extent to which such learning will endure beyond the end of U.S. involvement in its campaigns in Afghanistan and Iraq. To be enduring, change will need to be supported over an extended period of time by key leaders within the organization who ensure that it is institutionalized in doctrine, training, organizational structures, equipment acquisition, and personnel incentive systems.[56]

The Ground Force Capacity of the U.S. All-Volunteer Military. According to the 2006 counterinsurgency manual, "maintaining security in an unstable environment requires vast resources, whether host nation, U.S., or multinational."[57] This requirement applies not only to counterinsurgency but also to other forms of U.S. military operations against irregular challenges in which stability is a desired goal. Depending on the contributions of allies or coalition partners and the status of a supported country's security institutions, the required U.S. contribution may be significant. In the absence of a U.S. national police force, this requirement falls primarily on U.S. ground forces.

The U.S. armed forces that have to meet this requirement have, until very recently, been shrinking for the past thirty-five years. Since the Vietnam War, the overall number of American men and women on active duty has fallen from 3.5 million to 1.4 million. The U.S. Army, the country's primary force for protracted land campaigns, declined from 1.6 million troops in 1968 to just over four hundred eighty thousand at the time of the September 11, 2001, attacks. These cuts in the U.S. armed forces have been a nonpartisan affair, with the Army shrinking from eighteen divisions to twelve under President George H. W. Bush and then to ten under President Bill Clinton.

Although the end of the Cold War made these force reductions understandable, U.S. military operations abroad accelerated in the 1990s, with commensurate strain on a smaller force. As discussed in Chapter 3, this strain and resulting military readiness problems became an issue in the 2000 presidential campaign. Questions about the adequacy of ground forces to support the U.S. national security strategy became even more frequent after the U.S.-led invasions of Afghanistan and Iraq. In January 2007, newly confirmed Secretary of Defense Robert Gates announced a recommended increase of ninety-two thousand ground forces—a number that would bring the Army and Marine Corps to end strengths of "547,000 and 202,000, respectively, by 2012."[58]

Although these additions will help the Army and Marine Corps manage future requirements, U.S. national security commitments have currently placed major strains on U.S. ground forces. Most of the Army's forty-four combat brigades have seen two or more combat tours between late 2001 and 2008, with many units having four combat tours. This strain was exacerbated when tours were lengthened to fifteen months and the "dwell time" between combat tours was reduced to only twelve months.[59] The standard had previously been that a soldier should have at least twenty-four months at home between twelve-month deployments.

Due to these on-going requirements, the Army and Marine Corps have enormous challenges in the retaining of junior officers (especially at the rank of captain), recruitment, training, readiness, and equipment maintenance.[60] The United States also faces strategic risk because, as many have observed, "[a]ll 'fully combat ready' active-duty and reserve combat units are now deployed or deploying to Iraq or Afghanistan. No fully-trained national strategic reserve brigades are now prepared to deploy to new combat operations."[61]

Existing constraints on ground forces have accelerated the use of civilian contractors, with problematic repercussions:

> The Defense Department estimates that roughly 20,000 security contractors operate in Iraq alone, the equivalent of over three Army combat brigades. . . . Unlike our soldiers and marines, these contractors are subjected to little in the way of oversight, despite the fact that counterinsurgency operations demand the highest levels of restraint on the part of counterinsurgent forces.[62]

Contractor security forces are more likely to focus on their specific purposes, such as providing security to a particular dignitary, than on the broad requirements of the overall mission, which requires that the legitimacy of the supported government and the political effects of all actions must remain foremost considerations. A heated controversy caused by the killing of nine Iraqi civilians by Blackwater contractors in Baghdad in September 2007 is representative of the problematic effect that these contractors can have on an overall U.S. counterinsurgency effort.[63]

Though the U.S. Army and Marine Corps are still among the most capable ground force organizations in the world, some analysts have begun to ask the question: "What is the maximum force utilization rate we can sustain before degrading a first rate military?"[64] According to Major General (retired) Robert Scales, "No one from the Vietnam generation would ever have foreseen that America's ground forces would be so stretched for so long without breaking."[65]

An increase in force size is one possible response to this situation, though this option is very expensive, takes time to implement, and will be a challenge to execute without unacceptably lowering recruiting standards. Further, some argue that merely increasing existing force structure constitutes an inadequate response to the requirements of today's complex contingency operations. These analysts argue that the United States should invest instead in capabilities, such as advisor units, optimized to help the Army succeed in irregular warfare operations.[66]

As an alternative, the country's political leaders could recognize the constraints posed by the size of U.S. ground forces and adjust the goals of U.S. national security strategy and policy to better reconcile ends, ways, and means. However, the nature of the current strategic environment could make that difficult. In the words of one review of alternative futures:

> One of the major problems affecting global security—failed or failing states that could or do nurture terrorist organizations—is unlikely to disappear in the future. Although chastened by the Iraq experience, U.S. policymakers may nonetheless feel compelled to engage in stability operations or counterinsurgency, just as Bush, who promised in 2000 to get U.S. military forces out of the "nation-building" business, felt compelled to send forces into Afghanistan after the terrorist attacks of 11 September 2001.[67]

Without a renewal of conscription, which will not occur absent a major catastrophe, American policy makers will need to keep limitations in available ground forces in mind as they make decisions regarding future large-scale or long-term military interventions.

U.S. Government Agency Capability and Capacity and the Interagency Process. A recurring theme in current U.S. military doctrine is that military force may be necessary, but will alone be insufficient, in planning and executing successful U.S. responses to many irregular challenges to American national security. Instead, the United States must also bring diplomatic, informational, and economic instruments of power to bear to be successful in interventions, such as peace operations, stability operations, and counterinsurgency. In an apparent affirmation of this perspective, the 2006 Iraq Study Group's "most important recommendations" were for "enhanced diplomatic and political efforts in Iraq and the region."[68]

To play their needed role, organizations and agencies across the U.S. government must have the *capability* to operationally deploy and the *capacity* to perform these functions at the required scale. As one study states: "While the U.S. military is unmatched in terms of its effectiveness, capabilities, and reach, the U.S. government lacks a standing, deployable capacity for stability operations in non-DoD agencies."[69] The study goes on to note that "recent changes in U.S. interventions—increased operational tempo, rapid success on the battlefield, and an ever-expanding list of post-conflict objectives—have dramatically increased the need for rapid civilian deployments."[70] In the absence of civilian agency capability, military units are often put in charge of performing a broad array of tasks, relating to economic, social, and political development, for which they may not have the requisite expertise and which further stretches military resources.[71]

This dynamic helps explain why emphasis on the need to develop civilian capabilities and capacity in these areas often comes from the U.S. military and defense analysts.[72] Gates made this a personal priority. In a November 2007 speech, he said:

> My message is that if we are to meet the myriad challenges around the world in the coming decades, the country must strengthen other important elements of national power both institutionally and financially, and create the capability to integrate all the elements of national power to problems and challenges abroad. . . . One of the most important lessons of the wars in Afghanistan and Iraq is that military success is not sufficient to win: economic development, institution-building and the rule of law, promoting internal reconciliation, good governance, providing basic services to the people, training and equipping indigenous military and police forces, strategic communications, and more—these, along with security, are essential ingredients for long-term success.[73]

Gates went on to note that the U.S. military had sought to meet many of these needs in the absence of civilian partners and argued that much of the resulting organizational learning on the part of the military would need to be retained and institutionalized. Nevertheless, these efforts were "no replacement for the real thing—civilian involvement and expertise."[74] Though the State Department responded positively to Gates's ideas and increased the number of diplomats assigned to partner with military commanders, significant needs remain unmet.[75]

Beyond organizational capability and capacity, the effectiveness of the interagency process is also essential. Interagency coordination in response to crises or even in the management of ongoing operations still largely takes place on an ad hoc basis. As discussed in Chapter 9, there is no single, unified national security apparatus with the capability to plan, manage, and control all national security-related spending. Also, as discussed in Chapter 10, the interagency process has continued to expand and grow more complex over time as new functions and entities have been added to the U.S. government to respond to new national security needs. Recommendations to improve U.S. government effectiveness in interagency cooperation have included proposals to further institutionalize strategic planning, to clarify presidential national security guidance, to define interagency roles and responsibilities, and to develop more robust mechanisms to strengthen connections among "policy, resource allocation, and execution."[76]

Costs of Operations.   As discussed above, counterinsurgency operations may require the devotion of enormous resources. Through Fiscal Year 2008, funding for the Iraq War alone reached $608 billion.[77] As of 2009, U.S. military casualties included over four thousand two hundred dead and over thirty thousand wounded.[78] Among the wounded are many who have suffered life-changing injuries and face long-term disability. These numbers do not include the much smaller number of U.S. civilian or contractor personnel casualties.

As important as these budgetary and casualty figures are, they do not capture the full range of costs that are associated with a large-scale American military intervention. Additional important costs include: diplomatic costs in the event that an American military intervention lacks strong multilateral support; the time and focus required of U.S. national security policy makers, which may come at the expense of other national security priorities; domestic costs relating to public trust in political leaders and government institutions if interventions do not succeed; possible stresses on the Constitutional balance between government institutions created by a long war; the effect of a U.S. intervention on international or regional peace and stability; the impact on lives or government finances of U.S. coalition partners; and the impact on lives and property in the target country. These costs will vary in every conflict. For example, successful interventions could have beneficial effects on the reputation and influence of the U.S. government abroad or the domestic political standing of the country's leaders. Nevertheless, the potential importance of such costs is worthy of evaluation as national security policy makers seek to choose between various courses of action.

Public Support.   One of the principles of counterinsurgency operations, discussed above, is the need for a long-term commitment. Regarding the U.S. intervention in Iraq, Ryan Crocker, U.S. Ambassador to Iraq, reaffirmed this general principle in his September 2007 testimony to Congress, stating that, although it would be possible for the United States to achieve its goal of a "secure, stable democratic Iraq at peace with its neighbors," the "process will not be quick, it will be uneven, punctuated by setbacks as well as achievements, and it will require substantial U.S. resolve and commitment."[79] Although the link between domestic public opinion and government policy is not simple or direct, a major challenge for policy makers is sustaining U.S. commitment over the long term as a majority of Americans oppose the Iraq War.[80]

In Chapter 2, it was suggested that Americans have traditionally approached national security affairs with a degree of impatience and that protracted limited wars do not fit this temper. The U.S. historical experience provides some interesting precedents for sustaining protracted military interventions abroad. Declining U.S. public support was a driving factor in the U.S. military withdrawal from Vietnam in 1973 and the U.S. withdrawal from Somalia in 1994. On the other hand, even after policy makers claimed that the operation would last for only one year, the United States sustained a military commitment in Bosnia for ten years beginning in 1995 with little public attention or opposition. Similarly, an extended U.S. intervention in Afghanistan that began in 2001 still received approval from a majority of Americans near the end of 2007.[81] Of course, in a prime example of patience, the American public stood fast in the Cold War confrontation with the Soviet Union for more than forty years. This brief survey suggests that, although sustained U.S. public support should not be taken for granted, it may be achievable, depending on the circumstances.

Conflict Termination.   A final challenge, related to many of those above, is *conflict termination.* Successful conflict termination is necessary because, to paraphrase Carl von Clausewitz, the best way to judge military operations is by the success of the whole. Tactical and operational victories may not be adequate to the achievement of the country's political purposes; planning for and resourcing those actions necessary to bring a particular intervention to a successful close are also critical.[82]

U.S. military doctrine published in 2006 makes it clear that the supported commander "must work closely with the civilian leadership to ensure a clearly defined national end state is established." This end state should be "the broadly expressed diplomatic, informational, military, and economic conditions that should exist after the conclusion of a campaign or operation." With regard to the effect of this end state on military planning, "[t]ermination of operations must be considered from the outset of planning and should be a coordinated OGA [Other Government Agency], IGO [intergovernmental organization], NGO [nongovernmental organization], and multinational effort that is refined as operations move toward advantageous termination." Finally, with regard to setting expectations, U.S. military doctrine argues that "military operations will normally continue after the conclusion of sustained combat operations. Stability operations will be required to enable legitimate civil authority and attain the national strategic end state. These stability operations historically have required an extended presence by U.S. military forces."[83]

Though U.S. military doctrine seems closely attuned to the requirements of conflict termination, doctrine itself may be more or less meaningful according to the extent to which it is embodied in the actual practices of the organizations it is meant to guide. Realization of this doctrinal vision will also require cooperative involvement by the country's political leaders and other agencies within the U.S. government, as well as compliance by the DoD and the military services.

The Beginnings of Reform

Since 2004, the U.S. government has made deliberate efforts toward reorganizing U.S. intervention capacity and capabilities, particularly within the State Department and DoD. One of the major efforts has been a collaborative effort between the State Department and DoD to develop common tasks and objectives for stability and reconstruction operations. In 2004, the Office of the Coordinator for Reconstruction and Stabilization (S/CRS) was formed in the Department of State with the mission to "lead, coordinate and institutionalize U.S. Government civilian capacity to prevent or prepare for post-conflict situations, and to help stabilize and reconstruct societies in transition from conflict or civil strife, so that they can reach a sustainable path toward peace, democracy and a market economy."[84] Despite the potential value of its functions, to date, limited resources have mostly restricted its efforts to improve coordination and planning.[85]

Change within the DoD has been perhaps more significant. In February 2005, President George W. Bush issued an Executive Directive to the DoD that ordered all armed services to improve their stability and reconstruction capabilities and capacities to levels commensurate with their traditional prowess at major combat operations.[86] In response, the DoD developed and issued Directive 3000.05, which states that stability operations are a "core U.S. military mission that the Department of Defense shall be prepared to conduct and support."[87]

In spite of these notable efforts to reform and reorganize for more effective U.S. intervention policy, many challenges remain in seeking to create more effective intervention capabilities within the U.S. government. In particular, anemic funding and resource allocations to U.S. government agencies other than the DoD have limited the effectiveness of efforts to create expanded civilian capabilities. As a consequence, U.S. intervention policy still largely relies on the military—an approach that seems increasingly unable to respond to the national security challenges of the twenty-first century.

Looking Ahead

In the decades since the end of the Cold War, limitations in U.S. intervention capability have become all too apparent. Failures to secure, stabilize, and reconstruct in the wake of otherwise successful initial combat operations have been matched by failures to adequately perform similar functions at home in the aftermath of such disasters as Hurricane Katrina in 2005 (see Chapter 6). Unfortunately, these challenges seem unlikely to diminish in the future. As the 2005 Council on Foreign Relations task force report notes, "In today's world of failed states, terrorism, proliferation, and civil conflict, the trend is clear: The United States will often be drawn into complex situations when they affect its national security or its conscience."[88] The United States has taken initial steps to create more robust intervention capabilities, but the effectiveness of even these initial steps remains unproven. There is undoubtedly still a long way to go.

Discussion Questions

1. What is an *irregular challenge* to U.S. national security? How is this category of threats useful to defense policy makers?

2. To what extent are irregular challenges to U.S. national security of increasing importance in the early twenty-first century? Why or why not?

3. What types of military operations might the United States employ against irregular challenges? Under what circumstances is each likely to be appropriate?

4. How has the nature of insurgency changed over time? What are some of the important characteristics of contemporary insurgencies?

5. What does historical experience suggest are principles of counterinsurgency operations? Which of these are most important? Under what circumstances do these factors vary?

6. What challenges are the United States likely to continue to face in counterinsurgency operations? Are these challenges relevant to other types of military operations? Why or why not?

7. Does the United States have adequate nonmilitary capabilities to deal with the irregular national security challenges of the twenty-first century? What could be done to improve these capabilities?

Recommended Reading

Beckett, Ian F. W. *Modern Insurgencies and Counter-Insurgencies: Guerrillas and Their Opponents Since 1750.* New York: Routledge, 2001.

Cassidy, Robert M. *Counterinsurgency and the Global War on Terror: Military Culture and Irregular War.* Westport, CT: Praeger Security International, 2006.

Covey, Jock, Michael Dziedzic, and Leonard Hawley. *The Quest for Viable Peace: International Intervention and Strategies for Conflict Transformation.* Washington, DC: U.S. Institute of Peace Press, 2005.

Damrosch, Lori Fisler, ed., *Enforcing Restraint: Collective Intervention in Internal Conflicts.* New York: Council on Foreign Relations Press, 1993.

Galula, David. *Counterinsurgency Warfare: Theory and Practice.* Westport, CT: Praeger, 2006.

Haass, Richard N. *Intervention: The Use of American Military Force in the Post-Cold War World.* Washington, DC: Carnegie Endowment for International Peace, 1994.

Harkavy, Robert E., and Stephanie G. Neuman. *Warfare in the Third World.* New York: Palgrave, 2001.

Hashim, Ahmed. *Insurgency and Counter-Insurgency in Iraq.* Ithaca, NY: Cornell University Press, 2006.

Joes, Anthony. *Resisting Rebellion.* Lexington: University Press of Kentucky, 2006.

Lomperis, Timothy. *From People's War to People's Rule.* Raleigh: University of North Carolina Press, 1996.

Mandel, Robert. *The Meaning of Military Victory.* Boulder, CO: Lynne Reiner, 2006.

Merom, Gil. *How Democracies Lose Small Wars.* Cambridge: Cambridge University Press, 2003.

Nagl, John. *Learning to Eat Soup with a Knife: Counterinsurgency Lessons from Malaysia and Vietnam.* Chicago: University of Chicago Press, 2005.

Osgood, Robert E. *Limited War: The Challenges to American Strategy.* Chicago: University of Chicago Press, 1957.

Paret, Peter, ed., with Gordon A. Craig and Felix Gilbert. *Makers of Modern Strategy: From Machiavelli to the Nuclear Age.* Princeton, NJ: Princeton University Press, 1986.

Wilson, Isaiah. *Thinking Beyond War: Why America Fails to Win the Peace.* New York: Palgrave Macmillan, 2007.

Internet Resources

Council on Foreign Relations, *In the Wake of War: Improving U.S. Post-Conflict Capabilities,* www.cfr.org /content/publications/attachments/Post-Conflict_Capabilities_final.pdf

U.S. Department of the Army, Field Manual (FM) No. 3-24/Marine Corps Warfighting Publication (MCWP) No. 3-33.5, *Counterinsurgency,* 2006, http://usacac.army.mil/cac/repository/materials/coin-fm3-24.pdf

U.S. Department of Defense, Directive 3000.05, November 2005, "Military Support for Stability, Security, Transition, and Reconstruction (SSTR) Operations," www.dtic.mil/whs/directives/corres/html/300005.htm

U.S. Department of Defense, *The National Defense Strategy of the United States of America,* March 2005, www.defenselink.mil/news/Mar2005/d20050318nds.pdf

17

Nuclear Policy

Throughout the Cold War, nuclear weapons formed the backbone of Western defense policy. Unable to fully match the conventional military strength of the former Soviet Union and the Warsaw Pact, the United States and its North Atlantic Treaty Organization (NATO) allies used the threat of nuclear retaliation to help avert what U.S. policy makers believed to be a serious risk of Soviet military adventurism as well as to deter the use of the Soviet nuclear arsenal. In support of this policy, the United States and its allies built tens of thousands of strategic and tactical nuclear weapons and deployed them in Europe, the Far East, and at sea. The policy was fraught with risks—indeed some believed that the nuclear arms race placed the very survival of the human race in jeopardy—but Western leaders thought the Soviet threat justified those risks.

In the years since the end of the Cold War, the Soviet nuclear threat has been replaced by a range of challenges posed by new or aspiring nuclear weapons states, such as North Korea and Iran, as well as by nonstate actors looking to acquire a nuclear weapon or a nuclear device to strike at Western targets. Particularly in the case of nonstate actors, U.S. strategic planners confront an enemy that most analysts believe cannot be deterred or contained by threats of nuclear reprisal (see Chapter 14). This chapter primarily focuses on what defense planners have termed *catastrophic challenges*, as shown in the upper right box in the diagram of threats identified in Figure 13.1 in Chapter 13 (though it also has implications for traditional and disruptive challenges). It examines the role of nuclear weapons in the post–Cold War security environment and measures to prevent the spread of nuclear weapons to states and nonstate actors that might use them against the United States or its allies.

U.S. Nuclear Strategy during the Cold War

As the leader of the Free World during the Cold War, the United States was the principal guardian of western Europe, the Middle East, northeast Asia, and other regions against communist incursions. Its nuclear arsenal was the keystone of containment, providing military strength and deterrence that buttressed U.S. and NATO conventional military strength and political unity. On many occasions, the United States enunciated or became party to doctrines explicitly relying on the threat of nuclear war to achieve U.S. strategic aims (see Chapter 3). The predictable result was the deployment of a vast U.S. nuclear arsenal that included more than twelve thousand strategic warheads, thousands of tactical nuclear weapons at locations throughout Europe and the Far East, extremely accurate counterforce nuclear weapons, the satellites and command systems to help guide them, intercontinental ballistic missiles (ICBMs), submarine launched missiles, and heavy bombers to penetrate enemy airspace. The United States spent trillions of dollars on the strategic triad—the combination of nuclear missiles, bombers, and submarines—that comprised the U.S. nuclear posture.

Nuclear Deterrence.   At different times, U.S. policy during the Cold War reflected two basic theories regarding how to deter an opponent from starting a nuclear war. One theory, known as *assured destruction*, holds that as long as a nuclear power is capable of responding in kind to a nuclear attack, any aggressor state would know that an attack would be suicidal and would therefore be deterred from making such an attack. Assured destruction requires a secure, second-strike capability—a nuclear force capable of withstanding an enemy attack and responding. If both sides have this capability, a situation known as *mutually assured destruction* (MAD) exists. Neither side can rationally start a war, because both sides are vulnerable to planned and credible retaliation. This threatened retaliation is often aimed at civilian targets, such as cities and industries, in what is called a *countervalue* approach to targeting. Assured destruction does not require a large or extremely accurate nuclear arsenal, but one that is certainly survivable and capable, after an enemy attack, of inflicting an unacceptably high level of punishment. The emphasis on credibility requires not merely the existence of nuclear weapons but the command, control, training, and exercising of nuclear weapon delivery systems so that an adversary will conclude that it could and would suffer devastating retaliation if it launched a nuclear attack.

A warfighting theory supported by a *counterforce* nuclear strategy, on the other hand, is much more ambitious than a countervalue, assured destruction approach. It holds that to deter an opponent, whose leaders might believe a nuclear war could be fought and won, military forces must have the ability to go beyond retaliation and be able to prevail over an opponent in a nuclear conflict. Such a strategy requires numerous accurate weapons capable of destroying enemy nuclear forces, well beyond the relatively few nuclear weapons required to hold enemy population centers or factories at risk. Counterforce strikes could be aimed at either nuclear or non-nuclear targets, such as command nodes or radar sites, but it is most commonly associated with counternuclear strikes. This approach seeks to deter by denying the attacker the ability to prevail in a nuclear attack.

One common analogy for the nuclear superpowers during the Cold War is of two people with guns pointed at one another's heads. In the context of this image, assured destruction would have each side merely watch and wait and promise to pull the trigger if the other side does. Counterforce advocates say such a mutual suicide pact may not be credible and argue that each side must be prepared to win a gun duel rather than merely fire back. The distinction is between deterrence by threatening punishment and deterrence by demonstrating the capability to win a nuclear conflict.

History of U.S. Nuclear Weapons Strategy.   To properly understand nuclear strategy today, the evolution of U.S. nuclear weapons policy must be considered, because previous approaches provide the theory, context, weapons, and precedents that affect current decision making. The earliest U.S. nuclear war plans emphasized countervalue targeting of Soviet cities because of the small number of bombs available and because of their unprecedented destructiveness. President Harry Truman saw little value in nuclear weapons and placed emphasis on arms control with such initiatives as the 1946 Baruch Plan—a proposal for total nuclear disarmament. Civilian control of nuclear weapons was absolute; it was not until 1948 that the military was allowed to formulate plans for the use of nuclear weapons.[1]

Eventually, however, Truman redoubled U.S. production of nuclear weapons and began to permit some military control.[2] Once given the right to formulate nuclear options, the new Strategic Air Command began to immediately develop plans to destroy Soviet war-making potential. The Soviet Union's August 1949 test of an atomic bomb lent new urgency to efforts to target Soviet military assets. By 1956–1957, the Soviet Union was expected to possess up to two hundred fifty bombs, and Soviet nuclear stockpiles, production facilities, and bomber delivery vehicles became the chief targets of the U.S. nuclear force.[3]

This targeting policy was not publicly announced, however. Secretary of State John Foster Dulles formally endorsed massive retaliation in 1954, and official U.S. statements still stressed general retaliation against Soviet society. Yet counterforce targeting had already begun, and target priorities would remain largely unchanged for decades. By the late 1950s, the push to target the Soviet military was in full force, and Defense Secretary Thomas Gates spelled out the implications: "We are adjusting our power to a counterforce theory," he said. "We are not basing our requirements on just bombing Russia for retaliatory purposes."[4]

From the beginning, U.S. military planners sought two primary goals with counterforce strategies. One was damage limitation. By destroying Soviet nuclear assets, planners contended that those weapons could not be launched against the United States. A second rationale for counterforce targeting was tied to the American policy of threatening nuclear escalation in Europe's defense. Early on, U.S. and NATO officials recognized that they would be unable to match Soviet conventional force levels in Europe, and they looked to American nuclear weapons as the absolute deterrent. Though committed to this policy, American policy makers also sought options that would not necessarily cause immediate Soviet retaliation on U.S. cities. The ability to selectively target with nuclear weapons military formations moving toward western Europe could deter a Soviet attack without necessarily escalating to a major strategic nuclear exchange.[5] A policy of extended deterrence—where U.S. nuclear weapons deterred not only a Soviet nuclear strike but also protected allies against a Soviet conventional attack—began as early as 1948, with the deployment of B-29 bombers to Germany, and emerged fully during the Eisenhower administration.

The Kennedy administration and Secretary of Defense Robert McNamara pursued this same strategy and did so in part by downplaying the threat of massive retaliation and emphasizing flexible strategies of counterforce targeting as well as conventional force development. Domestic and international opinion quickly forced the Kennedy administration to retreat from public statements on flexible nuclear options. Some observers in the United States viewed counterforce strategy as problematic, because it suggested the possibility of launching a first strike at the Soviet Union. As might be expected, Moscow condemned the doctrine as provocative and dangerous. American allies also expressed doubts about a strategy that contemplated fighting limited nuclear wars. While such a policy could make the threat of nuclear use more credible, it might also make nuclear war more conceivable, and the territory of allied countries could become nuclear battlegrounds.

Given the destructiveness of nuclear weapons, the potential damage of even limited nuclear wars—let alone the ever-present possibility of further escalation—made U.S. discussion of making nuclear weapons "usable" unpopular at best and, for many, an unacceptable policy option. Development of means other than nuclear weapons to deter or defeat limited threats became the hallmark of the "flexible response" strategy.

During the Nixon administration, a distinction again emerged between publicly stated strategies and actual ones. Public opposition to counterforce targeting strategies and the Soviet's major buildup of strategic nuclear weapons induced President Richard Nixon to adhere to a policy of *strategic sufficiency*—a more limited doctrine that aimed at some notion of adequacy rather than superiority—but, in fact, his administration accelerated the trend toward counterforce targeting. Secretary of State Henry Kissinger's National Security Study Memorandum 3, requested the day after Nixon's inauguration in 1969, was partly designed, as Kissinger put it, to "kill assured destruction" and establish the need for limited nuclear options and escalation control. A series of Nixon directives and decisions on the development of nuclear weapons as well as their employment reflected this goal.[6] Secretary of Defense James Schlesinger, the architect of this shift, sought a robust but limited and discriminatory nuclear counterforce.

For the remainder of the Cold War, counterforce targeting strategies continued to dominate U.S. nuclear policy. During the Carter administration, senior officials

held the view that an ability to *fight* a nuclear war had become an integral component of deterrence.[7] By the late 1970s, influential Western experts on the Soviet
Union were convinced that Soviet military officers believed that their combination
of heavy intercontinental ballistic missiles and an evolving strategic defense allowed them to fight and win a nuclear war against the United States. American
planners concluded that they must threaten Soviet leaders with death and defeat,
not just post-attack destruction, to deter them adequately. Counterforce capabilities would promote those goals.

By 1983, when the Reagan administration instituted its nuclear war plan, counterforce targets dominated U.S. retaliatory plans. As documented in numerous
books and articles during the early 1980s, U.S. planning to fight, survive, and ultimately win a nuclear war reached a peak during the early Reagan years.[8] Some
of the proponents of Ronald Reagan's policy to begin building defenses against
missile attacks (the so-called Strategic Defense Initiative or SDI) made their case
in a counterforce context, arguing that missile defenses were necessary to deny
Soviet war aims. Even today, the United States continues to pursue some form of
counterforce targeting as part of its comprehensive nuclear weapons posture,
which is discussed later in this chapter.

U.S. Nuclear Policy after the Cold War

The end of the Cold War brought with it the demise of the past central focus of
U.S. nuclear policy—the Soviet Union. Theoretically, Russia still possesses
the capability to destroy the United States in a matter of hours with its huge nuclear arsenal, but despite recurring tensions in relations between the two countries, few observers believe that Russia intends to wage nuclear war against the
United States or poses the military threat to NATO or other U.S. allies that it
did during the Cold War (see Chapter 22). Nevertheless, since Russia still has
the ability to devastate the U.S., a nuclear deterrence hedge continues to be
essential.

This change in context requires a complete re-examination of the role of nuclear weapons in U.S. national security policy. There are two related, and yet distinct, issues to be considered. The first challenge facing U.S. strategic planners is
the threats created by the proliferation of nuclear weapons and technology to additional states or nonstate actors. The second issue concerns the overall nuclear
capabilities that will best enhance U.S. national security in the current and probable future strategic environment.

Current and Future Threats.   While the end of the Cold War has diminished
though not entirely eliminated the threat of an all-out nuclear war involving the
United States, the threat of nuclear weapons, possessed by a handful of states and
coveted by other states and nonstate actors hostile to the West, is highly dangerous. Considering each of these potential threats illustrates the complexity and interconnected nature of U.S. nuclear policy.

Russia.   Despite Russia's continuing nuclear capabilities, improved relations between the United States and Russia since the end of the Cold War have dramatically reduced the risk of nuclear war. In the minds of some experts, concern over the potential for nuclear conflict has now been largely displaced by fear of the deteriorating condition of the Russian nuclear arsenal. Russia's nuclear forces did not entirely escape the general collapse that occurred in all the country's armed forces. Horror stories of broken equipment, lax security, Strategic Rocket Forces personnel not being paid for months at a time, and rumors of attempted black-market sales of nuclear warheads had become commonplace by the late 1990s. Many analysts believe that the greatest threat from Russia stems not from deliberate government action but rather from a lack of effective control, which could lead to an accidental, unintentional, or unauthorized use of nuclear weapons.[9]

China.   As of 2008, China's nuclear arsenal remains modest. China has an estimated twenty nuclear-tipped missiles with truly intercontinental range, and another twenty-two long-range missiles. It also deploys another estimated one hundred intermediate range missiles and at least one nuclear-armed submarine. The balance of China's nuclear arsenal is composed of hundreds of gravity bombs or tactical nuclear weapons.[10]

This relatively small force has long been adequate to China's traditional nuclear strategy of minimum deterrence. During the Cold War, China never sought to match the nuclear arsenals of the United States or the Soviet Union. Instead, China built a force large enough to destroy a number of major cities of any state that attacked its homeland. The question remains whether Chinese military leaders will remain content with this approach or will seek to expand their nuclear arsenal to achieve parity with the reduced forces of the United States and Russia. As far as can be determined, China's current nuclear plans, similar to those for the rest of the People's Liberation Army, point to more of the same—it has declared a preference for modernizing its relatively small force rather than substantially increasing its size. Of course, changes in U.S. nuclear policy could influence China's choice. Surprisingly, some American analysts argue that the United States should seek dramatic reductions in U.S. and Russian nuclear forces to emphasize to Chinese policy makers that a further nuclear buildup is not necessary.[11]

North Korea.   On October 9, 2006, North Korea detonated a nuclear device. This detonation came after years of negotiations among six parties: the United States, North Korea, South Korea, China, Japan, and Russia. Throughout the long diplomatic process, North Korea, despite promises to the contrary, continued to secretly pursue nuclear weapons.

According to an authoritative 2006 Congressional Research Service report, North Korea is estimated to have enough plutonium for six to ten atomic bombs and enough highly enriched uranium (HEU) for between two and six additional weapons.[12] Likely targets of a North Korean nuclear weapon would be South Korea or Japan, as well as U.S. forces deployed in the region. It is unclear whether North Korea has been able to miniaturize a nuclear device to fit on the tip of a missile. Current North Korean ballistic missile technology is not capable of targeting cities in the United States.[13]

One worrisome side effect of a nuclear North Korea is the specter of a nuclear arms race in Asia. It is possible that South Korea and Japan would want to acquire nuclear weapons to deter a North Korean attack. In turn, the possibility of South Korea and Japan acquiring nuclear weapons could cause China to create more robust nuclear capabilities in response. Also, given the nuclear status of India and Pakistan, a destabilizing arms race could spread beyond the immediate region and engulf most of Asia.

India and Pakistan.　In 1998, India and Pakistan conducted underground nuclear tests and became declared nuclear weapons states. This situation raises at least three significant concerns. First, relations between the two states are still marked by sharp tensions—particularly over the contested region of Kashmir—and they have already fought one minor war since becoming nuclear powers.[14] Second, the nuclear programs of these states could become a source of proliferation of nuclear technologies to additional state or nonstate actors, as has already occurred through the network that Pakistani nuclear scientist Abdul Qadeer Khan admitted to having established in 2004 (see Chapters 19 and 26). Third, domestic political instability in the region—particularly in Pakistan—could result in risky nuclear posturing or loss of control over the country's nuclear arsenal, constituting another possible source of nuclear anarchy. The bilateral relationship between India and Pakistan and their nuclear postures will remain serious concerns for U.S. national security policy makers.

Iran.　The 2006 U.S. National Security Strategy identifies Iran as the single most dangerous state-centered threat to U.S. security.[15] Iran pursued nuclear weapons in secret for nearly twenty years until 2002, when the National Council of Resistance of Iran blew the whistle on nuclear activities at Natanz and Arak.[16] Despite these covert nuclear programs, Iran proclaims that its nuclear ambitions are peaceful, claiming that nuclear energy is required to meet rising domestic energy requirements. However, the November 2007 U.S. National Intelligence Estimate (NIE) on Iranian nuclear intentions and capabilities reports that Iranian military entities were "working under government direction to develop nuclear weapons" until the fall of 2003, when they stopped their nuclear weapons program "in response to international pressure."[17] The NIE further judges that if Iranian policy changed, it could restart the nuclear program, and Iran could produce a nuclear weapon some time between 2010 and 2015.[18] The difficulty of assessing the intentions and capabilities of a covert nuclear weapons program in Iran highlights the difficulty and importance of using intelligence assessments as a guide for national security policy making.

Copyright 1985 CARTOONEWS INTERNATIONAL Syndicate, N.Y.C., USA. Reprinted with permission of Ranan Lurie.

The regional implications of a nuclear Iran are similar to those of Asia. Should Iran successfully acquire nuclear weapons, it would create numerous problems, including the possibility of touching off a nuclear arms race in the region. Israel in particular has reason for concern; Iranian President Mahmoud Ahmadinejad has stated many times that Israel should be wiped off the map. Should Iran nearly or actually complete a nuclear device, Israel might decide to take action, much as it did in 1981 when the Israeli air force conducted a successful preemptive strike against the Osiraq nuclear reactor in Iraq. Whether such a raid would succeed against hardened buried facilities in Iran is unclear. Additionally, a Shiite Iran with nuclear weapons would likely make the Sunni Arab states feel dangerously threatened, perhaps leading them to seek their own nuclear weapons. Finally, Iranian sponsorship of terrorist groups, such as Hezbollah and Hamas, leads to the possibility of terrorists gaining access to nuclear weapons. This would raise the specter of some of the most dangerous people being armed with the world's most dangerous weapons. Each of these consequences highlights the importance of precluding Iranian nuclear weapons, if that is possible.

Nonstate Actors. The rise of terrorism in the post–Cold War era has been marked by an increase in violence toward nonmilitary targets, such as civilians. Many terrorism experts agree that nuclear weapons especially lend themselves to this purpose (see Chapter 14). Once terrorists acquire a weapon, deterring its use is highly problematic. Perhaps the most promising deterrence policy is to focus on preventing the acquisition of a device or the nuclear material for it in the first place.

The obstacles that a terrorist organization, such as al-Qa'ida, would have to overcome to attain nuclear capability include the acquisition of a weapon and the ability to employ it. A more likely related scenario would be for a nonstate actor to acquire sufficient radiological and explosive material to fashion a *radiological dispersion device*, or what is more commonly referred to as a *dirty bomb*, for use against targets in the United States or abroad.[19] This type of device would be easier for a non-state actor to acquire, transport, and use than a nuclear weapon, yet it would still inflict significant physical and even greater psychological damage. The danger of this scenario developing is far from negligible.

Managing the Nuclear Challenge in a New Era. As this brief survey reflects, the challenges to U.S. national security created by nuclear technology have grown far more diverse in the twenty-first century. U.S. policy makers can no longer focus on the threat posed by a single, rival superpower; instead, they must seek effective ways to deter the threat posed by new and aspiring nuclear weapons states as well as nonstate actors. Deterring this hosts of threats requires understanding of the values, motives, fears, risk tolerance, and priorities for each and tailoring policies for each without confusing the differing messages that must be sent.[20] These traditional nuclear deterrence strategies cannot be discarded but must be supplemented with other foreign policy tools, such as arms control, nonproliferation strategies, and counterproliferation measures.

Arms Control. In 1961, the United States established the Arms Control and Disarmament Agency (ACDA) to advise the president on arms control, to regulate nuclear activities, and to build expertise on negotiated measures for dealing with international conflict. For a United States focused on the problems of military strategy and international conflict in a nuclear age, *arms control* was defined as having three purposes: to reduce the likelihood of war by enhancing communication and crisis stability, to limit the damage if war were to occur, and to lessen the economic burdens of preparing for war.[21] While these purposes continue, in 1999 ACDA was dissolved as an independent agency, and its bureaus and functions were incorporated into the State Department.

During the Cold War, arms control agreements were an important component of U.S. nuclear policy. They can broadly be grouped into three categories: confidence-building measures, restrictions on the development and testing of weapons, and limitations on the weapons themselves. Examples of *confidence-building measures* include the "Hot Line Agreement" that established a direct communications link between the leadership of the United States and the Soviet Union (1963) and the on-site inspections by foreign teams that were instituted by the Stockholm Conference on Confidence and Security-Building Measures and Disarmament in Europe (1986). Examples of *testing restrictions* include the Limited Test Ban Treaty that banned nuclear tests in the atmosphere, outer space, and under water (1963); and the Threshold Test Ban Treaty that committed the superpowers to limit the size of underground nuclear weapons tests (1974). *Weapons limitations* include: the Nuclear Non-Proliferation Treaty (NPT; 1970), which is discussed below; the Strategic Arms Limitation Talks (SALT I), which constrained certain offensive strategic systems (1972); the Anti-Ballistic Missile (ABM) Treaty, which limited the superpowers' development of defensive capabilities (1972); SALT II, which sought arms reductions between the superpowers (1979; although the U.S. Senate never ratified it, the United States followed its restrictions); the Intermediate-Range Nuclear Forces Treaty, which eliminated U.S. and Soviet intermediate-range nuclear systems (1989); and the Strategic Arms Reduction Treaty (START), which reduced U.S.- and Soviet-deployed nuclear forces and established robust verification measures (1991).

In the early twenty-first century, it is not clear what role bilateral arms control agreements will play in U.S.-Russia relations. In May 2002, U.S. President George W. Bush and Russian President Vladimir Putin signed the Strategic Offensive Reductions Treaty (SORT), which committed each side to reduce its forces to not more than 2,200 operationally deployed warheads by the end of 2012. However, the treaty lacks verification measures and allows the storage rather than destruction of warheads that are not operationally deployed. The SORT treaty is scheduled to expire on the same day its limits must be reached, unless it is extended by both nations. The George W. Bush administration preferred flexible and informal arrangements, while the Russian leadership preferred another formal agreement cutting strategic nuclear forces.[22]

Another dynamic in the U.S.-Russia relationship has been created by the U.S. withdrawal from the ABM Treaty in 2002, followed by U.S. proposals in 2007 to put ground-based missile interceptors in Poland and a new radar system in the Czech Republic. From the U.S. perspective, these initiatives merely recognize the end of the Cold War and the existence of new threats—such as the possibility of Iranian missile launches—in a new strategic environment. However, Russian officials have expressed strong opposition to these developments. According to one Russian foreign ministry statement, "one cannot ignore the fact that U.S. offensive weapons, combined with the missile defense being created, can turn into a strategic complex capable of delivering an incapacitating blow."[23] Whether the United States and Russia continue to turn to arms control as a way to manage the nuclear arsenals each side developed during the Cold War remains to be seen.

Nuclear Non-Proliferation Treaty.   The most significant multilateral agreement regarding nuclear weapons is the treaty commonly referred to as the NPT. This treaty was signed by the United States in 1968 and entered into force in 1970. As of 2008, 188 states were party to the treaty, including the five recognized nuclear weapons states (the United States, Russia, the United Kingdom, France, and China) and 183 non–nuclear weapons states. The only states that are not signatories to the treaty are India, Pakistan, Israel, and North Korea (North Korea withdrew from the NPT in January 2003, but this action has not been recognized by the United Nations [UN]).[24] India, Pakistan, and North Korea possess nuclear weapons, and Israel is an undeclared nuclear weapons state.

The NPT commits the non–nuclear weapons states to not build or use nuclear weapons and commits the nuclear weapons states (the five states that had exploded a nuclear device by January 1, 1967) to the eventual elimination of their own weapons. In addition, all parties to the NPT agree to accept International Atomic Energy Agency (IAEA) safeguards on all nuclear activities; to not export nuclear equipment or materials to non–nuclear weapons states except under IAEA safeguards; and to give ninety days' notice when withdrawing from the NPT. The NPT has undoubtedly played an important role in limiting the spread of nuclear weapons to only four states in the nearly forty years since its inception. (South Africa had a nuclear weapons program from 1977 to 1989 but later dismantled it, destroyed the six weapons it had reportedly produced, and signed the NPT in 1991.)[25] The relatively small growth in nuclear weapons states is particularly impressive in light of the fact that the NPT has no means, aside from referring the matter to the UN Security Council, of punishing those who violate its provisions.

Though the NPT is the centerpiece of the global nonproliferation regime, it has faced numerous trials over time and remains under stress. One tension results because the NPT enshrines the status of the five nuclear weapons states and therefore can be seen as preserving their long-term military dominance. This aspect of the treaty was partially mitigated by the fact that these nuclear weapons states committed to eventual nuclear disarmament by signing the NPT. However, they are regularly criticized "for not disarming fast enough and for abandoning nuclear arms control, increasing reliance on nuclear weapons, and especially for developing new types of weapons."[26] A second source of tension relates to compliance. A particularly unpleasant surprise occurred after the Persian Gulf War in 1991, when it was discovered that Iraq had managed to begin a nuclear weapons program despite the oversight of IAEA inspectors. Iran's case, discussed above, is another compliance problem. Other current tensions include safeguarding the nuclear fuel cycle to support the use of nuclear energy for peaceful purposes while stemming the diversion of material to weapons programs; and recent U.S. initiatives to support India's nuclear energy program despite the fact that India's facilities are not all subject to IAEA safeguards (see Chapter 19).[27]

Cooperative Threat Reduction.   In November 1991, in response to deteriorating conditions in the former Soviet Union, the U.S. Senate passed the Nunn-Lugar Act, with the intent "to assist the states of the former Soviet Union in dismantling weapons of mass destruction and establishing verifiable safeguards against the proliferation of those weapons."[28] The objectives of cooperative threat reduction (CTR) are to:

- Destroy nuclear, chemical, and other weapons of mass destruction (WMDs).
- Transport, store, disable, and safeguard weapons in connection with their destruction.
- Establish verifiable safeguards against proliferation of such weapons.
- Prevent diversion of weapons-related expertise.
- Facilitate demilitarization of defense industries and conversion of military capabilities and technologies.
- Expand defense and military contacts between the United States and the former Soviet Union.[29]

Initial CTR support included assisting in the transport of nuclear warheads from Kazakhstan, Ukraine, and Belarus back to Russia; converting the Soviet-era method of tracking nuclear warheads from a time-consuming and often inaccurate manual system to a rapid, automated system; and providing upgraded security equipment at weapons storage sites.[30]

In addition to securing nuclear weapons, CTR efforts focused on securing the material necessary to construct a nuclear weapon. Russia possesses the world's largest stock of fissile material (highly enriched uranium [HEU] and plutonium).[31] Keeping this material out of the hands of terrorists became even more pressing after the events of September 11, 2001. By April 2005, Senator Sam Nunn estimated that, since 1991, the United States and Russia had "completed between 25 and 50 percent of the job of securing nuclear weapons and materials, depending on definitions."[32] In recent years, CTR programs have continued and have expanded beyond the former Soviet Union into other states in eastern Europe.

The Nuclear Suppliers Group.   The Nuclear Suppliers Group (NSG) is a forty-five-state association that has agreed to coordinate export controls to prevent the sale or transfer of nuclear-related equipment, materials, or technology to non–nuclear weapons states. Its aim is to preclude nuclear exports for such commercial, peaceful purposes as medicine and agriculture from being diverted to production of nuclear weapons. Its formation in 1975 was in response to the 1974 explosion by India, which had diverted commercial materials to build its nuclear device. To be eligible for nuclear imports, non–nuclear weapons states have to agree to IAEA safeguards on the imports. Among the nuclear weapons states that have not joined the NSG are India, Pakistan, Israel, and North Korea. In addition to the problem of lack of universal membership, the NSG faces the difficulty that, as a voluntary organization, it cannot compel compliance with its guidelines. Russia, for instance, despite opposition by other members, transferred nuclear fuel to India in 2001.

The Proliferation Security Initiative.   Originally launched in 2003, the Proliferation Security Initiative (PSI) is designed to stop the international shipment of nuclear weapons, weapons materials, and related technology. The focus of PSI is interdicting nuclear materials during transit between the country of origin and the country or nonstate actor that is the intended recipient. States that are party to PSI voluntarily agree to provide intelligence, law enforcement, and diplomatic cooperation to combat the spread of nuclear weapons, utilizing force if necessary. Membership in the PSI, as well as levels of participation by the signatories, is not widely publicized because of the political sensitivity of these activities.

Reviews of the effectiveness of PSI are mixed. On the one hand, it has raised awareness of illicit trafficking in WMD-related materials, probably constrained traffickers, and "increased national capacities for coordinated detection and interdiction of suspect shipments" through its exercises.[33] On the other hand, the initiative is characterized by a lack of transparency that reflects the political sensitivity of interdiction activities and the ambivalent status of such interdiction under international law. These characteristics make claims of its success difficult to verify.[34]

Counterproliferation.   In addition to the various measures to stem proliferation, such as the NPT, PSI, and NSG, in recent years the United States has begun to focus on actions that can minimize the impact of weapons that have been proliferated. Offsetting the dangers of state and nonstate actors that have already acquired or may acquire nuclear weapons is at least as difficult as stopping the proliferation in the first place; however, several steps can be taken. First, missile defense, discussed below, is a measure that, if successful, would address one dimension of the problem. Second, strengthening the IAEA, expanding arms control initiatives, and increasing international pressure on actors with nuclear weapons minimizes the prospect of their proliferation. Third, development of sensors that can locate nuclear weapons and their production facilities as well as conventional weapons that can destroy them are important to counterproliferation. Finally, various defensive steps, which are analogous to the civil defense programs that were aimed at mitigating the damage of a nuclear attack during the Cold War, can be part of a comprehensive counterproliferation strategy. These include homeland security measures, such as improvements in detection, vaccines, antidotes, communications, medical responses, and protective equipment. Known collectively as *consequence management*, such measures comprise a system that organizes, trains, and exercises government agencies and ordinary citizens to respond to a nuclear weapons or other major disaster can minimize the impact of such an event. While no government action can fully negate the proliferation of nuclear weapons, several steps pursued as part of a comprehensive counterproliferation strategy may be effective at limiting the impact that such weapons can have on national security.

Missile Defense

Given the security challenges posed by nuclear weapons, as well as the difficulty each of the approaches mentioned above faces in meeting those challenges, a perennial issue is the development of an effective defense against nuclear weapons. This has been an issue since the development of nuclear weapons and has become increasingly important with the proliferation and the progress of missile defense technology.

In the context of the superpower rivalry of the Cold War, the United States accepted limits on the creation of ABM defenses, which are enshrined in the 1972 ABM Treaty. By becoming a party to this treaty, the United States acknowledged the situation of MAD and accepted vulnerability as a means of preserving stability in its nuclear competition with the Soviet Union. The first significant challenge to this situation came in January 1984, when Reagan issued Presidential National Security Decision Directive (PNSDD) 119. The purpose of PNSDD 119 was to establish the SDI (which became known as "Star Wars") to "investigate the feasibility of eventually shifting toward reliance upon a defensive concept. Future deterrence should, if possible, be underwritten by a capability to defeat a hostile attack."[35] Reagan's proposal has evolved since its inception because of budgetary constraints, the evolution of technology, and the changing nature of the threat.

A realistic test for missile defense technology came during the 1991 Gulf War with Iraq. U.S. Patriot missiles were used to shoot down incoming Iraqi Scud missiles aimed at Saudi Arabia and Israel. Although the Scud missiles carried only conventional warheads and were not very accurate, and the Patriot missiles had limited success in actually defeating them, these engagements demonstrated the possibility of defeating ballistic missiles while in flight. Each subsequent administration has continued to develop a missile defense program. These efforts have been a great deal more successful for theater weapons than for strategic ones.

On December 17, 2002, George W. Bush directed the Department of Defense (DoD) to develop a system "to protect our homeland, deployed forces, and our friends and allies from ballistic missile attack."[36] The resulting Ballistic Missile Defense System (BMDS) is a layered network of systems that is designed to eventually be able to destroy ballistic missiles in all three stages of flight: the boost phase, the midcourse phase, and the terminal phase.[37] In fiscal year 2008, the United States spent $8.7 billion on BMDS.[38]

The Case for Ballistic Missile Defense.   The primary reason for the United States to acquire a defense against ballistic missiles is the threat of missile-delivered nuclear weapons on the United States, on deployed U.S. troops, or on U.S. allies and interests abroad. According to a 2001 State Department report entitled "The Emerging Ballistic Missile Threat," some twenty-seven states currently possess or are in the process of obtaining ballistic missiles.[39] A handful of these states also have nuclear weapons programs. The report cites missile technology in North Korea and Iran as the greatest threat to the "U.S., its forces deployed abroad, and allies and friends."[40] The report further states that the preeminence of the United States in the world's political affairs may cause its adversaries to seek ballistic missiles as a means to deliver chemical, biological, radiological, or nuclear weapons (CBRN). These adversaries would seek to use CBRN weapons to "deter the U.S. from intervening in, or leading coalitions against, their efforts at regional aggression, or these states may believe that such capabilities would give them the ability to threaten allied countries in order to dissuade them from joining such coalitions."[41] A viable BMDS not only would confront the threat posed by states or nonstate actors possessing ballistic missiles but also would protect the United States and its allies against an accidental nuclear launch by any other state.

The Case against Ballistic Missile Defense. Opponents of the BMDS argue that such a system cannot protect the United States, provides a false sense of security, and requires great expenditures for a program of uncertain effectiveness. If BMDS works by destroying a hostile warhead with an interceptor, to achieve certainty the United States would need to launch multiple interceptors for every single hostile warhead. For example, if a country were to launch one thousand warheads, then the United States would need to launch many more than one thousand interceptors to defeat each warhead as well as to confront any decoy warheads or other countermeasures that would likely accompany any attack.

Because the BMDS is a layered network of systems that consists of elements that acquire targets, computer systems that analyze the data, and interceptor missiles that destroy the incoming missiles, it is difficult to test such a system. Even if a very expensive missile defense may be effective in theory or simulations, it would be difficult or impossible to ever know if it would work perfectly in practice. Moreover, some believe a successful strategic BMDS could even be destabilizing; other states may perceive U.S. strategic invulnerability to portend greater U.S. aggression vis-à-vis other states.

In addition to these concerns, two additional issues are opportunity cost and appropriateness to current threats. With regard to opportunity cost, investments in missile defense systems come at the expense of other defense or homeland security priorities. A second and related issue concerns the nature of the threat. Some analysts argue that other homeland security measures, such as cargo inspection at U.S. ports, might actually be more effective than missile defense in providing protection against the most probable delivery method of CBRN against the United States.

Whether to deploy strategic or theater ballistic missile defenses and, if so, which kind of defense to deploy will continue to be a central issue in U.S. nuclear policy. The allure of defensive weapons integrated into a system that reduces vulnerability will always be appealing, despite costs, technical challenges, and potential strategic ramifications.

Toward a New Nuclear Posture and Strategy

Despite repeated efforts at arms control, membership in the NPT, and less formal arrangements, such as CTR, PSI, and NSG, the United States continues to maintain the essentiality of nuclear weapons. Nuclear weapons are the ultimate deterrent. Many experts believe that Saddam Hussein did not use chemical or biological weapons during the 1991 Persian Gulf War because he feared threatened nuclear retaliation by the United States.

Maintaining a credible deterrent means that the United States must continue to invest in nuclear technology, inevitably at the expense of other weapons or other critical programs. Nuclear weapons, much like conventional weapons, become obsolete over time and require investment in basic sustainment and modernization. Current American nuclear weapons are decades old and in the absence of testing will be increasingly difficult to certify as reliable. Congress has been very reluctant to appropriate the funds necessary for sustainment, let alone modernization. As the strategic situation changes over time, new threats to national security may require new types of weapons. Debates over new weapons are likely to travel through familiar territory, requiring answers to such questions as their continuing deterrence role their political and strategic utility for purposes beyond deterrence and projections about the ability to control escalation in the event of nuclear weapons use.[42]

In January 2002, at the direction of Congress, the DoD released the classified Nuclear Posture Review (NPR). The intent of the NPR was to develop a road map for the future development of strategic weapons. The NPR recognizes that the U.S. Cold War nuclear arsenal is no longer appropriate in light of twenty-first century threats. The DoD therefore developed a new strategic triad to replace the old model. The new triad incorporates the previous triad (nuclear weapons launched from ballistic missiles, strategic bombers, and submarines) while also adding non-kinetic and non-nuclear weapons as part of the offensive strike capabilities on the first leg of the triad. These offensive capabilities allow the United States to use a spectrum of weapons when responding to a threat against its interests, reserving nuclear weapons as the highest level of response the United States could take. The first leg of the new triad is reminiscent of the flexible response policy of the Kennedy administration and clearly recognizes that nuclear weapons have a major role, although they need not be the initial weapon of choice, in future military planning.

The second leg of the new triad consists of passive and active defensive measures (such as the BMDS and the PSI). These methods seek to deter adversaries from the pursuit of nuclear weapons technology, dissuade those states (and potentially nonstate actors) that seek to possess nuclear weapons from acquiring them, and deny or reduce the effectiveness of nuclear attacks if they occur. The aim is to add deterrence by denial to deterrence by retaliation.

The third leg is an improved nuclear weapons infrastructure designed to improve the development and procurement of weapons systems as well as to improve communications and intelligence capabilities. This leg of the triad acknowledges the need to modernize the Cold War nuclear force using current technologies that make nuclear forces safer and more effective. Additionally, the new triad, according to the NPR, should allow the United States to reduce its nuclear arsenal to between 1,700 and 2,200 operationally deployed nuclear warheads by the year 2012.[43] This would make the U.S. nuclear posture consistent with that proposed as part of the SORT, discussed above.

To maintain a strong viable nuclear arsenal, despite obsolescence and shrinking numbers, the Secretaries of Energy, Defense, and State, in July 2007, urged the Congress to support initiation of the Reliable Replacement Warhead (RRW) Program. This program is designed to improve the safety of the U.S. arsenal by replacing older warheads with new similar yield warheads that contain state-of-the-art security systems. These systems are designed to augment prevention of unauthorized use or accidental launch of a nuclear weapon. Additionally, the RRW Program is designed to improve weapons reliability by offsetting the natural effects of age while also eliminating the need to test weapons to measure their output.[44] The Congress was not, however, persuaded and the program has not been funded as of late 2008.

For a variety of reasons, U.S. spending on the further development of its nuclear arsenal is seen with a critical eye in many quarters. One issue is scale. In 2006, two national security scholars, Kier Lieber and Daryl Press, argued that U.S. investment in more or improved nuclear weapons—especially given the status of the arsenals of major nuclear rivals Russia and China—could reasonably be seen as an effort by the United States to obtain a first-strike capability. In other words, a degree of U.S. nuclear superiority had the potential to enable the United States to inflict such a devastating nuclear first strike that an adversary would be unable to retaliate.[45] (This argument disregards the fact that both Russia and China are modernizing and enlarging their nuclear arsenals.) Some policy advocates, concerned about the effect of continued U.S. nuclear weapons development upon arms control and nonproliferation efforts, argue against modernization on the grounds that, even before modernization, the current U.S. nuclear arsenal is more than capable of meeting contemporary and future threats to national security. On the other hand, experts on the actual status of our weapons argue that, given obsolescence, without modernization the U.S. is on the path to unilateral nuclear disarmament. Some believe that the United States has an obligation not to pursue new nuclear technology, especially in light of its NPT obligations and its commitment to limit the spread of nuclear weapons. A final argument relates to resources, with some analysts believing that money spent on researching and developing new nuclear weapons would make a more effective contribution to U.S. national security if it were spent on securing "loose" nuclear weapons in the former Soviet Union or funding other CTR programs. Collectively, these and similar anti arguments have produced a national nuclear allergy in the U.S that makes it difficult to maintain a viable nuclear deterrent.

Clearly, the end of the Cold War has reduced the profile of nuclear weapons in international politics, at least among the major powers. Yet despite currently planned arms reductions in the U.S. and Russian arsenals, many policy makers around the globe continue to push for new nuclear weapons to replace the old, outdated models. Whether the impetus for denuclearization will continue and build or nuclear arsenals will increase in the future is an open question. What is clear is that nuclear weapons cannot be uninvented and that any scheme to eliminate them once and for all would require climbing a verification mountain of unprecedented height.

Looking Ahead

After the end of the Cold War, the United States faced a new strategic environment in which the role of its nuclear arsenal became less central. If anything, this trend accelerated after the terrorist attacks of 9/11 and the U.S. wars began in Afghanistan and Iraq. Policy makers and analysts consumed with diverse new challenges have generally paid less attention to matters of nuclear policy. Indicative of that inattention is the fact that deep reductions in the U.S. nuclear arsenal since the end of the Cold War have gone almost unnoticed.

The serious issues that the United States should address in the nuclear area would benefit from broad-ranging, vigorous debate, which to this point has been lacking. A discussion of the size and characteristics of the future U.S. nuclear arsenal should include the likely impact of such weapons on nonproliferation efforts, arms control, crisis stability, deterrence, military budgets, and other political and economic factors.

The vision of a world in which nuclear weapons play a diminishing and ultimately nonexistent role has had broad, worldwide appeal for decades. But nuclear weapons are spreading. The extent to which their elimination is achievable and the extent to which the United States should pursue that goal are issues U.S. policy makers will have to confront in the years ahead.

Discussion Questions

1. What is the difference between a *countervalue* and a *counterforce* nuclear strategy? Which strategy requires more nuclear weapons? Which strategy would better suit U.S. national security needs? Why?

2. What is *counterproliferation*? What is *nonproliferation*? What are the similarities and differences between the two policies?

3. Will traditional methods of deterrence used during the Cold War work on modern adversaries, such as Iran, North Korea, and such nonstate actors as al-Qa'ida? Why or why not?

4. What did the U.S. strategic triad include during the Cold War? What does it include today? What are the reasons for the changes?

5. Which poses the greater threat to U.S. security: possession of nuclear weapons by rogue states (such as North Korea and Iran) or by nonstate actors (such as al-Qa'ida or Hezbollah)? Why?

6. Has the NPT been a success, or does the spread of weapons to at least four states since 1970 constitute a failure?

7. How does North Korea's acquisition of nuclear weapons affect security in Asia? Does the threat posed by Iran's nuclear program have similar consequences for the Middle East?

8. Should the United States focus its efforts on preventing the spread of nuclear weapons or on defending itself and its allies from a nuclear attack?

9. What is the role of nuclear weapons in U.S. defense policy today? Should the United States develop new nuclear weapons as new threats emerge? Why or why not?

Recommended Reading

Ball, Desmond, and Jeffrey Richelson, eds. *Strategic Nuclear Targeting.* Ithaca, NY: Cornell University Press, 1986.

Brown, Michael E., ed. *Grave New World: Security Challenges in the 21st Century.* Washington, DC: Georgetown University Press, 2003.

Campbell, Kurt M., Robert J. Einhorn, and Mitchell B. Reiss, eds. *The Nuclear Tipping Point: Why States Reconsider Their Nuclear Choices.* Washington, DC: Brookings Institution Press, 2004.

Cirincione, Joseph, Jon B. Wolfsthal, and Miriam Rajkumar. *Deadly Arsenals: Nuclear, Biological, and Chemical Threats.* Washington DC: Carnegie Endowment for International Peace, 2005.

Cordesman, Anthony H. *Terrorism, Asymmetric Warfare, and Weapons of Mass Destruction: Defending the U.S. Homeland.* Westport, CT: Praeger, 2002.

Drell, Sidney D., and James E. Goodby. *The Gravest Danger: Nuclear Weapons.* Stanford: Hoover Institution Press, 2003.

Feldman, Shai. *Nuclear Weapons and Arms Control in the Middle East.* Cambridge, MA: MIT Press, 1997.

Knopf, Jeffrey W. "Wrestling with Deterrence: Bush Administration Strategy After 9/11." *Contemporary Security Policy,* 29: 2, August 2008

Lieber, Keir A., and Daryl G. Press. "The End of MAD? The Nuclear Dimension of U.S. Primacy." *International Security* 30, no. 4 (Spring 2006): 7–44.

Sagan, Scott D., and Kenneth N. Waltz. *The Spread of Nuclear Weapons: A Debate Renewed.* New York: W. W. Norton & Company, 2003.

The White House, Nolan, Janne E., Bernard I. Finel, and Brian D. Finlay, eds. *Ultimate Security: Combating Weapons of Mass Destruction.* New York: Century Foundation Press, 2003.

The White House. National Security Strategy of the United States of America, March 2006.

The White House. National Strategy to Combat Weapons of Mass Destruction, December 2002.

Wirtz, James J., and James A. Russell. "A Quiet Revolution: Nuclear Strategy for the 21st Century." *Joint Forces Quarterly* (Winter 2002/2003): 9–15.

Internet Resources

Arms Control Association, www.armscontrol.org

Carnegie Endowment for International Peace, www.carnegieendowment.org

International Atomic Energy Agency, www.iaea.org

Missile Defense Agency, www.mda.mil

The Nuclear Files Web site, www.nuclearfiles.org.
Nuclear Posture Review, www.globalsecurity.org/wmd/library/policy/dod/npr.htm
Nuclear Suppliers Group, www.nuclearsuppliersgroup.org
Nuclear Threat Initiative, www.nti.org
Programme for Promoting Nuclear Non-Proliferation, www.ppnn.soton.ac.uk
U.S. Air Force Counterproliferation Center, http://cpc.au.af.mil

IV

International and Regional Security Issues

18

East Asia

East Asia is one of the few regions of the world in which the possibility of great power conflict remains substantial. The countries that make up Northeast Asia—defined here as including Russia, China, Taiwan, North Korea, South Korea, and Japan—all have significant military capabilities and are in close proximity to the large contingent of military force that the United States maintains in the area. (Note: Despite disagreement over its sovereign status and Washington's "One China" policy, Taiwan is treated as a country for the purpose of this discussion.) Southeast Asia, which includes the Philippines and Indonesia as well as peninsular Southeast Asia, is also discussed briefly toward the end of this chapter. All the Northeast Asian countries, with the exception of North Korea, rank in the top ten countries of the world in terms of military spending. Russia, China, and perhaps North Korea have already demonstrated nuclear weapons capabilities. Taiwan, South Korea, and Japan have robust civilian nuclear power industries and the technological capability to rapidly become nuclear weapons states if they so desire. (See Map 18.1 for a map of the region.)

In addition to these sobering facts, the legacy of World War II and the Cold War have fostered the continuing possibility of great power conflict. In Northeast Asia, many of the security challenges that divided the region throughout the Cold War remain salient. These include the security standoff between China and Taiwan, the absence of a permanent peace on the Korean peninsula, ongoing territorial disputes, China's continuing defense buildup across the range of forces and weapons systems, and an incipient arms race fueled by deep-rooted mistrust and nationalism among the countries of the region. Northeast Asia's lack of strong international institutions to handle these security challenges makes the region even more volatile.

MAP 18.1 East Asia

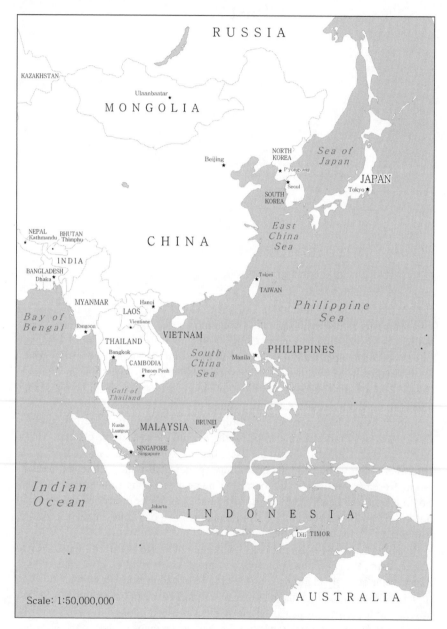

Table 18.1 United States Trade Figures in 2006 (in Thousands of $ and % of World Total)

	U.S. Exports		U.S. Imports	
China	65,238,310	5.6%	321,507,785	16.5%
Japan	62,664,976	5.4%	145,463,648	7.4%
South Korea	34,702,985	3.0%	47,566,302	2.4%
Taiwan	26,358,532	2.3%	38,301,899	2.0%
Russia	7,365,345	0.6%	19,360,240	1.0%
Northeast Asia Subtotal	196,330,148	16.9%	572,199,874	29.3%
ASEAN	60,559,700	5.2%	111,170,613	5.7%
World	1,162,708,293	100%	1,953,698,801	100%

Source: U.S. Department of Commerce, http://tse.export.gov/.

American Interests

In the mid-1800s, before the United States even had a West Coast and before the arrival of the "black ships" of Commodore Matthew Perry that are credited with opening Japan to the West, the U.S. Navy had a presence in East Asia. Why has the United States demonstrated this prolonged interest in a region on the other side of the world? The answer lies in four key U.S. interests that have remained largely consistent over time.

Maintain Economic Access. Since the dawn of the industrial age, the huge potential of Asian economic markets has held special appeal for the United States. Recent trade figures highlight Asia's current economic importance to the United States. Table 18.1 presents data for U.S. trade with countries in Northeast Asia, the Association of Southeast Asian Nations (ASEAN), and the world in 2005. U.S. exports to the Northeast Asia accounted for over 16% of total exports—a percentage that rises to over 22% with the inclusion of ASEAN-member states. Imports also reveal a robust trade relationship. In 2005, over 29% of total U.S. imports came from Northeast Asia. The number grows to 35% when U.S. imports from other ASEAN countries are also included.

In addition to the strictly economic benefits from trade, U.S. leaders have also hoped that economic ties with countries in the region would help contribute to political reform. This is especially true in the case of China. For instance, an important reason that the United States actively supported China's entry into the World Trade Organization (WTO) in 1999 was the hope that WTO membership would provide incentives for China to continue economic and political reforms.

Deter the Rise of a Regional Hegemon. To maintain its access to and influence in the region, the United States has sought to prevent the rise of a great power that would dominate the region—a regional hegemon. In addition to constraining U.S. freedom of action, the rise of such a power could disrupt regional stability as other countries could be expected to resist domination. During the Cold War, this objective of preventing a regional hegemonic power essentially meant containing Soviet influence. In the post–Cold War era, the potential hegemon of concern has been China. (See Table 18.2 for more information on relative power within the region.)

Discourage Conflict and Maintain Regional Stability.   Stability within East Asia is important not only for long-term economic growth for the United States and for the countries in the region but also for continuing regional peace. One key concern is the potential for conflict between China and Taiwan. Another serious potential source of conflict or instability is the continuing standoff on the Korean peninsula. Since the Korean War in the early 1950s, the United States has been concerned about a possible resumption of hostilities. In addition, in the wake of the September 11, 2001, terrorist attacks in the United States, regional manifestations of transnational security issues, such as nuclear proliferation and terrorism, have increased in salience.

Promote Human Rights and Democracy.   Yet another American interest is the promotion of democracy and human rights in East Asia. As the U.S. Department of State's 1998 Foreign Policy Agenda report on the Asia-Pacific states:

> [W]e must not neglect our historic commitment to the fundamental principles of democracy, pluralism, and respect for human rights. Any . . . policy that is merely based on realpolitik and is devoid of moral grounding will ultimately not sustain the support of the American people.[1]

The importance of human rights was reaffirmed in the 2002 and 2006 National Security Strategies. In the 2002 document, for example, the United States commits to making "freedom and the development of democratic institutions key themes in our bilateral institutions . . . while we press governments that deny human rights to move toward a better future."[2]

History of U.S. Policy Toward East Asia

Although the United States has had a sustained interest in East Asia since well before the twentieth century, it long faced stiff competition from other Western powers for regional influence. It did not emerge as the primary power in the region until the end of World War II, which brought with it three developments: the defeat of Imperial Japan, the resurgence of civil war in China, and the eclipse of European colonization.

The Origins of Containment in East Asia.   After Japan surrendered on September 2, 1945, the United States became engaged in supporting the transition of former European and Japanese colonies to self-rule throughout Asia, with the important exception of French Indochina. The United States also became involved in efforts to end the civil war in China between Mao Zedong's Chinese Communist Party (CCP) and Chiang Kai-shek's Nationalist Kuomintang (KMT) Party. These competing forces—each of which claimed all of China—presented a significant policy dilemma for the United States. On the one hand, Chiang Kai-shek had been an ally during World War II, and thus the United States sought to continue to provide support. On the other hand, the KMT had established a consistent pattern of

Table 18.2 East Asia Key Statistics

Country	Total Population (millions)	Average Life Expectancy	GDP US$ (billions)	GDP/Capita (US$)	Population Living in Poverty (%)	Military Spending % of GDP	Military Spending US$ (millions)	Human Development Index Ranking (out of 177)
Cambodia	14	61.3	6.6	2,800	35	3	111	131
China	1,322	72.88	2,527.0	7,800	10	4.3 (d)	103,956 (e)	81
Hong Kong, China	7	81.7	188.8	37,300	—	(a)	(a)	21
Indonesia	234.7	70.2	264.7	3,900	17.8	3	8,437	107
Japan	127.4	82	4,883.0	33,100	—	0.8	43,910	8
Korea, Democratic People's Republic of	23.3	71.92	(b)	1,800 (c)	—	—	—	—
Korea, Republic of	49	77.2	897.4	24,500	15	2.7	20,313	26
Lao People's Democratic Republic	6.5	55.9	2.8	2,200	30.7	0.5	12	130
Malaysia	24.8	72.8	132.3	12,800	5.1	2	2,930	63
Myanmar	50	60.5	—	—	—	—	6,944	132
Papua New Guinea	5.8	65.6	4.2	2,700	37	1.4	26	145
Philippines	91.1	70.5	116.9	5,000	40	0.9	837	90
Singapore	4.5	81.8	122.1	31,400	—	4.9	5,578	25
Taiwan	22.9	77.6	346.7	29,600	0.9	2.85	7,978	—
Thailand	65.1	72.55	197.7	9,200	10	1.8	2,021	78
Timor-Leste	1.1	66.6	0.3	800	42	—	—	150
Vietnam	85.3	71	48.4	3,100	19.5	2.5	3,153	105

Sources: CIA World Factbook, updated December 13, 2007, UNHDR Human Development Index 2007/2008; IISS Military Balance 2007.

Notes:

(a) Military responsibilities fall under China

(b) North Korea does not publish any reliable National Income Accounts data

(c) Data derived from OECD 1999 study extrapolated to 2006

(d) China's military spending known to exceed declared data

(e) Defense expenditure figure includes PPP estimates and extra budgetary expenditure corruption and harsh governance that weakened China's claims on U.S. support. Mao ultimately drove Chiang and the KMT off the mainland and onto the island of Taiwan; Mao officially proclaimed the People's Republic of China (PRC) as a unified communist state for all of China on October 1, 1949. Staking a competing claim, Chiang Kai-shek proclaimed his government in Taiwan—the Republic of China (ROC)—to be the official government for all of China.

Initially, the United States did not take an official position on which government it would recognize. This ambiguity ended when North Korea invaded South Korea in June 1950. This attack, and the PRC's support of it, served as a catalyst for the United States to extend into East Asia the main containment principles of the Truman Doctrine that had originated primarily from a U.S. fear of the spread of communism in Europe. The United States deployed vessels from the U.S. Navy's Seventh Fleet to the Taiwan Straits and publicly announced its willingness to support Taiwan and assist in its defense. The schism with the PRC deepened in late 1950 when Chinese communist forces entered the Korean War, attacking U.S. forces that were then deep in North Korea and approaching the Chinese border.

The Truman Doctrine also affected U.S. policy toward Japan and South Korea. Prior to the Korean War, General Douglas MacArthur, commander of U.S. occupation forces in Japan, focused on the promotion of liberal democracy and on comprehensively demilitarizing Japan. Testament to this is Article 9 of the U.S.-drafted 1947 Japanese Constitution, which states that the Japanese "forever renounce war as a sovereign right of the nation and the threat or use of force as means of settling international disputes."[3] However, American enthusiasm for Article 9 diminished with the onset of the Korean War. The United States came to perceive Japan as a bulwark against the spread of communism and as a potentially useful ally rather than as a possible future threat. Accordingly, the United States concentrated on strengthening Japan economically, politically, and militarily. With security concerns similarly at the forefront, after the Korean War the United States gave priority to strong governance in South Korea over liberal democratic reform.

These policies formed the foundation of a broad containment strategy to deter Soviet and Chinese aggression and to stop various communist revolutionary movements in the region, many of which were emboldened or supported outright by Mao's government in China. Ho Chi Minh launched the Viet Minh guerrilla forces against French colonists in Indochina; the Hukbalahap rebellion simmered in the Philippines; and other communist insurgencies occurred in Indonesia, Malaya, and Burma (now Myanmar). The U.S. pursuit of containment in the region was based on an underlying assumption that if communist states emerged throughout Asia, they would be linked ideologically, militarily, and politically with the Soviet Union and China. Regional containment set the stage for increased security assistance to and alliances in East Asia and ultimately led to U.S. military involvement in Vietnam.

The primary diplomatic dimension of containment policy in East Asia was the foundation of a system of bilateral alliances that came to be known as the *San Francisco System.*[4] The name originated because many of these alliances were created during the Japan peace conference convened in San Francisco in September 1951. At that conference, separate defense accords were signed with Australia,

Japan, and the Philippines. Over the next few years, these treaties were supplemented by additional treaties with South Korea, Taiwan, and Thailand. In each of these alliances, American interests in political reform aimed at liberal democratic ideals were discounted, and emphasis was instead given to the development of strong, stable, and anti-communist states willing and able to support U.S. interests.

In addition to these bilateral alliances, the United States actively encouraged the development of regional security pacts. The first of these was the 1951 Australia, New Zealand, and United States (ANZUS) treaty, which provided for mutual aid in the event of aggression. The second was the Southeast Asian Treaty Organization (SEATO), established in 1954 by the United States, the United Kingdom, Australia, New Zealand, France, Pakistan, the Philippines, and Thailand. SEATO was created as a direct response to the perceived threat of communist expansion in Southeast Asia.

Meanwhile, China continued to openly support communist insurgencies in Asia and to engage in various military ventures. It invaded Tibet in 1950, fought the United States and United Nations (UN) forces during the Korean War (1950–1953), conducted operations against Taiwan over the smaller islands of Quemoy and Matsu in 1954 and 1958, and fought a brief war with India over border disputes in 1962. It later attacked Vietnam in 1979. Furthermore, China became a nuclear state in 1964 when it conducted its first successful nuclear test. All these developments contributed to a growing U.S. perception of China as an aggressive military power in much the same way that it had long viewed the Soviet Union. Moreover, military cooperation between the two communist states and the seemingly close personal relationship between Mao and Soviet leader Joseph Stalin contributed to the appearance of a unified Sino-Soviet bloc. The so-called bloc began to unravel into Sino-Soviet rivalry after Stalin's death in 1953, eventually providing the opportunity for a new direction for U.S. foreign policy in the region.

Evolution of the U.S. Containment Policy.   By the late 1960s, the United States was ready to re-examine its policy of containment in Asia. Sino-Soviet rivalry had evolved into a Sino-Soviet split, as tensions between the two states escalated into military conflict along their shared borders. Domestic factors in the United States, such as growing public discontent with the Vietnam War, provided further impetus for a new approach. President Richard Nixon, elected with the understanding that he would end U.S. military involvement in Vietnam, was in effect given an electoral mandate to look for other ways to pursue the policy of containment in Asia.

Regional factors also played a role in promoting a change in U.S. policy, including the successful economic development of Japan and, increasingly, of South Korea. As these important regional allies became major economic powers, the perception of the danger of communist expansion decreased, and the ability of others to share the burden of regional defense increased. In this context, Nixon announced a new policy for the region, the Nixon Doctrine. According to this doctrine, the United States would keep its treaty commitments but, should a security threat arise, it would henceforth look first to the threatened state to assume primary responsibility for its own defense, assisted by regional neighbors. This emphasis on burden sharing set the stage for the withdrawal of approximately twenty thousand troops from South Korea, leaving only two combat divisions as the main U.S. ground force component in Korea.

In furtherance of this new doctrine and to exploit the now evident Sino-Soviet split, Nixon ushered in a new era of détente in Sino-U.S. relations with his visit to Beijing in 1972. This meeting and future visits by other U.S. presidents produced three communiqués (released in 1972, 1979, and 1986) that continue to form the foundation of U.S. policy toward China and Taiwan. Although each communiqué dealt with the issue on an incremental basis, in the aggregate they proclaim: (1) that the United States acknowledges that Chinese on both sides of the Taiwan Strait claim there is only one China and that Taiwan is part of China; (2) that the PRC government is the sole *legal* government of China; and (3) that the United States will continue to maintain cultural, commercial, and "other unofficial relations" with Taiwan.[5] The United States closed its official embassy in Taiwan in 1979 and established one in Beijing.

It is important to note that these communiqués do not necessarily mean that the United States officially recognizes that Taiwan is part of the PRC, only that it acknowledges that both sides claim all of China and Taiwan. The vagueness of this wording was intentional and formed the basis for what came to be known as America's *one-China policy*. The strategic ambiguity inherent in this approach is intended to deter both sides from taking unilateral steps that could provoke a renewal of conflict. Although the United States proclaimed its legal recognition of the PRC in 1979, it also made clear that same year through the passage of the Taiwan Relations Act that this recognition did not imply that the United States would tolerate the use of military force by the PRC against Taiwan. This legislation authorized the U.S. government to sell arms to Taiwan for its defense and also stated that the United States would maintain the capacity of Taiwan to resist any use of force by China that would jeopardize Taiwan's security.[6]

Although this piece of legislation did much to quell Taiwan's fears of abandonment by the United States, other developments, including the withdrawal of U.S. forces from Vietnam and the downsizing of U.S. forces in South Korea, created a growing sense of anxiety within states in the region that relied on U.S. security commitments. This anxiety increased when President Jimmy Carter ordered the withdrawal of additional forces from Korea in 1979.[7]

But it was not long until other events diminished these concerns. After the failure of Mao's policies, such as the dramatic effort to industrialize China's agrarian economy in the Great Leap Forward in 1958 that resulted in the death of approximately 30 million Chinese people, and the chaotic upheaval of Mao's effort to establish political and social control in the Cultural Revolution in the 1960s, the PRC instituted major changes to its economic and foreign policies. After Mao's death in 1976, Deng Xiaoping and subsequent Chinese leaders initiated a wave of remarkable reforms that stressed capitalist principles, initially in designated economic zones. They also gradually reshaped China's foreign policy from one that actively promoted revolutionary movements throughout the developing world to one that promoted regional stability for the purpose of furthering China's economic growth.

Meanwhile, in 1986, Soviet leader Mikhail Gorbachev initiated a major set of political and economic reforms known as *glasnost* and *perestroika* and adopted a new approach toward East Asia that emphasized mutual security, balanced force reductions, and economic cooperation. This approach resulted in improved relations with China, South Korea, and Japan, as well as with the United States. Then, just five years later, the Soviet Union disintegrated, and the Cold War ended.

Post–Cold War Period: Fleeting Euphoria.   With the collapse of the Soviet threat and improved relations with China, along with growing demands for a peace dividend, the United States began cutting its defense budget and reducing the number of military forces forward deployed in the region. President George H. W. Bush ordered steep reductions in defense spending and a further withdrawal of thirty-three thousand service members from East Asia. This was a 25% decrease, which left approximately one hundred thousand U.S. forces in the region.

The downward trend in defense spending and forward presence stopped, however, when the initial euphoria brought about by the end of the Cold War was overtaken by new regional developments. Of central import, China was achieving an astonishing 8% to 10% rate of annual growth in its gross domestic product (GDP), leading many experts to predict that its GDP could become larger than that of the United States by 2015.[8] China's defense budget was correspondingly increasing at an alarming rate. Japan, which had entered into a decade-long economic slump in 1990, became increasingly worried about the intent and commitment of the United States to its security, especially in light of China's growing power and other problematic developments in North Korea.

A number of crises in the 1990s further degraded the initial euphoria after the end of the Cold War. In 1993, a standoff escalated over North Korea's nuclear program, creating tensions that the Clinton administration temporarily eased in 1994 with a negotiated compromise called the Agreed Framework.[9] In June 1995 and again in July 1996, China conducted a series of missile tests and military exercises in Fujian, the province opposite Taiwan. The United States responded by deploying two aircraft carrier battle groups to the area as a deterrent show of force. These developments convinced the United States that, unlike the situation in Europe, many of the prominent Cold War security issues in East Asia persisted in the post–Cold War era. In response, the United States stopped further reductions of its military presence in the region, maintaining the force at about one hundred thousand.[10] The United States also made clear its intentions to maintain its security commitments as outlined in its "San Francisco" system of bilateral alliances that were formed in the 1950s.

The Terrorist Attacks of September 11, 2001, and Their Impact on U.S. Policy.
The terrorist attacks against the United States on 9/11 fundamentally changed U.S. perceptions of the world. The approach of the administration of President George W. Bush to this new security situation came to be known as the Bush Doctrine.[11] (For a more detailed discussion of the Bush Doctrine, see Chapter 3.)

This doctrine's focus on combating terrorism and nuclear proliferation, and its embrace of the use of preventive—even preemptive—military force, affected East

Asia's security environment in several ways. One impact was that it created increased demands on U.S. allies in the region and, in the case of South Korea, it contributed to emerging strains in relations between the two longtime allies. The United States reduced its troop presence on the Korean peninsula by approximately twelve thousand to better support operations in the Middle East and Central Asia and also requested military support from South Korea and Japan for contributions to military operations in Afghanistan and Iraq.

The Bush Doctrine also affected the Korean peninsula by elevating concerns about North Korea's nuclear program and by influencing North Korea's perception of the threat from the United States. Given that George W. Bush had already named North Korea a member of an "Axis of Evil," along with Iraq and Iran, the Bush Doctrine's focus on rogue states and nuclear proliferation caused many in South Korea and North Korea to fear U.S. military action on the peninsula.[12]

Emerging Trends Affecting East Asia's Security Environment

East Asia has always held the possibility for great power conflict because it is a nexus where major powers physically intersect: China, Japan, Russia, and the United States. As mentioned earlier, it is also a region characterized by significant defense spending and military rivalry.[13] Four key trends will have a particularly important impact on the character of the region's future security environment: (1) the rise of China; (2) Taiwan's democratization; (3) changes in Japan's national security policy; and (4) security developments on the Korean peninsula, to include North Korea's nuclear program.

The Rise of China.   China's transformation is massive in scope and nature. Indeed, some analysts believe its transformation may eclipse the twentieth-century transformations of the United States, Germany, Japan, or even the Soviet Union.[14] Rising in terms of economic power, military power, and foreign influence, China is at the same time also struggling to master growing domestic challenges. How the CCP handles these challenges while maintaining stability and economic growth will have a major impact on the regional security environment, as well as on its relations with the United States and the West.

Economic Growth.   After the discrediting of communism, marked especially by the catastrophic failures of Mao's economic policy under the Great Leap Forward and the Cultural Revolution, the CCP leadership under Deng initiated a bold set of economic reforms in 1978–1979. These reforms strayed far from the original ideological underpinnings of Maoism, representing a more pragmatic capitalistic approach that stressed the importance of effectiveness over political ideology. This sentiment is captured by Deng's use of the cat analogy: "[A] cat, whether it is white or black, is a good one as long as it is able to catch mice."[15]

To improve government performance, especially in the area of economics, Deng initially developed Special Economic Zones along China's coastline where state controls were relaxed and capitalism was allowed to flourish. This produced dramatic results, and China's economy has over the last three decades grown at a truly extraordinary rate of roughly 8% to 10% per year. As of 2006, China boasted the second-highest GDP in the world in terms of purchasing power parity, a GDP that is more than twice that of Japan.

One relatively recent factor that has contributed to this growth has been China's 2001 entry into the ranks of the WTO. Although this membership gave Chinese exports better access than before into other markets, it has also created a number of challenges. It has, for example, committed China to the implementation of further economic and legal reforms that promote transparency and accountability while also requiring it to lower trade barriers in virtually every sector of its economy. Such commitments add to the already daunting set of domestic challenges facing the CCP.

The breakneck pace of China's economic growth has resulted in a major scramble worldwide for oil and other materials and has produced a number of associated problems, especially environmental degradation. Sixteen of the twenty most air-polluted cities on the planet are Chinese, and more than three fourths of the water flowing through China's cities is unfit for fishing or drinking.[16] China's public health system is overburdened, with HIV, SARS, tuberculosis, and other communicable diseases threatening it. The growing income gulf between rich and poor adds to these problems.

Domestic Challenges.   The CCP's embrace of capitalism to bolster its legitimacy provides a continuous challenge. The ideological shift away from the ideals of Marxism and socialism has undercut the original ideological base of CCP legitimacy, which now has come to rest increasingly on economic growth. The Tiananmen Square demonstrations in 1989 are a poignant reminder of the legitimacy challenge. Since then, the CCP has methodically cracked down on demonstrations and weathered the ensuing diplomatic backlash from abroad. The size and seriousness of subsequent demonstrations have not repeated those of Tiananmen, but the frequency of these occurrences has increased. "According to official PRC sources, 'public order disturbances' grew from 58,000 incidents in 2003 to 87,000 in 2005," becoming broader in scope and larger in average size, as well as greater in frequency.[17]

These demonstrations are in large part reflections of deep-seated major social issues, including the growing income gap between the rich and the poor, the associated economic gulf between the coastal and interior provinces, the spread of AIDS and other health issues, political corruption, environmental degradation, a migrant workforce of perhaps 140 million individuals who have left the countryside hoping to find employment in the cities, expansion of the number of nongovernmental organizations (NGOs) operating in Chinese society, and the explosive growth of information available through the Internet. In 2006, the number of Internet users was estimated to be 111 million, increasing annually at a rate of about 25%. Despite the government's efforts, not all Internet usage can be effectively censored.

In addition to economic performance, the CCP has also increasingly resorted to nationalism to bolster its legitimacy. Of course, relying on nationalism carries its own set of risks. If populist nationalism were to grow too powerful, the CCP could lose its ability to control it, risking its relations with other countries. Resurgent nationalism could, for example, necessitate overly strong policy reactions to future regional security challenges, such as another Taiwan crisis.[18]

Military Modernization.   China is actively modernizing and strengthening its military, the People's Liberation Army (PLA). The largest military force in the world, the PLA is comprised of four services: ground forces (PLA); naval forces (PLAN), which include the marines and naval aviation; air forces (PLAAF); and strategic missile forces (Second Artillery), which include nuclear weapons. The active force totals approximately 2.3 million personnel, and another 10 million are enlisted in the reserves, armed police, and militia forces.[19]

Military reform has been an issue throughout China's post–World War II history, but the perceived need to change intensified in the 1990s. This was largely due to China's observations of U.S. military performance during the 1991 Gulf War—performance that apparently had a profound effect on PLA leaders.[20] Although they had known that the PLA was not yet a modern force, they were not prepared for just how wide the performance gap between their forces and those of the United States had become. The ability of the United States to project such a massive force over long distances, to incorporate high technology in adverse terrain, and to perform deep surgical strikes supported by aerial and space reconnaissance was alarming for Deng and the PLA. The relative ease with which the United States toppled the Taliban's regime in Afghanistan in 2001 and Saddam Hussein's regime in Iraq in 2003 only served to heighten China's sense of urgency about military modernization.

The large gap in capabilities between the Chinese military and that of the United States is also reflected in the huge difference in defense expenditures between the two countries. In 2007, the United States spent $603 billion on its military, while the official Chinese defense spending figure was approximately $45 billion.[21] Consequently, rather than competing directly with the United States, the PLA is focused on preparing to fight and win short-duration, high-intensity conflicts along China's periphery in defense of its territorial sovereignty.[22] What China also seeks "are niche capabilities to exploit U.S. vulnerabilities to deter, complicate, and delay, if not defeat, U.S. (or other) intervention in a Taiwan scenario."[23]

Although China still maintains its claims regarding various territorial disputes, the PLA appears to be primarily focused on preventing Taiwanese independence or compelling Taiwan to negotiate a settlement on Beijing's terms. In March 2005, China's National People's Congress passed an anti-secession law to deter Taiwan's leaders from taking steps to proclaim independence. The PLA also regularly holds amphibious exercises that deal explicitly or implicitly with a Taiwan scenario and has deployed over seven hundred short-range ballistic missiles in the region directly opposite Taiwan. These missiles give the mainland the capability to launch punitive missile strikes to threaten Taiwan without having to launch an amphibious assault, which the Chinese still lack the ability to execute successfully with any degree of certainty. The PLA is also developing asymmetric means to isolate or blockade the island of Taiwan by increasing its naval capability with more modern diesel submarines, GPS-guided munitions, and Su-27 and Su-30 fighter/bomber aircraft to bolster its combat air capability.[24]

With regard to potential military rivalry with the United States, China's military modernization efforts do not reflect a Chinese intent to compete with the United States on a symmetric basis. Instead, China is focusing on asymmetric capabilities that can operate against U.S. weaknesses, especially in the areas of information technology and space. The Chinese interception/destruction of a Chinese satellite in 2007 is indicative of this latter priority. Additionally, China appears to be focused on developing concepts and weapons that will enable it to conduct anti-access and area denial operations against the United States.

Diplomatic Initiatives. Although Chinese military power has certainly grown, its greatest gains have recently come in the realm of diplomacy and foreign relations. During the past decade, it has enhanced ties with important countries in virtually every region of the world and has resolved or diminished a number of border disputes with its regional neighbors. This success is all the more extraordinary when one considers China's history of troubled relations within the region. During the 1960s and 1970s, China engaged in land wars with the Soviet Union, India, and Vietnam and supported Maoist insurgencies in Southeast Asia.[25] But, with Mao's death, his successors have focused on building a peaceful regional environment in which China could pursue its economic development and modernization efforts.

During the Asian financial crisis of 1997–1998, China enhanced its reputation as a regional player when it resisted devaluing its currency and provided capital to various Southeast Asian countries without many of the conditions demanded by the International Monetary Fund (IMF) and the United States. In the aftermath of this crisis, the organization ASEAN+3 (the ASEAN-member states plus China, Japan, and South Korea) was created to build on the goodwill generated by China's actions as well as to avert a future occurrence of the crisis. At the 2004 ASEAN summit, Chinese Premier Wen Jiabao launched two proposals, one for the development of a China-ASEAN Free Trade Area, and the other for the establishment of an East Asian community to discuss political and security issues.[26]

China has also greatly increased its diplomatic activity in Central Asia. In 1996, China and Russia declared a "strategic partnership" between the two countries and created the Shanghai Five, a new multilateral organization that included China, Russia, Kazakhstan, Kyrgyzstan, and Tajikistan as members. This organization has since grown to what is now known as the Shanghai Cooperation Organization (SCO). In 2001, Uzbekistan was granted membership, and India, Pakistan, Iran, and Mongolia were granted observer status in 2006.[27] In 2005, the SCO sponsored the first combined/joint military exercise between China and Russia, which involved about ten thousand troops in an amphibious operation.

China has also been a central player in the multinational diplomatic effort to convince North Korea to dismantle its nuclear program. The latest nuclear crisis on the Korean peninsula, which began in 2002, prompted the initiation of the Six-Party Talks in 2003 as a means to stop North Korea's development of nuclear weapons. This forum, which met repeatedly in China, included representatives from the United States, Japan, China, Russia, South Korea, and North Korea. The talks provided China an opportunity to play a leadership role in East Asian affairs and also became a venue through which China improved its relations with the United States, Russia, Japan, and especially South Korea.[28] On February 13, 2007, a deal was reached in which North Korea agreed to freeze its nuclear program for economic and energy incentives. This was followed by a further agreement on October 3, 2007, which raised hopes for eventual denuclearization, although it did not specifically state the manner in which North Korea would dismantle its nuclear program. The issue had not been permanently resolved by late 2008.

These various diplomatic initiatives by China have both positive and negative implications for the United States. On the one hand, they may signal an increased readiness for multilateral cooperation and a decreased willingness to resort to military force to pursue security interests. On the other hand, they may only represent a pragmatic use of national power to influence the region to support certain interests that may conflict with those of the United States. As an example of the latter, China has been using its growing influence to successfully pressure more countries to cease their relationships with Taiwan.

Democratization in Taiwan.   The danger of war across the Taiwan Strait has existed ever since Chiang Kai-shek fled to the island of Taiwan with his KMT Party in 1949. As noted earlier, the United States has pursued a policy of "strategic ambiguity" to deter conflict by providing assurances to China and Taiwan simultaneously. This strategic ambiguity has two primary elements: "(1) clear, credible commitments to transfer defensive capabilities to Taiwan and, if necessary, to intervene on Taiwan's behalf; and (2) political reassurances that the United States does not plan to use its superiority now or in the future to harm Beijing's core security interests by promoting the independence of Taiwan."[29] The first element works to ensure that China does not unilaterally attack Taiwan, and the second element works to ensure that Taiwan does not unilaterally provoke a change in the status quo.

However, this policy of dual deterrence faces challenges arising out of Taiwan's successful democratization. Since 1949, Taiwan had essentially been a one-party, authoritarian state ruled by the KMT. From the 1950s through the 1970s, the KMT ruled with absolute power, oppressing aboriginal natives and the Han people who inhabited the island prior to 1949. It was not until the emergence of opposition parties in the late 1980s and a series of political reforms that a new national assembly was elected in 1991. This new legislative body passed a number of further reforms, leading to Taiwan's first direct presidential election in 1996. These elections alarmed China to the point that it resorted to military provocations, which triggered the 1995–1996 Taiwan Straits crisis.

China considers Taiwan to be a renegade province within its sovereign domain, so any words or actions in Taiwan or elsewhere that could lead to Taiwanese independence are stridently opposed. For this reason friction between China and Taiwan increased when Chen Shui-bian, a public advocate for Taiwanese independence, won Taiwan's 2000 presidential election. During his campaign and at various times during his presidency, President Chen expressed support for constitutional reforms or referenda that would present what mainland China views as an unacceptable political challenge.

Chen's interest in Taiwanese independence reflects the views of a growing segment of the population who deem the objective of reclaiming the mainland no longer feasible. These Taiwanese, therefore, have abandoned the historic ROC goal of reunification under the ROC in favor of the establishment of an independent Taiwan divorced from the mainland. It remains unclear how hard the democratically empowered Taiwanese people might, over time, push to realize this vision. At risk is provocation of the mounting military threat posed by the mainland, as well as trade with and investment in China.

Taiwan's democratization presents a significant challenge to U.S. efforts to maintain cross-straits stability. As Taiwan continues its democratization, its policies will increasingly have to reflect the will of its people, possibly presenting a political challenge to China that could lead to miscalculations and provocations. Such uncertainties promise to make Taiwan's security dilemma more dangerous and complex in the future.

Japan's Evolving Approach to National Security.   After catastrophic defeat in World War II, which saw the psychologically and physically devastating atomic bombing of Hiroshima and Nagasaki, Japan took drastic steps to ensure that its former aggressive nature would not re-emerge. The legal foundation for this was Article 9 of Chapter 2, "The Renunciation of War," of the 1947 Japanese Constitution:

> Aspiring sincerely to an international peace based on justice and order, the Japanese people forever renounce war as a sovereign right of the nation and the threat or use of force as means of settling international disputes.
>
> In order to accomplish the aim of the preceding paragraph, land, sea, and air forces, as well as other war potential, will never be maintained. The right of belligerency of the state will not be recognized.[30]

At first glance, this article provides an impressive legal obstacle against the creation of any military capability. However, the second portion of the article, which starts with the words, "In order to accomplish the aim of the preceding paragraph," allows for an interpretation that permits Japan to maintain military forces as long as they are not for the purpose of settling international disputes. Japanese governments have subsequently interpreted Article 9 as allowing Japan to exercise the right of self-defense and to develop and maintain the Japanese Self-Defense Force for that purpose. This interpretation has evolved over time from a narrow one that concentrated on territorial self-defense toward a broader concept of collective defense.

During the first half of the Cold War, the narrow interpretation was favored. This was consistent with the Yoshida Doctrine, named after Japan's first postwar prime minister, Shigeru Yoshida. That doctrine stressed the primacy of economic development while making only limited military improvements to reduce the possibility of entanglement in security issues that did not directly threaten Japan's sovereignty. An important concern was that Japan's provision of bases to U.S. forces, a key obligation of the U.S.-Japan alliance, could make Japan a proxy target for enemies of the United States.[31] Japanese leaders were also concerned that the United States might pressure them to assume a greater role in support of the U.S.-led strategy of containment—a role that would extend beyond strict national defense.

Japan's perspective changed rather significantly as a result of the Nixon Doctrine. Because the Nixon administration stressed détente with China and the Soviet Union and greater burden sharing between the United States and its allies, Japanese fears of entanglement were largely replaced by fears of abandonment. These concerns were further aggravated by growing trade and economic disputes between the United States and Japan that peaked during the 1980s.

As a result of these various developments, Japan began a qualitative buildup of its defense forces and published its first National Defense Program Outline in 1976.[32] For the first time, Japan not only identified its security strategy but also outlined the military force structure needed to resource it. This and subsequent plans provided added impetus and focus for the development of a sophisticated defense industrial complex and a small but relatively advanced military force.

Japanese concern over a declining U.S. commitment toward its security rose even higher after the 1991 Gulf War. Japan's decision not to make a military contribution to coalition forces during that conflict was derided by many in the United States and by many of America's coalition partners. At the time, the United States was also under significant domestic pressure to decrease its forward military presence and reduce defense spending to cash in on a post–Cold War "peace dividend." Although these factors hinted at a lesser U.S. commitment, the rise of China and North Korea's developing missile and nuclear weapons programs served as powerful reminders to Japan of the dangers it still faced. Such concerns provided the necessary impetus for a shift away from focusing only on territorial self-defense and toward an acceptance of the need for collective defense.

In June 1992, the Japanese Diet passed the International Peace and Cooperation Law, which permitted the deployment of Japanese troops in support of UN peacekeeping operations. The law allowed the deployment of Japanese Self-Defense Forces to Cambodia and to East Timor. Although these forces did not take part in combat, their deployment signaled Japan's increased willingness to contribute militarily to the resolution of collective security issues.

This trend accelerated following the 9/11 terrorist attacks in the United States. Just a few months afterward, the Japanese Diet passed the Anti-Terrorism Special Measures Law. This law enabled the dispatch of Japanese Maritime Self-Defense Forces to the Indian Ocean to provide support to U.S. and coalition forces engaged in Operation Enduring Freedom in Afghanistan. In 2003, the Diet passed the Law Concerning Special Measures on Humanitarian and Reconstruction Assistance to enable the deployment of Japanese Ground Self-Defense Forces to Iraq.[33]

In 2005, the United States and Japan issued a joint "Security Guidelines" statement, which proclaimed that their alliance plays "a vital role in ensuring the security and prosperity of both the United States and Japan, as well as in enhancing regional and global peace and stability."[34] The joint security guidelines listed twelve common regional and six common global strategic objectives that both countries share as a further testament of Japan's willingness to embrace collective defense. The list even included the peaceful resolution of the Taiwan Straits security dilemma, a provision that did not go unnoticed by China.

It is not altogether clear how far Japan will go with its new security outlook and its corresponding development of military forces. To a large extent, this will depend on a number of factors, including the nature of China's rise; North Korea's nuclear and other military capability and intentions; Japan-U.S. relations; Japanese relations with other countries, especially China and South Korea; and domestic political support for such policies. One thing does seem clear: Japan will continue to develop its military capability for the foreseeable future.

Changing Security Conditions on the Korean Peninsula.   At first glance, the Korean peninsula remains caught in the military stalemate created during the Korean War, a war that has not—as of late 2008—officially been concluded with a peace treaty. Yet numerous changes are underway, such as the changing military balance between the two Koreas, North Korea's pursuit of nuclear weapons, growing challenges to the U.S.–South Korean alliance, and a gradual thawing of North-South relations.

The Changing Military Balance on the Peninsula.   The conventional military balance on the Korean peninsula has changed from one that favored North Korea during the early part of the Cold War to one that is now far less favorable to the North—if it is favorable at all (though the North's nuclear weapons capability could be a great equalizer). Currently, North Korea is the world's most militarized nation, with more than 1 million troops on active duty from a population of only just over 20 million. Two thirds of these troops are deployed fewer than sixty miles away from the demilitarized zone separating the two Koreas. Despite the fact that most of its population lives in abject poverty, the North Korean government under Kim Jong Il is estimated to spend well over 20% of its gross national product (GNP) on its military. Kim oversees a Stalinist political system and command economy with a political ideology known as *Juche*, which emphasizes socialism, extreme nationalism, and self-reliance.[35]

North Korea lost one of its two major patrons, the Soviet Union, with the end of the Cold War and has since become increasingly isolated from the rest of the international community. Its remaining patron is China, which regularly provides as much as two thirds of the fuel and one third of the food North Korea consumes. Despite Kim's continued bellicosity and the political leverage one would expect to accompany this supply relationship, China has been reluctant to pressure Kim for fear such action would destabilize North Korea, with consequent chaos, massive refugee flows into China, and perhaps a peninsular war. Still, North Korea has to worry about China's reliability, for Beijing has improved political and economic relations with North Korea's main adversaries—South Korea and the United States. China normalized relations with South Korea in 1992, and by 2005 it had become the number-one destination for South Korean exports.[36] China's warming relations with the United States have been noted above.

On the other side of the demilitarized zone, South Korea's political system evolved from an authoritarian republic into a flourishing liberal democracy. Its economic development has been equally dramatic. South Korea has a GDP more than twenty-four times that of the North and roughly twice the population. Although smaller in size, South Korea's military presents an increasingly formidable challenge to North Korea's military when the quality of training and weapons and the availability of energy resources are taken into account.[37] Although it has renounced the development of nuclear weapons, South Korea has experimented with nuclear technology in the past and could probably become a nuclear state rapidly if it so desired.[38]

Many experts conclude that although North Korea still presents a formidable conventional threat, especially to the city of Seoul, which is in range of North Korean artillery and short-range rockets and missiles, it no longer has the ability to unify the peninsula by force. This is not only because of South Korea's increased military capabilities, augmented by U.S. forces, but also because North Korea would not have the needed external support for such an operation.

North Korea's Pursuit of Nuclear Weapons.   Over the past three decades, North Korea has sought to acquire nuclear weapons to offset its shrinking conventional military advantage and to deter possible U.S. attack. In the 1970s, North Korea received technical assistance on nuclear power from the Soviet Union, including the provision of a research reactor. This reactor was subsequently placed under International Atomic Energy Agency (IAEA) safeguards in 1977, but by then North Korea had already begun developing a small 5-megawatt (MWe) nuclear reactor of its own at Yongbyon.[39] It finished the Yongbyon reactor in 1987 and began construction of two more reactors, a 50-MWe reactor at Yongbyon and a 200-MWe reactor at Taechon. It claims that these reactors are dedicated solely to the production of energy for peaceful civilian use.

These developments raised serious concerns in the United States and among its regional allies and sowed the seeds for the first nuclear crisis in 1994. Despite being a signatory of the Nuclear Non-Proliferation Treaty (NPT) in 1985, it was not until 1992, when the Yongbyon reactor had already been operational for five years, that North Korea allowed IAEA inspectors into its reactor sites. Western intelligence agencies estimated that by that time, North Korea could probably have produced enough fissile material for one or two nuclear weapons.[40]

When the inspections finally began in 1992, the inspectors encountered numerous discrepancies and challenges. In 1993, North Korea responded by blocking further inspections and threatening withdrawal from the NPT. After protracted negotiations, an agreement was reached in 1994, the so-called Agreed Framework, which stated that North Korea would freeze any further production of fissile material in return for a number of energy and economic concessions.[41] Over time, it became increasingly clear that North Korea was not honoring the Agreed

Framework; by early 2003, these escalating suspicions resulted in U.S. nullification of the Agreed Framework, a public statement by North Korea that it had resumed reprocessing spent nuclear fuel rods to extract plutonium, and North Korea's official withdrawal from the NPT.

These developments alarmed not only the United States but also other states in the region, and diplomatic negotiations began in 2003 to resolve the crisis. Over the next four years, these Six-Party Talks (discussed above) generated multiple, largely fruitless rounds of negotiations, during which time Western intelligence officials estimated that North Korea could have produced enough fissile material for six to eight additional nuclear weapons.[42] The crisis reached a new peak on October 9, 2006, when North Korea apparently conducted its first successful nuclear test.

Despite these discouraging developments, the Six-Party Talks continued, and a deal was announced on February 13, 2007. It featured another freeze of North Korea's nuclear program in return for energy and economic aid, much like the previous Agreed Framework. Subsequently, the promise that North Korea would cease all nuclear operations by the end of 2007 was added. Weaknesses of the deal include its lack of specifics about the disposition or disposal of any weapons already produced. Given these limitations—as well as Kim Jong Il's typical tactics—it seems highly unlikely that North Korea is genuinely on the path to foregoing nuclear weapons.

The U.S.–South Korean Alliance.   Although the 1954 U.S.–South Korea mutual defense treaty remains in effect, the North Korean nuclear weapons threat has highlighted an important division between the allies. The United States assumes that North Korea has already produced nuclear weapons and is primarily concerned about its further nuclear production and possible diversion of nuclear weapons to other rogue states or terrorists. South Korea, on the other hand, is more concerned with the stability of its northern neighbor. South Korea fears that any vigorous action to check the North's nuclear ambitions could bring about the untimely collapse of the regime, which would likely bring significant economic, social, and political fallout.

Following the Korean War, South Korea's emphasis was defense against the North and early reunification. In the post–Cold War period, South Korea's policy toward North Korea came to emphasize economic engagement in order to promote gradual change in the North's political and economic policies. In part, this reflects vast differences in wealth between the two halves of the peninsula. In 2005 for example, North Korea's estimated per-capita GDP was $1,700, while South Korea's was $20,400. The gap has widened since. The high cost of German reunification has reminded South Korea of the likely expense that would be associated with reunification with North Korea and dampened enthusiasm for it.

In pursuit of its policy of engagement with North Korea, known as the *Sunshine Policy* (the name refers to one of Aesop's fables in which only warm sunlight, and not harsh wind, was able to convince a traveler to take off his coat), South Korea has become a major aid provider to the North, significantly augmenting assistance allocations over the past decade. According to the South Korean government, total humanitarian aid provided to the North rose to $185 million in 2006 from $4.6

Bridging the gap

Copyright 2000 CARTOONEWS INTERNATIONAL Syndicate, N.Y.C., USA. Reprinted with permission of Ranan Lurie.

million in 1996.[43] In 2003, after the joint construction of a major industrial park in Kaesong, North Korea, just north of the demilitarized zone (DMZ) in 2002, North-South trade reached $724 million.[44] In this industrial park, fifteen South Korean firms produce manufactured goods, largely for South Korean markets, employing approximately eight thousand North Korean workers.[45] By the end of 2006, North-South trade reached almost $1.35 billion.[46] A relatively successful North-South summit meeting and the opening of limited rail links across the DMZ in 2007 signaled further possible warming. This policy of engagement has become a source of friction between the United States and South Korea, as the former has sought to organize pressure on North Korea to renounce nuclear weapons.[47]

These tensions in the U.S.–South Korean alliance have surfaced as the United States has been in the process of further downsizing its military presence, repositioning its forces south of Seoul, and negotiating the transfer of wartime control of South Korean forces from the United States to South Korea. Although it would be hazardous to estimate a specific time frame, with all these developments underway it is unlikely that the status quo of recent decades on the Korean peninsula will continue indefinitely.

Southeast Asia

Comprised of ten nations with about 570 million people, Southeast Asia is so diverse and complex that it defies generalizations. From tiny, urban Singapore—with about 4 million people and a per-capita GDP of more than $12,000—to vast Indonesia—sprawling across six thousand inhabited islands, with about 230 million people and a per-capita GDP of nearly $4,000—these states have only one thing in common: a sense of vulnerability. Each lives in a dangerous neighborhood and each (with the exception of Thailand) remembers generations of being dominated by colonial powers.

With the 1945 defeat of the Japanese, who had overrun the region during World War II, and with the withdrawal of the colonial powers shortly thereafter, the regional states were confronted by the daunting challenges of creating new institutions, suppressing communist insurgencies, and building viable economies. Progress was periodically interrupted by regional conflicts (Vietnam's invasion of Cambodia and China's assault on Vietnam), by a number of coups (most notably in Indonesia and the Philippines), and by the protracted and ultimately unsuccessful American-led defense of South Vietnam, which embroiled Cambodia and Laos as well as North and South Vietnam.

Nevertheless, the necessities of nation building and the talents of their hardworking people have resulted in staggering economic and political progress across the region. Conscious of their individual vulnerabilities and believing their interests would be served by intensifying cooperation, in 1967, five of the regional states—Thailand, Malaysia, Singapore, Indonesia, and the Philippines—formed ASEAN. As the value of organization became clear and as inter-regional tensions subsided, all ten of the region's states became members, with Cambodia being the last to join in 1999. In the 1970s, the members of ASEAN invited Japan, China, and South Korea to join in its deliberations, producing what became known as ASEAN+3. In 1994, a further cooperation process was launched, the ASEAN Region Forum (ARF), which included the ASEAN states, Japan, China, South Korea, the United States, Canada, Russia, New Zealand, and Australia, as well as the European Union. With twenty-six participants as of early 2008, ARF's focus has thus far been on confidence building and environmental measures.

During its forty years of existence, ASEAN has been slowly evolving from a loose economic and political grouping toward a more cohesive, rules-based organization with security and sociocultural dimensions as well as economic interests. Its lofty goals of a nuclear-weapons-free zone in Southeast Asia and a fully integrated economic region are still far from realized. (However, an ASEAN-wide free trade area by 2015 continues to be a goal.) The ARF is still focused on confidence building, and discussions of ASEAN peacekeeping forces for such local crises as East Timor have not progressed.

To confront these challenges and to create a more relevant, effective organization, in late 2007, ASEAN's leaders adopted a formal ASEAN Charter. The charter streamlines the structure and decision-making processes of the organization and creates several new institutions within it. However, the charter does not fundamentally change the requirement that decisions must be by consensus—the "ASEAN Way." Though it has provided a useful forum for networking, consultations, and negotiations, it seems unlikely to become an action-oriented body until the consensus rule is substantially modified.

Although other states in the region, particularly Thailand, Singapore, and Malaysia, are also in varying degrees important to U.S. national security, there is only space here to discuss, even briefly, the three most populous and powerful: Vietnam, the Philippines, and Indonesia. Each is likely to grow in political and security importance to the United States, and each is undergoing economic reforms that should further strengthen it.

Despite being the smallest of the big three, with a population of about 85 million people, Vietnam is nevertheless of significant concern to the United States. Not only has it demonstrated its military prowess through its defeat of invading Chinese forces in 1979, but it has also shown its determination to dominate the other states of former French Indochina—namely, Cambodia and Laos. Depending on how responsibly it uses its military power in the future—in Indochina and elsewhere—it can become a major contributor to regional stability or instability. Given its continuing concern about its giant northern neighbor—China—some degree of military cooperation with the United States may become possible in the future.

Vietnam is also a significant actor in terms of economic potential. Although handicapped for a time by war damage, the loss of Soviet aid, and inefficiencies stemming from its communist ideology and institutions, it had managed by the 1990s to attain annual growth rates of more than 8%; from 2005 to 2007, it averaged 8.3% to 8.4%, echoing the Chinese experience.[48] Indeed its approach toward economic and political liberalization—slow but persistent in the former, very slow and very hesitant in the latter—resembles China's.

With 90 million people spread over about seven thousand islands (but 95% of them on the eleven largest islands), the Philippines is a difficult country to govern effectively. Plagued by widespread corruption and an unstable political system, its economy has lagged far behind its potential, despite its educated (95% literate) and industrious people. By 2008, it had not fully recovered from the extended (1968–1986), corrupt, dictatorial rule of Ferdinand Marcos, but political and economic progress was discernable by the turn of the century. From 2005 to 2007, its economic growth rate averaged 4.9% to 6.7%.[49]

In 1992, the Philippines evicted the United States from its two principal regional bases, Clark Field and Subic Bay. Still, the long-standing military alliance has held, and overall relations have remained warm. Military relationships have continued but on a smaller scale in recent years—and with an express prohibition on American participation in a combat role in counterinsurgency operations in the Philippines. U.S. troops can only provide intelligence and logistical assistance.

The long-simmering Muslim insurgency on the southern island of Mindanao is a major continuing challenge. Not only does the situation test the government's ability to rule and suppress economic development in one of the least developed parts of the country, but it also provides a training base and recruits for radical Islamists. A decades-long communist insurgency also continues, but at a relatively low level. By late 2007, there was substantial hope that ongoing negotiations would succeed in ending that insurgency in 2008. But even with progress in dealing with both insurgencies, the Philippines is likely to continue to lag in meeting the expectations of its people until its dysfunctional leadership can alter its ways.

Indonesia's vast geographic reach, its large population of 235 million (more than 40% of the region's total), and its economic potential make it a key player in the region. After suffering through more than five decades of strongman rule under Sukarno (1946–1966) and Suharto (1966–1998), with accompanying unbridled corruption and maladministration, as of 2008, the country appears to be settling in as a vibrant democracy, though natural disasters, provincial separatism, ethnic tensions, and a badly skewed distribution of wealth continue to be major problems.

With the world's largest Muslim population (almost 205 million, more than in all the Middle Eastern states combined), Indonesia has the potential to be an important moderating influence on Islam worldwide. Although a number of terrorist cells have been discovered there, Indonesia's Muslims have been overwhelmingly tolerant and moderate. Since the 2002 disastrous terrorist bombing in Bali (two hundred dead), the government has been vigorously clamping down on the political, educational, and terrorist operations of the country's relatively few Islamist radicals.

Generally rated as one of the world's most corrupt countries in which to do business, Indonesia has, until lately, largely failed to attract needed foreign investment. Moreover, its economy was particularly hard hit by the Southeast Asian economic crisis that began in 1997 with the deep devaluation of the Thai baht. Currency devaluations spread across Southeast Asia and beyond. After a $40-billion bailout by the IMF, a major devaluation of its own currency, and considerable pain, Indonesia's economy stabilized. From 2005 through 2007, it averaged 5.7% to 6.3% growth.[50]

Although no longer in the dominant position it was during the Suharto era, Indonesia's military continues to play an important role in national political life. Largely pro-Western in orientation, it has particularly sought cooperation with the United States. After being interrupted for a period as a result of alleged human rights abuses by the Indonesian military, American military assistance, training, and sales of equipment resumed, initially on a small scale, in 2001. Future prospects for deeper and stronger U.S.-Indonesian military-to-military ties and enhanced cooperation in counterterrorism, sea lane security, counterproliferation, and other broad security matters seem reasonably bright as of late 2008.

Challenges and Choices for Future U.S. Policy

The key challenge for U.S. policy makers in East Asia is deciding how to respond to a rising, powerful China. The two broad choices are containment or engagement. Proponents of containment seek to prevent China from gaining strategic preponderance in the region, wary that it will try to undermine the U.S. military presence in the area, and are skeptical about Chinese involvement in multilateral regimes, such as the SCO and ASEAN+3. The containment approach emphasizes the value of a strong U.S.-Japan alliance, a strengthened U.S.-ROK alliance, and improved relations with India and the ASEAN countries.

Alternatively, the United States could pursue engagement with China. Proponents of this view believe that containment policies will ensure that a hostile relationship will develop and that the more China interacts with the United States and multilateral organizations, the more its government will move in a liberal direction. Proponents of engagement argue that a China that is fully integrated in the international community will become dependent on international cooperation to maintain its economy and will not threaten important U.S. interests or support measures that could disrupt regional stability.

In addition to U.S. policy choices, the future of U.S.-Chinese relations will also depend upon developments across the Taiwan Straits. The U.S. policy of "strategic ambiguity" has worked in past decades in deterring China and Taiwan from taking unilateral steps that would overturn the status quo.[51] However, the policy of ambiguity may be losing its effectiveness. As Taiwan continues democratizing, a political compromise with the mainland that would be acceptable to both governments seems less likely, and it also becomes increasingly difficult to predict what path the Taiwanese government will take in terms of promoting independence. Furthermore, the military balance between China and Taiwan is clearly tipping in the mainland's favor. Not only is China deploying increasing numbers of ballistic missiles immediately opposite Taiwan, but it is also acquiring and developing precision-strike munitions, including land-based cruise missiles. As already noted, it is focusing on submarines and missile launch platforms and has deployed more than seven hundred aircraft within operational range of Taiwan.[52] Its doctrine, training, procurement, and developments seem geared primarily to a

Taiwan Straits scenario. Meanwhile, Taiwanese defense spending has steadily declined in real terms over the past decade. Of course, capabilities that China develops for the Straits could well be directed elsewhere—for example, to settle territorial disputes with other neighbors. But peaceful resolution of the Taiwan Straits issue will continue to be an important U.S. strategic goal.

The United States also faces a choice concerning how to respond to the evolution of Japan's increasingly activist national security policy. The U.S.-Japan alliance has been critical to enhancing regional stability and in providing U.S. forces with bases from which to deploy American power in the Asia-Pacific region. But there are dangers in relying too heavily on this strategic relationship, for Japan still lacks the legitimacy it would need to play a leadership role in East Asia. Should the United States pressure Japan to make greater efforts to achieve regional reconciliation as it continues to develop its military capabilities? Should it press for further military responsibility by Japan in the international arena, or would U.S. pressure come at too high a price in terms of U.S.-Japanese relations or other U.S. relations in the region? In particular, would American efforts to encourage greater Japanese military strength unnecessarily damage U.S.-Chinese relations?

As China increases its regional influence and its diplomatic activity within regional associations, the United States needs to increase its multilateral profile in East Asia as well as strengthen its bilateral efforts. The threat posed by North Korea's nuclear program may ultimately serve as a catalyst for this, as the Six-Party Talks continue to be a useful venue for efforts to check Pyongyang's nuclear ambitions. Proponents of the Six-Party Talks argue that this process should become the first step toward the development of a more formal regional institution.

Of key importance is the challenge of dealing with the transnational issue of nuclear proliferation. Toward this end, the United States will need to continue to wrestle with the problem of North Korea's nuclear weapons. One option would be to denuclearize North Korea by whatever means necessary; a less ambitious, more realistic alternative would be to focus on preventing further proliferation to other states and to nonstate actors. Both in the nuclear context and, more broadly, in seeking regional stability, the U.S.–South Korean relationship will have to be strengthened as well. The election of a more conservative ROK administration in December 2007 should help facilitate this, but a revitalization of the alliance will require increased sensitivity to Seoul's preoccupation with the sunshine approach to the North.

Given the importance of the Southeast Asian region and the fact that China is actively pushing regional diplomatic and economic initiatives, a strong case can be made for more robust American involvement in the region as well. The kinds of measures needed include the bolstering of trade through free trade agreements, the deepening of military cooperation through increased military aid and training programs, and a more extensive engagement with ASEAN on a range of issues.

Continuing American concern about human rights, which has sometimes set back relations with various regional states (most recently with Thailand in 2006, when the military ousted an elected civilian government), will likely also surface in the future. As of 2008, the prime regional violator is ASEAN member Myanmar. Its ongoing flagrant abuses of opposition elements, including Buddhist clergy, is likely to undercut near-term prospects that the United States will intensify its cooperation with ASEAN because ASEAN members have responded to these incidents with mere scolding. Conditions in Myanmar are made even worse by periodic natural disasters such as the Cyclone Nargis that killed over 140,000 people and devastated large swaths of the country in May 2008. American pursuit of broader, deeper regional engagement via ASEAN is doubtful in the next few years. However, given that the logic of intensified cooperation is so compelling, it is likely that bilateral paths will be chosen until and unless multilateral ways are unclogged.

Discussion Questions

1. To what extent does China's rise in power present a strategic threat to the United States?

2. Should the United States seek to contain or engage China? Why? Can the two approaches be pursued simultaneously?

3. Given the rise in China's military power and a simultaneous rise in pro-independence sentiments in an increasingly democratic Taiwan, should the United States change its policy toward Taiwan?

4. How strongly should the United States support Japan's changing national security policy? Is a Japan that is focused on broader regional security issues better for the United States and for the region as a whole?

5. How can the United States prevent a strategic arms race in the region, especially between China and Japan?

6. Can the United States live with a nuclear North Korea? What will be the impact of a nuclear North Korea on other states in the region?

7. Should the United States change its alliance relationship with South Korea? If so, how?

8. Should the United States adjust its traditional bilateral approach to a more multilateral approach to foreign policy in the region?

9. Should the United States lead or actively support the creation of an East Asian security organization?

10. How can the United States influence the political systems in China and North Korea?

11. What are the prospects for further meaningful ASEAN integration?

Recommended Reading

Abramowitz, Morton, and Stephen Bosworth. "Adjusting to the New Asia." *Foreign Affairs* 82, no. 4 (July/August 2003): 119–131.

Betts, Richard K. "Wealth, Power, and Instability: East Asia and the United States after the Cold War." *International Security* 18, no. 3 (Winter 1993/1994): 34–77.

Campbell, Kurt M., and Derek J. Mitchell. "Crisis in the Taiwan Strait?" *Foreign Affairs* 80, no. 4 (July/August 2001): 14–25.

Cha, Victor. *Alignment Despite Antagonism: The US-Korea-Japan Security Triangle.* Stanford: Stanford University Press, 1999.

———. *Nuclear North Korea: A Debate on Engagement Strategies.* New York: Columbia University Press, 2005.

Christensen, Thomas J. "China, the US-Japan Alliance and the Security Dilemma in East Asia." *International Security* 23, no. 4 (Spring 1999): 49–80.

———. "The Contemporary Security Dilemma: Deterring a Taiwan Conflict." *Washington Quarterly* 25, no. 4 (Autumn 2002): 7–21.

Dittmer, Lowell. "Taiwan and the Issue of National Identity." *Asian Survey* 44, no. 4 (August 2004): 475–483.

Ganesan, N. "Thai-Myanmar-ASEAN Relations: The Politics of Face and Grace," *Asian Affairs: An American Review* 33, no. 3 (Fall 2006): 131–149.

Green, Michael J. *Japan's Reluctant Realism: Foreign Policy Challenges in an Era of Uncertain Power.* New York: Palgrave for the Council on Foreign Relations, 2001.

Haacke, Jurgen. "'Enhanced Interaction' with Myanmar and the Project of a Security Community: Is ASEAN Refining or Breaking with Its Diplomatic and Security Culture?" *Contemporary Southeast Asia: A Journal of International & Strategic Affairs* 27, no. 2 (August 2005): 188–216.

Hemmer, Christopher, and Peter J. Katzenstein. "Why Is There No NATO in Asia? Collective Identity, Regionalism, and the Origins of Multilateralism." *International Organization* 56, no. 3 (Summer 2002): 575–607.

Johnston, Alastair I. *Cultural Realism: Strategic Culture and Grand Strategy in Chinese History.* Princeton: Princeton University Press, 1995.

———. "Is China a Status Quo Power?" *International Security* 27, no. 4 (Spring 2003): 5–56.

Katzenstein, Peter, and Nobuo Okawara. "Japan's National Security: Structures, Norms and Policies." *International Security* 17, no. 4 (Spring 1993): 84–118.

Khoo, Nicholas. "Constructing Southeast Asian Security: The Pitfalls of Imagining a Security Community and the Temptations of Orthodoxy." *Cambridge Review of International Affairs* 17, no. 1 (April 2004): 137–153.

Lampton, David. *The Making of Chinese Foreign and Security Policy in the Era of Reform 1978-2000.* Stanford: Stanford University Press, 2001.

Oberdorfer, Don. *The Two Koreas: A Contemporary History.* New York: Basic Books, 2001.

Oh, Kong Dan, and Ralph C. Hassig. *North Korea Through the Looking Glass.* Washington, DC: Brookings Institution Press, 2000.

Pollack, Jonathan D. "The United States, North Korea, and the End of the Agreed Framework." *Naval War College Review* 56, no. 3 (Summer 2003): 10–49.

Shambaugh, David. "China and the Korean Peninsula: Playing for the Long Term." *Washington Quarterly* 26, no. 2 (Spring 2003): 43–56.

———. *Modernizing China's Military: Progress, Problems, and Prospects.* Berkeley: University of California Press, 2003.

Squassoni, Sharon A. *North Korea's Nuclear Weapon.* CRS Report No. S21391, February 2, 2004.

To, Lee Lai. "China's Relations with ASEAN: Partners in the 21st Century?" *Pacifica Review: Peace, Security & Global Change* 13, no. (February 2001): 61–71.

Vogel, Steven K. *US-Japan Relations in a Changing World.* Washington, DC: Brookings Institution Press, 2002.

Internet Resources

Asian Military Balance, http://www.csis.org/burke/mb/asia/
Asia News Network, www.asianewsnet.net
Asia-Pacific Area Network, www1.apan-info.net
Comparative Connections, www.csis.org/pacfor/ccejournal.html
East-West Center, www.eastwestcenter.org
Internet Resources for East Asian Studies, www2.lib.udel.edu/subj/eastasia/internet.htm
The National Bureau of Asian Research, www.nbr.org
Open Source Center, www.opensource.gov
Portal to Asian Internet Resources, http://digicoll.library.wisc.edu/PAIR/index.html

19

South Asia

Since World War II, U.S. policy toward South Asia has been largely shaped by U.S. global strategic interests rather than by developments within the region itself. The American perspective was influenced first by the Cold War struggle against the Soviet Union and later by rivalry with China's burgeoning economic and political power. South Asia's secondary importance began to change in the late 1990s as India became increasingly integrated into the global economy and Pakistan and India achieved nuclear weapons capability. Although these relatively recent developments have been significant, as of yet, they have not entirely altered the trend of the previous fifty years in which America's role in the region was primarily driven by its global priorities.

The Indus Valley peoples and their modern descendents represent some of the world's oldest civilizations. America's relatively recent arrival on the region's stage has injected a powerful element into the local mix, but one that has had, so far, a surprisingly limited impact. This is in large part because America's influence has yet to radically alter the fundamental dynamics that animate the region's states: religious rivalry between Hinduism and Islam, political and military struggle between India and Pakistan, India's huge population, and Pakistan's geostrategic centrality and political volatility. However, the impact of the United States on South Asia, as well as the impact of South Asia on the United States, has begun to grow in response to increasing globalization and the escalation of transnational threats, including nuclear proliferation and terrorism.

For the purposes of this chapter, South Asia includes India, Pakistan, the Maldives, Sri Lanka, Bangladesh, Bhutan, and Nepal (see Map 19.1). The focus here will be on U.S. interactions with and developments within India and Pakistan, the largest and most powerful regional actors. Although not usually considered part of

MAP 19.1   South Asia

South Asia, neighboring Afghanistan will also be discussed here because of the intimacy and intensity of its relations with Pakistan.

U.S. Interests in South Asia

American global priorities clearly dominated U.S. policy regarding South Asia for decades following World War II. This was evident in the early 1950s when America warmed to Pakistan's founding fathers, Muhammad Ali Jinnah and Liaquat Ali Khan, with the intent of enlisting their support for the U.S. strategy of Soviet containment at a time when India was championing nonalignment but often cooperating with the Soviet Union. Likewise, U.S. saber rattling in 1971 aimed at India during its support of East Pakistan's struggle to emerge as independent Bangladesh was designed to support a Pakistan that was providing critical support to President Richard Nixon's overtures to China. In 1979, the United States intensified relations with Pakistan after the Soviet Union invaded neighboring Afghanistan, but U.S. interest and involvement declined again as the withdrawal of Soviet forces from Afghanistan began in 1988.[1]

In the early twenty-first century, the United States has had several reasons to focus more directly on its interests in South Asia. First, the terrorist attacks in the United States on September 11, 2001, brought the importance of nonstate actors and South Asian states into sharp relief. This is unlikely to be a transient U.S. interest, as instability in Afghanistan or worsening security conditions in Pakistan would recreate conditions in which al-Qa'ida or similar groups could thrive. More broadly, the willingness and ability of Pakistan and India to respond to transnational threats, such as terrorism or disease pandemics, will significantly influence the effectiveness of global responses to these threats. Second, South Asia's developing economies present important financial opportunities and challenges. Growing South Asian demand for raw materials is affecting global commodity prices and international transportation patterns. India in particular is clearly rising in economic significance, and an increasingly diverse group of Americans (including government policy makers, investment managers, and directors of large corporations) are taking note of the opportunities and challenges that stem from India's rise in global affairs. Third, now that Pakistan and India have become declared nuclear weapons states, the potential cost of future conflict between them has escalated dramatically. Moreover, their actions regarding nuclear weapons technology are likely to continue to have significant implications for the global nonproliferation regime.

Into the foreseeable future, American interests in South Asia are likely to include political stability within the major states, regional peace and stability, economic opportunities, nuclear proliferation, and transnational threats.

Internal Political Stability.   The cohesiveness and effective functioning of the region's major states, India and Pakistan, are of key importance to the United States. Pakistan's political system is chronically fragile, yet a "stable Pakistan at peace with itself and its neighbors" is a crucial American interest.[2] It is hard to exaggerate the destabilizing effect, regionally and globally, of a failed, chaotic, nuclear-armed, Islamic state on Afghanistan's and India's borders.

Founded during partition as a home for British India's Muslims, Pakistan has had great difficulty in marrying Islam and democracy. Military and civilian governments have alternated in power, with no elected government completing its term of office before being ousted by a military coup. Neither civilian nor military government has been able to extend its writ over the fractious tribal areas in the northwest. In early September 2008, Asif Ali Zardari (the widower of former Pakistani Prime Minister Benazir Bhutto) replaced former General Pervez Musharaff as President, returning Pakistan to rule by a civilian leader brought to power by a democratic process. Nevertheless, the new President immediately faced significant challenges associated with responding to the legal and political legacies of Musharaff's rule (which began with a military coup in 1999), lagging economic growth, and rising Islamist militancy.

Crippled by deep ethnic divisions as well as by the defense spending needed to confront an India seven times its size, Pakistan has been unable to create the conditions for stable, sustainable, and politically acceptable levels of economic growth. High levels of defense spending (some 25% of the national budget) have diverted resources needed to feed undernourished educational, medical, and other social programs. Economic progress is also dependent on Pakistan's internal stability, which is clearly tenuous. As Musharraf expressed in 2002, the choice before Pakistan is between a turbulent, nuclear armed "theocracy or a modern, progressive and dynamic state."[3]

With decades of experience as a democratic, economically progressing, multiethnic state, India has a more promising and predictable future than Pakistan. Despite continuing major problems, its political stability seems reasonably assured. Yet the grinding poverty of the hitherto passive hundreds of millions of its one billion people who live below the poverty line; the continuing, though diminishing, drag of the caste system; virulent insurgencies in Kashmir and northeastern tribal areas; the challenge of containing continual, flaring antagonisms between its large (about 150 million) Muslim population and Hindu extremists; and its ongoing disputes with Pakistan, which could well erupt into open warfare, all indicate caution in projecting a thriving, stable state contributing to regional and international peace and stability.

Regional Peace and Stability.   As the British ended their colonial presence on the South Asian subcontinent in 1947, India and Pakistan separated into two rival states. Since this partition, India and Pakistan have fought four wars with one another. The key source of contention has been the disputed territory of Kashmir. Although at partition the province of Kashmir had a majority Muslim population, its Hindu leader chose to become part of India. Disputes over the status of Kashmir sparked wars that began in 1947, 1965, and 1999.[4] The fourth war, which took place in 1971, was primarily a product of East Pakistan's successful attempt to secede from the Muslim successor state that originally had included West and East Pakistan as territories. India entered that conflict on the side of East Pakistan and helped it to become the independent state of Bangladesh. As further discussed below, Kashmir will likely continue to be a source of simmering instability and possible open warfare into the indefinite future. Always costly in human terms, the potential devastation of future wars between India and Pakistan rose tremendously in 1998 as the two states exploded nuclear devices, raising the possibility that nuclear weapons would again be used in war for the first time since 1945.

India's great power ambitions and increasing political and economic clout could lead to further regional volatility beyond periodic clashes with Pakistan. Its growing navy and increasing influence in Southeast Asia provide further fuel for Hindu chauvinists who aspire to regional hegemonic status for India.

Bangladesh may also become a source of regional instability. With nearly 150 million people crowded into an area about the size of Illinois and situated on the deltas of the great Ganges and Brahmaputra rivers, it is always on the brink of natural disasters. In 1991, a cyclone killed more than one hundred thirty thousand

Table 19.1 South Asia Key Statistics

Country	Total Population (millions)	Average Life Expectancy	GDP US$ (billions)	GDP/Capita (US$)	Population Living in Poverty (%)	Military Spending % of GDP	Military Spending US$ (millions)	Human Development Index Ranking (out of 177)
Sri Lanka	20.9	74.8	27.4	4,700	22	2.6	564	99
Maldives	0.37	64.8	0.9	3,900	21	5.5*	41	100
India	1,129.9	68.6	805.5	3,800	28.6	2.5	21,726	128
Bhutan	2.3	55.2	0.8	1,400	31.7	1	—	133
Pakistan	164.7	63.8	124	2,600	24	3	4,050	136
Bangladesh	150.4	62.8	69.2	2,300	45	1.5	841	140
Nepal	28.9	60.56	6.9	1,500	30.9	1.6	—	142
Afghanistan	31.9	43.77	8.8	800	53	1.9	—	—

Sources: CIA World Factbook, updated December 13, 2007, UNHDR Human Development Index 2007/2008; IISS Military Balance 2007.

*Maldives has no regular armed forces and funding used largely to reinforce Maldives Police Service.

people; in 1998, massive floods put two thirds of the country under water and made 30 million people homeless. In 2007, the weather continued its terrible toll; flooding covered most of the country, leaving thousands dead and millions homeless.

Since it became independent in 1971, having earlier been part of Pakistan, Bangladesh's politics have been as unsettled as its weather. Ineffective, corrupt civilian rule has been periodically ended by military coups, with the army widely believed to be behind the emergency transition government that took power in early 2007. Whether this caretaker government will ensure that the promised, fair parliamentary elections are held by the end of 2008 is unclear. What is clear is that greatly improved civilian governance is essential if adequate economic development is to proceed and growing Islamic extremism is to be checked.[5]

Although the vast majority of Bangladesh's more than 120 million Muslims have long practiced a relatively moderate form of Islam, extremism has grown significantly in recent years. Two of the more radical Islamist parties were banned in early 2005, but later that year a widespread series of bombings signaled that the militants were far from neutralized. If major natural catastrophes continue to occur, as is likely, and if civilian governments continue to be as disastrous as in the past (leading, perhaps, to further military interventions), the Islamist radicals may well grow into a major destabilizing force in the region. With its large Muslim minority, India is unlikely to remain indifferent to serious turbulence within its next-door "little brother"—which also contains a Hindu minority of about 25 million.

Economic Opportunities and Concerns.   The United States faces significant emerging economic opportunities and challenges in South Asia. Although Pakistan's relatively small economy presents limited prospects, India's far larger and more sophisticated economy is a growing focus for many U.S. commercial interests. India has the world's twelfth largest economy, with an estimated gross domestic product (GDP) of $796 billion in 2006, and it achieved an average annual growth rate of more than 7% between 1996 and 2005. The United States is India's largest trading partner—bilateral trade was $26.8 billion in 2005—and also India's largest investor.[6] Shared commercial interests are growing; examples include Boeing seeking to sell its commercial aircraft to India's expanding private sector airlines and American high-technology firms seeking to expand their already considerable access to India's knowledge workers and information technology infrastructure.

Although the U.S.-India economic relationship benefits both parties, it also poses challenges. Politically sensitive issues include the competition of low-cost Indian manufacturers with American firms and the outsourcing of business processes to well-educated, English-speaking Indian engineers, call-center operators, and high-technology firms. In addition, economic growth is increasing global competition for raw materials, which boosts commodity prices. Finally, continued South Asian, largely Indian, economic growth is leading to greater energy demand. Between 1993 and 2003, commercial energy consumption grew by 52% in South Asia, even as the region continued to face shortfalls and chronic electricity outages. Consumption of oil, driven by increased transportation and industrial demand, more than doubled between 1990 and 2005. Greater demand for energy influences not only global markets but also the environment. India is the third-largest coal producer in the world after the United States and China and relies on coal for more than 50% of its energy, with consequent polluting carbon emissions.[7]

Nuclear Nonproliferation. U.S. interests in stemming the proliferation of nuclear technologies and weapons to non-nuclear states and violent nonstate actors face significant challenges in South Asia. Along with Cuba and Israel, India and Pakistan are among the very few countries in the world that have refused to sign the Nuclear Non-Proliferation Treaty (NPT)—which entered into force in 1970—and have since remained outside the global nonproliferation regime.[8] India has long argued that the NPT is an unjust arrangement that legitimizes the status of the five declared nuclear weapons states (United States, United Kingdom, France, Soviet Union, and China) while preventing others from taking similar measures to ensure their own security. India was also influenced in its rejection of the NPT by the specifics of its own security situation. China became a nuclear power in 1964, a mere two years after its 1962 border war with India. As a leader of the non-aligned movement during the Cold War, India had no superpower patron to protect it from this Chinese capability.[9] India was also concerned about China's strategic partnership with Pakistan, with whom India had just fought another war. In 1974, India conducted its first underground nuclear test. Decades later, in May 1998, India conducted two more tests. Before the end of that month, Pakistan had also conducted nuclear tests, and the two adversaries had declared themselves members of the nuclear club.

Because the two states are not parties to the NPT, their nuclear facilities and programs are not subject to the International Atomic Energy Agency (IAEA) safeguards which govern the nuclear programs of the five declared nuclear weapons states. The risks were brought into stark relief in January 2004, when Abdul Qadeer Khan, the "father" of Pakistan's nuclear weapons program, admitted on television that he had been involved in transferring uranium enrichment technologies to Libya, Iran, and North Korea.[10] Since that time, India and Pakistan have taken measures to convey that they are responsible nuclear weapons states that will not engage in proliferation-related activities, but significant portions of both of their nuclear programs remain ungoverned by IAEA safeguards.[11] Particularly in relation to Pakistan, with its established history of proliferation, there is the additional concern that members of its nuclear bureaucracy or military might transfer additional nuclear technology or material to another state or violent nonstate actor. Important, too, given the chronic political instability in Pakistan, is the possibility that control over its own nuclear weapons would fall into irresponsible hands. Because of these concerns, Pakistan has been called "the most crucial node of the nexus of terrorism and weapons of mass destruction proliferation."[12]

Transnational Threats. The 9/11 attacks on U.S. soil catapulted India and particularly Pakistan into the status of front-line states in America's counterterrorism campaign. Since the 2001 U.S.-led invasion of Afghanistan, Pakistan's support has been critical to U.S. military operations in Central Asia.

Pakistan officially withdrew its support for the Afghan Taliban, allowed limited use of its air space and territory for U.S. counterterrorism efforts, and provided active support in the form of intelligence and extradition of suspected terrorists. However, powerful factions within Pakistan resent the country's close alliance with the United States and would like to redefine Pakistan's national interests along more Islamic lines. Some within Pakistan identify with such Islamist groups as the Taliban and their ethnic and ideological allies. As of 2008, difficult-to-govern areas in Pakistan's northwest tribal areas were continuing to serve as sanctuaries for allies of the Taliban and members of al-Qa'ida.[13]

In Pakistan's northeast region, violent separatist groups operating in Kashmir could also pose a long-term security problem that extends beyond that disputed territory. India has estimated that "about 40 percent of the militants in Kashmir today are Pakistani or Afghan" and that there are approximately "3,000 to 4,000" self-styled "mujahedeen" ("those who participate in Islamic Holy War") usually present in Kashmir. Although the short-term goal of Islamist groups operating in Kashmir is secession from India, there is also concern that "their next objective is to turn Pakistan into a truly Islamic state."[14]

Emerging transnational threats in South Asia are not limited to terrorism. Analysts have reported a possible link between bovine spongiform encephalopathy ("mad cow disease") in European cattle and Indian fertilizer.[15] More deadly is the growth of the AIDS pandemic, especially among poor Indians. This pandemic carries a growing human and economic cost, burdening India's budget and social services. Given India's status as the world's second-most populous country, with 15% of the global population, the rise in its AIDS-infection rate challenges global efforts to contain the spread of this disease. The United Nations (UN) estimates that, as of 2004, India has surpassed South Africa as having the largest number of AIDS cases. American efforts to eradicate AIDS (including support from governmental and private organizations, such as the Bill and Melinda Gates Foundation) play an often overlooked role in protecting U.S. security interests and in limiting the human and economic costs of this transnational threat.[16]

History of U.S. Policy in the Region

As noted earlier, U.S. foreign policy in South Asia has historically been shaped by many factors external to the region itself. This has led to misunderstandings as well as a lack of consistency in U.S. policy, creating frustration and limiting confidence on all sides.

The Immediate Post–World War II Period.   After World War II, the United States looked to Pakistan and to democratic India for support in its struggle against the spread of communism and the global influence of the Soviet Union. Pakistan proved an eager and willing ally, primarily because it sought help from the most powerful country in the world against the most powerful country in its region—India. Pakistan's search for a protective patron was constant throughout the Cold War and continues to this day. In contrast, due to its size and relative military advantage, India was mostly concerned with preserving its national prerogatives against any who would infringe upon them. Its continuing obstruction of UN and other efforts to resolve the Kashmir dispute, its cooperative relations with the Soviet Union, and its self-appointed role as spokesperson for developing countries combined to alienate successive American administrations. The results were a growing commonality of security positions between the United States and Pakistan and a growing diplomatic chill between the United States and India.

The 1950s, 1960s, and the Formation of Cold War Alliances.   One Eisenhower administration initiative of particular importance to U.S. relations with the countries of South Asia was the creation of Cold War alliances in the region. The two alliances that involved Pakistan were the Southeast Asian Treaty Organization (SEATO) and the Baghdad Pact, which became the Central Treaty Organization (CENTO) in 1958.

In 1954, after the French departure from Vietnam, SEATO was formed by the United States, Pakistan, and six other countries to oppose further communist expansion into South and Southeast Asia. At the time, Pakistan sought an explicit wording within SEATO's organizing documents that mutual defense obligations would be invoked upon the attack of a member from any quarter.[17] The United States, however, limited the obligation solely to an attack by communist forces.

In 1955, the United States organized the creation of what was to become CENTO to deter Soviet expansion toward the southwest. The initial members were the United Kingdom, Turkey, Iraq, Iran, and Pakistan, with the United States joining the military committee in 1958. One practical benefit for the United States was Pakistan's willingness to allow intelligence operations on its territory. It was from a Pakistani airbase, for example, that U.S. Air Force pilot Gary Powers took off in his U2 surveillance aircraft in 1960 on his way to being shot down over the Soviet Union—an incident that exposed these U.S. intelligence operations to international scrutiny.

Although neither SEATO nor CENTO survived beyond the 1970s, both arrangements made evident a U.S. tilt toward Pakistan, based on its support of the U.S. policy of containment. As Pakistani military ruler Ayub Khan phrased it in his autobiography, Pakistan had become America's "most allied ally in Asia."[18] To reward Pakistan for joining the fight against communism and ostensibly to better prepare it for that struggle, in 1954, President Dwight Eisenhower approved the first sale of military hardware to Pakistan. India reacted with anger and predicted that arms given to Pakistan by the United States would be used against India rather than against communist adversaries. Although Eisenhower made a similar arms offer to India, Prime Minister Jawaharlal Nehru rejected it to preserve India's independent foreign policy stance and amicable relations with the Soviet Union.

Although U.S. relations with Pakistan were generally good through the 1950s and early 1960s, U.S. relations with India were not. In addition to Indian dislike of the U.S. arms flow to Pakistan, the colonial experience had made India's leaders particularly sensitive to any paternalistic actions by Western powers or infringements upon its sovereignty. One reflection of these sentiments was Nehru's 1958 proclamation that inspired the Non-Aligned Movement, of which India became a leader. This grouping of newly independent states declared its desire not to become involved in the struggles between the West and communism. For their part, U.S. policy makers were also troubled by India's military cooperation with the Soviet Union.

Despite these dynamics, the United States responded to Indian requests for military aid after its brief, disastrous 1962 border war with China. Its erstwhile military equipment supplier, the Soviet Union, refused help. From the U.S. perspective, this experience showed that India could be a useful if limited ally in its global struggles against communism. India, however, took away a different lesson. Its rough handling by China and the necessity of requesting U.S. aid indicated the need for nuclear weapons capability—a need that was only reinforced by China's nuclear test in 1964.

In the mid-1960s, American relations with Pakistan deteriorated. In 1965, Pakistan launched an invasion into the Indian-controlled portion of Kashmir. Though Pakistan benefitted at first from having the initiative, the conflict quickly turned in India's favor, and the resulting ceasefire saw the pre-conflict status quo restored. The subsequent decision by President Lyndon Johnson to end ten years of U.S. military aid revealed Pakistan's dependence on that aid and left the country at a serious disadvantage relative to India. As a result, Pakistan turned to China and deepened a security relationship that has since flourished.[19]

The 1970s.   The beginning of the 1970s saw Pakistan serving as an interlocutor for the United States as the Nixon administration made overtures to China. However, Pakistan's attentions were soon drawn inward. Long dis-satisfied with their relationship with West Pakistan, the people of East Pakistan, encouraged by India, declared their separation and independence in March 1971. As the situation escalated, India intervened in November 1971. Nixon ordered a U.S. carrier battle group to stand off the Bengali coast as a futile warning to India to curtail its military operations. In December 1971, India forced the surrender of the Pakistani army in East Pakistan, thus guaranteeing the emergence of the new state of Bangladesh. Washington's "carrier diplomacy" increased the animosity between Indian and U.S. leaders, with little benefit to relations with the remaining Pakistani state.[20]

In 1979, U.S. relations with Pakistan were buffeted by a number of policy issues. The United States finally ceased the support begun by the Eisenhower administration to Pakistan's nuclear energy program due to intelligence assessments indicating that Pakistan was actively developing nuclear weapons. However, this blow to the bilateral relationship was reversed by the Soviet invasion of Afghanistan on Christmas Eve 1979. This Soviet effort to restore stability in a bordering country, as well as to restrain what it viewed as the dangerous and erratic leadership of a shaky communist government, led to a decade-long insurgency by Afghan resistance fighters.[21] The United States sought, successfully, to gain Pakistan's help in its aid to these fighters, and thus Pakistan regained its status as a "front-line" state and aid recipient within America's anti-Soviet alliances.[22]

The 1980s and the End of the Cold War. By 1989, the Soviets had withdrawn from Afghanistan, and shortly thereafter the Soviet Union collapsed. The end of the Cold War again changed the manner in which the United States viewed its interests in South Asia. In 1985, the Pressler Amendment to the Foreign Assistance Act was passed, which required the president to certify that a country was not actively seeking nuclear weapons before that country could receive U.S. aid. In 1990, President George H. W. Bush determined that he could not certify Pakistan, ending a substantial U.S. aid program. The effect of this reversal was similar to that of America's earlier decision to end aid in 1979. Once again, Pakistan perceived that the United States was a fickle and ultimately untrustworthy ally.[23]

The Clinton Administration and U.S. Policy in the 1990s. As already noted, in May 1998, India and Pakistan conducted a series of nuclear tests and declared themselves the newest members of the nuclear arms club. The Clinton administration reacted quickly against both states by suspending aid and launching an intense diplomatic effort to sanction and curtail the two countries' weapons programs. Strobe Talbott, the U.S. deputy secretary of state, conducted protracted but futile shuttle diplomacy for two years by frequently traveling between the Pakistani and Indian capitals and meeting with senior officials of both countries in an attempt to restrain both countries from escalating the regional arms race.

As the twentieth century came to a close, U.S. policy toward South Asia was shaped by several additional developments and dynamics. First, in May 1999, insurgents supported by Pakistani troops (though this was denied by Pakistan) crossed the Line of Control in Kashmir and sparked the Kargil War with India. (The *Line of Control* is the de facto border separating the portions of Kasmir administered by India and Pakistan.) In July 1999, the conflict ended with a restoration of the Line of Control, but almost five hundred Indians and eight hundred Pakistanis had died.[24] In October, an attempt by Pakistani Prime Minister Nawaz Sharif to replace Chief of the Army Staff Musharraf ended instead in a military takeover of the government, led by Musharraf. This coup resulted in additional U.S. sanctions against Pakistan. As these developments increasingly jeopardized U.S.-Pakistan relations, an improved U.S. dialogue with India was occurring as bilateral commercial ties deepened and the Indian-American community became an increasingly important U.S. domestic political voice.[25] As a reflection of the status of U.S. relations with the region, President Bill Clinton's 2000 visit to the subcontinent included five festival-like days in India and five constrained and difficult hours in Pakistan. During the visit, Clinton and Indian Prime Minister Atal Behari Vajpayee signed a five-page "Vision for the 21st Century" to create a "closer and qualitatively new relationship" between the two countries.

The Impact of the Terrorist Attacks of September 11, 2001, on U.S. Policy toward Pakistan. After the 9/11 terrorist attacks in New York City and Washington, D.C., U.S. policy toward South Asia underwent another dramatic shift. Within a matter of weeks, the ties became clear between the attacks, the al-Qa'ida terrorist network, and the Taliban government that was serving as al-Qa'ida's host in Afghanistan. As in 1979 after the Soviet invasion of Afghanistan, Pakistan once again became a crucial U.S. ally in the fight against undesirable forces within Afghanistan's borders.

As U.S. demands to the Taliban to hand over their al-Qa'ida guests looked unlikely to be fulfilled and America's preparations for war went into high gear, Musharraf was quick to offer Pakistan's full support to the coming U.S.-led assault. This alignment gained Pakistan rich rewards in terms of U.S. aid. In 2002, the U.S. Agency for International Development (USAID) re-entered Pakistan, disbursing large amounts of funds in an attempt to support the legitimacy of Musharraf's regime and decrease the attractiveness of radical Islamist groups. In 2003, U.S. support to Pakistan expanded to include a five-year, $3-billion military aid and sovereign debt-relief package.[26]

Despite this aid, U.S. relations have been complicated by important divisions within Pakistan. Though many Pakistanis support a foreign policy favorable to U.S. interests, many others identify with their ethnic kin within the Pashtun tribe on which the Taliban is based and whose traditional homeland straddles the Afghan-Pakistan border. Some of those holding this latter view identify Pakistan's national interests with the Taliban and a pan-Islamic struggle against perceived Western domination of the Muslim world. These elements not only jeopardize relations with the United States but also threaten Pakistan's internal political stability.

U.S.-India Relations Since 2001.   U.S. relations with India have continued to improve since Clinton's visit in 2000, and the aftermath of the 9/11 attacks saw an outpouring of sympathy from India. Though India condemned the U.S. invasion of Iraq in 2003, Indian leaders were circumspect in their criticism to avoid significant damage to U.S.-India relations.

A key component of U.S. efforts to strengthen the nation's strategic partnership with India has been an effort by the administration of President George W. Bush to resume nuclear energy cooperation with India while stopping short of supporting India's accession to the NPT as a sixth recognized nuclear weapons state. India's robust democracy, the country's growing economy and population, and its rivalry with China all suggest that India could become an increasingly valuable U.S. partner. Indian support could be crucial in dealing with such global issues as trade and investment, competition for raw materials, transnational threats, and the economic, political, and military rise of China.

In December 2006, at the administration's urging, Congress approved a bill to allow cooperation with India on civilian nuclear issues in return for India's agreement to allow international monitoring of its civilian nuclear plants. The Bush administration justified this policy departure as helping to "alter the strategic advantage in Asia and South Asia to the benefit of the U.S." and called U.S. relations with India since 1947 the "ultimate unfulfilled relationship."[27] The Bush administration gambled that India's value as a strategic partner would offset the potential damage that this special exemption would do to the global nonproliferation regime and to the incentives of such other nuclear aspirants as Iran.

Key Developments within South Asia's Security Environment

Kashmir: Covert Hostilities, Conventional and Possibly Nuclear War. One consequence of the 1947 partition of British India into two predominantly Hindu and Muslim states was that millions on both sides were massacred as scattered Hindus and Muslims moved to their new homelands. Another consequence was that one of the so-called princely states within British India, Kashmir, was acrimoniously divided. At the end of 1947, India and Pakistan fought their first war over Kashmir, with India gaining the largest and wealthiest share. A second inconclusive war followed in 1965. In 1971, a third Pakistani-Indian war was ignited by the violent internal division of Pakistan between its western (Pakistan) and its eastern (Bangladesh) halves. A fourth eruption between the two states occurred in 1999, around the Kashmiri mountain town of Kargil. Each of these conflicts has been a contained affair due to mutual restraint often reinforced by outside pressure. However, Pakistan and India continue to jockey for advantage to satisfy domestic constituencies and to exert regional influence.

One of the reasons that the issue of Kashmir has been so intractable is that it is fundamentally related to the identities of the two states. At the time of partition, the majority Hindu Congress Party sought a future multiethnic India ruled by a secular government. The Muslim league, in contrast, argued that the distinct religious and social identity of Muslims, as well as their minority status, required that they have their own state. Kashmir was particularly contentious because it was located next to Pakistan and had a majority Muslim population but a Hindu leader who chose to join India.[28] Although India retains a rhetorical claim over the portion of Kashmir on the Pakistani side of the Line of Control that currently divides Kashmir, it has been willing to recognize this line as a permanent international boundary. Pakistan, however, is not satisfied with the current division and still lays claim to all of Kashmir. Due to its military advantage, India is in no danger of losing its portion of Kashmir. This situation is a cause of Pakistan's perennial search for allies, such as the United States or China, who are willing to materially support Pakistani claims.[29]

Kashmir is dangerous not only as a source of interstate conflict but also as an operating area for violent nonstate actors. Kashmiri efforts from 1947 onward to achieve self-governance, or at least increased autonomy, were systematically crushed by India, resulting in a continuing, low-level insurgency. This insurgency took on increased substance toward the end of the 1980s, at the same time as the Soviet withdrawal from Afghanistan. It attracted battle-hardened mujahedeen grown accustomed to, and successful at, waging what they considered to be holy war against the Soviets occupying Afghanistan. The direct role of the Pakistani government has never been proven, but strong links are believed to exist between Pakistan's Inter-Services Intelligence Directorate and the mujahideen.[30]

Lurie's NewsCartoon

"Call me once you conclude a peace treaty."

Reprinted with permission of Ranan Lurie.

The years 2006 and 2007 witnessed a glimmer of rapprochement, with India and Pakistan actively exploring avenues to mitigate the problem of Kashmir. A critical component of this new understanding has been the long-needed, partial devolution of power from New Delhi to Srinagar, the capital of Indian Kashmir.

This has led to increased legitimacy of the provincial government in the eyes of locals and removed some of the pressure on Pakistani officials to actively support their coreligionists. Though criminal activity by elements within the Indian security apparatus as well as abuses stemming from India's counterinsurgency campaign continue, India has promised zero tolerance of such activities.[31] For its part, Pakistan has taken steps to rein in the most militant Kashmir separatists and has increased efforts to seal the Line of Control from infiltration by outside groups.

Domestic Divisions within India and Pakistan. As the world's most populous democracy and one of the few new states to remain consistently democratic since independence, India is a seemingly healthy cauldron of interests and ethnicities competing within the confines of a democratic political system. Successive civilian leaders have maintained control of the country and its political system, while the military has remained clearly subordinate and has held limited political influence. Nonetheless, India continues to face internal challenges, particularly the barely contained hostility between its Hindu majority and its 150 million Muslim citizens—hostility that continually threatens the fabric of the nation.

Pakistan's political system has not proven as resilient as India's. Within a few years of its emergence as a state, Pakistan suffered the unfortunate loss of its founding father, Mohammed Jinnah, and saw the assassination of its first prime minister, Liaquat Ali Khan, in 1951 by Syed Akhbar, an Afghan national, whose motives have never been fully clarified. Democracy suffered as the civil and military bureaucracies maintained centralized control over the country and its political processes. As already noted, Pakistan's political history has been marked by military coups and lengthy periods of military rule—a situation that seems likely to recur.[32]

The Afghanistan Dimension. A critical, lingering problem for the government of Pakistan stems from developments in neighboring Afghanistan. After being defeated by U.S. forces in 2001–2002, the Taliban and their al-Qa'ida allies retreated to the tribally ruled, mountainous Afghan-Pakistan border region. From havens on both sides of the border, the resurgent Taliban have fought a deadly insurgency, threatening to destabilize the newly installed Afghan regime and Pakistan's central government. Continuing deadly turbulence in Afghanistan, with inevitable spillover into Pakistan, seems highly likely. Although the Texas-size, arid, mountainous land (only 12% arable) has been unified since the eighteenth century, it has been continually rent by ethnic and tribal conflict and military coups. When the decade-long Soviet effort to bring communist order to the country aborted in 1989, civil war again erupted. The extremist fundamentalist Taliban finally succeeded, after nearly a decade of fighting, in taking over 90% of the nation's territory and its government. But it made the mistake of harboring Osama bin Laden and his al-Qa'ida cohorts, who set up headquarters and training camps in the countryside.

Given mounting evidence of al-Qa'ida's terrorist activities, the UN Security Council imposed sanctions on Afghanistan in 1999 when the Taliban refused to turn bin Laden over to the United States for prosecution. After the 9/11 terrorist attacks on American soil, readily traced to al-Qa'ida, on October 7, 2001, the United States and the United Kingdom launched an air assault against the country.

With U.S. ground and air support, the opposition Northern Alliance—a religiously and ethnically diverse association of rebel groups—then attacked southward, routed the Taliban, and retook Kabul in little more than a month of fighting. Shortly thereafter, the anti-Taliban factions were able to agree on a coalition government under Hamid Karzai, who was later elected president in 2004.

Although the UN authorized a small international security force (of which the North Atlantic Treaty Organization [NATO] took control in 2003) in support of the Karzai government, and the United States also augmented its forces, the Taliban were able to reconstitute and increasingly carry out offensive operations and suicide bombings. As of this writing, despite continuing allied efforts, bin Laden and Taliban leaders had continued to evade capture (probably in the rugged terrain straddling the Afghan-Pakistan border). Meanwhile, in 2005, the Afghan people managed to write a new constitution and hold parliamentary elections, in which millions voted in spite of the Taliban's disruptive efforts.

By late 2008, an effective Afghan national army was well into the process of development, and approximately forty-three thousand foreign troops (twenty-five thousand American and eighteen thousand NATO) were available to train it and conduct operations. Despite allied efforts, the resilient Taliban, operating from their safe haven on the Afghan-Pakistan border and drawing support from the Pashtun tribes on which it is based (about 43% of the nation's 31 million people are Pashtun), continues its insurgency.

On the broader issue of nation building, progress has also been halting, at best. A 2007 report by the Center for Strategic and International Studies summarized the discouraging situation at this point as follows:

> Afghans are losing trust in their government because of an escalation in violence; public expectations are neither being met nor managed; conditions in Afghanistan have deteriorated in all key areas targeted for development, except for the economy and human rights.[33]

In September 2008, Chairman of the Joint Chiefs of Staff Admiral Michael Mullen admitted that he was not convinced that the United States and its allies were winning in Afghanistan and announced that he had ordered a major review of U.S. strategy.[34]

Nuclear Proliferation and Cooperation.   The question of how to deal with India and Pakistan as nuclear weapons states is an exceptionally difficult one for America. The United States is concerned that nuclear weapons could be used to devastating effect in a future India-Pakistan war and that the weapons or the underlying technology could be transferred to terrorist groups or (again in the case of Pakistan) to other states who aspire to possess nuclear weapons. Since the nuclear tests in the region in 1998, the United States has gradually come to recognize that no amount of negotiation or arm twisting will result in complete nuclear disarmament in India or Pakistan. Even if all security concerns in South Asia were magically resolved, nuclear weapons programs have evoked national pride and tremendous popular support in both countries.

From the beginning, the U.S. response to the status of Pakistan and India as nuclear weapons states has been decisively shaped by other national security priorities. Even after the 2004 admission by Pakistani scientist Abdul Qadeer Khan that he had run an international black market trade in nuclear secrets, the U.S. government carefully avoided accusing the Pakistani government of direct involvement and sought to prevent the situation from damaging U.S.-Pakistan relations.[35] The U.S. action was limited despite the grave consequences of this proliferation, including its probable contributions to the current status of North Korean and Iranian nuclear programs. After the 2004 revelations, Musharraf pardoned the enormously popular Khan. Shortly thereafter, grateful for Pakistani support in Afghanistan, the United States declared Musharraf's Pakistan to be a "major, non-NATO ally."[36]

In December 2006, the nuclear issue in South Asia again resurfaced when George W. Bush signed the agreement to allowing civil nuclear cooperation with India for the first time since the 1970s.[37] As suggested earlier, this arrangement runs the risk of damaging the NPT, which sets rules governing the nuclear programs of its 187 members. As part of the NPT bargain, non–nuclear weapons states agree not to pursue nuclear weapons in exchange for promises that the existing nuclear weapons states will provide assistance with nuclear energy programs and pursue nuclear disarmament. India is now gaining assistance with its nuclear energy program while retaining nuclear weapons and avoiding the full range of international controls associated with the NPT.

South Asia and China.   Never far removed from any calculation of U.S. regional interest in South Asia is consideration of China's rising importance. Commercial rivalry between India and China naturally swings between cooperation and competition but for the most part is based on the established rules of the marketplace. Despite a common interest between the two in stability, tensions may yet resurface over the once fought over and still disputed border between them. This dispute will in all likelihood remain nonviolent, but its existence is part of the reason that the United States sees India as a potentially valuable partner in offsetting China's growing power. U.S. expectations of its relationship with India should be tempered, however, by India's demonstrated preference for an independent foreign policy. The United States cannot expect Indian support unless India's regional and increasingly global aspirations are also furthered by U.S. policies.

China's role in U.S.-Pakistan relations has been and will continue to be complicated. In developments growing out of the security cooperation which began in the late 1960's, China was implicated in the early sale of nuclear and missile technology to Pakistan. China will likely continue to supply such weapons technology as long as Pakistan is willing to side with China when called upon. For its part, Pakistan will undoubtedly continue to seek political and material support from China to strengthen its position in its continuing rivalry with India.[38]

India's Economic Growth and Great Power Aspirations.   As the world's largest democracy and second-most populous state, India has long held high aspirations concerning its rightful place in the world. Although India's ambition has not been supported by its economic and military capabilities, this is changing. Particularly since its adoption of economic reforms in the early 1990s, India's fortunes have improved dramatically. It has emerged as a critical player in the global information technology business, a source of world-leading industrial firms, and a consumer whose demand for raw materials is having an appreciable impact on global commodity prices.

The growing global importance of India's economy invites comparisons with the rise of China. Between 2000 and 2004, India's GDP grew at an average rate of more than 6% annually; this rate rose to 8.1% in 2005 and 9.4% in 2006. In comparison, China's economy has grown at a rate of approximately 9% to 10% throughout the past 3 decades.[39]

Despite indicators of strength, India faces significant challenges in sustaining rapid economic progress. First, India will need to enact changes in its domestic market; including reforming its sclerotic bureaucracy; loosening tight labor rules; and removing inefficiencies in its finance, housing, and educational sectors.[40] Second, India will need to take measures to ensure that more Indians benefit from economic growth. As evident from the following statistics, deep poverty is still a tremendous problem in India:

> China ranks at number 81 of 177 countries on the latest United Nations Human Development Index (in the neighborhood of Armenia or Peru), while India is 126 (below Namibia and just ahead of Cambodia). In China, a person's chance of dying before the age of 40 is just under 7 percent. In India it's over 16 percent, higher than in Pakistan or Bangladesh. Eighty percent of Indians live on $2 a day or less, compared with about 46 percent of the Chinese. Almost half the children under 5 in India are malnourished, compared with 8 percent in China.[41]

Many Indians are paying a heavy price in economic as well as human terms as India transitions from a primarily agrarian economy to industrial and even postindustrial forms of production.

As India's economy has grown, so has its relationship with the United States. The United States is India's largest export market and a lucrative source of financial and technological support. The Indian community in the United States has become increasingly important to this bilateral relationship. An estimated thirty thousand Indian information technology professionals work in Silicon Valley, many of whom exercise political influence either as American citizens or as leaders of an industry that is a pillar of U.S. economic health. Indians enjoying success in the United States also have an impact on developments back in India, with some running parallel business operations in both countries. American and Indian firms work to influence their governments to prevent political obstacles from unduly interfering in these burgeoning business ties.[42]

The strength and growth of India's economy has fueled its longstanding ambitions in the global diplomatic arena. As recognition of its great power status, India has long pursued a permanent seat on the UN Security Council. Its efforts have not met with success, for reorganizing the Security Council is a politically charged and extremely complex undertaking. The 2006 nuclear cooperation deal between the United States and India is an indication that the U.S. attitude toward India's attempts to become a permanent member may be changing as the United States seeks new allies to help it meet the challenges of the twenty-first century.

Pakistan as an Emerging Market. Although there are indications of progress, Pakistan is not yet an emerging market that has a significant impact on global commerce. On the positive side, its GDP has been recently growing at the robust annual rate of approximately 6%, its central bank has been playing an active and constructive role in macroeconomic management, and new funds are flowing into the country. In early 2005, Pakistan took steps to create more room for private business by privatizing key sectors of the economy, including banking and power generation, and has limited political interference in the workings of the central bank.

Despite this progress, the challenges confronting Pakistan are enormous. Its political economy is still dominated by agricultural products, textiles, and the political interests these sectors represent.[43] In addition, its recent economic successes and growth have been closely tied to unsustainable or one-time stimuli. Examples include massive debt forgiveness (sponsored by the United States as compensation for Pakistan's support after the 9/11 terrorist attacks); increased International Monetary Fund lending, and the entrée to private lending that such funds support (again at the instigation of the United States); and a surge in remittances from Pakistanis living abroad.[44] These developments could help Pakistan to address long-term problems stemming from uncompetitive industries, an overly rigid economy, and severe market inefficiencies, or they could be only short-term gains. The importance of the U.S. role is also an issue. Should history repeat itself and Pakistan fall from U.S. favor, Pakistan's economy would likely suffer again.

There are also several troubling aspects of Pakistan's current economic growth. One measure Pakistan has undertaken to enhance its economic resilience is the development of its state-owned conventional arms industry. Much of the basic technology for the industry comes from China; the target market is the Middle East and Africa.[45] A second concern is the growing importance of the Afghan opium trade within Pakistan. One of the unintended consequences of the U.S.-led removal of the Taliban has been an explosion in opium production. Formerly harshly repressed by the puritanical Sunni Taliban, Afghan poppy growers have enjoyed the patronage and protection of the multitude of Afghan warlords who have exploited the weakness of the Kabul government after the Taliban's fall from power. Afghanistan produces an estimated 90% of the world's opium poppy supply and, according to former U.S. drug control officials, "Afghanistan and Pakistan are the number one export and transit nations in the world for opium used for heroin."[46] According to the U.S. Department of State, the activity in Pakistan consists of more than just the transit of drugs as "Pakistan is part of the massive Afghan opium production/refining 'system.'"[47] As the State Department report also points out, "with government salaries low and societal and government corruption endemic, narcotics related corruption is likely to be associated with the movement of large quantities of narcotics and pre-cursor chemicals." The longer the trade continues and the larger it grows, the more deleterious its effect will be on the Pakistani government, local rule of law, and U.S. interests.

Future South Asia Challenges Facing U.S. Policy Makers

Future U.S. relationships with the region face numerous challenges. A key one is the U.S. interest in a successful, stable, and moderate Pakistani government. Conflict in Afghanistan, the rise of the narcotics trade, and the split between radical and moderate Islamic forces have increased the difficulty of the balancing act that Pakistan's leaders must perform to maintain national stability. Strong and consistent U.S. support to moderate political elements in the civilian and military bureaucracies is needed to improve the effectiveness of the government's ability to deliver enhanced services and standards of living.

A second major regional challenge facing the United States is the need to appropriately support India's integration as a great power into the global political and economic system. As they strive to forge a new strategic partnership with India, U.S. policy makers will need to pay greater heed to India's perspective and national interests. American interests need not, however, extend to supporting Indian ambitions to become a regional hegemon in South and Southeast Asia.

American relations with Pakistan and India will continue to be shaped by developments in Kashmir, terrorism, and nuclear proliferation. Only negotiation, accompanied by occasional arm twisting by outsiders, seems likely to mitigate the Kashmir problem to the point that it no longer poisons every dimension of India-Pakistan relations. America has a strong interest in helping, in any way feasible, the two states to develop a process "that would result in less acrimonious bilateral relations and ultimately create an atmosphere conducive to working out a Kashmir settlement."[48]

The presence of terrorist groups and acts of terrorism in South Asia, whether inspired by pan-Islamic zeal or the more local Kashmir dispute, will continue to jeopardize security within the region and beyond. U.S. policy makers will be challenged, particularly in relations with Pakistan, to develop collaborative and effective responses to terrorist threats. Finally, nuclear proliferation will long remain a significant concern. The United States will have to continually weigh its interest in the credibility and effectiveness of the global nonproliferation regime as it interacts with Pakistan and India while they pursue their nuclear ambitions.

Discussion Questions

1. How did the U.S. policy of containment affect the country's relations with India and Pakistan during the Cold War? Have there been lasting effects stemming from U.S. Cold War policies?

2. What is the origin of the conflict between India and Pakistan? What is the most likely flash point for a renewal of armed conflict today?

3. What dynamics have shaped the relationships between China and the countries of South Asia?

4. How would you characterize the nature of the alliance between the United States and Pakistan? What factors have shaped this alliance over time?

5. What are some of the critical differences between the political systems of India and Pakistan as they have evolved since the 1947 partition?

6. How can the United States best contribute to strengthening moderate forces in Bangladesh?

7. Can the United States promote stability in Pakistan? If so, how?

8. How are U.S. national security interests in South Asia affected by the rise of China?

9. Does the tacit U.S. acknowledgment of India and Pakistan as nuclear weapons states represent the end of the international nonproliferation regime? Why or why not?

10. What policies should the United States adopt toward India and Pakistan to minimize the risk of further proliferation of nuclear weapons technology?

11. Is Pakistan taking adequate action to reduce the threat of international terrorism?

12. What additional U.S. and allied measures are necessary to help stabilize Afghanistan?

Recommended Reading

Blank, Stephen. *Natural Allies? Regional Security in Asia and Prospects for Indo-American Strategic Cooperation*. Carlisle, PA: U.S. Army War College, September 2005.

Chambers, Michael, ed. *South Asia in 2020: Future Strategic Balances and Alliances*. Carlisle, PA: U.S. Army War College, November 2002.

Gupta, Amit. *Strategic Effects of the Conflict with Iraq: South Asia*. Carlisle, PA: U.S. Army War College, March 2003.

———. *The U.S.-India Relationship: Strategic Partnership or Complementary Interests?* Carlisle, PA: U.S. Army War College, February 2005.

Kapur, Ashok, Yogendra K. Malik, Arthur G. Rubinoff, and Harold Gould, eds. *India and the United States in a Changing World*. Thousand Oaks, CA: Sage Publications, Inc., 2002.

Kux, Dennis. *Pakistan, Flawed Not Failed State*. New York: Foreign Policy Association, 2001.

———. *The United States and Pakistan, 1947–2000: Disenchanted Allies*. Baltimore, MD: Johns Hopkins University Press, 2001.

———. "India's Fine Balance." *Foreign Affairs* 81, no. 3 (May/June 2002): 93–106.

Raju, Subramanyam. *Democracies at Loggerheads: Security Aspects of U.S.-India Relations*. Denver, CO: International Academic Publishers, Ltd., 2001.

SarDesai, D. R., and Raju Thomas, eds. *Nuclear India in the Twenty-First Century*. New York: Palgrave-Macmillan, 2002.

Schaffer, Teresita. *Kashmir: The Economics of Peace Building*. Washington, DC: Center for Strategic & International Studies, 2004.

———. *Pakistan's Future and U.S. Policy Options*. Washington, DC: Center for Strategic & International Studies, 2004.

———. *Bangladesh in the Balance*. Washington, DC: Center for Strategic & International Studies, 2007.

Stewart, Andrew. *Friction in U.S. Foreign Policy: Cultural Difficulties with the World*. Carlisle, PA: U.S. Army War College, June 2006.

Talbott, Strobe. *Engaging India: Diplomacy, Democracy, and the Bomb*. Rev. ed. Washington, DC: Brookings Institution Press, 2004.

Wisner, Frank, Nicholas Platt, Marshall M. Bouton, Dennis Kux, and Mahnaz Z. Ispahani. *New Priorities in South Asia: U.S. Policy Toward India, Pakistan, and Afghanistan*. New York: Council on Foreign Relations, 2003.

Internet Resources

International Atomic Energy Agency, www.iaea.org
The International Institute for Strategic Studies, www.iiss.org
The Library of Congress Country Studies, http://lcweb2.loc.gov/frd/cs/cshome.html
The Library of Congress Thomas, http://thomas.loc.gov
Near East South Asia Center for Strategic Studies, www.ndu.edu/nesa
U.S. Agency for International Development, www.usaid.gov
U.S. State Department Bureau of South and Central Asian Affairs, www.state.gov/p/sca

20

The Middle East

The new millennium ushered in momentous transformations in the Middle East that have significantly affected key U.S. interests. The Israeli-Palestinian Peace Process again stalled; the terrorist attacks of September 11, 2001, served as an impetus for the U.S. invasions of Afghanistan and Iraq; and international concern grew over Iran's possible pursuit of nuclear weapons. The confluence of these events has increased the turbulence in an already unstable Middle East (see Figure 20.1). (Note: The term *Middle East* in this chapter includes Egypt, Israel, Jordan, Lebanon, Syria, Turkey, Iraq, Saudi Arabia, Kuwait, Bahrain, Qatar, the United Arab Emirates, Iran, Oman, Yemen, and Sudan.)

In 1993, through their signatures on the Oslo Accords, Israel and the Palestinians indicated their acceptance of a peace settlement based on the concept of a two-state solution. However, a lack of tangible progress produced a Palestinian rebellion in September 2000 against the continued Israeli occupation and the corrupt Palestinian Authority (PA), which had gained control of newly autonomous Palestinian areas. This second Palestinian uprising, known as the *Al Aqsa Intifada* ("Al Aqsa" after the mosque in Jerusalem, and "Intifada" for uprising), unraveled previous progress and left the peace process in tatters.[1]

A year after this renewal of violence between Israelis and Palestinians, deadly terrorist attacks in the United States triggered events that led to enormous changes in the Middle East. To root out al-Qa'ida operatives who were behind the attacks and who had established training camps in Afghanistan with the assistance of its fundamentalist Taliban regime, the United States attacked Afghanistan in October 2001. With the stated intent of finding and destroying weapons of mass destruction (WMDs), in March 2003 the

MAP 20.1   The Middle East

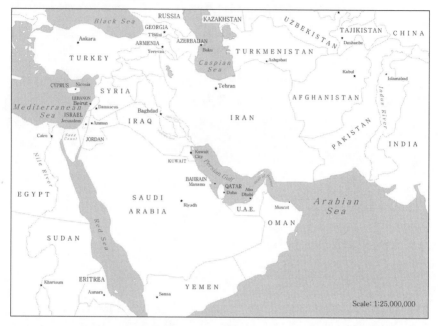

Scale: 1:25,000,000

United States launched an invasion of Iraq that toppled its brutal dictator, Saddam Hussein. An additional goal of the invasion was to establish a democracy in Iraq that would serve as an exemplar to other societies in the Middle East. It was posited that a successful democracy in Iraq could help stem the growth of regional extremism by addressing what many believed to be one of its important root causes—political disaffection and unrepresentative governance. In the years after 2003, however, violence and political instability in Iraq diminished prospects for the successful establishment of a representative democracy and upset the regional balance of power by eliminating Iraq as a counterbalance to Iran.

The deep and increasingly difficult U.S. involvement in Iraq and the creation of a Shiite majority government in Iraq have emboldened Iran to take a more assertive stance in the region. Elected in 2005, Iranian President Mahmoud Ahmadinejad, supported by the powerful religious establishment, has pursued strongly anti-Western foreign policies. Iran has continued to pursue its national interests by supporting terrorist groups, such as the Shiite Hezbollah that operates primarily in southern Lebanon. On July 12, 2006, Hezbollah kidnapped two Israeli soldiers and killed six others across the border in Israel, precipitating a thirty-three-day war in which Israel's air strikes killed numerous Lebanese civilians and massively damaged Lebanese infrastructure without significantly hurting Hezbollah. In return, Hezbollah launched hundreds of rockets against mainly civilian targets in northern Israel and emerged from the inconclusive conflict claiming victory. Despite pressure from the international community, Iran has also continued to advance its uranium enrichment program, prompting fears that its true goal is the development of nuclear weapons. Further, by 2007 it had become clear that Iran was providing arms and training to Shiite militias and extremists in Iraq.[2]

U.S. Interests

Despite these new and challenging dynamics, two enduring U.S. interests in the region remain reliable access to energy and the security of Israel. In the early twenty-first century, additional important U.S. interests include securing stability and security in Iraq, preventing Iran from developing nuclear weapons, containing Islamist radicalism, and maintaining influence in a strategically important region of high volatility.

Oil. The Middle East is the world's most important source of oil exports. Persian Gulf countries produce 28% of the world's oil, retain more than 70% of the world's excess oil production capacity, and hold 65% of the world's oil reserves.[3] The importance of the Middle East as an oil-producing region has continued to increase over time as the U.S. dependence on imported oil and global demand have continued to grow. Whereas 35% of U.S. oil consumption came from foreign imports in 1973, by 2006 the number had grown to 60%. Although only 17% of U.S. imports come from the Gulf area, the global oil market is essentially an integrated whole; the loss of Persian Gulf oil due to armed conflict or terrorism would greatly affect world energy supplies and lead to increased competition for resources located elsewhere.[4] Three fourths of Japan's and two thirds of western Europe's oil imports originate in the vicinity of the Persian Gulf. Without these supplies, consumers in these countries would be required to seek other sources. Additionally, China's demand for oil has increased tremendously since the 1990s; it has overtaken Japan as the world's second-largest consumer of oil, after the United States. It imports 32% of its oil, with 58% originating in the Middle East.[5] Absent highly unlikely dramatic progress in the development of alternative fuel sources, the rapid development of such countries as India and China will continue to fuel increased global demand for oil for at least several decades to come.

The Security of Israel. U.S. relations with Israel have always been complicated. Prior to Israel's creation in 1948, members of the U.S. government clashed over whether recognizing the nascent Jewish state would be a liability, given the U.S. relationship with the Arab world and especially the Persian Gulf states.[6] Despite competing interests, President Harry Truman ultimately decided to back the creation of the new state.

Since 1948, commitment to the security of Israel has been one of the most enduring features of U.S. policy in the Middle East. This is true despite periodic

Table 20.1 Middle East Key Statistics

Country	Total Population (millions)	Average Life Expectancy	GDP US$ (billions)	GDP/Capita (US$)	Population Living in Poverty (%)	Military Spending % of GDP	Military Spending US$ (millions)	Human Development Index Ranking (out of 177)
Israel	6.4	79.6	140.3	26,800	21.6	7.3	9,826	23
Kuwait	2.5	77.4	60.8	23,100	—	5.3	4,403	33
Qatar	0.9	74	30.8	29,800	—	10	2,198	35
United Arab Emirates	4.4	75.7	109.3	49,700	19.5	3.1	2,561	39
Bahrain	0.7	74.7	12.1	25,600	—	4.5	500	41
Oman	3.2	73.6	27.3	14,400	—	11.4	3,695	58
Saudi Arabia	27.6	75.9	282	13,800	—	10	25,372	61
Turkey	71.2	72.9	361.1	9,100	20	5.3	11,728*	84
Jordan	5.6	71.6	11.5	2,117	11.7	8.2	973	86
Lebanon	3.9	73.2	20.6	5,900	28	3.1	638	88
Iran, Islamic Republic of	65.4	70.6	193.5	8,700	40	2.5	5,223	94
Syrian Arab Republic	19.3	70.6	24.3	4,100	12.5	5.9	1,257	108
Egypt	80.3	71.6	85.4	4,200	20	3.4	3,834	112
Yemen	22.2	62.5	15.1	1,000	45.2	6.6	584	153
Iraq	27.5	69.3	40.7	1,900	—	8.6	—	—

Sources: CIA World Factbook, updated December 13, 2007, UNHDR Human Development Index 2007/2008; IISS Military Balance 2007.
*Datum for Turkey found under NATO Europe section in the Military Balance 2007.

disputes between the two states, including Israel's participation with Britain and France in the Suez War in 1956 and Israel's continued settlement of the West Bank and Gaza after its occupation of the Palestinian territories in 1967. An important motivation for continuing U.S. support is that Israel is the only democracy in the Middle East. That support is consistently and persuasively bolstered by the unflagging efforts of the American-Israel Political Action Committee (AIPAC), which is widely recognized as the most powerful lobbying organization in the United States. AIPAC's efforts are seconded by various influential Christian groups.

Despite the early political support provided by Truman during Israel's founding, U.S. materiel support for Israel did not become truly significant until the mid-1960s. Until then, France and Britain had been its major suppliers of arms. In 1966, responding to Israel's fears of increased Soviet arms deliveries to Egypt and Syria, the United States agreed to provide it with large quantities of modern military equipment. Due to this continuing arms relationship, as well as to the terms of the 1979 Camp David Peace Accords (which are discussed later in this chapter), Israel remains the largest single recipient of U.S. foreign aid.

The Stability and Security of Iraq.   Since the 2003 invasion, the United States has been heavily engaged politically, economically, and militarily in Iraq. Although successful in toppling Saddam, it was still debatable in late 2008 whether the U.S.-led invasion had led to a stable, effective successor regime capable of maintaining internal order and protecting Iraq from external interference. Indeed, the continued U.S. presence in Iraq itself proved to be a problem because it served as a source of Arab humiliation and bolstered perceptions that the United States intends to dominate and exploit the region. Yet premature withdrawal could create a catastrophe. According to the 2006 bipartisan Iraq Study Group, failure of U.S. policy in Iraq could lead to ethnic cleansing, a large-scale humanitarian crisis, a violent sectarian partition of the state, a brutal successor regime, a broader regional conflict, and the possibility of "Sunni-Shia clashes across the Islamic world."[7]

As a consequence of deterioration in security conditions within Iraq in 2006, American strategy shifted in early 2007. From a focus on finding and fighting insurgents, U.S. forces switched to a "clear and hold" approach—i.e., clearing selected areas (Baghdad initially) of insurgents and then holding those areas with a continuing troop presence. The additional troops needed to execute the new strategy were provided by additional Iraqi units but also by the United States. Accordingly, about thirty thousand more U.S. troops were "surged" to Iraq, bringing the total there to more than one hundred sixty thousand. As of late 2008, the surge was proving successful, though the durability of improved security conditions was far from assured. Critics pointed out that the Iraqi political reconciliation necessary for long-term stability and progress in Iraq was proceeding at an unacceptably slow pace.

Iran and the Proliferation of Weapons of Mass Destruction.   Regarding Iran's nuclear program, the U.S. National Security Strategy of 2006 states:

> For almost 20 years, the Iranian regime hid many of its key nuclear efforts from the international community. Yet the regime continues to claim that it does not seek to develop nuclear weapons. The Iranian regime's true intentions are clearly revealed by the regime's refusal to negotiate in good faith; its refusal to come into compliance with its international obligations by providing the [International Atomic Energy Agency] access to nuclear sites and resolving troubling questions; and the aggressive statements of its President calling for Israel to be "wiped off the face of the Earth."[8]

If Iran were to develop nuclear weapons, it seems likely (though hardly certain) that it could be deterred from their deliberate use through the threat of retaliation, just as nuclear-armed states have been deterred in the past. However, Iran's possession of nuclear weapons could lead to their use by miscalculation or accident. Moreover, there are at least three other significant concerns. First, Iran may deliberately, or accidentally through an inadequate system of controls, transfer a nuclear device to a nonstate actor who cannot be deterred in the same fashion. Second, Iran's possession of a nuclear arsenal may spark an effort at military preemption by another state, such as Israel. Third, Iran may set off a dangerous regional nuclear arms race among Sunni-dominated states distressed by Shia Iran's possession of nuclear weapons.

Political Islam and Countering Radical Islamist Ideology.   U.S. interests in the Middle East include protecting the United States and its citizens wherever they might be from acts of terrorism inspired by an extreme ideology that justifies public violence—even the targeting of noncombatants—in the name of jihad. (*Jihad* is often translated as *struggle*, which may imply nonviolent means but is also used in the context of violent action.) Countering radical extremists requires the capturing or killing of Islamist terrorists as well as ending the willingness of states, such as Iran and Syria, to harbor and support such terrorist groups. An even more difficult, but essential, task necessary to long-term success is the delegitimization of radical Islamists' claims and violent acts. That effort must begin with an understanding of Islam, including differentiating between its extreme interpretations and its liberal interpretations. These interpretations compete for legitimacy and popular support throughout the Muslim world.

Islam, the world's second-largest religion, implores its followers to submit to the will and ultimate sovereignty of God (Allah) as communicated through Muhammad, the final prophet of God, in its holy book, the Koran.[9] Muhammad's proclamation in Mecca in AD 622 that there is only one God and that all humanity is subject to God's authority ultimately had a unifying effect on the previously fractured, tribal cultures of pre-Islamic Arabia. The subsequent rapid spread of the Islamic caliphate throughout the region and into Europe and Asia serves, for many Muslims, as historical validation of the truth and authenticity of God's revelations. Inherent in this sense of authenticity is the belief that the early generations of Muslims flourished (were blessed by God) because of their devoutness and adherence to Islamic law and traditions.[10] The fact that the Muslim world today lives in relative powerlessness and poverty—especially compared with the West—constitutes a serious, ever-present source of humiliation for some believers. They ask, as scholar Bernard Lewis suggests in a classic text about Islam, "What Went Wrong?"[11]

One answer, within the fundamentalist strain of Islamic political thought, holds that diminished devoutness among subsequent generations of Muslims led to eventual Western exploitation and domination of the region.[12] Accordingly, restoring the Muslim world to its rightful state of societal justice and strength will require a return to first principles. Dutiful Muslims must reject corrupting Western influences and man-made political institutions and rise up and wage jihad against corrupt regional regimes and the West.[13] The United States is a particular target; radical Islamists argue that the United States is at war with Islam. Many Muslims see U.S. political, economic, and military engagement in the Middle East—particularly U.S. support for Israel and military interventions in Afghanistan and Iraq—as confirmation of this narrative.

However, a competing approach exists that is considered by many to be legitimate within the İslamic tradition. Sometimes termed *Liberal Islam*, this approach promotes pluralism, liberalization, freedom of conscience and political participation, rights for women and non-Muslims, and interpretation of Islamic law in light of modern political, economic, and social conditions.[14] Liberal Islam upholds the personal and political sovereignty of God (not popular sovereignty as in the West) and insists that the restoration of societal justice, vitality, and strength in the Muslim world will require a return to Islam's true first principles (which include liberal principles), but in the context of modern political and economic institutions. Dutiful Muslims, it is held, should rise up publicly and oppose radical Islamists, who are misguided practitioners of an illegitimate doctrine and therefore acting in opposition to God. Unfortunately, these liberal voices are too often drowned out by the sounds of the fundamentalists' suicide bombers.

Clearly, the United States has an interest in combating violent religious extremists and in countering the ideology from which violence stems. A challenge for the United States is to protect its interests while refining its political, economic, and military engagement in the Middle East to strengthen liberal Islamic thought and institutions and to encourage the delegitimization of extremism. Of course, the United States has a limited capacity to directly facilitate the delegitimization process, so much will depend upon developments within the region and between extremist and moderate Muslims. The continued intractability of the Israeli-Palestinian issue, America's unwavering alignment with Israel, U.S. support of some repressive regimes in the Middle East, and the continued presence of U.S. troops in the region all combine to limit American influence in meeting this challenge.

Continuing Regional Influence.   With the 1968 withdrawal of British forces from the area, the United States and the Soviet Union became the region's principal external influences. Using U.S. support for Israel as the area's anvil, the Soviets continually sought to hammer out a solid anti-American Arab bloc. Military aid and advisers were the principal means used, although trade and civilian aid projects, such as support for Egypt's high-profile Aswan Dam, were also employed. The Soviet Union's strategy yielded mixed results but was relatively successful in Iraq and Syria.

The disappearance of the Soviet Union left the United States as the only major external actor in the region. In the absence of the Soviets, American military power was dramatically demonstrated by the 1990–1991 Gulf War and in late 2001–2002, in Afghanistan. Awareness of and respect for that power lingers on, although the setbacks in the Iraq War demonstrated its limits. The attractiveness of America and the perceived legitimacy of American leadership have been drastically reduced by the travails in Iraq. Although for decades U.S. policy in the region has been mostly distrusted by the Arab world, those negative views reached new peaks with the American invasion of Iraq. Even in countries with strong intergovernmental ties with the U.S., such as Saudi Arabia, Egypt, Jordan, and Morocco, the "street" was overwhelmingly negative, with its conclusion that the invasion was "to control oil, protect Israel, and weaken the Muslim world."[15] Clearly, it will be essential to mount a major public diplomacy effort to offset these views. It is equally clear that substantive policy modifications and new initiatives will also be needed, or the public diplomacy effort will founder. In this context, successful handling of Iran's defiance on the nuclear issue and its meddling in Iraq will be especially significant.

History of U.S. Involvement in the Region

Increased U.S. Engagement and the Importance of Oil.   Starting in the mid-1960s, a series of political and economic changes in the Middle East and the rest of the world combined to increase the importance of the region to U.S. national security. These trends and developments included an enormous increase in global oil consumption, the Israeli occupation of the West Bank and Gaza during the 1967 war, the British withdrawal from the Persian Gulf area in 1968, and the broadening influence of the Soviet Union in the region.

These changes affected the relationships between the United States and the states of the Middle East in three important ways. First, several U.S. interests in the region that previously had been of only marginal concern were elevated to the level of important or even vital. Second, the growing Soviet presence and declining British power made it crucial to find new means to protect these newly important interests. Third, U.S. interests in the Middle East, such as the security of Israel and of Persian Gulf oil, which had been treated by policy makers as essentially separate, became increasingly intertwined.

The rapid increase in world oil consumption after 1965 fundamentally altered the conditions governing the production and distribution of oil. Before then, the major oil companies had been able to ensure that the supply of oil met or slightly exceeded demand. By 1970, however, the supply of oil was not increasing fast enough to keep pace with escalating demand, and competition among consumers for available oil intensified. Furthermore, in 1970, first Libya and then others began to pressure oil companies for improved concessions and payments. As producing states gradually realized that the market for oil had become a seller's market, they nationalized the oil business and raised prices.

Between 1968 and 1975, the average price of oil increased from less than $2 per barrel to roughly $11 per barrel. Most of this increase occurred at the end of 1973 and early in 1974, when prices were quadrupled following an embargo by Arab producers against the United States and the Netherlands because of their support for Israel during the 1973 Arab-Israeli War. In the United States and other importing states, such steep increases led to serious balance-of-payments problems and contributed to inflation. The realization was driven home that America had a strong interest in ensuring reliable access to Middle Eastern oil at acceptable prices.

The 1980–1988 Iran-Iraq War posed a renewed threat to oil supplies as each side attacked the other's production and refinery facilities. Despite the consequent loss of about 3 million barrels per day of exports, oil was initially plentiful due to unprecedented standby production capacity, primarily in Saudi Arabia. Nor did the years of conflict, including Iraq's and Iran's targeting of tanker ships in the Persian Gulf beginning in 1984, seriously threaten overall oil flows from the Gulf. Pipelines could, to a limited extent, divert Saudi and Iraqi oil to the Red Sea. However, it should be noted that the 8 million barrels per day or more exported through the Gulf accounted for more than 40% of world trade in oil; effective closure of the Gulf's 28-mile wide Strait of Hormuz would have wreaked havoc on the global economy.

The risk during the Persian Gulf crisis of 1990–1991 was not only that the conflict would interrupt the supply of oil but also that if Saddam were to control most Persian Gulf oil reserves and the choke point of the Strait of Hormuz, he would have been in a position to set a monopoly price on the world's oil. The resulting U.S. intervention stemmed not only from a desire to return sovereignty to Kuwait but also from an American appreciation of the potential threat to the health of the U.S. and international economy.

By 2005, the price per barrel of oil had spiked to $70 as a product of increased demand and limitations in refining capability throughout the global oil industry.[16] In July 2008, the figure reached a record of $147 with continuing market volatility.

Such terrorist groups as al-Qa'ida decry U.S. efforts to ensure access to the region's oil through support for "un-Islamic governments." But regional disengagement is simply not a viable U.S. option. Given the decades that would be needed to develop sufficient alternative liquid fuels, dependence of the U.S. and the global economy on oil will mandate continued U.S. efforts to establish partnerships with friendly governments in the Middle East into the foreseeable future.

Support for Israel.   As noted above, it was not until the mid-1960s that Jerusalem began to receive large amounts of military and financial aid from Washington. In response to Soviet support for Egypt and Syria prior to the 1967 war, the United States began providing substantial military arms and equipment to

Israel. Since that time, a continuing challenge for U.S. foreign policy in the Middle East has been to balance its relations with Israel and the Arab states.

In 1973, Egyptian President Anwar Sadat launched a surprise attack against Israel, jeopardizing the existence of the small state. After being informed of a Soviet airlift to Syria, President Richard Nixon authorized a full-scale U.S. airlift to Israel.[17] All told, Israel received an emergency package of $2 billion worth of U.S. arms during the crisis. Although the Arab states initially inflicted severe casualties on the Israelis, they were unable to retain control of the territory they gained early in the war.

Despite the continuing flow of U.S. arms, Israel came to recognize that excessive reliance on U.S. goodwill could restrict its freedom of action. As a result, it embarked on a program to acquire and manufacture enough military equipment to enable its forces to wage a war against the combined forces of Egypt, Syria, Jordan, Iraq, and Saudi Arabia for three weeks without exhausting their supplies. Strategically, the Camp David Accords and the Egyptian-Israeli peace treaty of 1979 helped Israel achieve this goal. The United States facilitated the acceptance of the 1979 peace treaty with pledges of massive financial and military aid to Egypt and Israel. This assurance of supply, combined with Israel's own production and military predominance in the region, seriously reduced the possibility that the United States would be able to pressure Israel in a future crisis. Importantly, Israel also gained flexibility through the removal of Egypt as a possible opponent.

An important test came when Israel preemptively and successfully struck Iraq's Osirak nuclear facility in 1981. Although President Ronald Reagan condemned Israel's attack in the United Nations (UN) Security Council and temporarily suspended the delivery of F16 aircraft that Israel had already purchased, the Arab world was outraged at what they perceived to be a mild American response to an attack on Iraq's sovereignty. Israel also demonstrated its strategic independence by invading Lebanon in June 1982 in response to Palestinian guerilla attacks launched into Israel from southern Lebanon. Eventually Israeli troops laid siege to West Beirut, forcing the Palestinian Liberation Organization (PLO) to withdraw from its sanctuary in Lebanon. Only after the Reagan administration threatened a breach in relations did the Israelis call off their siege. Nevertheless, Israel and the United States were drawn into the quagmire of Lebanon's civil war, and both incurred serious human and political costs before they were able to withdraw. Israel's troops did not leave Lebanon completely until Israeli Prime Minister Ehud Barak's unilateral withdrawal in 2000.

Reagan's successor, President George H. W. Bush, sought to distance himself somewhat from the right-wing Likud government of Israeli Prime Minister Yitzhak Shamir. Moreover, the first Gulf War in 1991 and America's aid to Kuwait restored some U.S. credibility in the Arab world. Consequently, George H. W. Bush was able to convince key Arab states to participate in the Madrid Conference, discussed below, and to undertake bilateral and multilateral negotiations with Israel. He also opened talks with the Palestinians and threatened to withhold financial aid from Israel in a fruitless effort to pressure Shamir to cease constructing Israeli settlements in the West Bank and Gaza Strip.

Following his predecessor's acrimonious relationship with Israel's leadership, President Bill Clinton fostered warm ties with Israeli Prime Minister Yitzhak Rabin. Building on the 1993 Oslo Accords between Israel and the Palestinians, Clinton actively sought to build a sustained peace. His efforts culminated in the U.S.-sponsored Camp David summit in July 2000 between Barak and Palestinian Chairman Yassir Arafat. Unfortunately these leaders failed at the summit to resolve final status issues for the creation of a Palestinian state.

When President George W. Bush assumed office in January 2001, he initially neglected the Israeli-Palestinian peace process and then moved firmly into backing Israel following the terrorist attacks on the United States later that year. To many in the Bush administration, Israel's war against suicide bombers and the U.S. struggle against international terrorists constituted the basis for even deeper cooperation between the two countries. An added complication later arose when Hamas, an organization that refused to recognize Israel and renounce violence, won a majority in the January 2006 Palestinian parliamentary elections. Despite these challenges, Secretary of State Condoleezza Rice increased U.S. activism in the peace process during the second four years of the George W. Bush administration. It remains to be seen whether these and subsequent efforts will result in real progress on the establishment of a Palestinian state.

Operation Desert Storm: The First Gulf War and Its Aftermath. On August 2, 1990, still reeling from the manpower losses and economic dislocations of a stalemated eight-year war with Iran, Iraq invaded the tiny sheikdom of Kuwait. Led by the United States, most of the world responded with condemnations and a variety of economic sanctions. By the end of 1990, most countries supported military action if Iraq failed to immediately and unconditionally withdraw. Last-minute diplomatic efforts failed to resolve the crisis, and a U.S.-led coalition attacked Iraq on January 16, 1991. Coalition forces from thirty-four countries, numbering more than seven hundred fifty thousand thousands of aircraft, and nearly two hundred warships, liberated Kuwait in a forty-four-day campaign.

Within two weeks of the start of hostilities, the Iraqi army in Kuwait was cut off from its command and control linkages and most of its logistical lifelines. Only the continuing threat of Iraqi Scud missiles aimed at key Israeli and Saudi cities remained a danger, but, by the third week of the air campaign, actual launches of Iraqi Scud missiles were reduced to zero. The complex ground campaign began on February 23, 1991, and in a one-hundred-hour assault and flanking maneuver, allied forces encircled and defeated the Iraqi army.

Concerned with maintaining the coalition and fearful that complete destruction of Iraq's forces would result in chaos and create a power vacuum that Iran could exploit, the U.S.-led coalition allowed a substantial portion of the Iraqi army to escape. As a consequence, and in defiance of ceasefire agreements, Saddam was able to reconstitute a sizable force that he used a few months later to quell uprisings of internal opponents, including Kurds in the north and Shiites in the south. After much Kurdish suffering, the UN imposed a protective area in Iraqi Kurdistan and provided humanitarian relief there. Further, in 1992, the international community imposed a no-fly zone over Iraqi territory south of the 36th parallel to protect the mostly Shiite local communities from Saddam's air power. Despite these measures and continuing economic sanctions that proved painful to Iraq's people and damaging to its economy, Saddam resisted full compliance with the cease-fire agreement's call for the destruction of all of Iraq's missiles and chemical, biological, and nuclear weapons manufacturing facilities.

The UN sanctions against Baghdad were an important component of Washington's overall policy of *dual-containment* in the Persian Gulf. This policy, articulated in 1993, was designed to contain and isolate Iran and Iraq. Although U.S. policy toward these two states fell under the same framework, Washington's objectives for each were different. Whereas a change in regime became virtually a prerequisite for a resumption of U.S.-Iraq relations, the United States demanded only that Tehran alter its behavior by terminating its support for terrorism and its efforts to develop WMDs.

To many contemporary observers, the Gulf War of 1991 marked the beginning of a new era. For the first time, the United States became massively involved militarily on the ground in the Middle East. Some Western observers contended that the war's end provided an opportunity for a new world order of cooperation among the great powers after the demise of the Soviet Union. Others saw the war's conclusion as an opportunity to transform traditional political structures in the Middle East through the spread of pluralism and democracy. One immediate effect was that Americans achieved new credibility within the region. The United States took advantage of this opportunity to press for an international peace conference to resolve the Arab-Israeli conflict and eventually arranged the October 1991 Madrid Conference.

Except for Egypt, which had signed a peace agreement with Israel in March 1979, this regional peace conference saw the first direct negotiations between Israel and its Arab neighbors. This Arab recognition of Israel's right to exist, although only implicit, set the stage for agreements between Jerusalem and a number of regional actors and states, most notably the Oslo Accords with the PLO in 1993 and a treaty of peace with Jordan in 1994. In addition, Arab states in the Gulf and North Africa established commercial relations with Israel.

U.S. Military Operations in Afghanistan and Iraq.   Following the 9/11 attacks, George W. Bush declared a "war on terrorism." It soon emerged that fifteen of the nineteen terrorist hijackers were from Saudi Arabia, which resulted in consequent deterioration of relations between the United States and Saudi Arabia. Further, under pressure from militant Islamic groups and the Saudis themselves, the United States removed its troops from Saudi Arabia. As covered further in Chapter 19, in October 2001, the United States attacked Afghanistan to force from power the Taliban regime that had supported al-Qa'ida with finances and training bases. By spring 2002, U.S. and Afghan forces had largely suppressed Taliban and al-Qa'ida elements and had succeeded in establishing a pro-American government in Kabul headed by Mohammed Karzai.

After this apparent success in Afghanistan, the United States again turned its attention to Saddam in Iraq. Although Saddam's ouster was considered during the first Gulf War, George H. W. Bush had opted to end the war once Saddam was driven from Kuwait. The primary considerations behind that decision were the status of the international coalition that had fought the war and the obligations that the United States would assume if it decided to overthrow the Iraqi government.[18] Slightly more than a decade later, in the wake of the large-scale terrorist attacks on U.S. soil, the calculus had changed. George W. Bush was convinced that Saddam's noncompliance with UN resolutions on the elimination of WMDs meant Saddam had such weapons; moreover, George W. Bush was more willing to accept the risks associated with changing the Iraqi regime.

In his 2002 State of the Union address, George W. Bush labeled Iran, Iraq, and North Korea an "axis of evil," alleging that those states supported terrorist groups and were pursuing WMDs. His administration spent the next year making the case that Iraq possessed WMDs and had connections with al-Qa'ida and other terrorist organizations. While seeking international support, the United States made it clear that it would act unilaterally if necessary.

After considerable internal debate, the George W. Bush administration opted to present its case to the UN. The Security Council passed Resolution 1441, which called on Saddam to admit UN weapons inspectors and threatened severe repercussions in the event of his refusal to comply. Saddam then permitted UN inspectors access to purported weapon sites and delivered some documents that ostensibly revealed the status of Iraq's weapons programs. The United States, however, pointed to Saddam's repeated noncompliance with earlier UN resolutions and limitations in his current compliance, emphasizing his untrustworthiness.

On March 17, 2003, in a televised address, George W. Bush gave Saddam and his sons forty-eight hours to leave Iraq. When the deadline passed and Saddam remained, the United States and the United Kingdom moved pre-positioned troops from Kuwait into southern Iraq and began air strikes on key targets. Within two weeks, the United States and other coalition forces had gained control of southern Iraq and were preparing to move on to Baghdad. Despite limited resistance that slightly slowed the advance, including opposition from irregular fedayeen fighters, Baghdad fell on April 9, 2003. In the north, Kurdish militia took over key cities, such as Mosul, Kirkuk, and Erbil. George W. Bush declared the end of major combat operations in a dramatic speech on an aircraft carrier in the Persian Gulf on May 1, 2003.

With this declaration, postconflict requirements, such as sealing borders, maintaining order, rebuilding Iraqi infrastructure, and administering the country until a new Iraqi government could be established, rose to the fore. With insufficient numbers of forces in country, the initial U.S. response to these requirements was grossly inadequate.[19] The first civilian entity charged with establishing an administration until the Iraqis were prepared to take over the governance of their country was the Office of Reconstruction and Humanitarian Assistance (ORHA). This organization was established on January 20, 2003, and led by retired Lieutenant General Jay Garner. Garner's prewar understanding that his work in Iraq would

Lurie's NewsCartoon

Expecting the newly-born Iraqi government

Reprinted with permission of Ranan Lurie.

take only three months lends credence to a pervasive view that the George W. Bush administration did not plan sufficiently for "worst-case scenarios" for post-war Iraq.[20] Garner arrived in Baghdad on April 21 after a significant amount of destruction had already occurred from widespread looting. He left Baghdad on June 1, and ORHA was dissolved on June 16, 2003.

By May 2003, the president had selected former Ambassador L. Paul Bremer III to head the Coalition Provisional Authority (CPA), which would replace ORHA and assume responsibility for reconstruction and political transition. Arriving in Iraq on May 12, 2003, Bremer made two key, controversial decisions within his first thirty days in Baghdad: to disband the Iraqi Army and to engage in a "de-Baathification" of the Iraqi government—i.e., purge Saddam loyalists from all positions of authority. Although there were arguments in favor of both of these decisions, their impact proved to be disastrous, increasing the number of opponents of the occupation and vastly heightening the difficulty of creating order and stability. After little more than a year, on June 28, 2004, the CPA handed sovereignty back to the Iraqis.

As postinvasion challenges in Iraq grew, the George W. Bush administration hoped that Saddam's capture and Iraqi elections would limit the violence. On December 13, 2003, Saddam was captured in a dirt hole near his hometown of Tikrit. In December 2005, elections were held to select the Iraqi legislature. Although these elections indicated progress, most people voted along sectarian lines, and after the elections it took almost five months for a government to form.

Meanwhile, violence increased in scale and complexity. In addition to the mostly Sunni insurgents, other violent actors—including Shiite militias, foreign fighters, and criminals—entered the fray.

By 2009, U.S. casualties numbered more than 4,200. Estimates of the number of Iraqi insurgents and civilians killed ranged from one to six hundred thousand.[21] American popular support for the war plummeted, and Congress sought to restrict the president's capability to continue American involvement by attaching various exit requirements to funding provisions. Though specific exit dates were eliminated from funding bills, public debate over enduring U.S. military involvement in Iraq continued to escalate.

Factors Affecting Regional Stability

The ability of the United States to protect its national interests in the Middle East has been significantly affected by the regional issues already mentioned. However, such highly visible specific issues are only part of the challenge. An important underlying contributor can be found in the sources of political and social instability that continue to characterize much of the region.

State Strength.   Many Middle Eastern states were either created or significantly altered after World War I in a highly arbitrary fashion by the European powers that dominated the region. The political systems established to govern the new entities reflected European rather than local interests and values, and borders were drawn largely to satisfy the interests of the European powers. As a result, some ethnic or cultural groups who conceived of themselves as separate were incorporated into a single state. In other cases, cohesive linguistic or religious groups were divided into several states dominated by their traditional antagonists. Most prominent among these are the Kurds, who are dispersed in a large geographic area cutting across parts of Turkey, Iraq, Syria, and Iran.

As a result of these artificial boundaries, once the states of the Middle East achieved independence, the level of national cohesion and political solidarity tended to be low. In all parts of the region, the focal points of loyalty were the family, village, tribe, and ethnic group. Ties of regionalism, ethnic and cultural solidarity, and religion competed vigorously with the new state governments for popular allegiance.

Complicating these internal political dynamics was the widespread appeal of Arab nationalism. Egypt's charismatic leader, Gamal Abd al-Nasser, used Arab nationalist rhetoric in the 1950s and 1960s to galvanize Arab masses across the Middle East against "reactionary" regimes in Jordan and Saudi Arabia, Zionism, and continued Western colonialism. The allure of Arab nationalism led to experiments with Arab unity, the most prominent of which was the "United Arab Republic" formed in 1958 between Egypt and Syria. This union lasted only three and a half years, collapsing from political differences between Nasser and Syria's leadership.

In the competition among Arab states in the Middle East, Arab nationalism itself became a source of contention. Border clashes and attempts to subvert rival regimes, either through propaganda or the distribution of arms and subsidies to potential dissidents, were common.[22] Conflicts between Arab states were further exacerbated by tensions stemming from rapid economic change. After World War II, countries of the Middle East saw land reforms, the development of heavy industry, and the growth of state ownership and bureaucratic controls over the economy. Increased taxes, scarcities, and heavy inflation seemed to accompany the new economic policies. Economic dissatisfaction was easily converted into political unrest.

In the oil-producing countries, the problems caused by economic development were different but no less acute. The vast funds generated by the oil industry enabled them to initiate major economic development programs, although the required technical expertise was largely absent. As a result, by the late 1970s, Americans, Europeans, Egyptians, and Palestinians played key roles in the economies, bureaucracies, and educational systems of the oil-producing countries of the Arabian peninsula. Yemenis, Pakistanis, and Indians made up much of the unskilled labor force. This foreign presence became a politically sensitive issue and a source of grievance. For example, in Iran prior to the 1979 revolution, the Islamic opposition was able to use highly visible Westerners as a symbol of the corrupt Pahlavi regime. To this day, American relationships with regimes that are friendly to U.S. interests and the continued presence of U.S. forces in the region are sources of widespread resentment. As merely the most dramatic example, Osama bin Laden proclaimed in 1996 that the U.S. troop presence in Saudi Arabia was a justification for Muslims to attack Americans and U.S. interests worldwide.[23]

Arab-Israeli Conflict.   As outlined above, one of the most profound and persistent of the many regional problems in the Middle East is the Arab-Israeli conflict. In 1947, the UN called for the partition of Palestine to create a Jewish and Arab state in an attempt by the international community to alleviate the tensions between the two groups. The United States voted in favor of the UN partition plan of a two-state solution with Jerusalem under international administration. On May 14, 1948, David Ben-Gurion proclaimed the formation of the state of Israel and became its first prime minister. Full-scale war promptly broke out, with the armies of five neighboring Arab states intervening haphazardly on the side of the Palestinians.

By April 1949, Israel had defeated the combined Arab forces and gained control of additional territory that had not been assigned to it in the original partition plan. More than seven hundred thousand Palestinian Arabs had been expelled or fled from their homes and were living as stateless refugees in neighboring Arab countries. Jordan took control of the West Bank, and Egypt maintained authority over the Gaza Strip—both areas assigned to the Palestinians in the original plan.

Arab-Israeli hostility was deepened by Israel's inconclusive 1956 attack on Egypt, in concert with the British and French, following Nasser's nationalization of the Suez Canal. A number of hostile Arab moves in the spring of 1967—including Nasser's ejection of UN peacekeeping forces that had been present in the Sinai since 1956, Egypt's closing of the Straits of Tiran at the Gulf of Aqaba to Israeli shipping, and the massing of Syrian forces on the Golan Heights— precipitated a surprise preemptive strike by the Israeli air force on the morning of June 5. The June 1967 war, in which Israel defeated Egypt, Syria, and Jordan on three fronts in six days, radically altered the political and military balance in the Middle East. The combined Arab forces suffered a humiliating defeat as Israel occupied the Sinai Peninsula, the Gaza Strip, West Bank, and Syria's Golan Heights. Continued Israeli occupation of those lands increased antagonism toward Israel to the point that this animosity took precedence over various inter-Arab disputes.

The resulting inter-Arab rapprochement was demonstrated by the joint Egyptian-Syrian surprise attack on Israel in October 1973. The Saudis and other oil-producing states in the region supported the Arab cause with oil embargoes against the United States and the Netherlands. Despite early Arab successes, once again the Israelis were victorious.

On the Arab side, the Egyptian-Israeli peace treaty, signed in March 1979 in Washington, D.C., signaled Egypt's shift from further support of pan-Arab military confrontation to policies of political accommodation and economic cooperation with Israel. In return, Egypt regained control over the Sinai, captured by Israel in 1967, and gained an Israeli promise of autonomy for the predominantly Palestinian West Bank area. The Saudis joined the other Arab states in opposing Egypt's separate peace with Israel.

No serious progress was made in the 1980s in resolving the thorny Palestinian problem. On December 8, 1987, an Israeli army vehicle hit a car and killed four Palestinian passengers. This incident sparked the first *intifada*—a spontaneous wave of mass demonstrations and violent riots in the Israeli-occupied territories that lasted in varying degrees of intensity for several years.[24] Despite these developments, in December 1988, PLO Chairman Yasir Arafat recognized Israel's existence and renounced the use of terrorism, satisfying U.S. preconditions for talks with the PLO. Over the objections of the Israeli government and the American Jewish community, the Reagan administration began meeting with PLO leaders in Tunis. But the talks, which were intended to lay the groundwork for Israeli-Palestinian negotiations, broke down in March 1989 after a planned Palestinian attack on a Tel Aviv beach was thwarted at the last moment by an Israeli coastal patrol.

Beyond the Israeli-Palestinian track, the overall record on reconciliation between Israel and its Arab neighbors has been mixed. The 1994 Jordan-Israel peace agreement set out an ambitious agenda of cooperative relations between the two countries in diverse fields, including economic development, tourism, environmental protection, cultural exchanges, and even security.[25] Although official relations have developed, popular Jordanian opposition to the agreement remains strong. Because a majority of Jordanians are of Palestinian origin, Jordanians are resistant to the development of normal relations with Israel until the Israeli-Palestinian conflict is resolved.

In May 1999, Barak became the Israeli prime minister and formed a coalition that championed a final resolution of the Arab-Israeli conflict. He began direct negotiations with Syria on the future of the Golan Heights, but those talks were suspended when Israel and Syria hit a key obstacle: Israel wanted security guarantees, while Syria required Israel to agree to full withdrawal from the Golan Heights before it would make any concessions.

On Israel's northern border, Syria controlled Lebanon's foreign policy and limited Lebanon's ability to make a separate peace treaty with Israel. After the assassination of former Lebanese Prime Minister Rafik Hariri in February 2005, Lebanese protesters poured into the streets, demanding the withdrawal of Syrian troops that had been present in Lebanon since 1976.[26] By April 2005, Syria had withdrawn its troops, and it appeared that Lebanon was on the road to building a new, more independent parliamentary democracy. Yet Hezbollah's continued control of Lebanon's southern border, as well as the July 2006 kidnapping of two Israeli soldiers, prompted a destructive war fought on Lebanese soil. Due to the tremendous destruction Israeli air strikes caused in Lebanon (an estimated $4 billion of damage) and the more than seven hundred fifty thousand refugees created by the conflict, it seems unlikely that Lebanon will respond positively in the near term to any efforts to create a peace treaty between the two countries.

The Israeli-Palestinian Peace Process.   Israel's national election of June 1992 returned the left-of-center Labor Party to power after fifteen years in opposition. The new prime minister, Rabin, a hero of the June 1967 war with impeccable credentials as a tough-minded security hawk, represented the mainstream of an Israeli electorate who wanted peace but did not want to compromise security or capitulate to Arab terror. Eventually, the lack of progress of other efforts convinced a number of leading political figures in Israel that the path to peace lay in direct negotiations with the PLO, which had been designated by the Arab League in 1974 to be the "sole, legitimate representative of the Palestinian people." With Labor's victory, the Israeli parliament was persuaded to lift the ban on private contacts with the PLO.[27] Direct negotiations between the PLO and Israel began in earnest in a secluded farmhouse outside the Norwegian city of Oslo in January 1993.

The Oslo negotiations resulted in the *Declaration of Principles*, also known as the Oslo Accords, signed by Rabin and Arafat in an extraordinary ceremony on the White House lawn on September 13, 1993. The agreement worked out in Oslo was a framework for negotiation intended to build trust between the two parties through incremental steps, the most prominent of which would be an Israeli withdrawal from significant portions of the West Bank and Gaza Strip. These redeployments did not include relinquishing control of external security or the security of the one hundred forty Jewish settlements in the occupied territories. The Oslo Accords were followed by the Cairo Agreement in May 1994, which committed Israel to withdraw from the Gaza Strip and the West Bank town of Jericho, paving the way for Arafat's first return to Palestine since the late 1960s. Further negotiations yielded a third agreement in September 1995, dubbed *Oslo B*. Cumulatively, these agreements promised the Palestinians limited autonomy, with authority over 90% of the Palestinian population in the West Bank and Gaza Strip. But by early 1998, Israel had ceded full control over only about 3% of the territory and shared control over an additional 24%.

Despite progress, extremists on both sides continued to oppose reconciliation. Terrorism and retaliation continued unabated. Israeli extremists made their opposition known through the assassination of Rabin in November 1995. In May 1996 elections, the Israeli public returned the Likud Party to power under the leadership of hard-liner Binyamin Netanyahu, who ran on a platform of "peace with security." Netanyahu demanded that the PA root out and destroy Palestinian extremist organizations. In Netanyahu's first year in power, the peace process ground to a halt. The Palestinians lacked faith in an Israeli political party that was inexorably opposed to the Oslo Accords and that advocated the continuation of Jewish settlement in disputed areas, including East Jerusalem, which the Palestinians considered their future capital.

By 2000, two years after the Palestinians were supposed to have reached final status agreements with Israel, they still lacked an independent state. The slow pace of the peace process along with the deteriorating economic and political situation of Palestinians set the stage for another rebellion. It was in this charged environment that the head of the Likud Party, Ariel Sharon, entered the mosque enclave above the Temple Mount on September 28, 2000, despite warnings that his visit would exacerbate tensions.[28] Sharon's aggressive assertion of Israeli sovereignty over one of the most holy places in Islam as well as Judaism at a sensitive stage in negotiations triggered a new escalation in violence. In contrast to the first intifada, the Palestinians embraced more violent means, including the use of firearms. It was clear that the Oslo Accords were dead.

To stem the heightened violence in the Middle East, the United States, Russia, European Union (EU), and the UN—known as the Middle East Quartet—drafted a road map for peace in December 2002. Although deferring complex issues, such as the return of refugees or the status of Jerusalem, the proposal called for a Palestinian state by 2005.[29] The road map led to a ceasefire that began on June 29, 2003. However, on August 14, 2003, Israel assassinated a Palestinian militant—a member of Islamic jihad—who Israel claimed was responsible for planning suicide attacks and who was in the midst of planning a new assault.[30] In response, the Islamic resistance movement Hamas carried out an attack on August 19 that killed twenty Israelis. The ceasefire was over, and the peace process was again in tatters. Two years later, however, Israel began to withdraw from Gaza and parts of the West Bank, reflecting Sharon's new acceptance of a two-state solution to the continuing crisis.

The death of Palestinian leader and national symbol Arafat in November 2004, coupled with the waning of the *Al Aqsa intifada* that had begun in September 2000, ushered in a period with the potential for peace and the consolidation of a democratic Palestine. The PA sought to stem the appeal of more violent organizations, such as Hamas, the Islamic jihad, and a secular group known as the Al Aksa Martyrs Brigade. Unfortunately, the PA did not reform sufficiently before the January 2006 elections, leading to Hamas's victory at the polls. Israel, the United States, and the EU have all refused to negotiate with Hamas until the organization recognizes Israel's right to exist, honors all previous agreements between the PA and Israel, and renounces terrorism. Despite enormous financial pressure (the

United States and the EU refuse to aid the PA until these conditions are met), Hamas has held firm in its refusal to comply with the aforementioned conditions.

Fresh American efforts to reinvigorate the road map were launched toward the end of the second George W. Bush administration. These led to the convening in Annapolis, Maryland, at the end of 2007 of a major conference attended not only by Israelis, Palestinians, and the Middle East Quartet, but also by a number of Arab states. However, the resulting minimal progress toward peace reaffirms that the conflict is likely to endure.

The Role of Iran.   Arabs and Iranians have coexisted uneasily within the framework of Islam since the Arab conquest of Persia in the AD seventh century. When subsequent Iranian empires were strong, they dominated Arab lands on both sides of the Persian Gulf. In contrast, when such empires were weak, local Arabs quickly threw off Iranian control. Arab-Iranian tension in recent decades stems partly from Arab fears that an increasingly strong Iran will seek to reassert its past hegemony over the Gulf.

After World War II, U.S. military assistance to thwart Soviet influence in Iran enabled the Shah, Mohammad Reza Shah Pahlavi, to expand and strengthen his armed forces considerably. In the late 1960s, the Shah began to purchase large quantities of arms designed to provide Iranian forces with a significant offensive capability. To the Arabs, and most significantly to Iraq, it seemed that these forces were oriented directly at them. From the Iranian point of view, such a military buildup was necessary to provide security for vital Persian Gulf oil fields and tanker facilities. Iranian diplomats went to great lengths to convince Arab rulers that Iran's military power posed no threat. At the same time, however, the Shah did not hesitate to use force to seize three Arab islands in the Persian Gulf in 1971 or to give military support to Kurdish rebels in Iraq.[31]

The Iranian revolution of 1978–1979 upset all the old assumptions, in Iran and elsewhere in the region. The Shah's accelerated economic development program was carried out with a heavy infusion of Western values and Western technicians to work on projects in infrastructure, industry, and health care. Though some Iranians were in favor of these developments, others criticized what they saw as a Westernizing effort and the slow pace of change, persistent inequality, government corruption, and authoritarian nature of the Shah's rule The precipitating cause of the Shah's downfall was his attempt to crush religious opposition to his regime. Although Iran's rulers had traditionally shared power with religious leaders, the Shah was convinced that the mosque stood against his modernization efforts. The Shah found himself confronted with a genuine popular revolution under the banners of resurgent Islam. Contributing to the Shah's demise was his increasingly repressive and authoritarian rule in the face of a sizable, politicized middle class.

Unwilling to share power with the middle class and alienated from traditional sources of support, the Shah relied more heavily on repression to maintain control. As a result, Tehran and other major cities saw massive demonstrations and street riots. This instability culminated in the Shah's flight from Iran in early 1979 and the Ayatollah Khomeini's triumphant return from exile in France to establish a "pure Islamic state."[32] The new government also antagonized and humiliated the United States. In November 1979, a group of several hundred students stormed the U.S. embassy in Tehran, taking more than fifty American diplomats and Marine guards hostage for 444 days. The United States was able to rally international opinion and law to its side, but the Iranians ignored the pressure. Western technicians, essential to maintaining the advanced weapons systems the Shah had purchased, were pushed out of the country and the once-large and well-armed Iranian military went into decline.

To exploit Iran's weakened, isolated condition and also to preempt possible Iranian incitement of Iraq's large Shiite population, Iraq launched a series of ground and air assaults against Iran in late September 1980. The resulting Iran-Iraq War lasted for eight years. Despite some initial territorial gains, Iraq was unable to prevail over Iran's weakened forces and was forced to withdraw in 1982. Iranian counteroffensives, which resulted in massive casualties particularly on the Iranian side, began immediately. The credibility of U.S. attempts to help terminate the war suffered sharply with the revelation of covert U.S. arms sales to Iran in 1985 and 1986 (the Iran-Contra affair). Both exhausted and with casualties in the hundreds of thousands, Iran and Iraq finally agreed in August 1988 to halt the fighting.

When the Ayatollah Khomeini died in 1989, the climate in Iran began to change. Prior to his death, Khomeini was able to use his charisma as well as growing repression to stave off the opposition. However, once he passed from the scene, reformist tendencies began to surface. Elected in 1989, President Ali Rafsanjani embarked on policies to ameliorate Iran's relations with Western powers. In 1997, Iran elected reformist President Muhammed Khatami, who ran on a platform that called for liberalization of the mass media, freedom of expression, civil rights, and pluralism. Relations between Iran and the United States finally began to thaw. Unfortunately, this trend proved short lived. The slow pace of domestic reforms, as well as the manipulation of the electoral system by the hard-line mullahs in the Guardian Council, who banned reformist candidates from running, brought hard-liner Ahmadinejad to power in the 2004 elections.

Ahmadinejad took an antagonistic approach to the West, called for Israel to be "wiped off the map," and accelerated aspects of Iran's nuclear program. In December 2006, the UN agreed to sanctions against Iran for its pursuit of uranium enrichment. The sanctions were strengthened in March 2007 by UN Resolution 1747, which banned Iranian arms exports and levied financial and travel restrictions on Iranians involved in suspected proliferation-related activities. Yet the effect of these sanctions was weakened by the lack of uniform support. As one important example, China had signed an energy contract with Iran in 2005 that made it reluctant to implement effective sanctions. Support for sanctions was further eroded by the late 2007 release of American intelligence finding that Iran had, in 2003, stopped its program to weaponize uranium. Because Iran continues an expanded uranium enrichment program that could readily be adapted to produce weapons-grade material, and because it could quickly revive its weapons program, the danger of a nuclear-armed Iran persists.

Conflict in Iraq.   As noted earlier, Operation Iraqi Freedom in 2003, lauded initially as an effective high-tech military operation against Saddam's conventional forces, bogged down into a counterinsurgency war for which U.S. national security decision makers and military forces were not prepared. The new Iraqi government executed Saddam on December 30, 2006, but the insurgency continued and grew in intensity, taking a large toll in U.S. and Iraqi casualties. Opposition to the war grew rapidly in the American public and abroad, but tended to subside in 2008 under the impact of a new and effective counterinsurgency strategy led by General David Petraeus.

By late 2008, Washington and a functioning, reasonably secure, democratic government in Baghdad had agreed upon a Status of Forces Agreement that would extend a U.S. military presence in Iraq through 2011. Iraqi provincial elections were scheduled for January 2009. Estimates of both the outgoing Bush administration and the incoming Barack Obama administration were that troop reductions could be made in Iraq and that U.S. and NATO troops should be significantly augmented in Afghanistan. Whether the apparently successful counterinsurgency strategy adopted for Iraq was appropriate for use against Taliban warlords and al-Qa'ida in Afghanistan was an open question.

Whether a viable constitutional democracy can be maintained in Iraq will be a key factor affecting Middle East regional stability as U.S. decision makers confront threats from Iran.

Developments in Turkey.   Turkey occupies a key position in the Middle East, geographically and functionally. It is a bridge between Europe and Asia, and during the Cold War it was also a barrier between the Soviet Union and the Mediterranean. Since 1951, Turkey has been an important component of the North Atlantic Treaty Organization, serving as a security bulwark on the alliance's southeastern flank. Although Turkey's strategic significance to the United States temporarily waned after the demise of the Soviet Union, it was restored following the catastrophic attacks of 9/11.

In 2003, Turkey's parliament voted to refuse to allow U.S. forces to transit the country to invade Iraq from the north, souring relations across the board. Tensions persist between the two countries over the growing independence of the Iraqi Kurds and over Turkey's anxiety about the aspirations of its own Kurdish population. The Bush administration attempted to repair relations in November 2007 by declaring the Turkish separatist group, the PKK, as a "common enemy" and by providing to Ankara "actionable intelligence" on the PKK. Turkey remains an important U.S. strategic partner. The continued value that the United States places on this relationship is reflected in U.S. efforts to pressure Europe into accepting Turkey as a member of the EU. From the U.S. perspective, the EU's admittance of a Muslim country would have profound positive effects on U.S. security and other regional interests.[33]

Looking Ahead

Undoubtedly, the Middle East will be turbulent for years to come. The lack of progress on the Palestinian-Israeli front, the tension between Israel and Hezbollah, the violent conflict in Iraq, and Iran's insistence on enriching uranium provide ample grounds for pessimism. Clearly, the United States will continue to have important national security interests in the Middle East and will stay engaged in the region's affairs. Yet U.S. engagement, direct and indirect, has the potential to backfire into regional resentment and to further fuel instability.

Political leaders in the region recognize U.S. economic and political power and in many cases aim to retain close relationships with America. Virtually every significant political group in the Middle East has found some area—economic, political, scientific, or military—from which it can derive benefits from maintaining good relations with the United States. The resulting U.S. ability to exert influence on both sides of regional disputes has been a major diplomatic and security asset. Nevertheless, the legitimacy of U.S. involvement in the region is increasingly treated with great skepticism by much of the population of the region, and this skepticism will be difficult for the United States to overcome.

The conjunction of high stakes and persistent instability makes the Middle East the single most critical and difficult region for U.S. national security policy makers. However, the United States still possesses formidable assets with which it can further its interests in this region. Using these assets wisely to promote peaceful change will be a major continuing challenge.

Discussion Questions

1. How have U.S. economic interests in the Middle East changed during the past thirty years?

2. What policies could the United States pursue to prevent further large increases in the price of oil?

3. What advantages and disadvantages does Iran possess in its relationships with other countries in the Middle East? Will Iran become a regional superpower in the twenty-first century? What are the implications for the national security interests of the United States in the region?

4. What non–Middle Eastern powers, other than the United States, have major interests in the Middle East? How do you expect them to attempt to exert their influence?

5. How important is it for the United States to be closely involved in searching for a settlement to the Israeli-Palestinian conflict? Can the United States be an honest broker in the dispute?

6. How did the 9/11 terrorist attacks affect U.S. interests in the region?

7. Has the U.S. intervention in Iraq in 2003 made regional stability more or less likely?

8. Does the history of colonial rule still affect Middle Eastern politics today? If so, how?

9. Discuss the advantages and disadvantages for the United States of relying on Israel and Saudi Arabia to further U.S. interests in the Middle East. What advantages or disadvantages would those countries derive from such an arrangement?

Recommended Reading

Abbas Milani, Abbas. "U.S. Foreign Policy and the Future of Democracy in Iran." *Washington Quarterly* 28, no. 3 (Summer 2005): 41–56.

Ajami, Fouad. *The Arab Predicament: Arab Political Thought and Practice Since 1967.* New York: Cambridge University Press, 1992.

Andersen, Roy R., Robert F. Seibert, and Jon G. Wagner. *Politics and Change in the Middle East.* 8th ed. Upper Saddle River, NJ: Pearson Prentice-Hall, 2006.

Ayoob, Mohammed, Robert Springborg, Ann Lesch, Ziya Önis, and Shireen Hunter. "The Middle East in 2025: Implications for U.S. Policy." *Middle East Policy* 13, no. 2 (Summer 2006): 148–176.

Diamond, Larry. "Lessons from Iraq." *Journal of Democracy* 16, no. 1 (2005): 9–234

Hen-Tov, Elliot. "Understanding Iran's New Authoritarianism." *Washington Quarterly* 30, no. 1 (Winter 2006/2007): 163–179.

Hourani, Albert. *A History of the Arab Peoples.* Cambridge, MA: Harvard University Press, 1991.

Hunter, Shireen T. *Iran and the World: Continuity in a Revolutionary Decade.* Bloomington: Indiana University Press, 1990.

Karsh, Ephraim. "Geopolitical Determinism: The Origins of the Iran-Iraq War." *Middle East Journal* 44, no. 2 (Spring 1990): 256–268.

Milani, Mohsen M. *The Making of Iran's Islamic Revolution: From Monarchy to Islamic Republic.* 2nd ed. Boulder, CO: Westview Press, 1994.

Piscatori, James, and Dale Eikelman. *Muslim Politics.* Princeton, NJ: Princeton University Press, 1996.

Quandt, William B. *Decade of Decisions: American Policy toward the Arab-Israeli Conflict, 1967-1976.* Berkeley and Los Angeles: University of California Press, 1977.

Robinson, Glenn E. *Building a Palestinian State: The Incomplete Revolution.* Bloomington: Indiana University Press, 1997.

Rose, Euclid. "OPEC's Dominance of the Global Oil Market: The Rise of the World's Dependency on Oil." *Middle East Journal* 58, no. 3 (Summer 2004): 424–443.

Sterner, Michael. "Closing the Gate: The Persian Gulf War Revisited." *Current History* 96, no. 106 (January 1997): 13–19.

Waxman, Dov. "Between Victory and Defeat: Israel after the War with Hizballah." *Washington Quarterly* 30, no. 1 (Winter 2006/2007): 27–43.

Internet Resources

Cooperation Council for the Arab States of the Gulf, www.gcc-sg.org/eng/
Energy Information Administration, www.eia.doe.gov
International Atomic Energy Agency, www.iaea.org
United States Central Command, www.centcom.mil
U.S. Department of State Bureau of Near Eastern Affairs, www.state.gov/p/nea

21

Sub-Saharan Africa

The continent of Africa is four times larger than the United States, and it is home to a vast array of resources and more than 940 million people.[1] With thousands of languages, unique tribal histories, and diverse political systems organized into forty-six states, Africa is an incredibly difficult and complicated place about which to generalize (see Map 21.1). No single state or coalition on the African continent poses a significant security threat to the United States and its allies. Yet, there are many reasons why the United States will be increasingly engaged in the affairs of sub-Saharan Africa in the twenty-first century. (Note: Though this chapter gives some attention to states from throughout Africa, the focus of this chapter is on *sub-Saharan Africa*, a term used herein to denote all of Africa except the North African States of Egypt, Libya, Tunisia, Algeria, and Morocco.)

Primary U.S. interests in the subcontinent can be loosely organized into two intersecting categories—security and economics—which are underscored by basic humanitarian concerns. In both categories, the United States competes with several nations in Europe and Asia for greater strategic influence in sub-Saharan Africa. Nevertheless, U.S. policy makers have only recently demonstrated a significant commitment to providing security and economic assistance to the subcontinent, partly in response to the threat that transnational terrorist organizations pose to American interests in the region and at home.

During the Cold War, U.S. involvement in the security affairs of Africa was sporadic at best, usually driven by ideological and military competition with the Soviet Union. In the early post–Cold War years, U.S. interventions in Africa, such as in Somalia in 1993, were usually conducted as part of humanitarian relief missions. By the early twenty-first century, the United States had begun to focus on the development of greater security and economic opportunities for Africans for

MAP 21.1 Africa

Scale: 1:75,000,000

financial and humanitarian reasons, but this attention was also driven in part by the conviction that addressing the major conditions behind the rise of (and support for) worldwide transnational terrorist organizations is in the best interests of the United States. This conviction continues to underscore a variety of security and economic assistance initiatives that the United States either leads directly or supports with military, diplomatic, and financial assistance.

U.S. Interests

Local Governance and U.S. Security Concerns.   It is widely understood that sub-Saharan Africa contains some of the largest regions of insecurity, instability, and lawlessness anywhere in the world. According to a 2006 World Bank report, thirty-eight of the forty-six countries of Africa were poorer and had worse governance than the world average.[2] Roughly one fourth of the world's national governments do not have complete control over all the territory defined by their state's boundaries, and the majority of these are in sub-Saharan Africa. Such terms as *fragile states, failed states, ungoverned spaces,* and *zones of competing governance* have been used interchangeably to describe how the security environment in sub-Saharan Africa offers safe havens for the activities of transnational criminal and terrorist organizations.[3] The 2006 *Report on Global Terrorism* released by the U.S. Department of State defines a *terrorist safe haven* as "an area of relative security exploited by terrorists to indoctrinate, recruit, coalesce, train, and regroup, as well as prepare and support their operations."[4] In sub-Saharan Africa, adversaries of the United States can exploit safe havens created by lack of effective local governance to cause harm to U.S. citizens and commercial interests throughout the subcontinent, from U.S. embassies in Kenya and Tanzania to vital oil pipelines in Nigeria. Throughout the region, weak or nonexistent coastal security and border controls further facilitate trafficking in weapons, drugs, and people. As scholar Robert Rotberg has asserted, "in the wake of September 11, the threat of terrorism has given the problem of failed nation-states an immediacy and importance that transcends its previous humanitarian dimension. . . . The existence of these kinds of countries, and the instability that they harbor, not only threatens the lives and livelihoods of their own peoples but endangers world peace."[5]

The same impoverished or corrupt regimes that lack complete control over the territory of their respective countries also generally lack either the capability or the will to address issues that impact human security. Important threats to the survival and welfare of individual human beings include civil wars, disease, famine, poverty, political oppression, and lack of housing. These problems cross state borders, affect the physical environment, put enormous pressure on political systems and societies, and present vulnerabilities for criminal and terrorist organizations to exploit.[6] These issues also often create a population that tends to direct its loyalties toward local warlords or criminal gangs instead of the government. (For more on human security, see Chapter 25.)

Endemic poverty is a large part of the problem. In most countries of sub-Saharan Africa, large portions of the population live below the poverty line; per-capita gross domestic product and average life expectancy are far lower than those of industrialized countries (see Table 21.1). The United Nation's (UN) annual Human Development Index consistently rates African countries as having the worst living conditions in the world, and the number of people estimated to be living in extreme poverty on the continent has doubled in the last two decades.[7] Indeed, in 2004, British Prime Minister Tony Blair observed that Africa was the only continent to have grown poorer in the last twenty-five years.[8] Threats to human security in poor countries have the potential to affect U.S. national security; if people are insecure, then problems stemming from and fostered by that insecurity can quickly spread in today's globalizing world.

Domestic Security Challenges and U.S. Economic Interests. Human security challenges also affect America's economic interests in the region. Major U.S. trading partners in Africa include Algeria, Angola, Egypt, Nigeria, and South

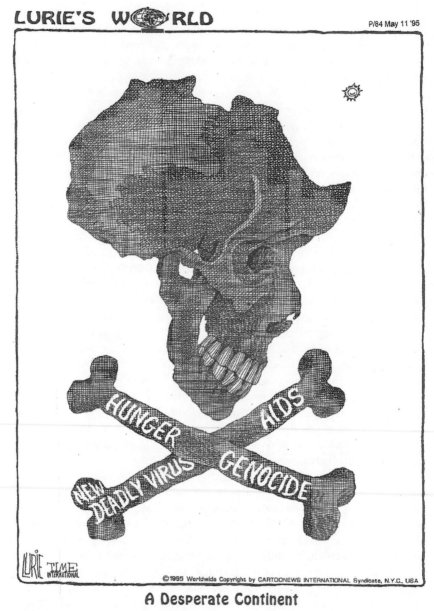

A Desperate Continent

Reprinted with permission of Ranan Lurie.

Africa. U.S. economic interests are affected by conditions in African states with considerable wealth in natural resources, such as minerals, natural gas, and oil. Africa produces between one quarter and two thirds of many of the world's essential minerals, including chromium, cobalt, diamonds, manganese, platinum, and vanadium. In addition, nearly 18% of U.S. oil imports come from Africa—almost as much as from Saudi Arabia. According to projections by the National

Table 21.1 Sub-Saharan Africa Key Statistics

Country	Total Population (millions)	Average Life Expectancy	GDP US$ (billions)	GDP/ Capita (US$)	Population Living in Poverty (%)	Military Spending % of GDP	Military Spending US$ (millions)	Human Development Index Ranking (out of 177)
Angola	12.1	37.9	80.1	6,500	70	5.7	4566	162
Burkina Faso	14.3	49.2	5.9	1,400	46.4	1.2	76	176
Chad	9.9	47.2	5	1,500	80	4.2	56	170
Congo, Democratic Republic of the	65.8	57.2	8	700	—	2.5	150	168
Congo, Republic of	3.8	53.3	5.1	1,400	—	3.1	61	139
Djibouti	0.5	43.2	0.7	1,000	50	3.8	25	149
Eritrea	4.9	59.6	1.2	1,000	50	6.3	65	157
Ethiopia	76.5	49.2	13.3	1,000	38.7	3	300	169
Kenya	36.9	55.3	17.5	1,200	50	2.8	353	148
Liberia	3.2	40.4	0.9	900	80	1.3	—	—
Nigeria	135	47.4	83.4	1,500	60	1.5	854	158
Rwanda	9.9	49	2	1,600	60	2.9	56	161
Sierra Leone	6.1	40.6	1.2	900	70.2	2.3	26	177
Somalia	9.1	48.8	2.5	600	—	0.9	—	—
South Africa	44	42.5	201.4	13,300	50	1.7	3,697	121
Sudan	39.4	49.1	25.4	2,400	40	3	453	147
Tanzania, United Republic of	39.4	50.7	13.1	800	36	0.2	122*	159
Uganda	30.3	51.8	8.5	1,900	35	2.2	196	154
Zimbabwe	12.3	39.5	3.2	2,100	68	3.8	136	151

Sources: CIA World Factbook, updated December 13, 2007, UNHDR Human Development Index 2007/2008; IISS Military Balance 2007.
*Figures of Tanzania's 2005 military expenditures were unavailable; the datum provided is the 2004 figure.

Intelligence Council, that proportion will likely reach 25% by 2015. The vast majority of this oil will come from a stretch of western Africa's coastline between Nigeria and Angola called the Gulf of Guinea, where an estimated 50 billion barrels of oil reserves are located.[9] Already, Nigeria is the fifth largest supplier of U.S. oil, Angola is the ninth largest, and such countries as Equatorial Guinea, Gabon, and the Republic of Congo are becoming increasingly important to U.S. energy security.[10] Threats to the stability of these important trading partners impact U.S. economic and security interests.

The History of U.S. Involvement in Africa

Africa's many challenges partly stem from the border delineation scheme agreed upon by the major European powers at the Berlin Conference of 1815. To avoid major clashes over competing colonial claims, the leaders of England, France, Spain, Portugal, Germany, and Belgium carved up a continent about which they knew almost nothing and then proceeded to subjugate the peoples of Africa and to plunder the continent's resources. By the early 1800s, the Arab and European slave trade had already drained the continent of a significant part of its productive labor. Throughout the next century, Africa's resources were systematically exploited, while very little investment was made in developing local human capital or infrastructure.

In some cases, the colonial powers imported educational and political systems, social and religious customs, and modern approaches to economic production that are still evident in the independent countries of Africa today. In other cases—particularly the former Belgian Congo, now the Democratic Republic of Congo—the exclusive focus of the colonial power was the extraction of resources. In all areas that were colonized, the arbitrary assignment of borders at the Berlin Conference ignored ancestral tribal territories, historical migration patterns, and local customs, creating a variety of conflicts that still influence African politics today.[11]

During World War I and World War II, African colonies provided manpower for the armies of their rulers. In some cases, whole brigades of African soldiers fought alongside their European counterparts. After World War II, African veterans returned home with a greater awareness of living conditions in other countries and were better able to recognize just how impoverished and underdeveloped their own countries were by comparison. Meanwhile, World War II had severely weakened the ability of European countries to project power overseas and thus ensure their colonies' continued subjugation. The distribution of power in the world had also changed dramatically. The United States and the Soviet Union emerged as the world's two superpowers, and neither was inclined to support European aspirations to retain colonial possessions. As a result of these and other factors, a number of independence movements arose within Africa during the late 1950s and early 1960s. In 1955, only five independent countries existed on the whole of the African continent. Ten years later, there were thirty-eight.

Africa during the Cold War.   For the most part, the United States warmly embraced these independence movements. As France, Belgium, Portugal, and the

United Kingdom granted sovereignty to some three dozen states, the United States offered goodwill and modest amounts of aid and investment. However, an underlying motivation behind U.S. involvement in Africa was its Cold War ideological struggle with the Soviet Union. Indeed, by the early 1960s, U.S. policies toward sub-Saharan Africa had taken on the dual nature that they were to maintain for well over two decades. The United States would support socioeconomic development in sovereign states (preferably democratic ones) linked to the West and oppose intrusion by communist powers. As the colonial powers left Africa, the United States and the Soviet Union vied for influence and resources in a series of proxy conflicts.

As the U.S. preoccupation with Southeast Asia (and particularly Vietnam) began to grow in the mid-1960s, the attention that the United States paid to Africa waned. Along with its Cuban ally, the Soviet Union moved in to fill the gap through direct intervention and by actively seeking influence wherever it could be gained. Marxist regimes assumed power in Ethiopia in 1974 and Mozambique in 1975. The most dramatic Soviet involvement, however, occurred in Angola, where three liberation movements struggled for power. Although the Ford administration attempted to influence the outcome of this conflict, Congress voted to end clandestine support for the two non-Marxist groups. Meanwhile, more than fifteen thousand Cuban troops and Soviet advisors poured into Angola, enabling the Soviet-aligned Marxist faction to defeat its opponents and declare itself the official government of Angola in February 1976. In October, the new regime signed a treaty of friendship and cooperation with the Soviet Union, and in December 1977, the ruling party formally proclaimed its adherence to Marxism-Leninism.

Although these and other conflicts in Africa were seen as opportunities by the United States and Soviet Union to enlarge their respective spheres of influence, the predominant geopolitical trend was neither pro-Western nor anti-Western. As diverse as the new states were domestically, a distinctive African style in international affairs emerged, represented most prominently by the Organization of African Unity. Created in 1963, the core principles of this organization were African unity (internally and internationally), socioeconomic development, respect for the territorial integrity of all member states, independence from external influence, elimination of all forms of colonialism, and support for the principles of the UN. Apart from the exceptional case of Eritrea's successful secession from Ethiopia, the organization achieved acceptance of boundaries inherited from the colonial era and successfully moderated several African disputes.[12] Its successor organization, the African Union (AU), has slowly developed a capacity for addressing local and regional conflicts. Unfortunately, its military and peacekeeping capabilities are still wholly dependent upon other organizations (for example, the Economic Community of West African States) and wealthy industrialized states, such as France, England, and the United States, particularly in terms of airlift and force projection. Overall, however, the existence of the AU and its commitment to addressing security threats throughout the continent are encouraging signs for the future.

Post–Cold War Africa. At the risk of oversimplifying a complex history, it can be said that the African component of the Cold War symbolically ended on

December 22, 1988. It was on this date that officials of South Africa, Cuba, and Angola met in New York to sign the agreements that initiated the phased departure of all fifty thousand or so Cuban troops in Angola, as well as Namibia's UN-monitored transition to independence. These agreements, largely negotiated over a period of several years by U.S. Assistant Secretary of State for African Affairs Chester Crocker (with critical Soviet support in the latter stages), embodied an implicit recognition on the part of Washington and Moscow that neither would gain from further military competition in Africa.[13]

The impact of the Cold War on Africa's development cannot be overstated. During the critical early years of independent statehood, the focus of the world's most powerful countries was less on the development of African economies and political systems than on ideological support for either Western liberal democracy or Soviet communism. As a result, many corrupt regimes took for themselves whatever development aid was offered, along with revenues gleaned from their countries' exports (most notably, oil in Nigeria). Billions have been plundered from the state coffers in many countries, including Nigeria, Congo, Kenya, and many others. Transparency International has consistently ranked the countries of sub-Saharan Africa as having among the most corrupt regimes in the world. In addition to corruption, the states of this region are plagued with widespread border insecurity; massive amounts of small arms and light weapons scattered throughout the continent (a legacy of decades of independence struggles, ethnic disputes, and other political conflicts); political instability (over ninety coups have occurred in sub-Saharan Africa since 1960); and—as described earlier—extreme poverty and human insecurity.

Nevertheless, since the end of the Cold War, democracy in Africa has expanded rapidly. The number of democracies in Africa quadrupled between 1990 and 2000, while economic growth hovered around 2% (rising to more than 5% by 2006).[14] U.S. policy has remained focused on democratization, and, as scholars have noted, fledgling democracies can be expected to experience slow economic growth.[15] However, this is not to suggest that the United States has ignored altogether the economic dimension of the continent's security challenges. Rather, much of U.S. recent policy has focused on economic development as well as on security.

Contemporary U.S. Policies.   The 2002 U.S. National Security Strategy set forth several overarching goals, including the promotion of political and economic freedom, peaceful relations with other states, and respect for human dignity.[16] The need to advance security, democracy, and economic development in Africa was explicitly addressed:

> In Africa, promise and opportunity sit side by side with disease, war, and desperate poverty. This threatens both a core value of the United States—preserving human dignity—and our strategic priority—combating global terror. American interests and American principles, therefore, lead in the same direction: we will work with others for an African continent that lives in liberty, peace, and growing prosperity. Together with our European allies, we must help strengthen Africa's fragile states, help build indigenous capability to secure porous borders, and help build up the law enforcement and intelligence infrastructure to deny havens for terrorists.[17]

The 2006 edition of the same document describes a number of initiatives meant to address Africa's many human security challenges, including disease, poverty, and hunger:

> Our strategy is to promote economic development and the expansion of effective, democratic governance so that African states can take the lead in addressing African challenges. Through improved governance, reduced corruption, and market reforms, African nations can lift themselves toward a better future. We are committed to working with African nations to strengthen their domestic capabilities and the regional capacity of the African Union to support post-conflict transformations, consolidate democratic transitions, and improve peacekeeping and disaster responses.[18]

The framework articulated here has informed a number of policies and security programs specifically focused on Africa since the end of the Cold War.

Peacekeeping. During the 1990s, the Clinton administration established the African Crisis Response Initiative to bolster Africa's indigenous peacekeeping capabilities. This initiative trained and equipped more than six thousand troops from seven African states between 1997 and 2000. Before being terminated, about nine thousand troops from eight countries were trained, and some of these forces participated in UN peacekeeping operations in the region. After President Bill Clinton was succeeded by President George W. Bush, this initiative was replaced by the African Contingency Operations Training and Assistance program. This program emphasizes a more robust Chapter VII[19] approach that allows UN forces to conduct nonconsensual peace operations.[20] In 2004, this program trained and helped equip approximately nine thousand African soldiers for emergency use as peacekeepers for missions in sub-Saharan Africa. Recent training missions have included Mozambique, Senegal, Botswana, and Nigeria.

Due to other priorities, U.S. funding for African peacekeeping in general shrank from $41 million in 2002 to $30 million in 2003.[21] However, the U.S. financial commitment was renewed with the Bush administration's introduction of the Global Peace Operations Initiative in 2005. This program was intended to provide $660 million over five years to train, equip, and support forces in states willing to participate in peace operations.[22] The plan calls for fifteen battalions to be trained per year: ten in Africa and five in Europe or the United States. The plan also calls for increased coordination with the UN, the European Union (EU), and the AU and an improvement in regional training centers. The United States has also offered support for an Italian initiative, the Center of Excellence for Stability Police Units, collocated with the European Gendarme Force Headquarters in Vicenza, Italy.

The goals of this initiative were endorsed by Global Eight Forum (G8) leaders at their June 2004 summit meeting at Sea Island, Georgia, where they adopted an "Action Plan on Expanding Global Capability for Peace Support Operations."[23] This was actually the third G8 Action Plan concerning peacekeeping in Africa. In June 2002, the G8 Summit at Kananaskis, Canada, adopted a broad Africa Action Plan that contained sections on conflict resolution and peace-building efforts. A more specific plan was then developed over the next year and presented at the

June 2003 Summit at Evian-les-Baines, France.[24] The United States is clearly not alone in recognizing the need to provide training to African militaries. France and the United Kingdom have also done significant work in this area.

Multilateral help is likely to remain important in addressing Africa's security challenges. In 2004, for example, the UN led sixteen peace operations, and seven were in Africa: Burundi, Côte d'Ivoire, Liberia, Ethiopia-Eritrea, Democratic Republic of Congo, Sierra Leone, and the Western Sahara. These African missions accounted for more than 80% of all UN peacekeepers deployed worldwide that year.[25] Given continuing civil strife in the Congo and elsewhere, conflict and hardship in the Darfur region of Sudan, as well as the challenges of violent nonstate actors operating in Africa—including the Lords Resistance Army, a group that has been carrying out a vicious campaign of banditry and terrorism in Uganda and the Sudan for more than twenty years—even greater peacekeeping efforts will likely be needed on the continent in the future.

In recognition of this, the United States has also offered its support to the AU's planned African Standby Force, a multinational force empowered to intervene in serious conflicts in Africa. With an eventual capacity of twenty thousand peacekeepers, these troops will deploy under the auspices of the AU to intervene in border wars and internal conflicts.[26] Although this is a seemingly important initiative, it is likely to be a number of years before the AU can truly offer this capability to its members without outside assistance.

The United States has also supported the establishment of the Kofi Annan International Peacekeeping Training Center. This center was first proposed by Ghana in 1997 and was originally intended to provide training for that country's substantial force contributions to Peace Support Operations worldwide. However, the center's first few years of existence were hampered by a severe lack of funding. In November 2003, in coordination with the Pearson Peacekeeping Center of Canada, the center conducted its first course on disarmament, demobilization, and reintegration. The center launched its first full annual training and education cycle in March 2004.

By training African peacekeepers and constabulary forces, as well as by providing equipment, transport, and logistical support, the United States and its allies are laying the groundwork for increased coordination among the UN, the United States, the EU, and the AU. If plans succeed, this training will eventually result in a substantial indigenous capability to address Africa's pressing security concerns.

Countering Violent Nonstate Entities.   Since the terrorist attacks of September 11, 2001, the United States has invested in improving the security environment on every continent of the world.[27] This focus has also shaped much of U.S. foreign policy toward Africa. Although al-Qa'ida is the most well known of the violent nonstate actors, U.S. policy makers are concerned about an array of armed entities—affiliated or not affiliated with al-Qa'ida—that pose a threat to the security of American political and economic interests throughout the subcontinent. The United States demonstrates its commitment to enhancing the counterterrorism capabilities of African militaries through a number of programs managed by the State Department, including the Anti-Terrorism Assistance program, the

African Coastal Security Program, the Pan Sahel Initiative (which grew into a more robust program, the Trans-Saharan Counter Terrorism Initiative), and the East Africa Counterterrorism Initiative. In addition, the State Department's Bureau of African Affairs is involved in Foreign Military Financing and International Military Education Training programs that are jointly coordinated with the Department of Defense (DoD).

The Department of State's Anti-Terrorism Assistance Program was initiated in 1983 as a means of providing specialized training and equipment to states facing terrorist threats.[28] Authorization for the program stems from the Foreign Assistance Act of 1961, which governs how the United States provides training services and equipment to other countries. This particular program provides training and equipment related to bomb detection and disposal; management of hostage situations; senior leadership crisis management exercises; physical security; and other matters relating to the detection, deterrence, and prevention of acts of terrorism; the resolution of terrorist incidents; and the apprehension of those involved in such acts.[29] The program is implemented by the Department of State's Bureau of Diplomatic Security, which works closely with the department's Regional Security Officers in each embassy.[30] However, section 573(b) of the Foreign Assistance Act also requires that the assistant secretary of state for Democracy, Human Rights, and Labor be consulted when choosing countries that will receive antiterrorism assistance and when determining the nature of the assistance to be provided.

Another potentially important American initiative is the African Coastal Security Program, launched in 1985 as part of the U.S.-sponsored African Civic Action Program, which sought to strengthen regional cooperation in search and rescue, pollution control, and training operations. This program was specifically designed to help West African states patrol and defend their Exclusive Economic Zones against treaty violations, illegal fishing, and smuggling. By 1995, however, funding for the program had dried up, and the program lay dormant until April 2003, when the Bush administration announced plans to relaunch it. The new version was intended to improve the capability of African governments to combat piracy, terrorism, trafficking in narcotics, trafficking in persons and immigrant smuggling, and general smuggling. The program was also intended build the capacity of these countries to respond effectively to possible threats of violence to offshore drilling rigs and similar kinds of operations.

A further security-related program is the Pan Sahel Initiative, which was launched by the Department of State in October 2002 to assist Mali, Niger, Chad, and Mauritania in detecting and responding to suspicious movement of people and goods across and within their borders through training, equipment, and cooperation. The Sahel is a dry stretch of land from east to west Africa that contains nine of the world's poorest countries (Burkina Faso, Cape Verde, Chad, Gambia, Guinea-Bissau, Mali, Mauritania, Niger, and Senegal) and approximately 47 million inhabitants. The primary goal of this initiative is to provide training and equipment to enhance the border security capabilities of these countries and to encourage better regional cooperation and coordination in combating arms smuggling, drug trafficking, and the movement of transnational terrorists. As part of this initiative, teams from the 1st Battalion, 10th Special Forces Group (Airborne) were sent from the United States in March 2004 to Mali and Mauritania to provide training on mobility, communications, land navigation, and small-unit tactics.

Despite its successes, the Pan Sahel Initiative was constrained from its inception by limited funding and a limited focus, leading to its replacement in 2005 by the more ambitious Trans-Saharan Counterterrorism Initiative, which was funded at about $100 million per year for five years. Under this program, U.S. special operations forces train their counterparts in seven Saharan countries, teaching military tactics critical for the enhancement of regional security and stability. At the same time, they encourage the participating nations to work collaboratively toward confronting regional issues. The real change is that, unlike the program it replaced, the Trans-Saharan Counterterrorism Initiative combined military efforts with a more comprehensive approach to regional security. The DoD will continue to focus on military operations but other U.S. government agencies also will be active players: The U.S. Agency for International Development, for example, will address educational initiatives; the State Department, airport security; and the Department of Treasury, efforts to tighten up money-handling controls in the region. While executing this interagency approach, representatives of the United States will continue efforts to convince participating nations to think regionally about their mutual security concerns.

A similar security assistance program, the East Africa Counterterrorism Initiative, is aimed at increasing the regional counterterrorism capacities of Kenya, Ethiopia, Djibouti, Uganda, Tanzania, and Eritrea. Formally announced in June 2003, this initiative sought to reduce the scope and capacity of terrorists to act in the region by focusing on such critical areas as military training for border and coastal security; immigration and customs; airport/seaport security; police and law enforcement training; terrorist tracking databases; disruption of terrorist financing; regional information sharing and cooperation; and community outreach through education, assistance, and public information. The initiative also included a strong public diplomacy and outreach component and provided training assistance for senior-level decision makers and legislators involved in drafting legislation on terrorist financing and money laundering. Although the effort involved in this and all the other security assistance programs just cited is substantial, given the depth of the region's problems, progress will likely come slowly and fitfully.

Fostering Economic Development and Addressing Other Human Security Needs. Security initiatives cannot on their own address the multitude of problems faced by sub-Saharan African states. In addition to security-related programs, U.S. government agencies cooperate in or administer a variety of economic development and human security–related programs. Key development initiatives include the African Growth and Opportunity Act; the Millennium Challenge Account; the Global Fund to Fight HIV, Malaria, and Tuberculosis (reinforced by the President's Emergency Fund for AIDS Relief); and the Mother and Child HIV Prevention Initiative.[31] The United States is the world's largest provider of emergency humanitarian assistance to Africa. Additionally, since 1960, it has provided more than $50 billion in official bilateral development assistance to sub-Saharan Africa to help relieve poverty, provide humanitarian assistance, and spur economic growth.[32] During the George W. Bush administration, American aid to Africa roughly tripled.[33]

Given Africa's challenges in the areas of stability, security, and development, a broad approach that seeks to strengthen security through improved governance and economic development is required. The International Law Enforcement Academy in Gaborone, Botswana, is an example of an American interagency program that directly contributes to strengthening governance by improving critical internal security institutions around the continent.[34] Economic development efforts must recognize the importance of policies that foster trade and private sector growth while combating corruption. Accordingly, the African Growth and Opportunity Act and the Millennium Challenge Account provide access to the U.S. market and aim to reward good governance by directing aid to the strongest and most responsible performers. Other initiatives, such as the President's Emergency Fund for AIDS Relief, the Initiative to End Hunger in Africa, and the Africa Education Initiative, are meant to contribute to a healthier and economically stronger Africa. The President's Emergency Fund for AIDS Relief was introduced at the State of the Union Address in January 2003 when George W. Bush announced his intention to commit $15 billion over five years to fight HIV/AIDS.[35] The Initiative to End Hunger in Africa, announced by Bush in August 2002, sought to reduce hunger in Africa by half by 2015, in keeping with the UN Development Goals of the Millennium Declaration.[36] And the Africa Education Initiative, announced by George W. Bush in June 2002, sought to increase access to basic educational opportunities in Africa and specifically to improve primary education by providing teacher training, textbooks and other learning materials, support for community involvement, and scholarships to girls.[37]

The massive debt-relief programs for Africa sponsored by the G8 are also intended to enable governments to more effectively address their underlying crises of human underdevelopment. African countries struggle under the burden of huge debts of more than $300 billion, and pay enormous sums for debt servicing each year. Recognizing the impact of these massive debts, the leaders of the world's most industrialized countries agreed at the July 2005 G8 Summit to an unprecedented $50 billion aid package for the developing world—the majority of it targeted toward the nations of Africa. These nations also agreed to cancel the multilateral debt of the eighteen poorest countries of the world—fourteen of which are in Africa.[38]

Despite the multiplicity of programs it offers to Africa, the United States is still regularly criticized as a lagging international donor. For example, a UN Development Report in 2005 noted that although the United States was the single-largest giver in terms of overall amount, it ranked second to last among the rich countries of the world in aid as a proportion of national income.[39] In 2004, for example, all U.S. official development assistance combined was only 0.16% of national income, and most of this did not go to the world's poorest countries.[40] Others have also pointed out that expanding free trade is not always the boon to developing countries that one would expect. In many cases, these countries lack the ability to shift resources and people into sectors of the economy in which the developing country might have a comparative advantage.[41]

Though these criticisms have merit, the U.S. government has nevertheless put forward an impressive array of programs and initiatives over the past several decades that are meant to address Africa's challenges and needs in areas ranging from security to health to economic growth. The formulation and implementation of these policies involves a number of organizations within the government, each with its own strategic mission, history, culture, and resources. Improving the effectiveness of these initiatives will require great attention to interagency coordination and multinational cooperation.

Recent Developments in Sub-Saharan Africa.   Despite some progress, the continent's security challenges remain significant. As of mid-2008, for example, Somalia has been without an effective central government since President Siad Barre was overthrown in 1991. In 2006, an armed Islamist group triumphed over several violent warlords and claimed control over the capital, Mogadishu. Simultaneously, pirates attacked dozens of vessels off the Somali coast, in one instance hijacking a ship carrying food aid on behalf of the UN. By early 2007, Ethiopian troops (with support from the United States) had routed the Islamist group, and the internationally recognized interim government of Abdullahi Yusuf was returned to power in Mogadishu. Whether Somalia will emerge from its failed-state status in the near future is an open question.

Moving to the west, Ethiopia's government has been grappling with a multiyear drought and famine, as well as the renewal of its conflict with Eritrea. Ethiopia's neighbor to the south, Kenya, has been embroiled in a continuing corruption scandal that reached the highest levels of government, and two of its major cities—Nairobi and Mombassa—are crime ridden and have been targets of multiple terror attacks by Islamic militants. In the territory of Kenya's neighbor, Sudan, a twenty-one-year civil war between the north and south came to a shaky close in 2004, but new violence erupted in its western Darfur region, causing millions to flee their homes. The government and the Arab militias it has hired (including the so-called Janjaweed) are accused of war crimes against the region's black African population, while two rebel groups—the Justice for Equality Movement and the larger Sudan Liberation Army—are said to have received at least moral support from neighboring (and recently oil-rich) Chad. Sudan's recent history as a safe haven for Osama bin Laden and al-Qa'ida also plays a role in strained U.S. relations with the regime of President Omar al-Bashir, who came to power in a 1989 coup.

Militias and refugees are scattered throughout the Democratic Republic of Congo (especially in the Ituri province in the northeast and the mineral-rich Katanga province in the southeast). Remnants of the Salafist Group for Preaching and Combat (an Algerian group with strong ties to al-Qa'ida) roam the Sahel, and rebel movements and internal instability continue to plague the Central African Republic. In southern Africa, an AIDS crisis has decimated much of once-thriving

Botswana, and several countries—including South Africa, Lesotho, and Namibia—have some of the highest infection rates (and deaths) in the world. A 2006 coup attempt in Chad and a successful coup that year in Mauritania underscore the impact of recent oil discoveries in these countries. In West Africa, Liberia's strongman dictator Charles Taylor was forced out of office and in 2006 was turned over to the International Criminal Court for war crimes, while Sierra Leone and Côte d'Ivoire (Ivory Coast) continue to teeter on the brink of renewed civil war.

Although these various events are deeply worrisome, perhaps the most troubling events have occurred in Nigeria, by far Africa's most populous country and one of the world's critical energy producers. In recent years, the country has seen numerous pipeline explosions (including one in the economically vital capitol city of Lagos, which killed more than one hundred fifty people in May 2006), as well as kidnappings and other forms of violence in the oil-rich Niger Delta. In fact, members of a militia led by one of Nigeria's more notorious local warlords actually triumphed over the Nigerian Army in a 2004 battle. Meanwhile, Nigeria has also been struggling to suppress a Taliban-style Islamic extremist uprising in the predominately Muslim north of the country. Hundreds of people have been killed, and thousands more have been forced to flee their homes due to the periodic religious violence there.

The criminal oil cartels operating boldly in the Niger Delta may pose a threat that is even greater than the religious violence. Roughly half of Nigeria's Army battalions are deployed internally for policing missions, but the military is not properly configured or trained to perform police functions. Reasonable estimates indicate that in the Niger Delta alone, close to twenty thousand (nongovernment) men are under arms, and "as many as 300,000 barrels of oil may be exported from the country illegally every day."[42] This criminal activity provides an estimated $3 billion to $4 billion per year in illegal oil revenue that finances continued theft, violence, and instability. Nigeria also serves as a busy transit point for the global trade in illegal weapons and drugs, making it all the more attractive to transnational criminal organizations.

Violence and insecurity in the Niger Delta region directly impact global oil markets and contributed to soaring prices beginning in 2005 For economic reasons alone, improving security in Nigeria is in America's best interest. However, the country also plays a vital role in U.S.-Africa policy because of its population size, regional economic activity, and—perhaps most importantly—its military power and force projection capabilities, which have been crucial in Africa's various peacekeeping missions.

Beyond helping to meet these local African challenges, the United States must also address growing competition to its policy influence in the region. The role of the Soviet Union as the strategic counterweight to the United States has, post–Cold War, been picked up by China. Some observers worry a growing Chinese presence and influence in Africa may lead the United States to turn once again to the approach to foreign policy seen during the Cold War: African states will again be wooed or coerced to choose between East and West.

Whereas the Soviets were interested in building ideological solidarity with African states, the Chinese are pursuing more pragmatic goals in the realms of trade, investment, and energy. In doing so, China has been willing to support and legitimize some of the continent's more corrupt, dictatorial regimes. For example, Zimbabwe—where President Robert Mugabe has ruled with an iron fist since coming to power in 1980, and where hyperinflation and destitution rage because of his administration's incompetence and corruption—is a major source of platinum and iron ore for China. In return, China provides Zimbabwe with weapons and military support, despite sanctions placed on Mugabe's regime by most Western countries. In another example, despite the continuation of extreme human rights abuses in the Darfur region, Sudan provides substantial oil exports to China and is the beneficiary of large amounts of Chinese investment. With Chinese assistance, the Sudanese government has built three weapons factories, complicating international arms embargoes against Khartoum.[43]

Other countries with which China has developed close ties include Angola, Nigeria, and Gabon—three of the continent's major oil producers. China is also pursuing stronger relations with several African states as a means to further isolate Taiwan. Five of the twenty-four countries that have full diplomatic relations with Taiwan are African (Burkina Faso, Gambia, Malawi, Sao Tome and Principe, and Swaziland). Other countries—including Japan, India, Brazil, and Venezuela—are also establishing stronger relationships in sub-Saharan Africa that warrant attention, while former colonial powers (particularly England and France) have maintained strategic relationships with many of their former colonies. These various relationships influence the receptivity of African countries to helping the United States achieve its national security objectives.

China has clearly embarked on a major expansion of its African efforts. The Forum on China and African Cooperation in November 2006 was an exceptionally high-profile event, attended not only by senior Chinese leaders but also by forty-three African heads of state. Given China's focus on acquiring African oil and minerals and on expanding trade and political influence there, it will be important for U.S. policy makers to avoid, insofar as possible, costly competition and clashes. Instead, if long-term wisdom prevails, complementary interests in peace, stability, and development offer the prospect of constructive collaboration.[44]

Future Challenges for U.S. Policy Makers

Africa not only is by far the poorest continent but also has the world's fastest rate of population growth. The continent's population has doubled since 1970, and it is expected to rise to almost 1.4 billion by 2025.[45] This total will be greater than the populations of North America and Europe combined. Africa is full of fragile states, whose leaders are dealing with a multitude of enormous challenges. As noted earlier, the confluence of these challenges creates an environment that violent nonstate actors (including transnational terrorist organizations) can use to develop the capacity attack the United States. The United States learned this lesson from Afghanistan in 2001.

To counter threats to themselves and to the United States, sub-Saharan African states need to develop the capacity to provide for their own security and economic prosperity. Improving the level of security throughout the subcontinent is an important U.S. objective that will require American policy makers to decide how much to invest to help create an environment in which real economic growth, political stability, and democratization can be realized. Equally or more important, given the fact that billions of dollars of aid to Africa from many sources have been squandered, U.S. policy makers must decide how to invest the limited resources available.

An additional challenge will be to bring all elements of U.S. national power to bear in addressing Africa's security and economic challenges. According to Henry Crumpton, the former U.S. Department of State ambassador-at-large for counterterrorism:

> Countering this multi-layered threat requires calibrated application of all the elements of U.S. national power: diplomacy, information, intelligence and covert action, economic power, military power, and the rule of law. . . . Our effort is structured at multiple levels—a global campaign to counter al-Qa'ida and associated networks; a series of regional cooperative efforts to deny terrorist safe havens; and numerous national security and development assistance operations designed to build liberal institutions, support the rule of law and enhance our partners' capacity to resist the threat and address the conditions that terrorists exploit—all focused on unique local conditions.[46]

Interagency coordination and multinational cooperation are essential to success. Unfortunately, these tasks are intrinsically difficult for governmental bureaucracies to perform well.

Policy makers within the DoD face the additional challenge of making a new operational command effective. Until recently, the U.S. military lacked a concerted focus on Africa. Responsibility had been divided among three of the five regional unified commands—U.S. European Command; U.S. Central Command (whose geographic boundaries included Djibouti, Egypt, Ethiopia, Eritrea, Kenya, Somalia, and Sudan); and U.S. Pacific Command, which had responsibility for Madagascar.[47] However, in February 2007, George W. Bush approved a Pentagon plan for a new combatant command for Africa and instructed Defense Secretary Robert Gates to get the new command up and running by the end of September 2008. According to Gates, this command would be responsible for cooperating with African countries, providing DoD support for nonmilitary missions, "building partnership capability . . . and, if directed, military operations."[48] A four-star combatant commander may be significant in increasing the salience of security-related Africa issues within the U.S. national security system.[49] Nevertheless, it will take time for this new command to refine its mission and become effective. Defining this role and determining the resource level for its efforts will be a challenge for U.S. policy makers in the decade to come.

Finally, as noted earlier, multilateral cooperation will be crucial in enabling African solutions to Africa's problems of transnational criminal and terrorist organizations, the cross-border flow of weapons and drugs, piracy, and other maritime security challenges. U.S. policy makers will have to decide how much support they are willing and able to provide to the network of multinational organizations that the Africans have established for themselves. If the AU takes the lead for the continent as a whole, subregional organizations may come to have an equally significant role to play within their respective areas. How can the United States best contribute to the future effectiveness of all these organizations, unilaterally and through cooperation with others? Whatever the answer, there is no avoiding the conclusion that U.S. national security interests will depend heavily on the unproven ability of the inhabitants of Africa to create for themselves a more positive future.

Discussion Questions

1. What are the national interests of the United States in Africa? How have these changed over time?

2. Who the key allies and adversaries of the United States in sub-Saharan Africa?

3. Should the United States build a stronger relationship with a country, such as Equatorial Guinea (an oil-rich regime in West Africa), despite its terrible record on human rights, corruption, and democracy?

4. During the Cold War, the United States and the Soviet Union competed for spheres of influence in Africa. What impact has this had on contemporary African security affairs?

5. Is regional integration among African countries important for economic development? If so, what are the key challenges to effective regional integration?

6. How is Africa important to the U.S. struggle against transnational terrorist groups? What priorities should U.S. policy makers adopt as they continue this struggle?

Recommended Reading

Akindele, R.A., ed. *Civil Society, Good Governance and the Challenges of Regional Security in West Africa.* Ibadan, Nigeria: Vantage Publishers, 2003.

Ayittey, George B. N. *Africa in Chaos.* New York: St. Martin's Press, 1999.

Ballentine, K., and J. Sherman, eds. *The Political Economy of Armed Conflict: Beyond Greed and Grievance.* Boulder, CO: Lynne Rienner, 2003.

Clough, Michael. *Free at Last? U.S. Policy Toward Africa and the End of the Cold War.* New York: Council on Foreign Relations Press, 1992.

Collier, Paul. *Economic Causes of Civil Conflict and Their Implications for Policy.* Washington, DC: World Bank, June 2000.

Commission for Africa. *Our Common Interest: Report of the Commission for Africa.* London: Commission on Africa (London, March 2005). www.commissionforafrica.org.

Congressional Research Service. *Nations Hospitable to Organized Crime and Terrorism.* Library of Congress, Federal Research Division (October, 2003). http://www.loc.gov/rr/frd/pdf-files/Nats_Hospitable.pdf.

Corporate Council on Africa. "A Ten-Year Strategy for Increasing Capital Flows to Africa" (June 2003). www.iie.com/publications/papers/africa-report.pdf.

Crocker, Chester A. *High Noon in Southern Africa: Making Peace in a Rough Neighborhood.* New York: W. W. Norton and Company, 1992.

———. "Engaging Failed States." *Foreign Affairs* 82, no. 5 (September/October 2003): 32–44.

Deng, Francis. *War of Visions: Conflict of Identities in the Sudan.* Washington, DC: Brookings Institution Press, 1995.

Forest, James J. F., and Matt V. Sousa. *Oil and Terrorism in the New Gulf: Framing U.S. Energy and Security Policies for the Gulf of Guinea.* Lanham, MD: Lexington Books, 2006.

Gill, Bates, Chin-Hao Huang, and J. Stephen Morrison. *China's Expanding Role in Africa.* Washington, DC: CSIS Report, 2007.

Hodges, Tony. *Angola from Afro-Stalinism to Petro-Diamond Capitalism.* Bloomington: Indiana University Press, 2001.

Institute for Advanced Strategic and Political Studies. *African Oil: A Priority for U.S. National Security and African Development.* Washington, DC: Institute for Advanced Strategic and Political Studies, 2002.

Klare, Michael T. *Resource Wars: The New Landscape of Global Conflict.* New York: Henry Holt and Company, LLC, 2001.

Laidi, Zahi. *The Superpowers and Africa.* Chicago: University of Chicago Press, 1990.

Libby, Ronald T. *The Politics of Economic Power in Southern Africa.* Princeton, NJ: Princeton University Press, 1987.

Rotberg, Robert I. "Strengthening African Leadership: There Is Another Way." *Foreign Affairs* 83, no. 4 (July/August 2004): 14–19.

Sachs, Jeffrey D. "The Development Challenge." *Foreign Affairs* 84, no. 2 (March/April 2005): 78–90.

United Nations Office on Drugs and Crime. *Transnational Organized Crime in the West African Region.* New York: United Nations, June 2005.

United Nations Office on Drugs and Crime. *Crime and Development in Africa.* New York: United Nations, June 2005.

Internet Resources

Africa Center for Strategic Studies, www.africacenter.org
African Union, www.africa-union.org
Kofi Annan International Peacekeeping Training Centre, www.kaiptc.org
Southern African Development Community, www.sadc.int
U.S. Department of State Bureau of African Affairs, www.state.gov/p/af
The World Bank Enhanced Heavily Indebted Poor Countries Initiative, www.worldbank.org/hipc

22

Russia

Relations between the United States and the Soviet Union, and then later between the United States and post-Soviet Russia, have played an essential, central role in American national security. Marked by confrontation after World War II, these relations shifted to expectations of partnership with the new Russian state after the Soviet collapse. However, the first decade of the twenty-first century brought renewed friction over Russia's behavior and its standing in the international political, economic, and strategic order. Across the different stages of its recent history, the changes in Russia's international power and influence have been dramatic.

The collapse of the Soviet Union eliminated what was arguably the single greatest external threat to the United States since its founding. The Soviet threat was not simply strategic in nature but encompassed a profoundly different set of values and institutions that formed an alternative political, economic, and cultural system. An appreciation for the history of this threat remains valuable for the perspective it provides on current U.S. national security challenges, including the problem of terrorism. As the primary heir of the Soviet Union, Russia is still shaped by this legacy. Moreover, it retains a nuclear arsenal that is still capable of destroying the United States.

Russia's failure to establish authentic democratic institutions and a market economy after the Soviet collapse means that cooperation between Washington and Moscow for the foreseeable future will rest less on common values than on perceptions of shared interests. Depending on how Moscow defines its interests, Russia can play the role of spoiler or supporter of U.S. foreign policy.

MAP. 22.1 Russia

The Cold War

The central dynamics in the history of U.S. national security policy during the Cold War, reviewed in Chapter 3, were the tension and competition between the United States and the Soviet Union. Although hundreds of books have been written on the origins of the Cold War, two main causes are worthy of mention here.[1]

The first, frequently listed as the chief among all causes, was a set of beliefs arising from Marxist and Soviet ideology. This ideology assumed inherent conflict between capitalism and communism and drastically skewed relations between the Soviet Union and the West. The brutal nature of Soviet domestic politics strengthened the ideological tendency of the Kremlin to see the world in zero-sum terms—any loss for one side was a gain for the other and vice versa. For example, Soviet leader Joseph Stalin accused his political rivals in the Communist Party of being "enemies of the people" who served foreign powers and were intent on destroying the new Soviet state from within. Soviet moderates who favored a less confrontational approach to the Western democracies, such as Nikolai Bukharin (communist theorist and leader during the 1917 Russian Revolution) were swept away. Yet careful observers understood that Soviet behavior was shaped not only by communist ideology and an authoritarian past but also by the tumultuous history of Russia, which had suffered numerous and devastating invasions from the Mongols to Napoleon Bonaparte and Adolf Hitler.

A second key origin of the Cold War arose from deep conflicts of interest. The first major area of friction was the fate of postwar Germany and Eastern Europe. Stalin wanted to establish a socialist "sphere of influence" in Eastern Europe and ultimately place Germany under Soviet domination. This policy was designed not only to increase the number of nations in the socialist camp (and thereby validate ideological predictions) but also to provide a friendly "buffer zone" for the territory of the Soviet Union.

The United States was willing to see the establishment of governments friendly to the Soviet Union in Eastern Europe but objected to the forcible imposition of communist regimes. The survival of European noncommunist states, especially a free Germany, gradually became a key concern for American leaders, who believed that the addition of any significant portion of western Europe to the newly expanded Soviet bloc would eventually tip the global balance of power. The resolve of the United States and its allies was tested by the Soviet Union on numerous occasions: in 1946, over the prolonged Soviet occupation of Iran; in 1946–1947, over threats to Greece and Turkey; in 1948, by the Soviet sponsored coup that installed a communist government in Czechoslovakia; and in 1948–1949, by the blockade of West Berlin by Soviet forces.

In 1947, President Harry Truman announced the Truman Doctrine, proclaiming America's intention "to support free people who are resisting attempted subjugation by armed minorities or by outside pressures." Shortly thereafter, U.S. diplomat George Kennan published an influential article titled "The Sources of Soviet Conduct" in the journal *Foreign Affairs* (using the pseudonym of "Mr. X") which argued that the United States should aim to contain the Soviet Union. Over time, this article came to be seen as one of the key statements of the emerging U.S. strategic doctrine of containment. In response to the Czech coup and the Berlin blockade in 1948, in 1949 ten western European states, Canada, and the United States signed the North Atlantic Treaty, a collective self-defense pact. This became the basis for the North Atlantic Treaty Organization (NATO) military alliance (see Chapter 23). After the rearming of West Germany, the Soviet Union and its Eastern European satellites responded by signing a treaty "On Friendship, Cooperation, and Mutual Aid" in May 1955, creating the Warsaw Treaty Organization. The countries of the Warsaw Pact, as this agreement came to be known, included the Soviet Union, Albania, Bulgaria, Czechoslovakia, East Germany, Hungary, Poland, and Romania.

Even as the United States was adapting to its new activist role, the international environment produced dramatic changes. First, the Soviet Union exploded its first atomic bomb in 1949, undercutting the heavy U.S. reliance on nuclear weapons to check potential Soviet aggression. Also in 1949, the Chinese Communists ejected the Chinese Nationalists, with whom the United States was allied, from mainland China. Finally, perhaps influenced by a speech given by U.S. Secretary of State Dean Acheson in which South Korea was left outside the U.S. security perimeter in Asia, Stalin gave his support to the North Korean Communist invasion of South Korea in 1950. When United Nations (UN) forces—led by the United States—made a successful counterattack and drove deep into North Korea, Communist

Chinese forces entered the war. This string of stimuli brought a series of strong U.S. responses. Work began on the next generation of nuclear weapons, containment was transformed into a global doctrine, and NATO conventional forces were strengthened.

The Movement Toward Détente.   Stalin died just before the end of the Korean War in July 1953. The policies of his successors (Georgy Malenkov and then Nikita Khrushchev) showed change as well as a degree of continuity with Stalin's policies. The changes in Soviet strategy were significant. First, realizing the awesome effects of nuclear weapons, both subsequent leaders shelved the rhetoric and perhaps even the idea of the inevitability of war between capitalist and socialist states. "Peaceful coexistence" between the United States and the Soviet Union became a goal, though perhaps not the dominant one, of post-Stalinist foreign policy. Second, after 1957, Khrushchev insisted on developing a nuclear-oriented force structure at the expense (temporarily, it proved) of the ground forces and the surface navy. Third, in an effort to "embarrass and outflank Western diplomacy," Khrushchev began a major effort to increase Soviet influence with the nonaligned nations of the Third World, many of which were former Western colonies.[2] The doctrine that it was the sacred duty of the Soviet Union to promote and support "wars of national liberation" was enunciated by Khrushchev in 1961.

Key elements of continuity in Soviet policy were the Soviet preoccupation with the settlement of the German question and with Western acceptance of Soviet domination of Eastern Europe. Khrushchev twice tried unsuccessfully to push the West into greater acceptance of the Soviet position on these issues, using Berlin as the fulcrum for his efforts. Khruschev's desire to achieve strategic parity with the United States, as well as his desire to ensure the security of a Third World communist ally, led to his decision to deploy nuclear weapons in Cuba. The result was the 1962 Cuban Missile Crisis, which was ultimately a dramatic Soviet psychological defeat.[3] Khrushchev's covert missile buildup was discovered while still underway; faced with U.S. nuclear as well as local conventional superiority, the Soviets backed down.

Although the Cuban Missile Crisis was a setback for the Soviet Union, three factors contributed to subsequent Soviet successes in the foreign policy realm. First, especially during the decade from 1965 to 1975, the Soviet economy prospered. Relative economic health enabled the regime of Leonid Brezhnev (successor to Khrushchev and leader of the Soviet Union until his death in 1982) to spend more on defense while simultaneously investing in an improved domestic standard of living.[4] Second, the United States became increasingly bogged down in Vietnam, with the result that U.S. spending on nuclear forces and conventional capabilities in Europe suffered. American policy makers and the general public turned increasingly against the notion of military power, and wider talk of "American imperialism" called into question the legitimacy of U.S. actions abroad. A third factor sprang from a re-evaluation of Soviet intentions on the part of many politicians and intellectuals in the West who came to view the Kremlin as less threatening and more worthy of accommodation.

The Soviets also wished to lessen tensions for strategic and economic reasons. Under President Richard Nixon, the United States made what to the Soviets were worrisome overtures to the People's Republic of China (which since the late 1950s had increasingly distanced itself from the Soviet Union). An accommodation between the United States and China had the potential to weaken the global influence and power position of the Soviet Union. With regard to economic incentives, the Soviets also saw an opportunity to gain from increased trade with the West. Increasingly, both sides saw value in seeking to limit strategic arms. Thus, the relatively short era of *détente* was born.

Return to Cold War.   The high point of détente occurred in 1972, when the United States and the Soviet Union signed agreements on anti-ballistic missiles and strategic arms at the conclusion of the first round of Strategic Arms Limitation Talks (SALT I). By 1973, however, it became obvious that the Cold War had not ended. In October of that year, the Soviets threatened intervention in the Arab-Israeli War. Unlike during the days of Khrushchev, this Soviet threat was not empty—six airborne divisions stood ready, and the Soviet Mediterranean fleet numbered a near-record eighty-five vessels.[5] In response, the United States found it necessary to alert its armed forces throughout the world.

From the American perspective, the Arab-Israeli War damaged but did not sink the ship of détente; subsequent Soviet operations in the Third World did. After 1973, with varying degrees of Soviet help, procommunist parties oriented toward Moscow seized power or de facto control in Vietnam, Laos, Angola, Ethiopia, Afghanistan, South Yemen, Cambodia, and Nicaragua. Unlike previous Soviet forays into the Third World, these activities seemed particularly ominous for two reasons. First, the Soviets were no longer content to work through nationalist movements but instead began to rely on proclaimed communist or socialist elements. Second, Soviet military moves became bolder. Beginning in 1975, Cuban troops and Soviet arms, advisors, and technicians became major, direct tools in Africa.[6] In 1979, a Soviet army of about one hundred fifteen thousand troops moved into Afghanistan, dramatically increasing Western perceptions of aggressive Soviet intent.

The Crisis of Afghanistan.   The December 1979 Soviet invasion of Afghanistan marked the first time since the end of World War II that Soviet ground forces had engaged in combat outside the Warsaw Pact countries of central and eastern Europe. No longer limiting intervention to arms, advisors, and proxies, the Soviet Union had now become directly involved in a Third World country.

Western governments were alarmed by the opportunities that the Soviet invasion seemed to create for Soviet policy. First, the Soviet Union had a better position than ever from which to exploit ethnic rivalries in the area. Turbulent Pakistan seemed an especially vulnerable target. Second, the possession of airfields around Afghanistan's Kandahar region put Soviet aircraft in closer proximity to the critical Strait of Hormuz in the Persian Gulf. Finally, a Soviet presence in Afghanistan could incentivize countries in the region to distance themselves from the United

States and its allies by subjecting governments to the Soviet mixture of "fear and seduction."[7]

Soviet operations in Afghanistan also had more general and disconcerting implications. Earlier operations in Angola and Ethiopia had given Soviet leaders confidence in their logistical capabilities and generalship. Success in Afghanistan increased the confidence of the Politburo (the central governing body of the Soviet Union) in the Soviet military establishment, making it more prone to use force in the future.[8] In the context of their intervention in Afghanistan, the Soviets extended the "protective custody" of the Brezhnev Doctrine (which guaranteed the perpetual "socialist" character of Soviet satellites) to all of the proclaimed Marxist states in the Third World. The Soviet Union had, in effect, created a rationale for using force in areas of the Third World wherever the correlation of forces would permit them to do so.[9]

To counter Soviet military adventures and proxy wars in the Third World, the American government began to support anti-Soviet insurgencies in a policy that became known as the Reagan Doctrine. This policy forced the Soviet Union to focus considerable resources on sustaining its clients as they waged difficult campaigns against insurgents supported by the United States.[10] As a tool to impose local defeats or higher costs on Soviet policy, the Reagan Doctrine was a significant innovation after a decade of relatively ineffective responses by the United States to Soviet activism in the Third World.

From Stalin's era to Brezhnev's, the Soviet Union evolved from a regional power with global pretensions to a global power with the ambition to at least equal the United States in virtually every category of military strength. In expanding its role, the Soviet Union increasingly relied on its strongest asset—its formidable military establishment. However, this reliance came at a political as well as an economic cost. Throughout much of its existence, the Soviet model of socialism with its emphasis on economic and social equality was often viewed within portions of the developing world and in Western Europe as a viable and even attractive alternative to capitalist democracy. However, the increasing Soviet reliance on military force, as demonstrated by its invasions of Hungary in 1956, Czechoslovakia in 1968, and Afghanistan in 1979, seriously undermined the international legitimacy of the Soviet system. The advent of authentic reform in Soviet domestic politics and in Soviet foreign policy in the mid-1980s can be traced in part to the recognition by a segment of the Soviet political elite that the Kremlin's reliance on military force would ultimately be self-defeating.

The Gorbachev Era and the Collapse of the Soviet Union. Brezhnev's death on November 10, 1982, ushered in a new era in Soviet politics. After a brief interregnum, in which first former Committee for State Security (KGB) chief Yuri Andropov and then Party Secretary Konstantin Chernenko were elevated to the position of general secretary, only to fall ill and die, Mikhail Gorbachev was selected by the Politburo to become the Communist Party's leader on March 11, 1985. By the time that Gorbachev assumed power, the declining economic performance of the Soviet economy had become so serious that Soviet leaders could no longer ignore it. Gorbachev's answer was to embark on an ambitious but piecemeal program of structural reform (*perestroika*) of key sectors of the economy. Faced by significant resistance to economic reforms from vested interests, especially the bureaucracy, Gorbachev launched the policy of *glasnost* (openness) and then *demokratizatsiia* (the infusion of competitive elements into the Soviet one-party system) as political tools to expose inefficiencies and failures.

As more controversial topics became the focus of attention in the official press, criticism of Soviet foreign and military policy—once taboo—became a more frequent feature of articles in the Soviet media. The war in Afghanistan, at first presented to Soviet citizens as a glorious effort to help a fraternal socialist revolution in an underdeveloped neighboring country, was for the first time presented in a new and disturbing light. Soviet television began to show footage of the fighting, and reports of casualties and deaths previously kept secret by censorship were more openly discussed. The rising chorus of criticism against the Afghan adventure rapidly spread to other areas, and the heavy share of the economy devoted to the military came under attack. The burden of supporting such faraway countries as Cuba, Angola, and Ethiopia at a time of mounting economic difficulties at home became the subject of public discussion, and the Soviet government was forced into a defensive stance. In light of serious military reversals, primarily at the hands of Afghans who were receiving covert assistance from the United States and Pakistan, Gorbachev declared victory and announced a withdrawal from Afghanistan in May 1988; the withdrawal was completed in February 1989.

Gorbachev's embrace of greater openness also led to the exposure of profound social problems at home, including rampant alcoholism and the decline in the growth of the Soviet work force, as well as irremediable structural problems in the centralized Stalinist economic model, such as widespread inefficiency and corruption. Gorbachev's economic reforms, poorly crafted and haphazardly implemented, seemed only to deepen these underlying problems. Most important, the disabilities of

"AT THIS POINT THE ARTIST RAN OUT OF PAINT."
Reprinted with permission of Ranan Lurie.

Soviet socioeconomic conditions assumed political relevance as a result of *glasnost* and the attendant policy of *demokratizatsiia* which freed Soviet society to organize against specific Soviet policies and, over time, against the Soviet system itself.

The mounting economic and political crises within the Soviet Union were compounded by acute political problems in the Soviet empire in Eastern Europe. Gorbachev encouraged the communist leadership there to embark upon a policy of liberalizing reforms similar to those he was pursuing at home. This triggered a series of changes that proved disastrous for the survival of communism in this key region of the empire. Gorbachev had hoped that a policy of reform would prove attractive and stabilizing in Eastern Europe. But the liberalization he encouraged only served to destabilize regimes that had been installed by Soviet force of arms and that continued to rest on the support of the secret police, communist penetration of all institutions of the societies, and, ultimately, the presence of Soviet troops. Deciding that the costs and uncertainties of intervention to preserve the status quo outweighed those of inaction, Gorbachev presided over the collapse of communism in the region, culminating in the fall of the Berlin Wall on November 11, 1989, which set the stage for the reunification of Germany.

In 1991, Gorbachev himself succumbed to the same political forces that had toppled communist regimes in Eastern Europe. His piecemeal economic reforms had only served to destabilize the Soviet Union's badly ailing economy, and the decline in the country's gross national product accelerated. His political thaw led to a rising chorus of criticism that spared not even the most sacred tenets of Marxist-Leninist ideology. The multinational, multiethnic complexion of the country contributed to the political crisis, as nationalism and separatism engulfed one region after another. The communist party apparatus tried to fight back, and, beginning in the fall of 1990, Gorbachev was prevailed upon to switch course and slow the pace of change. But conservatives remained fearful that Gorbachev's leadership would lead to the complete collapse of central Soviet authority.

On August 19, 1991, one day before a new treaty among the Soviet republics was to be signed, senior officials in the military, the communist party, and the KGB attempted a coup d'état against Gorbachev. Hastily planned and executed like a bad comic opera, the attempt failed within days. The only achievement was the very outcome the coup plotters had set out to avoid: the complete destruction of communist rule and the disintegration of the Soviet state. By December, Gorbachev, who was discredited at home by his failed economic policies as well as by his association with the very men who plotted against him, was pushed aside by Boris Yeltsin who was then serving as the elected president of the Russian republic within the Soviet Union. One republic within the Soviet Union after another, including Russia itself, declared independence from the Soviet state.

Although the Soviet Union proved unable to summon the coercive or normative power needed to ensure its survival, it had nevertheless clearly been viewed as legitimate by significant segments of the population, particularly Russians. The costly, seemingly miraculous victory in World War II; the remarkable economic recovery from the war; and the technological achievements exemplified by the 1957 launching of *Sputnik*, the first man-made satellite, all generated significant support for the Soviet system among the Soviet population and in many foreign countries as well. But Gorbachev's reforms allowed the Soviet citizen finally to evaluate more objectively the economic and political conditions of other countries, particularly the United States, which Soviet propaganda had long condemned as decadent, exploitative, and racist. In this sense, the United States contributed to the demise of the Soviet Union not only because of increased American spending on anti-Soviet "liberation" movements, military improvements, or regional alliances, but also because of the growing belief among Soviet citizens that Western values and institutions were more attractive. The Soviet Union officially ended its existence when the hammer and sickle flag was lowered for the last time over the Kremlin on December 31, 1991.

U.S.-Russian Relations in the Post-Soviet Period

U.S. foreign policy toward Russia in the post-Soviet period has sought to advance American values and interests. American values at stake in the U.S. relationship with Russia include the creation of democratic and free market institutions that could form the foundation for a pluralist Russian polity committed to respect for human freedom and prepared to contribute to a peaceful international order. American interests include arms control, nuclear nonproliferation, counterterrorism, trade, and U.S. influence in the *near abroad*, as the Russians termed the former Soviet republics.

U.S. foreign policy has yielded only mixed results in promoting these American values and interests. Perhaps the most important achievement, for which Washington can take partial credit, is that the U.S.-Russian relationship is no longer marked by the zero-sum ideological contest that characterized the Cold War; instead, it is now defined by "normal" interstate competition. The possibilities for cooperation are now much broader, and the prospect of severe political or even military conflict is much reduced. Nevertheless, by late 2008, some observers were forecasting a new Cold War between Russia and the West. Russian President Vladimir Putin helped fuel such speculation, making a veiled comparison between U.S. foreign policy and that of Nazi Germany and harshly criticizing Washington for planning to create "one single center of power . . . one single center of decision making" in world affairs.[11]

The gradual deterioration in U.S.-Russian relations in the post-Soviet period is due in part to the growth of negative conditions in Russian domestic politics. However, it is also attributable to the emergence of significant and seemingly irreconcilable conflicts of interests relating to Russia's international status that have helped generate significant grievances among Russia's elites and mass public. Three broad themes reflect the changing character of U.S.-Russian relations in the post-Soviet period: the gradual weakening of the integration of post-Soviet Russia into the West, including reversals in democratization; the revival of Russia as a regional power and international actor; and the declining ability, for a variety of reasons, of the United States to shape Russian behavior in the international and domestic spheres, despite America's superpower status.

The Yeltsin Era. The leadership of Yeltsin was an essential factor in the collapse of the Soviet Union and in the course of U.S.-Russian relations in the first post-Soviet decade. Yeltsin was the product of the Soviet communist system, having climbed the ladder of the Soviet bureauracy from provincial party leader to Politburo member in Moscow. After his break with Gorbachev and the communist party over the pace and nature of Soviet reform, Yeltsin was elected president of the Russian Soviet Federated Socialist Republic. From that position, he commanded enormous legitimacy and political power, enabling him to seal the fate of the Soviet Union and then emerge as the head of the newly born Russian Republic.

Achievements in U.S.-Russia Relations under Yeltsin (1991–1999). In the immediate post-Soviet period, Washington strongly supported Yeltsin, the first president of the new Russian state, as the most effective way to promote U.S. interests and values. On almost all foreign policy issues of importance to the United States, Yeltsin either backed Washington's initiatives or at least refused to obstruct them. Yeltsin's behavior was due in part to the realities of America's overwhelming power and the relative weakness of the new Russian state. Yet Yeltsin was also drawn to the United States, because he was ideologically comfortable with Western economic and political values. This comfort distinguished Yeltsin from Russian communists and ultranationalists, who were still a powerful force in Russian politics in the 1990s. Yeltsin also relied on Western political and economic aid to advance his political survival, further strengthening his ties to the West.

One of Yeltsin's most significant contributions to American interests was his rejection of the Russian and Soviet imperial mentality. He allowed eastern and central Europe to rejoin the West and permitted the new states of the former Soviet Union to establish their independence. It is conceivable that if the first Russian president had been an ultranationalist or an unreformed communist, Russian troops might still be in Poland and in the Baltic republics.[12]

Dramatic progress also occurred in arms control and disarmament during the years of Yeltsin's administration. International concern about the safety and security of the former Soviet nuclear stockpile, plus cost considerations, prompted a 1992 decision by the individual nuclear powers among the new post-Soviet states to have Russia retain centralized command and control over the vast former Soviet arsenal. With American encouragement and financial aid, particularly through the creation of the Nunn-Lugar Cooperative Threat Reduction (CTR) programs, the four nuclear successor states—Russia, Belarus, Kazakhstan, and Ukraine—signed a protocol in Lisbon in May 1992 assuming the responsibilities of the defunct Soviet Union under the 1991 Strategic Arms Reduction Treaty (START). Belarus, Kazakhstan, and Ukraine further committed themselves to joining the Nuclear Non-proliferation Treaty as non-nuclear weapons states. The denuclearization of Russia's neighbors was completed with the removal of the last Russian SS-25s from Belarus on June 30, 1997. Driven by concerns over the possible theft of nuclear materials and their sale to terrorists, CTR programs also created employment opportunities and better working conditions for former Soviet nuclear scientists and provided secure storage facilities for Russian nuclear materials.

Fears about smuggling, mishaps, and accidental launches of nuclear weapons stimulated and sustained interest in Moscow and Washington in continued strategic arms reduction. START and subsequent agreements reduced the levels of nuclear weapons drastically from the ten to twelve thousand warheads deployed at the end of the 1980s. START II, signed by Presidents George H. W. Bush and Yeltsin in January 1993, was ratified by the U.S. Senate in 1996 and by the Russian parliament in 2000. START II stipulates the elimination of all land-based missiles with multiple warheads and sets a limit of three thousand to thirty-five hundred deployed warheads for each side. As of mid-2007, negotiations were underway for START III, which would reduce active warheads to between two thousand and twenty-five hundred.

The high tide of U.S.-Russian cooperation occurred in 1997. In response to Washington's plans to expand NATO into eastern and central Europe, Yeltsin requested compensation. President Bill Clinton responded by offering the Russian president, who faced rising political opposition at home, significant inducements that moved Russia closer to integration with the West. Russia was made a partner in the prestigious annual Group of Seven (G7) summits, increasing Moscow's international influence and stature. Washington also promised the Kremlin that it would press for Russia's inclusion in important international institutions, such as the World Trade Organization and the Organization for Economic Cooperation and Development. Also significant, Russia and NATO signed the NATO-Russia Founding Act in Paris in May 1997, which established a formal mechanism to promote cooperation and to the "maximum extent possible . . . joint decisions and joint action with respect to security issues of common concern."[13]

The Failure to Establish Democracy in Russia.   Washington had thrown its support to Yeltsin largely because he was—at least initially—an effective advocate of Russian democratization. Russian progress toward democracy promised to advance American values and also to strengthen American security interests, given the widely held view that democracies do not fight wars with each other. Yet these expectations were confounded, and Russia is still struggling to determine its fundamental political values. For some observers, the problem of self-definition remains the "single greatest challenge" facing Russian society.[14]

The problematic nature of Russian political identity and the failure of democratization are due in large part to the extraordinary political, economic, and social upheavals that convulsed Russia in its first decade of independence. Perhaps most important, Yeltsin embarked on a wrenching economic program of marketization and privatization that helped impoverish many Russians while creating a small group of oligarchs who came to control much of Russia's national wealth.[15] As Russia descended further into economic and political instability and corruption in the 1990s, Yeltsin became isolated and dictatorial as he grew increasingly unpopular.

Changing Russian Assessments of U.S. Foreign Policy.   By the close of the twentieth century, Russia's elites and masses widely believed that the West, particularly the United States, opposed vital Russian interests. This perspective was fueled by accumulated grievances against the West and by Russian fears of international isolation and even encirclement by hostile powers. Against the backdrop of Russia's weakness and America's unchallenged global power, Russian elites (liberal and otherwise) broadly criticized the United States for its early advocacy of rapid Russian marketization and privatization and for its support for Yeltsin despite the rampant corruption and ineffectiveness of his regime.

The expansion of NATO during the 1990s and NATO's military campaign in support of the Kosovar Albanians against traditional Russian ally Serbia in 1999 were also especially contentious issues. NATO enlargement and the Kosovo campaign were stark reminders for Russia that it was simply too weak to have its objections to Western policies taken into account. This relative weakness was particularly painful for Russia's political and military elites, many of whom had recently stood at the helm of the Soviet superpower. Believing that the West had pledged at the end of the Cold War not to expand NATO, Russians were understandably concerned for their security as such countries as Poland, the Czech Republic, and Hungary (which had once provided a buffer between the Soviet Union and the West) became members of one of the most powerful alliances in history. Most Russian critics failed to acknowledge that the unfortunate history of these states as unwilling members of the oppressive Soviet "outer empire" had determined their foreign policy preferences and alliance choices. Even committed Russian democrats often believed that the United States was behaving like a "rogue hegemon," exploiting Russia's weakness, challenging its core national interests, and undermining the Russian state as a viable institution. The extent of anti-American and anti-Western attitudes was also influenced by a near collapse of the Russian economy in 1998. One 1999 Russian survey found that 41.1% of the respondents felt that the West was attempting to turn Russia into a Third World country; some 37.5% felt that Western nations were intent on breaking up and destroying Russia completely.[16] In other polls, 72% of the respondents described themselves as "hostile toward the United States,"[17] and 69% believed that the West desired the collapse of the Russian economy.[18] By then deeply unpopular with a collapsing political base, Yeltsin was less and less able to insulate Russian foreign policy from this rising tide of nationalist ferment.

The Advent of Putin and the Rise of the Militocracy.   Yeltsin's abrupt resignation in December 1999 elevated Putin, his prime minister and a former lieutenant colonel in the KGB, to acting president. This set the stage for Putin's election as president the following March. If Russian democratization under Yeltsin had suffered from mismanagement and frequent neglect, under Putin it suffered from direct assault.

An important development of the Yeltsin period had been the gradual acceptance by most Russian elites—at least in principle—of elections, markets, and private property. However, the most influential elites under Yeltsin—the oligarchs—did much to corrupt each of these, primarily by pressuring the Russian state to favor their private interests. Putin moved early to diminish the power of the oligarchs, in effect transferring their political influence to the *siloviki*, top state officials with backgrounds in the Interior Ministry, the military, and the Federal Security Service

(FSB; the successor to the KGB). These "uniformed bureaucrats" now formed a "militocracy" that shared Putin's desire to create a strong Russian state and revive Russian patriotism.[19] Largely hostile to political pluralism and highly vigilant against domestic and external enemies, real or imagined, this group reflected and supported Putin's worldview. Putin clamped down on the media, referring to his critics as "traitors," and worked to control and diminish Russian civil and political society across the board, including restricting the activities of nongovernmental organizations (NGOs). After the politicized arrest of the famous oil tycoon Mikhail Khodarkovsky in October 2003 for economic crimes, even the once-powerful Russian oligarchs were driven from any oppositional role in politics.

Despite Putin's assault on the political freedoms gained during the Yeltsin period, the Kremlin's efforts to restore the power of the Russian state, internally and externally, buoyed Putin's popularity among Russian elites and the mass public.[20] Many Russians regret the collapse of the Soviet Union not only for the loss of domestic economic and political stability but also for the collapse of Russian global power and prestige. When asked in a survey after the American-led invasion of Iraq in 2003—which Russia vocally and unsuccessfully opposed—how they wanted Russia to be perceived by other nations, 48% of survey respondents said "mighty, unbeatable, indestructible, a great world power." Only 3% of the respondents wanted Russia to be viewed as "peace-loving and friendly," and only 1% said "law-abiding and democratic."[21] Although other surveys reveal strong support for democratic values among most Russians, in practice, democratization in Russia suffered significant setbacks under Putin, in part because of the acquiescence of much of Russian society to his authoritarian style.[22] This Russian acquiescence to authoritarianism was also shaped by a rising tide of Russian nationalism, stoked by the Kremlin's control of Russian mass media, which maintains that the Kremlin is protecting Russia from Western—particularly American—attempts at "regime change" in Russia.

The Continuing Crisis in Chechnya.   Putin's approach to the crisis in Chechnya, which reflected his efforts to rebuild the power of the Russian state, was a primary source of his initial popularity and authority.[23] The secessionist movement in Chechnya and Moscow's brutal and ineffective efforts to reign it in sharpened Russia's sense of insecurity in the 1990s and even sparked fears of the collapse of the newborn Russian state. Under Yeltsin, the weakness of the Russian state was on full display during the disastrous Russian-Chechen war of 1994–1996, in which the well-organized and highly motivated Chechen rebels fought the ill-prepared, conscripted Russian Army to a humiliating standstill and eventually forced the Russian Army's withdrawal from Chechen soil. The war left Chechnya in ruins, wracked by violent feuds among rival warlords, the collapse of social order, and the rise of Islamic radicalism and terrorism.

Convinced that Russia was a paper tiger after the defeat in Afghanistan and the humiliation of the first Chechen War, Chechen radicals believed that a second war would destroy the political center in Chechen politics and propel them to power at the head of an independent trans-Caucasus Islamic state. To this end, Chechen militants launched terror campaigns, including deadly bombings of residential buildings in Moscow and an armed incursion into neighboring Dagestan. These provocations prompted Moscow to launch the second Russian-Chechen War in 1999 during Putin's brief tenure as Yeltsin's prime minister. This time Russian forces, better organized and facing a badly divided Chechen opposition, scored significant successes in the field, eventually pacifying most of the countryside. Although Chechen separatists led by Shamil Basayev committed several spectacular and brutal acts of terrorism during 2003 and 2004, by 2006 Basayev had been killed, and many other radicals had been killed or captured or had accepted amnesty. Moscow installed an oppressive and corrupt government in Chechnya, led by Ramzan Kadyrov, the leader of a prominent and rapacious Chechen militia.[24]

Although in 2007 Moscow claimed victory in the Chechen conflict, which the Kremlin had framed as Russia's battle against international terrorism, the entire North Caucasus region remains unstable. It seems likely that popular support in Chechnya for secession will reignite if its profound socioeconomic problems continue to fester. Also, as insurgency has waned in Chechnya, it has grown in its neighbors. Chechen militants have assisted in this development, but local Islamic radicals have taken the lead in Ingushetia, North Ossetia, and Kabardino-Balkariya (see Map 22.2). Russian authorities have aggravated this growing potential for instability and terrorism by persecuting observant Muslims as likely insurgents,

MAP 22.2   The North Caucuses and Chechnya

Source: Central Intelligence Agency.

by failing to address endemic poverty and joblessness, and by condoning widespread corruption.

Clearly, the Chechen wars have damaged the prospects for Russian democratization. The brutalities and failures of the first Chechen War generated a groundswell of criticism in Russian society, throwing Yeltsin off balance and severely damaging his authority. The Putin administration learned from this experience and effectively used the specter of Chechen terrorism and separatism to muzzle criticism of the second Chechen War and to build public support for further empowerment of the Russian state. Due primarily to its competing foreign policy priorities, the United States has been unwilling to level consistent or significant criticism against the Kremlin for the extreme violations of Chechen human rights by Russian security forces and their proxies.

Russian Foreign Policy under Putin.   Despite some worsening of relations as the 1990s drew to a close, the United States and Russia once again seemed to be on a path toward cooperation after the tragic events of September 11, 2001. Putin was the first foreign leader to contact President George W. Bush after the traumatic terrorist attacks on U.S. soil. Putin offered Bush a partnership based on Russian support for U.S. global leadership, the U.S. invasion of Afghanistan, and the establishment of U.S. bases in former Soviet Central Asia. In exchange, the United States would embrace Russia as a major ally and recognize the post-Soviet space as Russia's legitimate sphere of influence.

Although Moscow provided significant aid to the United States and the Afghan Northern Alliance in defeating the Taliban in Afghanistan, Washington's response to Putin's overtures fell well short of the full partnership sought by the Kremlin. Putin's discomfort deepened when George W. Bush decided in December 2001 to pull out of the 1972 Anti-Ballistic Missile Treaty, the arms control agreement designed to prevent either signatory from gaining a decisive advantage through the deployment of antiballistic missile (ABM) systems. In 2007, Washington announced plans to field a limited ABM system, including a radar installation and ten interceptor missiles, in Poland and the Czech Republic. Although Washington argued that the system was intended to defend Europe against the missiles of a "rogue" state, such as Iran or North Korea, the Kremlin strongly condemned the proposal and warned that, as a consequence, Russia might again target Europe with its nuclear arsenal.

Opposition to American foreign policy goals gradually crystallized in the run-up to the second Iraq war. In 2002, Russia joined Germany and France in opposing Washington's efforts to obtain UN support for an invasion of Iraq. Moscow's opposition was likely based on two factors. First was Putin's concern that the unilateralism of the Bush administration, within the context of American unipolarity and in the absence of a strategic partnership with the United States, was undercutting his efforts to restore Russia's status as a great power.

The second likely factor was Moscow's long-standing relationship with Baghdad. Iraq had been a Soviet client during the Cold War, and the resounding defeat of Saddam Hussein's Soviet-equipped army in 1991 was viewed as a humiliation by the Soviet political elite and the leadership of the Red Army. Moscow maintained close ties with Baghdad in the post-Soviet period, largely due to economic motivations, particularly arms sales. In the 2003 crisis over Iraq, Russia sought to support its old client and to resist the expansion of U.S. power in the Middle East.

In 2004, Russia suffered another reversal, again at the hands of NATO, when Estonia, Latvia, Lithuania, Bulgaria, Romania, Slovakia, and Slovenia were admitted into the alliance. Although NATO officials maintained that the latest round of enlargement did not threaten Russian security, the incorporation of the Baltic states, which had been constituent republics of the Soviet Union from 1940 to 1991, brought the alliance to Russia's doorstep.[25]

The Near Abroad: The "Color Revolutions."   In addition to the entry of Lithuania, Latvia, and Estonia into NATO, other developments complicated Russia's relationship with the "near abroad." Even under Yeltsin, Russian elites assumed that the former Soviet space would be part of Russia's sphere of interest. This assumption was based on the history of Russian imperialism in Eurasia and the long-standing socioeconomic and cultural ties between Russia and the peoples of the new post-Soviet states. The diaspora in the near abroad of up to 25 million ethnic Russians reinforced Russia's strong interest in the region.

Although Russia was profoundly weak in comparison to the United States, it overshadowed other post-Soviet countries in economic and military terms and so could continue to view itself as the dominant regional power. This self-image was challenged by the enlargement of NATO and the establishment of American bases in Central Asia after 9/11 and, most importantly, by an unexpected wave of democratization in Georgia (the "Rose Revolution," 2003), Ukraine ("The Orange Revolution," 2004), and Kyrgyzstan (the "Tulip Revolution," 2005). The events in Ukraine and Georgia, where electoral fraud by the semiauthoritarian regimes mobilized broad-based opposition, were of particular concern because of their proximity to Russia, Russia's unsuccessful efforts to tilt the elections, the distinctly pro-Western tenor of the political upheavals, and the important role that Western assistance played in supporting democratic forces in those countries. This assistance included the direct aid of Western governments to local actors in civil society, as well as the careful work of Western NGOs devoted to civic and political education.[26]

The "color revolutions" in Ukraine, Georgia, and even Kyrgyzstan may very well produce stable democracies on Russia's borders that may one day have positive effects on domestic politics in Russia.[27] In any case, the color revolutions have already served as stark reminders to Russia's elites of the eastward spread of Western influence and Russia's questionable ability to control events in contiguous states.

Fearing democratic contagion in Russia itself, the Kremlin characterized the political upheavals as meddling by an unsavory alliance of domestic opposition groups and foreign interests seeking to destabilize the region. On this basis, Moscow denounced the Organization for Security and Cooperation in Europe, which had uncovered and publicized electoral fraud in the pivotal elections in Ukraine. Within Russia, more stringent controls were placed on the freedom of the media, civic organizations, NGOs, and opposition groups and parties. These

Table 22.1   Major Russian Military Forces

Air Force (160,000 personnel)	
Bombers	124
Transports, tankers	50
Tactical aircraft	1,677
Helicopters	60
Aircraft for training	980
Army (395,000 personnel, of which 190,000 are conscripts)	
Main battle tanks	22,831
Armored combat vehicles	26,990
Artillery	30,045
Helicopters	771
Navy (142,000 personnel)	
Aircraft carriers	1
Cruisers, destroyers, frigates	44
Tactical submarines	53
Amphibious ships	71
Logistics and support ships	371
Aircraft	245
Helicopters	311
Coastal Defense and Naval Infantry (11,500 personnel)	
Main battle tanks	510
Armored combat vehicles	660
Artillery	819
Strategic Deterrent Forces (80,000 personnel)	
Strategic nuclear submarines	15
Intercontinental ballistic missiles	506
Antiballistic missiles	100
Long-range strategic bombers	80
Space Forces (40,000 personnel)	

Source: International Institute for Strategic Studies, *The Military Balance, 2007* (London: Routledge, 2007).

preventive, authoritarian measures prompted Western criticism, leading to a further cycle of mutual recrimination.

Russia Resurgent.   Russia's increasing assertiveness in the near abroad and on the international stage became a mark of Putin's leadership.[28] Having pacified Chechnya and neutralized Chechen terrorism by 2005 (if only temporarily), Moscow moved to roll back Western influence in Central Asia. In May 2005, the authoritarian regime in Uzbekistan put down protests in the provincial city of Andijan, leading to the deaths of hundreds of civilians. Criticized by the West, Uzbekistan sought Russia's support, arguing that it was battling the mutual threat of Islamic radicalism. The Kremlin sided with the Uzbek government, emboldening it to terminate basing rights that the United States had used to support military operations in Afghanistan. In 2006, Uzbekistan joined the Moscow-led Collective Security Treaty Organization, whose membership includes many of the new states of the former Soviet Union.

As a further example of Russia's assertiveness, Russia has not only repeatedly used its natural gas monopoly in the Ukraine to remind the former Soviet Republic of the wisdom of accommodating Moscow's interests, but it has also laid claim (via a capsule containing a Russian flag it planted in the Arctic sea floor) to the Arctic's potential oil and gas reserves.

Perhaps the most significant examples of Russian resurgence in the foreign policy arena come from Russian-Georgian relations. Moscow has continued to put pressure on Georgia, led by a strongly pro-Western government after its "Rose Revolution" of 2003, using its support for the separatist regions of Abkhazia and South Ossetia within Georgia to force the country to conform to Russian interests in the Caucasus.[29] Georgia's President Mikheil Saakashvili refused to yield ground and appealed to the United States. Moscow revealed its increased willingness to oppose U.S. interests when Putin warned Washington not to interfere in the diplomatic furor that erupted after Georgia arrested four Russian Army officers in late 2006 on charges of espionage. Russia imposed a full-scale transport and trade embargo on Georgia, and the officers were eventually released.

Conflict in Georgia reached a new level of intensity in 2008, with the spark being developments in South Ossetia. In response to a series of violent incidents including some against ethnically Georgian residents of South Ossetia, Saakashvili launched a military operation in South Ossetia in August 2008. The response by Russia, which had stationed peacekeepers in South Ossetia since the early 1990s, was dramatic. "Russia's disproportionate counter-attack" involved not only the reinforcement of Russian peacekeepers in South Ossetia but also the "movement of large forces into Abkhazia and deep into Georgia, accompanied by the widespread destruction of economic infrastructure, damage to the economy, and disruption of communications and movement between different regions of [Georgia]."[30] According to U.S. Secretary of State Condoleezza Rice, Russia's actions amounted to a "full scale invasion across an internationally-recognized border."[31] Russia subsequently recognized the independence of Abkhazia and South Ossetia, citing the aspirations of the peoples of these regions as well as its responsibility to protect Russian citizens living outside the borders of the Russian state (see also Chapter 23). Throughout this crisis, Putin—who had yielded the Russian Presidency to Dmitry Medvedev after 2008 presidential elections—appeared still to be decisively in charge from his new position as Russia's Prime Minister.[32]

The scope, scale, and immediacy of the Russian actions in this crisis suggest that Russia had motivations as well as intended effects beyond the situation in South Ossetia. With regard to motivations, these probably included "pushback against the decade-long eastward expansion of the NATO alliance" and "anger over issues ranging from the independence of Kosovo" to U.S. initiatives to place missile defense systems in eastern Europe.[33] The intended effects of Russia's actions in Georgia appear to include sending a message to former Soviet Republics such as Georgia and Ukraine that Russia still intends to exercise a degree of control in what Russia considers its rightful sphere of influence, and that it is not permissible for these two countries to obtain the NATO memberships that both Georgia and Ukraine have expressed interest in obtaining.[34]

Russia has also increasingly charted its own course outside its own perceived sphere of influence. It invited the Hamas leadership in Palestine to visit Moscow and offered financial assistance to the group after the United States and the European Union (EU) withdrew economic support. Russia has also declared that it opposes any sanctions against Iran for its program of uranium enrichment and has asserted that it would continue its arms trade and nuclear cooperation with Tehran in the face of European and American opposition. Moscow joined Beijing in calling for the withdrawal of the U.S. military from Central Asia, and China and Russia have begun to conduct joint military exercises.

A number of factors explain Russia's willingness and ability to disagree with or actively confront the Western powers, particularly the United States. For the near abroad, one factor is that Russia's influence in the former Soviet space, except for the Baltic region, has risen because U.S. influence has declined. Despite their spectacular electoral victories in the color revolutions, pro-Western forces in Georgia and particularly in the Ukraine have yet to consolidate their power. For these two countries, and even more for other post-Soviet governments, the economic and political presence of the West is limited because of geographical distance and because of the heavy American focus on the Middle East. Much of the region is still tied together by Soviet-era economic and energy infrastructures and by common knowledge of the Russian language. Given that significant Western investment, let alone membership in the EU and NATO, is not yet a viable option, a number of these countries are drawn to Russia as they seek development and security. In addition to the occasional use of military power, Russia has also sought to enhance its "soft power" by increasing regional investment and serving as an economic magnet for its post-Soviet neighbors.[35]

The rise of Russia as a dominant regional power also rests on its remarkable recovery since its economic collapse of 1998. Russia possesses vast natural resources that account for 80% of its exports. It is the world's largest exporter of natural gas and second-largest exporter of oil. The dramatic rise in the price of oil, from $11 a barrel in 1998 to more than $100 a barrel in 2008 has been the driving force behind Russian economic growth, which has averaged between 6% and 7% per year. Russia has also increased exports of other natural resources, particularly metals, and of manufactured goods, such as machinery.

Russia's emergence as an energy superpower under Putin has clear implications for global and regional security. On the one hand, Russia has used its newfound wealth primarily to support greater state-led economic modernization and not to strengthen its military power, which has grown only modestly. Although Russia's defense budget was $31 billion in 2007, up from $8 billion in 2001, Russian military spending was still far less than that of the United States.[36] On the other hand, Russia has not always used its economic power responsibly. In January 2006, Gazprom, the Russian government-controlled energy giant, abruptly turned off natural gas supplies to the Ukraine in a disagreement over prices, inadvertently creating shortages in western Europe. Efforts by the West to have Russia ratify the European Energy Charter, which calls for good governance and transparency, were turned back by Moscow. Russia's influence in global and regional energy security is likely to increase over at least the next decade or two. In mid-2007, Russia signed an agreement with Turkmenistan and Kazakhstan for the construction of a gas pipeline that would tie these countries to the European gas supply network. The agreement was an important coup for Russia in its efforts to check the power of the United States, which had sought for fifteen years to divert regional energy supplies in Central Asia away from Russian control. Equally important, as demonstrated by the just-cited case of the Ukraine, Russia has shown its willingness to wield oil and gas as a political weapon. Moscow believes, in the words of an influential Russian politician, that "Europe's reliance on Russian energy" will force the West to acquiesce in Russia's attempts to increase its political weight in the near abroad.[37]

U.S. Policy Challenges for the Future

U.S.-Russian relations in the twenty-first century demonstrate the limits of American power and influence in the former Soviet space. These limits are evident as the United States seeks to promote democracy, regional stability, and Russia's integration into global institutions.[38] If a state is self-sufficient or nearly so (as is Russia) and possesses vast natural resources, its rulers can more easily refuse to consider political reforms that might improve state capacity (including authentic democratization) but that might also weaken their power. Such rulers can also skillfully exploit the reliance of external actors on trade or strategic cooperation with their country. In Russia's case, European reliance on its energy resources and America's desire for Russian support for nonproliferation regimes enable Moscow to fend off international demands for political liberalization or foreign policy moderation.

Furthermore, location and size matter, even in the era of globalization. Leadership, of course, also matters. Although Moscow was closer to American political values during the Yeltsin period and was also more sensitive to Western pressure and foreign policy preferences, those proclivities have now faded. The ascendance of nationalistic and frequently anti-American elites within an increasingly authoritarian political setting, coupled with Russia's burgeoning energy wealth, has hardened the Kremlin's stance toward the West. On certain fundamental political and economic issues, Russia and the United States are now divided and are likely to remain so for the foreseeable future. The United States wants Russia to be a liberal democracy with a transparent market economy, and it also wants much the same for the countries in Russia's sphere of influence. For its part, Russia wants the United States to treat it as an equal and on its own terms.[39] Russia will resist Western influence in the former Soviet space and turn a deaf ear to Western calls for democratization in Russia itself. Flush with oil wealth and emboldened by U.S. difficulties in Iraq and Afghanistan, the Kremlin is critical of what it sees as a hegemonic U.S. foreign policy only thinly disguised by the rhetoric of democracy promotion.

Russian observers, such as Dmitri Trenin, criticize Russia's slide into authoritarianism, seeing it as akin to tsarism, and feel that "traditional" Russian liberalism, which was supported in the late 1980s and early 1990s by intellectuals who were disinterested in Russian nationalism and patriotism, has run its course. In this view, Russia must now wait for the growth of a new kind of liberalism that integrates democracy and nationalism as core values. Trenin hopes that the growing urban middle class in Russia will eventually become the standard bearer of this new ideology but also maintains that this process of ideological renovation will take years and may produce unanticipated and unwelcome results.[40]

This assessment does not mean that the United States will be unable to advance its core values and interests in its relations with Russia. The strongest checks on full-blown authoritarianism in Russia and on significant and sustained confrontation between Russia and the United States are twofold. First, Russia is no longer guided, as it was under communism, by a messianic ideology that seeks to create a new civilization in opposition to Western institutions and values. Russia's elites are not ideologically hostile to civil and political freedoms, although they are certainly opposed to the constraints that authentic democratic institutions would place on their power. Second, those elites embrace strong, albeit selective, relationships with the West for instrumental reasons. The Kremlin's conceptualization of Russian modernization is shaped in large measure by a view of the external world—and particularly the global economy—that is at best wary. But Russia's political elites also believe that Russia's membership in key Western institutions and its integration into the world economy are necessary for Russian modernization, which over the long term will ensure Russia's status as a great power.

Under these conditions, Russia for the foreseeable future will likely be neither for nor against the West but rather a partner or an opponent, depending on the issue at hand. The content of U.S. policy and the quality of U.S. diplomacy by the new Obama administration will play an important role, for unwise policies and pressure can ensure opposition. The challenge for the United States is to craft policies that blend and balance restraint, cooperation, and activism. Increasing economic investment in Russia can also be important in helping nurture an independent Russian middle class and by injecting Western managerial expertise, with its attendant emphasis on transparency and good governance in the marketplace.

In the end, Russia will determine its own future. It is significant that Russia's attempts to secure its position as a great power have focused primarily on the development of its economic, rather than military, assets. This shift in national perspective on the part of Russia's elites, which marks a sea change from the reliance of the Soviet Union on military power, contributes to American national security. Nevertheless, if Russia slips further into autocracy and continues to rely on its energy resources as the primary source of its economic strength, it will remain a one-dimensional power very much like the Soviet Union, lacking strong, pluralist institutions and possessing relatively few durable ties to the West.

Discussion Questions

1. Compare Soviet foreign policy under Stalin, Khrushchev, Brezhnev, and Gorbachev; identify elements of continuity and change.
2. Did Marxist-Leninist ideology lead or follow Soviet foreign policy?
3. What developments best explain the collapse of the Soviet Union in 1991?

4. What aspects of U.S. national security policy now call for enhanced cooperation between the United States and the states of the former Soviet Union? What, specifically, are American interests in the region?

5. In what way has the foreign policy of Russia and the other former Soviet republics changed as a result of the end of the Cold War?

6. How might the United States enhance its influence in former Soviet space, particularly in the strategically important area of Central Asia?

7. What are the most effective U.S. instruments for supporting stability in former Soviet space?

8. To what extent—and with what instruments—should the United States promote democratization in the post-Soviet region?

9. How might Russian influence in Eurasia and the world increase in the next decade?

Recommended Reading

Barkey, Karen, and Mark von Hagen, eds. *After Empire: Multiethnic Societies and Nation-Building: The Soviet Union and the Russian, Ottoman, and Habsburg Empires.* Boulder, CO: Westview Press, 1997.

Blank, Stephen J. *U.S. Interests in Central Asia and the Challenges to Them.* Carlisle, PA: U.S. Army War College, 2007.

Bugajski, Janusz. *Cold Peace: Russia's New Imperialism.* Westport, CT: Praeger, 2004.

Coleman, Fred. *Decline and Fall of the Soviet Union: 40 Years That Shook the World.* New York: St. Martin's Press, 1996.

Cornell, Svante. *Georgia after the Rose Revolution: Geopolitical Predicament and the Implications for U.S. Policy.* Carlisle, PA: U.S. Army War College, 2007.

Ellison, Herbert J. *Boris Yeltsin and Russia's Democratic Transformation.* Seattle: University of Washington Press, 2006.

Garthoff, Raymond. *The Great Transition: American-Soviet Relations and the End of the Cold War.* Washington, DC: Brookings Institution Press, 1994.

Goldgier, James, and Michael McFaul. *Power and Purpose: U.S. Policy toward Russia after the Cold War.* Washington, DC: Brookings Institution Press, 2003.

Herspring, Dale R., ed. *Putin's Russia: Past Imperfect, Future Uncertain.* Lanham, MD: Rowman & Littlefield, 2007.

Larson, Deborah. *Anatomy of Mistrust: U.S.-Soviet Relations during the Cold War.* Ithaca, NY: Cornell University Press, 1997.

Legvold, Robert. *Russian Foreign Policy in the Twenty-First Century and the Shadow of the Past.* New York: Columbia University Press, 2007.

Mandelbaum, Michael, and Strobe Talbott. *Reagan and Gorbachev.* New York: Vintage Books, 1987.

Matlock, Jack. *Reagan and Gorbachev: How the Cold War Ended.* New York: Random House, 2004.

Mendelson, Sarah, and Theodore P. Gerber. "Soviet Nostalgia: An Impediment to Russian Democratization." *Washington Quarterly* 29, no. 1 (Winter 2005/2006): 83–96.

Motyl, Alexander, ed. *The Post-Soviet Nations: Perspectives on the Demise of the USSR.* New York: Columbia University Press, 1992.

McFaul, Michael, Nikolai Petrov, and Andrei Ryabov. *Between Dictatorship and Democracy: Russian Post-Communist Political Reform.* Washington, DC: Carnegie Endowment for International Peace, 2004.

Sakwa, Richard. *Chechnya: From Past to Future.* London: Anthem Press, 2005.

Suny, Ronald Grigor. *Nationalism, Revolution, and the Collapse of the Soviet Union.* Palo Alto, CA: Stanford University Press, 1994.

Tsygankov, Andrei P. *Russia's Foreign Policy: Change and Continuity in National Identity.* Lanham, MD: Rowman & Littlefield, 2006.

Zimmerman, William. *The Russian People and Foreign Policy: Russian Elite and Mass Perspectives, 1993–2000.* Princeton, NJ: Princeton University Press, 2002.

Internet Resources

Carnegie Moscow Center, www.carnegie.ru/en

The Collective Security Treaty Organization, www.cagateway.org/en/topics/23/84

Eurasia Daily Monitor, www.jamestown.org/edm

Founding Act on Mutual Relations, Cooperation and Security Between NATO and the Russian Federation, NATO On-line Library, http://www.nato.int/docu/basictxt/fndact-a.htm

Johnson's Russia List, www.cdi.org/russia/johnson/default.cfm

Radio Free Europe/Radio Liberty, www.rferl.org

Russia's presidential Web site, www.kremlin.ru/eng/

Russia, U.S. Department of State, www.state.gov/p/eur/ci/rs

Strategic Studies Institute of the U.S. Army War College, www.strategicstudiesinstitute.army.mil

23

Europe

For more than four decades after World War II, U.S. security policy toward Europe focused on the East-West confrontation with the Soviet Union and the implementation of the policy of containment. The dissolution of the Soviet Union in 1991, the expansion of the North Atlantic Treaty Organization (NATO) and the European Union (EU), conflicts in the Balkans (especially in Bosnia-Herzegovina and Kosovo), al-Qa'ida terrorist attacks within the United States and European countries, and military operations in Afghanistan and Iraq have all combined to cause a fundamental realignment of U.S. foreign policy toward the European continent.

Today, U.S. security interests in Europe continue to be shaped by shared values and a shared history. From mature democratic political systems to developed capitalist economies, the similarities between the United States and Europe offer a foundation for sustaining and building upon the close network of cooperation that developed over the years of Cold War. Yet in recent years, significant transatlantic rifts have developed; without attention, these disagreements will adversely affect the ability of the United States to continue to partner with the countries of Europe to advance common interests.

U.S. Interests in Europe

The dramatic transformations on the European continent since the fall of the Berlin Wall in 1989 and the large-scale terrorist attacks in the United States and Europe in the early twenty-first century have quite logically led the United States to reassess its security interests in Europe. Five major topics deserve attention in looking to the future.

MAP 23.1   Europe

First, the United States has a continuing interest in the North Atlantic Treaty Organization (NATO) as an entity that promotes the security and stability of twenty-four European states (plus Canada) and contributes broadly to international peace and security. The collective defense provision of the alliance (Article 5) indicates that an attack on a member state will be considered an attack against the entire group of members. NATO successfully ensured the freedom of its members and prevented war in Europe during the forty years of the Cold War. However, some argue that with this success, NATO also ended the reason for its existence. Ongoing NATO operations in the Balkans, Afghanistan, and the Mediterranean Sea provide a counterargument and highlight the potential usefulness of continued U.S. participation in the alliance and transformation of its capabilities. Since its founding, The NATO alliance has served as the foremost means through which the United States cooperates with foreign partners in its initiatives relating to international peace and security and its continuing operations suggest that it will remain a useful treaty organization into the foreseeable future.

Second, because of the large volume of trade and investment across the Atlantic, the stability of this region and security of transatlantic lines of communication remain key U.S. interests for economic reasons. In 2005, 21% of all U.S. exports went to the EU, while 19% of total U.S. imports were from the EU.[1] Yet trade disputes between the United States and the EU (often aired in the World Trade Organization) are frequent, and the existence of various tariffs and subsidies (particularly regarding agricultural products and the aircraft industry) strain this economic relationship.

Third, the United States has an interest in remaining engaged in the region to serve as a counterweight to the influence of the major successor state to the former Soviet Union, Russia. Despite arms reductions, Russia retains a large conventional arsenal and nuclear weapons capable of threatening its neighbors and the United States. Because intentions can change, and because of the possibility that these capabilities could fall into the hands of terrorists or be sold to other states openly hostile to the United States, Russia's military arsenal remains a major U.S. security concern. In addition, many countries in eastern and central Europe and central Asia fear the threat that a resurgent Russia could pose to their security and autonomy. The United States has an interest in the continued political and economic development of these countries and long-term peace and stability in Eurasia. (For more on Russia, see Chapter 22.)

Fourth, Europe's geographic proximity to other regions in which U.S. vital interests lie—particularly the Middle East—also makes it strategically valuable to the United States. Continued close cooperation with the countries of Europe can help the United States address security concerns beyond the European continent.

Finally, the global fight against terrorism necessitates cooperation against the extremist threat. The September 11, 2001, attacks were planned in Hamburg, Germany, highlighting the transnational nature of the threat. Furthermore, the difficulty many European countries are having in integrating large Muslim immigrant populations has led some analysts to raise concerns that some European environments serve as breeding grounds for extremists. The United States has a continuing national security interest in coordinating diplomatic, military, financial, and law enforcement approaches to combating international terrorist groups with European partners.

In sum, despite the transformation in East-West relations that began with the end of the Cold War, European security will continue to be extremely important to the United States. Nevertheless, it will be appropriate for specific policies—such as the U.S. military posture in Europe—to continue to evolve. To have the necessary context to evaluate contemporary policy options, it is useful to review briefly the history of U.S. involvement in Europe since the end of World War II.

History of U.S. Involvement in Europe

After World War II, Europe faced a bipolar world: Only the United States and the Soviet Union had sufficient capabilities to play significant leadership roles. When

Table 23.1 Europe Key Statistics

Country	Total Population (millions)	GDP US$ (billions)	GDP/Capita (US$)	GDP Real Growth Rate	Unemployment Rate	Military Spending % of GDP	Military Spending 2005 (US$ millions)	Education Spending % of GDP	Research & Development Spending % of GDP	Foreign Aid Dispersed 2005	Human Development Index Ranking 2007/2008 (out of 177)
Albania	3.6	9.3	5,700	5	13.8	1.5	116	2.9	—	—	68
Austria	8.2	310.4	34,700	3.3	4.9	0.9	2,263	5.5	2.33	1,573	15
Belarus	9.7	28.98	8,100	9.9	1.6	1.4	2,700	6	0.62	—	64
Belgium	10.4	369.6	33,000	3	8.1	1.3	4,620	6.1	1.9	1,963	17
Bosnia and Herzegovina	4.5	9.2	5,600	6.2	45.5	4.5	175	—	—	—	66
Bulgaria	7.3	28	10,700	6.1	9.6	2.6	652	4.2	0.51	—	53
Croatia	4.5	37.5	13,400	4.8	17.2	2.4	600	4.7	1.14	—	47
Czech Republic	10.2	119.1	22,000	6.4	8.4	1.8	2,237	4.4	1.28	—	32
Denmark	5.5	258	37,100	3.5	3.8	1.5	3,557	8.5	2.63	2,109	14
Estonia	1.3	13.9	20,300	11.4	4.5	2	214	5.3	0.91	—	44
Finland	5.2	197.9	33,500	4.9	7	2	2,758	6.5	3.46	902	11
France	63.7	2,151	31,200	2.2	8.7	2.6	53,128	5.9	2.16	10,026	10
Germany	82.4	2,875	31,900	2.8	7.1	1.5	38,044	4.6	2.49	10,082	22
Greece	10.7	224	24,000	4.3	9.2	4.3	6,860	4.3	0.58	384	24
Hungary	10	113.2	17,500	3.9	7.4	1.8	1,453	5.5	0.88	—	36
Iceland	0.3	13.7	38,000	2.6	—	0	—	8.1	3.01	—	1
Ireland	4.1	203.8	44,500	5.7	4.3	0.9	948	4.8	1.21	719	5
Italy	58.1	1,785	30,200	1.9	7	1.8	31,384	4.7	1.14	5,091	20
Latvia	2.3	16.5	16,000	11.9	6.5	1.2	204	5.3	0.42	—	45
Lithuania	3.6	30.2	15,300	7.5	3.7	1.2	308	5.2	0.76	—	43
Luxembourg	0.5	34.53	71,400	6.2	4.1	0.9	264	3.6	1.81	256	18
Macedonia, Former Yugoslav Republic (FYR)	2.1	5.6	8,300	3.1	36	6	128	3.5	0.26	—	69

Malta	0.4	5.473	21,300	2.9	6.8	0.7	49	4.5	0.29	—	34
Netherlands	16.6	613.3	32,100	3	5.5	1.6	9,946	5.4	1.85	5,115	9
Norway	4.6	264.4	46,300	4.6	3.5	1.9	4,867	7.7	1.75	2,786	2
Poland	38.5	337	14,400	6.1	14.9	1.71	5,578	5.4	0.58	—	37
Portugal	10.6	176.8	19,800	1.3	7.6	2.3	2,966	5.7	0.78	377	29
Romania	22.3	80.1	9,100	7.7	6.1	2.5	1,948	3.4	0.4	—	60
Slovakia	5.4	47.72	18,200	8.3	10.2	1.9	838	4.3	0.53	—	42
Slovenia	2	37.92	23,400	5.2	9.6	1.7	574	6	1.61	—	27
Spain	40.4	1,084	27,400	3.9	8.1	1.2	13,175	4.3	1.1	3,018	13
Sweden	9	372.5	32,200	4.5	5.6	1.5	5,896	7.4	3.74	3,362	6
Switzerland	7.6	386.1	34,000	2.7	3.3	1	3,606	6	2.57	1,767	7
Ukraine	46.3	82.36	7,800	7.1	6.7	1.4	6,000	6.4	1.16	—	76
United Kingdom	60.8	2,346	31,800	2.8	2.9	2.4	51,696	5.4	1.89	10,767	16

Sources: CIA World Factbook, updated December 13, 2007, UNHDR Human Development Index 2007/2008; IISS Military Balance 2007.

victory ended the anti-fascist wartime alliance, conflicting ideologies and interests led to direct U.S.-Soviet competition in Europe. Faced with growing Soviet expansionism and bellicosity in central and eastern Europe, combined with Soviet threats directed against western and southern Europe, the United States responded strongly.

A first important American commitment was in reaction to the growing threat of communist insurgency within Greece and Turkey. On March 12, 1947, President Harry Truman announced what came to be known as the Truman Doctrine in a speech before a joint session of Congress. The Truman Doctrine identified the expansion of totalitarianism to be a threat to U.S. security and international peace and committed the United States to helping free peoples resist subjugation from militant minority groups and outside pressure. Within a year, the United States backed its words with action by sending military assistance and military advisors to Greece and Turkey.

As discussed in Chapter 3, the Truman Doctrine was the opening move in a strategy of worldwide containment through which the United States sought to confine the Soviet Union to its existing boundaries and limit its influence abroad. Recognizing that economic recovery from the effects of World War II would be vital to political stability and security in western Europe, the United States set forth the Marshall Plan in 1947. This plan played an important role in creating the conditions that allowed countries to recover from the massive physical devastation of the war and still stands today as an oft-cited model for how to facilitate a postwar recovery.[2]

The Formation of NATO and Its Evolution during the Cold War.   Although economic measures were important, they were by themselves insufficient. The Soviet-sponsored coup in Czechoslovakia in 1948 and the Soviet blockade of Berlin in 1948–1949 convinced Americans and Europeans alike of the need for a defensive military alliance. In 1949, twelve countries (Belgium, Canada, Denmark, France, Iceland, Italy, Luxembourg, the Netherlands, Norway, Portugal, the United Kingdom, and the United States) signed and ratified the treaty that created NATO. NATO was designed as a collective defense organization in which an attack on one would be considered an attack on all. The new alliance's strategic policy stressed deterrence of Soviet aggression by alliance forces on the ground, supported by U.S. strategic nuclear weapons. NATO also provided for a joint command structure with joint planning capabilities and forces-in-being.

Except for the 1947 Rio Pact (see Chapter 24), which allied the United States with its Latin American neighbors, NATO represented America's first peacetime military alliance. The alliance was at first focused on deterring a Soviet attack by increasing the Soviet perception of the costs of such a venture. However, this deterrence strategy rapidly evolved, beginning with the North Korean invasion of South Korea in 1950. Many believed that the invasion was instigated by the Soviet Union and feared that this portended a similar Soviet move within Europe. NATO strategy began to emphasize defense as well as deterrence, and NATO countries sought—with limited success—to develop a substantial force on the European continent, one capable of repelling a massive attack with conventional as well as nuclear means.

NATO has been a successful, if not always harmonious, alliance. At different times in its history, geopolitical developments have tested intra-alliance relations; at each such juncture, the alliance has been able to adapt and survive. An early and serious cause of intra-alliance debate centered on the credibility of the U.S. commitment to European security in the face of growing Soviet nuclear capability in the late 1950s. Europeans became concerned about U.S. willingness to use its nuclear arsenal in the event of a Soviet attack on Europe and attempted to gather multiple strategic assurances to ensure that a credible deterrent was indeed in place.[3] To solve this strategic dilemma, the NATO allies repeatedly searched for a credible nuclear policy. However, the search itself became a source of more intra-alliance problems. An attempt at building a European multilateral nuclear force failed in the mid-1960s, leading to a NATO nuclear deterrent composed primarily of U.S. theater nuclear forces as well as the U.S. strategic deterrent. The presence of on-the-ground nuclear forces in Europe achieved an essential goal for the European allies in that it linked the conventional defenses along the East-West frontier with American strategic forces.

The later modernization of theater nuclear systems, made necessary by the introduction of Soviet intermediate-range nuclear missiles aimed at western Europe, caused renewed friction within the alliance. As a result, NATO adopted in 1979 a two-track policy by which it would modernize its theater nuclear forces while the United States negotiated with the Soviet Union to achieve reductions. The resulting talks on intermediate-range nuclear forces began in 1981 and concluded in 1987 with the signing of the Intermediate-Range Nuclear Forces Treaty (INF) by President Ronald Reagan and Soviet General Secretary Mikhail Gorbachev.

NATO's shift from a *massive retaliation* strategy to a strategy of *flexible response* beginning in the 1960s also generated alliance problems (see Chapter 3 for a discussion of this strategy). Flexible response included the option of meeting a Soviet conventional attack, at least initially, by fighting a large-scale conventional war in Europe. The prospect of such a war naturally raised great concern in the countries whose territories stood to be devastated by it.[4] Flexible response also raised again the nuclear dilemma of the alliance. An increase in capability for conventional defense could imply less-than-full readiness to escalate to the use of nuclear weapons, thus undermining the credibility of nuclear deterrence.

As NATO coped with changes in doctrine necessitated by technology and an ever-shifting geopolitical environment, another common issue of debate was the fair distribution among the allies of the burden of providing for the common defense. It was a problem that was seemingly unavoidable for an alliance composed of a superpower, some medium powers, and smaller powers, with sometimes divergent goals.[5] The smaller NATO nations generally let their larger neighbors take the lead and pay the costs. Adding another dynamic to the situation, the French developed and deployed their own strategic weapons, the *force de frappe* and withdrew their forces from the military command of NATO in 1966, thus diminishing the capabilities of a concerted flexible defense in Europe. The Greeks and Turks engaged in a longstanding dispute over Cyprus and at times decreased their cooperation with NATO. Increasingly, the initiatives and the financial burdens shifted to Germany, the United Kingdom, and the United States.

The End of the Cold War.   European security planners in the late 1980s appeared prepared to continue on the path of intra-alliance negotiation and fine-tuning of NATO's conventional and nuclear strategies when the European security land-scape began to be significantly affected by Soviet "new thinking." The first demonstration of change in Soviet intentions occurred in the field of conventional arms control, an area that had languished in East-West relations. Negotiations to limit conventional military forces in Europe had occupied NATO and the Warsaw Pact for thirteen years with little result until 1986, when, in response to a NATO proposal, Gorbachev called for phased reduction of ground and air forces in Eu-rope. The Conventional Forces in Europe Treaty (CFE), signed by the 16 member countries of NATO and the six countries that had belonged to the Warsaw Pact in November 1990, reflected the rapid transformation of the European security envi-ronment; more than one hundred twenty-five thousand battle tanks, armored com-bat vehicles, artillery pieces, combat aircraft, and attack helicopters would be re-moved or destroyed. This removal greatly reduced the threat of large-scale, surprise conventional attack by limiting the weapons systems most capable of it.

However, this promising CFE Treaty was rapidly overcome by events. By the conclusion of the conventional force negotiations, the Warsaw Pact dissolved, and Germany was approaching unification. These developments made the ceilings arranged by the negotiations too high. The collapse of the Soviet Union itself fur-ther challenged the conventional arms control regime established in 1990, requir-ing additional negotiations among seven of the former republics—Russia, Be-larus, Ukraine, Moldova, Georgia, Armenia, and Azerbaijan—before the CFE Treaty could be ratified and come into force in 1992. In July 1997, the thirty state parties to the original treaty agreed to reopen negotiations, with the intention of adapting the treaty to the new environment. The aim was to lower significantly the total amount of conventional weaponry allowed under the existing treaty and to replace the old system of East-West parity with new national and territorial ceil-ings that limited national forces and foreign forces stationed in a country.[6] An adaptation agreement taking these new requirements into account was signed on November 19, 1999, but it has not yet been ratified by all parties.[7]

Just as the arms control process was forced to adapt to the changing political and security environment, so was the Western security framework that had evolved over more than four decades of East-West confrontation and the Cold War. In view of the sharply declining threat from the Soviet Union caused by con-ventional arms control arrangements, unilateral Soviet military withdrawals, the dissolution of the Warsaw Pact, and the unification of East and West Germany, the policy of stationing military forces along the former border between NATO and the Warsaw Pact was growing increasingly inappropriate. The Soviet military withdrawals extended the warning time available to the West to organize a defense should a threat from the former Soviet Union re-emerge. In addition, it was in-congruous to maintain forces positioned along the old East-West border that now ran through an allied country. Moving the border eastward would also be an inap-propriate solution, because it would imply that the non-Soviet former Warsaw Pact states were still the enemy at a time when they were trying to democratize their political systems. NATO needed to undertake a basic reassessment of its military and political strategy.

Evolution of NATO in the Early Post–Cold War Years.   NATO responded to the challenge created by the new environment by extending diplomatic liaison with the states of central and eastern Europe and announcing a fundamental political and military review at the London Summit of July 1990. The process of change begun with this summit had two major consequences. First, a new relationship was defined with the alliance's former enemies in the now-defunct Warsaw Pact. Second, a new strategic concept would have to be formulated for an alliance that found itself without an apparent adversary. The essence of NATO's political approach to the former Warsaw Pact states was encapsulated in the 1991 NATO Copenhagen communiqué:

> Our own security is inseparably linked to that of all other states in Europe. The consolidation and preservation throughout the continent of democratic societies and their freedom from any form of coercion or intimidation are therefore of direct and material concern to us.[8]

Although NATO initially stopped short of providing a security guarantee to the states of central and eastern Europe, it gradually became clear that the alliance was open to eventual expansion eastward.

By 1994, NATO had formulated the Partnership for Peace (PfP) to promote official military contact at all levels among the former enemies, as well as with traditionally neutral states. The PfP has focused on military matters, including transparency in defense planning; the democratic control of armed forces; the development of cooperative military ventures, such as peacekeeping and training exercises with NATO; and the training of troops better able to operate in the field with NATO forces.[9] For a variety of individual reasons, twenty-seven countries signed onto the program. Many undoubtedly hoped that membership in the PfP would lead to eventual membership in NATO itself. The PfP evolved until it became clear, at least unofficially, that it served two purposes: to prepare countries for membership in NATO and to enhance cooperation between NATO and those partners not likely to be admitted. Throughout 1996 and 1997, political debate raged over the possibility of expansion of NATO. Russia, in particular, was a stumbling block. Unsurprisingly, Russia saw eastward expansion of the alliance as a threat to its national security. Believing that enlargement would produce a stronger, more stable Europe and that it should not cave in to Russian concerns, NATO eventually decided to admit new members.

When the Soviet Union collapsed in 1991, NATO had sixteen member states; the original twelve members had been joined by Greece and Turkey in 1952, West Germany in 1955, and Spain in 1982. Since the end of the Cold War, ten additional countries have become NATO members in two waves of enlargement. The alliance's ranks first grew to nineteen when the Czech Republic, Hungary, and Poland joined in 1999. In March 2004, seven additional countries—Bulgaria, Estonia, Latvia, Lithuania, Romania, Slovakia, and Slovenia—formally joined the alliance, bringing the total membership to twenty-six. This latter expansion may not be NATO's last. As of 2007, three countries—Albania, Croatia, and the former Yugoslav Republic of Macedonia—are members of NATO's Membership Action Plan. In contrast to the PfP, which was broadly focused on enhancing security partnerships and not explicitly tied to future NATO membership, this plan is specifically designed to assist aspiring partner countries in meeting NATO standards and in preparing for possible future membership. Other states, such as the Ukraine and Georgia, have also indicated interest in joining. Some observers argue that expansion should not stop there. Because NATO has taken on global missions, they question why the alliance should limit its membership to countries from Europe or North America.[10]

Even as NATO was redefining its relationship with former adversaries and its basic security concept in the 1990s, it was also participating in an increasing number of operations. Beginning with involvement in Bosnia-Herzegovina in the wake of the Dayton Accords in 1995, the alliance moved beyond its Cold War task of defending member states and into crisis management outside its borders. NATO's new strategic concept, defined at the Washington Summit in April 1999, acknowledged the need for alliance participation in out-of-area peace support operations. This provided the underpinnings for NATO's intervention in Kosovo in the spring of 1999 to halt a humanitarian catastrophe and to restore stability in a strategic region. Despite strains, the alliance held together during seventy-eight days of air strikes encompassing more than thirty-eight thousand sorties.[11] (NATO missions in the Balkans are further discussed under "Disintegration in the East," below.)

Key Developments in the Twenty-First Century.   The 9/11 terrorist attacks within the United States forced the alliance to come to terms with the implications of collective defense in a new era.[12] On September 12, the alliance invoked Article 5 of the North Atlantic Treaty for the first time in its history, declaring "that an armed attack against one or more NATO member countries will be considered an attack against all."[13] The support that NATO provided to the United States in the aftermath of the terrorist attacks included five Airborne Warning and Control Systems aircraft and the deployment of the Standing Naval Force Mediterranean to the Eastern Mediterranean to begin a counterterrorism mission.[14]

NATO's Prague Summit of 2002 introduced the Prague Capabilities Commitment as well as the NATO Response Force, both adopted to improve military capabilities within the alliance.[15] Under the Prague Capabilities Commitment, NATO member countries agreed to improve their military capabilities in a wide range of specific areas. The development of the NATO Response Force was particularly noteworthy in that it created a force that can number up to twenty-five thousand designed to deploy within five days to crises anywhere in the world. Such a capability for worldwide force projection had never before existed within NATO. The Prague Summit also committed NATO to a leadership role in the United Nations–(UN-) mandated International Security Assistance Force operating in Afghanistan, marking the start of NATO's first and largest ground operation

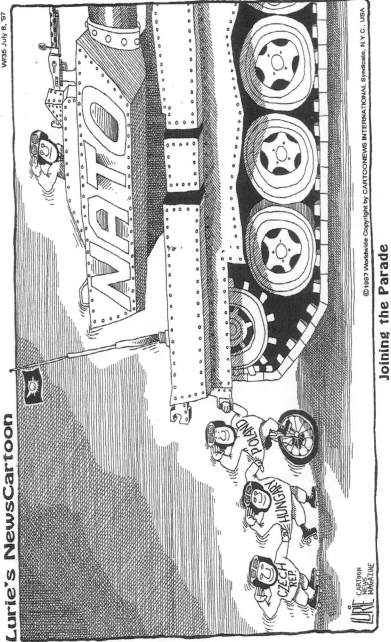

Joining the Parade

(*News Item:* The former East Bloc countries of Poland, Hungary and The Czech Republic are beginning talks leading to their entry into NATO during the organization's annual meeting in Madrid.)

Reprinted with permission of Ranan Lurie.

outside Europe. In October 2006, in another landmark step, the NATO Headquarters in Afghanistan took command of the international military forces in eastern Afghanistan from the U.S.-led coalition, expanding the alliance mission to the whole of Afghanistan.

Meanwhile, NATO's establishment of relationships with countries in other regions continued. The Istanbul Summit held in June 2004 opened the door to increased NATO responsibilities in Iraq. Though NATO has not assumed a combat role, NATO is supporting a training mission within Iraq that provides equipment, training, and technical assistance designed to support the creation of effective Iraqi security forces. The summit also placed a renewed emphasis on NATO's contacts in the Mediterranean and established the Istanbul Cooperation Initiative, which offers countries of the broader Middle East bilateral security cooperation with NATO. Further reforms sought to streamline and "Europeanize" the alliance. The number of commands within NATO underwent a drastic reduction under the NATO Command Structure streamlining initiative, and European officers were given more consideration for major commands that traditionally had gone to U.S. officers.

Debate over the Future of NATO.   Underlying the reforms has been an ongoing debate over the future of NATO and the value of NATO expansion.[16] Is there a real need for NATO now that the Soviet Union is gone? Is NATO expansion beneficial? On the first of these issues, the end of the Cold War and the dissolution of the Soviet Union undoubtedly removed the overarching rationale for cooperation. This over-riding purpose had always superseded even contentious security policy differences among NATO members. In the absence of such an overarching threat, members began to probe their way through an entirely new environment. This led to questions about the transatlantic cooperation that had formed the bedrock of the NATO alliance.

On the issue of NATO expansion, the two sides in the debate have squared off on a fairly common set of issues. On the one hand, proponents argue for two positive side effects of NATO expansion. First, by admitting eastern and central European states, NATO will foster democracy and the development of market economies. Second, the expansion will increase security in Eastern Europe by serving as a stabilizing force in the region. In addition, some analysts have argued that expanding NATO not only hedges against a return of Russian hegemony but also locks in alliance partners who might otherwise be attracted to alternative arrangements.

The case against NATO expansion essentially argues that the merits presented are illusionary and that the EU is a better instrument for fostering democracy and market economies. Critics argue that expansion could easily result in decreased security in the region.[17] For example, expansion could increase Russian hostility toward the West at a time of renewed potential for cooperation. Although estimates vary widely, monetary costs to current members of expansion also could prove significant. An additional powerful argument made against adding new members is the decreasing ability of an expanding alliance to achieve consensus. The larger NATO grows, the more difficult decision making will become.

Another dynamic that will affect the future of transatlantic security cooperation arises from efforts by the EU to strengthen its institutions and play a more important international role. To this end, the EU has recently sought to develop its military capabilities (separate and distinct from those of NATO, although there is acknowledged overlap) through the European Security and Defense Program (ESDP). As the Supreme Commander of Allied Forces Europe General Bantz Craddock has commented, "The United States has supported ESDP with the understanding that it will create real additional military capabilities and conduct missions where NATO is not engaged while working in a manner that is cooperative, and not competitive, with NATO."[18] Recent EU operations in Bosnia, Macedonia, and the Democratic Republic of the Congo have shown that this capability is real, although severe shortcomings still exist. Given its strategic lift shortfalls and hesitance to commit the force over an extended period of time, the EU's ability to project and sustain the force is questionable. The EU has also suffered internal political setbacks, the most notable of which was the 2005 failure to ratify a new constitution that was in part intended to increase its ability to set a common foreign policy (see the discussion of the EU in the "Integration in the West" section later in this chapter). Despite these limitations, the EU has acquired sufficient prominence to affect the calculus of U.S. security policy.

For the time being, NATO still appears to be the institution of choice for European nations to resolve matters involving the use of military force. The response to the Balkan crises, first in Bosnia-Herzegovina and then in Kosovo, showed the search for an effective institutional response eluded the UN and the Europeans acting alone. Fissures existed, but ultimately the NATO alliance committed itself to intervene in both troubled areas of the former Yugoslavia.

The Impact of the Iraq War on Transatlantic Relations.   Although the attacks of 9/11 provided a unifying moment, this unity became severely tested in 2003, when the United States led an invasion of Iraq. Several European allies vocally disagreed with U.S. assertions that this military action was connected to mitigating the dual threats of weapons of mass destruction (WMD) and global terrorism. The failure to find WMD in Iraq after the invasion gave further credence to critics within Europe who had questioned the U.S. case for war. A divide between those European countries that supported the U.S. action (such as Poland and Romania) and those that did not (France and Germany) appeared to form largely along earlier East-West lines (with the important exception, of course, of the United Kingdom, which supported the United States). Highlighting this divide, Secretary of Defense Donald Rumsfeld referred to the "new" European allies of the United States in contrast to the "old" Europe, with the clear message that the United States sought to bypass the old to engage the new.[19]

The fact that the invasion of Iraq occurred without support from the UN greatly affected European perceptions of the war, with large antiwar protests occurring even in countries whose governments supported the intervention. An overwhelming majority of the European public believed that the U.S. policies on Iraq were wrong (see Table 23.1), and this conviction only deepened in the first few years after the fall of Saddam Hussein.[20]

Table 23.2   European Opinion on Iraq War

Are you in favor of military action against Iraq?				If military action goes ahead against Iraq, should your country support this action?		
	No	Only with U.N. Approval	If just U.S. & Allies		Yes	No
Spain	74%	13%	4%	Finland	5%	79%
France	60	27	7	Spain	16	73
Luxembourg	59	34	5	Germany	24	71
Portugal	53	29	10	Ireland	29	69
Germany	50	39	9	Luxembourg	32	62
Denmark	45	38	10	France	29	61
Finland	44	37	6	Portugal	37	52
United Kingdom	41	39	10	Netherlands	35	52
Ireland	39	50	8	Denmark	42	41
Netherlands	38	51	7	United Kingdom	44	41

Source: Gallup International Poll Showing European Opposition to Iraq War in January 2003. Totals may not equal 100 percent because some responses have been excluded.

Key European Concerns and Developments

Analysis of future U.S. national security policies relevant to Europe has to take into account not only the history of U.S. engagement since World War II, discussed above, but also two parallel and defining processes on the continent: disintegration in the East and integration in the West.

Disintegration in the East.   The demise of the Soviet Union, the improved climate between the United States and successor governments in Russia, and the conventional arms control and verification regime negotiated in the early 1990s removed the threat of a massive attack on the territories of the Western allies by a single, well-defined enemy. With the end of the Cold War, however, new challenges to European security emerged. The end of the Soviet Union produced a lower level of threat but also introduced new instabilities into the strategic environment.

Four major potential sources of post–Cold War European instability were of concern.[21] First was the possibility of a residual threat from the Soviet Union— and then Russia—whose military capabilities remained substantial. The second involved the future of the united German state. One fear was that a newly reunified Germany would reassert itself on the European continent, either as a result of insecurity stemming from regional instability or in a conscious attempt to exploit the power vacuum left by the end of the superpower rivalry. Other analysts were concerned that Germany might render NATO ineffective by building new, more exclusive relationships with eastern European states.[22] The third threat to the European security environment was the potential for conflict arising from ethnic and nationalist tensions in Eastern Europe, which stood to be heightened by the economic strain of transforming centrally planned economies to free market systems.

The fourth area of concern was the potential for mass migration from areas east and south of western Europe as a result of regional political and economic instability.

Russia and Germany as Early Post–Cold War Concerns. Over time, the first two of these concerns—scenarios for instability involving Russia or Germany—appeared considerably less threatening. The prospect of an aggressive Soviet successor state grew less ominous during the course of the 1990s. The Soviet Union formally dissolved in December 1991, leaving the Soviet military machine under the control of the newly established Commonwealth of Independent States. Then, in June 1992, the conventional military assets of the former Soviet Union were divided among seven former Soviet republics. Though the vast bulk of the Soviet Union's conventional capability went to Russia, the deterioration of the Russian economy meant that resources once devoted to the Soviet military largely dried up. Although Russia's nuclear arsenal is still formidable, sizeable portions of its conventional armed forces are underpaid, underfed, and undertrained.[23] Of continuing and most immediate concern is Russia's potential contribution to the proliferation of WMDs. Many analysts are concerned that nuclear material could slip from Russian control due to a lack of proper security measures.[24] Importantly, too, Russia has recently been bolstered by high prices for its energy exports and, under President Vladimir Putin, has become increasingly confrontational as it attempts to reassert its status as a great power.[25] Particularly worrisome is Russia's use of energy policy to bully its neighbors, and its assertiveness in dealing with former Soviet Republics on its borders (see, for example, discussion of Georgia below and also Chapter 22).[26] Despite these developments, early fears of a "Weimar Russia" (a reference to Germany's Weimar Republic in the years between the two world wars) in which political instability and a sense of victimization would lead to the rise of nationalist leaders and bellicose policies in Europe have fortunately not been fully realized.[27]

A second early concern that has more completely vanished over time was Germany's role in post–Cold War Europe. The enormity of the commitment that the Federal Republic of Germany (West Germany) had to make to absorb the German Democratic Republic (East Germany) in 1990 was felt in the unified German state in the form of worrisome inflation and a widening fiscal deficit. These problems, along with the economic pressures of preparing for monetary union, preoccupied the German leadership. More importantly over the long run, with the signing of the 1992 Maastricht Treaty creating the EU, Germany became even more completely integrated into Europe.

Ethnic Nationalism as a Source of Conflict. Though the first two security concerns listed above either somewhat or almost totally dissolved, the third has proven to be significant. Regional instability arising from ethnic and nationalist tensions became a reality with the dissolution of Yugoslavia and from events on the territory of the former Soviet Union in such places as Nagorno-Karabakh, South Ossetia, Moldova, and Chechnya. Even the peaceful division of Czechoslovakia into the Czech Republic and Slovakia in 1993 was a result of nationalist and ethnic disputes. The processes of political and economic transition have in many cases been accompanied by sharp political, economic, and ethnic tensions.

From 1991 to 1995, fighting in the former Yugoslavia epitomized the dangers of ethnic conflict. The UN and the EU made several attempts to broker peace as war raged in Croatia and later in Bosnia-Herzegovina. Even with a large peace-keeping contingent, the UN proved unable either to separate the combatants or to negotiate sustainable cease-fires. At first the United States was content to let the EU and the UN handle the problem. However, as genocide and conflict fueled domestic political pressure to act, the Clinton administration began air strikes against Serb military targets. These strikes caused dissension between the United States and several European countries whose ground forces were participating in UN peacekeeping efforts. France and The United Kingdom, for example, believed that air strikes could threaten the lives of their peacekeepers. Briefly, it even seemed that disagreement over policy in Bosnia threatened the integrity of NATO.[28] Instead, the United States took a major part in resolving the conflict by pressuring the combatants to sign the Dayton Accords in 1995—an agreement which maintained the integrity of Bosnia and Herzegovina while creating semi-autonomous regions within it–and by providing American peace enforcement troops. Backed initially by a NATO-led Implementation Force of sixty thousand soldiers, the Dayton agreement resulted in a fragile peace.

The ethnic conflict and killings in Kosovo also provoked a NATO reaction. Here, fighting between President Slobodan Milosevic's Serbian and Yugoslav security forces and the Kosovo Liberation Army, an Albanian guerilla group seeking independence for the province, resulted in approximately eight hundred fifty thousand displaced persons and numerous accounts of atrocities against civilians. Despite international calls for a cease-fire, Milosevic pointed to security concerns raised by Serbs living within Kosovo and refused to remove his forces from the province. Ultimately, NATO decided to use military force. When NATO began an air campaign on March 24, 1999, it marked the first time the alliance had engaged in offensive military operations designed to force compliance with international agreements. After seventy-seven days of bombing, Milosevic agreed to withdraw Yugoslav forces from Kosovo. Immediately, a NATO-led Kosovo Force entered Kosovo under a UN mandate. As of mid-2008, approximately eight years after the end of the conflict, the sixteen-thousand member NATO Kosovo Force is still responsible for establishing and maintaining a safe and secure environment in Kosovo.

NATO did not possess a UN Security Council resolution authorizing the use of force against Serbia over Kosovo, but the alliance justified its actions on the basis of an "international humanitarian emergency." Critics charged that NATO attacked a nonmember country that was not a direct threat, and Russia in particular sought to support the claim of its long-standing ally Serbia that the NATO intervention constituted an unjustified intrusion in its sovereign affairs. NATO countered by claiming that instability in the Balkans was a direct threat to the security interests of NATO members, and military action was therefore justified. For years after the war, the status of Kosovo remained unresolved, and a UN protectorate ran the day-to-day affairs of the province in conjunction with local authorities.

Simultaneously, a contact group consisting of the United States, the United Kingdom, France, Germany, Italy, and Russia worked on a long-term solution.

In February 2008, Kosovo declared its independence and by mid-2008 Kosovo's status as an independent country had been recognized by almost 50 countries including the United States and a majority of NATO and EU countries. However, these actions were accompanied by concerns that Kosovo's independence and subsequent international recognition of it would encourage separatist movements everywhere and result in an increase in violence in areas around the world still plagued by ethnic conflict. These concerns seemed to be somewhat validated in August 2008 when Russia intervened militarily in Abkhazia and South Ossetia—two conflict-torn regions in Georgia—and in September 2008 recognized these regions as independent states. Russian President Putin specifically cited the Kosovo precedent when justifying Russia's actions in recognizing the sovereign independence of these two areas along Russia's southern border, arguing that "it was not we who opened this Pandora's box."[29] As of September 2008, only Nicaragua had joined Russia in its recognition of these two regions while the United States and many of its allies sought to buttress the claims of Georgia and support its desire to preserve the integrity of its international borders. The challenges that still remain in establishing a secure and enduring peace in the Balkans as well as resolving conflict in Georgia reveal the difficulties that have been associated with efforts to defuse post-Cold War ethnic tensions in Europe.

Kosovo may have been a turning point for NATO and for European security in general. Future armed conflicts in Europe seem more likely to occur within national borders, making intervention problematic. Although UN actions to protect the Kurds in Iraq in the 1990s set a precedent for international intervention against a government's abuse of its citizens, and although the principles established by the Helsinki Final Act and the Organization for Security and Cooperation in Europe (OSCE) embracing human rights and the self-determination of peoples could be taken to justify intervention, such interference holds dangers of its own.[30] Intervention in intrastate conflicts could, for example, lead to greater instability if it draws in outside participants with competing objectives. Lack of intervention, however, creates or contributes to other problems. First, the conflict could spill over national borders—a particularly potent threat in eastern Europe and the Balkans, where ethnic ties cross national boundaries. Second, the stability of neighboring nations can be affected even if they do not enter the conflict. Refugees from conflict-torn areas in eastern Europe could strain the capacity of western European nations to absorb them and potentially destabilize eastern European countries.

The international community—and U.S. security policy—must come to terms with a number of issues generated by the Yugoslav experience and subsequent developments along Russia's southern border. How should the United States respond to conflicts involving ethnically based claims of sovereignty? When does this type of conflict cease to be purely an intrastate matter and become an international concern? What are the costs of nonintervention in conflicts that may spread across borders? Limiting intervention to the provision of peacekeeping forces once a cease-fire has been achieved, in some cases, will merely amount to endorsement of the territorial gains of the aggressor.[31] In effect, by not intervening to stop aggression in the first place, the international community is sending a signal to other potential aggressors that violation of the sovereign claims or rights of others will be condoned.

But has intervention in Bosnia and Kosovo achieved its aims? Although NATO interventions there were successful in establishing and keeping the peace, can they ensure the development of Bosnia as a cohesive, democratic entity and provide an atmosphere in Kosovo that respects minority rights even as Kosovo seeks to exercise its newly claimed independence? The lessons of the Balkans for European security are twofold: the value of conflict avoidance and the importance of conflict containment. In this twin context, the evolution of the EU and of European and transatlantic political and security institutions will play an important role.

Immigration.   Finally, the fourth immediate post–Cold War concern—demographic trends and immigrant integration issues—has the potential to create major long-term security issues for the European continent. A declining birth rate and aging population, coupled with increased immigration from outside Europe, have created economic strains that have led to numerous political and social issues. These strains may also manifest themselves in relation to population movements within the EU, as resentment against the possibility that eastern European workers could reduce wages in western European countries was reflected in the 2005 debates over the EU constitution. Even more divisive is the EU candidacy of Turkey. Concern over Muslim immigration led former French President Valery Giscard d'Estaing to declare that Turkish EU membership would lead to the "end of Europe." Such comments suggest that Europe is a "Christian Club" that Muslims are not welcome to join.[32]

Indeed, the problem of integrating Muslims in Europe has profound security implications for Europe and for the United States. Some have even gone so far as to call it "critical to the future of Europe."[33] Most Muslim extremists in Europe are second- or third-generation immigrants who still do not identify with their country of residence. The less integrated people feel, the more attractive extremist groups with transnational identities and interests seem. Some assert that this alarming scenario is not entirely accurate: The "vast majority" of Europe's 15 to 20 million Muslims have nothing to do with radical Islamism and struggle to integrate into European society.[34] Still, the involvement of Europe's Muslims in the 2004 terrorist train bombings in Madrid, the 2005 terrorist attacks on the London subway system, the 2005 civil unrest and riots in Paris, and the 2007 attempted attacks at airports in London and Scotland have shown, even if just a small percentage of the overall European Muslim population feels separated from the society around it, this can have very large security implications. How Europe deals with this situation will affect the United States and the broader global struggle against international terrorism.

Integration in the West.   Even as the end of the Cold War promoted the forces of disintegration in eastern Europe as discussed in the previous section, western

Europe continued to advance toward greater economic and political integration. Progress in the integration process has meant the elimination of all barriers to the free flow of goods, services, capital, and labor among the fifteen EU members—introduced by the Single European Act of 1986—and agreement on the modalities for monetary union and greater political integration through the signing of the Maastricht Treaty in 1992. The process of European integration has shaped and will continue to shape the European political and security landscape in two significant ways: by acting as a magnet for the eastern European economies and by aligning the foreign as well as domestic policies of the member states. Analysis of the development and future prospects of the EU, therefore, must be an integral part of the continuing process of U.S. foreign and security policy formulation.

In the broadest sense, European integration may render an important verdict on one of the critical questions about international security writ large: whether a group of once-hostile states can transcend the risk of interstate conflict. If western Europe, an important engine powering the twentieth century's world wars, can make war a phenomenon of the past, it could point the way for other regions as well. But though the prospects are favorable, the jury is still out on whether Europe has made such a transition and, if so, whether the experience is transferable. Either way, much is at stake in European integration.

The EU had its origins in the European Coal and Steel Community developed in 1951 as part of a plan by Jean Monnet. Monnet, an economist and French public official, had two purposes in advancing his plan: first, to revitalize the steel industry in post–World War II France by ensuring access to German coal and coke; and second, to end centuries of Franco-German competition by organizing joint control of key mineral resources. The European Coal and Steel Community, which included Italy, Belgium, Luxembourg, the Netherlands, France, and Germany, created an impetus for a common internal market among its members, leading to the European Economic Community that was instituted for this purpose by the Treaty of Rome (1957). The further development of the European Economic Community from this organization of six members to a common market of twelve countries occurred incrementally and falteringly.

By the early 1990s, the European Economic Community appeared positioned to become a significant international actor as a result of the prospects for expansion and the development of a common foreign and security policy. Renamed the EU in 1994 as the Maastricht Treaty went into effect, it has thus far had limited success with regard to the forging of a common foreign and security policy. The additions of Austria, Finland, and Sweden in 1995 increased the political stature of the EU, but the development of a common foreign and security policy floundered. Still, even this qualified success proved to be a strong magnet for the rest of Europe. During the Copenhagen Summit in December 2002, the EU again embraced enlargement. Ten countries—Cyprus, the Czech Republic, Estonia, Hungary, Latvia, Lithuania, Malta, Poland, Slovakia, and Slovenia—officially joined in 2004, and Romania and Bulgaria joined in 2007, bringing the EU total to twenty-seven members.

Looking to the future of the EU, the candidacy of Turkey and its possible future accession has created heated controversy. The controversy stems from

Turkey's striking difference from the European norm in terms of economics, demography, culture, religion, and even basic geography, and it has exposed deep disagreements within the EU regarding the definition of "European." As journalist Mark Rice-Oxley writes:

> The crucial question is whether these differences will enhance or undermine the EU. Proponents say incorporating a Muslim-majority country for the first time will help the EU reach out to the Islamic world, and see Turkey's young, growing population and economy as a boon. . . . But opponents fret that a new member as large and poor as Turkey would adulterate European values. Lingering concern persists about the incorporation of 10 mostly East European countries . . . which some feared would dilute EU prosperity. Many feel that EU enlargement has run its course and that further extensions would make it unwieldy.[35]

On balance, it appears that Turkey's domestic, political, and economic life would be strengthened by association, as would its role as a bridge between Europe and the Middle East. Even so, it does not seem likely that Turkey will be admitted to the EU anytime soon.

Some analysts believe that the key challenge created by the end of the Cold War is one of choosing between enlargement (*widening*) or the creation of a stronger set of central EU institutions (*deepening*). Another perspective holds that in order to prepare for widening, the EU should first deepen by strengthening its institutions and shoring up its decision-making authority. Development of a common foreign and security policy is held to be a key aspect of this process of deepening.

In the last several years, the EU has made progress toward achieving a credible autonomous defense capability. The European Security and Defense Policy is the cornerstone of this effort, which seeks the capability to accomplish tasks ranging from humanitarian assistance to the rapid deployment of combat forces. The EU formally adopted these tasks with the 1997 signing of the Amsterdam Treaty and then with the 1999 creation of a European Rapid Reaction Force. These advances did not occur without vigorous debate. The British were at first reluctant but finally endorsed the plan in a 1999 joint declaration issued by French President Jacques Chirac and British Prime Minister Tony Blair. These two leaders affirmed that "the Union must have the capacity for autonomous action, backed up by credible military forces, the means to decide to use them, and a readiness to do so, in order to respond to international crises."[36]

To achieve this, European governments would have to bring into accord their force obligations to NATO and potential future commitments to the European Security and Defense Policy, coming to an understanding regarding which organization would lead an operation. At the 1996 NATO summit in Berlin, a short-lived Western European Union emerged as the overseer of the creation of a European Security and Defense Identity within NATO structures. The Berlin agreement allowed European countries (through the Western European Union) to use NATO assets if it so wished. By 2002, NATO and the EU had worked out a partnership regarding crisis management activities. In institutional terms, the partnership is reflected by the March 2003 Berlin-plus Agreement that allows the EU to use

NATO structures, mechanisms, and assets to carry out military operations if NATO declines to act.

Other developments changed the structure of the institutions involved in EU efforts to develop a common approach to foreign and security policy. In June 1999, the European Council incorporated the role of the Western European Union within the EU, effectively shutting down the Western European Union. Since then, the EU has taken steps to develop common policy agendas as well as an enhanced military capability, but most of these initiatives have not progressed beyond declarations of stated goals. For example, the EU failed to achieve on schedule (by 2003) the objective of creating a capability to rapidly deploy and sustain fifty thousand troops. The EU defense ministers approved "Headline Goal 2010" in May 2004, extending the timelines for this project, timelines that will likely continue to be extended.

The European Security Strategy overlaps strikingly with NATO's mission, leading to concerns that an independent European security pillar might result in the declining importance of NATO as a transatlantic forum. In 1998, Secretary of State Madeleine Albright outlined American expectations toward ESDP using the "three Ds": no duplication of what was done effectively under NATO; no decoupling from the United States and NATO; and no discrimination against non-EU members, such as Turkey. Since 2003, the EU has assumed the police mission in Bosnia from the UN, worked in cooperation with NATO in Macedonia from March to December 2003 (Operation Concordia), taken over NATO peacekeeping duties in Bosnia in December 2004 (Operation Althea), and embarked on a peacekeeping mission in the Democratic Republic of Congo conducted autonomously from NATO.

The proposed EU constitution sought to further the development of an EU political and security identity with the creation of an EU president, foreign minister, and External Relations Service. However, advocates for a stronger EU hit a significant stumbling block with the rejection of the constitution by French and Dutch voters in May 2005 and June 2005, respectively. It appears that many Europeans want the EU to pause before expanding or deepening further. As of mid-2008, fresh efforts were underway to produce a marginally weaker, less centralizing constitution; still, the prospects of EU-wide ratification are uncertain. The EU's development will shape the future division of labor across the Atlantic on a variety of international security tasks.

Another institution that plays a role in the future of European security deserves attention. The OSCE traces its origin back to the 1975 Helsinki Final Act and currently has fifty-six member states. Early hopes for a contribution by the OSCE to European security faded after 1992, as the organization demonstrated its limitations in dealing with the violent disintegration of Yugoslavia. The OSCE's decision-making structures and procedures, which require unanimity, prevented it from acting decisively and in a timely fashion in response to the crisis in Yugoslavia. The OSCE officially sponsored observer teams in Yugoslavia, but it delegated most of the mediation efforts among the parties in Yugoslavia to the EU and peacekeeping duties to the UN. The OSCE is caught in a dilemma: Its inclusivity imbues it with legitimacy but also limits its capacity for action.

The overall future of European integration remains uncertain. One possibility is that centrifugal tendencies will become increasingly prevalent among European countries and within the EU. If this were to happen, Europe would not be able to create its own autonomous defense capability and to play a more active role in world politics. However, many analysts think the opposite trend will occur: U.S. unilateral tendencies will be a catalyst for further European integration. It should be noted that an EU strengthened by these dynamics may be as inclined to seek subtle ways to work against the United States as it would be to work with the United States in common collaborative ventures.

Other Regional Trends and Security Issues.   Two additional issues deserve special mention: out-of-area military operations and access to energy. The decisions that Europeans make regarding these two issues will help shape their concept of security in the twenty-first century and will affect their relationship with the United States.

First, since the end of the Cold War, Europeans have shown a willingness to become involved outside the continent in peacekeeping, stability, and reconstruction operations. As evidenced by NATO's leadership in military operations in Afghanistan, the capability exists for fairly large-scale deployments at a strategic distance. Also, the political will to sustain these operations, even in the face of casualties, so far appears to exist. However, although these are encouraging developments from the perspective of the United States, NATO's involvement in Afghanistan has also highlighted shortfalls within the alliance. Many troop-contributing nations have placed caveats on their soldiers' involvement, limiting the commander's ability to call on them to perform certain actions. In addition, European nations have pressed to keep defense spending limited. Social programs remain the priority for many Europeans, and an unwillingness to fund military programs has created serious concerns about NATO's ability to execute the missions that its members have politically agreed upon. Increasingly, too, observers are calling for a restructuring of the common funding program to allow for greater flexibility in how NATO finances its operations. The current system of letting "costs lie where they fall," which mandates that member countries pay their own way during operations, needs review. NATO Secretary General Jaap de Hoop Scheffer described the current arrangement as "a reverse lottery," noting that "[i]f your numbers come up, you lose money. If the [NATO Response Force] deploys while you happen to be in the rotation, you pay the full costs of the deployment of your forces."[37]

Second, energy and energy infrastructure security is another topic that will challenge Europe in the coming decades. As the economies of such larger developing countries as China and India grow, competition for scarce natural resources, especially oil, will become increasingly fierce. Unless and until it develops alternative energy sources, the West will remain dependent on imports of vast quantities of fossil fuels. This situation cannot change quickly and does not appear likely to change for the foreseeable future.

Conscious of their vulnerability as energy importers, European states are generally unwilling to confront energy-rich countries, from Saudi Arabia to Russia. The failure of Europe to condemn Russia's brutal treatment of the Muslim Chechens, in part because Europe leans heavily on Russia's oil and gas, has enabled Islamic radicals to paint the West as complicit in the repression of an Islamic population. Of course, the U.S. invasion of Iraq has also enabled radicals to portray the Americans as repressing Muslims on behalf of oil. Despite their interventions to safeguard Muslim communities in Bosnia and Kosovo, Europe and the United States have not been successful in the crucial fight for Muslim public opinion.

Energy dependence could make it more difficult for Europe and the United States to find common ground when dealing with Russia, which has shown a readiness to use its energy exports as a political weapon. The January 2006 gas pipeline disruptions that Russia created over a dispute with Ukraine brought into stark relief questions about the reliability of the source of much of Europe's fuel. Europe obtains a quarter of its gas from Russia and and most of this supply crosses Ukraine by pipeline—a vulnerability that is impossible to counter in a short time.[38] Because of this, Europe's calculus when dealing with Russia on a wide array of policy issues will undoubtedly be affected by fears of a potential disruption in fuel supply. Under these conditions, U.S. and European priorities and perspectives on an array of Russian policy issues could diverge.

U.S. Policy Challenges for the Future

Although the Iraq War has contributed to a deep divide between the United States and Europe, the war may not be the only important dynamic at work. According to historian Niall Ferguson:

> As for Europe, one must not underestimate the extent to which the recent diplomatic "widening of the Atlantic" reflects profound changes in Europe, rather than an alteration in U.S. foreign policy. The combination of economic sclerosis and social senescence means that Europe is bound to stagnate, if not decline. Meanwhile, Muslim immigration and the prospect of Turkey's accession to the European Union are changing the very character of Europe. And the division between Americans and Europeans on Middle Eastern questions is only going to get wider.[39]

As Europe itself changes, and as Europe's attitudes toward the U.S. evolve, both sides of the Atlantic need to come to terms with the role and relevance of NATO. Should the United States continue to rely on NATO as the bedrock of the transatlantic relationship, or should American policy makers pursue "coalitions of the willing" when seeking allies in the foreign and security policy realms? The ad hoc arrangement of the latter option presents advantages and challenges. Although it does not tie the United States to any set of countries, it also creates less capability because an ad hoc coalition has not been working to create interoperability during peacetime.

The interoperability issue is one that also plagues the NATO alliance. Advances in military technology, supported by large amounts of U.S. defense spending, have left many European militaries struggling to operate effectively in a coalition with the United States without substantial assistance in training and materiel. Some argue that this gap in military capabilities between the United States and its European allies inevitably limits interoperability, while others point to new arrangements that would allow alliance members to specialize in one niche area of need, thus benefiting all while simultaneously reducing national military costs.[40]

Although the rift over Iraq was not the first time that Europeans and Americans have disagreed, it is particularly significant. By not supporting the Iraq War, Germany vehemently opposed a major U.S. foreign policy decision for the first time since World War II. In the past, if The United Kingdom supported an American initiative and France opposed it, Germany would often play the role of intermediary. In the case of Iraq, however, Germany completely threw its weight behind the French-led opposition. Second, German assertiveness may be indicative of a larger generational change occurring in Europe. As *68-ers* (the generation associated with the often violent social protests of 1968), German Chancellor Gerhard Schroeder and his foreign minister, Joschka Fischer, not only were less willing to go along with U.S. initiatives but were willing to forcefully oppose them.

More broadly, as the collective memory of the American role in World War II and the reconstruction of Europe fades among younger Europeans, the European commitment to the transatlantic alliance may continue to diminish. Acrimony over troop commitments to the NATO mission in Afghanistan makes this diminution a priority for the United States. A related concern stems from potential European reactions to other possible future terrorist attacks; Europe could either adopt a unified front with the United States or blame the United States and its foreign policies. The quite different strategic responses of the Spain and the United Kingdom to the 2004 terrorist attack in Madrid and the 2005 attack in London, with the Spanish deciding to retrench and end their commitment in Iraq and the government of the United Kingdom reaffirming its international commitments and strategic partnership with the United States, reveal the range of possible reactions terrorist attacks on European soil could provoke.

Ultimately, the United States will necessarily continue to involve itself with and in Europe, but the form and structure of transatlantic cooperation will continue to evolve. Although NATO will clearly be the key near-term element in the overall transatlantic security relationship, over the long run it seems possible that NATO will mutate into a different institution or will be displaced from its position of primacy as other European institutions develop. If and when this occurs, the United States will find itself relying more on bilateral relationships or ad hoc coalitions than on established multilateral arrangements.

Discussion Questions

1. What are U.S. security commitments under NATO?
2. Given the dissolution of the Soviet Union and the end of the Cold War, is NATO still relevant today?
3. What factors have enhanced or limited the credibility of NATO?
4. How does the EU's desire for common foreign and defense policies (and an autonomous defense capability) affect U.S. interests?

5. What are the arguments for and against the expansion of NATO and the EU? How are U.S. security interests affected if either organization expands?

6. What role should the United States play in preventing and responding to ethnic- or nationality-based conflicts on the European continent? Does the U.S. still have an interest in maintaining a security presence in the Balkans?

7. When dealing with such global security concerns as terrorism, should the United States approach European states on a bilateral basis or through international organizations, such as NATO or the EU? What are the advantages and disadvantages to each approach?

8. How might the changing demographics of Europe affect U.S. security policies?

9. What does the future hold for transatlantic relations? Will the U.S. continue to view European states as key allies that are instrumental to American security interests?

Recommended Reading

Ash, Timothy Garton. *Free World: America, Europe, and the Surprising Future of the West.* New York: Vintage Books, 2005.

Calleo, David P. *Rethinking Europe's Future.* Princeton, NJ: Princeton University Press, 2001.

———. "Power, Wealth, and Wisdom: The United States and Europe after Iraq." *National Interest*, no. 72 (Summer 2003): 5–15.

Clark, Wesley K. *Waging Modern War: Bosnia, Kosovo, and the Future of Combat.* New York: Public Affairs, 2001.

Coonen, Steven J. "The Widening Military Capabilities Gap Between the United States and Europe: Does it Matter?" *Parameters* 36, no. 3 (Fall 2006): 67–84.

Everts, Steven, Lawrence Freedman, Charles Grant, François Heisbourg, Daniel Keohane, and Michael O'Hanlon. *A European Way of War.* London: Centre for European Reform, 2004.

Giry, Stéphanie. "France and Its Muslims." *Foreign Affairs* 85, no. 6 (September/October 2006): 75–85.

Judt, Tony. *Postwar: A History of Europe Since 1945.* New York: Penguin Press, 2005.

Kagan, Robert. *Of Paradise and Power: America and Europe in the New World Order.* New York: Alfred A. Knopf, 2003.

Lindberg, Tod, ed. *Beyond Paradise and Power: Europe, America, and the Future of a Troubled Partnership.* New York: Routledge, 2004.

Moravcsik, Andrew. *Social Purpose and State Power from Messina to Maastrict.* Ithaca, NY: Cornell University Press, 1998.

Rühle, Michael. "NATO after Prague: Learning the Lessons of 9/11." *Parameters* 33, no. 2 (Summer 2003): 89–97.

Sloan, Stanley R. *NATO, the European Union, and the Atlantic Community: The Transatlantic Bargain Reconsidered.* Lanham, MD: Rowman & Littlefield, 2003.

Whitman, Richard. "NATO, the EU, and ESDP: An Emerging Division of Labor?" *Contemporary Security Policy* 25, no. 3 (2004): 430–451.

Internet Resources

Commission on Security & Cooperation in Europe, www.csce.gov
Europa: Gateway to the European Union, http://europa.eu/index_en.htm
North Atlantic Treaty Organization, www.nato.int

24

Latin America

Geography makes Latin America the neighbor of the United States, and by 2006 Hispanic or Latino Americans were America's largest single minority group at 14.8% of the U.S. population.[1] Driven by the search for jobs, opportunity, and security, Hispanics are bringing their culture and a complex set of issues to urban and rural areas of the United States. Due to Latin America's growing importance, the U.S. government has undertaken many initiatives in recent years to promote democracy, free trade, and security in the region. However, partially because the U.S. agenda has not always matched that of key countries in the region, progress has not been consistent. U.S. presidents emphasize free trade, counternarcotics initiatives, and ending illegal immigration; Latin leaders often have a different list of priorities. In addition to economic growth and development, key issues of Latino concern include U.S. immigration reform and continuing the flow of remittances from workers in the United States to relatives back home. To illustrate the scale of the remittances issue, the Inter-American Development Bank projected that 2006 remittances from the 12.6 million Latin Americans living in the United States would exceed $45 billion, dwarfing all sources of multilateral and bilateral aid flowing into these countries.[2] Without remittances from their citizens working in the United States, many countries in the region would lose a vital source of hard currency.

Long-standing political and economic challenges to U.S.–Latin American relations persist. The decades-old U.S. hope that competitive elections free from violence and corruption would produce a new generation of leaders committed to liberal democracy and free markets has yet to be fully realized. This is true despite the fact that by 1990 almost every country in Central and South America except Cuba had experienced a transition to democratic rule. Subsequent disappointments with liberal democracy and free market reforms led to what scholar Jorge G. Castanda labeled in 2006 "Latin America's Left Turn."[3] The appeal of a leftist agenda is natural in countries that face the level of poverty that still plagues Latin America. Unfortunately, the leaders of this left turn in several important Latin American countries resemble the old-style *caudillo* (military-political authoritarian ruler) more than they resemble modern social democrats.

One example of a leftist, populist leader with authoritarian tendencies is Hugo Chavez, the president of Venezuela who was first elected in 1998. The leader of a failed military coup in 1992, Chavez nevertheless achieved power six years later by advocating a "Bolivarian Revolution." Named in honor of Venezuelan Simón Bolivar, a famous figure in the liberation of South America from colonial rule, key elements of this revolution included changing the composition of the dominant class in Venezuela, greater military involvement in the government, nationalization of industries, wealth redistribution, and a nationalist foreign policy that encourages solidarity among underdeveloped countries against the United States and the West.[4] Chavez advocated this revolution as the answer to the region's problems and sought to counter U.S. initiatives with his own programs. Although Chavez highlighted and prioritized several real problems, such as persistent poverty, critics pointed out the similarities between Chavez's actions and those of failed former authoritarian leaders in the region: the transformation of the Venezuelan military into a praetorian guard, the concentration of power in the executive at the expense of other branches of government, the packing of electoral institutions with Chavez partisans, his division of Venezuelans into "patriots" and "traitors" (those who do not support him), the suppression of media critical of his government, and his open commitment to retaining power until 2030. In terms of economic policies, Chavez's early efforts to improve income equality in Venezuela actually resulted in a shrinking of the national economy and an increase in poverty by 10 percentage points between 1999 and 2004.[5]

Some observers fear that Chavez could be an indicator of the potential for "another wave of the populist *caudillismo* that has done [Latin America] so much damage in the past."[6] Several Latin American countries remain vulnerable to such developments due to the mixed track record of liberal democrats who have attained political power as well as the failure of free market economic reforms to improve more rapidly the welfare of many of the poorest of the region's citizens. In many ways, Latin America still appears to be shackled to its history.[7]

What Is Latin America?

Although it is convenient for Americans to think of Latin America as a whole, it is a highly diverse region with many cultures and heritages. "Latin" Mexico is geographically part of North America, along with the United States and Canada. The Caribbean Basin includes the islands of the Caribbean Sea and nearby Atlantic Ocean as well as four non-island countries: Belize, Panama, Colombia, and Venezuela. Among the Caribbean islands, one finds the French, English, Spanish, and Creole languages spoken, a linguistic fact that unites the Caribbean with

MAP 24.1   Latin America

Guyana, Surinam, and French Guiana on the northern coast of South America. Panama and Belize are often also included among the Central American nations, along with Guatemala, El Salvador, Honduras, Nicaragua, and Costa Rica.

Further divisions exist within the continent of South America. The Andean nations consist of Venezuela, Colombia, Ecuador, Peru, and Bolivia. Brazil has long been regarded as a unique entity within the region because of its size, Portuguese language and heritage, and independent economic and foreign policy. Finally, the countries of Paraguay, Uruguay, Argentina, and Chile make up the Southern Cone.

Latin America has tremendous economic and political potential. Brazil has become a major trading nation that in 2006 had the eleventh-largest economy in the world in terms of purchasing power parity.[8] With a market of more than 100 million consumers, Mexico was the third-largest trading partner of the United States in 2006.[9] In that same year, Venezuela was the world's sixth-largest net oil exporter, and it has substantial proven reserves of oil and natural gas.[10] Collectively, trade with Latin American states amounts to about one fifth of total U.S. trade. Unfortunately, these indicators of inherent dynamism and strength are accompanied by significant regional problems of political instability, corruption, structural adjustment, and stark income inequality.

U.S. Interests in Latin America

Since the early nineteenth century, the primary interest of the United States in Latin America has been to maintain a secure and peaceful southern flank. This objective led directly to President James Monroe's official warning against incursion by European powers into the Western Hemisphere: "The American continents . . . are henceforth not to be considered as subjects for future colonization by any European power."[11] This Monroe Doctrine, originally issued in 1823, served as the foundation of U.S. relations with Latin America for more than one hundred fifty years.

American fears about European interventions were not unjustified. In 1861, in the midst of civil wars in Mexico and the United States, a combined force from Spain, France, and Great Britain intervened in Mexico to ensure repayment of debts. The French eventually occupied all of Mexico, installing Archduke Maximilian, brother of the Austro-Hungarian emperor, and his wife, Charlotte, the daughter of the Belgian king, as emperor and empress. The Mexicans finally defeated the French and reclaimed their sovereignty in 1867.

The Monroe Doctrine is not invoked today because the current challenges to U.S. interests come from sources indigenous to the region rather than from European intervention. Examples include homegrown ideologies, such as Chavez's *chavismo* in Venezuela (an eclectic collection of principles mostly grounded in self-reliance and socialism), and the persistent problems caused by authoritarianism, corruption, and poverty.

Despite the altered global and regional circumstances of the twenty-first century, U.S. national interests in Latin America have remained relatively stable: peace on the U.S. southern flank, political stability in Central America and the Caribbean Basin, trade and investment opportunities, illegal drugs, democracy and human rights, the Panama Canal, and immigration.

Defending the Southern Flank.   Reaffirming the Monroe Doctrine in 1845, President James Polk added a corollary forbidding the voluntary transfer of territory by an American state to a European power. As the rivalries between European empires heated up in the last decades of the nineteenth century, competition between European navies for colonies, spheres of influence, and coaling stations for their new steam-driven fleets became a source of potential conflict. France, Great

Table 24.1 Latin America Key Statistics

Country	Total Population (millions)	Average Life Expectancy	GDP US$ (billions)	GDP/ Capita (US$)	Population Living in Poverty (%)	Military Spending % of GDP	Military Spending US$ (millions)	Human Development Index Ranking (out of 177)
Argentina	40.3	76.3	210	15,200	26.9	1.3	1,780	38
Belize	0.3	68.3	1.1	8,400	33.5	1.4	16	80
Bolivia	9.1	66.2	10.3	3,100	7.8	1.9	147	117
Brazil	190	72.2	967	8,800	9.6	2.6	13,281	70
Chile	16.3	77	99.6	12,600	18.2	2.7	4,143	40
Colombia	44.4	72.3	106.8	8,600	11.1	3.4	4,937	75
Costa Rica	4.1	77.2	21.4	12,500	18	0.4	95	48
Cuba	11.4	77.1	40	4,100	11.1	3.8	1,416	51
Dominican Republic	9.4	73.1	20.6	8,400	42.2	0.8	219	79
Ecuador	13.8	76.6	32.7	4,500	38.5	2.8	593	89
El Salvador	6.9	71.8	15.2	4,900	35.2	5	106	103
Guatemala	12.7	69.7	35.3	5,000	56.2	0.4	131	118
Guyana	0.8	66.2	0.8	4,900	—	1.8	—	—
Haiti	8.7	57	6	1,800	80	0.4	—	146
Honduras	7.5	69.4	8.5	3,100	50.7	0.6	53	115
Jamaica	2.8	73.1	9.2	4,700	14.8	0.6	56	101
Mexico	108.7	75.6	743.5	10,700	17.6	0.5	3,123	52
Nicaragua	5.7	71	4.9	3,100	48	0.6	34	110
Panama	3.2	75.2	16.5	8,200	37	1	158	62
Paraguay	6.7	75.3	7.8	4,800	9.4	1	58	95
Peru	28.7	70.1	77.1	6,600	53.1	1.5	1,097	87
Suriname	0.5	73.2	1.4	7,100	9.5	0.6	21	85
Uruguay	3.5	75.9	14.5	10,900	27.4	1.6	240	46
Venezuela	26	73.3	149.9	7,200	10.3	1.2	1,675	74

Sources: CIA World Factbook, updated December 13, 2007, UNHDR Human Development Index 2007/2008; IISS Military Balance 2007.

Britain, Spain, Holland, and Denmark all held territory in the Caribbean Basin, and newly united Germany was building a transoceanic fleet and seeking its own colonies. Moreover, long-standing international convention allowed creditor nations to intervene militarily in debtor nations to collect on unpaid debts.

Subsequent U.S. administrations continued to avow and to interpret even more expansively the Monroe Doctrine. For instance, Secretary of State Richard Olney famously claimed in 1895, "Today the United States is practically sovereign on this continent and its fiat is law upon the subjects to which it confines its interposition."[12] Against the backdrop of European intrigues in the closing years of the nineteenth century, the United States became more assertive. In 1895, the United States finally acceded to a longstanding Venezuelan request to become involved in a simmering border dispute between that country and British Guyana. Invoking the Monroe Doctrine, the United States demanded that Great Britain submit the dispute to arbitration, to which the British reluctantly agreed.[13] The bloody insurgency by Cuban rebels against Spain and the sinking of the USS *Maine* in Havana propelled the United States into a war against Spain in 1898 that ultimately resulted in the U.S. occupation of Cuba and the acquisition of Puerto Rico. In late 1902, warships from Great Britain, Germany, and Italy blockaded Venezuelan ports to demand debt repayments, with the German ships shelling one port in early 1903. Also in 1903, Germany threatened military action to collect debts in the Dominican Republic. Consequently, in 1904, President Theodore Roosevelt asserted that the United States might "exercise an international police power" in order to ensure that obligations to international creditors were met and to restore internal stability within the countries of Latin America in order to avoid any pretext for European interventions. This "Roosevelt Corollary" to the original Monroe Doctrine was subsequently used to justify several U.S. military interventions in the region.[14]

Although many Latin Americans originally welcomed the Monroe Doctrine (and at the Lima Conference in 1847 effectively endorsed it), disenchantment set in over the decades, and it was not until after World War II that the countries of the Western Hemisphere came together in a formal collective defense arrangement. In the 1947 Inter-American Treaty of Reciprocal Assistance (also known as the *Rio Pact*), these countries agreed that an assault by a non-American nation upon the territory or independence of any American state would be considered "an act of aggression against all the other American states."[15] The Rio Pact reflected a desire by the signatories to codify and strengthen complementary interests at least as much as it stemmed from any concern over the evolving U.S. confrontation with the Soviet Union. The U.S. interest in the pact was in preserving order and the status quo. Although the Latin American nations were also concerned with protecting the status quo, they were equally concerned with institutionalizing their special relationship with the United States. These countries hoped that increased U.S. attention would mean more financial resources to assist in addressing long-standing economic and social problems. They also hoped to be able to restrain the interventionist impulse of the United States. A year after the Rio Pact was signed, the Charter of Bogotá created the Organization of American States (OAS) in 1948.

Almost before the ink was dry, Latin American governments began to distance themselves from these arrangements that seemed to license American interference. Covert action by the United States to overthrow a popularly elected but left-leaning government in Guatemala in 1954, the failed Bay of Pigs operation in 1961, and the 1965 U.S.-led OAS military intervention designed to prevent the establishment of a communist government in the Dominican Republic reinforced Latin American wariness. The general ineffectiveness of the OAS as an organization for resolving regional conflicts is largely a consequence of Latin American suspicions regarding U.S. intentions.

Despite these tensions, the long-standing lack of a significant military threat in and from Latin America has been valuable to the United States in facilitating the deployment of U.S. power in other regions. Particularly during the Cold War, the absence of a Western Hemisphere–based opponent enabled the United States to concentrate on the defense of such regions as Europe and East Asia. To preserve this situation, the United States strongly resisted Soviet efforts to place nuclear weapons in Cuba in 1962 (the Cuban Missile Crisis) and viewed with deep suspicion any efforts by Latin American governments to seek closer ties with the Soviet Union and other Eastern bloc countries. In fact, after Cuban dictator Fidel Castro's successful 1959 revolution and his subsequent embrace of communism and alignment with the Soviet Union, a paramount concern for U.S. policy became avoiding a "second Cuba" in Latin America. The U.S. desire to keep the southern flank secure also explains continuing efforts to prevent historic rivalries among Latin American countries from degenerating into armed conflict and U.S. mediation efforts when conflict does arise, as it did briefly between Peru and Ecuador in 1995.

The U.S. entity that currently holds primary responsibility for securing the southern flank is the U.S. military's Southern Command, headquartered in Miami, Florida. According to this Command:

> Although border tensions have not been completely eliminated, the traditional threat of nations attacking neighbors with military force has diminished dramatically. Increasingly, asymmetric threats posed by non-state actors attempting to exploit nations' vulnerabilities have supplanted conventional force-on-force challenges.[16]

To deal with these concerns, Southern Command focuses heavily on building strong relationships with countries in the region in order to protect U.S. and partner security interests.

Political Stability in Central America and the Caribbean Basin.   The small island nations of the Caribbean and the republics of Central America have witnessed repeated interventions by U.S. troops. Between 1900 and 1933, U.S. armed forces intervened in Panama, Cuba, Nicaragua, Honduras, Mexico, Haiti, and the Dominican Republic. President Franklin D. Roosevelt's Good Neighbor Policy, announced in 1933, was an effort to move U.S. foreign policy away from its previous interventionist tendencies and to emphasize "cooperation and trade rather than military force to maintain stability in the hemisphere."[17] Despite this effort to change course, the United States intervened militarily on numerous occasions in the subsequent decades, including in the Dominican Republic (1965), Grenada (1983), Panama (1989), and Haiti (1994 and 2004). The United States also intervened using more indirect methods. For example, the United States provided clandestine support to the forces that overthrew Guatemalan President Jacobo Arbenz Guzmán in 1954, and it trained and deployed Cuban expatriates to attempt to overthrow Castro in the 1961 Bay of Pigs invasion. In the 1980s, U.S. military advisors trained and supported government forces in El Salvador, Honduras, and Guatemala when these countries were facing leftist insurgencies. Finally, the United States extended official and unofficial military support to rebels seeking to overthrow the communist regime in Nicaragua in the 1980s.

The end of the Cold War removed a significant source of regional military competition and an important motivation for U.S. military intervention. The United States no longer had to focus on the threat that communist regimes would gain an important foothold in the Western Hemisphere. In the early twenty-first century, the most likely scenarios for substantial U.S. military intervention in Central America and the Caribbean Basin relate to political instability in Cuba or Haiti that could result in widespread human suffering and mass illegal immigration to the United States.

Economic Interests.   The economic health of Latin American countries and trade between these countries and the United States are important to U.S. interests. Because it would eliminate an important root cause, economic development with Latin American countries is the most promising long-term answer to tensions between these countries and the United States over immigration. In addition, the United States has important economic interests in the region. As a recent study completed for Congress states, "Latin America, although not the largest, is the fastest growing U.S. regional trade partner."[18] Between 1992 and 2003, U.S. exports to Latin America grew by approximately 98%, while U.S. imports grew by 215%.[19] In 2006, Latin America accounted for more than 19% of total U.S. trade.[20] Latin America is also a major supplier of raw materials to the United States.

Venezuela's Chavez is leading the challenge to U.S. trade relations within the region, but, despite his rhetoric, Venezuela's state-owned petroleum company, PDVSA, continues to ship oil to the United States and continues to own several important U.S. refineries. This demonstrates the ambivalence of many Latin Americans about their economic ties with their northern neighbor. The countries of Latin America fear U.S. economic domination, yet they desire access to the large and profitable U.S. market. For their part, many U.S. companies view Latin America as a region of uncertain political stability but substantial potential for investment and trade.

Recognition of the mutual benefits to be gained from strengthening economic relationships among the countries in the hemisphere has led to the expansion of free trade proposals. Canada, the United States, and Mexico signed the North American Free Trade Agreement (NAFTA) in 1993; in the following decade, the overall level of trade among these three countries more than doubled.[21] A broader Free Trade

Area of the Americas (FTAA) has been in intermittent negotiation since the initial Summit of the Americas in 1994 but has foundered over differences in agricultural policy and several other issues. Despite continuing U.S. interest, prospects for the FTAA dimmed in 2005 when the MERCOSUR (Spanish for "Common Market of the South") countries—Argentina, Brazil, Paraguay, Uruguay, and Venezuela—failed to affirm the support that they had originally expressed in 1994.[22]

While awaiting the outcome of these broader multilateral trade negotiations, the United States, five Central American nations, and the Dominican Republic signed the Central America–Dominican Republic Free Trade Agreement (CAFTA-DR) in 2004. The United States was motivated by economic reasons and its democracy promotion agenda, arguing that CAFTA-DR "is a way for America to support freedom, democracy and economic reform in our neighborhood."[23] The United States also signed bilateral Free Trade Agreements with Chile in 2003 and with Columbia, Ecuador, Panama, and Peru in 2006. These agreements constitute an important component of the U.S. "strategy of opening markets in the Hemisphere through competitive liberalization."[24] The expansion of free trade agreements with Latin American countries represents a significant U.S. accomplishment, resulting from many years of diplomacy focused on a stable set of liberal economic principles.

Illegal Drugs.   Another specific U.S. interest in the region concerns the cultivation, production, and trafficking of illegal drugs. In recent years, the United States has focused particular attention on Colombia, the source of an estimated 80% of the cocaine shipped to the United States. The United States has invested billions of dollars in aid and posted up to eight hundred soldiers and hundreds of contractors in Colombia to assist in eradicating the coca trade and defeating the FARC (Colombian Armed Revolutionary Forces, a Marxist revolutionary movement accused of controlling an increasing share of the drug trade).[25] After the terrorist attacks of September 11, 2001, potential connections between the illegal drug trade and international terrorist groups grew in salience. U.S. counternarcotics initiatives that seek to strengthen law enforcement capacity and enhance the rule of law abroad may also contribute to political stability and counterterrorism.[26] Unfortunately, despite substantial American and local efforts to stem the tide, the flood of drugs from the south continues. Over the long term, this supply seems likely to subside only if demand in the United States contracts.

Promotion of Democracy and Human Rights in Latin America.   By the 1960s, the three traditional pillars of most Latin American societies—the church, the oligarchy, and the military—were no longer monolithic institutions upholding the status quo and enforcing a common ideology. Moreover, new social groups and new educational, demographic, and economic forces were growing up beside, and in some cases eclipsing, the traditional pillars. The resulting diffusion of power meant that many Latin American countries acquired a broader, more secure base for democracy. By the late 1980s, a tide of democratization had swept the area. Unfortunately, although a few countries such as Chile had long-standing democratic traditions, in most countries the institutions and practices of democracy were immature and weak.

The broad embrace of democratic practices by Latin countries in the 1980s and early 1990s resulted in the expansion of political and social rights to populations that had never before enjoyed them. However, this process also carried with it limitations and weaknesses. One key limitation was that uneven application of the rule of law impaired gains in individual civil rights. According to scholar Kenneth Roberts, "large swaths of the population in many countries lived on the margins of legal and administrative structures that could enforce equal rights of citizenship, from access to the courts to protection against police brutality."[27] In addition to this limitation, a key weakness has been that liberal democracy carried with it in the minds of many unrealistic expectations of greater national and personal prosperity. Instead of seeing a positive relationship between political and economic change, many of the least well off in Latin America felt the reverse, as structural adjustment policies and free market reforms lessened the social safety net in many countries. Even after two decades of market-oriented reforms, "in 2004 . . . more than 40 percent of Latin Americans continued to live below the poverty line."[28] There are, however, important tangible indications of progress. In the past twenty-five years in Latin America, infant mortality has gone down, life expectancy has gone up, and hunger and poverty have been reduced. However the pace of change has clearly not kept up with popular expectations.[29]

As of the early twenty-first century, it appears that the preservation and deepening of liberal democracy continues to be at risk in a number of countries in the region. This is clearly of concern to the United States; as articulated in the 2006 National Security Strategy, the U.S.

> goal remains a hemisphere fully democratic, bound together by good will, security cooperation, and the opportunity for all our citizens to prosper. . . . The deceptive appeal of anti-free market populism must not be allowed to erode political freedoms and trap the Hemisphere's poorest in cycles of poverty. If America's nearest neighbors are not secure and stable, then Americans will be less secure.[30]

A challenge for the United States is to continue promoting democratic and economic development without inciting traditional regional resentment against U.S. interference.[31]

The Panama Canal.   Although its strategic importance has diminished over the decades, the uninterrupted operation of the Panama Canal remains a U.S. interest. The opening of the canal in 1914 was the culmination of a long U.S. diplomatic and engineering effort to enable U.S. warships to move readily between the Atlantic and Pacific oceans and to enable commercial shipping to move all types of cargo inexpensively between the two oceans. To protect the canal, the United States acquired territory and built bases over the course of three decades, beginning in 1900. The importance of these investments was shown by the great utility of the canal in World War II and the Korean War in the 1950s. However, the potential wartime role of the canal subsequently declined as U.S. aircraft carriers became too large for the canal locks to handle and as the Soviet Union developed nuclear missiles capable of reaching the vulnerable locks. In 1999, operational control of the canal was transferred to Panama, and U.S. military installations reverted to Panamanian sovereignty.

Although the canal is extremely busy and continues to support approximately 5% of global shipping traffic, its inability to handle supertankers and large container ships limits its utility. In October 2006, in a demonstration of confidence about the future of the canal and the ability of the Panamanian state to manage a huge construction project, Panamanian voters approved by referendum a plan to add a new channel and a third set of locks to the canal.[32] This expansion will not only increase capacity but will also allow the passage of large, modern ships that cannot be accommodated by the original canal.

Illegal Immigration.   Another major U.S. interest in Latin America lies in stopping the flood of illegal immigration from the region. Although immigration was a mounting concern in the last decades of the twentieth century, the matter only came to a political boil in the United States at the outset of the twenty-first century. With an estimated twelve to fourteen million illegal Latino immigrants—overwhelmingly from Mexico—already in the United States; with the number growing daily; and with many Americans convinced that illegal immigrants depress wages, overload educational and welfare systems, commit disproportionate crime, and are the source of other assorted ills, the subject became a central political issue during President George W. Bush's administration.

Despite broad agreement that the immigration system was broken and that the flood of illegals must be checked—and, especially, that the "undocumented" already here must somehow be dealt with—as of late 2008, there was no consensus on how to proceed. All agree that enhanced border control is essential, which also helps mitigate the dangers of cross-border terrorism, but how best to secure thousands miles of land and sea borders remains controversial. Similarly, because many sectors of the American economy, especially agriculture and construction, depend heavily on immigrant labor, there is widespread agreement that a legal guest worker program is needed; but how many workers and how their status and presence can be regulated are unanswered questions. Thorniest of all, what is to be done with the large number of illegals (and, in many cases, their legal children) already in country? Amnesty for lawbreakers may be unacceptable, but so is mass deportation. Efforts to resolve these issues in a comprehensive immigration bill failed in 2007 and may well continue to fail. Piecemeal, cumulative reform—though less desirable—will likely prove more workable.

Obviously, Mexico has a critical interest in how its northern neighbor handles this bundle of issues. Badly handled U.S. immigration reform has the potential to sour key relationships between the two countries as well as to inflict needless hardships and costs and to crimp remittances. Yet, ultimately the resolution of the immigration problem rests on Mexico's shoulders as well as those of the United

States. Until there are major improvements in Mexico's own economy, especially for the desperately poor, the matter will continue to fester well into the twenty-first century.

Changing Patterns of Hemispheric Interaction

The period between 1978 and 1990 was a time of extraordinary political change in Latin America. In the late 1970s and early 1980s, even as Argentina, Guatemala, Nicaragua, and El Salvador were in the throes of bloody internal conflicts, there were elections in the Dominican Republic and a return to democratic government in Peru and Ecuador. By the end of 1990, democratic transitions had taken place in virtually every country in Central and South America. In 1993, the signing of NAFTA seemed to mark the beginning of a growing trend toward free trade and a sense of optimism about future economic growth.

Unfortunately, as already noted, the optimism created by these trends has been diminished by subsequent developments that have created doubts about the future of liberal democracy and free trade. The 1998 election of Chavez, followed by the success of populist politicians in several other Latin American countries, has marked a return toward more personalized leadership by charismatic figures with authoritarian tendencies. These leaders tend to portray free trade agreements between the United States and countries of the region as indicative of renewed U.S. economic dominance and imperialism rather than as expressions of hope about regional economic growth and prosperity.

Nowhere has the change in relations and the challenge to U.S. influence in the hemisphere been starker than in Venezuela. Chavez's inflammatory rhetoric extended to calling the president of the United States the "spokesperson for imperialism" and "the Devil" in a speech to the United Nations (UN).[33] Chavez also supported such populist leaders as Evo Morales in his successful bid to become the president of Bolivia in January 2006. But, possibly as a reaction to his interference, populist candidates Chavez endorsed were defeated in Mexico and Peru in 2006. Nevertheless, unstable political and economic patterns in the region and the wealth generated by Venezuela's energy exports continue to provide a foundation for Chavez's diplomatic efforts.

Liberalizing economic reforms in Latin America in the 1990s created growing wealth in many countries. Gains in prosperity, however, were not widely shared, and national elites and foreign partners were seen by many as receiving most of the benefits. This situation made the consensus behind liberal economic policies fragile and less able to persist in the face of economic difficulties.

Despite the high profile of Chavez and the prominence of his Bolivarian Revolution, it is important to note that many of the new leaders on the left in Latin America have sustained agendas of economic reform even as they have sought to improve social programs and address the needs of the poorest citizens in their respective countries. One prominent leader who has tried with some success to strike this balance is President Luiz Inacio Lula da Silva (known as "Lula") of Brazil.[34] It is important for the United States to distinguish between antidemocratic populism and other variants of leftist politics as it seeks regional partners in furthering democratic reform and economic development.[35]

Subregional Review

Central America.   During the 1970s and earlier, the United States paid scant attention to developments in Central America, even as tensions within several countries mounted ominously. This changed in the 1980s, when the United States became intensely focused on Central America as a strategic interest. One country of particular concern was Nicaragua. An eleven-year confrontation began when the repressive Somoza political dynasty was toppled in 1979 and was succeeded by the Sandinista National Liberation Front. Because of the Sandinistas' leftist politics, the Reagan administration terminated all aid to Nicaragua and began to support an opposition group known as the *Contras*. Over the next eight years, U.S. support for the Contras became a highly contentious issue, not only in Latin America, but also between President Ronald Reagan and Congress.

The Iran-Contra scandal that erupted in the United States in the mid-1980s sparked growing uncertainty about the future of U.S. policy in the region. Faced with this uncertainty and an increasing flow of Nicaraguan refugees, Costa Rican President Oscar Arias formulated a fresh approach. He called for the suspension of all external aid to insurgents, across-the-board cease-fires, democratization, refugee repatriation, and regional arms reduction. In August 1987, Arias and the leaders of the other four Central American countries—Guatemala, El Salvador, Honduras, and Nicaragua—signed an accord that included these provisions. In 1988 and 1989, under UN auspices, steps were taken to implement this peace process, and the Nicaraguan civil war came to an end. In February 1990, the candidate of the United Nicaraguan Opposition, Violeta Chamorro, was elected president of Nicaragua in a surprise victory over Sandinista National Liberation Front leader Daniel Ortega, who had served as president of Nicaragua since the overthrow of Somoza. Center-right candidates were elected in 1997 and 2002, but in 2006, Ortega won a plurality of the votes and was re-elected president on his fourth attempt. Although Ortega has disavowed his revolutionary past, the impact of his administration on democratic development and economic progress in Nicaragua remains to be seen.

After its success in Nicaragua, the Arias Peace Plan also became the basis for an agreement to end the bloody civil war in El Salvador. In January 1992, the democratically elected government of Alfredo Cristiani signed a peace accord with the leaders of the Farabundo Marti National Liberation Front (FMLN), the coalition of leftist insurgency groups that had been at war with the government since 1980. The Salvadoran accord has been successful in bringing peace to a small country that experienced more than seventy-five thousand deaths from internal conflict in the 1980s. El Salvador has elected presidents from the conservative Arena party since 1992, and it has become a strong U.S. ally. It was one of a handful of Central American countries to contribute forces to the U.S.-led coalition in Iraq beginning in August 2003 and the only Central American country to sustain that commitment through mid-2008.

In neighboring Guatemala, more than thirty-five years of armed internal conflict came to an official close with a peace treaty signed in late 1996 by the Guatemalan National Revolutionary Unity (UNRG) guerrilla movement and the government of President Alvaro Arzu. This accord ended a civil war that had killed more than one hundred thousand people and created as many as 1 million refugees in a country of only 12 million citizens. Although the civil war is over, Guatemala has continued to struggle with overwhelming problems of poverty and corruption and remains a major transit country for illegal narcotics. Its continuing problem of economic development is revealed by the fact that its primary source of foreign income consists of remittance payments sent back to Guatemala by expatriates living in the United States.[36]

In 1988, the Panamanian strongman Manuel Noriega, who had in the past cooperated with the U.S. Central Intelligence Agency, began to pose a serious problem because of his involvement in drug trafficking and other illegal activities. After various unsuccessful attempts to remove Noriega from office, including the provision of support to an election that he nullified, the United States mounted a military operation in December 1989 to capture him and bring him to the United States, where he was successfully tried on charges of drug smuggling. More than fifteen years after these events, this U.S. intervention does not appear to have adversely affected the long-term security relationship between the United States and Panama. As already noted, positive developments since that time have included the return of the canal zone to Panamanian sovereignty, a U.S.-Panama bilateral free trade agreement, and Panama's decision to expand the canal.

In contrast to the violent struggles and U.S. interventions of the 1980s, by the early twenty-first century, prevailing Central American dynamics had evolved in a positive direction. The CAFTA-DR trade agreement exemplifies the current relations of calm and cooperation that now exist between the United States and the countries of Central America, based on democratic governance and liberalizing economic relationships.

The Caribbean.   The Caribbean subregion is characterized by small states with large humanitarian and economic problems. Overall, these countries are poorly endowed economically. Fluctuating tourism revenues, relatively high energy prices, and a drop in the demand and prices for major exports, such as sugar and bauxite, have put a tremendous strain on Caribbean economies. Severe income disparities and rapid demographic growth have added to an already depressed socioeconomic situation, resulting in political turbulence and major population outflows. In a few cases, such as in Haiti and Cuba, refugee flows have attained dramatic proportions.

Cuba remains in many ways the subregion's focal point in terms of U.S. national security, primarily because it is governed by a repressive Marxist regime and lies only ninety miles off the coast of Florida. Although it has a population of only 10 million and is about the size of the state of Virginia, Cuba enjoyed considerable global influence during the 1960s, 1970s, and early 1980s. In that period, Castro actively supported numerous leftist movements and regimes throughout the region and in Africa, with Cuba serving as an agent of the Soviet Union and as a safe haven and center of coordination for assorted revolutionary movements. The level of such activities declined dramatically, however, as financial support from the Soviet Union dwindled severely during the late 1980s, and Cuba's domestic problems deepened. In response, Cuba turned to international investment in the 1990s in such industries as tourism. Despite the continuing U.S. economic embargo, which Congress strengthened in 1992 and again in 1996, these Cuban initiatives met with some success. In 2004, the George W. Bush administration imposed new restrictions on U.S. travel and financial transfers to Cuba to eliminate a major source of income for the Castro regime. Since 2006, Castro's apparently poor medical condition and the appointment of his brother Raúl as acting president has heightened speculation that Castro's days are numbered. An unresolved question is whether institutionalized Communist Party rule will prevail in Cuba after Castro's death.

Although transition in Cuba is uncertain, the situation in Haiti is a source of significant concern. For decades, Haiti has been the poorest country in the Western Hemisphere, and the ruthless and despotic misrule of the Duvalier era (1957–1986) guaranteed that the road to economic viability and democratic governance would be long and difficult. After the 1991 military overthrow of elected-President Jean-Bertrand Aristide, the United States intervened in 1994 to restore his government. After being re-elected in 2001, Aristide resigned in 2004 as armed insurgents threatened Haiti's capital and the U.S. expressed a lack of confidence in his presidency, and once again U.S. troops intervened. In a sign of increased regional cooperation, Brazil assumed leadership of an international peacekeeping force drawn largely from Latin American countries later that year. Although Haiti inaugurated a democratically elected government in 2006, Haiti's legacy of poverty and political violence remains a continuing curse. It is still dependent on external armed forces and financial aid to guarantee domestic peace and civil order.

Mexico.   The two-thousand-mile border between the United States and Mexico is the longest border between a developing country and a country with an advanced post-industrial economy anywhere in the world. As a result, there is an extensive and delicate network of interaction between the two states. Under the leadership of President Carlos Salinas de Gortari (1988–1994), Mexico began a program of economic liberalization and restructuring that was successful in greatly improving social and political stability as well as economic prosperity. Partially in recognition of this success, the administrations of Presidents George H. W. Bush and Bill Clinton committed to achieving a regional free trade zone in North America, which they argued would deepen and strengthen the prosperity of all parties. The culmination of this process was the ratification of NAFTA in 1993.

Unfortunately, the Salinas administration that had begun so promisingly unraveled in its final months. Social stability and economic equity were increasingly brought into question with the emergence of the Zapatista guerrilla group in the southern state of Chiapas. Political stability was challenged with the assassinations of key officials in the ruling party, which eventually led to the uncovering of

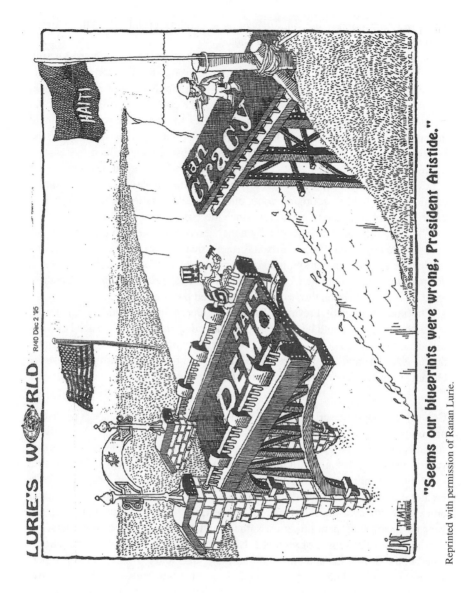

"Seems our blueprints were wrong, President Aristide."

Reprinted with permission of Ranan Lurie.

high-level corruption. And, finally, economic stability crumbled as the Mexico peso underwent a severe crisis in late 1994.

Since those dark days, however, Mexico's prospects have brightened again. President Ernesto Zedillo, who assumed office in late 1994 under difficult circumstances, moved to liberalize a political system that had kept his Institutional Revolutionary Party (PRI) in absolute control of the country since 1929. Regional elections in July 1997 brought sweeping victories to opposition parties and held the promise of competition at all levels of Mexican politics. In the aftermath of the peso crisis, Zedillo was also able to negotiate a substantial U.S. loan, underscoring recognition in the United States that a serious and prolonged deterioration of Mexico's economy and political stability would be disastrous. Genuine multiparty elections were held in 2000 and 2006, ending the domination of the PRI, which had ruled Mexico as a one-party state since the 1930s.

The United States has traditionally been viewed with suspicion by Mexicans, and, despite hopes that Vicente Fox, a former Coca-Cola executive, would bring a productive era of cooperation, his six-year presidency that began in 2000 was a disappointment on both sides of the border. Drugs, immigration, and security were all issues on which the two countries talked past one another.

The inauguration of President Ricardo Calderon in 2007 once again raised hopes that progress could be made on the bilateral agenda. Despite social and political turbulence, Mexico continues to advance economically, at least partially due to NAFTA, and as of yet remains the only Latin American member of the Organization for Economic Cooperation and Development.

Colombia.   Despite serious foreign debt pressures, insurgency, and a persistent narcotics industry, Colombia maintains a democratic government. A relatively sound economy, strengthened civilian institutions, and the firm leadership of Alvaro Uribe—who became Colombia's president in 2002 and was re-elected to a second four-year term in 2006—have enabled the government in Bogotá to assert greater control over the countryside and to reduce the level of violence in major cities. Nevertheless, the FARC, although reduced, remains an unvanquished adversary. Right-wing paramilitaries, some of whom contain Uribe supporters, are another important source of violence. Like the FARC, these groups have participated in the drug trade and engaged in kidnappings and assassinations. The persistence of these armed groups, as well as suspected links between the Uribe government and the paramilitaries, continue to challenge efforts by Colombians to end the violence and corruption that have plagued their country.[37]

Venezuela.   No relationship between the United States and Latin America is more vexing than that with Venezuela. For years, Venezuela was a stable democracy and a reliable trading partner. As Chavez has forced through constitutional changes, personalized the institutions of state, and sought to restrict the media, it has become possible that he could achieve his stated goal of remaining president for another twenty years.[38] He is a master showman and seizes every opportunity to demonstrate his contempt for George W. Bush. Despite his antics and propaganda, he continues to sell his heavy crude to the United States, and the United States remains a willing buyer.

The Andean Countries: Peru, Bolivia, Ecuador. The transition to democracy has also been tested in the Andes. One important recent development there has been Chavez's efforts to influence domestic politics in the Andean countries. In 2006, he endorsed politician Ollanta Humala in his bid for national leadership. In what was widely seen as a protest against this meddling, Peruvians instead elected Allan Garcia, a politician who had left the presidency in disgrace in 1990. Results differed in Bolivia and Ecuador, however, where Chavez-endorsed candidates were successful in their bids for the presidency in 2005 and 2006, respectively. However, it is not clear what role Chavez played in this outcome. Prior to 2006, massive street protests led by indigenous activists were responsible for multiple presidential resignations in both countries. Since their elections, Evo Morales in Bolivia and Eduardo Correa in Ecuador have sought constitutional changes to strengthen presidential power.

Bolivia and Peru have unsettled claims with their neighbor, Chile, which seized its now extremely valuable copper-rich northern territories from them after victory in a 1879–1884 war. Bolivia continues to seek the access to the Pacific that it lost, and Peru continues to dispute its maritime boundary with Chile. Notwithstanding these simmering disputes, further hostilities seem unlikely since both countries are focused internally on more pressing challenges related to economic development and political stability.

The Southern Cone. Until recently, Chile and Argentina were the most distant partners of the United States in the hemisphere, politically and geographically. However, Argentina was declared a major U.S. ally in 1998, and, in 2003, Chile was the first country in South America to sign a bilateral free trade agreement with the United States.

An example of the less-than-warm historical relationship between the United States and Argentina occurred in 1982, when the military government in Buenos Aires decided to act on Argentina's long-standing claim to the Malvinas/Falkland Islands. By doing so, it provoked a war with Great Britain and placed Washington in an awkward diplomatic position. Given the importance of the U.S.-U.K. alliance, Washington supported Great Britain's successful campaign against Argentina, much to Argentina's chagrin. Elected in 1983, one year after Argentina's defeat, President Raúl Alfonsin was faced with the virtual reconstruction of a once-prosperous state shattered by forty years of irresponsible rule. Over the next six years, Alfonsin made significant strides in implementing democracy, including putting former military leaders on trial for gross human rights violations. However, a series of rebellions by military officers during his last two years in office, though unsuccessful, made the democratic transition more uncertain. His 1989 successor, Carlos Menem, brought with him a measure of political stability and an agenda of free market reform. Under his leadership, the size and budgets of the armed forces were reduced significantly, and their mission was reoriented toward international peacekeeping efforts. These changes permitted Argentina to focus on infrastructure modernization and monetary stabilization.

After a half century of economic profligacy and political chaos, Argentina seemed poised to re-emerge as an economic power in the Southern Cone until a financial crisis erupted in 2001, forcing a devaluation of 75% in the value of the peso and suspension of payments to the country's creditors. Under the leadership of populist President Nestor Kirchner, elected in 2003, Argentina's economic situation once again stabilized. Argentina achieved at least an 8% growth rate between the first year of Kirchner's presidency in 2003 and early 2007. A question for the future is whether this economic growth is sustainable in view of inflationary pressures caused by Kirchner's manipulation of price controls and export taxes.[39] Argentina also continues to owe $24 billion to disgruntled debtors harmed by the 2001 suspension and faces dozens of international arbitration cases from foreign investors resulting from Argentine government actions during the crisis. Until resolved, these outstanding issues will limit the realization of Argentina's considerable economic potential.

After the return of democracy to neighboring Argentina in 1983, American attention shifted to Chile and its deplorable human rights record. Since the overthrow of Salvador Allende's Marxist government in 1973, Chile had been governed by the authoritarian General Augusto Pinochet. Events took a surprising turn in 1988, however, when Pinochet was defeated in a national referendum on his rule, leading to democratic elections at year's end. Although Pinochet tried to keep tight control of the transition, he nonetheless honored the mandate to return to democratic rule. Since Pinochet's departure, Chile has held four presidential elections, which have all been judged to be "free and fair."[40] Since this return to democracy, Chile has benefited from a broad, multiparty consensus behind the liberal economic reforms and fiscal prudence instituted in the Pinochet era.

At the December 1994 Miami Summit of the Americas, Chile was invited to become the fourth member of NAFTA, but its potential accession subsequently became embroiled in the U.S. domestic debate over trade. In the late 1990s, the resulting inability of the United States to solidify its trading relationship caused Chile to seek trading partners elsewhere in South America, in the European Union, and in Asia. After years of negotiation, a U.S.-Chile Free Trade Agreement was finally signed in 2003 and implemented in 2004.

Brazil. Brazil is the sole Latin American nation capable of aspiring to a major global role on its own. Its population of 190 million dwarfs that of its neighbors. Geographically the fifth largest state in the international system, it is endowed with plentiful resources, including uranium, bauxite, copper, iron, and some of the world's best farmland. This former Portuguese colony is second only to the United States as the world's largest agricultural exporter. Also a major exporter of weapons, Brazil has sold aircraft, tanks, and missiles to more than thirty countries. Brazil's development has transformed the balance of power in the southern portion of Latin America, historically an area of intense Brazilian-Argentine rivalry. The century-old parity between Argentina and Brazil has given way to clear and growing Brazilian superiority.

Until 1982, Brazil was justly pointed to as a model of rapid growth. But this "miracle" began to fade during the 1980s, as the country struggled under an enormous external debt burden and growing domestic political uncertainties. By 1985, inflation had jumped to 200% annually, and new foreign investment in the country had virtually come to a halt. With the 1990 return to electoral democracy, renewed efforts to rejuvenate the economy began to bear fruit. Despite the impeachment in 1992 of President Fernando Collor de Mello and the accompanying political crisis, economic stabilization and improved international credibility were achieved under Fernando Cardoso, who assumed the presidency in late 1994.

Unlike Argentina, which suspended debt payments during the 2001–2002 financial crisis, Brazil accepted and received a bailout from the International Monetary Fund and has since stabilized its financial situation by reducing its foreign debt exposure while simultaneously reducing its overall indebtedness. Trade has been a contentious issue between Brazil and the United States, with Brazil pressuring the United States for greater access for its agricultural products and the U.S. demanding more and better protection for intellectual property such as copyrights and patents. Nevertheless, relations between the two countries have generally remained amicable. A pragmatic Brazilian foreign policy is one of the strongest regional counters to the growing influence of Chavez in the region.

Extrahemispheric Relations

The search for technology, foreign investments, and financial credits from diverse sources has long been central to the foreign economic policies of many Latin American countries. During the 1970s, in order to reduce the gap between themselves and the advanced industrialized world, many of the region's countries borrowed heavily and not always wisely. The changing economic realities of the 1980s forced most of them to take a much more pragmatic, though economically and politically painful, approach to economic stability and growth. Debt repayment, even with generous rescheduling by creditors, has been particularly difficult. In 2002, the countries of Latin America still had an external debt of $694 billion and the highest debt service ratio among the regions of the world.[41]

In recent decades, the region's countries have begun diversifying their trade, investment, and security relationships in order to reduce their dependence upon the United States. In their search for technology and associated foreign investment, they have looked to Europe and Asia, asking in return that these foreign markets be opened to Latin American finished goods as well as raw materials. In addition, there has been a significant increase in their trade with China and other developing countries and less reliance on the more economically advanced states. Regional trade agreements are also altering Latin American economic and political dynamics, stimulating growth and in turn introducing new opportunities and new tensions.

Military Issues

Although Latin America is not nearly as militarized as Northeast Asia or the Middle East, internal security threats and historic conflicts have left the region with often overly large military establishments armed with relatively sophisticated weapons. New tasks for many Latin American countries include streamlining and professionalizing their armed forces, reorienting force missions from internal to external security and peacekeeping, and establishing new norms that institutionalize civilian control over the military. Three primary security issues in Latin America, discussed in turn below, continue to involve military considerations.

Challenges to Internal Order.   Although less pressing than in earlier decades, challenges to internal order persist. The Castro revolution of 1959 demonstrated that small, efficiently organized forces could employ irregular warfare to defeat established armed forces and create the opportunity for total societal reorganization. The United States and most Latin American governments have long assigned high priority to preventing another guerrilla movement from repeating the Cuban experience. Despite past successes against insurgents, Latin American leaders have not discounted the possibility that irregular warfare might again seriously threaten their countries. Many are paying increased attention to some of the root causes of this type of warfare, such as racial discrimination and deep poverty, and to solutions that emphasize negotiation and increased opportunities for political participation.

Border Disputes and Conflicting Territorial Ambitions.   Since the Chaco War between Bolivia and Paraguay in the 1930s, no Latin American territory has changed hands in the course of a war. Nevertheless, disputes remain between several countries of the region. As noted earlier, tensions between Peru and Chile have persisted since the latter's territorial conquests in the War of the Pacific (1879–1884). Bolivia, forced to surrender its outlet to the sea in that conflict, has continually pressed Chile and Peru for a Pacific port.[42] In northern South America, Colombia and Venezuela remain at odds over the location of their boundary in the potentially oil-rich Gulf of Venezuela. Despite the already-cited flare-up between Peru and Ecuador in 1995, however, the number of disputes among nations of the hemisphere is low, given their contentious histories.

Hemispheric Security Cooperation.   The need to defend Latin America against interstate war gave rise to institutions and arrangements known collectively as the Inter-American Defense System. Until the election of Brazilian Lieutenant General Jorge Armando de Almeida Ribeiro in 2006, the system's governing Inter-American Defense Board (IADB) had always been headed by a U.S. general officer. Traditionally weak due to lack of U.S. interest as well as Latin American concern about U.S. interventionism, the IADB may gain more support as a result of the change to Latin American leadership. With its status as an agency of the

OAS formalized in 2006, key programs through which the IADB contributes to hemispheric security include the removal of landmines to protect populations and promote agriculture and economic development, national disaster preparation, confidence and security building measures, and the operation of the Inter-American Defense College.[43]

Since the end of World War II, thousands of Latin American officers have attended U.S. military service schools, and U.S. military training missions have operated in many Latin American countries. During the Cold War, the U.S. expectation was that these efforts would help deliver Latin American support for the United States. After the Cold War, these programs persisted as mechanisms for enhancing security cooperation. One of the most important of these programs has been the Western Hemisphere Institute for Security Cooperation (formerly known as the School of the Americas), now located at Fort Benning, Georgia. Although the school has been the target of protests because of alumni who have been accused of human rights abuses, it remains an important vehicle for fostering productive military-to-military contacts in the region. At sea, the Annual U.S.–South American Allied Exercise, held since 1958 in the south Atlantic and Pacific oceans, has facilitated naval cooperation between the United States and Latin America. The U.S. Southern Command particularly focuses on providing training for and coordinating peacekeeping and stability operations, conducting humanitarian relief missions, and ensuring that friendly nations in the region can conduct joint operations with U.S. forces.

A significant challenge that Latin American militaries have met successfully is the 2004 peacekeeping deployment to Haiti, known by its French acronym MINUSTAH (UN Stabilization Mission to Haiti). As of early 2007, MINUSTAH has been consistently led by a Brazilian general with forces drawn from Argentina, Bolivia, Brazil, Chile, Ecuador, Guatemala, Paraguay, Peru, Uruguay, and other partner states. This Latin American–led peacekeeping mission has enabled U.S. forces to concentrate on other U.S. national security challenges around the world.

Future Latin American Challenges to U.S. National Security

In April 2001, George W. Bush laid out his agenda for Latin America at the Third Summit of the Americas in Quebec, Canada, with these words:

> We have a great vision before us: a fully democratic hemisphere, bound together by good will and free trade. That is a tall order. It is also the chance of a lifetime. And it is the responsibility we share.[44]

George W. Bush's vision to make the twenty-first century the "Century of the Americas" included proposals to strengthen democratic governance in the region; to complete the Free Trade Area of the Americas agreement; to enhance cooperation with Caribbean countries; and to increase development and counternarcotics assistance to the Andean countries; as well as initiatives relating to education, intergovernmental cooperation, business, and the environment. Although some progress has been made on this agenda, after the 9/11 terrorist attacks, other U.S.

national security priorities reduced the attention given to Latin American affairs. Such issues as fragile democracies, ongoing insurgent movements, drug trafficking, economic growth and equality, economically driven immigration, and clashing environmental and economic interests remain significant challenges for U.S. policy makers into the twenty-first century.

Four countries that are likely to be of particular concern to U.S. policy makers in the years ahead are Mexico, Cuba, Haiti, and Venezuela. The U.S.-Mexico relationship was particularly affected by the terrorist attacks on the United States on 9/11. On September 6, less than a week before the terrorist attacks, President Vincente Fox of Mexico and George W. Bush issued a joint statement expressing their agreement that "U.S.-Mexican relations [had] entered their most promising moment in history."[45] As of early 2008, much of this promise remains unrealized. Mexico's differences with U.S. foreign policy, including the U.S. response to the 2001 terrorist attacks, led Mexico to withdraw formally from the Rio Pact in 2002. More recently, the debate in the United States over immigration reform has made an already-contentious relationship even more difficult. A key challenge for U.S. policy makers will be to overcome these tensions and to cooperate effectively with the Mexican government to make progress in areas of mutual interest.

Developments within Cuba are a second major source of concern. Although Castro was able to retain unchallenged control of the political, economic, and military structures of Cuban society from 1959 to 2006, the transition to a post-Castro Cuba has begun. Whether this transition will bring large or small changes, or whether it will be violent or peaceful, remains to be seen. The United States should be ready to adjust its Cuban policy to respond appropriately to this inevitable process.

Haiti is a third country that will remain a continuing concern of U.S. policy makers. Although it is not the only country in the Caribbean to face internal political strains and severe economic problems, Haiti has been the most dramatic example and has demanded the most international attention. A peacekeeping presence is likely to be needed indefinitely if Haiti is to overcome chronic instability and to create a truly democratic government. Ultimately the eventual solutions to the problems in Haiti and the rest of the Caribbean will be political and economic, not military. A comprehensive program of coordinated aid will be essential to reducing the likelihood that widespread suffering and political upheaval will lead to future refugee flows and other threats to U.S. and Latin American security.

Venezuela will remain a fourth focus of particular concern. As already noted, Chavez has actively sought to thwart U.S. policy initiatives in the region through his deep and active opposition to the FTAA and his use of oil revenues to support populist politicians and U.S. opponents. A continuing challenge for the United States will be to manage its dependence on imported oil while seeking to limit Chavez's negative impact on the institutions of democracy in Venezuela and other countries in the hemisphere.

With the exception of the 2004 U.S. military intervention in Haiti, there has been a clear regional trend in recent years away from confrontation and toward negotiated settlements of longstanding conflicts—a trend that seems likely to continue. The principal challenge ahead for the United States will be to work with the various regional powers to bring political and economic stability to the entire hemisphere. A secure southern flank, based on democratic governance and economic growth, still remains fundamental to the security of the United States. The preservation of a secure southern flank will require continuing, even increasing, effort and understanding on the part of the American public and American policy makers.

Discussion Questions

1. What are the national security interests that the United States has historically had in Latin America? How have these changed in the twenty-first century?

2. Is the early-twenty-first-century trend of the success of leftist politicians in Latin America a political dynamic that should be embraced or confronted by the United States? Are there important distinctions among leftist governments that U.S. policy makers should keep in mind?

3. What problems in Latin America involve military considerations? How do these problems affect existing security arrangements with the United States?

4. In the 1980s, many countries in Latin America transitioned to democracy. What subsequent challenges have these young democracies faced?

5. Should the United States play a role in supporting democratic consolidation in Latin America? If so, what specific policies should the United States adopt?

6. How did the end of the Cold War affect U.S. relations with the countries of Latin America?

7. What traditional security concerns remain for the United States in Latin America? What security concerns have diminished during the past decade? What new concerns have emerged?

8. What kind of relationship with Mexico will be most supportive of U.S. interests in the short term as well as in the long run?

9. Can the Rio Pact and the OAS be made to serve the mutual interests of the United States and the countries of Latin America? What would it take to create an effective regional security arrangement?

Recommended Reading

Adams, Francis. *Deepening Democracy: Global Governance and Political Reform in Latin America.* Westport, CT: Praeger, 2003.

Appelbaum, Nancy P., Anne S. Macpherson, and Karin Alejandra Rosemblatt. *Race and Nation in Modern Latin America.* Chapel Hill: University of North Carolina Press, 2003.

Arceneaux, Craig L., and David Pion-Berlin. *Transforming Latin America: The International and Domestic Origins of Change.* Pittsburgh: University of Pittsburgh Press, 2005.

Buvinic, Mayra, and Jacqueline Mazza, eds. *Social Inclusion and Economic Development in Latin America.* New York: Inster-American Development Bank (distributed by Johns Hopkins University Press), May 2004.

Campbell, Tim. *The Quiet Revolution: Decentralization and the Rise of Political Participation in Latin American Cities.* Pittsburgh: University of Pittsburgh Press, 2003.

Cleary, Edward L., and Timothy J. Steigenga. *Resurgent Voices in Latin America: Indigenous Peoples, Political Mobilization, and Religious Change.* New Brunswick, NJ: Rutgers University Press, 2004.

Domínguez, Jorge I., and Michael Shifter. *Constructing Democratic Governance in Latin America.* 2nd ed. Baltimore: Johns Hopkins University Press, 2003.

Eckstein, Susan, and Timothy P. Wickham-Crowley. *What Justice? Whose Justice? Fighting for Fairness in Latin America.* Berkeley: University of California Press, 2003.

Feinberg, Richard E., Carlos H. Waisman, and León Zamosc. *Civil Society and Democracy in Latin America.* 1st ed. New York: Palgrave Macmillan, 2006.

Franko, Patrice M. *The Puzzle of Latin American Economic Development.* 2nd ed. Lanham, MD: Rowman & Littlefield, 2003.

Frühling, Hugo, Joseph S. Tulchin, and Heather A. Golding. *Crime and Violence in Latin America: Citizen Security, Democracy, and the State.* Baltimore: Johns Hopkins University Press, 2003.

Gibson, Edward L. *Federalism and Democracy in Latin America.* Baltimore: Johns Hopkins University Press, 2004.

Gwynne, Robert N., and Cristóbal Kay. *Latin America Transformed: Globalization and Modernity.* 2nd ed. New York: Oxford University Press, 2004.

Hite, Katherine, and Paola Cesarini, Eds. *Authoritarian Legacies and Democracy in Latin America and Southern Europe.* Notre Dame, IN: University of Notre Dame Press, 2004.

Kacowicz, Arie Marcelo. *The Impact of Norms in International Society: The Latin American Experience, 1881–2001.* Notre Dame, IN: University of Notre Dame Press, 2005.

Kirby, Peadar. *Introduction to Latin America: Twenty-First Century Challenges.* Thousand Oaks, CA: Sage Publications, 2003.

Koonings, Kees, and Dirk Kruijt. *Armed Actors: Organised Violence and State Failure in Latin America.* London; New York: Zed Books, 2004.

Menjívar, Cecilia, and Néstor Rodriguez. *When States Kill: Latin America, the U.S., and Technologies of Terror.* 1st ed. Austin: University of Texas Press, 2005.

Nun, Jose. *Democracy: Government of the People or Government of the Politicians? Critical Currents in Latin American Perspective.* Lanham, MD: Rowman & Littlefield, 2003.

Yeats, Guillermo M. *The Roots of Poverty in Latin America.* Jefferson, NC: McFarland & Co., 2005.

Internet Resources

Inter-American Development Bank, www.iadb.org
Inter-American Dialogue, www.thedialogue.org
Latinamerica Press, www.latinamericapress.org
LatinFocus, www.latin-focus.com
Organization of American States, www.oas.org
Pew Hispanic Center, http://pewhispanic.org
U.S. Department of State Bureau of Western Hemisphere Affairs, www.state.gov/p/wha

V

National Security Policy: Current and Future Issues in American National Security Policy

25

Globalization and Human Security

Although it is necessary to examine U.S. national security interests and challenges in particular regional and country contexts, it is no longer sufficient. Many important actors and issues are now global or transnational in nature. This important trend is now widely analyzed and discussed in terms of the impact of globalization on the international system.[1] Although there is no single agreed-upon definition, *globalization* is generally described as an ongoing multidimensional process that is decreasing the significance of state borders. National security policy makers have to be aware of the implications of this process as they analyze policy options.

One effect of globalization is that nonstate actors are playing increasingly significant roles in an international system previously dominated by states. A second implication is that the permeable nature of state borders and the phenomenon of weak and failing states make it more and more necessary to look beyond traditional state-centric conceptions of security. Analysts have to look at intrastate violence and transnational problems, such as disease, environmental degradation, and resource scarcity, as human security issues that deserve more attention than they have traditionally been given. After reviewing nonstate actors and the issues highlighted by a human security perspective, this chapter concludes by examining some of the challenges and opportunities created by a globalizing world.

The Global Security Environment

Enabled by reductions in transport and communication costs, new technologies, and the policy choices of many of the world's political leaders, international trade is increasing, international flows of capital are on the rise, the nature of international business activity is changing, and there is a tremendous, transnational diffusion of cultural forms. Although these manifestations of globalization have a tendency to lessen the significance of state borders, international relations scholar James Rosenau has argued that they are accompanied by a related process known as *localization*. Localization responds to individuals' needs for a stable sense of identity and stems from the value that human beings place on traditional cultural practices and community. As globalization "allows people, goods, information, norms, practices and institutions to move about oblivious to or despite boundaries," localization "derives from all those pressures that lead individuals, groups and institutions to narrow their horizons."[2] As the changes brought by globalization threaten and disrupt political, economic, and social life in many countries, localizing tendencies may gain force as a reaction.

As a result of diverse choices by national political leaders, as well as the varying abilities of different countries to prosper from globalization, the impact of globalization varies widely across regions and states.[3] Although globalization can create new and vastly expanded opportunities for economic growth and development, it can also place new pressures on leaders, institutions, and societal structures. It can therefore lead to instability as well as to progress.

The process of globalization has caused "a novel redistribution of power among states, markets, and civil society" and led to a situation in which "resources and threats that matter, including money, information, pollution, and popular culture," are less and less restricted by state borders.[4] As this diffusion of power occurs, even "individual actions may have dramatic consequences for international relations."[5] Perhaps there is no single better example of this than the impact that nineteen hijackers had on the United States and its national security policy through their attacks on September 11, 2001. The actions of these hijackers were enabled by many of the same advances in information technology and transportation that underpin other dimensions of globalization. It is clear that in this environment, challenges to U.S. national security can no longer be seen as stemming solely from the actions of other states. Similarly, responses that emphasize only state-centric solutions may be insufficient.

Nonstate Actors

Key nonstate actors include intergovernmental organizations (IGOs), nongovernmental organizations (NGOs), multinational corporations, the media, and religious groups. This category also includes groups once primarily thought of as "subnational," such as labor unions and political parties. Many of these formerly subnational actors now have extensive international connections. Finally, nonstate actors include violent entities, such as criminal organizations and terrorist groups. American national security is likely to be increasingly affected by some or all these actors in the years to come.

Intergovernmental Organizations.   An *IGO* is a multinational body whose members are states. These organizations may be relatively global in scale, as exemplified by the United Nations (UN; 192 members), the World Bank (185 members), the International Monetary Fund (IMF; 185 members), and the World Trade Organization (WTO; 150 members). However, IGOs can also be regional organizations, such as the European Union (EU; twenty-seven members), the African Union (AU; fifty-three members), and the Association of Southeast Asian Nations (ASEAN; ten members).[6] The purposes of IGOs can vary widely, including the coordination of policies relating to security, trade, currency exchange, communications, and economic development.

The UN and its affiliated organizations were created by the United States and its allies following World War II to promote global peace and stability. The UN provides a forum for all countries to meet together to address global problems. Although in theory all UN member states are equal, in practice some states have more power than others; the composition of the UN's most important body, the Security Council, reflects this reality. There has been pressure in recent years to expand the number of countries seated on the Security Council to balance the influence of the five permanent members who each hold veto power, but these proposals are unlikely to result in substantive change anytime soon.

IGOs such as the IMF and the World Bank provide supranational mechanisms for meeting common goals related to currency stability and economic development and growth. Each IGO has its own decision-making process and procedures for determining the best available solution for a given problem. Although the world's international financial institutions have had successes, some solutions have proven to be less effective than anticipated, and others have produced unintended negative consequences. For example, efforts to privatize state-owned industries have in some instances undermined confidence in governments and exacerbated corruption as political elites gained control of newly privatized companies.[7]

It is not surprising that powerful countries seek to manipulate decision-making processes within IGOs to support their own interests. During the Cold War, for example, the UN became an ideological battleground for the United States and the Soviet Union as the two superpowers competed for the loyalty of other states. It is still the case that the effectiveness of an IGO will depend not only on the capabilities of its member states but also on its decision-making procedures and the degree of consensus underlying its core purposes.

Regional IGOs, such as the AU, have come to play increasingly important roles in recent decades. Whereas the UN is large and often slow to react, regional IGOs can have the ability to respond more rapidly and, in some cases, more appropriately. Regional associations of states may also enjoy greater local legitimacy. These characteristics make regional IGOs an attractive vehicle for developed states as they seek to distribute the global burden for peacekeeping and humanitarian actions, particularly in the less developed world. An important constraint, however, is that in many cases the military forces available to regional associations, such as the AU, are very limited in terms of their capabilities, training, and professionalism.

A number of Western nations are attempting to redress this deficiency through sponsorship of regional military training. France's Reinforcement of African Peace-Keeping Capacities program coordinates with the AU and the UN to provide training. The U.S. Trans-Saharan Counterterrorism Program promotes regional security cooperation and provides training to facilitate local responses to security crises. Such programs seek to build trust between participating nations as a basis for future cooperation in international peacekeeping operations.

Expanding the capacity of regional organizations benefits developed and underdeveloped states: Underdeveloped states gain capabilities that allow them to manage regional problems themselves, and developed states do not have to shoulder as much of the responsibility and costs of crisis response. In supporting these multilateral capacity-building initiatives, donor states also avoid the appearance of favoritism that often accompanies bilateral aid relationships. However, regional organizations also come with drawbacks. In cases where the strongest state in a given region is also the leader, smaller states may feel that their interests are threatened or may believe that the organization is merely a proxy for this state. Despite these limitations, increasingly capable regional organizations have the potential to make important contributions to the resolution of regional economic and security challenges in the years to come.

Nongovernmental Organizations.   *NGOs* are nonstate entities that often operate both domestically and abroad. Some NGOs rely on financial support from donor states, while others raise funds through individual and corporate donations. Well-known NGOs include humanitarian aid organizations, such as *Médecins Sans Frontières* (Doctors Without Borders) and the International Committee of the Red Cross. Many NGOs focus on specific goals, such as providing vaccinations for children, reducing communicable diseases, or expanding educational opportunities for girls. NGOs play a critical role in international development, as they often address problems that less-developed states are unable or unwilling to tackle on their own. NGOs may also disburse funds on behalf of a developed state when local authorities are too corrupt to be trusted to spend foreign aid appropriately.

In their contributions to development as well as to other issue areas, NGOs have strengths and limitations. Turning first to strengths, most NGOs approach their work with a wisdom acquired from experience. They seek to promote solutions that are time tested and locally appropriate. Most also emphasize the development of local capacity—collaborative programs rather than donations—because sustainable development only takes place when the target audience is committed to the value of the project. In most cases, NGOs attempt to hire local employees, a policy that increases their legitimacy while reducing operating costs.

Though these strengths are invaluable, NGOs also have important limitations. Like all actors, NGOs can make mistakes, but they are not generally held accountable for their actions in the same way that IGOs may be. NGOs may have conflicting constituencies they have to satisfy, including private and state donors, government partners, and the people whose lives they seek to improve. Moreover, NGOs are sometimes as vulnerable to corruption as any other organization. A few use development work as a cover to promote radical or divisive political goals, such as the promotion of the interests of one ethnic or religious group at the expense of another, thereby generating suspicion among local populations and complicating the work of other NGOs. In addition, NGOs can only operate with the permission of the host country and must therefore avoid the appearance of taking sides in local political contests. In some cases, host governments that become uncomfortable with the work of an NGO will accuse it (rightly or not) of political activity to force it to leave its territory. Finally, NGOs are generally focused on a single issue or problem, which makes them less capable than governments at prioritizing among all the needs of a given community.

The United States Agency for International Development (USAID) is the primary liaison between the United States government and a number of NGOs that it supports. Working closely with U.S. embassies, USAID sets American development priorities to ensure that U.S. taxpayer dollars are put to the best possible use, based on the judgment of career professionals with local expertise. Though USAID has considerable latitude in determining the most appropriate uses for its limited budget, the agency is not completely safe from domestic controversy.[8] As one example, USAID programs relating to the promotion of reproductive health care abroad may touch on issues currently the subject of intense religious, social, and political debates within the United States.

Multinational Corporations.   *Multinational corporations* (MNCs), such as Coca-Cola, Royal Dutch Shell, and De Beers, are primarily motivated by profits. Accordingly, it is important to recognize that the loyalties of MNCs are to their shareholders and not to the states in which they operate. Due to their sheer size and wealth, MNCs can be powerful actors, and many underdeveloped states will provide tax benefits and waive financial restrictions, environmental regulations, and labor laws to attract them. As an unfortunate side effect, the resulting arrangement can spark local resentment at the power of the MNC and constrain the local government's ability to pursue other socially desirable goals.

To be sure, some MNCs attempt to give something back to the societies in which they operate through such activities as building schools, subsidizing health clinics, or repairing damaged environments. Whether these initiatives are mere token gestures meant to deflect local resentment is often difficult to determine. In any case, such philanthropic initiatives do improve the quality of life for some local people, but it would be a mistake to expect MNCs to replace the state in providing social services or to serve as an adequate replacement for international development organizations.

MNCs also bring needed technology and employment opportunities that frequently pay better than indigenous sectors of the economy; they often offer prestigious jobs to well-educated elites who might otherwise seek jobs abroad. Unfortunately, such interactions can also lead to corruption. MNCs may employ family members of political elites, or government officials may be given shares in the company as an incentive for supporting the corporation's operations.

MNCs are rarely held accountable in local courts, creating an enormous potential for civil rights abuses. Local populations may become angry at the presence of the MNCs because of perceived corruption and the appearance (or existence) of an exploitative relationship. Also, the presence of an MNC can sometimes attract predatory attention from local criminal groups. For example, Shell's foreign workers in Nigeria have been kidnapped and held for ransom, and there is a large black market for oil stolen directly from Shell's pipelines. MNCs that require physical protection may hire security contractors or form private paramilitary groups, either with or without the consent of the host government. These armed groups may be above the law, again creating the potential for abuse. Host governments are often reluctant to pressure MNCs to alter their behavior, because the MNCs may then simply relocate to a less demanding host.

Although accountability to host governments is often problematic, some MNCs may be held accountable in their home countries. For example, Nike has been sued in U.S. courts for allegedly using false advertising to describe working conditions at its foreign factories.[9] In another example, the U.S. Supreme Court ruled in 2001 that Shell (which is based in the United Kingdom) could be sued in a New York court over accusations that the company manufactured evidence to support murder charges against Nigerian activist Ken Saro-Wiwa, accusations that resulted in Saro-Wiwa's execution by Nigeria in 1995.[10]

The Media.   The media play an important role in raising awareness of transnational security issues in the United States. Television coverage of humanitarian disasters is critical for mobilizing private donations to relief organizations, such as the International Committee of the Red Cross. Considering that relief organizations often arrive on the ground long before any other form of international response, the media's role in attracting attention to a brewing crisis is critical. Media coverage can often spur donor states into action as well, as voters exert political pressure on their government to "do something" about the horrendous images of starving children or devastated villages appearing on their televisions. The media is a fickle presence, however, as broadcasters must keep their viewers interested. Coverage will decline rapidly once the initial reporting begins to lose its impact.

The media also plays a role in framing issues, which can affect policy response. Media expert Susan Moeller describes the way in which the media uses "frames" to facilitate reporting by drawing on familiar reporting themes.[11] For example, the public is familiar with the "famine frame," so most reports on famines begin with the image of a thin African child, crying and covered in flies. The audience will instantly fill in the rest of the story based on similar stories they have seen in the past, the report will have the desired emotional impact, and the network does not have to spend time providing contextual details. The lack of contextual understanding encourages cookie-cutter responses to crises that are not at all similar in either source or scope. Again, using famine as an example, the implication is that if children are starving, sending food to them will solve the problem. Policy makers may be as likely as average viewers to fall victim to the attractive simplicity of such solutions. Although the media may oversimplify and be biased, its role cannot be discounted, and it is important to recognize its potential impact on policy making.

In some cases, the media becomes an actor in its own story. An example of this has been the Pentagon's program to "embed" reporters in various military units to facilitate reporters' access to breaking events in the war in Iraq that began in 2003. This program provided the news networks with an intimate, visceral, and at times highly emotional stream of news reports that proved extremely popular with viewing audiences. The reporters sometimes found themselves in dangerous situations, and their personal security was dependent on the actions of the American troops on whom they were reporting. Many reporters developed close bonds with the units they covered, which necessarily altered their views of events.

Religious Groups.   Religion will likely continue to play an important role in international affairs, as well as in the domestic affairs of various states. An obvious and very relevant example from the perspective of U.S. national security is the fact that al-Qa'ida is using appeals to a particular interpretation of Islam as the justification for its actions. As a second example, prior to the end of the Cold War, the Catholic Church in Poland played a critical role in the de-legitimization of communism in that country. As a third example, competing claims over treasured holy sites is part of what makes competing Israeli and Palestinian claims over Jerusalem so seemingly irreconcilable (see Chapter 20 for more on this conflict).

The processes of modernization and globalization inevitably bring social changes that are disruptive to traditional community and family structures, creating fear that traditions and even identity will be lost. Religious authorities can provide an alternate source of inspiration and guidance.[12] Consistent with the localizing tendency discussed early in this chapter, religious and other social groups may reassure people facing change by revitalizing traditional norms and practices. In a vacuum of authority or capacity, religious figures may step up or be pushed forward to fill the void. In certain cases, religious groups have provided social services, including education, health care, insurance, small business loans, job training, and employment opportunities. For example, Hezbollah has demonstrated that it is more effective than the state in providing social services in portions of southern Lebanon, seriously undermining the state's legitimacy and authority. In certain areas, Hezbollah functions as a parallel government that cannot be ignored.

Religion can also be used to define one group's identity in opposition to that of another. Many fledgling independence movements have used religion as a basis for mobilization, because it serves as a clear way to differentiate indigenous culture from that of an occupying colonial power.[13] Mobilization based on religion can be extremely problematic, because throughout human history religion has been used to sanction extreme forms of violence. People who believe they are acting on the will of a god or gods may feel less guilt and personal responsibility for their actions. Scholars believe that religious violence is substantively different from other kinds of violence in that it has facilitated greater acceptance of "civilian" casualties.[14] Additionally, whereas traditional political violence is assumed to have an achievable goal, religious violence may not need to achieve anything within the participants' lifetimes to be considered successful. Obviously, this complicates any security response, as such groups may not negotiate and may be difficult to deter. Clerics play a critical role, because their sanction of violent action absolves perpetrators of responsibility and assures them that their actions will be rewarded. Clerics also affect public opinion, and their support for violence may convince the greater community that violent actions are acceptable or even admirable.

Subnational Groups.   Multiple interest groups exist in every state, large or small. These groups may be organized around social or economic class, ethnicity, religion, geography, or trade. Some of these interest groups fit neatly within the borders of a particular state, but many do not. Ethnic groups are often dispersed through several states, and in some cases an individual's sense of ethnic identity may be stronger than his or her identity as a citizen of any state. When the majority of people in an interest group feel that their group identity is more important than their national identity, this can become a source of social unrest and political instability. In some cases, the actions of such interest groups may undermine state sovereignty.

Ethnic Groups.   Particularly in the case of states that gained their independence after colonization, political borders were often determined by negotiation between great powers with no consideration of ethnic groups. As a result, the traditional homelands of many ethnic groups now sit astride two or more states or have been combined into a common political entity. (See Chapter 20 for the impact of this in the Middle East and Chapter 21 for a discussion of sub-Saharan Africa.) Some states have been able to create a national identity that encompasses all the diverse ethnic groups within their territories, but this is no easy task. Even a country as stable as the United States has difficulty assimilating and accommodating its diverse ethnic minorities. States that never develop a strong national identity face a perpetual risk of instability, particularly if one group dominates others. The risk of instability increases when these states are in unstable regions and when ethnic cleavages overlap with socioeconomic status or other social divisions, such as class or religion, as is the case in Iraq.

Professional, Labor, and Migrant Groups.   Labor unions and professional associations are examples of interest groups that are organized around a shared trade or occupation. These groups tend to be most powerful in developed states, where they have played a key role in forcing governments to enact legislation to protect workers' rights. Examples include restrictions on child labor, limits on mandatory overtime, and workplace health and safety regulations. Generally, these groups work within their domestic political systems, using legal mobilization techniques to negotiate solutions with business and the government. A small number of labor groups have also been able to generate pressure to improve working conditions abroad at the factories of MNCs through negative publicity campaigns.

There are also unorganized or informal labor groups, and these groups may also become transnational actors. When the economic environment in one state deteriorates, people may migrate elsewhere to seek employment. Environmental triggers, such as drought, crop failure, loss of grazing lands, or the death of livestock, may also trigger mass migrations. Labor migrations may be legal or illegal, but, in either case, these labor migrations have the potential to cause social and economic disruption. For example, states obviously cannot tax illegal workers, yet these workers may have access to costly social services, such as hospital care. In addition, even a relatively small number of instances of crime or prostitution by migrants may become politically salient. Even worse would be instances in which labor migration accelerated the transmission of an infectious disease, such as HIV/AIDS.

In addition to problems in the receiving state, labor migrations represent a loss of potential productive capability in the state of origin. Prolonged separation of workers from their homes may also cause severe disruption to communities and families, such as occurs in many instances in Mexico, for example. States may not have the capacity to monitor the scope of labor movements (and some are unwilling to acknowledge the issue), yet few states are able to ignore these migrations completely.

Violent Nonstate Actors: Political Opposition, Terrorism, and Crime.   It is critical to understand the role of violent nonstate actors, because the very existence of such groups poses a direct challenge to international stability and state authority.[15] Globalization has facilitated the growth of such groups, which like businesses have benefited from advances in information technology and transportation. Secure communications, ready availability of arms and other supplies, access to global financial markets, global recruitment opportunities, and the increasing ease of international travel have allowed these groups to operate as transnational entities. The increasing sophistication of violent nonstate actors has created new dangers and a greater need for cooperation among states. Although there are commonalities among violent nonstate actors, each poses a slightly different security threat based on its strategic motivations. Nevertheless, these groups often overlap, and their boundaries can shift over time.

Violent Political Opposition Groups.   Violent political opposition groups, a category that includes guerillas, revolutionaries, insurgents, and terrorists, are motivated by deeply held political convictions and seek to change the political order in either a local or global context. By contrast, criminals are motivated simply by profit. Successfully limiting violent activity—criminal or political—requires that states respond on strategic and operational levels. Strategic responses undercut motivations for violence by removing personal or organizational incentives for violent action. Operational responses prevent violent activity by disrupting the operating environment and by removing individual actors where possible.

To achieve their goal of altering the existing political or social order, violent political groups need support or at least acquiescence from the general population. For this reason, such groups are often engaged in an ideological battle with the state, using messages based on religion, ethnicity, or social class to challenge the legitimacy of state authority. Violent political groups may use intimidation to coerce support from the population while also providing some level of social services in an attempt to demonstrate that the state is ineffective in responding to the opposition group's challenge and in providing for the people. If the state responds in a heavy-handed manner, this may alienate the population and further support the opposition group's assertion that the state is illegitimate.

Today's violent political groups pose a greater threat to peace and stability than their predecessors, because their capacity for violence is exponentially greater and because their range of movement has expanded. It has become much more difficult for states to contain violent political groups within their borders. In some cases, even formal cease-fires and peace agreements may not end the violence. Any time that large numbers of combatants are disarmed and demobilized, a small number of fighters inevitably refuse to cease fighting. These individuals may become mercenary fighters who travel from one conflict zone to another, bringing their skills and social networks with them. Africa has been particularly cursed by this phenomenon.

Terrorism.   Terrorism is a tactic used by politically motivated groups that, for whatever reason, feel that there is no other way to achieve their goals. Terrorists emerge from the radical fringe of a political movement, using violence to draw attention to a cause that has been unable to generate mass support. Political terrorist groups use violence for specific purposes, such as attracting attention, mobilizing support, undermining the authority of the state, and reducing the political will of the target population.[16] Individuals join terrorist groups for a variety of reasons, which may include spiritual absolution, revenge, fanaticism, camaraderie, or even in some cases money.[17] It is important to acknowledge that not all terrorist groups are political in the common sense of the term. An apocalyptic group may conceive of violence as an end in itself rather than merely a means to an end. In any case, long-term success in combating terrorism requires capturing or killing leadership elements and countering the ideologies that support violence, while also providing socioeconomic alternatives to terrorist activity.

Al-Qa'ida provides an excellent example of how violent groups can take advantage of the benefits of globalization. Al-Qa'ida has capitalized on advances in communications technology to spread its political and religious messages while creating a vast network of suppliers, financiers, and logisticians. It has taken advantage of weak states and gaps in international oversight and has proven to be flexible in its associations, making common cause with drug traffickers, diamond smugglers, warlords, and petty criminals. It is one of the first truly global terrorist groups in that it has an ideology that emphasizes loyalty to the group over loyalty to a national identity, and it has a truly global recruitment network. (For more on the origins and evolution of al-Qa'ida, see Chapter 14)

Transnational Crime.   Transnational crime is not a new phenomenon, but globalization has allowed criminal groups to expand their activities by capitalizing on international black markets for counterfeit currency, drugs, human trafficking, and small arms and light weapons. In extreme cases, powerful criminal groups may even hold territory (undermining one of the fundamental principles of state sovereignty, which is territorial control). Groups may conduct criminal activity in one state, launder their money in a second, and bank in a third. Given the mobility of criminals and the diversification of their activities, robust international cooperation is often the only way to seriously reduce the capability of such groups.

The Complex Relationship between Crime and Terrorism.   Although scholars have often considered that mutually exclusive goals would prevent substantive cooperation between criminals and terrorists, growing evidence shows that this is not always the case. One key difference is that criminal groups are motivated by profit and desire secrecy above all else, whereas terrorist groups must attract media attention to be successful. Despite this and other differences, instances of cooperation and organizational learning between criminal and violent political groups have increased.[18]

Successful terrorist groups have many of the same operational requirements as criminal groups. All violent nonstate actors must move money, goods, and people without detection, and they have similar logistical requirements, such as access to false documents, arms, and transportation. Trading in drugs and precious stones is a good way for any illegal organization to launder money, and, in many cases, it is just as easy to move these items across international borders as it is to move cash.[19] Violent groups of all kinds benefit from "ungoverned spaces" where law enforcement is unable to monitor their activities or where the state simply lacks the capability or authority to enforce its will.

Individuals with certain criminal skills, such as an ability to forge documents or smuggle goods, can be useful to terrorist groups. Terrorist groups take a risk in hiring criminals, as they may draw the attention of security services to a group that was previously unknown. Scholars have also cited this increased risk of discovery or interference as a reason why cooperation between terrorists and criminals is likely to remain the exception rather than the rule. However, it is becoming increasingly apparent that certain kinds of terrorists—in particular, self-directed cells that have had little formal training—benefit enormously from criminal associations, as demonstrated by the importance of criminal networks in the 2004 train bombings in Madrid. The attacks were made possible by an "in-kind" trade of illegal materials; drugs and a stolen car were exchanged for stolen explosives. In addition, there has been a rise in terrorist recruitment from within prisons as radical extremists have used their incarcerations as opportunities to attract skilled criminals to their causes. The United States has not yet experienced this problem on a large scale, but the potential certainly exists.

State Responses to Violent Nonstate Actors.   Government responses to armed political opposition groups, terrorists, and criminals will, in many cases, require similar types of solutions, including sharing of intelligence, monitoring of financial flows, arrests, and prosecutions. Since the attacks of 9/11, the U.S. government has brought more resources to bear against criminal actions that facilitate terrorist activities out of an appreciation that today's drug smuggler may be tomorrow's terrorist financier. For any state, devising a national strategy requires an intricate understanding of the enemy (or enemies) and how they evolve and adapt.

Many governments have increased their level of cooperation with the United States to respond to these actors, at times incurring harsh criticism at home from citizens who fear that human rights may be violated in the pursuit of terrorists. Moreover, given the increased levels of foreign aid available for fighting terrorism, there is an incentive on the part of governments to frame any security problem as "terrorism." International cooperation has been complicated by the fact that the United States is most concerned with international terrorism, whereas many states view terrorism as primarily a domestic problem. Even in the best of circumstances, international security cooperation is beset with rivalries and suspicions, because it requires security services to share some of their most sensitive intelligence. However, there is simply no other option. Information sharing and coordinated action is absolutely essential to respond effectively to these threats.

These threats are growing as violent groups effectively exploit not only bureaucratic seams within the United States, and among the United States and its allies, but also areas beyond the reach of these countries and even local governments. These ungoverned spaces serve as potential havens for terrorists and also may contain populations vulnerable to the appeal of radical ideologies. When states are weak and cannot meet even the basic needs of their populations, people look elsewhere for relief. Consequently, countering terrorism requires a comprehensive understanding of the security environment in ungoverned spaces and an ability to address effectively the basic needs of vulnerable societies.

Regional Variation in the Impact of Globalization

As noted earlier, due to a variety of factors, the impact of globalization has varied across the different regions and countries of the world. States and societies that are unwilling or unable to participate in the process of globalization are likely to fall behind the rest of the world by all indicators—politically, socially, and economically. These less-developed regions are most likely to contain the ungoverned spaces alluded to above.[20] Many less-developed regions consist of weak states that have porous borders, overlapping ethnicities, and colonial histories. Many of these weak states entered the international system late, attaining legitimacy more from the international system than from their own citizenry. Moreover, the threats facing these states have historically been internal, many times reflecting weak institutions, a weak state identity, a lack of state capacity, and a bankrupt economy, as well as dangerous neighbors.[21] Unfortunately, the gap between the "haves" of the developed world and the "have-nots" in the less-developed world is growing.[22] As a result of political corruption and persistent underdevelopment, the number of failing and failed states has been on the rise. Where states have failed, violent nonstate actors will find a natural sanctuary.

Transnational Issues and Human Security[23]

Because the circumstances that tend to create ungoverned spaces are complex, policy makers have to consider complex multidimensional solutions. *Human security* is a concept that provides a useful approach to understanding these issues. Due to variations among regions and localities, a first step is to understand the dynamics and circumstances at the ground level. The UN recognized this approach in 1994:

> The concept of security has far too long been interpreted narrowly. . . . Forgotten were the legitimate concerns of ordinary people who sought security in their daily lives.

For many of them, security symbolized protection from the threat of disease, hunger, unemployment, crime [or terrorism], social conflict, political repression and environmental hazards. With the dark shadows of the Cold War receding, one can see that many conflicts are within nations rather than between nations.[24]

Although human insecurities may occur primarily in weak and failing states, such insecurities can quickly spread. Global effects, such as migrations, reverberations in diaspora communities, environmental impacts, and the exportation of terrorism, are possible.[25] A current example is the northwestern region of Pakistan along the border with Afghanistan. In a poor region, which the central government has long had difficulty controlling, local tribes and foreign militants engage in a complex and violent struggle that claims the lives of combatants and civilians.[26] Unsurprisingly, al-Qa'ida members are reportedly finding refuge and regrouping there, illustrating this statement from a 2006 UN study: "In an era of globalization, the concern with human security is linked to interdependence and the fact that no state can insulate itself any longer from insecurity in other parts of the world."[27]

The human security paradigm has important implications for traditional notions of state sovereignty. Recognizing this, the UN has argued for a new conception of sovereignty that reflects the realities of today's challenging security environment:

In signing the Charter of the United Nations, States not only benefit from the privileges of sovereignty but also accept its responsibilities. Whatever perceptions may have prevailed when the Westphalian system first gave rise to the notion of State sovereignty, today it clearly carries with it the obligation of a State to protect the welfare of its own peoples and meet the obligations to the wider international community.[28]

According to this formulation, some will argue that when a state cannot or will not protect its citizens, the international community has an obligation to engage.[29] Scholars have described this forward-leaning definition of security as the "duty to protect."[30] Although laudable from a humanitarian perspective, this is a shift with important implications, and specific applications of this doctrine are likely to be met with less-than-universal acceptance. What some see as an appropriate intervention can be seen by others as interference or even cloaked neocolonialism.

Operationalizing Human Security: Understanding Its Transnational Components. An advantage of focusing on human security is that this perspective requires an examination of the specific characteristics of each situation and recognition of the inter-relationships among complex factors that need to be addressed if security is to be enhanced. Most regions of the world suffering from human insecurities are facing several or all of the following issues: economic underdevelopment; environmental degradation; food scarcity; health insecurities; political and/or civil inequalities; and violence, including human trafficking, terrorism, crime, and armed conflict.[31] Many insecure populations also are vulnerable to radical ideologies that stifle development and exacerbate social tensions. Not all areas face the same insecurities or combination of insecurities, and therefore there is no common strategy for all situations.

Economic Insecurities.   In combating human insecurity, a first goal is to eradicate hunger and limit poverty. Basic subsistence requirements include the necessities of life, such as food, clean water, and other basic requirements of good health.[32] Unfortunately, globalization has tended to harden the distinction between haves and have-nots; the UN Development Program's global income distribution model reveals a huge gap between the very rich and very poor on a global scale that is greater than the inequalities within any one country.[33] Although rising incomes in the extremely populous countries of China and India have contributed to a positive global picture, they have masked the deep inequalities that exist across regions.[34] Particularly within twenty-five sub-Saharan African countries and ten Latin American countries, stagnation has been a prevalent accompaniment to globalization. When faced with chronic poverty, people look for relief by migrating to cities or to other countries. The social dislocations stemming from economic insecurities affect social, political, and economic development not only within the particular state but also often within the region.

Environmental Degradation.   To be sustainable over the long term, economic development must be accompanied by preservation of the environment.[35] Scholar Thomas Homer-Dixon warns:

> Within the next fifty years, the planet's human population will probably pass 9 billion, and global economic output may quintuple. Largely as a result, scarcities of renewable sources will increase sharply. The total area of high quality agricultural land will drop, as will the extent of forests and the number of species they sustain. Coming generations will also see the widespread depletion and degradation of aquifers, rivers, and other water resources; the decline of many fisheries; and perhaps significant climate change.[36]

Many areas in Africa are already witnessing the impact of environmental instabilities, such as arable land degradation, drought, and deforestation. Widespread migration, refugee flows, and conflict have set in, as in Sudan's drought-plagued Darfur region, putting great pressure on already weak states. Although countries in the developed world may not directly feel the impact of this situation, they are not likely to be immune to its consequences.[37]

Food Shortages.   Recent estimates suggest that 1 billion of the world's people are undernourished, and challenges in this area are only likely to grow because the world's population is projected to increase by three billion by 2050—mostly in less-developed states.[38] Former Chairman of the United Nations Commission on Sustainable Development Henrique Cavalcanti defines *food security* as "practices and measures related to the assurance of a regular supply and adequate stocks of foodstuffs of guaranteed quality and nutritional value."[39] He identifies the three pillars of food security as availability, access, and stability. Between 1950 and 1984, availability was increased as grain production outpaced population growth. However, since 1984, grain harvests have declined. Some of the major causes include soil erosion, desertification, transfer of cropland to nonfarm purposes, falling water tables, and rising temperatures. Shocks, such as natural disasters, droughts, and disease, also contribute to food insecurities. These conditions may reveal themselves globally in the form of higher food prices, but at local and regional levels, these conditions can develop into catastrophic shortages and conflict.[40]

Health Insecurities.   Poverty, environmental degradation, and food shortages all can have a negative impact on health. Given that about 1 billion people in the world lack access to clean water, for example, it is not surprising that water-related diseases account for millions of deaths per year.[41] One issue that particularly highlights the inter-relationships among human security challenges is HIV/AIDS. In some African countries, HIV/AIDS has infected 20% to 30% of the adult population.[42] It should be no surprise that the prevalence of HIV/AIDS in Africa directly exacerbates food insecurities, as the loss of workers due to AIDS adversely affects the ability to harvest crops.[43] Unfortunately, Africa is not alone—"major epidemics are already underway in China, India, and Russia."[44] Inadequate state actions as well as local social mores inhibit adequate responses to the spread of this disease.

There is also a clear connection between the rise of infectious diseases and the degradation of the environment. According to the World Health Organization (WHO):

> Poor environmental health quality is directly responsible for some 25 percent of all preventable ill health, with diarrheal diseases and acute respiratory infections heading the list. Two-thirds of all preventable health due to environmental conditions occurs among children, particularly the increase in asthma. Air pollution is a major contributor to a number of diseases and to a lowering of the quality of life in general.[45]

Moreover, the 2005 Millennium Ecosystem Assessment report claims that continued degradation of ecosystems may increase the spread of common diseases, such as malaria, as well as facilitating the evolution of new diseases.[46] States that have inadequate health public support systems will be most vulnerable and least able to respond. Even developed states that do have such systems could be severely challenged in reacting adequately to a serious global health crisis.

Human Security and U.S. National Security

In a globalized world, meeting basic needs at the individual level has important security implications at the state, regional, and global levels. The challenges are most acute in weak or developing states and their regional neighborhoods. Without state support in meeting basic human security needs, people lose faith and look for other ways to survive. Although sometimes people turn toward ethnic groups, kin, and other subnational entities, they may also turn to violent groups that offer hope and tangible support. Security policy requires a holistic approach that views human security as critical to building state capacity and legitimacy vis-à-vis these other groups.

Somalia provides a useful example—though by no means the only one—of the nexus between the rising importance of nonstate actors, human security challenges,

Copyright 1992 CARTOONEWS Inc., N.Y.C., USA.
Reprinted with permission of Ranan Lurie.

and threats to international peace and security. Somalia has been without an effective government since President Siad Barre was overthrown in 1991. According to the United Nations, this situation has led

> to the destruction of infrastructure, the disintegration of basic health and social services and widespread human rights abuses. The country also has some of the worst human development indicators in the world. At the start of 2006, the country was experiencing an aggravated humanitarian emergency brought on by the worst drought in a decade. Of an estimated population of 7.7 million, around 2.1 million people countrywide were in need of critical assistance including an estimated 400,000 internally displaced persons.[47]

As mentioned in Chapter 21, in 2006, an armed group Islamic group claimed control over the capital, Mogadishu, but it had been expelled by early 2007 by Ethiopian troops with support from the United States. This intervention returned the leader of the internationally recognized Somali Transitional Federal Government, Abdullahi Yusuf, to power to serve out the rest of his five-year mandate, which began in 2004—if he can manage to stay in office.

The weakness of Somalia as a state has long had an effect on regional security as well as the condition of its own people. Civil strive, starvation, and the flow of refugees into neighboring Ethiopia, Djibouti, and Kenya led the UN to respond by establishing a task force that included U.S. involvement from 1992–1994. The UN has since continued its nonmilitary involvement in cooperation with a wide variety of NGOs to meet basic human needs and to foster development.

After the terrorist attacks of 9/11, Somalia again received the attention of U.S. policy makers concerned that it could become a potential base for international terrorist organizations, such as al-Qa'ida. In addition to providing assistance in expelling the Islamic Courts Union government, U.S. involvement in 2007 also included military strikes against suspected terrorists living in Somalia.[48] Though these military actions may make a contribution, the assessment of the U.S. State Department is that "the long-term terrorist threat in Somalia . . . can only be addressed through the establishment of a functioning central government."[49] In order for a Somali government to be effective and to attain legitimacy, it will have to address some of the critical human security challenges discussed in the preceding section. To gain the capacity to make progress, the Somali government will undoubtedly need partnerships with such IGOs as the UN and the AU, a variety of NGOs, and other states. The new U.S. Africa Command (AFRICOM) may enable the United States to be a more consistent partner, though some fear that its establishment reflects an overly militarized approach to Africa's many challenges.[50] The optimal relationship between AFRICOM and its programs and State Department efforts in the region will have to be worked out in practice over time.

Challenges for U.S. Policy Makers

The preceding discussion suggests that those concerned with U.S. national security policy have to be concerned with the capacity and legitimacy of states around the world. Only a legitimate and effective government can adequately address the human insecurities that exist in many states, especially in underdeveloped countries. Accordingly, U.S. national security policy makers must craft effective approaches to fostering good governance abroad, as well as activate institutions of the U.S. government that may not previously have seen this function as one of their core tasks. They also must overcome the political challenge of creating support for policies that lack natural constituencies within the United States but that may be necessary to long-term success.

One example of a nontraditional national security policy that may be needed in this new environment relates to educational systems in underdeveloped countries. Better education is an essential element of any sustainable development program. Some *Madrassas* (religious schools in Muslim lands), for example, not only fail to prepare students for the modern world but also often serve as incubators of extremism. A cornerstone of the needed education process is likely to be the inclusion of women. The education of women doubles the talent pool of a society— Mao Zedong's aphorism phrased it as "women hold up half the heavens"—but also brings numerous other beneficial effects. Educated women tend, for example, to have fewer children, which reduces pressures stemming from overpopulation. In addition, educated women who know how to prevent diseases, understand nutrition, and send their children to school can positively influence the direction of a society and its state. U.S. policy makers who wish to further these dynamics will have to seek ways to increase the limited resources available for such programs and create effective partnerships with other states and nonstate actors.

The cultivation of legitimacy within another state is likely to be a very challenging task, because it requires an understanding of local culture and historical context, as well as an appreciation of formal and informal governing institutions. Similar painstaking analysis must precede efforts to counter violent nonstate actors, such as terrorist groups. Local terrorist groups have specific goals and ideologies that must be understood in the context of a specific region. In some cases, there may be little that the United States can accomplish directly. However, it may be able to shape the incentives of local governments and at least ensure that U.S. actions do not inadvertently undercut the governments it seeks to support.

Unfortunately, many of the regions that suffer from grave human insecurities have harsh and extreme climates, as well as geographical features and environmental challenges that affect local populations in significant ways. This is important on several counts. First, environments change over time, thus contributing to the dynamic nature of human insecurity challenges. Infrastructure is also critical. It is hard enough to grow crops in some vulnerable regions, but food insecurity is often compounded by the difficult task of getting crops and goods to market. Understanding the environment is essential when seeking to understand the totality of challenges faced by the local population, the government, and external actors.

These complexities must be understood as policy makers try to anticipate the direct and indirect effects of their decisions and actions. Cultivating the development of stable and legitimate states that are capable of good governance will take time, and progress is not inevitable. If U.S. policy makers are to succeed, they will need to acquire local political support, enhance interagency cooperation within the U.S. government, and effectively collaborate with a broad array of state partners and nonstate actors—and avoid the hubris to which the helpful outsider is often prone.

Discussion Questions

1. Should the UN be restructured to more effectively address current and future security challenges? If so, how?

2. When and under what conditions can regional organizations be more effective in promoting peace and stability than organizations that are global in scale?

3. What impact can the global media have on U.S. national security policy?

4. Is the presence of an MNC beneficial to a developing country? Explain.

5. What is the relationship between *poverty* and *instability*?

6. Should the United States try to counter all terrorism or just terrorism that threatens U.S. interests?

7. Why should U.S. strategists be concerned with human insecurities occurring halfway across the globe?

8. How should the United States prioritize its efforts toward ungoverned spaces? Which U.S. government agencies should be involved?

9. Is the U.S. government taking adequate measures to foster the international cooperation necessary to global governance in an environment of increasingly important transnational security challenges? Give examples to support your answer.

10. What steps must the United States take to leverage its interagency talents and expertise?

Recommended Reading

Brown, Michael, ed. *New Global Dangers: Changing Dimensions of International Security.* Cambridge, MA: MIT Press, 2004.

Crenshaw, Martha, ed. *Terrorism in Context.* University Park: Pennsylvania State University Press, 1995.

Faksh, Mahmud A., *The Future of Islam in the Middle East: Fundamentalism in Egypt, Algeria, and Saudi Arabia.* Westport, CT: Praeger, 1997.

Hoffman, Bruce. *Inside Terrorism.* Rev. and exp. ed. New York: Columbia University Press, 2006.

Holm, Hans-Henrik, and Georg Sorensen. *Whose World Order? Uneven Globalization and the End of the Cold War.* Boulder, CO: Westview Press, 1995.

Human Security Centre. *Human Security Report 2005: War and Peace in the 21st Century.* Oxford: Oxford University Press, 2006.

Jebb, Cindy R., P. H. Liotta, Thomas Sherlock, and Ruth Margolies Beitler. *The Fight for Legitimacy: Democracy vs. Terrorism.* Westport, CT: Praeger Security International, 2006.

Reich, Walter, ed. *Origins of Terrorism: Psychologies, Ideologies, Theologies, States of Mind.* Washington, DC: Woodrow Wilson Center Press, 1998.

Sachs, Jeffrey D. *The End of Poverty: Economic Possibilities of Our Time.* New York: Penguin Books, 2005.

Sen, Amartya. *Development as Freedom.* New York: Alfred A. Knopf, 1999.

Watkins, Kevin. *Human Development Report 2005: International Cooperation at a Cross-roads: Aid, Trade and Security in an Unequal World.* New York: United Nations Development Programme, 2005.

Internet Resources

African Union, www.africa-union.org
International Committee of the Red Cross, www.icrc.org
INTERPOL, www.interpol.int
Memorial Institute for the Prevention of Terrorism, www.tkb.org
United Nations Development Programme, www.undp.org
The World Bank, www.worldbank.org
World Health Organization, www.who.int

26

Looking Ahead

As this book goes to the printer, the United States is in the middle of the presidential transition from George W. Bush to Barack Obama. Reports abound in the media about new government appointments and forthcoming domestic and foreign policy changes. This final chapter briefly examines seven national security issues that will face U.S. policy makers in the Obama administration and beyond: relations with China, nuclear proliferation, energy security, radical Islamist terrorism, the tension between unilateralism and multilateralism, national security restructuring, and the balance between security and liberty within the United States. This list is not exhaustive—many other issues are likely to become important as well. Climate change, cyberterrorism, and resource conflicts that involve the United States are examples of issues that could evolve into serious security threats. The continued expansion of globalization with attendant frictions, rising fundamentalism, increased anti-Western sentiment, and proliferation of failed states are other threats that could generate major security problems in the future. While these possibilities are important, the seven areas discussed in this chapter pose current or near-term challenges that national security policy makers will doubtless have to address in the next one to five years.

U.S. Relations with China

Accommodating China's dramatic rise is a central challenge. As discussed in Chapter 18, China has achieved impressive economic growth in the last two decades. From 2000 to 2005, for example, China's economy grew by 86%, while the U.S. economy grew by only 27%.[1] If U.S. growth remains relatively stable at its customary 3% to 4% per year, and if China continues to grow at its recent brisk annual rate of 9% to 10%, the size of the Chinese economy will surpass that of the United States around midcentury.[2] Given the importance of economic strength to military power, some analysts point to these trends with consternation.[3]

As China's economy has expanded, so has its military investment. Over the past decade, China's military budget has grown by 300% in real terms. In 2007, China announced a 17.8% increase in its military budget, bringing the total amount of China's military spending to approximately $45 billion. This was the seventeenth consecutive year China's military budget grew by more than 10%.[4] Increased financial resources have allowed China to modernize its military and become a much more capable potential adversary. Furthermore, the opacity of Chinese defense spending has exacerbated international concern. To improve transparency, the Chinese government released its first "White Paper on China's National Defence" in 1998 and has since updated the document every two years. Although these documents provide official figures on spending, major accounting items, such as the procurement of weapons from abroad, state subsidies to the defense industry, select research and development programs, and the funding of paramilitaries, are not included. Taking these areas into account, the Defense Intelligence Agency estimates that China's total military spending could be as much as $85 to $125 billion.[5]

On the surface, the dramatic growth in the Chinese economy and the associated increase in military spending represent a serious development from the perspective of U.S. national security. However, a detailed analysis paints a less dire and more nuanced picture. In terms of economics, three points are important. First, despite China's impressive growth, the U.S. economy still dwarfs the Chinese economy at present, reinforcing the fact that concerns about relative strength rely on projections that become increasingly uncertain the further into the future they reach. Second, it is helpful to remember that newly industrializing countries typically go through a period of dramatic economic growth followed by a period in which growth rates moderate and stabilize. It is highly unlikely that the Chinese economy will continue to grow at annual rates of 9% to 10% percent for the next twenty to thirty years. Finally, China faces a number of significant internal challenges, as discussed in Chapter 18.[6] To sustain the record of growth that China has established in recent decades, China will have to carefully manage and successfully address these internal challenges to sustainable economic development.

A more detailed analysis of Chinese military spending also calls into question China's ability to compete militarily with the United States as a peer anytime soon. Though Chinese defense expenditures have expanded rapidly over the last decade, China only spends about one fifth as much the United States.[7] Certain characteristics of the Chinese military also provide a revealing glimpse of Chinese strategy, intentions, and capabilities. China has no aircraft carrier battle groups or long-range bombers in production, it has few destroyers capable of operating in the open ocean, and it is not yet acquiring military bases abroad or conducting large-scale exercises far from China's shores.[8] These traits do not represent the military program of a power bent on challenging U.S. global leadership in the near term.

Given the anarchic and uncertain nature of the international system, the fact that China has used a portion of its growing wealth to increase its military capability should not be surprising. China seeks to build a military capacity that reflects its status as a great power and that provides a host of options with respect to Taiwan.[9] To achieve these goals, the Chinese may be developing military capabilities specifically designed to counter U.S. strengths and to improve China's freedom of action within the region.[10] As discussed in Chapter 18, the United States has an important interest in retaining access to East Asia, and therefore these developments are of concern. However, current Chinese efforts will not enable power projection at a great distance and thus do not seem designed to challenge the U.S. position worldwide.[11]

Despite concerns expressed within the United States, China's diplomacy has led many within Asia to view its re-emergence as a great power in a more benign light. According to expert David Shambaugh, "most nations in the region now see China as a good neighbor, a constructive partner, a careful listener, and a non-threatening regional power."[12] China now actively participates in regional diplomatic associations, such as the Association of Southeast Asian Nations+3 and the Shanghai Cooperation Organization, enjoying a constructive regional reputation. Having successfully hosted the 2008 Olympics, China is also scheduled to host the World Expo in 2010. Beijing can be expected to use events such as these to project a positive international image in the coming years.[13]

Because the two countries have differing perspectives on a number of issues in East Asia, the most dangerous of which is Taiwan, tensions between the United States and a stronger China seem inevitable. However, outright conflict is not. The Chinese Communist Party leadership is focused on maintaining economic growth, which is important to economic development, political stability, and the long-term enhancement of China's status as a great power. In the near term, the pursuit of economic growth leads China's leaders to place a premium on regional peace and stability.

In addition to the ruling Chinese Communist Party's reasons for valuing a calm international situation, those who argue that China's emergence as a great power could have a generally benign impact usually rely on one of two sets of arguments. A first perspective holds that the more China becomes integrated into a global system of trade and investment and the supporting network of international financial institutions, the more costly and thus less likely an aggressive Chinese foreign policy becomes.[14] Although this perspective has merit, history is replete with examples of countries that have pursued economically destructive policies out of nationalist fervor. U.S. policy makers cannot afford to underestimate the importance of growing nationalism in China, particularly as it applies to Taiwan, and the effect that it may have on the decision making of China's leaders.[15]

A second perspective flows from democratic peace theory, introduced in Chapter 1, which argues that liberal democracies are less likely to go to war with one another. Seeming to accept the logic of this approach, successive U.S. administrations have promoted economic growth and liberalization in China as a means of encouraging political liberalization. The 2006 U.S. National Security Strategy (NSS) states, "As economic growth continues, China will face a growing demand from its own people to follow the path of East Asia's many modern democracies, adding political freedom to economic freedom."[16] However, many scholars question this logic and argue that many authoritarian regimes have managed to achieve economic growth while stifling political liberalization.[17]

Regardless of whether the optimists or pessimists prove correct regarding the above dynamics, it would be costly and difficult for the United States to seek to restrain China's growth. The two countries are now so economically interdependent that any U.S. efforts to dampen Chinese economic growth would simultaneously damage the U.S. economy. According to a report recently prepared for Congress, in 2003 China "surpassed Japan to become America's third largest trading partner, after Canada and Mexico, while the United States is China's second largest trading partner after the expanded European Union."[18] China received almost $4 billion in foreign direct investment from the United States in 2004, and, as of early 2006, the Chinese central bank owned $476 billion in U.S. Treasury securities.[19] In light of this intertwined relationship, negative developments within the economies of either the United States or China would have a deleterious effect on the other country.

China's extraordinary rise in recent decades, in virtually every dimension, poses enormous challenges not only for the United States but also for the world as other countries also adjust to that rise. Vital American strategic and economic interests are at stake in how the relationship develops. Preventing the rise from generating a dangerous or irresponsible China will be a primary policy goal for decades to come. Neither "panda huggers" nor "China hawks" should be permitted to dominate the needed dialogue. As policy makers work through the complexities of the bilateral relationship between the United States and China, it will be imperative to build on common interests, to cultivate allies and friends in the region, and to avoid needless confrontations that could make conflict a self-fulfilling prophecy.

Nuclear Proliferation

The proliferation of weapons of mass destruction (WMDs) represents an immediate, serious threat to U.S. national security that will likely only intensify in the coming years. Although the threats posed by biological and chemical weapons also warrant the attention of policy makers, nuclear weapons are unique in their ability to inflict casualties on a catastrophic scale.[20] Depending on the size of the nuclear device, a detonation in a major American city could kill several hundred thousand people, exponentially surpassing the September 11, 2001, death toll.[21]

A nuclear attack against the U.S. homeland or U.S. interests overseas could be perpetrated directly by a state or by a terrorist group, such as al-Qa'ida. Russia, China, and North Korea are all examples of states that possess nuclear weapons and could theoretically attack the United States. However, although a nuclear attack from one of these countries as a result of accident or miscalculation is conceivable, a deliberate nuclear attack is highly unlikely, because the United States would almost certainly launch a devastating response.

A more realistic scenario would involve the transfer of nuclear technology, materials, or weapons from North Korea, Pakistan, or potentially Iran to a terrorist group. This transfer could result from a deliberate policy choice or from the actions of a disenchanted, corrupt, or ideologically motivated group that enjoys access to key nuclear technology, materials, or weapons. As discussed in Chapter 17, the 2004 acknowledgment that Pakistani scientist Abdul Qadeer Khan sold nuclear material and expertise to Iran, Libya, and North Korea demonstrates the damage that can be done by a small group of willing individuals within a government bureaucracy. As more states obtain nuclear weapons, and as nuclear technology and expertise become increasingly available, the chance that a nuclear transfer could lead to a successful attack against the United States increases.

This situation is made more threatening due to the existence of hostile nonstate actors, such as al-Qa'ida. Al-Qa'ida has expressed a desire to obtain nuclear weapons and inflict "maximum casualties" on the United States (see also Chapter 14).[22] Rohan Gunaratna, a leading expert on al-Qa'ida, asserts that al-Qa'ida "will have no compunction about employing chemical, biological, and nuclear weapons against population centers."[23] Osama bin Laden himself has said, "It would be a sin for Muslims not to try to possess the weapons that would prevent the infidels from inflicting harm on Muslims."[24] Based on al-Qa'ida's stated intentions and the multiple plausible scenarios through which terrorists could obtain nuclear weapons, some experts predict that a nuclear terrorist attack in America is more likely than not in the coming decade.[25] Although this notion may seem alarmist, the threat is significant. Future U.S. administrations should seriously promote further efforts to help other countries properly secure nuclear material and technology. In particular, the Nunn-Lugar Cooperative Threat Reduction program should be extended and strengthened. Building on Nunn-Lugar and working with the Nuclear Threat Initiative, the American and Russian governments "spirited more than 100 pounds of nuclear weapons-grade material out of Serbia" in 2002. It is noteworthy, too, that "through Nunn-Lugar, Albania recently got U.S. help to destroy a secret Cold War-era stockpile of chemical weapons."[26]

As discussed in Chapter 17, the United States needs to strengthen its own and international efforts to prevent additional states from developing nuclear weapons—and perhaps subsequently passing them on to terrorists. Pursuing this nonproliferation end, it is important to understand what motivates particular regimes to seek such weapons. Policies should be tailored to counter motivation and capability to obtain nuclear weapons.

Why States Want Nuclear Weapons.   Four primary reasons encourage states to pursue nuclear weapons. First, and perhaps most importantly, nuclear weapons serve as a powerful and relatively inexpensive means to deter aggressive action by militarily superior states. Unfortunately, recent U.S. actions toward Iraq and North Korea may have bolstered this incentive. By late 2002, the North Koreans had developed a secret nuclear program, and the CIA estimated that they had already produced one or two nuclear weapons.[27] During that same time, it was widely believed that while Iraq was pursuing the development of WMDs, Iraq did not yet have operational nuclear weapons. In the case of nuclear North Korea, the United States relied on multilateral talks. In the case of Iraq, the United States invaded the country and overthrew the regime. Though significant differences exist between the two situations, one possible lesson observers could draw is that the United States may be less likely to attack a country believed to have an existing nuclear weapons capability. Leaders in such countries as Iran could conclude that they should get nuclear weapons as soon as possible.[28]

Not only do nuclear weapons provide a relatively inexpensive and effective deterrent, they also often provide regimes with a tremendous amount of domestic support and prestige. The pursuit or possession of nuclear weapons may rally nationalist sentiment behind a strong leader who is perceived by the country's citizens to be building the nation's defenses. To a large degree, Iran's Mahmoud Ahmadinejad has benefited from this phenomenon, and the hostile U.S. response to Iran's program may have enhanced this effect.[29] The more aggressive the United States becomes in confronting the Iranian regime, the more popular Ahmadinejad likely becomes in Iran and much of the Islamic world. With U.S. military forces on Iran's eastern and western borders and a significant U.S. presence to Iran's south in the Persian Gulf region, it should not be a surprise that Ahmadinejad's demagoguery has resonated with many Iranians.[30]

A regime's pursuit or possession of nuclear weapons also yields important benefits in terms of international prestige. As negotiations with North Korea and Iran reflect, North Korea, a country roughly the size of the state of Mississippi whose entire economy is roughly a tenth of the size of the U.S. defense budget, has maneuvered its way into formal and highly publicized negotiations with the United States. Similarly, Iran's apparent pursuit of nuclear weapons has allowed it to directly or indirectly bargain with the United Kingdom, France, Germany, China, and Russia, as well as the United States. For North Korea and Iran, the possession or pursuit of nuclear weapons seems to have increased international stature.

Finally, pursuing nuclear weapons can lead to valuable concessions. In 1994, as part of the Agreed Framework, the United States and its allies offered North Korea two light-water nuclear reactors, as well as food and fuel assistance, in return for a North Korean promise to freeze its plutonium production.[31] More recently, in 2003, Libya earned significant political and economic benefits by ending its pursuit of nuclear weapons. Libya would not have gained these valuable concessions if it did not have a nuclear program to relinquish. Although each of these bargains may be worthwhile, they have created problematic incentives for future nuclear aspirants.

Nuclear Proliferation as an Enduring Challenge.   The danger presented by nuclear proliferation is not likely to subside anytime soon. Countries or terrorist movements that seek to quickly redress the balance of power in their favor or to shock the United States to achieve dramatic changes in U.S. policy will continue to try to take advantage of porous borders, weak international controls, and the Internet to obtain nuclear technology. Though the 1968 Nuclear Non-Proliferation Treaty (NPT) likely slowed the rate of proliferation, developments in India, Pakistan, North Korea, and Iran over the last decade have exposed its shortcomings. In addition, the fact that some of the leading dangers related to nuclear material

and weapons come from nonstate actors suggests that the NPT must be strengthened, updated, and expanded to be effective in the future.

Until the United States and the other major nuclear powers develop the political will to work cooperatively toward a new international consensus on developing more effective and comprehensive nonproliferation and counterproliferation
programs, future U.S. policy makers will find themselves wrestling with the increasing likelihood of a nuclear attack against the United States. Even with enhanced efforts to meet the threat, the danger will always be significant.

Energy Security

The United States faces, now and for at least the next two decades, an energy
crisis—or, more accurately, an oil crisis. An important study in 2006 concludes:

> Major energy suppliers—from Russia to Iran to Venezuela—have been increasingly
> able and willing to use their energy resources to pursue their strategic and political ob-
> jectives. Major energy consumers—notably the United States, but other countries as
> well—are finding that their growing dependence on imported energy increases their
> strategic vulnerability and constrains their ability to pursue a broad range of foreign
> policy and national security objectives.[32]

For many years, the United States produced the vast majority of the oil it consumed. After 1970, U.S. oil consumption continued to increase while U.S. domestic oil production leveled off, requiring the United States to increase imports.
The risks inherent in this growing dependence on foreign oil were highlighted in
1973. U.S. support for Israel in the 1973 Arab-Israeli war prompted Arab oil-producing states to implement an oil embargo against the United States, quadrupling
the domestic price of oil. The situation became so dire that Secretary of State
Henry Kissinger spoke openly about Pentagon plans to invade Middle Eastern
countries to gain access to coveted supplies. He later remarked, "Never before in
history has a group of such relatively weak nations been able to impose with so little protest such a dramatic change in the way of life of the overwhelming majority of the rest of mankind."[33] The trauma of these events motivated President
Richard Nixon to issue a November 1973 call for the United States to free itself of
the need to import energy by the end of the decade.[34] However, neither Nixon's
call for action nor the trauma of another oil crisis in 1979 reversed the trend of increasing U.S. reliance on imported oil. Today, thirty-five years after the embargo
of 1973, the United States imports 60% of the petroleum it consumes.[35]

Indeed, America consumes and imports more crude oil and petroleum products
now than at any time in history (see Figure 26.1).[36] As noted in Chapter 12, the
United States accounts for 5% of the world's population but consumes roughly
one quarter of the world's oil.[37] This voracious American energy appetite and the
associated dependence on imported oil simply will not subside any time soon.[38] In
fact, the Department of Energy predicts that U.S. petroleum demand will increase
over the next two decades, with imports reaching as much as 67% of consumption
by 2030.[39] Increased U.S. demand mirrors larger global trends. The worldwide

FIG. 26.1   Petroleum Overview, 1949–2007

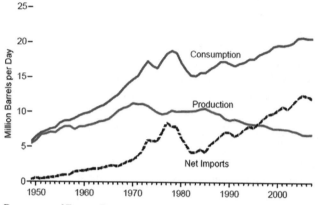

Source: U.S. Department of Energy, Energy Information Administration, *Annual Energy Review* 2007, www.eia.doe.gov/emeu/aer/petro.html

consumption of primarily petroleum-based liquid fuels is expected to increase 42% in the next twenty-five years, from 83 million barrels per day in 2004 to 118 million barrels per day in 2030.[40]

Predictable future increases in U.S. and global oil consumption would not represent such a serious development if the world's oil-producing countries were postured to produce enough oil to meet the burgeoning demand. Unfortunately, in recent years, the global oil market has operated with supply near its maximum capacity. Unused global production capacity has generally hovered around five hundred thousand to 1 million barrels per day, with all of the slack located in Saudi Arabia.[41] Although the United States enjoys relatively good relations with the Saudi government, the Saudi regime presides over a large number of citizens who harbor great animosity toward the United States and could potentially wield the "oil weapon." Other leading suppliers of U.S. oil include countries of questionable reliability, such as Venezuela, Nigeria, Angola, Iraq, and Russia (see Figure 26.2).[42]

These oil market realities present U.S. decision makers with several difficult dilemmas. If gasoline prices remain consistently high, natural market mechanisms will increase the incentives for conservation and the development of alternate energy sources. Over the long term, the United States could thus, theoretically, substantially reduce the amount of oil it imports. However, history teaches us that, unless oil prices remain consistently high, they will provide inadequate incentives to motivate energy conservation and alternate fuel innovation. For example, once prices abated after the oil shocks of 1973 and 1979, public angst subsided, and political will evaporated. An energy policy that goes beyond intermittent prices shocks is required.

Many leaders have called for government intervention to reduce or even eliminate U.S. dependence on foreign oil, but policies have been inadequate to

FIG. 26.2   2007 U.S. Petroleum Imports by Country of Origin

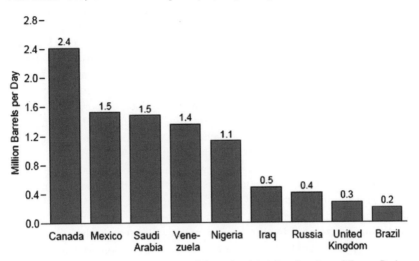

Source: U.S. Department of Energy, Energy Information Administration, *Annual Energy Review* 2007, www.eia.doe.gov/emeu/aer/petro.html

accomplish that objective. Proposed policies include increased domestic drilling, subsidized development of domestic oil shale and oil sands, increased ethanol production, increased gas mileage requirements for cars, enhanced incentives for hybrids and flex-fuel vehicles, and increased utilization of coal and nuclear energy for electric power generation. Each of these proposals inspires passionate responses from various interest groups that have a financial or political stake in the outcome. Yet, some mix of these and other measures is clearly essential.

To enable Americans to meet their liquid fuel needs reliably, given the characteristics of the global oil market and the realities of American domestic life, at least three responses are required. First, as discussed in Chapter 20, the United States must continue to protect the flow of oil from the world's major source of exports—primarily the Persian Gulf—for at least the next two decades. Unfortunately, the U.S. military presence in the region has served as a significant catalyst for radicalization and Islamist terrorism.[43] A key challenge will be to develop U.S. policies and a military posture that protect the flow of oil while minimizing negative side effects.

Second, as just explained, a major, robustly funded effort to induce conservation and to produce alternative fuels should be promptly initiated. This will require a determined, extended, bipartisan campaign to convince Americans of the dangers of the status quo and the consequent sacrifices required. Without such a campaign, it is unlikely that U.S. consumers will cure their collective national addiction to relatively cheap gasoline. With prices having risen over $4 a gallon for extended periods of time in the United States in 2008, it may be easier than it has been in the past for such a campaign to gain traction.

Third, U.S. policy makers must focus on the risk that terrorist groups, such as al-Qa'ida and associated movements, pose to the international oil supply chain. Captured al-Qa'ida documents suggest that the terrorist movement has been interested in attacking oil-related targets for several years.[44] Al-Qa'ida has already demonstrated a willingness to attack key nodes, claiming credit for a February 2006 attempted suicide attack on the Saudi Abqaiq plant near Dammam, which is one of the most important oil-processing facilities in the world.[45] Successive large-scale attacks on oil fields, pipelines, processing facilities, or shipping lanes could devastate Western economies. The situation is aggravated by the fact that the international oil supply chain contains a virtually unlimited number of "soft targets," or relatively unprotected nodes, which will likely become an increasingly attractive focus for potential attacks as Western countries continue to increase domestic security measures. The United States needs to take the lead in international efforts to protect infrastructure and secure transit routes.

One of al-Qa'ida's preeminent goals is to overthrow the House of Saud in Saudi Arabia. The Central Intelligence Agency (CIA) estimates that oil accounts for roughly 75% of Saudi budget revenues, 45% of its gross domestic product, and 90% of its export earnings.[46] An al-Qa'ida attack that severely curtailed oil exports from Saudi Arabia could destabilize the Saudi regime and dramatically affect the global economy. Enhanced U.S.-Saudi relationships are needed to help secure oil supplies, encourage political reforms, and moderate the religious fundamentalism that can destabilize the region.

Islamist Terrorism and Al-Qa'ida

Though the United States has improved homeland security and has captured or killed many terrorist operatives since the attacks of 9/11, al-Qa'ida and its associated movements are hardly on the verge of defeat. On the contrary, many analysts believed al-Qa'ida "is on the march."[47] Experts outside the government are not alone in this dire assessment. The September 2006 U.S. National Intelligence Estimate acknowledges U.S. successes against al-Qa'ida but describes al-Qa'ida as the "greatest threat to the homeland and U.S. interests." The estimate further states that an increasing number of Muslims in more diverse geographic areas are describing themselves as *jihadists* (a term adopted by those using violence to advance their struggle). It is clear from developments over the past few years, most recently in Great Britain, that radical Islamist cells only loosely affiliated with al-Qa'ida exist in various European and Asian states. Though not as sophisticated or as experienced as al-Qa'ida, they have nevertheless proven deadly. If unabated, this expansionist trend will likely lead to an increased number of attacks worldwide.[48]

Although most observers acknowledge the continuing, even growing dangers of radical Islam, there is less agreement on explanations for the resonance of its message or the vitality of its movement. The United States and the West as a whole cannot address all the radicals' grievances, but it is essential to move expeditiously to address and to ameliorate as many of them as is feasible. Ultimately, however, the main means for defeating the danger lies within the Islamic world.

Unless moderate Muslim forces effectively turn away from and isolate the radical extremists, there is substantial danger that the extremists could enhance their power in a number of states with large Muslim populations, which would add an entirely new dimension to the threat.

The Enduring Nature of the Terrorist Challenge. Al-Qa'ida and its associated movements will continue to pose a serious threat to the United States for the foreseeable future. Al-Qa'ida continues its efforts to plan and conduct terrorist attacks against the United States and its allies. As noted in the previous sections of this chapter, the challenges of energy security and nuclear proliferation are U.S. vulnerabilities that al-Qa'ida has identified and will likely seek to exploit. In some respects, U.S. actions to combat terrorists and secure the homeland have made the country safer than it was the day before the 2001 terrorist attacks, but maladies in the Muslim world and some U.S. policy choices continue to replenish the ranks of al-Qa'ida operatives, supporters, and like-minded affiliated terrorists.

Critical challenges that the United States will need to address include developing a military posture in the Middle East that is capable of protecting U.S. interests while minimizing negative side effects; addressing sources of Islamic grievance, such as the Israeli-Palestinian conflict and U.S. actions in Iraq; seeking ways to encourage political and educational reform in Muslim states; and creating a U.S. approach to the problem of international terrorism that strengthens international cooperation and effectively leverages all agencies of the U.S. government and instruments of power.

Even if the United States successfully addresses these significant challenges, it will not fully or immediately remove the threat. Now that al-Qa'ida has become an amorphous global movement, any quick solution is impossible. Killing a handful of al-Qa'ida leaders or incarcerating members of a terrorist cell will not change the fact that thousands of Muslims around the world empathize with or directly ascribe to the group's ideology. On the other hand, it would be unwise to succumb to the seductive logic that al-Qa'ida opposes the United States for its core values and identity, and therefore Americans can do little to reduce the threat.

If the United States understands the enemy and the nature of the conflict, develops the necessary capabilities, makes difficult—yet necessary—policy changes, and promotes positive and gradual change in the Middle East, it can begin to deprive al-Qa'ida of the new recruits and supporters it needs. But, progress may have to be measured in decades, not years. The struggle will undoubtedly be rough, requiring strong political leadership and popular endurance. In the absence of this combination of leadership and support, the status quo will continue to create the next generation of terrorists and will further endanger American national security.

Unilateralism and Multilateralism

As noted in earlier chapters, American national security policy has long been torn between going it alone and proceeding *multilaterally*—that is, in concert with other states. Multilateralism is more than simply policy coordination among three or more states. At its core, it concerns efforts by states to develop and to comply with a set of general principles or rules that define how they should act on specific issues. By doing so, states attempt to organize their interactions in a way that softens the most dangerous consequences of anarchy, moving away from unilateral raw power and armed conflict as the route to security. Multilateralism is not about subordinating an individual state's particular interests to help foster the greater good of the international community. Instead, it is an alternative way to meet a state's particular interests—even its most important need for physical security—in a potentially dangerous world.

There has generally been a continuing strong impulse toward multilateralism in U.S. foreign policy starting in the mid-1940s, which can be traced back at least to President Woodrow Wilson's attempt to build a new multilateral security system through the League of Nations after World War I. Although Wilson's ambitious efforts toward this goal ended in failure, just two decades later, the principles of multilateralism again formed the core of the American vision for a more progressive postwar order. In recent years, however, key policy makers and analysts have challenged the multilateral approach, contending that multilateralism constrains America's freedom of action and that America's power means that it does not need help to meet a number of policy goals. Although the nation cannot, in extremis, forgo proceeding alone, it can generally choose between unilateralism and multilateralism. The debate over these two approaches will likely shape American national security policy for decades to come.

Multilateralism offers three key advantages: (1) it provides a framework for organizing interstate relations and fostering stability, (2) it allows for sharing the burdens of meeting common goals, and (3) it generates international legitimacy for a state's foreign policy. The ultimate goal for any state that accepts multilateral principles is to serve its own interests by supporting a system that regulates the behavior of the other participating states, establishes certain rights others should respect, and reduces uncertainty.[49]

Perhaps as important as the advantages of burden sharing and collaboration on common goals, a state's compliance with multilateral principles helps to establish the legitimacy of its foreign policy. With a broad set of interests and an activist foreign policy that spans the globe and cuts across virtually every major international issue area, the United States frequently faces a world that is suspicious of its motives and inclined to counter its initiatives. The legitimacy that comes from respecting multilateral mechanisms can make it easier for the United States to achieve its goals. Compliance with multilateral principles can also help to sustain international tolerance for the considerable power America wields in the international system.[50]

U.S. Multilateralism after the Cold War.   Several key events, such as the first Gulf War and the Somalia intervention in the early 1990s, illustrate the advantages and drawbacks of multilateralism. According to Brent Scowcroft, President George H. W. Bush's national security advisor, the administration's "core premise" from August 1990 forward was that the United States "would be obligated to lead the world community to an unprecedented degree, as demonstrated by the

Iraqi crisis, and that we should attempt to pursue our national interests, whenever possible, within a framework of concert with our friends and the international community."[51] *Concert* in this context meant multilateralism.

The Gulf War, 1990–1991. The Gulf War following Iraq's invasion of Kuwait was only the second multilateral security operation authorized explicitly by Chapter VII of the United Nations (UN) Charter.[52] From the American perspective, the invasion of Kuwait was not just a threat to international peace and security. Iraq's 1990 seizure of Kuwait gave it control over about 20% of the world's proven petroleum reserves. If its offensive had continued into eastern Saudi Arabia to seize its oil fields, Iraq would have controlled nearly 50% of world oil reserves, thus dominating the global market.[53]

Within days, George H. W. Bush ordered a light defensive force into Saudi Arabia, with the acquiescence of the Saudi king. Although the United States remained firmly in the lead, Bush enthusiastically embraced the UN Security Council as the proper international body to authorize this operation. On August 2, 1990, the Security Council unanimously declared the invasion of Kuwait to be a "breach of international peace and security," and on August 6, 1990, the Security Council unanimously imposed a full economic and financial embargo on Iraq. On November 29, 1990, the Bush administration managed to gain Security Council authorization by a 12 to 2 vote (with China abstaining) for the use of "all necessary means, including the use of force," to remove Iraq from Kuwait.

As former Secretary of State James Baker recalls, some influential Americans argued that the United States could simply declare its right to come to Kuwait's aid under Article 51 of the UN Charter, which grants states the right to individual or collective self-defense, without having to go through the UN Security Council. But, he asserts, the administration "recognized the importance of doing this in a way that was not seen to be America and the West against the Arab world and that it was not seen to be a cowboy operation."[54] At home, the UN vote led to a jump in public support for taking the offensive.[55] The UN vote helped the president win congressional approval, especially in the Senate, which approved of the use of force by a close 52 to 47 vote. Globally, the UN Security Council authorization was instrumental in helping George H. W. Bush assemble an unprecedented international coalition of states willing to join the fight against Iraq. Overall, thirty-four countries from literally around the world contributed 25% of the military forces, while $54 billion of the $61 billion cost of the war was covered by other states.[56]

This case also revealed that multilateralism imposes constraints. As Iraqi forces fled Kuwait, U.S. commander General Norman Schwarzkopf considered pursuing units deep into Iraq to destroy them, and some analysts argued for taking the fight to Baghdad to overthrow Saddam Hussein's regime.[57] The president, however, not only ordered the end of the ground campaign after one hundred hours, leaving the Iraqi military defeated but not destroyed, but he also refused to consider a drive to the Iraqi capital to bring down the government. As he and his national security advisor described the problem, if the U.S. tried "to eliminate Saddam, extending the ground war into an occupation of Iraq . . . the coalition would instantly have collapsed, the Arabs deserting it in anger and other allies pulling out as well."[58] Despite the strategic logic of driving on Baghdad, George H. W. Bush was willing to accept limits on the use of American power to uphold multilateralism and sustain the international legitimacy of U.S. actions.

Somalia, 1992–1993.   A year and a half after the Gulf War, the United States again faced the multilateral impulse to respond to a stark situation in Somalia. By the summer of 1992, the civil war had produced the potential for a catastrophic humanitarian crisis. By November, three hundred thousand were already dead, and between 2 and 4.5 million Somalis were at risk of starvation. Fighting between rival clan militias and drought had combined to cause the collapse of the Somali agricultural system and normal food distribution within the country.[59]

As the humanitarian disaster grew, so did international pressure on the United States to lead a forceful intervention. Despite the great scale of the suffering, the United States had no direct interests at stake. Nevertheless, the president authorized a U.S. military operation to secure food supplies, feeding centers, and the convoys supplying them, which the UN Security Council unanimously approved on December 3, 1992.[60] George H. W. Bush did not want American military forces to be dragged into Somali politics and would only engage the warlords directly if necessary to secure food supplies,[61] but by mid-December U.S. forces were raiding arms caches to weaken the warlords.[62]

With the inauguration of President Bill Clinton in late January 1993, the new administration approached the ongoing Somalia mission with a burst of enthusiasm for this type of multilateralism. During the first nine months of the Clinton administration, however, the Somalia mission and the logic of multilateralism forced the president to reassess just how "assertive" UN multilateralism should be.[63]

By September 1993, the Clinton administration recognized that, for all its benefits, multilateralism meant that America would be called on time after time to fill the vacuum of capabilities that existed internationally. In an extraordinary turnaround, Clinton, in an address to the UN General Assembly in September 1993, stated that the UN "must learn to say 'no.'" The United States, he was declaring, could not be counted on if the UN's multilateral ambitions outpaced the capabilities of other member states.[64]

Despite this September retrenchment, in a bad example of "mission creep" (the expansion of a mission beyond its original goals without a full evaluation of the consequences), American forces were increasingly drawn into the Somalian anarchy. On October 3, 1993, eighteen U.S. soldiers were killed and seventy-eight were wounded in a battle in Mogadishu.[65] This "Black Hawk Down" disaster led to the Clinton administration's disenchantment with the Somalia mission as it had evolved and to a precipitate withdrawal of all U.S. forces.

The Iraq War, 2003.   Perhaps the most dramatic example of the dilemma inherent in the multilateralism debate is the 2003 Iraq war. In early 2003, the administration of President George W. Bush confronted a stark choice over how to move forward toward its goal of removing Hussein and his regime from power in Iraq and disarming Iraq of suspected WMDs. In November 2002, the UN Security Council had unanimously demanded Iraqi compliance with disarmament obligations stretching back to the Gulf War of 1991 and cooperation with international weapons inspectors who would verify the state of Iraq's weapons programs. This collective demand, which threatened "serious [yet unspecified] consequences" if Iraq refused to cooperate, was a powerful symbol of international support of the administration's objectives. The Arab League, North Atlantic Treaty Organization, and the European Union all endorsed the international demand for Iraqi compliance with the multilateral nonproliferation system.[66]

By January 2003, however, the George W. Bush administration had grown impatient with what it deemed continuing deception by the Iraqi regime and with the ongoing inspections that had yet to reveal evidence that Iraq actually had WMD stockpiles or a capability to manufacture them. Despite pressure from the United States, other key members of the Security Council, including France, Germany, China and Russia, refused to agree with the United States that the time had come for military action.[67] Instead, these other states demanded inspections continue before any next steps were considered.

The basic choice American policy makers faced was: Should the United States continue working through the UN; or should it break free from the restraints imposed by multilateralism, form an ad hoc coalition of states willing to follow America's lead, and initiate the military action it preferred? After several fruitless attempts to persuade the Security Council of the necessity for force, the George W. Bush administration gave up on multilateralism and invaded Iraq in March 2003.

Although the United States and the ad hoc coalition it assembled easily brought down Hussein's regime, the debate over the war continues. In large part because of its unilateralism on Iraq, America's international prestige has suffered. Although the United States could technically claim several dozen states as coalition partners, very few actually helped fund the reconstruction effort. The military forces in Iraq have been overwhelmingly American, and over time coalition contributions have eroded. America has carried the vast burden of this effort.

The Continuing Multilateralism-Unilateralism Debate.   The administration of George W. Bush has challenged the multilateral impulse in American foreign policy more directly than any administration since World War II. The desire for an unhampered military response to post-9/11 security challenges certainly accounts for a portion of the administration's resistance to multilateralism. However, even before 9/11, Bush sought to maximize America's freedom of action by eschewing established multilateral commitments. For example, the administration withdrew from or declined to approve the Anti-Ballistic Missile Treaty, the International Criminal Court, and the Kyoto protocol that sought to further international cooperation on the prevention of climate change.[68].

On the other hand, the administration chose multilateral approaches for two pressing security problems: North Korean nuclear weapons and Iranian aspirations for nuclear weapons. As these Korean and Iranian cases suggest, policy makers will continually confront the same basic multilateral versus unilateral dilemmas and must weigh the benefits of multilateralism (an agreed framework for action, burden sharing with other states, and international legitimacy) against the added costs of constraints on U.S. power and freedom of action.

National Security Restructuring

A perennial problem of national security policy is how to organize the U.S. government to best develop and execute it. At the end of World War II, the National Security Act of 1947 was passed, which fundamentally restructured organizational relationships within the defense and national security community. In addition to creating the Air Force and linking all services under a single Department of Defense (DoD), the act established the CIA and the National Security Council (NSC). That basic structure has remained in place until today, with amendments to the act making moderate adjustments in 1949, 1958, and, most recently, in 1986.[69] In response to recommendations after the 9/11 attacks, two new cabinet-level posts have been created: the secretary of homeland security, who leads an associated department, and the director of national intelligence, who supervises the intelligence community. In spite of these changes, many analysts have pointed out significant flaws in the development, coordination, and execution of policy.

To attempt to facilitate a strategic defense perspective, Congress has mandated that the DoD conduct a Quadrennial Defense Review (QDR), which is:

> A comprehensive examination of the national defense strategy, force structure, force modernization plans, infrastructure, budget plan, and other elements of the defense program and policies of the United States with a view toward determining and expressing the defense strategy of the United States and establishing a defense program for the next 20 years.[70]

This assessment reorients decision makers away from the annual budget process and is intended to provide a better match between the ends, ways, and means of defense strategy over the long term. The QDR reports published in 1997, 2001, and 2006 identify some areas for change, but they have frequently been criticized as being primarily bureaucratic exercises that have not resulted in aggressive transformation of defense strategy, forces, or policies.[71] In spite of its shortcomings, however, the QDR process does provide a systematic method to link resources with programs and then programs with missions that accomplish national security objectives. With more robust direction and innovation, the QDR has the potential to be a useful tool to drive future defense polices.

In fact, the contribution of the QDR has led many to argue that the entire government should adopt a similar process to address all the elements of power and departments of government that are involved in national security policy. There is an understandable bureaucratic tendency for each department and agency to concentrate on its specific mission, resources, and political constituency, without proposing tradeoffs among departments that might more effectively accomplish U.S. national security objectives. Theoretically, the president and the NSC staff might make such tradeoffs, but they are invariably consumed with the ongoing crisis of the moment. They are more likely to align U.S. government resources for the immediate challenges, which may not best influence long-terms strategic interests. Congress does require that the president submit an annual national security strategy, but this document, at best, describes the U.S. objectives (ends) and does not go though a robust process of matching the national security instruments (means) and a particular strategy (ways) to those objectives.

A potentially useful reform, which was proposed by defense analysts Michele Flournoy and Shawn Brimley, would be the creation of a Quadrennial National Security Review, which would be an interagency process to develop a strategy and to identify the capabilities required from all elements of power and all departments of government to best achieve that strategy.[72] They argue that this type of review was accomplished once already, by the Eisenhower administration in 1953, in a comprehensive review of U.S. strategy. The 1953 review, dubbed "Project Solarium" because it was first discussed by President Dwight Eisenhower in the White House solarium, took almost two months and included working groups from all relevant agencies of government. They vigorously debated alternative allocations of budgets, forces, diplomatic efforts, information strategies, economic policies, and other components of national security policy. The results of the review were presented—and debated—at the cabinet level, and, eventually, the decisions based on this comprehensive review were incorporated into policy in NSC 162/2.[73] This kind of comprehensive review across all elements of power and departments of government could significantly improve resource allocation in support of national strategy.

Beyond changing the development of strategy, there have been additional proposals for restructuring government to improve effectiveness. The sixty-year history of the DoD has entailed a gradual progress toward greater service unification, or *jointness*, among the services of the U.S. military. Although there are occasionally problems, the interoperability of military forces in combat operations in Iraq and Afghanistan has generally been successful and is a function of training, education, and personnel policies, such as those mandated as part of the Goldwater-Nichols Department of Defense Reorganization Act (described in more detail in Chapters 5 and 8). The relative success of the Goldwater-Nichols Act has led policy makers to argue that the U.S. government should extrapolate from that example and have a similar reform to the entire national security structure.

In 2004, the Center for Strategic and International Studies (CSIS) completed a report titled "Beyond Goldwater-Nichols: Defense Reform for a New Strategic Era."[74] This report identifies structural changes that should be made to the American national security apparatus. It agrees that the DoD requires change, but it goes further and recommends that the entire structure in the Executive and Legislative branches also requires adjustment. Without change, the study argues, the U.S. "ability to conduct successful political-military contingency operations will continue to be fundamentally impaired."[75] Although these CSIS recommendations may not be the exact steps needed, they highlight the kinds of change that policy makers should consider.

One important change recommended by the CSIS study is the creation of structures to facilitate the interagency process. The pinnacle of an interagency national security infrastructure should be the Office of the Deputy Assistant to the President in the NSC. This office would facilitate the integration of interagency strategies and plans and would supervise the execution phase on behalf of the president. Each cabinet secretary should in turn appoint similar offices within his or her bureaucratic structure to engage in robust coordination.[76] Currently, the NSC staff is neither large enough nor empowered enough to provide much of an integration role, nor does it have significant capacity to monitor or supervise the execution of policies.

According to CSIS, Congress has a dual charge in the restructuring of the national security environment: to create a professional corps of national security experts and to increase oversight of the national security process. To ensure that any new organization is operated by competent, trained individuals, Congress should authorize the creation of a National Security Professional Corps.[77] This group of civil servants would eliminate the revolving door of expertise and excessive reliance on contractors that currently reduces the ability of different national security agencies to provide strategic guidance.[78] These new experts would be trained at the new Training Center for Interagency and Coalition Operations, also to be established by Congress.[79] Congressional oversight is imperative to ensure that, instead of simply creating another level of bureaucracy, the interagency process is made more efficient and responsive to future threats.

Massive challenges face any effort to transform the U.S. government. Bureaucracies are notoriously resilient. Reform attempts are constrained by the nature of the American political system, which calls for separation of powers and is inherently biased against concentration of authority.[80] Nevertheless, the challenges that the nation faces today, which have been identified throughout each of the areas discussed in this book, contribute to growing calls for reform within the overall national security system.

National Security versus Civil Liberty

Protecting and promoting American "life, liberty, and the pursuit of happiness" is the fundamental task of the U.S. government. Yet, these cherished American values may conflict with one another, especially during times of war. The requirements of national security may require some curtailment of personal freedoms, and to a certain extent U.S. citizens may be willing to accept this bargain. A central challenge in developing American national security policy is, therefore, to protect the United States and its citizens in a physical sense while minimizing any adverse effect on the U.S. system of limited government and core U.S. values.

Current debates regarding the balance between security and liberty are not new. In ancient Greece, Pericles commemorated Athenian dead in the war against Sparta by celebrating the open and democratic character of Athens. Acknowledging that the freedoms enjoyed by Athenians also made Athens vulnerable to its enemies, Pericles asserted, "We throw open our city to the world, and never by alien acts exclude foreigners from any opportunity of learning or observing, although the eyes of an enemy may occasionally profit by our liberality; trusting less in system and policy than to the native spirit of our citizens."[81] In the timeless debate between safety and freedom, Pericles was willing to accept some security risk to maintain the free and open character of Athens that he cherished.

More than two thousand years later, the Framers of the U.S. Constitution struggled with the same dilemma. In the Federalist Papers, which were written to explain and support ratification of the Constitution, Alexander Hamilton expressed fears that American disunity and the subsequent militarization of society would endanger the liberties that were at the core of the Constitution:

> Safety from external danger is the most powerful director of national conduct. Even the ardent love of liberty will, after a time, give way to its dictates. The violent destruction of life and property incident to war, the continual effort and alarm attendant on a state of continual danger, will compel nations the most attached to liberty to resort for repose and security to institutions which have a tendency to destroy their civil and political rights. To be more safe, they at length become willing to run the risk of being less free.[82]

American history demonstrates Hamilton's foresight. During the U.S. Civil War, in response to secessionist riots and sabotage in and around Baltimore, President Abraham Lincoln suspended the writ of habeas corpus. He also interfered with freedom of speech and of the press and tried suspected political criminals before military commissions.[83] During World War II, in response to fears of espionage or worse, President Franklin Roosevelt ordered thousands of Japanese immigrants and U.S. citizens of Japanese descent to be interned in detention camps. Lincoln and Roosevelt believed the urgency and nature of possible threats justified the extraordinary, ultimately unconstitutional curtailment of civil liberty in the pursuit of national security.

These and other examples in U.S. history demonstrate that U.S. presidents may recast the balance between civil liberty and national security to do what they believe is necessary to shepherd the country through dangerous times. Francis Biddle, an observer of Roosevelt and his World War II detention program, wrote: "The Constitution has not greatly bothered any wartime President. That was a question of law, which ultimately the Supreme Court must decide. And meanwhile—probably a long meanwhile—we must get on with the war."[84]

However, presidents would not be able to push the limits of American liberty for very long if they did not receive the deference or even support of the Supreme Court and Congress. Although Cicero's maxim that laws are silent in war may be an exaggeration, the Supreme Court has been reluctant to over-rule controversial presidential actions during times of war.[85] During the most dangerous days of World War II, the Supreme Court upheld Roosevelt's unconstitutional curfew and relocation program of Japanese citizens and immigrants in the June 1943 *Hirabayashi* and December 1944 *Korematsu* cases. Congress has also been willing to respond to what it has seen as the exigencies of war. In 1917, for example, Congress passed the Espionage Act, making many forms of antiwar activism illegal. Subsequently, the U.S. Supreme Court upheld the indictment and conviction of Eugene V. Debs under this new law for his multiple remarks opposing U.S.

involvement in World War I. In short, through acts of omission and commission, the other two branches of the federal government have, at least in the short term, deferred to the president's executive leadership when he has sacrificed some amount of liberty for increased security.

In wars and crises of short to medium duration, a temporary sacrifice of civil liberty in the name of security may be tolerable to many. Former Supreme Court Chief Justice William Rehnquist argued, "It is neither desirable nor is it remotely likely that civil liberty will occupy as favored a position in wartime as it does in peacetime."[86] Although individuals deprived of liberty would undoubtedly disagree, a significant percentage of Americans appear to concur with Rehnquist. For example, in the wake of 9/11, the George W. Bush administration began a covert program of wiretapping calls from suspected terrorists abroad to individuals in the United States. A September 2006 Gallup Poll asked more than one thousand respondents, "Do you think the Bush administration was right or wrong in wiretapping these conversations without obtaining a court order?" Fifty-five percent of the respondents felt that the policy was right.[87]

Many Americans appear willing to defer to the president during times of crisis because of the gravity of the threat. Although Pericles may have been able to accept the risks inherent in free society, it is becoming increasingly difficult for modern states to do so. The proliferation of WMDs has dramatically increased the damage terrorist organizations could inflict on the United States. This reality has shifted the thinking of many regarding the balance between liberty and security. If the wiretapping of the communications between American citizens and suspect foreigners is necessary to the prevention of a nuclear detonation in the United States, many argue that this action is not only permissible but essential. As some have observed, "the Constitution is not a suicide pact."[88] Of Lincoln's decision regarding habeas corpus, Rehnquist rhetorically asks, "Should [Lincoln] . . . have risked losing the Union that gave life to the Constitution because that charter denied him the necessary authority to preserve the Union?"[89]

In an age of terrorism, porous borders, and nuclear weapons, this logic is appealing at least on a superficial level. However, the fact that the threat posed by al-Qa'ida and other terrorists will likely last for generations is a particular challenge. This is not a short war. Under these circumstances, it is not clear that any expansion of executive power or curtailment of civil liberties will be only temporary and minimal. As Alexis de Tocqueville wrote in the 1830s, "Any long war always entails great hazards to liberty in a democracy."[90] In the years ahead, the Supreme Court, Congress, and the American people must find an approach toward executive power that is characterized by a healthy combination of skepticism and deference. Diligence will be needed to ensure that national security policies do not destroy the liberty they are designed to protect.

Conclusion

It is impossible to forecast all the challenges the United States and the Obama administration will confront in a dynamic future. Although existing trends enable one to venture educated estimates, major historic events, such as the fall of the Berlin Wall in 1989 or the terrorist attacks of 2001, have often taken Americans by surprise. Nevertheless, and despite the likelihood of future surprises, the seven issues discussed in this chapter are likely to remain central concerns: the emergence of China as a great power, the proliferation of nuclear weapons, U.S. dependence on foreign sources of energy, Islamist terrorism, unilateralism versus multilateralism, national security reform, and protection of the domestic balance between liberty and security. How well the United States addresses these challenges will largely determine American national security in the years ahead.

Discussion Questions

1. In what ways, if any, do China's expanding economy and improving military capabilities represent a threat to American national security? What are China's likely grand strategic objectives? Will Chinese economic growth and liberalization lead to political liberalization?

2. Can the United States peacefully coexist with an authoritarian China that possesses an economy and military capability equal to that of the United States?

3. How serious a threat to American national security does the proliferation of WMDs represent? Why do such states as North Korea and Iran seek nuclear weapons?

4. What policy or institutional reforms are required to protect the United States from a potential nuclear attack by a terrorist organization or rogue regime?

5. Why has the United States been unable or unwilling to reduce its dependence on foreign oil since 1973?

6. What can be done to reduce U.S. dependence on foreign oil? Can that dependence be eliminated entirely?

7. What are the most important actions the United States should take to reduce the threat posed by al-Qa'ida and associated movements?

8. In what situations might a state pursue a multilateral approach to national security? What advantages does it offer? What constraints does it impose?

9. Will the conditions that the United States faces in the future more likely lead to greater or less use of multilateralism in its approach to foreign policy? Why?

10. What are the circumstances that lead to calls for changes in national security structures?

11. Which reforms to defense and national security organizations are most important and most likely to succeed?

12. How has the United States managed the precarious balance between security and liberty in the wake of the terrorist attacks of 9/11?

13. Other than the several prospective American national security challenges discussed, what other major challenges will the United States likely confront in coming years?

Recommended Reading

Allison, Graham T. *Nuclear Terrorism: The Ultimate Preventable Catastrophe.* New York: Times Books/Henry Holt, 2004.

Brzezinski, Zbigniew. *The Choice: Global Domination or Global Leadership.* Cambridge, MA: Basic Books, 2004.

Brzezinski, Zbigniew, and John J. Mearsheimer. "Clash of the Titans." *Foreign Policy* 146 (January/February 2005): 46–50.

Bueno de Mesquita, Bruce, and George W. Downs. "Development and Democracy." *Foreign Affairs* 84, no. 5 (September/October 2005): 77–86.

Deutch, John, and James R. Schlesinger, chairs. *National Security Consequences of U.S. Oil Dependency*. Independent Task Force Report no. 58. New York: Council on Foreign Relations, 2006.

Deutch, Philip J. "Energy Independence." *Foreign Policy* 151 (November/December 2005): 20–25.

Foot, Rosemary, S. Neil MacFarlane, and Michael Mastanduno, eds. *US Hegemony and International Organizations: The United States and Multilateral Institutions*. New York: Oxford University Press, 2003.

Fukuyama, Francis. *America at the Crossroads: Democracy, Power, and the Neoconservative Legacy*. New Haven, CT: Yale University Press, 2006.

Gries, Peter Hays. "Chinese Nationalism: Challenging the State?" *Current History* 104, no. 683 (September 2005): 251–256.

Haass, Richard N. *The Opportunity: America's Moment to Alter History's Course*. New York: Public Affairs, 2005.

Ikenberry, G. John. *After Victory: Institutions, Strategic Restraint, and the Rebuilding of Order After Major Wars*. Princeton, NJ: Princeton University Press, 2001.

Institute for Strategic Studies. *The Military Balance 2006*. London: International Institute for Strategic Studies, 2006.

Mearsheimer, John J. "China's Unpeaceful Rise." *Current History* 105, no. 690 (April 2006): 160–162.

Posner, Richard A. *Not a Suicide Pact: The Constitution in a Time of National Emergency*. New York: Oxford University Press, 2006.

Rosen, Stephen P. "After Proliferation: What to Do If More States Go Nuclear." *Foreign Affairs* 85, no. 5 (September/October 2006): 9–14.

Sagan, Scott D. "How to Keep the Bomb from Iran." *Foreign Affairs* 85, no. 5 (September/October 2006): 45–59.

Shambaugh, David. "China Engages Asia: Reshaping the Regional Order." *International Security* 29, no. 3 (Winter 2004): 64–99.

Yergin, Daniel. "Ensuring Energy Security." *Foreign Affairs* 85, no. 2 (March/April 2006): 69–82.

Internet Resources

Annual Report to Congress: Military Power of the People's Republic of China, 2006, www.defenselink.mil/pubs/pdfs/China%20Report%202006.pdf

Combating Terrorism Center at West Point, www.ctc.usma.edu

Energy Information Adminstration, www.eia.doe.gov

Quadrennial Defense Review Report, 2006, www.defenselink.mil/qdr/report/Report20060203.pdf

Notes

Chapter 1: The International Setting

1. J. Boone Bartholomees, Jr., ed., "Guidelines for Strategy Formulation," in *U.S. Army War College Guide to National Security Policy and Strategy*, 2nd ed. (Carlisle Barracks, PA: Strategic Studies Institute, 2006), 388.

2. See also Joseph S. Nye, Jr., "Redefining the National Interest," *Foreign Affairs* 78, no. 4 (July/August 1999): 22–35; and the Commission on America's National Interests, *America's National Interests* (Cambridge, MA: The Commission on America's National Interests, 2000), esp. 5–8.

3. See, for example, Thomas F. Homer-Dixon, *Environment, Scarcity, and Violence* (Princeton, NJ: Princeton University Press, 1999); Ole Waever et al., *Identity, Migration, and the New Security Agenda in Europe* (New York: St. Martin's Press, 1993); and National Intelligence Council, *Global Trends 2015: A Dialogue About the Future with Nongovernment Experts*, NIC 2000-02, December 2000.

4. Human Security Centre, *Human Security Report 2005: War and Peace in the 21st Century* (New York: Oxford University Press, 2005), *viii*.

5. George W. Bush, *Department of Homeland Security* (Washington, DC: The White House, June 2002), 8.

6. In the interests of space, and because of its decline over time, not discussed here is Marxism. For its basic tenets, see Robert Gilpin, "Three Ideologies of Political Economy," in *Understanding International Relations*, 5th ed., ed. Daniel J. Kaufman et al. (New York: McGraw-Hill, 2004), 426–428. For its translation into a theory of international relations, see V. I. Lenin, *Imperialism: The Highest Stage of Capitalism* (New York: International Publishers, 1939). Perhaps the Marxist perspective persists most strongly among dependency theorists who examine the role of the capitalist developed world in contributing to underdevelopment in other parts of the world. See Theotonio Dos Santos, "The Structure of Dependence," *American Economic Review: Papers and Proceedings* 9, no. 2 (May 1970): 231–236. For a more recent view, see Kema Irogbe, "Globalization and the Development

of Underdevelopment of the Third World," *Journal of Third World Studies* 22, no. 1 (2005): 41–68.

7. Kenneth N. Waltz, *Theory of International Politics* (New York: McGraw-Hill, 1979), 131.

8. Ibid., 117.

9. Stephen M. Walt, *Origins of Alliances* (Ithaca, NY: Cornell University Press, 1987), 21–26.

10. See, for example, John J. Mearsheimer, *The Tragedy of Great Power Politics* (New York: W. W. Norton, 2001).

11. Peter J. Katzenstein, Robert O. Keohane, and Stephen D. Krasner, "International Organization and the Study of World Politics," *International Organization* 52, no. 4 (Autumn 1998): 684–685.

12. Thucydides, *History of the Peloponnesian War*, trans. Rex Warner (New York: Penguin, 1972), 49.

13. John Locke, *The Second Treatise of Government*, ed. Thomas P. Peardon (New York: Macmillan, 1952), esp. 119–139.

14. Andrew Moravcsik, "Taking Preferences Seriously: A Liberal Theory of International Politics," *International Organization* 50, no. 4 (Autumn 1997): 516.

15. Bruce Russett, *Grasping the Democratic Peace* (Princeton, NJ: Princeton University Press, 1993), 24–42.

16. Hans Morgenthau, *Politics among Nations: The Struggle for Power and Peace*, 2nd ed., rev. and enlarged (New York: Knopf, 1954), 10.

17. Immanuel Kant, *Political Writings*, ed. Hans Reiss (Cambridge: Cambridge University Press, 1970, 1991), 41–53 and 93–130.

18. See Robert O. Keohane and Joseph S. Nye, *Power and Interdependence*, 3rd ed. (New York: Pearson Education, 2001).

19. Declaration of Independence, www.archives.gov/national-archives-experience/charters/declaration_transcript.html.

20. United Nations, Universal Declaration of Human Rights, www.un.org/Overview/rights.html; for a discussion of current challenges to the law of war, see Kenneth Roth, "The Law of War in the War on Terror," *Foreign Affairs* 83, no. 1 (January/February 2004): 2–7.

21. See Edward D. Mansfield and Jack Snyder, "Democratization and the Danger of War," *International Security* 20, no. 1 (Summer 1995): 5–38; and see Edward D. Mansfield and Jack Snyder, "Democratic Transitions, Institutional Strength, and War," *International Organization* 56, no. 2 (Spring 2002): 297–337.

22. Charles Krauthammer, "The Unipolar Moment," *Foreign Affairs* 70, no. 1 (Winter 1990/1991): 29.

23. Ibid., 25.

24. William Kristol and Robert Kagan, "Toward a Neo-Reaganite Foreign Policy," *Foreign Affairs* 75, no. 4 (July/August 1996): 27.

25. Charles Krauthammer, "The Unipolar Moment Revisited," *The National Interest* 70 (Winter 2002/2003): 16.

26. Ibid., 14.

27. Francis Fukuyama, "The Neoconservative Moment," *The National Interest*, no. 76 (Summer 2004): 57–68. See also the response, Charles Krauthammer, "In Defense of Democratic Realism," *The National Interest*, no. 77 (Fall 2004): 15–25.

28. Alexander Wendt, "Constructing International Politics," *International Security* 20, no. 1 (Summer 1995): 77–78.

29. As one example, see Alastair Iain Johnston, *Cultural Realism: Strategic Culture and Grand Strategy in Chinese History* (Princeton, NJ: Princeton University Press, 1995).

30. Martha Finnemore, *The Purpose of Intervention: Changing Beliefs about the Use of Force* (Ithaca, NY: Cornell University Press, 2003); for another examination of the role of international norms, see Jeffrey W. Legro, *Cooperation Under Fire: Anglo-German Restraint during World War II* (Ithaca, NY: Cornell University Press, 1995).

31. For a case study that tests this, see Alastair Iain Johnston, "Learning versus Adaptation: Explaining Change in Chinese Arms Control Policy in the 1980s and 1990s," *China Journal* no. 35 (January 1996): 27–61.

32. Thomas Hobbes, *Leviathan*, ed. Michael Oakeshott (New York: Macmillan Publishing Company, 1962), 101.

33. Charter of the United Nations, www.un.org/aboutun/charter.

34. Convention on the Prevention and Punishment of the Crime of Genocide, www.un.org/millennium/law/iv-1.htm.

35. Kenneth N. Waltz, *Man, the State, and War* (New York: Columbia University Press, 1959), 12.

36. Kevin Woods, James Lacey, and Williamson Murray, "Saddam's Delusions: The View from the Inside," *Foreign Affairs* 85, no. 3 (May/June 2006): 2–26.

37. Lenin, *Imperialism*. See also John Hobson, *Imperialism* (London: Allen & Unwin, 1916).

38. Jerome D. Frank, *Sanity and Survival: Psychological Aspects of War and Peace* (New York: Random House, 1967), 109.

39. For example, see the bureaucratic politics and organizational process models in Graham T. Allison and Philip Zelikow, *Essence of Decision: Explaining the Cuban Missile Crisis* (New York: Longman, 1999).

40. Robert Axelrod and Robert O. Keohane, "Achieving Cooperation under Anarchy: Strategies and Institutions," *World Politics* 38, no. 1 (October 1985): 226–254.

41. James Rosenau, "The Complexities and Contradictions of Globalization," *Current History* (November 1997): 360–364.

42. Waltz, *Theory of International Politics*, 118.

43. Kenneth N. Waltz, "Structural Realism after the Cold War," *International Security* 25, no. 1 (Summer 2000): 5–41.

44. Morgenthau, *Politics Among Nations*, 102–137.

45. Ibid., 138–152.

46. Joseph S. Nye, Jr., and William A. Owens, "America's Information Edge," *Foreign Affairs* 75, no. 2 (March/April 1996): 21, fn. 1. See also Joseph S. Nye, Jr., *Bound to Lead* (New York: Basic Books, 1990).

47. Klaus Knorr, *Military Power and Potential* (Lexington, MA: Heath, 1970), 143.

48. It should be noted that the theory of hegemonic stability has both realist and liberal variants.

49. Stephen M. Walt, "The Relationship Between Theory and Policy in International Relations," *Annual Review of Political Science* 8, no. 1 (2005): 23.

50. Ibid., 28–29. See also David A. Baldwin, "Success and Failure in Foreign Policy," *Annual Review of Political Science* 3, no. 1 (2000): 167–182.

51. Jeffrey W. Legro, "What China Will Want: The Future Intentions of a Rising Power," *Perspectives on Politics* 5, no. 3 (September 2007): 516.

52. Globalization's foremost enthusiast may be journalist Thomas L. Friedman. See his *The World Is Flat: A Brief History of the Twenty-First Century* (New York: Farrar, Straus, and Giroux, 2005). For a discussion of the limitations and risks associated with globali-

zation, see Stanley Hoffmann, "Clash of Globalizations," *Foreign Affairs* 81, no. 4 (July/ August 2002): 104–115.

53. For an examination of increased intergovernmental cooperation as a response to globalization, see Anne-Marie Slaughter, *A New World Order* (Princeton, NJ: Princeton University Press, 2004).

54. Robert Jervis, *American Foreign Policy in a New Era* (New York: Routledge, 2005), 12.

55. See, for example, Stephen M. Walt, *Taming American Power: The Global Response to U.S. Primacy* (New York: W. W. Norton & Company, 2005), esp. 109–179.

56. This is consistent with Robert Gilpin, *The Political Economy of International Relations* (Princeton, NJ: Princeton University Press, 1987), 72–80.

57. For the U.S. role after World War II, see G. John Ikenberry, *After Victory: Institutions, Strategic Restraint, and the Rebuilding of Order after Major Wars* (Princeton, NJ: Princeton University Press, 2001), esp. 163–175. For policy recommendations for the current era, see Joseph S. Nye, *The Paradox of American Power: Why the World's Only Superpower Can't Go It Alone* (New York: Oxford University Press, 2002).

58. Jervis, *American Foreign Policy in a New Era*, 2.

Chapter 2: Traditional American Approaches to National Security

1. Gabriel A. Almond, *The American People and Foreign Policy*, 2nd ed. (New York: Praeger, 1977), 54.

2. Gabriel A. Almond, "Public Opinion and National Security Policy," *Public Opinion Quarterly* 20, no. 2 (1956): 371–373.

3. Ole R. Holsti, "Public Opinion and Foreign Policy: Challenges to the Almond-Lippmann Consensus Mershon Series: Research Programs and Debates," *International Studies Quarterly* 36 (1992): 440.

4. Ibid.

5. Benjamin I. Page and Robert Y. Shapiro, *The Rational Public: Fifty Years of Trends in Americans' Policy Preferences* (Chicago: University of Chicago Press, 1992), 1.

6. Philip J. Powlick, "The Sources of Public Opinion for American Foreign Policy Officials," *International Studies Quarterly* 39, no. 4 (1995): 428.

7. Joseph S. Nye, Jr., "Redefining the National Interest," *Foreign Affairs* 78, no. 4 (July/August 1999): 24.

8. The White House, *National Security Strategy of the United States of America* (Washington, DC: The White House, September 2002), v.

9. Charles B. Cushman, Jr., *An Introduction to the U.S. Congress* (Armonk, NY: M. E. Sharpe, 2006), 41.

10. Douglas C. Foyle, "Public Opinion and Foreign Policy: Elite Beliefs as a Mediating Variable," *International Studies Quarterly* 41, no. 1 (1997): 141–142.

11. See Nye, "Redefining the National Interest," 22–35.

12. Ralph B. Levering, *The Public and American Foreign Policy, 1918–1978* (New York: Morrow, 1978), 134–137.

13. Associated Press-Ipsos poll conducted by Ipsos Public Affairs, April 2–4, 2007, www.pollingreport.com/iraq5.htm.

14. Eric V. Larson, *Casualties and Consensus: The Historical Role of Casualties in Domestic Support for U.S. Military Operations* (Santa Monica, CA: RAND, 1996), xix.

15. Powlick, "The Sources of Public Opinion for American Foreign Policy Officials," 430.

16. See Wallace Earl Walker, "Domesticating Foreign Policy: Congress and the Vietnam War," in *Democracy, Strategy, and Vietnam*, eds. George R. Osborn et al. (Lexington, MA: Lexington Books, 1987), 106–110.

17. Richard F. Grimmett, *War Powers Resolution: Presidential Compliance* (Washington, DC: Congressional Research Service, 2004), CRS-1.

18. Carl Becker, *The Declaration of Independence: A Study in the History of Political Ideas* (New York: Knopf, 1942), 76–78.

19. Lee Ward, "Locke on the Moral Basis of International Relations," *American Journal of Political Science* 50, no. 3 (2006): 692.

20. Thomas Hobbes, *Leviathan* (New York: Collier Books, 1962), 100.

21. Ibid.

22. Ibid., 101.

23. Robert E. Osgood, *Ideals and Self-Interest in America's Foreign Relations* (Chicago: University of Chicago Press, 1953), 433.

24. Frederick H. Hartmann, *The Relations of Nations*, 4th ed. (New York: Macmillan, 1973), 101–102; and Kenneth W. Thompson, *American Diplomacy and Emergent Patterns* (New York: New York University Press, 1962), 45–46.

25. Hartmann, *Relations of Nations*, 102.

26. Harry R. Davis and Robert C. Good, *Reinhold Niebuhr on Politics* (New York: Scribner, 1960), 308–313.

27. See Frederick Merk, *Manifest Destiny and Mission in American History* (New York: Knopf, 1963), 261.

28. Albert Gallatin, quoted in ibid., 262–263.

29. See Charles O. Lerche, Jr., *Foreign Policy of the American People*, 3rd ed. (Englewood Cliffs, NJ: Prentice-Hall, 1967), 110–111.

30. See Davis and Good, *Reinhold Niebuhr on Politics*, 140.

31. Carl von Clausewitz, *On War*, trans. and ed. Michael Howard and Peter Paret (Princeton, NJ: Princeton University Press, 1976), 87.

32. Lerche, *Foreign Policy*, 117.

33. Robert E. Osgood, *Limited War: The Challenge to American Strategy* (Chicago: University of Chicago Press, 1957), 31

34. Robert W. Tucker, *The Just War: A Study in Contemporary American Doctrine*, 2nd ed. (Baltimore: Johns Hopkins University Press, 1979), 11.

35. See also Michael Walzer, *Just and Unjust Wars* (New York: Basic Books, 1977), 76–78.

36. Harry S. Truman, quoted in ibid., 15.

37. For an expression of this position, see Samuel P. Huntington, *The Soldier and the State* (Cambridge, MA: Harvard University Press, Belknap Press, 1957).

38. George Washington, quoted in Daniel J. Boorstin, *The Americans: The Colonial Experience* (New York: Random House, 1958), 368.

39. James Gerhardt, *The Draft and Public Policy* (Columbus: Ohio State University Press, 1971), 83–122.

40. Resolution, Continental Congress, quoted in Huntington, *The Soldier and the State*, 144.

41. The White House, *The National Security Strategy of the United States of America* (Washington, DC: The White House, March 2006), i.

42. John W. Shy, *A People Numerous and Armed: Reflections on the Military Struggle for American Independence* (Ann Arbor: University of Michigan Press, 1990), 238–242.

43. Almond, *American People and Foreign Policy*, 30–31, 48–50.

44. Ibid., 51.

45. Dafna Hochman, "Rehabilitating a Rogue: Libya's WMD Reversal and Lessons for US Policy," *Parameters* 36, no. 1 (Spring 2006): 63. For an example of a call to action on the nuclear threat, see Graham T. Allison, *Avoiding Nuclear Anarchy: Containing the Threat of Loose Russian Nuclear Weapons and Fissile Materials* (Cambridge, MA: MIT Press, 1996).

46. Andrew Newman, "Arms Control, Proliferation, and Terrorism: The Bush Administration's Post–September 11 Security Strategy," *Journal of Strategic Studies* 27, no. 1 (March 2004): 59.

47. John A. Thompson, "Conceptions of National Security and American Entry into World War II," *Diplomacy and Statecraft* 16, no. 4 (December 2005): 671–672.

48. "Confidence in Institutions," Gallup Poll, June 9–12, 2008, www.gallup.com/poll/1597/Confidence-Institutions.aspx.

49. Ibid. The survey did not ask about the police as an institution until 1993.

50. Andrew J. Bacevich, *The New American Militarism: How Americans Are Seduced by War* (New York: Oxford University Press, 2005).

51. Stephen Kosiak, "National Defense Budget Authority and Outlays," *Historical and Projected Funding for Defense: Presentation of the FY 2009 Request in Tables and Charts*, Center for Strategic and Budgetary Assessments, March 31, 2008, www.csbaonline.org/4Publications/PubLibrary/U.20080331.FY_09_Request_in_T/U.20080331.FY_09_Request_in_T.pdf. All numbers are in current 2008 dollars.

52. See, for example, "World Military Spending," Global Issues, www.globalissues.org/article/75/world-military-spending#InContextUSMilitarySpendingVersusRestofthe World.

53. For both sides of the debate, see Charles Rangel, "Should the All Volunteer Force Be Replaced by Universal Mandatory Military Service?" *Congressional Digest* 85, no. 7 (September 2006): 206–208.

54. Finnemore, 129.

55. See, for example, Scott A. Silverstone, *Preventive War and American Democracy* (London: Routledge, 2007). For a challenge to the idea that the consideration of preventive war is new to the American experience, see John Lewis Gaddis, *Surprise, Security, and the American Experience* (Cambridge, MA: Harvard University Press, 2004).

56. The White House, *The National Security Strategy of the United States of America* (Washington, DC: The White House, September 2002), 14–15.

57. George Shultz, "Address before the Trilateral Commission on April 3, 1984," *Department of State Bulletin* 84, no. 2086 (May 1984): 13.

58. See Gaddis, *Surprise, Security, and the American Experience*, for a discussion of these developments.

59. Robert Jervis, *American Foreign Policy in a New Era* (New York: Routledge, 2005), 87. For a different perspective that argues that the national security strategy of President George W. Bush is actually more multilateral than that of his predecessor, see John Lewis Gaddis, "A Grand Strategy of Transformation," *Foreign Policy* 285, no. 4 (April 2000): 50–57.

60. For a critical perspective, see Barbara Bodine, "Channel Surfing: Non-Engagement as Foreign Policy," *Audit of the Conventional Wisdom* (August 2006): 1–3.

61. The White House, *The National Security Strategy of the United States of America* (Washington, DC: March 2006), 1.

62. Stanley Hoffmann, "Clash of Globalizations," *Foreign Affairs* 81, no. 4 (2002): 105.

63. Ana Maria Arumi et al., *Americans Wary of Creating Democracies Abroad* (New York: Public Agenda, 2006), 18.

64. Gallup Poll, April 23-26, 2007, www.pollingreport.com/prioriti2.htm.

Chapter 3: The Evolution of American National Security Policy

1. DOD Dictionary of Terms, "strategy," www.dtic.mil/doctrine/jel/doddict/data/s/05200.html.

2. DOD Dictionary of Terms, "national policy," www.dtic.mil/doctrine/jel/doddict/data/n/03629.html.

3. Walter Lippmann, *U.S. Foreign Policy: Shield of the Republic* (Boston: Little, Brown, 1943), 51.

4. Henry Kissinger, *American Foreign Policy* (New York: W. W. Norton, 1974), 13.

5. *Report of the President's Commission on Strategic Forces* (Washington, DC: U.S. Government Printing Office, April 1983), passim.

6. Samuel P. Huntington, *The Common Defense* (New York: Columbia University Press, 1961), 3–4.

7. Henry T. Nash, *American Foreign Policy: Response to a Sense of Threat* (Homewood, IL: Dorsey Press, 1973), 19.

8. Huntington, *Common Defense*, 41.

9. Nash, *American Foreign Policy*, 19.

10. George Kennan, "The Sources of Soviet Conduct," *Foreign Affairs* 25, no. 4 (1947): 575–576.

11. Walter Millis, ed., *The Forrestal Diaries* (New York: Viking Press, 1951), 350.

12. Huntington, *Common Defense*, 41.

13. Ibid., 43.

14. Chief of Staff, *Final Report*, United States Army, February 7, 1948, 11–12.

15. Huntington, *Common Defense*, 45.

16. Ibid., 47.

17. President Harry S. Truman, address delivered to a joint session of Congress, March 12, 1947, reprinted in Joseph M. Jones, *The Fifteen Weeks* (New York: Harcourt, Brace & World, 1955), 272.

18. Nash, *American Foreign Policy*, 25.

19. Ibid., 29.

20. Warner Schilling, Paul Hammond, and Glenn Snyder, *Strategy, Politics, and the Defense Budget* (New York: Columbia University Press, 1962), 292.

21. Paul H. Nitze, "The Need for a National Strategy" (address delivered at Army War College, Carlisle Barracks, Pennsylvania, August 27, 1958).

22. Huntington, *Common Defense*, 54.

23. For a discussion of U.S. perceptions of communist intentions, see Morton Halperin, *Limited War in the Nuclear Age* (New York: John Wiley & Sons, 1963), chap. 3.

24. Huntington, *Common Defense*, 88.

25. Ibid., 56.

26. Ibid., 73–74.

27. Jerome Kahan, *Security in the Nuclear Age* (Washington, DC: Brookings Institution Press, 1975), 28.

28. "Text of Dulles' Statement on Foreign Policy of Eisenhower Administration," *New York Times*, January 13, 1954, 2.

29. John Foster Dulles, "The Evolution of Foreign Policy," *Department of State Bulletin* 30 (January 25, 1954): 108.

30. Huntington, *Common Defense*, 88.

31. Ibid., 92.

32. Ibid., 96–97.

33. Morton Halperin, *Defense Strategies for the Seventies* (Boston: Little, Brown, 1971), 46.

34. Huntington, *Common Defense*, 105.

35. John Foster Dulles, "Challenge and Response in U.S. Foreign Policy," *Foreign Affairs* 36, no. 1 (October 1951): 31.

36. Maxwell D. Taylor, *The Uncertain Trumpet* (New York: Harper, 1959), 82–83.

37. William W. Kaufmann, *The McNamara Strategy* (New York: Harper & Row, 1964), 29.

38. Alain C. Enthoven and K. Wayne Smith, *How Much Is Enough?* (New York: Harper & Row, 1971), 21.

39. House Committee on Armed Services, *Hearings on Military Posture*, 85th Cong., 2nd sess., 1962, 3162.

40. Kaufmann, *McNamara Strategy*, 53–54.

41. Ibid., 71.

42. What constituted unacceptable damage to an adversary could not be measured precisely. However, the planning figure accepted by U.S. authorities was 25% to 33% of Soviet population and about 75% of Soviet industrial capacity. This judgment was influenced primarily by the demographics of Soviet population distribution and by the rapidly diminishing marginal returns beyond a certain level of retaliatory attack. For a more complete explanation of assured destruction criteria, see Enthoven and Smith, *How Much Is Enough?*, 207.

43. John F. Kennedy, Inaugural Address given in Washington, D.C., January 20, 1961, www.jfklibrary.org/Historical+Resources/Archives/Reference+Desk/Speeches/JFK/003P OF03Inaugural01201961.htm.

44. Edward R. Fried et al., *Setting National Priorities: The 1974 Budget* (Washington, DC: Brookings Institution Press, 1973), 292.

45. *U.S. Department of Defense Annual Report, Fiscal Year 1975* (Washington, DC: U.S. Government Printing Office), 22.

46. Halperin, *Defense Strategies for the Seventies*, 52.

47. Alton H. Quanback and Barry M. Blechman, *Strategic Forces: Issues for the Mid-Seventies* (Washington, DC: Brookings Institution Press, 1973), 6–7.

48. Ibid., 9.

49. Halperin, *Defense Strategies for the Seventies*, 126.

50. Ibid.

51. Ibid., 127.

52. Bernard Brodie, "Technology, Politics, and Strategy," *Adelphi Papers*, 9, no. 55 (March 1969): 22.

53. See John Lewis Gaddis, *How Relevant Was U.S. Strategy in Winning the Cold War?* (Carlisle Barracks, PA: Strategic Studies Institute, 1992), 14.

54. John Lewis Gaddis, "A Grand Strategy of Transformation," *Foreign Policy* 133 (November/December 2002): 53.

55. See Don M. Snider, *The National Security Strategy: Documenting Strategic Vision* (Carlisle Barracks, PA: Strategic Studies Institute, 1992), 14.

56. See "Statement of the Secretary of Defense Dick Cheney before the Senate Budget Committee, February 3, 1992," 1.

57. See *National Military Strategy of the United States* (Washington, DC: U.S. Government Printing Office, January 1992), 6–10.

58. William J. Perry, "Defense in an Age of Hope," *Foreign Affairs* 75, no. 6 (November/December 1996): 64–79.

59. See for example, Don M. Snider, "The Coming Defense Train Wreck," *Washington Quarterly* 19, no. 1 (Winter 1996): 89–102.

60. For a defense of President Clinton's stewardship of the armed forces, see Michael O'Hanlon, "Clinton's Strong Defense Legacy," *Foreign Affairs* 82, no. 6 (November/December 2003): 126.

61. For a discussion reflecting campaign issues, see Lawrence Korb, Condoleezza Rice, and Robert B. Zoellick, "Money for Nothing: A Penny Saved, Not a Penny Earned, in the U.S. Military," *Foreign Affairs* 79, no. 2 (March/April 2000): 149–152.

62. Condoleezza Rice, "Promoting the National Interest," *Foreign Affairs* 79, no. 1 (January/February 2000): 51.

63. See the second presidential debate, *Online News Hour with Jim Lehrer*, PBS, October 11, 2000, www.pbs.org/newshour/bb/election/2000debates/2ndebate2.html.

64. Gaddis, "A Grand Strategy of Transformation," 50.

65. George W. Bush, "Address Delivered to the West Point Graduating Class" (June 1, 2002), www.whitehouse.gov/news/releases/2002/06/20020601-3.html.

66. The White House, *The National Security Strategy of the United States* (Washington, DC: The White House, September 2002), iv.

67. Ibid., 15.

68. Robert Jervis, *American Foreign Policy in a New Era* (New York: Routledge, 2005), 85.

69. See John Lewis Gaddis, "Grand Strategy in the Second Term," *Foreign Affairs* 84, no. 1 (January/February 2005): 2–15.

70. Stephen Biddle, *Afghanistan and the Future of Warfare: Implications for the Army and Defense Policy* (Carlisle, PA: U.S. Army Strategic Studies Institute, November 2002).

71. North Atlantic Treaty Organization, "NATO in Afghanistan," www.nato.int/issues/afghanistan/040628-factsheet.htm.

72. L. Paul Bremer, *My Year in Iraq: The Struggle to Build a Future of Hope* (New York: Threshold Editions, 2006)

73. Iraq Study Group, *The Iraq Study Group Report* (Washington, DC: U.S. Institute of Peace, 2006), www.usip.org/isg/.

74. David H. Petraeus, "Report to Congress on the Situation in Iraq," September 2007, www.defenselink.mil/pubs/pdfs/Petraeus-Testimony20070910.pdf.

75. *The National Security Strategy of the United States*, 2006, 22.

76. Keir A. Leiber and Daryl G. Press, "The Rise of U.S. Nuclear Primacy," *Foreign Affairs* 85, no. 2 (March/April 2006): 52–53.

77. Secretary of Defense Task Force on DoD Nuclear Weapons Management, *Report of the Secretary of Defense Task Force on DoD Nuclear Weapons Management*, (Washington: Department of Defense, September 2008), 2.

78. As quoted by Marc Kaufman, "Bush Sets Defense As Space Priority," *The Washington Post*, October 18, 2006, A01.

79. See Donald Rumsfeld, "Against the Unknown: Armed Forces Transformation for the 21st Century," *Hampton Roads International Security Quarterly* (Autum 2002): 6–15.

80. *Quadrennial Defense Review Report* (Washington, DC: U.S. Government Printing Office, February 6, 2006), v–vi.

81. *Budget of the United States Government, Fiscal Year 2007*, www.whitehouse.gov/omb/budget/fy2007/defense.html.

82. See "Beyond Goldwater-Nichols: U.S. Government and Defense Reform for a New Strategic Era, Phase II Report" (Washington, DC: CSIS, July 2005), www.csis.org/index.php?option=com_csis_pubs&task=view&id=1849.

Chapter 4: Presidential Leadership and the Executive Branch

1. Alexander Hamilton, *The Federalist No. 74*, in *Great Books of the Western World*, ed. Robert M. Hutchins, vol. 43 (Chicago: Encyclopedia Britannica, 1952), 21.

2. Arthur M. Schlesinger, Jr., *The Imperial Presidency* (Boston: Houghton Mifflin, 1973).

3. U.S. Constitution, art. 1, sec. 8.

4. Edwin S. Corwin, *The President: Office and Powers, 1787–1957* (New York: New York University Press, 1957), 171.

5. Schlesinger, *Imperial Presidency*, 291.

6. Robert A. Diamond and Patricia Ann O'Conner, eds., *Guide to Congress* (Washington, DC: Congressional Quarterly, 1976), 279.

7. Richard Lacayo, "A Reluctant Go Ahead," *Time*, January 21, 1991, 32.

8. *Use of Force Resolution*, 107th Cong., 1st sess., September 14, 2001, thomas.loc .gov/cgi-bin/query/z?c107:S.J.RES.23.ENR:.

9. The attacks against Afghanistan are discussed in Bob Woodward, *Bush at War* (Simon & Schuster, 2002).

10. The text of UN Security Council Resolution 1441, November 8, 2002, is available at daccessdds.un.org/doc/UNDOC/GEN/N02/682/26/PDF/N0268226.pdf?OpenElement.

11. For an analysis of the preinvasion planning for the war in Iraq as well as postwar re-construction, see Bob Woodward, *Plan of Attack* (New York: Simon & Schuster, 2004), and Woodward, *State of Denial: Bush at War Part III* (New York: Simon & Schuster, 2006).

12. For a thoughtful assessment of the expansion of presidential power in the George W. Bush administration after September 11, 2001, see Andrew Rudalevige, *The New Imperial Presidency: Renewing Presidential Power after Watergate* (University of Michigan Press: Ann Arbor, MI, 2005).

13. Clinton Rossiter, *The American Presidency* (New York: New American Library, 1960), 14–40.

14. Keith C. Clark and Laurence J. Legere, eds., *The President and the Management of National Security* (New York: Praeger, 1969), 19.

15. George Reedy, quoted in Doris Kearns, *Lyndon Johnson and the American Dream* (New York: New American Library, 1977), 339.

16. Richard E. Neustadt, "Approaches to Staffing the Presidency," in *The Presidential Advisory System*, ed. Thomas E. Cronin and Sanford D. Greenberg (New York: Harper & Row, 1969), 15.

17. Ibid., 19.

18. Starting with Henry Kissinger in 1969, "special" was dropped from the title.

19. Discussion of the Hoover staffing arrangements is from Henry T. Nash, *American Foreign Policy: Response to a Sense of Threat* (Dorsey Press: Homewood, IL, 1973), 113. The George W. Bush White House figure is from George C. Edwards III and Stephen J. Wayne, *Presidential Leadership: Politics and Policy Making*, 7th ed. (Florence: KY: Thomson-Wadsworth, 2006), 205. Comments on the proliferation of presidential assistants are derived from Harold Seidman, *Politics, Position, and Power: The Dynamics of Federal Organization* (New York: Oxford University Press, 1970), 213.

20. The functions of the Office of Civil and Defense Mobilization were absorbed in the late 1960s by the director of the Office of Emergency Preparedness until 1974, when the latter office was abolished and replaced by the Federal Emergency Management Agency.

21. Seidman, *Politics, Position, and Power*, 165. For current information on the National Security Council, see the council's Web site at www.whitehouse.gov/nsc.

22. Seidman, *Politics, Position, and Power*, 91.

23. For a discussion of presidential modus operandi, see Andrew J. Goodpaster, "Four Presidents and the Conduct of National Security Affairs: Impressions and Highlights," *Journal of International Relations* 2:2 (Spring 1977): 27–29.

24. Dwight D. Eisenhower, "The Central Role of the President in the Conduct of Security Affairs," in *Issues of National Security in the 1970s*, ed. Amos Jordan (New York: Praeger, 1967), 214.

25. For a discussion of the differences in national security policy making between Eisenhower and Kennedy, see Meena Bose, *Shaping and Signaling Presidential Policy: The National Security Decision Making of Eisenhower and Kennedy* (College Station, TX: Texas A&M University Press, 1998).

26. John F. Kennedy, quoted in Clark and Legere, *President and Management of National Security*, 70.

27. For detailed views of the Johnson presidency, see Kearns, *Lyndon Johnson*.

28. Ibid., 294.

29. Henry A. Kissinger, *The White House Years* (Boston: Little, Brown, 1979), 30.

30. The so-called "Iran-Contra" affair was the conflagration of two covert policies, one in which the U.S. government sold weapons to Iran and another in which the U.S. government supported Contra rebels, which opposed the government in Nicaragua. The two operations became linked when an NSC staff member, Marine Lt. Col. Oliver North, developed a plan to use profits from the arms sales to Iran in support of the Contras. The combination of these policies was not authorized by President Reagan and, when it was discovered, led to the firing of North, the resignation of the National Security Advisor, Admiral John Poindexter, and an investigation of the entire operation.

31. *Report of the President's Special Review Board* (Washington, DC: U.S. Government Printing Office, 1987), 11–15.

32. Bob Woodward, *The Commanders* (New York: Simon & Schuster, 1991), 41.

33. "History of the NSC, 1947–1997," August 1997 (Washington, DC: Office of the Historian, U.S. Department of State), www.whitehouse.gov/nsc/history.html.

34. Ibid.

35. Ivo H. Daalder and I. M. Destler, moderators, "The Clinton Administration National Security Council," *The National Security Project: Oral History Roundtables* (Washington, DC: Brookings Institution Press, September 27, 2000), esp. 19–20.

36. Fred I. Greenstein and Richard H. Immerman, "Effective National Security Advising: Recovering the Eisenhower Legacy," *Political Science Quarterly* 115, no. 3 (2000): 335.

37. For illustrations of how Rice ran NSC staff meetings, see Woodward, *Bush at War*, 85–91, 242–246.

38. For a detailed discussion of the functions and organizational culture of the Department of State, see Nash, *American Foreign Policy*, 65–99.

39. Kissinger, *White House Years*, 26–31.

40. Woodward, *Commanders*, and U.S. News and World Report, *Triumph Without Victory* (New York: Warner Books, 1992) provide the best descriptions of Bush's decisionmaking style.

41. Woodward discusses Powell's role in the decision making leading to the 2003 war in Iraq in *Plan of Attack*, 78–80.

42. Nash, *American Foreign Policy*, 71–72. See also Roger Hilsman, *The Politics of Policy Making in Defense and Foreign Affairs* (New York: Harper & Row, 1971), 47–48.

43. I. M. Destler, *Presidents, Bureaucrats, and Foreign Policy* (Princeton, NJ: Princeton University Press, 1972), 156–160.

44. Nash, *American Foreign Policy*, 91.

45. Ibid., 74.

46. Alain C. Enthoven and K. Wayne Smith, *How Much Is Enough?* (New York: Harper & Row, 1971), 3.

47. For example, see *Defense Organization: The Need for Change*, Staff Report to the Committee on Armed Services, United States Senate, 99th Cong., 1st sess., 1985, Senate Report 99-86, 422–423.

48. Henry Stimson, quoted in Miles Copeland, *Without Cloak or Dagger* (New York: Simon & Schuster, 1974), 36.

49. Nash, *American Foreign Policy*, 146–149. See also Marjorie Hunter, "Carter Won't Oppose CIA Cost Disclosure," *New York Times*, April 28, 1977, A-17.

50. For information on the Office of the Director of National Intelligence, see its Web site at www.dni.gov.

51. Theodore C. Sorensen, *Decision Making in the White House* (New York: Columbia University Press, 1963), 29–30.

52. For a detailed discussion of the origins of legislative central clearance, see Richard E. Neustadt, "Presidency and Legislation: The Growth of Central Clearance," *American Political Science Review* 48, no. 1 (1954): 641–671.

53. Richard E. Neustadt, *Presidential Power* (New York: New American Library, 1960), 42.

54. Roosevelt as quoted in by Arthur M. Schlesinger Jr., "State of the Vision Thing," *Los Angeles Times*, January 21, 2004.

55. Ibid., 53, 47.

56. Aaron Wildavsky, "The Two Presidencies," *Trans-Action* 4, no. 2 (December 1966), reprinted in *Perspectives on the Presidency*, ed. Wildavsky (Boston: Little, Brown and Company, 1975).

57. Kearns, *Lyndon Johnson*, 258–259.

58. U.S. News & World Report, *Triumph Without Victory*, 188, 206, 207.

59. James Schlesinger, "Fragmentation and Hubris: A Shaky Basis for American Leadership," *National Interest*, no. 49 (Fall 1997): 3-9 .

60. Theodore C. Sorensen, *Kennedy* (New York: Harper and Rowe, 1965), 296–297.

Chapter 5: Congress

1. Alexander Hamilton, "Federalist #75," Para. 3, www.yale.edu/lawweb/avalon/federal/fed75.htm.

2. George Washington, "The Writings of George Washington from the Original Manuscript Sources, 1745–1799," Para. 1, http://press-pubs.uchicago.edu/founders/documents/v1ch7s6.html.

3. Charles A. Stevenson, *Warriors and Politicians: U.S. Civil-Military Relations under Stress* (New York: Routledge, 2006), 6. Stevenson further writes, "In practice, the law now allows money for weapons procurement and research and development to be spent over a longer period of years."

4. *Congressional Record*, October 14, 1993, S13432, quoted in Barbara Hinckley, *Less Than Meets the Eye: Foreign Policy Making and the Myth of the Assertive Congress* (Chicago: University of Chicago Press, 1994), 199.

5. Richard F. Fenno, *Congressmen in Committees* (Boston: Little, Brown, 1973).

6. Roger H. Davidson and Walter J. Oleszek, *Congress and Its Members* (Washington: CQ Press 2006), 454.

7. Alexander Hamilton, "Federalist #70," Para. 7, www.yale.edu/lawweb/avalon/federal/fed70.htm.

8. Andrew Rudalevige, *The New Imperial Presidency* (Ann Arbor: University of Michigan Press, 2006), 30–32.

9. John Lehman, *Making War: The 200-Year-Old Battle between the President and Congress Over How America Goes to War* (New York: Charles Scribner's Sons, 1992), 66.

10. Cecil V. Crabb, Glenn J. Antizzo, and Leila E. Sarieddine, *Congress and the Foreign Policy Process* (Baton Rouge: Louisiana State University Press, 2000), 157–192.

11. Lehman, *Making War*, 72.

12. Davidson and Oleszek, *Congress and Its Members*, 453.

13. Charles B. Brownson, ed., *Congressional Staff Directory* (Mount Vernon, VA: Congressional Staff Directory, 1980), 579.

14. Blair S. Williams, "What's the Cavalry to Do with Economics? The Political and Economic Dynamics of Military Base Closures" (West Point, NY: U.S. Military Academy, Department of Social Sciences, working paper, 2006).

15. Mary T. Tyszkiewicz and Stephen Daggett, *A Defense Budget Primer*, U.S. Library of Congress, Congressional Research Service, CRS Report RL30002.

16. Williams, working paper.

17. Jacob B. Javits, "Congress and Foreign Relations: The Taiwan Relations Act," *Foreign Affairs* 60, no. 1 (Fall 1981): 54.

18. Davidson and Oleszek, *Congress and Its Members*, 454.

19. Paul F. Boller, *Congressional Anecdotes* (New York: Oxford University Press, 1991), 287.

20. U.S. Constitution, art. 4, sec. 3.

21. U.S. Constitution, art. 1, sec. 8.

22. Kenneth R. Mayer, "Closing Military Bases (Finally): Solving Collective Dilemmas Through Delegation," *Legislative Studies Quarterly* 20, no. 3 (1995): 393–416.

23. John Donnelly, "Troop Spending Trumps New Systems," *CQ Weekly*, May 1, 2006, 1171.

24. Ivan Eland, "Bush versus the Defense Establishment?" *Issues in Science and Technology* 17, no. 4 (2001), www.issues.org/17.4/index.html.

25. John Donnelly, "Defense Authorization Carries a Lot of Constituent Service from Home Districts," *CQ Today*, April 27, 2006, 1.

26. Lawrence Korb, *The Korb Report: A Realistic Defense for America*, Business Leaders for Sensible Priorities (2001), 7–8.

27. Dan Morgan, "Congress Backs Pentagon Budget Heavy on Future Weapons," *Washington Post*, June 11, 2004, A-23.

28. George Cahlink, "2006 Legislative Summary: Defense Appropriations," *CQ Weekly*, December 18, 2006, 3331.

29. Richard F. Grimmett, "Conventional Arms Transfers to Developing Nations, 1996–2003," U.S. Library of Congress, Congressional Research Service, CRS Report RL32547, 2004.

30. Directorate of Defense Trade Controls, Bureau of Political-Military Affairs, U.S. Department of State, *Defense Trade Controls Overview 2006*.

31. William D. Hartung, "Corporate Welfare for Weapons Makers: The Hidden Costs of Spending on Defense and Foreign Aid" (Washington, DC: CATO Institute in Policy Analysis, 1999), 5, www.cato.org/pubs/pas/pa350.pdf.

32. Powerful groups include the National Guard Association, the Association of the U.S. Army, and the Military Officers Association of America.

33. Williams, working paper.

34. Charles Henning, "The FY2007 National Defense Authorization Act: Selected Military Personnel Policy Issues," U.S. Library of Congress, Congressional Research Service, CRS Report RL33571, 2006.

35. David R. Mayhew, *Congress: The Electoral Connection* (New Haven, CT: Yale University Press, 1974), 61–62.

36. Amy B. Zegart, *Flawed by Design: The Evolution of the CIA, JCS, and NSC* (Stanford: Stanford University Press, 1999), 145.

37. For more, see Zegart, and also see James R. Locher, *Victory on the Potomac* (College Station: Texas A&M Press, 2002).

38. Office of Management and Budget, Budget of the U.S. Government: Summary Tables FY2008, www.whitehouse.gov/omb/budget/fy2008/summarytables.html.

39. Office of Management and Budget, Budget of the U.S. Government: Historical Tables FY2005, www.gpoaccess.gov/usbudget/fy05/hist.html.

40. National Defense Authorization Act, Public Law 104-201, 104th Cong, 2nd Sess. (September 23, 1996) section 923.

41. National Defense Authorization Act for Fiscal Year 2000, Public Law 106-65, 106th Cong, 1st Sess. (October 5, 1999) section 901.

42. *Congressional Record*, May 19, 1997, S4673.

43. See, for example, Andrew Krepinevich, "The Quadrennial Defense Review," testimony before Congress, Center for Strategic and Budgetary Assessments, March 14, 2006, www.csbaonline.org/4Publications/PubLibrary/T.20060314.QDRTestimony/T.20060314 .QDRTestimony.pdf.

44. U.S. Constitution, art. 2, sec. 2.

45. U.S. Senate, "Treaties," www.senate.gov/artandhistory/history/common/briefing/ Treaties.htm.

46. Jennifer Elsea, "U.S. Policy Regarding the International Criminal Court," U.S. Library of Congress, Congressional Research Service, CRS Report RL31495, 2006, 7.

47. Colum Lynch, "Congress Seeks to Curb International Court," *Washington Post*, November 26, 2004, A-2.

48. Eric S. Kraus and Mike O. Lacy, "Utilitarian vs. Humanitarian: The Battle over the Law of War," *Parameters* 32, no. 2 (Summer 2002): 83.

49. Richard F. Grimmett, *War Powers Resolution after Thirty Years*, U.S. Library of Congress, Congressional Research Service, CRS Report RL32267, 2004, 42–45.

50. U.S. Constitution, art. 1, sec. 8.

51. U.S. Constitution, art. 2, sec. 2.

52. Grimmett, *War Powers Resolution after Thirty Years*, 56–75.

53. Roger Simon, "Feingold Ups The Ante On Iraq Funding" *CBS News*, January 30, 2007, www.cbsnews.com/stories/2007/01/30/politics/main2413236.shtml.

54. Louis Fisher and David Gray Adler, "The War Powers Resolution: Time to Say Goodbye," *Political Science Quarterly* 113: 1 (Spring 1998): 1–20.

55. *War Powers Resolution*, Public Law 93-148, 93rd Cong., 1st sess. (November 7, 1973), section 4.

56. Fisher and Adler, "The War Powers Resolution," 1–10.

57. Louis Fisher, "Congressional Checks on Military Initiatives," *Political Science Quarterly* 109, no. 4 (1995): 749.

58. Grimmett, *War Powers Resolution after Thirty Years*, summary.

59. Grimmett, *War Powers Resolution after Thirty Years*, 12–13.

60. I. M. Destler, "Dateline Washington: Congress as Boss?" *Foreign Policy* 42 (Spring 1981): 168–169.

61. Lawrence Freedman and Efraim Karsh, "How Kuwait Was Won; Strategy in the Gulf War," *International Security* 16, no. 2 (Autumn 1991): 6–8.

62. Rudalevige, *The New Imperial Presidency*, 194–195.

63. Ryan C. Hendrickson, "War Powers, Bosnia, and the 104th Congress," *Political Science Quarterly* 113, no. 2 (Summer 1998): 241–258.

64. Davidson and Oleszek, *Congress and Its Members*, 346–347.

65. Nancy Pelosi, "Benchmarks Without Deadlines Are Just Words; After Four Years, Words Are Not Enough," remarks on the House floor, March 23, 2007, www.house .gov/pelosi/press/releases/March07/Supplemental.html.

Chapter 6: Homeland Security

1. U.S. Constitution, art. 1, sec. 8.

2. While *homeland security* could be broadly construed to include such issue areas as global warming, fossil fuel scarcity, or even economic opportunity and social justice, the term was narrowly defined by the July 2002 *National Strategy for Homeland Security* as "a concerted national effort to prevent terrorist attacks within the United States, reduce America's vulnerability to terrorism, and minimize the damage and recover from attacks that do occur." This chapter is in line with the more focused view, although it also considers natural and man-made disasters and possible attacks by nation-states as integral aspects of homeland security.

3. See Mark A. Sauter and James J. Carafano, *Homeland Security: A Complete Guide to Understanding, Preventing, and Surviving Terrorism* (New York: McGraw-Hill, 2005), 3–19, for a brief overview of the history of U.S. homeland security efforts.

4. United States Commission on National Security/21st Century, "New World Coming: American Security in the 21st Century" (September 1999), "Seeking a National Strategy: A Concert for Preserving Security and Promoting Freedom" (April 2000), and "Road Map for National Security: Imperative for Change" (February 2001); Advisory Panel to Assess Domestic Response Capabilities for Terrorism Involving Weapons of Mass Destruction, "Assessing the Threat" (December 1999), and "Toward a National Strategy for Combating Terrorism" (December 2000).

5. George W. Bush, The White House, "Message to the Congress of the United States," Office of the Press Secretary, June 18, 2002, www.whitehouse.gov/news/releases/2002/06/20020618-5.html.

6. Sauter and Carafano, *Homeland Security*, 53.

7. For an example of the debate over Patriot Act provisions, see Alice Fisher, "The PATRIOT Act Has Helped Prevent Terrorist Attacks," and Nancy Chang, "The PATRIOT Act Has Undermined Civil Liberties," in *Homeland Security*, ed. James D. Torr (San Diego: Greenhaven Press, 2004), 34–42 and 43–53, respectively.

8. Henry H. Willis et al., *Estimating Terrorism Risk* (Santa Monica, CA: RAND, 2005). The same logic is applicable to assessing risk from natural disasters.

9. See Government Accountability Office, "Review of Studies of the Economic Impact of the September 11, 2001, Terrorist Attacks on the World Trade Center" (GAO-02-700R; Washington, DC: Government Accountability Office, May 2002), for a discussion of factors involved in estimating costs of the 9/11 attacks on the World Trade Center.

10. Congressional Research Service, "Risk Management and Critical Infrastructure Protection: Assessing, Integrating, and Managing Threats, Vulnerabilities, and Consequences," September 2, 2004.

11. George W. Bush, *The National Security Strategy of the United States of America* (Washington, DC: The White House, 2002).

12. On preemption, see Karl P. Mueller et al. *Striking First: Preemptive and Preventive Attack in U.S. National Security Policy* (Santa Monica, CA: RAND, 2006).

13. On collective action problems and "public goods" (such as homeland security), see Mancur Olson, *The Logic of Collective Action: Public Goods and the Theory of Groups* (Cambridge, MA: Harvard University Press, 1965). Olson argues that in most cases, groups of "rational, self-interested individuals will not act to achieve their common or group interests."

14. Information on grant programs is from Peter Eisinger, "Imperfect Federalism: The Intergovernmental Partnership for Homeland Security," *Public Administration Review* 66, no. 4 (July/August 2006): 537–545. "The politics of distribution tend to prevail over allocation rules governed by vulnerability assessments and the presence of critical infrastructure."

15. Samuel P. Huntington, "American Ideals Versus American Institutions," in *American Foreign Policy: Theoretical Essays*, 2nd ed., ed. G. John Ikenberry (New York: HarperCollins College Publishers, 1996), 251–283. Huntington focuses on foreign policy institutions, but his discussion is clearly applicable to homeland security as well.

16. For example, see the 9/11 Public Discourse Project, "Final Report on 9/11 Commission Recommendations," December 5, 2005, www.9-11pdp.org/press/2005-12-05_report.pdf; Stephen E. Flynn, "The Neglected Home Front," *Foreign Affairs* 83, no. 5 (September/October 2004), 20–33; and Michael O'Hanlon and Jeremy Shapiro, "Introduction," in *Protecting the Homeland 2006/2007*, ed. Michael d'Arcy et al. (Washington, DC: Brookings Institution Press, 2006), 1–16.

17. A summary of these scenarios, which range from natural disasters to disease outbreaks to various types of terrorist attacks, is available at www.globalsecurity.org/security/library/report/2004/hsc-planning-scenarios-jul04_exec-sum.pdf.

18. For an example of this line of thinking, see Graham Allison, "The Will to Prevent," *Harvard International Review* 28, no. 3 (Fall 2006): 50–55.

19. For additional information on the threat posed by pandemic influenza, see U.S. Department of Health and Human Services pandemic flu Web site, www.pandemicflu.gov.

20. Scott D. Holmberg et al., "State Plans for Containment of Pandemic Influenza," *Emerging Infectious Diseases,* 12, no. 9 (September 2006): 1414–1417.

21. Hospital capacity is an example of an area where variation in planning approaches could be damaging to the effectiveness of pandemic influenza response. The financial incentive for hospitals is generally to increase efficiency by reducing excess capacity (currently, capacity is approximately nine hundred fifty thousand staffed beds in the United States), but excess capacity may be a key requirement in case of pandemic influenza or a mass-casualty attack or disaster. Without consistent across-the-board guidance tied to funding, hospitals' approaches to maintaining surge capacity are likely to be uneven.

22. On concerns with broadening the military's domestic role, see Richard H. Kohn, "Using the Military at Home: Yesterday, Today, and Tomorrow," *Chicago Journal of International Law* 4, no. 1 (Spring 2003): 165–192.

23. Homeland defense is defined by the *Department of Defense Strategy for Homeland Defense and Civil Support* as "the protection of U.S. sovereignty, territory, domestic population, and critical defense infrastructure against external threats and aggression or other threats as directed by the President." This definition includes some overlap with homeland security, and the distinction is not always clean. For example, the case of interdicting a terrorist-operated ship intending to attack a port could be seen as both preventing a terrorist attack (homeland security) and protecting U.S. territory and people against external threats and aggression (homeland defense). From a policy perspective, the critical challenge is determining whether the military or another agency (such as the Coast Guard, which is part of the DHS) will have the lead responsibility for particular types of actions to facilitate effective planning.

24. The act is extended by DoD policy to apply to the Department of the Navy (which includes the U.S. Marine Corps) as well. No one has ever been prosecuted under the act. On the history of the act and common misinterpretations, see John R. Brinkerhoff, "The Posse Comitatus Act and Homeland Security," *Journal of Homeland Security* (February 2002), www.homelandsecurity.org/newjournal/articles/brinkerhoffpossecomitatus.htm.

25. The 2006 change to the Insurrection Act expanded the circumstances in which the president may employ the active Armed Forces or the National Guard in federal service to restore order and enforce the law, including situations when, as a result of "natural disaster, epidemic, or other serious public health emergency, terrorist attack or incident, or other condition," "domestic violence has occurred to such an extent that the constituted authorities of the State or possession are incapable of maintaining public order." This broadens the original Insurrection Act, which listed "insurrection, domestic violence, unlawful combination, or conspiracy" as the factors that could justify presidential employment of Title 10 forces in a law enforcement role.

26. See James Q. Wilson, *Bureaucracy: What Government Agencies Do and Why They Do It* (New York: Basic Books, 1989), for a discussion of the causes of organizational action and the challenges of interorganizational cooperation.

27. For example, see the recommendations in *The Federal Response to Hurricane Katrina: Lessons Learned* (Washington, DC: The White House, February 2006).

Chapter 7: Intelligence and National Security

1. See Alexander Hamilton, *The Federalist No. 75*, in *Great Books of the Western World*, ed. Robert M. Hutchins, vol. 43 (Chicago: Encyclopedia Britannica, 1952).

2. See John Jay, *The Federalist No. 64*, in *Great Books of the Western World*, ed. Robert M. Hutchins, vol. 43 (Chicago: Encyclopedia Britannica, 1952).

3. Mark M. Lowenthal, *Intelligence: From Secrets to Policy*, 3rd ed. (Washington, DC: CQ Press, 2006), 1–2.

4. Abram N. Shulsky and Gary L. Schmitt, *Silent Warfare: Understanding the World of Intelligence*, 3rd ed. (Washington, DC: Brassey's, 2002), 1.

5. Lowenthal, *Intelligence*, 6.

6. Melanie M. H. Gutjahr, ed., *The Intelligence Archipelago: The Community's Struggle to Reform in the Globalized Era* (Washington, DC: Center for Strategic Intelligence Research, 2005), 8.

7. Ibid.

8. Frank J. Cilluffo, Ronald A. Marks, and George C. Salmoiraghi, "The Use and Limits of U.S. Intelligence," *Washington Quarterly* 25, no. 1 (2002): 61.

9. Lowenthal, *Intelligence*, 7.

10. Bob Woodward, *The Commanders* (New York: Simon & Schuster, 1991), 248.

11. Robert M. Clark, *Intelligence Analysis: A Target-Centric Approach* (Washington, DC: CQ Press, 2004), 15.

12. Lowenthal, *Intelligence*, 2.

13. Russell E. Travers, "Failures, Fallacies and Fixes: Posturing Intelligence for the Challenges of Globalization," in *The Intelligence Archipelago: The Community's Struggle to Reform in the Globalized Era*, ed. Melanie M. H. Gutjahr (Washington, DC: Center for Strategic Intelligence Research, 2005), xiii.

14. Ibid.

15. United States Intelligence Community, "Collection," www.intelligence.gov/2-business_cycle2.shtml.

16. Joseph S. Nye, Jr., *Soft Power: The Means to Success in World Politics* (New York: Public Affairs, 2004), 105–106.

17. United States Intelligence Community, "Collection," www.intelligence.gov/2-business_cycle2.shtml.

18. Cilluffo, Marks, and Salmoiraghi, "The Use and Limits of U.S. Intelligence," 68.

19. See, for example, Jarrett M. Brachman and William McCants, *Stealing Al-Qa'ida's Playbook* (West Point: Combating Terrorism Center, U.S. Military Academy, February 2006), ctc.usma.edu/publications/publications.asp.

20. Dan Elkins, *Managing Intelligence Resources* (Alexandria, VA: DWE Press, 2004), 1–2.

21. Cilluffo, Marks, and Salmoiraghi, "The Use and Limits of U.S. Intelligence," 68.

22. United States Intelligence Community, "Collection," www.intelligence.gov/2-business_cycle2.shtml.

23. Elkins, *Managing Intelligence Resources*, 1–2.

24. Roger Z. George and Robert D. Kline, *Intelligence and the National Security Strategist: Enduring Issues and Challenges* (Washington, DC: NDU Press, 2004), 148.

25. United States Intelligence Community, "Collection," www.intelligence.gov/2-business_cycle2.shtml.

26. Ibid.

27. Cilluffo, Marks, and Salmoiraghi, "The Use and Limits of U.S. Intelligence," 68.

28. United States Intelligence Community, "Collection," www.intelligence.gov/2-business_cycle2.shtml.

29. Ibid.

30. United States Intelligence Community, "Processing and Exploitation," www.intelligence.gov/2-business_cycle3.shtml.

31. Cilluffo, Marks, and Salmoiraghi, "The Use and Limits of U.S. Intelligence," 70.

32. United States Intelligence Community, "Processing and Exploitation," www.intelligence.gov/2-business_cycle3.shtml.

33. Ibid.

34. Cilluffo, Marks, and Salmoiraghi, "The Use and Limits of U.S. Intelligence," 70.

35. Robert M. Clark, *Intelligence Analysis: A Target-Centric Approach*, 2nd ed. (Washington, DC: CQ Press, 2007), 3–4.

36. Nye, *Soft Power*, 105–106.

37. Ibid.

38. Cilluffo, Marks, and Salmoiraghi, "The Use and Limits of U.S. Intelligence," 70.

39. Senate Select Committee on Intelligence, *Hearings on the Nomination of Mike McConnell to Be Director of National Intelligence*, 110th Cong., 1st sess., February 1, 2007, 8.

40. Lowenthal, *Intelligence*, 177.

41. Tyrus G. Fain, ed., *The Intelligence Community*, Public Document Series (New York: Bowker, 1977), 87.

42. Assistant Director of Central Intelligence for Analysis and Production, "The Role of Intelligence," (speech at the IC Colloquium, New Mexico State University, New Mexico, September 15, 2003).

43. Clark, *Intelligence Analysis*, 16.

44. Assistant Director of Central Intelligence for Analysis and Production, "The Role of Intelligence."

45. Martin Petersen, in *Intelligence and the National Security Strategist*, 427.

46. Assistant Director of Central Intelligence for Analysis and Production, "The Role of Intelligence."

47. Molly Moore, "Schwarzkopf: War Intelligence Flawed," *Washington Post*, June 13, 1991, A-1.

48. Assistant Director of Central Intelligence for Analysis and Production, "The Role of Intelligence."

49. Ibid.

50. See Frederic F. Manget, "Another System of Oversight: Intelligence and the Rise of Judicial Intervention," *Studies in Intelligence* 39, no. 5 (1996), www.CIA.gov/library/center-for-the-study-of-intelligence/csi-publications/csi-studies/studies/96unclass/magnet.htm.

51. Robin Wright, "Efforts to Halt Arms Race Called Limited," *Los Angeles Times*, June 21, 1992, A-2.

52. For a first-hand account, see Gary C. Schroen, *First In: An Insider's Account of How the CIA Spearheaded the War on Terror in Afghanistan* (New York: Presidio Press, 2005).

53. *National Security Act of 1947*, Public Law 253, 80th Cong., 1st sess. (July 26, 1947), Section 103.

54. See David F. Rudgers, "The Origins of Covert Action" *Journal of Contemporary History* 35, no. 2 (April 2000): 249–262.

55. George Lardner, "Restrictions Approved on Covert Action," *Washington Post*, August 16, 1991, A-22.

56. Demetri Sevastopulo and Patti Waldmeir, "Ruling on Secret Prisons May Affect Bush 'War on Terror.'" *Financial Times*, October 8, 2007, 10.

57. Roy Godson, ed., *Intelligence Requirements for the 1980s: Elements of Intelligence* (Washington, DC: National Strategy Information Center, 1983), 50.

58. Richard B. Schmitt, "FBI has some explaining to do; Senators question the bureau's director about abuses of power," *Los Angeles Times*, March 28, 2007, A-12.

59. United States Intelligence Community, "Definition of the Intelligence Community (IC)," www.intelligence.gov/1-definition.shtml.

60. The 9/11 Commision, *The 9/11 Commission Report*, 411, www.9-11commission.gov/report/911Report.pdf.

61. George W. Bush, "President Signs Intelligence Reform and Terrorism Prevention Act," Office of the Press Secretary, December 17, 2004, www.whitehouse.gov/news/releases/2004/12/20041217-1.html.

62. See, for example, the DNI's "joint duty" initiative, Office of the Director of National Intelligence, *United States Intelligence Community 100 Day Plan for Integration and Collaboration*, April 2007, 3.

63. Senate Select Committee on Intelligence, "The Nomination of Mike McConnell to be Director of National Intelligence," 110th Cong, 1st Sess., February 1, 2007, 3.

64. Department of Defense Directive 5143.01, SUBJECT: Undersecretary of Defense for Intelligence (USD(I)), November 23, 2005, fas.org/irp/doddir/dod/d5143_01.pdf.

65. National Security Agency/Central Security Service, "National Asset," www.nsa.gov/coremsgs/corem00001.cfm.

66. Office of the Director of National Intelligence (ODNI), *An Overview of the United States Intelligence Community*, 2007, 19, www.dni.gov/who_what/061222_DNIHandbook_Final.pdf.

67. Elkins, *Managing Intelligence Resources*, 2–4.

68. ODNI, *An Overview of the United States Intelligence Community*, 2007, 15.

69. Ibid.

70. Ibid., 14.

71. Ibid.

72. Ibid., 13.

73. Elaine Sciolino, "Conferees Agree to Curb President on Covert Action," *New York Times*, July 27, 1991, A1.

74. John Hedley, *Checklist for the Future of Intelligence* (Washington, DC: Institute for the Study of Diplomacy, 1995).

75. *The 9/11 Commission Report*, xv.

76. CSIS, Section 1061, PL 108-458, www.csis.org/media/csis/pubs/041201_irtpa_overview.pdf.

77. Privacy and Civil Liberties Oversight Board, "About the Board," www.white house.gov/privacyboard/.

78. U.S. Courts, "Cases Related to Intelligence Surveillance," www.uscourts.gov/outreach/topics/fisa/cases.html.

79. Federal Judicial Center, "Foreign Intelligence Surveillance Court," www.fjc.gov/history/home.nsf/page/fisc_bdy.

80. Van Wagenen, "Critics and Defenders," www.cia.gov/library/center-for-the-study-of-intelligence/csi-publications/csi-studies/studies/97unclass/wagenen.html.

81. Federal Judicial Center, "Foreign Intelligence Surveillance Court."

82. Ibid.

83. Manget, "Another System of Oversight."

84. "Final Report of the Commission on the Intelligence Capabilities of the United States Regarding Weapons of Mass Destruction," 3, www.fas.org/irp/offdocs/wmd comm.html; see also "Report of the Select Committee on Intelligence on the U.S. Intelligence Community's Prewar Intelligence Assessments on Iraq," July 7, 2004, www.gpo access.gov/serialset/creports/iraq.html.

85. Richard A. Best, Jr., "U.S. Intelligence and Policymaking: The Iraq Experience," CRS Report for Congress, updated December 2, 2005. One effort that does examine the role of policy makers in pre–Iraq War intelligence is Office of the Inspector General, "Review of Pre-Iraqi War Activities of the Office of the Undersecretary of Defense for Policy," Report No. 07-INTEL-04, Department of Defense, February 9, 2007.

Chapter 8: The Role of the Military in the Policy Process

1. U.S. Department of Defense, "Department of Defense 101," www.defenselink.mil/pubs/dod101/.

2. For a thorough discussion of the Framers' views and intense debate over the issue of standing armies, see Richard H. Kohn, ed., "The Constitution and National Security: The Intent of the Framers," in *The United States Military Under the Constitution of the United States, 1789–1989* (New York: New York University Press, 1991), 61-94.

3. Douglas Johnson and Steven Metz, *American Civil-Military Relations: New Issues, Enduring Problems,* April 24, 1995, www.strategicstudiesinstitute.army.mil/pdffiles/PUB 287.pdf.

4. Adapted from David F. Trask, "Democracy and Defense: Civilian Control of the Military in the United States," *Issues of Democracy* 2, no. 3 (July 1997), http://usinfo .state.gov/journals/itdhr/0797/ijde/trask.htm.

5. Forest Pogue, *Command Decisions,* 381, cited in Urs Schwarz, *American Strategy: A New Perspective* (New York: Doubleday, 1966), 48.

6. Walter Millis, *Arms and the State* (New York: Twentieth Century Fund, 1958), 124–132.

7. John C. Ries, *The Management of Defense* (Baltimore: Johns Hopkins University Press, 1964), 26–30.

8. Gerhard Loewenberg, "The Remaking of the German Party System," in *European Politics: A Reader,* ed. Mattei Dugan and Richard Rose (Boston: Little, Brown, 1971), 259–280.

9. Cordell Hull, *The Memoirs of Cordell Hull,* vol. 2 (New York: Macmillan, 1948), 1625–1713.

10. Hull opted out of political-military planning even before American direct involvement in World War II. During the war, he devoted a large part of his own and his department's energy and talents to planning the fledgling United Nations Organization.

11. Samuel P. Huntington, *The Common Defense* (New York: Columbia University Press, 1961), 35.

12. *National Security Act of 1947*, Public Law 253, 80th Cong., 1st sess. (July 26, 1947).

13. See Burton M. Sapin and Richard C. Snyder, *The Role of the Military in American Foreign Policy* (New York: Doubleday, 1954).

14. Lawrence M. Martin, "The American Decision to Rearm Germany," in *American Civil Military Decisions*, ed. Harold Stein (Birmingham: University of Alabama Press, 1963), 652–660.

15. Huntington, *Common Defense*, 54.

16. An excellent discussion surrounding the MacArthur case can be found in Millis, *Arms and the State*, 259–332.

17. Huntington, *Common Defense*, 380.

18. For a good discussion of the many postwar problems of interservice rivalry, see Ries, *Management of Defense*, 129–192. For a discussion of why defense issues frequently are resolved by political bargaining, see Huntington, *Common Defense*, 123–196.

19. See Alain C. Enthoven and K. Wayne Smith, *How Much Is Enough? Shaping the Defense Program, 1961–1969* (New York: Harper & Row, 1971).

20. See Leslie H. Gelb and Richard K. Betts, *The Irony of Vietnam: The System Worked* (Washington, DC: Brookings Institution Press, 1979).

21. See H. R. McMaster, *Dereliction of Duty: Lyndon Johnson, Robert McNamara, the Joint Chiefs of Staff, and the Lies That Led to Vietnam* (New York: HarperCollins, 1997).

22. Adam Yarmolinsky, *The Military Establishment* (New York: Perennial Library, 1973), 175–176.

23. Ibid., 138–140.

24. Richard K. Betts, "Are Civil-Military Relations Still a Problem" (unpublished paper prepared for Senior Conference 2007, West Point, New York, May 31–June 2, 2007), 14–15.

25. Christopher P. Gibson and Don M. Snider, "Civil-Military Relations and the Potential to Influence: A Look at the National Security Decision-Making Process," *Armed Forces and Society* 25, no. 2 (Winter 1999): 196.

26. Ibid., 207.

27. See Amos A. Jordan and William J. Taylor, Jr., "The Military Man in Academia," *Annals* 406 (March 1973): 129–145.

28. Gibson and Snider, "Civil-Military Relations and the Potential to Influence," 207.

29. See Bob Woodward, *The Commanders* (New York: Simon & Schuster, 1991); and U.S. News and World Report, *Triumph Without Victory* (New York: Warner Books, 1992).

30. Stephen Biddle, "Victory Misunderstood: What the Gulf War Tells About the Future of Conflict," *International Security* 21, no. 2 (Autumn 1996): 142.

31. See Mark Garrard, "War Termination in the Persian Gulf: Problems and Prospects," *Aerospace Power Journal* 15, no. 3 (Fall 2001): 42–50.

32. Eliot Cohen, "Supreme Command in the 21st Century," *Joint Force Quarterly* 31 (Summer 2002): 53–54.

33. Michael O'Hanlon, "Clinton's Strong Defense Legacy," *Foreign Affairs* 82, no. 6 (November 2003): 126–134.

34. Richard H. Kohn, "The Erosion of Civilian Control of the Military in the United States Today," *Naval War College Review* 55, no. 3 (2002): 10.

35. See Richard H. Kohn, "Out of Control: The Crisis in Civil-Military Relations," *National Interest* 35 (1994): 3–17; Russell F. Weigley, "The American Military and the Principle of Civilian Control from McClellan to Powell," *Journal of Military History* 57, no. 5 (1993): 27–58; and Eliot A. Cohen, "Playing Powell Politics," *Foreign Affairs* 74, no. 6 (1995): 102–110. This discussion of the 1990s "crisis" draws on Suzanne C. Nielsen, "Civil-Military Relations Theory and Military Effectiveness," *Public Administration and Management* 10, no. 2 (2005): 5.

36. Edward N. Luttwak, "Washington's Biggest Scandal," *Commentary* 97, no. 5 (1994): 29–33.

37. Deborah D. Avant, "Are the Reluctant Warriors Out of Control? Why the U.S. Military Is Averse to Responding to Post–Cold War Low-Level Threats," *Security Studies* 6, no. 2 (1996/1997): 51–90.

38. Deborah D. Avant, "Conflicting Indicators of 'Crisis' in American Civil-Military Relations," *Armed Forces and Society* 24, no. 3 (1998): 375–388; James Burk, "The Logic of Crisis and Civil-Military Relations Theory: A Comment on Desch, Feaver, and Dauber," *Armed Forces and Society* 24, no. 3 (1998): 455–462; and Kohn, "The Erosion of Civilian Control of the Military in the United States Today," 9.

39. Lyle J. Goldstein, "General John Shalikashvili and the Civil-Military Relations of Peacekeeping," *Armed Forces and Society* 26, no. 3 (2000): 387–411.

40. Colin L. Powell, "Why Generals Get Nervous," *New York Times*, October 8, 1992, A-35; Colin L. Powell, "U.S. Forces: Challenges Ahead," *Foreign Affairs* 71, no. 5 (Winter 1992): 3–41.

41. See, for example, Lieut. General Greg Newbold (Ret.), "Why Iraq Was a Mistake," *Time*, April 9, 2006, 42.

42. Mackubin Thomas Owens, "Rumsfeld, the Generals, and the State of U.S. Civil-Military Relations," *Naval War College Review* 59, no. 4 (Autumn 2006): 79.

43. See Risa A. Brooks, "Rethinking Objective Control: Political Activities of the Military in Democracies" (unpublished paper prepared for Senior Conference 2007, West Point, New York, May 31–June 2, 2007).

44. Peter D. Feaver and Richard H. Kohn, "The Gap: Soldiers, Civilians, and Their Mutual Misunderstandings," *National Interest* 61 (Fall 2000): 29.

45. Ibid., 31–32.

46. Ibid., 44.

47. See, for example, Michael C. Desch, "Bush and the Generals," *Foreign Affairs* 86, no. 3 (May/June 2007): 97–108. See also Richard B. Myers and Richard H. Kohn, Mackubin Thomas Owens, Lawrence J. Korb, and Michael C. Desch, "Salute and Disobey? The Civil-Military Balance, Before Iraq and After," *Foreign Affairs* 86, no. 5 (September/October 2007): 147–156.

48. Vernon Loeb and Thomas E. Ricks, "Rumsfeld's Style, Goals Strain Ties In Pentagon: 'Transformation' Effort Spawns Issues of Control," *Washington Post*, October 16, 2002, A-1.

49. Ibid.

50. See, for example, Al Kamen, "Donny, We Hardly Knew Ye," *Washington Post*, September 7, 2001, A-27. For a sympathetic view of Rumsfeld's difficulties, see David Ignatius, "Change Is Unwelcome in Washington, Rumsfeld Has Learned," *International Herald Tribune*, September 3, 2001, A-6.

51. See Donald H. Rumsfeld, "Transforming the Military," *Foreign Affairs* 81, no. 3 (May/June 2002): 20–32.

52. For an authoritative account, see Matthew Moten, "Several Hundred Thousand: Rumsfeld, Shinseki, and Civil-Military Tension" (unpublished paper prepared for Senior Conference 2007, West Point, New York, May 31–June 2, 2007).

53. Ibid., 13.

54. See Desch, "Bush and the Generals," 97–108

55. Owens, "Rumsfeld, the Generals, and the State of U.S. Civil-Military Relations," 78.

56. For accounts of the postwar planning effort, see Michael Gordon and Bernard Trainor, *Cobra II: The Inside Story of the Invasion and Occupation of Iraq* (New York: Pantheon, 2006); and Thomas Ricks, *Fiasco: The American Military Adventure in Iraq* (New York: Penguin Books, 2006).

57. James A. Baker III and Lee H. Hamilton, cochairs, *The Iraq Study Group Report*, December 2006, 52, http://bakerinstitute.org/files/pubs/iraqstudygroup_findings.pdf.

58. Ibid.

59. James R. Locher III, "Has It Worked? The Goldwater-Nichols Reorganization Act," *Naval War College Review* 54, no. 4 (Autumn 2001): 112.

60. Department of Defense Directive Number 5100.1, "SUBJECT: Functions of the Department of Defense and Its Major Components," August 1, 2002, 2, www.dtic.mil/whs/directives/corres/html/510001.htm.

61. These concerns are central to Samuel Huntington's classic text *The Soldier and the State*. See Samuel P. Huntington, *The Soldier and the State* (Cambridge, MA: Belknap Press of Harvard University Press, 1957), esp. 2–3.

62. Matthew Ridgway's "Farewell Letter" to Secretary of Defense Charles E. Wilson, June 27, 1955.

63. For a short summary and critique of the fusionist theory, see Huntington, *Common Defense*, 350–354.

64. John F. Kennedy, commencement address delivered at West Point, June 6, 1962.

65. Maxwell D. Taylor, address given at West Point, February 18, 1969.

66. Huntington, *Soldier and the State*, 83–85.

67. Morris Janowitz, *The Professional Soldier* (London: Collier-Macmillan Limited, 1960).

68. Ibid., 342.

69. Ibid., 342, 257–279.

70. Carl von Clausewitz, *On War*, as cited in Suzanne C. Nielsen, *Political Control Over the Use of Force* (Carlisle, PA: Strategic Studies Institute, May 2001), 17 and fn. 107; 44.

71. See Thomas L. McNaugher, "The Army and Operations Other Than War: Expanding Professional Jurisdiction," in *The Future of the Army Profession*, eds. Don M. Snider and Gayle L. Watkins (Boston: McGraw-Hill, 2002), 155–178.

72. John G. Kester, "The Future of the Joint Chiefs of Staff," *AEI Foreign Policy and Defense Review* 2, no. 1 (1980): 11.

73. From Richard H. Kohn, "Huntington's Challenge: Maximizing National Security and Civilian Control of the Military" (paper delivered at the U.S. Military Senior Conference, June 2007).

74. Marybeth Peterson Ulrich, "Infusing Normative Civil-Military Relations Principles in the Officer Corps," in *The Future of the Army Profession*, 2nd ed., ed. Don M. Snider and Lloyd J. Matthews (Boston: McGraw-Hill Custom Publishing, 2005), 663.

75. Gibson and Snider, "Civil-Military Relations and the Potential to Influence," 193–218.

76. Betts, "Are Civil-Military Relations Still a Problem?" 29–36.

77. See Gordon and Trainor, *Cobra II*; and Ricks, *Fiasco*.

78. The war colleges already have civilian students, so this would be a proposed expansion. See, for example, the "Vision of Mission" of the National Defense University at www.ndu.edu/info/mission.cfm.

Chapter 9: Planning, Budgeting, and Management

1. See Dwight D. Eisenhower, "The Chance for Peace," address delivered to the American Society of Newspaper Editors, April 16, 1953, contained in *Public Papers of the President.*

2. Allen Schick, *The Federal Budget: Politics, Policy, Process* (Washington, DC: Brookings Institution Press, 2000), 5.

3. George C. Edwards III, Martin P. Wattenberg, and Robert L. Lineberry, *Government in America: People, Politics, and Policy*, 12th ed. (New York: Pearson Longman, 2006), 453–460.

4. Ibid., 183.

5. Ibid., 272.

6. Ibid., 18.

7. Ibid., 19.

8. Mid-Session Review, Budget of the U.S. Government, Fiscal Year 2008, Office of Management and Budget, 32, www.whitehouse.gov/omb/budget/fy2008/pdf/08msr.pdf.

9. Among the most important of these were Arthur Smithies, *The Budgetary Process of the United States* (New York: McGraw-Hill, 1950); Maxwell Taylor, *The Uncertain Trumpet* (New York: Harper: 1959); and a series of articles for the RAND Corporation by David Novick, Charles Hitch, and Roland McKean.

10. See Taylor, *Uncertain Trumpet*, 123.

11. For a well-crafted criticism of PPBS, see Carl H. Builder, *Military Planning Today: Calculus or Charade?* (Santa Monica, CA: RAND Corporation, 1993).

12. See the Defense Acquisition University's "Planning, Programming, Budgeting, and Execution Process," http://akss.dau.mil/dag/Guidebook/IG_c1.2.asp.

13. Ibid.

14. Ibid.

15. Congressional Budget Office, *The Budget and Economic Outlook, Fiscal Years 2007–2016*, 2006, 69.

16. Jerry L. McCaffery and L. R. Jones, *Budgeting and Financial Management for National Defense* (Greenwich, CT: Information Age Publishing, 2004), 189.

17. Ibid., 183.

18. Stephen Daggett, "Military Operations: Precedents for Funding Contingency Operations in Regular or Supplemental Appropriations Bills," *CRS Report for Congress* (2006).

Chapter 10: Putting the Pieces Together: National Security Decision Making

1. Samuel P. Huntington, *The Common Defense* (New York: Columbia University Press, 1961), 1.

2. See, for example, Alan G. Whittaker, Frederick C. Smith, and Elizabeth McKune, *The National Security Policy Process: The National Security Council and Interagency System* (Washington, DC: National Defense University, 2005).

3. Richard E. Neustadt, *Presidential Power and the Modern Presidents*, 3d ed. (New York: Free Press, 1990), 8.

4. Ibid.

5. Robert L. Pfaltzgraff and Uri Ra'anan, *National Security Policy: The Decision-Making Process* (Hamden, CT: Archon Books, 1984), 291.

6. Neustadt, *Presidential Power*, 29.

7. Pfaltzgraff and Ra'anan, *National Security Policy*, 291.

8. Jeffrey H. Birnbaum, "Fat & Happy in D.C.," *Fortune* 143, no. 11 (May 28, 2001): 94–99. As of mid-2007, the most recent "Power 25" survey was in 2001.

9. Aaron Wildavsky, ed., *Perspectives on the Presidency* (Boston: Little, Brown, 1975), 448.

10. The 9/11 Commision, *The 9/11 Commission Report*, 400, www.9-11commission.gov/report/911Report.pdf.

11. Wildavsky, *Perspectives on the Presidency*, 448–449.

12. See Chris Hornbarger, "National Strategy: Building Capability for the Long Haul," in *Homeland Security and Terrorism: Readings and Interpretations*, eds. Russell Howard, James Forest, and Joanne Moore (New York: McGraw-Hill, 2005), 272–322.

13. Arthur H. Vandenberg, Jr., *The Private Papers of Senator Arthur Vandenberg*, (Boston: Houghton Mifflin, 1952) 552-553.

14. Richard Holbrooke, *To End a War* (New York: The Modern Library, 1999), 274.

15. Henry Kissinger, *Years of Upheaval* (Boston: Little, Brown and Company, 1982), 368.

16. Ibid.

17. Ernest R. May, *The Making of the Monroe Doctrine* (Cambridge, MA: Harvard University Press, 1975), *x*.

18. Pfaltzgraff and Ra'anan, *National Security Policy*, 292.

19. Roger B. Porter, *Presidential Decision Making: The Economic Policy Board* (Cambridge: Cambridge University Press, 1980), 10.

20. Neustadt, *Presidential Power*, 28.

21. Porter, *Presidential Decision Making*, 7.

22. Elliot Richardson, *The Creative Balance* (New York: Holt, Rinehart and Winston, 1976), 76.

23. Hugh Heclo, "Political Executives and the Washington Bureaucracy," *Political Science Quarterly* 92, no. 3 (Autumn 1977), 396.

24. I. M. Destler, *Presidents, Bureaucrats, and Foreign Policy* (Princeton, NJ: Princeton University Press, 1972), 56–57.

25. The best discussion of this can be found in James Q. Wilson, *Bureaucracy: What Government Agencies Do and Why They Do It* (New York: Basic Books, Inc., 1989), esp. 179–195.

26. Richard E. Neustadt and Graham T. Allison, "Afterword," in *Thirteen Days: A Memoir of the Cuban Missile Crisis*, Robert F. Kennedy (New York: W. W. Norton & Company, 1971), 133.

27. John Tower, Edmund Muskie, and Brent Scowcroft, *The Tower Commission Report: The Full Text of the President's Special Review Board* (New York: Bantam, Times Books, 1987), 79.

28. This section draws heavily from David Aidekman, "The National Security Act of 1947: Background, History, and Politics" (unpublished memorandum of the Harvard-Stanford Preventive Defense Project, October 26, 1999).

29. *National Security Act of 1947*, Public Law 253, 80th Cong., 1st sess. (July 26, 1947), section 402.

30. John E. Endicott, "The National Security Council: Formalized Coordination and Policy Planning," in Pfaltzgraff and Ra'anan, *National Security Policy*, 185.

31. Whittaker, Smith, and McKune, *National Security Policy Process*, 11.

32. See John P. Burke, *Becoming President: The Bush Transition, 2000–2003* (Boulder, CO: Lynne Rienner Publishers, 2004), 165.

33. While it is common convention to refer to the staff as the NSC, this chapter uses the terms NSC (the formal council) and NSC staff (the White House staff that supports it).

34. Porter, *Presidential Decision Making*, 213.

35. Whittaker, Smith, and McKune, *National Security Policy Process*, 16.

36. See John Deutch, Arnold Kanter, and Brent Scowcroft, with Christopher Hornbarger, "Strengthening the National Security Interagency Process," in *Keeping the Edge: Managing Defense for the Future*, ed. Ashton B. Carter and John P. White (Cambridge, MA: MIT Press, 2000), 265–283.

37. George W. Bush, *Executive Order 13228 of October 8, 2001: Establishing the Office of Homeland Security and the Homeland Security Council* (Washington, DC: Federal Register 66, no. 196, 2001).

38. Figure 10.2 depicts four of the five White House coordinating councils. Not shown is the Council on Environmental Quality (CEQ), created by Congress in 1969.

39. Whittaker, Smith, and McKune, *National Security Policy Process*, 23.

40. David J. Rothkopf, *Running the World: The Inside Story of the National Security Council and the Architects of American Power* (New York: Public Affairs, 2005), 267.

41. Whittaker, Smith, and McKune, *National Security Policy Process*, 12.

42. For 2001, see George W. Bush, *National Security Presidential Directive 1: Organization of the National Security Council System* (Washington, DC: White House, 2001). For 2005, see Whittaker, Smith, and McKune, *National Security Policy Process*, 13–14.

43. Sandy Berger, in "The Role of the National Security Advisor," moderated by Ivo H. Daalder and I. M. Destler (transcript of the Brookings Institution National Security Council Project: Oral History Roundtable, October 25, 1999), 79.

44. Federal Register, *Executive Orders Disposition Tables, 1937–Present* (Washington, DC: National Archives, 2007), www.archives.gov/federal-register/executive-orders/disposition.html.

45. See John P. Burke, "The Neutral/Honest Broker Role in Foreign-Policy Decision Making: A Reassessment," *Presidential Studies Quarterly* 35, no. 2 (June 2005): 233–235.

46. Kissinger, *Years of Upheaval*, 434.

47. Senator Henry M. Jackson, *The National Security Council: Jackson Subcommittee Papers on Policy-Making at the Presidential Level* (New York: Praeger Publishers, 1965), 19.

48. Philip Zelikow and Condoleezza Rice, *Germany Unified and Europe Transformed: A Study in Statecraft* (Cambridge, MA: Harvard University Press, 1997), 26–27.

49. Ibid., 25.

50. Ibid., 159–160.

51. Kissinger, *Years of Upheaval*, 996.

52. National Security Council, *Memorandum for the President's Files (Top Secret; declassified): Briefing of the White House Staff on the July 15 Announcement of the President's Trip to Peking* (Washington, DC: White House, 1971): 1.

53. Daalder and Destler, "Role of the National Security Advisor," 20–21.

54. See also Tower, Muskie, and Scowcroft, *Tower Commission Report*, 90.

55. Burke, "Neutral/Honest Broker Role," 242.

56. See Rothkopf, *Running the World*, 367, describing how Clinton National Security Advisor Tony Lake abandoned the honest broker role to pursue a solution in Bosnia in 1995.

57. John W. Kingdon, *Agendas, Alternatives, and Public Policies* (Boston: Little, Brown, 1984), 58. Porter, *Presidential Decision Making*, 27.

58. Patrick J. Haney, *Organizing for Foreign Policy Crises: Presidents, Advisers, and the Management of Decision Making* (Ann Arbor: University of Michigan Press, 1997), 128.

60. Neustadt and Allison, in *Thirteen Days*, Kennedy, 131.

61. Irving L. Janis, *Groupthink: Psychological Studies of Policy Decisions and Fiascoes* (Boston: Houghton Mifflin, 1972), 197–198.

62. See Richard Tanner Johnson, *Managing the White House: An Intimate Study of the Presidency* (New York: Harper & Row, 1974).

63. Ibid., 3.

64. Ibid., 236–237.

Chapter 11: Shaping the International Environment

1. Dean Acheson, as quoted in "Ends and Means," *Time*, December 18, 1964, www.time.com/time/magazine/article/0,9171,876455,00.html.

2. Virtually all scholars and national security policy makers acknowledge the four elements of power listed here, to the extent that they are frequently referred to as the "DIME" model. Especially since 9/11, additional elements of power have occasionally been added, which most often include law enforcement, intelligence, and financial elements of power. These areas are mentioned in Chapters 6, 7, and 12, respectively.

3. Harold Nicholson, *Diplomacy* (Oxford: Oxford University Press, 1939).

4. For a complete listing of the bilateral treaties in force between the United States and other countries, see the U.S. Department of State, "Bilateral Treaties and Other Agreements," www.state.gov/documents/organization/38406.pdf.

5. "Chapter I: Purposes and Principles," *Charter of the United Nations*, www.un.org/aboutun/charter.

6. International Monetary Fund, "IMF Executive Directors and Voting Power," www.imf.org/external/np/sec/memdir/eds.htm.

7. Map is adapted from Aris Katsaris, "Regional Organizations Map," available at en.wikipedia.org/wiki/File: Regional_Organizations_Map.png.

8. United States Trade Representative, "NAFTA: A Decade of Strengthening a Dynamic Relationship," www.ustr.gov/assets/Trade_Agreements/Regional/NAFTA/asset_upload_file606_3595.pdf.

9. Office of Management and Budget, "Budget of the United States Government, Fiscal Year 2008," www.whitehouse.gov/omb/budget/fy2008/budget.html.

10. See Robert D. Putnam, "Diplomacy and Domestic Politics: The Logic of Two-Level Games," *International Organization* 42: 3 (Summer 1988): 427–460.

11. Lloyd E. Ambrosius, "Woodrow Wilson, Alliances, and the League of Nations," *Journal of Gilded Age and Progressive Era* (April 2006), www.historycooperative.org/journals/jga/5.2/ambrosius.html.

12. The conferences included the Washington Naval Conference, the London Conference, and the "Pact of Paris."

13. Henry Kissinger, *Diplomacy* (New York: Simon and Schuster, 1994), 17–18.

14. See Joseph S. Nye, Jr., *Soft Power: The Means to Success in World Politics* (Cambridge, MA: Public Affairs, 2004).

15. See Torie Clark, *Lipstick on a Pig* (New York: Free Press, 2006).

16. Defense Science Board Task Force on Strategic Communication, *Final Report* (Washington: Department of Defense, September 2004).

17. See Wilson Dizard, Jr., "Remembering USIA," *Foreign Service Journal* (July/August 2003): 57.

18. The Joint Staff, *Information Operations*, Joint Publication 3-13 (Washington, DC: Joint Staff, February 13, 2006).

19. See Defense Science Board, 24–25.

20. The White House, "Executive Order: Establishing the Office of Global Communications," www.whitehouse.gov/news/releases/2003/01/20030121-3.html.

21. See House Committee on Armed Services, *Testimony of Wesley K. Clark*, 106th Cong., 1st sess., March 17, 1999, http://armedservices.house.gov/comdocs/testimony/106thcongress/99-03-17clark.htm.

22. Center for Strategic and Budgetary Assessments, *The Quadrennial Defense Review: Rethinking the U.S. Military Posture*,(Washington, DC: Center for Strategic and Budgetary Assessments 2005), 4, www.csbaonline.org/4Publications/Archive/R.20051024 .QDR06/R.20051024.QDR06.pdf.

23. Kurt M. Campbell and Celeste Johnson Ward, "New Battle Stations?" *Foreign Affairs* 80, no. 4 (July/August 2001): 95–103.

24. Center for Strategic and International Studies, *CSIS Commission on Smart Power* (Prepublication draft report), 430.

Chapter 12: Economics

1. Samuel Huntington, "America's Changing Strategic Interests," *Survival* (January/February 1991), 8.

2. Bureau of Economic Analysis, "Selected NIPA [National Income and Product Account] Tables," table 1.1.5 and 7.1, September, 2008, www.bea.gov/scb/pdf/2008/09% 20September/D-Pages/0908dpg_a.pdf.

3. Angus Maddison, *The World Economy:A Millennial Perspective* (Paris: Organization for Economic Co-operation and Development, 2001), table B-18.

4. See World Bank, *World Development Indicators Database 2006* (Washington, DC: World Bank, 2006); and Central Intelligence Agency (CIA), *The World Factbook* (Washington, DC: Central Intelligence Agency, 2007). Economic comparisons are calculated on a purchasing power parity (PPP) basis.

5. Exxon's market capitalization is from Jon D. Markman, "Exxon Proves Raw Stuff Is the Right Stuff," *MSN Money*, http://moneycentral.msn.com/content/P109915.asp. Swiss GDP is from World Bank, using authors' projections. Market capitalization captures the market value of the entire company; it measures the market value of all the company's productive assets. It is worth noting that GDP is a measure of the output produced in a year, not the entire value of all productive assets in the economy. The comparison is illustrative only.

6. See CIA, *World Factbook*, for military expenditures by country (on dollar basis, using PPP conversions). The Council of Economic Advisors reports a slightly higher number for total spending on national defense in 2005: $589 billion.

7. During the debate about awarding most favored nation status to China, Stanley Roth testified before the House Ways and Means Committee, Subcommittee on Trade: "There is no greater opportunity—or challenge—in U.S. foreign policy today than to encourage China's integration into the world community. President [Bill] Clinton's decision to extend MFN status to China reflects our commitment to this goal." See Stanley O. Roth, "Testimony before the House Ways and Means Committee: China's MFN Status," prepared remarks, June 17, 1998 (Washington, DC: Office of East Asian Affairs, U.S. Department of State, 1998).

8. WTO, *International Trade Statistics* (Geneva: World Trade Organization, 2006), www.wto.org/english/res_e/statis_e/statis_e.htm. World trade is measured in total merchandise exports (current U.S. dollars).

9. This chapter focuses primarily on the proximate determinants of economic growth: labor, capital, technology, and other inputs. Yet a large and growing body of literature addresses the deeper determinants of growth, including geography and institutions. The geography thesis is well articulated in Jeffrey D. Sachs, "Institutions Don't Rule: Direct Effects of Geography on Per Capita Income," *NBER Working Paper No. 9490* (Cambridge, MA: National Bureau of Economic Research, 2003). The institutions thesis is supported by several authors; among them, see Hernando de Soto, *The Mystery of Capital: Why Capitalism Triumphs in the West and Fails Everywhere Else* (New York: Basic Books, 2000).

10. Defense spending has been linked with technological innovations that may enhance long-term growth. See Vernon W. Ruttan, *Is War Necessary for Economic Growth? Military Procurement and Technology Development* (New York: Oxford University Press, 2006).

11. See Paul Collier, *Breaking the Conflict Trap: Civil War and Development Policy* (Washington, DC: International Bank for Reconstruction and Development/World Bank, 2003); and Paul Collier and Anke Haeffler, "Greed and Grievance in Civil War," *Oxford Economic Papers* 56, no. 4 (2004): 563–595.

12. "Crowding out" of private capital formation is known to become a particular risk during wartime. For example, Jeffrey Williamson suggests that crowding out created a drag on the British Industrial Revolution. See his article, "Why Was British Growth So Slow During the Industrial Revolution?" *Journal of Economic History* 44, no. 3 (1984): 687–712. In the United States, spending on the Vietnam War in conjunction with President Lyndon Johnson's Great Society programs created strong inflationary pressures and high interest rates.

13. Figures for income per capita are from the CIA, *World Factbook*, using PPP conversions.

14. Iwan W. Morgan, *Eisenhower versus "The Spenders": The Eisenhower Administration, the Democrats, and the Budget, 1953–60* (New York: St. Martin's Press, 1990), 22.

15. See Paul Kennedy, *The Rise and Fall of the Great Powers* (New York: Random House, 1987).

16. U.S. Department of Labor, *A Chartbook of International Labor Comparisons: The Americas, Asia and Europe* (Washington, DC: U.S. Department of Labor, 2006), chart 5.7.

17. WTO, "World Trade in 2005—Overview," 26, www.wto.org/English/res_e/statis_e/its2006_e/its06_overview_e.pdf.

18. Bank for International Settlements, *Triennial Central Bank Survey: Foreign Exchange and Derivatives Market Activity in 2004* (Basel: Bank for International Settlements, March 2005), 1.

19. Diana Farrell, Susan Lund, and Alexander Maasry, *Mapping the Global Market: Third Annual Report* (San Francisco: McKinsey Global Institute, 2007), 7.

20. Reported in Finfacts, "Global Foreign Direct Investment inflows grew by 34% in 2006," January 15, 2007, www.finfacts.com/irelandbusinessnews/publish/article_10008686.shtml.

21. Xavier Sala-i-Martin, "The World Distribution of Income: Falling Poverty and... Convergence, Period," *Quarterly Journal of Economics* 121, no. 2 (2006): 351–397.

22. U.S. National Intelligence Council, *Mapping the Global Future: Report of the National Intelligence Council 2020 Project*, NIC Report 2004-13 (Washington, DC: Government Printing Office, 2004), 29.

23. See David Dollar and Aart Kraay, "Trade, Growth, and Poverty," *World Bank Policy Research Working Paper No. 2615* (Washington, DC: World Bank, 2001), in which the authors explicitly link openness to trade with increased economic growth and a reduction of poverty among a group of developing countries.

24. See Mary E. Burfisher, Sherman Robinson, and Karen Theirfelder, "The Impact of NAFTA on the United States," *Journal of Economic Perspectives* 15, no. 1 (2001): 125–144.

25. The phrase "giant sucking sound" was used derisively by presidential candidate Ross Perot in the 1992 presidential election as he decried the potential negative effects of NAFTA.

26. See Philippe Martin, Thierry Mayer, and Mathias Thoenig, "Make Trade Not War?" *Discussion Paper No. 5218* (London: Centre for Economic Policy Research, 2005).

27. U.S. Bureau of Economic Analysis, "Value of Foreign Investments in the U.S. Rises More than Value of U.S. Investments Abroad in 2005" (Washington, D.C.: U.S. Department of Commerce, Press Release from June 29, 2006), table B-107.

28. Michael Kouparitsas, "How Worrisome Is the U.S. Net Foreign Debt Position?" *Chicago Fed Letter, Essays on Issues*, no. 202 (Chicago: Federal Reserve Bank of Chicago, 2004), 1-2. See also Robert E. Scott, "Increases in Foreign Liabilities Financed Through Sale of Government Securities," Economic Policy Institute, June 30, 2006, www.epinet.org/content.cfm/indicators_intlpict_20060630.

29. China held nearly $700 billion in U.S. long-term debt as of June 30, 2006. See U.S. Department of the Treasury, *Report on Foreign Portfolio Holdings of U.S. Securities, as of June 30, 2006* (Washington, DC: U.S. Department of the Treasury, 2007), www.treas.gov/tic/shl2006r.pdf.

30. Alan Heston, Robert Summers, and Bettina Aten, *Penn World Table Version 6.2* (Center for International Comparisons of Production, Income and Prices at the University of Pennsylvania, September 2006).

31. United Nations Economic and Social Commission for Asia and the Pacific, *Sustainable Social Development in a Period of Rapid Globalization* (New York: United Nations Publications, 2003).

32. Robert Manning, "Executive Summary of Report on the Proceedings of the 19th Annual National Defense University Pacific Symposium—'The Asian Financial Crisis: Security Risk and Opportunities'" (Washington, DC: National Defense University, 1998).

33. House Committee on Armed Services, *Testimony of Joseph W. Prueher, Admiral, Commander, U.S. Pacific Command*, 105th Cong., 2nd sess, 1998.

34. Klaus Schwab, closing remarks at the Annual Meeting of the New Champions 2008, September 28, 2008, "News from the Annual Meeting of the New Champions 2008," www.weforum.org/en/events/ArchivedEvents/AnnualMeetingoftheNewChampions2008/index.htm.

35. *Emergency Economic Stabilization Act of 2008*, H.R. 1424, 110th Cong., 2nd sess. (October 3, 2008).

36. "U.S. Sanctions against Russia: A Flop," *U.S. News and World Report*, June 16, 1980, 33–34.

37. Hirsh Goodman, "Pretoria Connection," *New Republic* 196, no. 16 (April 20, 1987): 20–21.

38. Independent Inquiry Committee into the United Nations Oil for Food Programme, *Report on Programme Manipulation* (New York: Independent Inquiry Committee, 2005), www.iic-offp.org/documents.htm.

39. Robert C. Byrd, "Administration Promises Made, Administration Promises Broken," remarks on December 9, 2003 (Washington, DC: U.S. Senate, Office of Robert C. Byrd, 2003).

40. See Michael Meese and Pat Buckley, "The Financial Front in the Global War on Terrorism," in *Defeating Terrorism: Shaping the New Security Environment*, ed. Russell Howard and Reid Sawyer (New York: McGraw-Hill, 2004), 51–61.

41. International Monetary Fund, "Islamic Republic of Iran: 2006 Article IV Consultation," *IMF Country Report Number 07/100* (Washington, DC: International Monetary Fund, March 2007), 17.

42. John McCain, "Andean Trade Act Important to National Security," April 30, 2002, mccain.senate.gov/public/index.cfm?FuseAction=PressOffice.PressReleases&ContentRecord_id=4949C65A-E961-4F5C-8005-C1765CE7424A.

43. George W. Bush, *The National Security Strategy of the United States* (Washington, DC: U.S. Government Printing Office, September 2002), 4.

44. The agencies in the U.S. government responsible for fostering economic and political development abroad are also less developed than those charged with ensuring U.S. military security. See Francis Fukuyama, *American at the Crossroads* (New Haven, CT: Yale University Press, 2006), esp. 149–154.

45. K. Alan Kronstadt, *Pakistan-U.S. Relations*, CRS Issue Brief for Congress (Washington, DC: Congressional Research Service, updated March 6, 2006), 16.

46. World Bank Lending to Iran," Subcommittee on Domestic and International Monetary Policy, Committee on Financial Services, U.S. House of Representatives, Washington, D.C., October 29, 2003.

Chapter 13: Military Power

1. Sun Tzu, *The Art of War*, trans. and ed. Samuel B. Griffith (Oxford: Oxford University Press Paperback, 1971), 63.

2. Carl von Clausewitz, *On War*, trans. and eds. Michael Howard and Peter Paret (Princeton: Princeton University Press, 1976), 86. For a more thorough discussion of this point, see Suzanne C. Nielsen, *Political Control Over the Use of Force* (Carlisle, PA: Strategic Studies Institute, May 2001).

3. Clausewitz, *On War*, 87.

4. Ibid. See also 605–607.

5. Ibid., 104.

6. Ibid., 149.

7. Ibid., 605.

8. Ibid., 579.

9. Ibid., 87

10. Ibid., 579.

11. Ibid., 112.

12. Ibid., 111.

13. Ibid., 585.

14. Ibid., 88–89.

15. Ibid., 604.

16. See Sun Tzu, *Art of War*, 71, for his views on the importance of making many calculations prior to deciding to go to war.

17. Clausewitz, *On War*, 87.

18. Sun Tzu, *Art of War*, 72–76.

19. Clausewitz, *On War*, 585–586.

20. Ibid., 78, 585.

21. Ibid., 81.

22. Ibid., 88.

23. Sun Tzu, *Art of War*, 143.

24. Kenneth N. Waltz, *Theory of International Politics* (New York: McGraw-Hill, Inc., 1979), 131.

25. K. J. Holsti, *International Politics: A Framework for Analysis*, 2nd ed. (Englewood Cliffs, NJ: Prentice-Hall, 1972), 77.

26. Henry Bienen, *The Military and Modernization* (New York: Aldine Atherton, 1971), 11–14.

27. See Barry R. Posen, "Command of the Commons: The Military Foundation of U.S. Hegemony," *International Security* 28, no. 1 (2003), 5–46.

28. See Bernard Brodie, *Strategy in the Missile Age* (Princeton, NJ: Princeton University Press, 1959), 319–321.

29. See Risa A. Brooks and Elizabeth A. Stanley, *Creating Military Power: The Sources of Military Effectiveness* (Stanford: Stanford University Press, 2007), 17–20.

30. Holsti, *International Politics*, 305.

31. Robert J. Art, "To What Ends Military Power?" *International Security* 4, no. 4 (Spring 1980), 5.

32. Ibid., 6.

33. Jerome D. Frank, *Sanity and Survival: Psychological Aspects of War and Peace* (New York: Random House, 1967), 139.

34. Art, "To What Ends Military Power?" 7. See also Thomas C. Schelling, *Arms and Influence* (New Haven, CT: Yale University Press, 1966), 69–86.

35. Art, "To What Ends Military Power?" 10.

36. See Peter Liberman, *Does Conquest Pay? The Exploitation of Occupied Industrial Societies* (Princeton, NJ: Princeton University Press, 1996).

37. Art, "To What Ends Military Power?" 25.

38. See J. I. Coffey, *Strategic Power and National Security* (Pittsburgh: University of Pittsburgh Press, 1971), 72–73.

39. See Roger W. Barnett, "Legal Constraints," and Michael Walzer, "The Triumph of Just War Theory (and the Dangers of Success)," in *American Defense Policy*, 8th ed., eds. Paul J. Bolt, Damon V. Coletta, and Collins G. Shackleford, Jr. (Baltimore: Johns Hopkins University Press, 2005), 117–125 and 24–30, respectively.

40. See Stanley Hoffmann, *The Ethics and Politics of Humanitarian Intervention* (Notre Dame: University of Notre Dame Press, 1996).

41. See David C. Gompert et al., *Nuclear Weapons and World Politics: Alternatives for the Future* (New York: McGraw-Hill, 1977), 83–88.

42. Klaus Knorr, *On the Uses of Military Power in the Nuclear Age* (Princeton, NJ: Princeton University Press, 1966), 67–68.

43. See Stanley Hoffman, *Gulliver's Troubles, or the Setting of American Foreign Policy* (New York: McGraw-Hill, 1968), 418–421; and Hanson W. Baldwin, *Strategy for Tomorrow* (New York: Harper & Row, 1970), 237–246. However, rearmament was again an issue of political debate in Japan in the early twenty-first century (see Chapter 18).

44. William M. Darley, "War Policy, Public Support, and the Media," *Parameters* 35, no. 2 (Summer 2005): 121–134.

45. Richard K. Betts, "A Disciplined Defense: How to Regain Strategic Solvency," *Foreign Affairs* 86, no. 6 (November/December 2007): 80.

46. Hans J. Morgenthau, *Politics among Nations: The Struggle for Power and Peace*, 5th ed. (New York: Knopf, 1973), 181.

47. Norman J. Padelford and George A. Lincoln, *The Dynamics of International Politics*, 2nd ed. (New York: Macmillan, 1967), 5.

48. Stephen M. Walt, *The Origins of Alliances* (Ithaca, NY: Cornell University Press, 1987).

49. This discussion of alliance motives is adapted from Raymond F. Hopkins and Richard W. Mansbach, *Structure and Process in International Politics* (New York: Harper & Row, 1973), 306–308.

50. *European Defence Agency: Building Capabilities for a Secure Europe*, www.eda .europa.eu/WebUtils/downloadfile.aspx?fileid=77.

51. Robert Endicott Osgood, *Alliances and American Foreign Policy* (Baltimore: Johns Hopkins University Press, 1968), 21–22.

52. See Wesley K. Clark, *Waging Modern War: Bosnia, Kosovo, and the Future of Combat* (New York: Public Affairs, 2001).

53. Nora Bensahel, "International Alliances and Military Effectiveness," in *Creating Military Power*, Brooks and Stanley, 200.

54. In response to Weinberger's statement that a domestic consensus must be reached before the use of U.S. forces, James Schlesinger remarked in February 1985, "Given the circumstances, that is indeed a demanding requirement. Were it to be rigorously implemented, it would virtually assure other powers that they can count on *not* facing American forces."

55. Casper W. Weinberger, "The Uses of Military Power," in *Defense '85* (Arlington, VA: American Forces Information Service, January 1985), 2–11.

56. Colin L. Powell, "U.S. Forces: Challenges Ahead," *Foreign Affairs* 71, no. 5 (Winter 1992): 32–45.

57. George Shultz, *Turmoil and Triumph* (New York: Charles Scribner's Sons, 1993), 650. A more thorough discussion of this debate can be found in Suzanne C. Nielsen, "Rules of the Game? The Weinberger Doctrine and the American Use of Force," in *The Future of the Army Profession*, proj. dir. Don M. Snider and Gayle L. Watkins, and ed. Lloyd J. Matthews (Boston: McGraw-Hill Companies, Inc., 2002), 212–214.

58. Kenneth J. Campbell, "Once Burned, Twice Cautious: Explaining the Weinberger-Powell Doctrine," *Armed Forces & Society* 24, no. 3 (Spring 1998): 357–374.

59. Harlan Ullman and James Wade Jr., *Shock and Awe: Achieving Rapid Dominance* (Washington, DC: National Defense University Institute for National Strategic Studies, 1996), *xxviii–xxix*.

60. Richard K. Betts, "Are Civil-Military Relations Still a Problem?" (unpublished paper prepared for Senior Conference 2007 held at West Point, New York, May 31–June 2, 2007), 10–11.

61. Robert Jervis, *American Foreign Policy in a New Era* (New York: Routledge, 2005), 12.

62. The Joint Chiefs of Staff, *The National Military Strategy of the United States of America*, 2004, 5, www.defenselink.mil/news/Mar2005/d20050318nms.pdf.

63. Figure 13.1 and the ensuing discussion are based on the following documents: The Joint Chiefs of Staff, *The National Military Strategy of the United States of America*, 2004, 4–6; Department of Defense, *The National Defense Strategy of the United States of America*, March 2005, 2–3, www.defenselink.mil/news/Mar2005/d20050318nds.pdf; and Department of Defense, *Quadrennial Defense Review Report*, February 6, 2006, www.defenselink.mil/pubs/pdfs/QDR20060203.pdf.

64. Association of the United States Army, *A Transformed and Modernized U.S. Army: A National Imperative* (Arlington, VA: Institute of Land Warfare, April 2007), 6.

65. *National Defense Strategy*, 2.

66. *Quadrennial Defense Review Report*, 19.

67. Ibid.

68. See George W. Bush, "President's Address to the Nation," The White House, Office of the Press Secretary, January 10, 2007, www.whitehouse.gov/news/releases/2007/01/20070110-7.html; and George W. Bush, "State of the Union 2007," The White House, Office of the Press Secretary, January 23, 2007, www.whitehouse.gov/news/releases/2007/01/20070123-2.html.

69. *Quadrennial Defense Review Report*, 20.

Chapter 14: Asymmetric Conflict, Terrorism, and Preemption

1. Sun Tzu, *The Art of War*, trans. Samuel B. Griffith (Oxford: Oxford University Press, 1971), 101.

2. This discussion of asymmetric attacks was informed by Steven Lambakis, James Kiras, and Kristin Kolet, *Understanding "Asymmetric" Threats to the United States* (Fairfax, VA: National Institute for Public Policy, 2002).

3. Secretary of Defense, *Quadrennial Defense Review 1997* (Washington: Department of Defense, 1997), fas.org/man/docs/qdr/index.html

4. The White House, *The National Security Strategy of the United States of America*, September 2002, 30., www.whitehouse.gov/nsc/nss/2002/.

5. Secretary of Defense, *Quadrennial Defense Review 1997*.

6. See Department of Justice, White Paper on "The Clinton Administration's Policy on Critical Infrastructure Protection: Presidential Decision Directive 63," May 22, 1998, www.usdoj.gov/criminal/cybercrime/white_pr.htm.

7. See Steven A. Hildreth, *Cyberwarfare* (Washington, DC: Congressional Research Service, updated June 19, 2001). A comprehensive reference is Lech J. Janczewski and Andrew M. Colarik, *Cyber Warfare and Cyber Terrorism* (London: IGI Global, 2008).

8. Reuven Paz, "Global Jihad and WMD: Between Martyrdom and Mass Destruction," in *Current Trends in Islamist Ideology*, vol. 2, eds. Hillel Fradkin, Husain Haqqani, and Eric Brown (Washington, DC: Hudson Institute, Inc., 2005), 78.

9. Robert Wesley, "Al-Qa'ida's WMD Strategy After the U.S. Intervention in Afghanistan," *Terrorism Monitor* 3, no. 20 (October 21, 2005) 1-10.

10. The value of asymmetry is stressed in the annual vision statements issued by each service. The Air Force states: "We are committed to sustaining our position of strength, the *asymmetric advantages* the Air Force gives our nation—America's edge." See Michael Wynne and Michael Moseley, *Air Force Posture Statement* (Washington, DC: U.S. Air Force, 2007), 1. The Navy states: "Our Navy must maintain its *asymmetric advantages* over any adversary: superior power, precision, advanced technology, information, and people." See U.S. Navy, *Sea Power for a New Era* (Washington, DC: U.S. Navy, 2007), 1.

11. Mao Zedong, "Problems of War and Strategy" (speech given at Sixth Plenary Session of the Sixth Central Committee of the Party, November 6, 1938), www.marxists.org/reference/archive/mao/selected-works/volume-2/mswv2_12.htm.

12. Sun Tzu, *Art of War*, 77.

13. The White House, *The National Security Strategy of the United States of America*, September 2002, 19., www.whitehouse.gov/nsc/nss/2006/.

14. 22 United States Code, Section 2656f (d). This definition is used for the annual counting of terrorism events. See also Paul R. Pillar, "The Dimensions of Terrorism and Counter Terrorism," in *Terrorism and Counterterrorism*, eds. Russell D. Howard and Reid L. Sawyer (New York: McGraw-Hill, 2005), 24–43.

15. Bruce Jenkins, "Will Terrorists Go Nuclear?" RAND Paper P-5541 (Santa Monica: RAND, 1974), 4.

16. There are reports of some internal conflict within al-Qa'ida concerning whether maximizing casualties should be their objective or whether that detracts from their efforts. Dr. Ayman al-Zawahiri, in a July 9, 2005, letter to the al-Qa'ida in Iraq leader at the time, Abu Musab Zarqawi, counsels him against "scenes of slaughtering the hostages," because "we are in a media battle in a race for the hearts and minds of our Umma." The letter is available at www.weeklystandard.com/Content/Public/Articles/000/000/006/203gpuul.asp. These specific objections not withstanding, the predominant approach of al-Qa'ida is to maximize casualties in most of their attacks.

17. Al-Suri, Abu Mus'ab, "Letter in Response to State Department," *Usamah's Memo Forum*, December 2004.

18. David J. Kilcullen, "Countering Global Insurgency" *Journal of Strategic Studies* 28: 4 (August 2005): 603.

19. House Committee on Armed Services, Subcommittee on Terrorism, Unconventional Threats and Capabilities, *Combating Al-Qa'ida and the Militant Islamic Threat: Testimony of Bruce Hoffman*, 199th Cong., 2nd sess., February 16, 2006, 3, www.rand.org/pubs/testimonies/2006/RAND_CT255.pdf.

20. Bruce Hoffman, "Islam and the West: Searching for Common Ground The Terrorist Threat and the Counter-Terrorism Effort," CT-263 (Santa Monica: RAND, 2006) 3.

21. Ibid., 4.

22. Ibid., 5–6.

23. Ibid., 6.

24. Andrew Bacevich (lecture at the United States Military Academy at West Point, New York, April 26, 2007).

25. Peter L. Bergen, *The Osama bin Laden I Know* (New York: Free Press, 2006), 50.

26. Ibid., 49.

27. Bruce Lawrence, ed., *Messages to the World: The Statements of Osama bin Laden* (New York: Verso, 2005), 50–51.

28. Ibid., 48.

29. Ibid., 49.

30. Ibid.

31. Ibid., 112–113.

32. Defense Manpower Data Center, Statistical Information Analysis Division. siadapp.dmdc.osd.mil; . CNN, "Gulf War Facts," www.cnn.com/SPECIALS/2001/gulf.war/facts/gulfwar/index.html.

33. Lawrence, *Messages to the World*, 25.

34. Lawrence, *Messages to the World*, 59–60.

35. Bergen, *Osama bin Laden I Know*, 60–61.

36. Hoffman, "Combating Al-Qa'ida and the Militant Islamic Threat," 7; Lawrence, *Messages to the World*, 162–172.

37. *National Strategy for Combating Terrorism*, September 2006, 9–10, www.white house.gov/nsc/nsct/2006.

38. Stephen M. Walt, *Taming American Power: The Global Response to U.S. Primacy* (New York: W. W. Norton , 2005), 62–108.

39. George W. Bush, "Graduation Speech" (at the U.S. Military Academy, June 1, 2002), www.whitehouse.gov/news/releases/2002/06/20020601-3.html.

40. The White House, *The National Security Strategy of the United States of America*, September 2002, 15., www.whitehouse.gov/nsc/nss/2002/.

41. George W. Bush, "Graduation Speech." June 1, 2002, West Point, NY.

42. Ibid.

43. Ibid.

44. Ibid.

45. Article 51 of the UN Charter states: "Nothing . . . shall impair the inherent right of individual or collective self-defense if an armed attack occurs against a Member of the United Nations." This has been extended to include attacks that are anticipatory self-defense against an imminent attack, but not one that would prevent the capability to wage an attack at some unspecified time in the future. See UN Charter, Article 51, www.un.org/aboutun/charter.

46. NSC-68, Section IX.C, www.mtholyoke.edu/acad/intrel/nsc-68/.

47. See, for example, Ivo H. Daalder and James Lindsay, "Bush's Flawed Revolution," *The American Prospect* 14, no. 10 (November 2003), 43–45.

48. Ibid.

Chapter 15: Conventional War

1. See Charles Krauthammer, "The Unipolar Moment," *Foreign Affairs* 70, no. 1 (1991): 23–33.

2. For an argument that wars in the future will not primarily be competitions between adversaries' military forces, see Thomas X. Hammes, "War Evolves into the Fourth Generation," *Contemporary Security Policy*, 26, no. 2 (August 2005): 189–221.

3. See John J. Mearsheimer, *The Tragedy of Great Power Politics* (New York: W. W. Norton, 2003).

4. For the United States, even the world wars were "limited" in the sense that not all material resources were mobilized. See Henry A. Kissinger, "The Problems of Limited War," in *The Use of Force*, eds. Robert J. Art and Kenneth N. Waltz (Boston: Little, Brown, 1971), 102.

5. Andre Beaufre, *An Introduction to Strategy, with Particular Reference to Problems of Defense, Politics, Economics, and Diplomacy in the Nuclear Age*, trans. R. H. Barry, with preface by B. H. Liddell Hart (New York: Praeger, 1965), 85.

6. While there has been no direct *general* conventional war, there have been at least two historical cases of *limited* conventional war between two nations possessing nuclear weapons. First, in the Korean War, American and Soviet pilots did engage in air-to-air combat. Second, between May and July 1999, Pakistan and India fought the Kargil conflict in Kashmir (see Chapter 19).

7. Kissinger, "The Problems of Limited War," 104.

8. The fact that the Korean War remained a limited war was due as much to chance as it was to design—the option of using nuclear weapons was never completely off the table—whereas in subsequent Cold War conflicts, nuclear weapons were never seriously considered.

9. See Samuel P. Huntington, *The Common Defense* (New York: Columbia University Press, 1961), 342–343.

10. Bruce Palmer, Jr., *The 25-Year War: America's Military Role in Vietnam* (New York: Simon & Schuster, 1984), 151.

11. W. Scott Thompson and D. Frizzel Donaldson, eds., *The Lessons of Vietnam* (New York: Crane, Russak, 1977), 279.

12. For a discussion of limited war, see Robert E. Osgood, "The Reappraisal of Limited War," in *American Defense Policy*, 3rd ed., eds. Richard G. Head and Ervin J. Rokke (Baltimore: Johns Hopkins University Press, 1973), 168–169.

13. See Stephen D. Biddle, *American Grand Strategy After 9/11: An Assessment* (Carlisle Barracks, PA: U.S. Army War College Strategic Studies Institute, April 2005), 11.

14. Ibid., 12. However, the U.S. preponderance of political, economic, and military power, as well as its unilateral tendencies, may prompt diplomatic and economic measures against the United States.

15. The White House, *The National Security Strategy of the United States of America*, March 2006, 14., www.whitehouse.gov/nsc/nss/2006/.

16. For a theoretical treatment of this point, see Klaus Knorr, *Military Power and Potential* (Lexington, MA: Health, 1970), 73–90.

17. Scott Pace et al., *The Global Positioning System: Assessing National Policies* (Santa Monica: RAND, 1995), 245.

18. For a more detailed explanation of the idea of hegemonic war, see Robert Gilpin, *War and Change in World Politics* (Cambridge: Cambridge University Press, 1981), chap. 5.

19. For details of this campaign, see Arnold L. Horelick and Myron Rush, *Strategic Power and Soviet Foreign Policy* (Chicago: University of Chicago Press, 1965), 58–70, passim.

20. Spiral development, as well as incremental development, is described and specified as "the preferred DoD strategy for rapid acquisition of technology." See Department of Defense, Instruction 5000.2, *Subject: Operation of the Defense Acquisition System*, May 12, 2003, https://akss.dau.mil/dag/DoD5000.asp?view=document&rf=DoD5002/DoD5002-3.3.asp.

21. For a review of current Department of Defense efforts to speed technology insertion into its programs and systems, see Sue C. Payton, "Nine Technology Insertion Programs That Can Speed Acquisition," *Defense AT&L* (January/February 2006): 10–13.

22. See Bruce R. Nardulli, et al., *Disjointed War: Military Operations in Kosovo* (Santa Monica: RAND, 1999).

23. Frederick W. Kagan, *Finding the Target: The Transformation of American Military Policy* (New York: Encounter Books, 2006), 253.

24. The term "Revolution in Military Affairs" is actually most commonly attributed to the Soviet Marshal Nikolai V. Ogarkov, who wrote about a "Military Technical Revolution" in the 1970s. See Steven Metz and James Kievit, *Strategy and the Revolution in Military Affairs: From Theory to Policy* (Carlisle Barracks, PA: U.S. Army War College Strategic Studies Institute, June 27, 1995).

25. See Department of Defense, *Transformation Planning Guidance* (Washington, DC: Department of Defense, April 2003).

26. Metz and Kievet, *Strategy and the Revolution in Military Affairs.*

27. Andrew F. Krepinevich, "Cavalry to Computer," *National Interest*, no. 37 (Fall 1994): 30.

28. For a discussion of "human software," see Eliot Cohen, "Change and Transformation in Military Affairs," *Journal of Strategic Studies* 27, no. 3 (September 2004): 395–407.

29. Donald Rumsfeld, "'21st Century' Transformation of the U.S. Armed Forces" (speech to the National Defense University, January 31, 2002), www.oft.osd.mil/library/library_files/speech_136_rumsfeld_speech_31_jan_2002.doc.

30. Whether a revolution in military affairs is even occurring is a debatable point. See Clifford J. Rogers, "'Military Revolutions' and 'Revolutions in Military Affairs': A Historian's Perspective," in *Toward a Revolution in Military Affairs? Defense and Security at the Dawn of the Twenty-First Century*, ed. Thierry Gongora and Harald von Riekhoff (Westport, CT: Greenwood Press, 2000), 21–36.

31. Jianxiang Bi, "The PLA's Revolution in Operational Art: Retrospects and Prospects," in *Toward a Revolution in Military Affairs?*, 115.

32. Ibid., 124.

33. Cohen, "Change and Transformation in Military Affairs," 402.

34. Ibid.

35. Michael G. Vickers, *Warfare in 2020: A Primer* (Washington, DC: Center for Strategic and Budgetary Assessments, October 1996).

36. Department of Defense, *Quadrennial Defense Review Report* (Washington, DC: Department of Defense, February 6, 2006), 27–28.

37. See Biddle, *American Grand Strategy After 9/11*, 16, for an excellent delimitation of the dilemma posed by aggressively fighting terrorism abroad.

38. Although many consider President George W. Bush's commencement speech at West Point in 2002 as the official proclamation of the "Bush Doctrine" of preemption, the notion of preemption has a much longer lineage in U.S. foreign policy. See John Lewis Gaddis, *Surprise, Security, and the American Experience* (Cambridge, MA: Harvard University Press, 2004), esp. 16–22.

39. Biddle, *American Grand Strategy After 9/11*, 16.

40. The White House, *The National Security Strategy of the United States of America*, March 2006, 15. www.whitehouse.gov/nsc/nss/2006/.

41. Although the Chinese government reports annual growth of 5% to 10%, many economists dispute these official statistics for several reasons: first, statistics are often released before the time period that they are supposed to cover; second, the growth rate rarely differs from earlier projected rates and until recently have not been subject to subsequent revision. See "China Country Profile," *Economist Intelligence Unit* (2006), 38–40.

42. C. Raja Mohan, "India and the Balance of Power," *Foreign Affairs* 85, no. 4 (July/August 2006): 19.

43. The incremental cost of the 1990–1991 Gulf War was only $4.7 billion. All other costs were either already included in the existing defense budget (e.g., personnel costs) or were paid for through contributions by allies. See Richard B. Cheney, *Annual Report to the President and Congress, Fiscal Year 1993* (Washington, DC: Department of Defense, January 1993).

44. Although never formally articulated by Powell as such, the "Powell Doctrine" is implicit in (among other sources) Colin L. Powell, "U.S. Forces: Challenges Ahead," *Foreign Affairs* 72, no. 5 (Winter 1992/1993): 32–45; and Powell, *My American Journey* (New York: Random House, 1995).

Chapter 16: Irregular Challenges, Military Intervention, and Counterinsurgency

1. The White House, *The National Security Strategy of the United States*, September 2002, 1.

2. Department of Defense, *The National Defense Strategy of the United States*, March 2005, 3.

3. Ibid., 3.

4. Ibid.

5. Colin S. Gray, "Irregular Warfare: One Nature, Many Characters," *Strategic Studies Quarterly* 1: 2 (Winter 2007): 42. The classic reference manual originally published in 1940 has been reprinted as *Marine Corps Small Wars Manual, United States Marine Corps, 1940* (Manhattan, KS: Sunflower Press, 1996).

6. Richard N. Haass, *Intervention: The Use of American Military Force in the Post-Cold War World* (Washington, DC: Carnegie Endowment for International Peace, 1994). Also see Bruce W. Jentleson and Ariel E. Levite, "The Analysis of Protracted Foreign Military Intervention," in *Foreign Military Intervention: The Dynamics of Protracted Conflict*, eds. Levite, Jentleson, and Larry Berman (New York: Columbia University Press, 1992), 1–22.

7. James Fearon and David Laitin, "Ethnicity, Insurgency, and Civil War," *American Political Science Review* 97, no. 1 (2003): 76 fn. 4.

8. Bard E. O'Neill, *Insurgency and Terrorism* (Washington, DC: Brassey's Inc., 1990), 17.

9. Department of the Army, Field Manual (FM) No. 3-24 / Marine Corps Warfighting Publication (MCWP) No. 3-33.5 *Counterinsurgency* (Washington, DC: Government Printing Office, 2006), 1-3. Hereafter, this document will be referenced as FM 3-24/MCWP 3-33.5.

10. See Haass, *Intervention*, esp. chap. 1 and 7. See also Howard M. Hensel, ed., *The Law of Armed Conflict: Constraints on the Contemporary Use of Military Force* (Burlington, VT: Ashgate Publishing, 2005).

11. Joint Chiefs of Staff, Joint Publication 1-02, *Department of Defense Dictionary of Military and Associated Terms* (Washington, DC: Government Printing Office, April 12, 2001, as amended through October 12, 2007), 128. Hereafter, this document will be referenced as JP 1-02.

12. Ian F. W. Beckett, *Modern Insurgencies and Counter-Insurgencies: Guerrillas and Their Opponents since 1750* (New York: Routledge, 2001), 24.

13. JP 1-02, 508.

14. JP 1-02, I-17.

15. Current U.S. Army and Marine Corps doctrine argues that stability operations, along with offense and defense, are an intrinsic part of counterinsurgency operations. See FM 3-24/MCWP 3-33.5, 1-19. See also Richard A. Lacquement, Jr., "Building Peace in the Wake of War: Appropriate Roles for Armed Forces and Civilians," in *American Defense Policy*, 8th ed., eds. Paul J. Bolt, Damon V. Coletta, and Collins G. Shackleford (Baltimore: Johns Hopkins University Press, 2005), 282–294.

16. Joint Chiefs of Staff, Joint Publication 3-0, *Joint Operations* (Washington, DC: Government Printing Office, February 13, 2008), VII-6. Hereafter, this document will be referenced as JP 3-0.

17. JP 3-0, VII-5.

18. JP 3-0, VII-6.

19. JP 1-02, 410.

20. Joint Chiefs of Staff, Joint Publication 3-07.3 *Peace Operations* (Washington, DC: Government Printing Office, October 17, 2007), x. Hereafter, this document will be referenced as JP 3-07.3.

21. Ibid.

22. Ibid.

23. See Julia Preston, "Rwanda Confounds UN Security Council," *Washington Post*, May 8, 1994, A25; "Why Not Rwanda?" *New Republic*, May 16, 1994, 7; Charles Krauthammer, "Stop the Genocide in Rwanda," *Washington Post*, May 27, 1994, A25; and Herman Cohen, "Getting Rwanda Wrong," *Washington Post*, June 3, 1994, A23.

24. See Michael J. Meese and Sean M. Morgan, "New Requirements for Army Expert Knowledge: Afghanistan and Iraq," in *The Future of the Army Profession*, 2nd ed., proj. dir. Don M. Snider (Boston: McGraw-Hill Publishing, Inc., 2005), 350.

25. As quoted in JP 3-07.3, II-1.

26. JP 3-0, VI-9 to VI-10.

27. Haass, *Intervention*, 63.

28. JP 3-0, I-14.

29. Haass, *Intervention*, 19.

30. Ibid., 64.

31. Beckett, *Modern Insurgencies and Counterinsurgencies*.

32. Robert Taber, *The War of the Flea: Guerilla Warfare in Theory and Practice* (New York: Lyle Stuart, Inc., 1965), 180.

33. Becket, *viii*.

34. FM 3-24/MCWP 3-33.5, 1-4.

35. Ibid.

36. Ibid.

37. See Donald L. Horowitz, "A Harvest of Hostility: Ethnic Conflict and Self Determination after the Cold War," *Defense Intelligence Journal* 1: 1 (1992): 137–163; and Chaim Kaufmann, "Possible and Impossible Solutions to Ethnic Civil Wars," *International Security* 20, no. 4 (Spring 1996): 136–175.

38. Ibid.

39. See Robert M. Cassidy, *Counterinsurgency and the Global War on Terror: Military Culture and Irregular War* (Westport, CT: Praeger Security International, 2006).

40. FM 3-24/MCWP 3-33.5, 1-4. See also David J. Kilcullen, "Countering Global Insurgency," *Journal of Strategic Studies* 28, no. 4 (August 2005): 596–617.

41. James A. Baker III and Lee H. Hamilton, cochairs, *The Iraq Study Group Report* (New York: Vintage Books, 2006), 32.

42. Ibid.

43. Ibid., 2.

44. Gray, "Irregular Warfare," 43.

45. The list of principles is from FM 3-24/MCWP 3-33.5, 1-21 to 1-24. Principles are verbatim, though descriptions of them are not. See also Eliot Cohen et al., "Principles, Imperatives, and Paradoxes of Counterinsurgency," *Military Review* 86, no. 2 (March/April 2006): esp. 49–51.

46. Cohen et al., 50.

47. Ibid.

48. Imperatives are drawn verbatim from FM 3-24/MCWP 3-33.5, 1-24 to 1-26.

49. For an example, see Chief of Naval Operations, *Navy Strategic Plan* (Washington, DC: Government Printing Office, May 2006), 1.

50. FM 3-24/MCWP 3-33.5, *vii.*

51. Carl Builder, *The Masks of War: American Military Styles in Strategy and Analysis* (Baltimore, MD: Johns Hopkins University Press, 1989), 192.

52. Andrew F. Krepinevich, Jr., *The Army and Vietnam* (Baltimore, MD: Johns Hopkins University Press, 1986), 4–7.

53. Nigel F. Aylwin-Foster, "Changing the Army for Counterinsurgency Operations," *Military Review* 86, no. 6 (November/December 2005): 2–3.

54. Ibid., 3–7.

55. See David H. Petraeus, "Learning Counterinsurgency: Observations from Soldiering in Iraq," *Military Review* 86, no. 1 (January/February 2006): 2–12; and Peter W. Chiarelli and Stephen M. Smith, "Learning from Our Modern Wars: The Imperatives of Preparing for a Dangerous Future," *Military Review* 87, no. 5 (September/October 2007): 2–15.

56. For the importance of personnel systems in sustaining military innovation, see Stephen Peter Rosen, *Winning the Next War* (Ithaca, NY: Cornell University Press, 1991).

57. FM 3-24/MCWP 3-33.5, 1-2.

58. International Institute for Strategic Studies (IISS), "Expanding the Army: Costs, Constraints, and Future Commitments," *IISS Strategic Comments* 13, no. 1 (February 2007): 1.

59. Senate Committee on Armed Services, *Testimony of Lawrence J. Korb*, XXth Cong., XX sess., April 17, 2007, 1–4; and Government Accountability Office, *Military Personnel: Strategic Plan Needed to Address Army's Emerging Officer Accession and Retention Challenges* (Washington, DC: GAO-07-224, January 2007), 27.

60. Ibid., 1–9.

61. Senate Committee on Armed Services, *Testimony of General Barry R. McCaffrey*, 110th Cong., 1st sess., April 17, 2007, 3.

62. Senate Committee on Armed Services, *Testimony of Andrew F. Krepinevich*, 110th Cong., 1st sess., April 17, 2007, 5.

63. See Robert Baer, "Why Blackwater—and More—Should Leave Iraq," *Time*, September 20, 2007, www.time.com/time/world/article/0,8599,1663937,00.html.

64. Ibid.

65. Senate Committee on Armed Services, *Statement for the Record of Major General (Ret.) Robert H. Scales*, 110th Cong., 1st sess., April 17, 2007, 1. See also Andrew F. Krepinevich, "The Thin Green Line," Center for Strategic and Budgetary Assessments Backgrounder, August 14, 2004.

66. Krepinevich testimony, 13; Korb testimony, 8; and John A. Nagl, *Institutionalizing Adaptation: It's Time for a Permanent Army Advisor Corps* (Washington, DC: Center for a New American Security, June 2007).

67. IISS, 1.

68. Baker and Hamilton, *Iraq Study Group Report*, xiii.

69. *Beyond Goldwater-Nichols: U.S. Government and Defense Reform for a New Strategic Era*, Phase II Report (Washington, DC: Center for Strategic and International Studies, July 2005), 55.

70. Ibid., 56.

71. In some cases, international governmental and nongovernmental organizations may help in fulfilling these functions, but their involvement cannot be guaranteed in advance, and their actions cannot be fully controlled by the United States.

72. Nina M. Serafino, "Peacekeeping and Related Stability Operations: Issues of U.S. Military Involvement," *CRS Issue Brief for Congress*, updated March 27, 2006, CRS-9.

73. Robert M. Gates, "Landon Lecture," (speech given at Kansas State University, November 26, 2007), www.defenselink.mil/speeches/speech.aspx?speechid=1199.

74. Ibid.

75. Nicholas Kralev, "State Doubles Military Advisors," *Washington Times*, January 18, 2008, A1.

76. *Beyond Goldwater-Nichols*, 6–7.

77. Congressional Research Service, "The Cost of Iraq, Afghanistan, and Other Global War on Terror Operations since 9/11," RL33110, updated November 9, 2007, CRS 5.

78. Casualty figures for Afghanistan and Iraq are posted by the Department of Defense, siadapp.dmdc.osd.mil/personnel/CASUALTY/castop.htm and www.defenselink.mil/news/casualty.pdf

79. House Joint Hearing of the Committee of Foreign Affairs and the Committee on Armed Services, *Testimony of Ambassador Ryan C. Crocker*, 110th Cong., 1st sess., September 10, 2007, 1.

80. As of December 2007, 65% of Americans opposed the U.S. war in Iraq. "Iraq," www.pollingreport.com/iraq.htm.

81. As of December 2007, 56% of Americans approved of U.S. military action in Afghanistan, and 41% disapproved. "Afghanistan," www.pollingreport.com/afghan.htm.

82. See Isaiah Wilson III, *Thinking Beyond War: Civil-Military Operations and Why America Fails to Win the Peace* (New York: Palgrave Macmillan, 2007).

83. JP 3-0, I-14 to I-15.

84. U.S. Department of State, "About S/CRS," www.state.gov/s/crs/c12936.htm.

85. *Beyond Goldwater-Nichols*, 59.

86. White House, Statement on Presidential Directive on U.S. Efforts for Reconstruction and Stabilization, December 14, 2005, www.whitehouse.gov/news/releases/2005/12/20051214.html www.whitehouse.gov/release/2005/12/20051214.html.

87. U.S. Department of Defense, Military Support for Stability, Security, Transition, and Reconstruction (SSTR), Department of Defense (DoD) Directive Number 3000.05 (Washington, DC: Department of Defense, 2005), 2.

88. Council on Foreign Relations Independent Task Force, *In the Wake of War: Improving U.S. Post-Conflict Capabilities* (New York: Council on Foreign Relations, 2005), *xiii*.

Chapter 17: Nuclear Policy

1. Michael Nacht, *The Age of Vulnerability* (Washington, DC: Brookings Institution Press, 1985), 85; Robert Jervis, *The Illogic of American Nuclear Strategy* (Ithaca, NY: Cornell University Press, 1984), 24; and Morton Halperin, *Nuclear Fallacy: Dispelling the Myth of Nuclear Strategy* (Cambridge, MA: Ballinger, 1987).

2. Janne E. Nolan, *Guardians of the Arsenal: The Politics of Nuclear Strategy* (New York: Basic Books, 1989), 35–38.

3. Desmond Ball, "Targeting for Strategic Deterrence," *Adelphi Papers*, no. 185 (Summer 1983): 2–6; and Lawrence Freedman, *The Evolution of Nuclear Strategy* (New York: St. Martin's Press, 1981), 1–224.

4. Quoted in Ball, "Targeting for Strategic Deterrence," 9–10.

5. Scott D. Sagan, *Moving Targets: Nuclear Strategy and Nuclear Security* (Princeton, NJ: Princeton University Press, 1989), 74. See also Earl Ravenal, "Counterforce and Alliance: The Ultimate Connection," *International Security* 6, no. 4 (Spring 1982): 26–43.

6. These directives included National Security Decision Memorandum 242 in January 1974 and the Nuclear Weapons Employment Policy Guide (NEWEP-1) in April 1974. See the essays by Daniel Allen Rosenberg and Desmond Ball in *Strategic Nuclear Targeting*, eds. Ball and Jeffrey Richelson (Ithaca, NY: Cornell University Press, 1986), 35–83.

7. Ball, "Targeting for Strategic Deterrence," 12–15; Freedman, *Evolution of Nuclear Strategy*, 331–371; Nolan, *Guardians of the Arsenal*, 89–117.

8. Robert Scheer, *With Enough Shovels: Reagan, Bush, and Nuclear War* (New York: Random House, 1982), 261–262.

9. Bruce G. Blair, "Lengthening the Fuse," *Brookings Review* 13, no. 3 (Summer 1995): 28–31.

10. Estimates of Chinese nuclear weapons capabilities vary, but these estimates are the most widely recognized. "Nuclear Threat Initiative." www.nti.org.

11. Joanne Tompkins, "How U.S. Strategic Policy Is Changing China's Nuclear Plans," *Arms Control Today* 33, no. 1 (January/February 2003): 11.

12. Larry K. Niksh, *North Korea's Nuclear Program*, CRS Report for Congress, October 5, 2006, summary and 11.

13. Stephen A. Hildreth, *North Korean Ballistic Missile Threat to the United States*, CRS Report for Congress, September 20, 2006, 2.

14. S. Paul Kapur, "Nuclear Proliferation, the Kargil Conflict, and South Asian Security," *Security Studies* 13, no. 1 (Autumn 2003): 80.

15. The White House, *The National Security Strategy of the United States of America*, March 2006, 14., www.whitehouse.gov/nsc/nss/2006/.

16. Sharon Squassoni, *Iran's Nuclear Program: Recent Developments*, CRS Report for Congress, 2.

17. National Intelligence Council, *Iran: Nuclear Intentions and Capabilities* (Washington, DC: U.S. Director of National Intelligence, November 2007), 6.

18. It should be noted that the weaponization efforts that were reportedly stopped in 2003 (but that could have been restarted since) were not the most important steps toward a weapon; rather, the principal danger is the continued uranium enrichment.

19. Charles D. Ferguson and William C. Potter, "Improvised Nuclear Devices and Nuclear Terrorism," Weapons of Mass Destruction Commission, Paper Number 2, 17, www.wmdcommission.org.

20. M. Elaine Bunn, "Can Deterrence Be Tailored?" *Strategic Forum,* Number 225, January 2007, www.ndu.edu/inss/press/NDUPress_StrFor.htm.

20. U.S. Arms Control and Disarmament Agency, *Arms Control Report* (Washington, DC: U.S. ACDA, 1976), 3. See also Bernard Brodie, "On the Objectives of Arms Control," *International Security* 1, no. 1 (Summer 1976): 17-36 .

22. Wade Boese, "U.S., Russia Exploring Post-START Options," *Arms Control Today* 37, no. 4 (May 2007): 34.

23. Quoted in Wade Boese, "Missile Defense Five Years After the ABM Treaty," *Arms Control Today* 37, no. 5 (June 2007): 34. See also, Daryl G. Kimball, "Missile Defense Collision Course," *Arms Control Today* 37, no. 6 (July/August 2007): 3.

24. Joseph B. Cirincione, Jon B. Wolfsthal, and Miriam Rajkumar, *Deadly Arsenals* (Washington, DC: Carnegie Endowment for International Peace, 2005), 27–29.

25. Roy E. Horton, *Out of (South) Africa: Pretoria's Nuclear Weapons Experience,* INSS Occasional Paper 27 (Colorado Springs: Institution for National Security Studies, August 1999), www.fas.org/nuke/guide/rsa/nuke/ocp27.htm.

26. Oliver Meier, "NPT Preparatory Meeting Scores Some Success," *Arms Control Today* 37, no. 5 (June 2007): 24.

27. Ibid., 25–26.

28. U.S. Congress. Senate. Congressional Record, 107th Cong. 2nd Sess., pp. S2009-S2014.

29. Edward L. Warner, III, "Nuclear Deterrence Force Still Essential," www.defenselink.mil/speeches/speech.aspx?speechid=683

30. Cirincione, Wolfsthal, and Rajkumar, *Deadly Arsenals,* 131.

31. Ibid., 132.

32. Sam Nunn, "The Race Between Cooperation and Catastrophe," *Vital Speeches of the Day* 71, no. 12 (April 1, 2005): 370.

33. Mark J. Valencia, "The Proliferation Security Initiative: A Glass Half-Full," *Arms Control Today* 37, no. 5 (June 2007): 18.

34. Ibid., 18–21.

35. The White House, National Security Decision Directive Number 119, January 6, 1984, www.fas.org/spp/starwars/offdocs/nsdd119.htm.

36. U.S. Department of Defense, Missile Defense Agency, "BMD Basics: An Overview," www.mda.mil/mdalink/html/basics.html.

37. Missile Defense Agency, "BMD Basics: An Overview."

38. U.S. Department of Defense, Missile Defense Agency, "Historical Funding for MDA FY85-08," www.mda.mil/mdalink/pdf/histfunds.pdf.

39. U.S. Department of State, "The Emerging Ballistic Missile Threat," September 1, 2001, www.state.gov/t/ac/rls/fs/2001/4892.htm.

40. Ibid.

41. Ibid.

42. See Michael A. Levi, "The Case Against New Nuclear Weapons," *Science and Technology* 19, no. 3 (Spring 2003): 63–68; and also James Kitfield, "The Pros and Cons of New Nuclear Weapons," *National Journal* 35 (August 9, 2003): 32–34.

43. U.S. Department of Defense, *Nuclear Posture Review* (unclassified portions), January 8, 2002, www.globalsecurity.org/wmd/library/policy/dod/npr.htm.

44. U.S. Secretary of Energy, Secretary of Defense, and Secretary of State, "National Security and Nuclear Weapons: Maintaining Deterrence in the 21st Century," July 2007, 4.

45. Keir A. Lieber and Daryl G. Press, "The End of MAD? The Nuclear Dimension of U.S. Primacy," *International Security* 30, no. 4 (Spring 2006): 7–44.

Chapter 18: East Asia

1. Rep. Doug Bereuter, "Congressional Priorities in East Asia," in *U.S. Foreign Policy Agenda: the United States and Asia- Pacific Security* (Washington DC: Department of State, 1998), 19.

2. The White House, *The National Security Strategy of the United States of America* (Washington DC: September 2002), 4.

3. Full text of the Japanese Constitution is available on the National Library of the Japanese Diet's Web site, www.ndl.go.jp/constitution/e/etc/co1.html.

4. For more information about the U.S. reliance on bilateral alliances, see Eric Heginbotham and Christopher P. Twomey, "America's Bismarckian Asia Policy," *Current History* 104, no. 683 (September 2005): 243–250; and Michael H. Armacost and Daniel I. Okimoto, eds., *The Future of America's Alliances in Northeast Asia* (Washington DC: Brookings Institution Press, 2004).

5. The text of all three communiqués are available at www.taiwandocuments.org/doc_com.htm.

6. *Taiwan Relations Act*, Public Law 96-8, 96th Cong., 1st sess. (April 10, 1979), www.taiwandocuments.org/tra02.htm.

7. President Carter actually wanted to order the complete withdrawal of all U.S. forces, a prominent campaign pledge he made during the 1976 presidential election, but the order was rescinded after protest from various policy advisors and security experts.

8. For more information about China's economic growth, see David Hale, "China Takes Off," *Foreign Affairs* 82, no. 6 (November/December 2003): 36–53.

9. In the Agreed Framework, North Korea agreed to freeze its nuclear program initially for a number of economic and energy concessions, including fuel shipments, talks toward normalization of relations, and the provision of two light-water reactors. The agreement also entailed a North Korean promise to dismantle its nuclear program once the promised light-water reactors were delivered. See Jonathan D. Pollack, "The United States, North Korea, and End of the Agreed Framework," *Naval War College Review* 56, no. 3 (Summer 2003): 10–49.

10. U.S. Department of Defense, "United States Security Strategy for the East Asia-Pacific Region," *East Asian Strategy Report 1998* (Washington DC: OSD, 1998).

11. For a more in-depth analysis of the Bush Doctrine, see Robert Jervis, "Understanding the Bush Doctrine," *Political Science Quarterly* 118, no. 3 (Fall 2003): 365–388.

12. President George W. Bush first used this term publicly in his 2002 State of the Union speech to Congress on January 29, 2002.

13. For annual statistics on the military balance in Northeast Asia, CSIS publishes a concise annual report; see Anthony H. Cordesman, "The Asian Conventional Military Balance in 2002: Northeast Asia," *CSIS* (February 2002), www.csis.org/burke/mb.

14. C. Fred Bergsten, Bates Gill, Nicholas R. Lardy, and Derek Mitchell, *China: The Balance Sheet* (New York: Public Affairs, 2006), 17.

15. Suisheng Zhao, "China's Pragmatic Nationalism: Is It Manageable?" *Washington Quarterly* 29, no. 1 (Winter 2005/2006): 134.

16. *China: The Balance Sheet*, 6.

17. Thomas Lum, *Social Unrest in China* (Washington, DC: Congressional Research Service, May 8, 2006), summary.

18. For more information about the potentially precarious relationship between CCP legitimacy and Chinese nationalism, see Peter Hayes Gries, "Chinese Nationalism: Challenging the State?" *Current History* 104, no. 683 (September 2005): 251–256.

19. Office of the Secretary of Defense, *Annual Report to Congress: The Military Power of the People's Republic of China 2005,*(Washington, DC: Office of the Secretary of Defense, 2005) 5, www.defenselink.mil/news/Jul2005/d20050719china.pdf.

20. For more information of the impact of the 1991 Gulf War on PLA reforms, see David Shambaugh, *Modernizing China's Military: Prospects, Problems, and Prospects* (Berkeley: University of California Press, 2004).

21. For the U.S. spending figure, see Stephen Kosiak, "National Defense Budget Authority and Outlays," *Historical and Projected Funding for Defense: Presentation of the FY 2009 Request in Tables and Charts,* Center for Strategic and Budgetary Assessments, March 31, 2008, www.csbaonline.org/4Publications/PubLibrary/U.20080331.FY_09_Request_in_T/U.20080331.FY_09_Request_in_T.pdf. The spending figure for China is from U.S. Department of Defense, *Military Power of the People's Republic of China 2007* (Washington, DC: Department of Defense), 25.

22. International Monetary Fund, World Economic Outlook Database (September 2006), data for the year 2005.

23. *China: The Balance Sheet,* C515, 15.

24. Office of the Secretary of Defense, *Annual Report to Congress: The Military Power of the People's Republic of China 2005,*(Washington, DC: Office of the Secretary of Defense, 2005) 33, www.defenselink.mil/news/Jul2005/d20050719china.pdf.

25. Graham Hutchings, *Modern China: A Guide to a Century of Change* (Cambridge, MA: Harvard University Press, 2001), 38.

26. Mohan Malik, "China and the East Asian Summit," *Asia Pacific Center for Security Studies* (February 2006), 2, www.apcss.org/Publications/APSSS/ChinaandEastAsiaSummit.pdf.

27. Lowell Dittmer, "Ghost of the Strategic Triangle: The Sino-Soviet Partnership," in *Chinese Foreign Policy,* ed. Suisheng Zhao (New York: East Gate, 2004), 213.

28. Jianwei Wang, "China's Multilateral Diplomacy in the New Millennium," in *China Rising,* eds. Yong Deng and Fei-Ling Wang (Lanham, MD: Rowman & Littlefield Publishers, Inc., 2005), 186.

29. Thomas J. Christensen, "The Contemporary Security Dilemma: Deterring a Taiwan Conflict," *Washington Quarterly* 25, no. 4 (Autumn 2002): 7.

30. Full text of the Japanese Constitution is available on the National Library of the Japanese Diet's Web site, www.ndl.go.jp/constitution/e/etc/c01.html.

31. For a more thorough discussion concerning the risks inherent to security alliances, see Glenn H. Snyder, "The Security Dilemma in Alliance Politics," *World Politics* 36, no. 4 (July 1984): 461–495.

32. David Fouse, "Japan's FY 2005 National Defense Program Outline: New Concepts, Old Promises," *Asia-Pacific Center for Security Studies* 4, no. 3 (March 2003).

33. James Przystup, "U.S.-Japan Relations: Progress Toward a Mature Relationship," *INSS Occasional Paper 2* (Washington DC: NDU Press, 2005).

34. "Joint Statement: U.S.-Japan Consultative Committee," available on the Japanese Ministry of Foreign Affairs Web site, www.mofa.go.jp/region/n-america/us/security/scc/joint0502.html.

35. For more information regarding the domestic political ideology of North Korea, see Kong Dan Oh and Ralph C. Hassig, *North Korea Through the Looking Glass* (Washington DC: Brookings Institution Press, 2000).

36. Denny Roy, "China and the Korean Peninsula: Beijing's Pyongyang Problem and Seoul Hope," *Asia-Pacific Center for Security Studies* 3, no. 1 (January 2004): 1–4.

37. Jin H. Pak and Michael Kim, "How Can the United States Take the Initiative in the Current North Korea Nuclear Crisis," *Pacific Focus* 20, 2 (Fall 2005): 112.

38. For more information regarding South Korea's history with nuclear weapons development, see Daniel Pinkston, "South Korea's Nuclear Experiment," *Center for Nonproliferation Studies Research Story* (November 9, 2004), http://cns.miis.edu/pubs/week/041109.htm#fnB14; Michael J. Siler, "U.S. Nuclear Nonproliferation Policy in the Northeast Asian Region During the Cold War: The South Korean Case," *East Asia: An International Quarterly* 16, no. 3/4 (Autumn/Winter 1998): 41–79.

39. *MWe* is a power rating that represents millions of watts of electricity produced every day. A 5-MWe rating is considered very small. Modern nuclear reactors typically yield about 500 to 2000 MWe.

40. Sharon A. Squassoni, "North Korea's Nuclear Weapons: How Soon an Arsenal?" *CRS Report RS21391*, February 2, 2004.

41. For an overview, see Jonathan D. Pollack, "The United States, North Korea, and the end of the Agreed Framework," *Naval War College Review*, 56, no. 3 (Summer 2003): 10-49.

42. Larry A. Niksch, "North Korea's Nuclear Weapons Program," *CRS Report RL33590*, August 1, 2006.

43. Ministry of Unification, Facts & Figures [Republic of Korea government Web site], "The Status of Humanitarian Assistance toward North Korea (as of June 30, 2006)," www.unikorea.go.kr/english/ENK/ENK0301R.jsp.

44. Mark E. Manyin, "Foreign Assistance to North Korea" *CRS Report RL31785* (May 2005).

45. Seongji Woo, "North Korea–South Korea Relations Under Kim Jong-Il," in *North Korea: The Politics of Regime Survival*, ed. Young Whan Kihl and Hong Nack Kim (New York: M. E. Sharpe, 2006), 227.

46. U.S. Department of State Bureau of East Asian and Pacific Affairs, "Background Note: South Korea," www.state.gov/r/pa/ei/bgn/2800.htm.

47. Larry A. Niksch, "Korea: U.S.-South Korean Relations—Issues for Congress," *CRS Report IB98045* (April 2002).

48. "Will Resilience Overcome Risk?" East Asia and Pacific Update (Washington, DC: World Bank, November 2007), http://siteresources.worldbank.org/INTEAPHALFYEARLYUPDATE/Resources/550192-1194982737018/Full-Report-EAP-Update-Nov2007.pdf.

49. Ibid.

50. Ibid.

51. Thomas J. Christensen, "The Contemporary Security Dilemma: Deterring a Taiwan Conflict," *Washington Quarterly* 25, no. 4 (Autumn 2002): 7.

52. Office of the Secretary of Defense, *Annual Report to Congress: The Military Power of the People's Republic of China 2005*,(Washington, DC: Office of the Secretary of Defense, 2005) 4, www.defenselink.mil/news/Jul2005/d20050719china.pdf.

Chapter 19: South Asia

1. Strobe Talbott, *Engaging India: Diplomacy, Democracy, and the Bomb*, rev. ed. (Washington, DC: Brookings Institution Press, 2006), 9.

2. Frank Wisner et al., eds. *New Priorities in South Asia: U.S. Policy Toward India, Pakistan, and Afghanistan* (New York: Council on Foreign Relations, 2003), 39.

3. Ibid., 80.

4. The Kargil conflict in 1999 is not always called a war, but it saw more than one thousand battle deaths and therefore met a common political science threshold criterion. S. Paul Kapur, "Nuclear Proliferation, the Kargil Conflict, and South Asian Security," *Security Studies* 13, no. 1 (Autumn 2003): 80.

5. Teresita Schaffer, *Bangladesh in the Balance* (Washington, DC: Center for Strategic & International Studies, 2007), 1.

6. Central Intelligence Agency, "India," *The World Factbook*, www.cia.gov/library/publications/the-world-factbook/geos/in.html; and U.S. Department of State, "Background Note: India," www.state.gov/r/pa/ei/bgn/3454.htm.

7. Energy Information Administration, "South Asia Overview," *Country Analysis Briefs*, last updated March 2006, 1, 2, 4, 7 www.eia.doe.gov/emeu/cabs/South_Asia/pdf.pdf.

8. George Bunn, "The Nuclear Nonproliferation Treaty: History and Current Problems," *Arms Control Today* 33, no. 10 (December 2003): 4.

9. Jaswant Singh, "Against Nuclear Apartheid," *Foreign Affairs* 77, no 5 (September/October 1998): 42.

10. Paul Kerr, "New Details Emerge on Pakistani Networks," *Arms Control Today* 35, no. 4 (May 2005): 35.

11. Paul Kerr, "India Passes Nonproliferation Legislation," *Arms Control Today* 35, no. 5 (June 2005): 27; "Pakistan forms body to approve export of nuclear-related items, technology," *BBC Monitoring South Asia*, May 2, 2007; Kenneth N. Luongo and Isabelle Williams, "Seizing the Moment: Using the U.S.-Indian Nuclear Deal to Improve Fissile Material Security," *Arms Control Today* 36, no. 4 (May 2006): 15.

12. Sharon Squassoni, "Nuclear Threat Reduction Measures for India and Pakistan," Congressional Research Service, May 5, 2003, cited in Luongo and Williams, "Seizing the Moment," 13.

13. Carlotta Gall, "At Border, Signs of Pakistani Role in Taliban Surge," *New York Times*, January 21, 2007, 1; Bruce Riedel, "Al-Qa'ida Strikes Back," *Foreign Affairs* 86, no. 3 (May/June 2007): 24–41.

14. Jessica Stern, "Pakistan's Jihad Culture," *Foreign Affairs* 79, no. 6 (November/December 2000): 118.

15. Alan C. F. Colchester and Nancy T. H. Colchester, "The Origin of Bovine Spongiform Encephalopathy: The Human Prion Disease Hypothesis," *Lancet* 366, no. 9488 (September 3–9, 2005): 856–861.

16. Todd Bullock, "U.S., India Cooperate in Fight Against HIV/AIDS," International Information Programs (Washington, DC: U.S. Department of State, June 9, 2005), http://news.findlaw.com/wash/s/20050609/20050609182452.html.

17. A. Subramanyam Raju, *Democracies at Loggerheads: Security Aspects of U.S.-India Relations* (Denver, CO: International Academic Publishers, 2001), 31.

18. Dennis Kux, *The United States and Pakistan: 1947-2000* (Baltimore, MD: Johns Hopkins University Press, 2001), 74.

19. Ibid., 343.

20. Raju, *Democracies at Loggerheads*, 64.

21. David N. Gibbs, "Reassessing Soviet Motives for Invading Afghanistan: A Declassified History," *Critical Asian Studies* 38, no. 2 (2006): 259.

22. Dennis Kux, *Pakistan, Flawed Not Failed State* (New York: Foreign Policy Association, 2001), 20.

23. Talbott, *Engaging India*, 57.

24. Kapur, "Nuclear Proliferation," 85.

25. Talbott, *Engaging India*, 57.

26. United States Agency for International Development, *U.S. Aid to Pakistan* (Washington, DC, 2004).

27. R. Nicholas Burns, Under-Secretary for Political Affairs, "India and Pakistan: On the Heels of President Bush's Visit" (remarks to the Heritage Foundation, Washington, DC, March 6, 2006).

28. Sumit Ganguly, "Avoiding War in Kashmir," *Foreign Affairs* 69, no. 5 (Winter 1990/1991): 57–58.

29. *New Priorities in South Asia: U.S. Policy Toward India, Pakistan, and Afghanistan* (New York: Council on Foreign Relations, 2003).

30. Khzem Merchant, "Three Arrested Over Mumbai Bombs Linked to Pakistan," *Financial Times*, July 22, 2006, 6.

31. Somini Sengupta, "Indian Army and Police Tied to Kashmir Killings," *New York Times*, February 6, 2007, A3.

32. Selig S. Harrison, Paul H. Kreisberg, and Dennis Kux, *India and Pakistan: The First Fifty Years* (Washington, DC: Woodrow Wilson Center Press, 1999), 91.

33. Post Conflict Resolution Project, *Breaking Point: Measuring Progress in Afghanistan* (Washington, DC: Center for Strategic and International Studies, February 23, 2007), 2.

34. Ann Scott Tyson, "Top Military Officer Urges Major Change in Afghanistan Strategy," *Washington Post*, September 11, 2008, p. A01.

35. See Sumit Ganguly, "Pakistan, the Other Rogue Nation," *Current History* 103, no. 162 (April 2004): 147–150.

36. Farhan Bokhari, Victoria Burnett, Stephen Fidler, and Edward Luce, "Pakistan's 'rogue nuclear scientist': what did Khan's government know about his deals?" *Financial Times*, April 6, 2004, 17.

37. Caroline Daniel, "Bush Signs India Nuclear Pact," *Financial Times*, December 19, 2006, 12.

38. Kux, *United States and Pakistan*, 333.

39. JPMorgan Services India, "India," JPMorgan Chase Bank, Economic Research, Global Data Watch, December 1, 2006.

40. "A Growing Indian Empire," *Economist.com/Global Agenda* (October 20, 2006): 1.

41. Barbara Crossette, "Think Again: India," *Foreign Policy* (January 2007), www.foreignpolicy.com/story/cms.php?story_id=3693.

42. Robert D. Hof, "India and Silicon Valley: Now the R&D Flows Both Ways," *Business Week*, December 8, 2003, 74.

43. JPMorgan Chase, "Pakistan's Economic Momentum Ahead of 2007 Elections," JPMorgan Chase Bank, Economic Research, Global Data Watch, September 8, 2006.

44. Ibid.

45. Farhan Bokhari, "Pakistan Stakes Claim to Join the World's Arms Exporters," *Financial Times*, November 21, 2006, 4.

46. "Pakistan Drugs Create Al Qaeda Chaos Under Bhutto Assassination Radar, Say ex-White House Drug Spokesman Robert Weiner and John Larmett; U.S. and Military, with 'No Plan,' Fail to Block bin Laden Funding Source," *PR Newswire*, January 14, 2008.

47. Bureau for International Narcotics and Law Enforcement Affairs, *International Narcotics Control Strategy Report* (Washington, DC: U.S. Department of State, March 2006), www.state.gov/p/inl/rls/nrcrpt/2006/vol1/html/62109.htm.

48. Wisner et al., *New Priorities in South Asia*, 73.

Chapter 20: The Middle East

1. The first uprising or *intifada* erupted in 1987 and ended after the Persian Gulf War in 1991.

2. General David H. Petraeus, Commander, Multi-National Force-Iraq, *Report to Congress on the Situation in Iraq*, September 10–11, 2007, www.foreignaffairs.house.gov/110/peto91007.pdf.

3. Phillip le Billon and Fouad al Khatib, "From Free Oil to 'Freedom Oil': Terrorism, War and US Geopolitics in the Persian Gulf," *Geopolitics* 9, no. 1 (Winter 2004): 114.

4. See Energy Information Administration, "Where Does My Gasoline Come From?" www.eia.doe.gov/bookshelf/brochures/gasoline/index.html.

5. Pak K. Lee, "China's Quest for Oil Security: Oil (Wars) in the Pipeline?" *Pacific Review* 18, no. 2 (June 2005): 266.

6. H. W. Brands, *Into the Labyrinth: The United States and the Middle East 1945-1993* (New York: McGraw-Hill, 1994), 19.

7. James A. Baker III and Lee H. Hamilton, cochairs, *The Iraq Study Group Report*, Section I.B., "Consequences of Continued Decline in Iraq," http://bakerinstitute.org/Pubs/iraqstudygroup_findings.pdf.

8. The White House, *The National Security Strategy of the United States of America* (Washington DC: March 2006), 20.

9. The Koran, formally compiled under Islam's third caliph, Uthman (AD 644–656), is said to be an exact translation of God's revelations to Mohammed without error or omission. Islamic law (sharia) is primarily comprised of dictates in the Koran, hadith (sayings of Mohammed), and the sunnah (examples or ways of Mohammed).

10. The seventh through thirteenth centuries represent a "Golden Age" of Islam. During the same period, Europe struggled during what is considered the Dark Ages and early Middle Ages.

11. See Bernard Lewis, *What Went Wrong: The Clash Between Islam and Modernity in the Middle East* (New York: Harper Perennial, 2002).

12. Prominent advocates of the strict-adherence approach in political Islam include Muhammad ibn Abd-al-Wahhab, Hassan Al Banna, Sayyid Abul Ala Mawdudi, and Sayyid Qutb.

13. For an overview, see William McCants, Ed., and Jarret Brachman, Project Director, *Military Ideology Atlas: Executive Report* (West Point, NY: Combating Terrorism Center, November 2006), http://ctc.usma.edu/atlas/Atlas-ExecutiveReport.pdf.

14. Charles Kurzman, ed., *Liberal Islam: A Sourcebook* (Oxford: Oxford University Press, 1998).

15. F. Gregory Gause III, "Can Democracy Stop Terror?" *Foreign Affairs* 84, no. 5 (September/October 2005): 72.

16. Leonardo Maugeri, "Two Cheers for Expensive Oil," *Foreign Affairs* 85, no. 2 (March/April 2006): 149–161.

17. Dana H. Allin and Steven Simon, "The Moral Psychology of US Support for Israel," *Survival* 45, no. 3 (September 1 2003): 126.

18. Michael Sterner, "Closing the Gate: The Persian Gulf War Revisited," *Current History* 96, no. 606 (January 1997): 15.

19. Larry Diamond, "Lessons from Iraq," *Journal of Democracy* 16, no. 1 (January 2005), 10.

20. See, for example, Thomas F. Ricks, *Fiasco: The American Military Adventure in Iraq* (New York: The Penguin Press, 2006), 3-4.

21. Brian MacQuarrie and Bryan Bender, "Disputed study says 600,000 Iraqis killed during war," *Boston Globe*, October 12, 2006, A16.

22. For complete coverage of this topic, see Malcolm Kerr, *The Arab Cold War*, 3rd ed. (London: Oxford University Press, 1971).

23. Osama bin Laden, "Declaration of War against the Americans Occupying the Land of the Two Holy Places," www.pbs.org/newshour/terrorism/international/fatwa_1996.html.

24. For more information on both the 1987 and 2000 intifadas, see Ruth Margolies Beitler, *The Path to Mass Rebellion: An Analysis of Two Intifadas* (Lanham, MD: Lexington Books, 2004).

25. See Steven A. Cook, *Jordan-Israel Peace, Year One: Laying the Foundation* (Washington, DC: Washington Institute for Near East Policy, 1995).

26. Syria is suspected to have carried out the assassination of Prime Minister Hariri, who called for the removal of Syrian troops and influence from Lebanon.

27. David Makovsky, *Making Peace with the PLO: The Rabin Government's Road to the Oslo Accord* (Boulder, CO: Westview Press, 1996), 14.

28. A day before Sharon's visit to the Temple Mount, Adnan Husseini, chairman of the Islamic trust, met with Jerusalem Police Chief Yair Yitzhaki to convince him to have the visit canceled. See Lee Hockstader, "Street Army Spearheads Arab Riots," *Washington Post*, October 4, 2000, A1. This area is the site of the Dome of the Rock and Al-Aqsa mosque as well as the Second Jewish Temple. It is sacred to both Muslims and Jews.

29. Neil King, Jr., and Jeanne Cummings, "Road Map Seeks Palestinian State Within a Year," *Wall Street Journal*, February 28, 2003, A7. For a full discussion of the roadmap, see U.S. Department of State, *A Performance-Based Roadmap to a Permanent Two-State Solution to the Iraeli-Palestinian Conflict*, April 30, 2003, www.state.gov/r/pa/prs/ps/2003/20062.htm.

30. Guy Chazan, "Militant is Killed, Further Clouding Truce in Mideast," *Wall Street Journal*, August 15, 2003, A6.

31. Sharham Chubin and Sepehr Zabih, *The Foreign Relations of Iran* (Berkeley and Los Angeles: University of California Press, 1974), 178–181.

32. Amos A. Jordan, "Saudi Pillar on Firmer Soil," *Washington Star*, February 18, 1979, D1.

33. Steve Wood and Wolfgang Quaisser, "Turkey's Road to the EU: Political Dynamics, Strategic Context and Implications for Europe," *European Foreign Affairs Review* 10, no. 2 (Summer 2005): 150.

Chapter 21: Sub-Saharan Africa

1. Population Reference Bureau, *2007 World Population Data Sheet* (Washington, DC: U.S. Agency for International Development, 2007), 11.

2. The World Bank, *World Development Report 2006: Equity and Development*, www-wds.worldbank.org/external/default/WDSContentServer/IW3P/IB/2005/09/20/000112742_20050920110826/Rendered/PDF/322040WorldoDevelopmentoReporto2006.pdf.

3. The term *zones of competing governance* is used to describe certain border areas of sub-Saharan Africa in James J. F. Forest and Matt Sousa, *Oil and Terrorism in the New Gulf: Framing U.S. Energy and Security Policies for the Gulf of Guinea* (Lanham, MD: Lexington, 2006).

4. U.S. Department of State, *Country Reports on Terrorism*, Office of the Coordinator for Counterterrorism (April 2006), 16.

5. Robert I. Rotberg, "Failed States in a World of Terror," *Foreign Affairs* 81, no. 4 (July/August 2002): 127.

6. For a thorough description and analysis of human security, see Madelfia A. Abb and Cindy R. Jebb, "Human Security and Good Governance: A Living Systems Approach to Understanding and Combating Terrorism," in *The Making of a Terrorist: Recruitment, Training and Root Causes*, ed. James J. F. Forest, (Westport, CT: Praeger, 2005).

7. Jagdish Bhagwati and Ibrahim Gambari, "Political Will, Not Just Aid, Can Lift Africa Out of Despair," *Financial Times*, July 5, 2005, 17.

8. Mark Doyle, "Blair Unveils Africa Action Plan," *BBC News*, February 27, 2004.

9. For more on this, see Forest and Sousa, *Oil and Terrorism in the New Gulf.*

10. Ibid.

11. For more on the history of Africa, particularly the precolonial and colonial periods, see John Reader, *Africa: A Biography of the Continent* (New York: Penguin, 1997); and George B. N. Ayittey, *Africa in Chaos* (New York: St. Martin's Press, 1999).

12. Abdul A. Said, *The African Phenomenon* (Boston: Allyn & Bacon, 1968), 120–122.

13. Chester Crocker, *High Noon in Southern Africa: Making Peace in a Rough Neighborhood* (New York: Norton, 1992).

14. "African Growth 'Steady but Frail,'" BBC News International, April 3, 2007, http://news.bbc.co.uk/2/hi/business/6522807.stm.

15. For example, see Forest and Sousa, *Oil and Terrorism in the New Gulf*, chap. 9.

16. Available at www.whitehouse.gov/nsc/nss/2006/.

17. The White House, *National Security Strategy of the United States of America* (Washington, DC: The White House, September 2002), 10–11.

18. Available at www.whitehouse.gov/nsc/nss/2006/.

19. Use of force to maintain international peace and security under Chapter VI of the UN Charter is generally done with the consensus of involved parties. Chapter VII authorizes forcible measures to deal with threats to international peace and security. For more information, see "Charter of the United Nations," www.un.org/aboutun/charter/.

20. More information on the African Contingency Operations Training and Assistance program is available at www.america.gov/st/washfile-english/2007/March/200703201240381EJrehsiFo.3458979.html.

21. Jonathan Stevenson, "Africa's Growing Strategic Resonance," *Survival* 45, no. 4 (Winter 2003): 166.

22. This discussion paraphrases Bradley Graham, "Bush Plans Aid to Build Foreign Peace Forces," *Washington Post*, April 19, 2004, A1. Also see Nina M. Serafino, *The Global Peace Operations Initiative: Background and Issues for Congress* (February 16, 2005), www.fas.org/sgp/crs/misc/RL32773.pdf.

23. G8 refers to the Group of Eight major industrialized countries: Canada, France, Germany, Italy, Japan, Russia, Great Britain, and the United States. The referenced document is available online at www.g8usa.gov/d_061004c.htm.

24. These documents are available at www.g8.gc.ca/2002Kananaskis/kananaskis/afraction-en.pdf and www.g8.gc.ca/AFRIQUE-01june-en.asp.

25. Victoria K. Holt, *Peacekeeping in Africa: Challenges and Opportunities: Testimony to the Subcommittee on Africa*, U.S. Committee on International Relations, U.S. House of Representatives, October 8, 2004 (Washington, DC: Henry L. Stimson Center, 2004), 1, www.stimson.org/fopo/pdf/Testimony-Holt-FINAL.pdf.

26. Theo Neethling, "Shaping the African Standby Force," *Military Review* 85, no. 3 (May/June 2005): 68.

27. Portions of this discussion are drawn from Forest and Sousa, *Oil and Terrorism in the New Gulf.*

28. See Anti-Terrorism Assistance, http://ciponline.org/facts/ata.htm.

29. House Committee on International Relations, *Fighting Terrorism in Africa*: Testimony of Karl Wycoff *to the Subcommittee on Africa*, 108th Congress, 2nd Session, April 1, 2004, 7

30. Ibid.

31. For more on these development initiatives, see Forest and Sousa, *Oil and Terrorism in the New Gulf*, 147–180.

32. Organization for Economic Cooperation and Development, International Development Statistics, www.oecd.org/dataoecd/50/17/5037721.htm.

33. Bates Gill, Chin-Hao Huang, and J. Stephen Morrison, *China's Expanding Role in Africa* (Washington, DC: CSIS Report, 2007), 14.

34. On October 22, 1995, President Clinton called for the establishment of a network of International Law Enforcement Academies throughout the world to combat international drug trafficking, criminality, and terrorism through strengthened international cooperation. As of 2007, the United States and participating nations have established academies to serve three regions—Europe (in Hungary), Asia (in Thailand), and Africa (in Botswana)—and a graduate facility in Roswell, New Mexico. An Academy for the Americas is currently under consideration.

35. *Engendering Bold Leadership: The President's Emergency Plan for AIDS Relief*, First Annual Report to Congress (March 2005), 5, www.state.gov/documents/organization/43885.pdf.

36. Bureau for Policy and Program Coordination, *Status of Presidential Initiatives FY 2003* (Washington, DC: U.S. Agency for International Development, 2004), 14.

37. Bureau for Policy and Program Coordination, *Status of Presidential Initiatives FY 2003* (Washington, DC: U.S. Agency for International Development, 2004), 7.

38. The debt relief agreement was approved by the International Monetary Fund and the World Bank in September 2005. However, it is important to note that this agreement focuses on multilateral debt and does not address the bilateral debt. In many African countries, particularly Nigeria, the majority of debt is actually bilateral.

39. Celia W. Dugger, "U.N. Report Cites U.S. and Japan as the 'Least Generous Donors,' " *New York Times*, September 8, 2005, 6.

40. Organization for Economic Cooperation and Development, *Official Development Assistance Increases Further—But 2006 Targets Still a Challenge*, April 11, 2005, www.oecd.org/document/3/0,2340,en_2649_201185_34700611_1_1_1_1,00.html.

41. Robert B. Reich, "The Poor Get Poorer," *New York Times*, April 2, 2006, Section 7, 21.

42. Forest and Sousa, *Oil and Terrorism in the New Gulf*, 99–100.

43. Peter Brookes and Ji Hye Shin, "China's Influence in Africa: Implications for the United States," *Heritage Foundation Backgrounder*, no. 1916 (February 22, 2006), www.heritage.org/Research/AsiaandthePacific/bg1916.cfm; and Peter Brookes, "Back to the Maoist Future: China's African Ambitions," *Heritage Foundation Commentary* (April 17, 2006), www.heritage.org/Press/Commentary/ed041706a.cfm.

44. Gill, Huang, and Morrison, *China's Expanding Role in Africa*, v.

45. Population Reference Bureau, *2007 World Population Data Sheet*, 11.

46. Henry A. Crumpton, Coordinator for Counterterrorism, Improving Interagency Coordination for the Global War on Terror and Beyond, Testimony before the House Armed Services Committee, Washington, D.C., April 4, 2006, www.america.gov/st/washfile-english/ 2006/April/20060404194541idybeekcmo.5748712.html.

47. For more on the challenges faced by this diffusion of responsibilities, see John E. Campbell, "Sub-Saharan Africa and the Unified Command Plan," *Joint Forces Quarterly* 29 (Autumn 2001): 72–75.

48. "US to Get Africa Command Center," BBC, February 6, 2007, http://news.bbc.co.uk/2/hi/americas/6336063.stm.

49. Richard Wilcox, "Four Stars for Africa," *New York Times*, October 14, 2004, A29.

Chapter 22: Russia

1. A selected bibliography of works on the Cold War can be found in Toby Trister, "Traditionalists, Revisionists, and the Cold War," in *Caging the Bear: Containment and the Cold War*, ed. Charles Gati (New York: Bobbs-Merrill, 1974), 211–222.

2. Adam Ulam, *Expansion and Coexistence: Soviet Foreign Policy, 1917-1973,* rev. ed. (New York: Praeger, 1974), 543–544.

3. For a complete record of the crisis, see Theodore C. Sorensen, *Kennedy* (New York: Harper & Row, 1965), 667–719

4. All estimates of the growth of the Soviet economy are subject to wide margins of error. According to some analysts from 1961 to 1970, the Soviet GNP grew at a respectable 5% per annum. In the 1970s, it declined to 4% and then to 3%; in the early 1980s, it was 2% or less, and by the mid-1980s it actually began to decline. Robert Byrnes, ed., *After Brezhnev: Sources of Soviet Conduct in the 1980s* (Bloomington: Indiana University Press, 1983). See also Central Intelligence Agency, *Gorbachev's Modernization Program: A Status Report,* presented to the joint Economic Committee of the U.S. Congress, March 19, 1987.

5. For a concise account of this crisis, see Scott D. Sagan, "Lessons of the Yom Kippur Alert," *Foreign Policy,* no. 36 (Autumn 1979): 160–177.

6. See Donald S. Zagoria, "Into the Breach: New Soviet Alliances in the Third World," *Foreign Affairs* 57, no. 4 (Spring 1979): 733–735; and Robert Legvold, "The Super Rivals: Conflict in the Third World," in the same issue.

7. These tactics are described in Kenneth L. Adelman, "Fear, Seduction, and Growing Soviet Strength," *Orbis* 21, no. 4 (Winter 1978): 743-765.

8. Edward Luttwak, "After Afghanistan, What?" *Commentary* 69, no. 4 (1980): 40–48.

9. The material on the Afghan invasion is adapted from Joseph Collins, "The Soviet Invasion of Afghanistan: Methods, Motives, and Ramifications," *Naval War College Review* 33, no. 6 (1980): 53–62.

10. David Ottaway, "Angola Gets Infusion of Soviet Arms," *Washington Post,* May 12, 1987, A27.

11. Andrew E. Kramer, "Putin Likens U.S. Policy to that of Third Reich," *International Herald Tribune,* May 9, 2007, www.iht.com/articles/2007/05/09/news/russia.php.

12. James M. Goldgeier and Michael McFaul, *Power and Purpose: U.S. Policy Toward Russia After the Cold War* (Washington, DC: Brookings Institution Press, 2003), 362.

13. For a discussion of the document, see Goldgeier and McFaul, *Power and Purpose,* 208.

14. Gail Lapidus, "Transforming Russia: American Policy in the 1990s," in *Eagle Rules? Foreign Policy and American Primacy in the Twenty-First Century,* ed. Robert J. Lieber (Upper Saddle River, NJ: Prentice-Hall, 2002), 108.

15. See Cynthia Roberts and Thomas Sherlock, "Bringing the Russian State Back in: Explanations for the Derailed Transition to Market Democracy," *Comparative Politics* 31, no. 4 (July 1999): 477–498.

16. Report on ROMIR poll, Reuters, November 23, 1999, published in *Johnson's Russia List,* November 23, 1999.

17. As cited in Vladimir Shlapentokh, "Aftermath of the Balkan War, the Rise of Anti-Americanism, and the End of Democracy in Russia," *The World and I* 14, no. 10 (October 1999): 310–325. See also Eric Shiraev and Vladislav Zubok, *Anti-Americanism in Russia from Stalin to Putin* (New York: Palgrave, 2000); and Theodore Gerber and Sarah Mendelson, "Young, Educated, Urban—and Anti-American: Recent Survey Data from Russia," PONARS Policy Memo #267 (October 2002), www.csis.org/ruseura/ponars/policymemos/pm_0267.pdf.

18. Mortimer B. Zuckerman, "A Paranoid Power," *U.S. News and World Report,* April 17, 2000, p. 68.

19. See Daniel Treisman, "Putin's Silovarchs," *Orbis,* 1, no. 1 (Winter 2007): 141–153.

20. See Thomas Sherlock, *Historical Narratives in the Soviet Union and Post-Soviet Russia* (New York: Palgrave-McMillan, 2007), chap. 7.

21. Richard Pipes, "Flight from Freedom," *Foreign Affairs* 83, no. 3 (May/June 2004): 14–15.

22. See Vladimir Petukhov and Andrei Ryabov, "Public Attitudes about Democracy," in Michael McFaul, Nikolai Petrov, and Andrei Ryabov, *Between Dictatorship and Democracy* (Washington, DC: Carnegie Endowment for International Peace, 2004), esp. 290–291.

23. For a more complete discussion of these issues, see the chapter on Russia in Cindy Jebb et al., *The Fight for Legitimacy: Democracy versus Terrorism* (Westport, CT: Praeger), 2006.

24. For an excellent, harrowing assessment of the Chechen tragedy, see Anna Politkovskaya, *A Small Corner of Hell: Dispatches from Chechnya* (Chicago: University of Chicago Press, 2003).

25. For the history of Russia-NATO relations in the post-Soviet period, see Martin A. Smith, *Russia and NATO Since 1991: From Cold War through Cold Peace to Partnership?* (London: Routledge, 2006).

26. Adrian Karatnycky, "Ukraine's Orange Revolution," *Foreign Affairs* 84, no. 2 (March/April 2005), 35.

27. For the obstacles to democratization in Kyrgyzstan, see Scott Radnitz, "What Really Happened in Kyrgyzstan," *Journal of Democracy* 17, no. 2 (April 2006): 132–146.

28. See Celeste Wallander, "Russian Transimperialism and Its Implications," *Washington Quarterly* 30, no. 2 (2007): 107–122.

29. See Svante Cornell, *Georgia After the Rose Revolution: Geopolitical Predicament and Implications for U.S. Policy* (Carlisle Barracks, PA: U.S. Army War College Strategic Studies Institute, 2007).

30. International Crisis Group, *Russia vs. Georgia: The Fallout* (Washington, DC: International Crisis Group, 22 August 2008), i.

31. Condoleezza Rice, "Secretary Rice Addresses U.S.-Russia Relations at the German Marshall Fund," September 18, 2008, www.state.gov/secretary/rm/2008/09/109954.htm.

32. Jim Nichol, *Russia-Georgia Conflict in South Ossetia: Context and Implications for U.S. Interests* (Washington, DC: Congressional Research Service, September 9, 2008), 12.

33. Ibid.

34. International Crisis Group, *Russia vs. Georgia: The Fallout,* 17.

35. Fionna Hill, "Moscow Discovers Soft Power," *Current History* 105, no. 693 (October 2006): 341–347.

36. Neil Buckley, Daniel Dombey, and Demetri Sevastopulo, "Russians accuse US of European military expansion," *Financial Times*, February 10, 2007, 5.

37. Marc Champion, "Moscow Trums West in Battle for Clout in Former Soviet States," *Wall Street Journal*, October 6, 2006, A1.

38. For a good discussion of U.S. policy prescriptions for Russia, see John Edwards and Jack Kemp, chairs, Stephen Sestanovich, project director, *Russia's Wrong Direction: What the United States Can and Should Do* (New York: Council on Foreign Relations, 2006).

39. See Celeste Wallander, "Suspended Animation: The US and Russia After the G-8," *Current History* 105, no. 693 (October 2006): 315–320.

40. Dmitri Trenin, "Reading Russia Right," Carnegie Endowment for International Peace, *Policy Brief*, no. 42 (October 2005).

Chapter 23: Europe

1. DG Trade, "EU Bilateral Trade and Trade with the U.S.," September 15, 2006, 4.

2. See Walt W. Rostow, "Lessons of the Plan: Looking Forward to the Next Century," in the Marshall Plan Commemorative Section, *Foreign Affairs* 76, no. 3 (May/June 1997): 205–212.

3. See Henry A. Kissinger, "The Future of NATO," *Washington Quarterly* 2, no. 4 (1979): 7.

4. For a brief but useful discussion of the military doctrine of flexible response, see Richard Hart Sinnreich, "NATO's Doctrinal Dilemma," *Orbis* 19 (Summer 1975): 461–477; see also Robert Kennedy, "NATO Defense Posture in an Environment of Strategic Parity and Precision Weaponry," in *Strategies, Alliances and Military Power: Changing Roles*, ed. James A. Kehlman (Leiden, the Netherlands: A.W. Sijthoff, 1977), 297–317.

5. For a discussion of the problems inherent in collective systems, see Mancur Olson, Jr., *The Logic of Collective Action: Public Goods and the Theory of Groups* (Cambridge, MA: Harvard University Press, 1965).

6. Wade Boese, "CFE Parties Agree on 'Basic Elements' For Negotiating Adaptation Accord," *Arms Control Today* (June/July 1997): 21, 23.

7. "Conventional Armed Forces in Europe (CFE) Treaty," Fact Sheet, State Department Bureau of Arms Control, Washington, D.C., June 18, 2002, www.state.gov/t/ac/rls/fs/11243.htm.

8. "Partnership with the Countries of Central and Eastern Europe," statement issued by the North Atlantic Council meeting in Ministerial Session in Copenhagen, June 6 and 7, 1991, Press Communique M-1(91)42 (Brussels: NATO, June 6, 1991).

9. Nick Williams, "Partnership for Peace: Permanent Fixture or Declining Asset?" *Survival* 38, no. 1 (Spring 1996): 102.

10. See Ivo Daalder and James Goldgeier, "Global NATO," *Foreign Affairs* 85, no. 5 (September/October 2006): 105–113.

11. NATO, "NATO's Role in Kosovo," www.nato.int/kosovo/kosovo.htm.

12. For a discussion of the events at NATO Headquarters on September 11 and 12, 2001, leading to the invoking of Article 5, see Edgar Buckley, "Invoking Article 5," *NATO Review* (Summer 2006), www.nato.int/docu/review/2006/issue2/english/art2.html.

13. NATO, "NATO and the fight against terrorism," www.nato.int/terrorism/index.htm.

14. Vice Admiral Roberto Cesaretti, "Combating Terrorism in the Mediterranean," *NATO Review* (Autumn 2005), www.nato.int/docu/review/2005/issue3/english/art4.html.

15. See NATO Press Release (2002) 127, "Prague Summit Declaration," November 21, 2002, www.nato.int/docu/pr/2002/p02-127e.htm.

16. See, for example, Ronald D. Asmus, Richard L. Kugler, and F. Stephen Larrabee "Building a New NATO," *Foreign Affairs* 72 , no. 4 (September/October 1993): 28–40; and Steve Weber, "Does NATO Have a Future?" in *The Future of European Security*, ed. Beverly Crawford (Berkeley, CA: Center for German and European Studies, 1992); 360-395. See also Peter van Ham, "Growing Pains," *NATO Review* (Autumn 2005), www.nato.int/docu/review/2005/issue3/english/analysis.html.

17. Jack Mendelsohn, "NATO Expansion: A Decision to Regret," *Arms Control Today* 27, no. 4 (June/July 1997): 2.

18. Advance Questions for General Bantz J. Craddock, USA, Nominee for Commander, United States European Command and Supreme Allied Commander, Europe. Confirmation Testimony available at http://armed-services.senate.gov/statemnt/2006/September/Craddock%2009-19-06.pdf.

19. During a briefing at the Foreign Press Center in January 2003, Defense Secretary Donald Rumsfeld responded to a question regarding the lack of European support for military action in Iraq: "Now, you're thinking of Europe as Germany and France. I don't. I think that's old Europe. If you look at the entire NATO Europe today, the center of gravity is shifting to the east. And there are a lot of new members." U.S. Department of Defense News Transcript, "Secretary Rumsfeld Briefs at the Foreign Press Center," January 22, 2003, www.defenselink.mil/Transcripts/Transcript.aspx?TranscriptID=1330.

20. See BBC World Services Poll conducted by GlobeScan in conjunction with the Program on International Policy Attitudes (PIPA) at the University of Maryland in February 2006, http://news.bbc.co.uk/1/shared/bsp/hi/pdfs/27_02_06world_poll.pdf. See also the January

2007 poll from BBC World Service conducted by GlobeScan and PIPA, www.worldpubli-copinion.org/pipa/articles/home_page/306.php?nid=&id=&pnt=306&lb=hmpg1.

21. Much of the ensuing discussion is based on Stanley Hoffmann, "Away from the Past: European Politics and Security 1990," in *Facing the Future: American Strategy in the 1990s*, Aspen Strategy Group Report (Lanham, MD: University Press of America, 1991): 119–141.

22. See, for example, Josef Joffe, "One and a Half Cheers for German Unification," *Commentary* 89, no. 6 (1990): 32.

23. See, for example, "Russia's in-the-red Army," *Economist*, August 2, 1997, 37. See also Aleksandr Golts, "The Social and Political Condition of the Russian Military," in *The Russian Military: Power and Purpose*, eds. Steven E. Miller and Dimitri V. Trenin (Cambridge, MA: MIT Press, 2004), 73–94.

24. See Matthew Bunn, "Loose Nukes Fears—Anecdotes of the Current Crisis," PBS *Frontline* report, December 5, 1998, www.pbs.org/wgbh/pages/frontline/shows/russia/readings/fears.html.

25. See Andrei P. Tsygankov, "Vladimir Putin's Vision of Russia as a Normal Great Power," *Post-Soviet Affairs* 21, no. 2 (April/June 2005): 132–158.

26. See, for example, Dan Bilefsky, "Russia-Ukraine Crisis Exposes Gaps in EU Energy Policies," *International Herald Tribune*, January 5, 2006, www.iht.com/articles/2006/01/05/business/eu.php.

27. For an early use of the Weimar Republic analogy to express concern over future developments in the Soviet Union, see Strobe Talbot, "The Fear of Weimar Russia," *Time*, June 4, 1990, 36.

28. William Drozdiak, "U.S. and Europe in Serious Rift Over Bosnia," *Washington Post*, November 27, 1994, A1.

29. Vladimir Putin as cited in, The Associated Press, "Putin: Georgia military presence up to regions," *International Herald Tribune,* September 20, 2008, accessed at: www.iht.com/articles/ap/2008/09/20/europe/EU-Russia-Georgia.php.

30. James E. Goodby, "Peacekeeping in the New Europe," *Washington Quarterly*, 15, no. 2 (1992): 154.

31. This is a point made by Blaine Harden, "Can the West Stop the Rape of Bosnia? Should It?" *Washington Post*, July 24, 1992, A30.

32. "Too big for Europe? The Turks are at the Gates of Brussels," *Economist*, November 16, 2002, p. 47.

33. Anthony Browne, "Threat of Islamic extremism that stretches across Europe," *TimesOnline*, July 26, 2005, www.timesonline.co.uk/tol/news/uk/article548063.ece.

34. See Stephanie Giry, "France and Its Muslims," *Foreign Affairs* 85, no. 5 (September/October 2006): 87–104.

35. Mark Rice-Oxley, "Bitter Debate over Turkey's EU Bid," *The Christian Science Monitor*, October 3, 2005, p. 6.

36. See Margarita Mathiopoulos and István Gyarmati, "Saint Malo and Beyond: Toward European Defense," *Washington Quarterly* 22, no. 4 (Autumn 1999): 65–76.

37. Nicholas Fiorenza, "NATO Response Force—ready for action," *Janes' Defense Weekly*, September 21, 2006, www.janes.com/defence/land_forces/news/jdw/jdw060921_1_n.shtml.

38. Neil Buckley and Catan, "What the clash means for Ukraine," *Financial Times*, January 3, 2006, p. 2.

39. Niall Ferguson, "Sinking Globalization," *Foreign Affairs* 84, no. 2 (March/April 2005): 64–77.

40. See Stephen J. Coonen, "The Widening Military Capabilities Gap between the United States and Europe: Does it Matter?" *Parameters* 36, no. 3 (Fall 2006): 67–84.

Chapter 24: Latin America

1. "Fact Sheet: 2006 American Community Survey," U.S. Census Bureau, factfinder.census.gov/servlet/ACSSAFFFacts?_submenuId=factsheet_1&_sse=on.

2. Inter-American Development Bank, Washington, D.C., www.iadb.org/news/articledetail.cfm?artid=3348&language=english.

3. Jorge G. Castanda, "Latin America's Left Turn," *Foreign Affairs* 85, no. 3 (May/June 2006): 28–43.

4. Jennifer McCoy, "One Act in an Unfinished Drama," *Journal of Democracy* 16, no. 1 (January 2005): 111.

5. Phil Gunson, "Chavez's Venezuela," *Current History* 105, no. 688 (February 2006): 59–61. For the rise of Chavez and a comparison to earlier Venezuelan caudillos, see Norman Gall, *Oil and Democracy in Venezuela*, parts 1 and 2 (Sao Paulo: Braudel Papers, 2006).

6. Gunson, 63.

7. See David Adelman, Ed., *Colonial Legacies: The Problem of Persistence in Latin American History* (New York: Routledge, 1999).

8. "Rank Order—GDP (purchasing power parity)," *The World Factbook*, www.cia.gov/library/publications/the-world-factbook/rankorder/2001rank.html (2007 estimate; page last updated October 2, 2008).

9. "Top Ten Countries with which the U.S. Trades," www.census.gov/foreign-trade/top/dst/2006/12/balance.html.

10. See "Top World Oil Net Exporters, 2006," www.eia.doe.gov/emeu/cabs/topworld-tables1_2.html; and "World Proved Reserves of Oil and Natural Gas, Most Recent Estimates," www.eia.doe.gov/emeu/international/reserves.html.

11. James Monroe, annual message delivered to Congress, December 2, 1823.

12. Quotation is from Wallace Thompson, "The Doctrine of the 'Special Interest' of the United States in the Region of the Caribbean Sea," *Annals of the American Academy of Political and Social Science* 132 (July 1927): 153.

13. U.S. Department of State, "Venezuela Boundary Dispute, 1895-1899," www.state.gov/r/pa/ho/time/gp/17463.htm.

14. See "Roosevelt Corollary to the Monroe Doctrine, 1904," www.state.gov/r/pa/ho/time/ip/17660.htm.

15. Article 3h, Charter of the Organization of American States, www.oas.org/juridico/English/charter.html.

16. "Theater Security Cooperation," U.S. Southern Command, www.southcom.mil/AppsSC/pages/theatersecurity.php.

17. "Good Neighbor Policy, 1933," www.state.gov/r/pa/ho/time/id/17341.htm.

18. J. F. Hornbeck, "U.S.-Latin American Trade: Recent Trends," Congressional Research Service Report for Congress, updated May 11, 2004, CRS-1.

19. Ibid., CRS-6.

20. J. F. Hornbeck, "U.S.-Latin American Trade: Recent Trends," Congressional Research Service Report for Congress, updated May 18, 2007, CRS-2.

21. Office of the United States Trade Representative, "North American Free Trade Agreement," www.ustr.gov/Trade_Agreements/Regional/NAFTA/Section_Index.html.

22. Edwin G. Corr, "Whither Bolivia?" *World Literature Today* 80, no. 2 (March/April 2006): 33.

23. Office of the United States Trade Representative, "The Case for CAFTA: Growth, Opportunity, and Democracy in our Neighborhood," February 2005, www.ustr.gov/assets/Trade_Agreements/Regional/CAFTA/Briefing_Book/asset_upload_file235_7178.pd.

24. Office of the United States Trade Representative, "Panama Trade Promotion Agreement," www.ustr.gov/Trade_Agreements/Bilateral/Panama_FTA/Section_Index.html.

25. U.S. Department of State, "Support for Plan Colombia," http://state.gov/p/wha/rt/plncol/.

26. Bureau for International Narcotics and Law Enforcement Affairs, *Fiscal Year 2007 Budget Congressional Justification* (Washington, DC: U.S. Department of State), 3.

27. Kenneth M. Roberts, "Latin America's Populist Revival," *SAIS Review* 27, no. 1 (Winter/Spring 2007): 9.

28. Ibid., 10.

29. See Indur M. Goklany, *The Improving State of the World: Why We're Living Longer, Healthier, More Comfortable Lives on a Cleaner Planet* (Washington, DC: Cato Institute, 2006).

30. The White House, *The National Security Strategy of the United States of America* (Washington DC: March 2006), 37.

31. Gunson, "Chavez's Venezuela," 63.

32. Peter T. Leach, "Voters OK Bigger Panama Canal," *Traffic World*, October 30, 2006, 1.

33. Hugo Chavez Frias, "Statement by H. E. Hugo Chavez Frias, President of the Bolivarian Republic of Venezuela," *Law and Business Review of the Americas* 12, no. 4 (Fall 2006): 431.

34. John Bellamy Foster, "'No Radical Change in the Model,'" *Monthly Review* 58, no. 9 (February 2007): 15–16.

35. Fernando Cardoso, "More than Ideology: The Conflation of Populism with the Left in Latin America," *Harvard International Review* 28, no. 2 (Summer 2006): 17. See also Castanda, "Latin America's Left Turn," esp. 42–43.

36. "Guatemala," *The World Factbook*, www.cia.gov/library/publications/the-world-factbook/geos/gt.html#Econ.

37. Simon Romero and Jenny Carolina Gonzalez, "Death-Squad Scandal Circles Closer to Colombia's President," *New York Times*, May 16, 2007, A6.

38. Simon Romero, "News Analysis: Chavez Looks at His Critics in the Media and Sees the Enemy," *New York Times* June 1, 2007, A6.

39. Larry Rohter, "Argentina Contemplates Shared Custody of Its Top Job," *New York Times*, March 3, 2007, p. A6.

40. U.S. Department of State, "Background Note: Chile," www.state.gov/r/pa/ei/bgn/1981.htm.

41. Latin Focus, Barcelona, Spain, www.latin-focus.com/latinfocus/countries/latam/latindex.htm.

42. Norman D. Arbazia, *Mars Moves South* (Jericho, N.Y.: Exhibition Press, 1974), pp.17-19.

43. See Inter-American Defense Board, "Overview," www.jid.org/en/programs/.

44. White House Office of the Press Secretary, "Fact Sheet President's Speech at the Summit of the Americas," April 21, 2001, www.whitehouse.gov/news/releases/2001/04/.

45. White House Office of the Press Secretary, "Joint Statement between the United States of America and the United Mexican States," September 6, 2001, www.whitehouse.gov/news/releases/2001/09/.

Chapter 25: Globalization and Human Security

1. A particularly important shaper of opinion regarding globalization has been *New York Times* columnist Thomas L. Friedman. See his *The Lexus and the Olive Tree* (New

York: Farrar, Straus, Giroux, 1999); and *The World Is Flat: A Brief History of the Twenty-First Century* (New York: Farrar, Straus, Giroux, 2005).

2. James N. Rosenau, "The Complexities and Contradictions of Globalization," *Current History* 96, no. 613 (November 1997): 361. This section draws on Cindy R. Jebb, *Bridging the Gap: Ethnicity, Legitimacy, and State Alignment in the International System* (Lanham, MD: Lexington Books, 2004), 241–265.

3. Hans-Henrik Holm and Georg Sorensen, *Whose World Order? Uneven Globalization and the End of the Cold War* (Boulder, CO: Westview Press, 1995), 6–7.

4. Jessica T. Mathews, "Power Shift," *Foreign Affairs* 76, no. 1 (January/February 1997): 50.

5. Holm and Sorensen, *Whose World Order?*, 5. For an examination of state adaptation to these challenges, see Anne-Marie Slaughter, "The Real New World Order," *Foreign Affairs* 76, no. 5 (September/October 1997): 183–197.

6. Membership numbers are as of June 2007.

7. Kurt Weyland, "Neoliberalism and Democracy in Latin America: A Mixed Record," *Latin American Politics and Society* 46, no. 1 (Spring 2004): 135–157. See also An Chen, "The New Inequality," *Journal of Democracy* 14, no. 1 (January 2003): 51–59.

8. See Holly Burkhalter, "The Politics of AIDS: Engaging Conservative Activists," *Foreign Affairs* 83, no. 1 (January/February 2004): 8–14.

9. Claire Cooper, "New Tack in Nike Lawsuit," *Sacramento Bee*, May 3, 2002, D1.

10. "US court backs anti-Shell lawsuit," BBC News, March 26, 2001.

11. See Susan D. Moeller, *Compassion Fatigue: How the Media Sell Disease, Famine, War and Death* (New York: Routledge, 1999).

12. Amartya Sen, *Development as Freedom* (New York: Alfred A. Knopf, 1999), 240–241.

13. See Noah Feldman, *After Jihad: America and the Struggle for Islamic Democracy* (New York: Farrar, Straus & Giroux, 2003).

14. Bruce Hoffman, *Inside Terrorism* (New York: Columbia University Press, 2006), 81–129. See also David C. Rapoport, "Fear and Trembling: Terrorism in Three Religious Traditions," *American Political Science Review* 78, no. 3 (September 1984): 658–677.

15. See Audrey Kurth Cronin, "Behind the Curve: Globalization and International Terrorism," *International Security* 27, no. 3 (Winter 2002/2003): 30–58.

16. For further discussions of strategic motivations for terrorism, see Walter Reich, ed., *Origins of Terrorism: Psychologies, Ideologies, Theologies, States of Mind* (Washington, DC: Woodrow Wilson Center Press, 1998), particularly chap. 1, 2, and 7, by Martha Crenshaw, Jerold M. Post, and David Rapoport, respectively.

17. For further discussion of the role of social networks in terrorism, see Marc Sageman, *Understanding Terror Networks* (Philadelphia: University of Pennsylvania Press, 2004).

18. Thomas Sanderson, "Transnational Terrorism and Organized Crime: Blurring the Line," *SAIS Review* 24, no. 1 (Winter 2004): 49–60.

19. Mark Basile, "Going to the Source: Why Al-Qa'ida's Financial Network Is Likely to Withstand the Current War on Terrorist Financing," *Studies in Conflict and Terrorism* 27, no. 3 (May/June 2004): 169–185. See also William F. Wechsler, "Strangling the Hydra," in *How Did This Happen*, eds. James F. Hogue and Gideon Rose (New York: Public Affairs, 2001), 129–143.

20. For one effort to examine the security implications of nonparticipation in globalization, see Thomas P. M. Barnett, *The Pentagon's New Map: War and Peace in the Twenty-First Century* (New York: G. P. Putnam's Sons, 2004).

21. See Mohammed Ayoob, *The Third World Security Predicament* (Boulder, CO: Lynne Reinner, 1995); Barry Buzan, *People, States, and Fear*, 2nd ed. (Chapel Hill: University of North Carolina, 1983); Charles Tilly, "War Making and State Making as

Organized Crime," in *Bringing the State Back In*, eds. Peter B. Evans, Dietrich Rueschmeyer, and Theda Skocpol (New York: Cambridge University Press, 1985): 169–191; and Mostafa Rejai and Cynthia H. Enloe, "Nation-States and State-Nations," *International Studies Quarterly* 13, no. 2 (June 1969): 140–158.

22. Secretary-General's High-Level Panel on Threats, Challenges, and Change, *A More Secure World: Our Shared Responsibility* (New York: United Nations Department of Public Information, 2004), 17.

23. This section on human security is modified from a similar discussion in Cindy R. Jebb et al., "Human and Environmental Security in the Sahel: A 'Modest' Strategy for Success," in *Environmental Change and Human Security: Recognizing and Acting on Hazard Impacts*, eds. William J. Kepner, et al. (NATO: Springer Books, forthcoming); and the general explanation is also found in Madelfia A. Abb and Cindy R. Jebb, "Human Security and Good Governance: A Living Systems Approach to Understanding and Combating Terrorism," in *The Making of a Terrorist: Recruitment, Training, and Root Causes*, ed. James J. F. Forest (Westport, CT: Praeger Security International, 2006): 220–237.

24. United Nations Development Program (UNDP) Report, 1994, 3, 22–23, as quoted by P. H. Liotta, *The Uncertain Certainty* (Lanham, MD: Lexington, 2004), 4–5.

25. Also see Tedd Robert Gurr, *Minorities at Risk: A Global View of Ethnopolitical Conflicts* (Washington, DC: United States Institute of Peace, 1993), 123–138; and Robert Kaplan, "The Coming Anarchy," *Atlantic Monthly* 273, no. 2 (February 1994): 44–76.

26. Ishtiaq Mahsud, "Tribesmen, Foreign Fighters Clash in Northwest Pakistan," *Washington Post*, March 21, 2007, A12.

27. United Nations Development Program, *Evaluation of UNDP Assistance to Conflict Afflicted Countries* (New York: UNDP, 2006), 2.

28. Secretary-General's High-Level Panel on Threats, Challenges, and Change, 21–22. See also Kofi Annan, *"We the Peoples": The Role of the United Nations in the 21st Century* (New York: United Nations Department of Public Information, 2000), esp. 5–6.

29. Ibid., 22. See also Cindy R. Jebb et al., *The Fight for Legitimacy: Democracy vs. Terrorism* (Westport, CT: Praeger Security International, 2006), 134–136.

30. See, for example, Morton H. Halperin, "Guaranteeing Democracy," *Foreign Policy* no. 91 (Summer 1993): 105–122; and Lee Feinstein and Anne-Marie Slaughter, "A Duty to Prevent," *Foreign Affairs* 83, no. 1 (January/February 2004): 136.

31. For a discussion of various definitions of human security, see P. H. Liotta and Taylor Owen, "Sense and Symbolism: Europe Takes on Human Security," *Parameters* 36, no. 3 (Autumn 2006): 87–93.

32. Jan Pronk, "Globalization, Poverty, and Security," in *Human and Environmental Security: An Agenda for Change*, eds. Felix Dodds and Tim Pippard (London: Earthscan, 2005), 84.

33. Kevin Watkins, *Human Development Report 2005: International Cooperation at a Crossroads: Aid, Trade and Security in an Unequal World* (New York: United Nations Development Programme, 2005), 37–38. The only country that measures a greater gap than the global scale between the very rich and the very poor is Namibia.

34. Watkins, *Human Development Report 2005*, 35–37.

35. Lester R. Brown, *Plan B 2.0: Rescuing a Planet Under Stress and a Civilization in Trouble* (New York: W. W. Norton, 2006), 3.

36. Thomas F. Homer-Dixon, "Environmental Scarcities and Violent Conflict," in *New Global Dangers: Changing Dimensions of International Security*, eds. Michael E. Brown, et al. (Cambridge, MA: MIT Press, 2004), 265.

37. For further discussion on resource driven conflicts, see Michael T. Klare, *Resource Wars: The New Landscape of Global Conflict* (New York: Henry Holt and Company, 2002).

38. Henrique B. Cavalcanti, "Globalization, Poverty, and Security," in *Human and Environmental Security*, eds. Dodds and Pippard, 156; and Brown, *Plan B 2.0*, 178.

39. Cavalcanti, "Globalization, Poverty, and Security," 153–154.

40. Lester R. Brown, *Outgrowing the Earth: The Food Security Challenge in an Age of Falling Water Tables and Rising Temperatures* (New York: W. W. Norton and Company, 2004), 4–9. See Cavalcanti, "Globalization, Poverty, and Security," 154, for a reference to the effects of shocks.

41. Christine K. Durbak and Claudia M. Strauss, "Securing a Healthier World," in *Human and Environmental Security*, eds. Dodds and Pippard, 128–129.

42. Stefan Elbe, "HIV/AIDS and the Changing landscape of War," in *New Global Dangers*, eds. Brown et al., 371.

43. Brown, *Plan B 2.0*, 19.

44. Nicholas Eberstadt, "The Future of AIDS," *Foreign Affairs* 81, no. 6 (November/December 2002): 42.

45. As cited in Durbak and Strauss, "Securing a Healthier World," 129.

46. Ibid., 129–130.

47. "Consolidated Appeal for Somalia 2007," November 30 2006, http://ochaonline.un.org/cap2005/webpage.asp?Page=1497.

48. Edmund Sanders, "10 Slain in U.S. Strike, Somalia Says," *Los Angeles Times*, June 4, 2007, A3.

49. U.S. Department of State, Bureau of African Affairs, "Background Note: Somalia," May 2007, www.state.gov/r/pa/ei/bgn/2863.htm.

50. Walter Pincus, "U.S. Africa Command Brings New Concerns; Fears of Militarization on Continent Cited," *Washington Post*, May 28, 2007, A13.

Chapter 26: Looking Ahead

1. These figures were derived using The World Bank, "World Development Indicators," http://devdata.worldbank.org/data-query/. (The query was done for each country, examining GDP (in current $) for both 2000 and 2005. The figures used are percentage increases for each country.)

2. "Chinese Economy Expected to Grow 10.4 percent in 2007—World Bank," *BBC Monitoring Asia Pacific*, August 15, 2006, 1.

3. John J. Mearsheimer, "China's Unpeaceful Rise," *Current History* 105, no. 690 (April 2006): 160.

4. See U.S. Department of Defense, *Military Power of the People's Republic of China 2007* (Washington, DC: Department of Defense), 25; and *The Military Balance 2006* (London: International Institute for Strategic Studies, 2006), 249.

5. U.S. Department of Defense, *Military Power of the People's Republic of China 2007* (Washington, DC: Department of Defense), 25.

6. Minxin Pei, "The Dark Side of China's Rise," *Foreign Policy* no. 153 (March/April 2006): 32–40.

7. Central Intelligence Agency, "China," *The World Factbook 2007*, www.cia.gov/library/publications/the-world-factbook/geos/ch.html.

8. David Shambaugh, "China Engages Asia: Reshaping the Regional Order," *International Security* 29, no. 3 (Winter 2004/2005): 85–86.

9. Ibid., 85.

10. Aaron L. Friedberg, "The Struggle for Mastery in Asia," *Commentary* 110, no. 4 (November 2000): 20–24.

11. Shambaugh, "China Engages Asia," 86.

12. Ibid., 64.

13. Zbigniew Brzezinski, "Make Money, Not War," *Foreign Policy* no. 146 (January/February 2005): 46–47

14. For an example of this reasoning, see Thomas L. Friedman, "This Is a Test," *New York Times*, March 21, 2000, A23.

15. Fei-Ling Wang, "Preservation, Prosperity, and Power: What Motivates China's Foreign Policy?" *Journal of Contemporary China* 14, no. 45 (2005): 691.

16. The White House, *The National Security Strategy of the United States of America* (Washington DC: March 2006), 41.

17. Bruce Bueno de Mesquita and George W. Downs, "Development and Democracy," *Foreign Affairs* 80, no. 6 (September/October 2005): 77–86.

18. Thomas Lum and Dick K. Nanto, "China's Trade with the United States and the World," Congressional Research Service Report for Congress, updated August 18, 2006, 5–6. At the time of this report, the EU had twenty-seven members; as of mid-2008, the EU has twenty-seven members.

19. "China Is Big Trouble for the U.S. Balance of Trade, Right? Well, Not So Fast," *New York Times*, September 7, 2006, www.nytimes.com/2006/09/07/business/worldbusiness/07scene.html; "Foreign Investment in China," U.S.-China Business Council, March 14, 2005, www.uschina.org/statistics/2005foreigninvestment.html.

20. See Ashton B. Carter, "How to Counter WMD," *Foreign Affairs* 83, no. 5 (September/October 2004), 72–85.

21. Graham T. Allison, *Nuclear Terrorism: The Ultimate Preventable Catastrophe* (New York: Times Books/Henry Holt, 2004), 3–4.

22. Ibid., 12–14; *Quadrennial Defense Review Report* (Washington, DC: U.S. Government Printing Office, February 6, 2006), 25.

23. Rohan Gunaratna, *Inside Al-Qa'ida: Global Network of Terror* (New York: Berkley Books, 2003), 15.

24. Ibid., 65.

25. Allison, *Nuclear Terrorism*, 203.

26. Jack Lugar and Sam Nunn, "The New Nuclear Threat," *Wall Street Journal*, August 18, 2007, p. A6.

27. Allison, *Nuclear Terrorism*, 80.

28. Kenneth Pollack and Ray Takeyh, "Taking on Tehran," *Foreign Affairs* 84, no. 2 (March/April 2005): 20–34.

29. Ibid.

30. The domestic impact of the pursuit of nuclear weapons is not uniform. In Iran, for example, moderates tend to have a less favorable view of Ahmadinejad's apparent pursuit of nuclear weapons and fear that Ahmadinejad's strategy will only result in increased economic isolation and hardship (Pollack and Takeyh, "Taking on Tehran," 20–34).

31. Allison, *Nuclear Terrorism*, 79.

32. John Deutch and James R. Schlesinger, chairs, *National Security Consequences of U.S. Oil Dependency*, Independent Task Force Report no. 58 (New York: Council on Foreign Relations, 2006), 3.

33. Henry Kissinger, *Years of Upheaval* (New York: Little, Brown and Co, 1982), 887.

34. Ibid., 874.

35. U.S. Department of Energy (DOE), Energy Information Administration, "Petroleum Products Consumption," www.eia.doe.gov/neic/infosheets/petroleumproductsconsumption.html.

36. DOE, Energy Information Administration, "U.S. Crude Oil and Petroleum Products Imports from All Countries," http://tonto.eia.doe.gov/dnav/pet/hist/mttimus2a.htm.

37. Senator Richard Lugar, "U.S. Energy Security—A New Realism" (speech at Brookings Institution, March 13, 2006), http://lugar.senate.gov/press/record.cfm?id=252509.

38. Philip J. Deutch, "Energy Independence," *Foreign Policy* no. 151 (November/December 2005): 20.

39. DOE, Energy Information Administration, *Annual Energy Outlook 2007*, 97, www.eia.doe.gov/oiaf/archive/aeo07/index.html.

40. DOE, Energy Information Administration, *International Energy Outlook 2007*, 96, www.eia.doe.gov/oiaf/archive/aeo07/index.html.

41. DOE, Energy Information Administration, "Persian Gulf Oil and Gas Exports Fact Sheet," Country Analysis Briefs, September 2004.

42. DOE, Energy Information Administration, "Crude Oil and Total Petroleum Imports Top 15 Countries," www.eia.doe.gov/pub/oil_gas/petroleum/data_publications/company_level_imports/current/import.html.

43. Bradley L. Bowman, "U.S. Grand Strategy for Countering Islamist Terrorism and Insurgency in the 21st Century," *Countering Terrorism and Insurgency in the 21st Century*, ed. James J. F. Forest (Westport, CT: Praeger Security International, 2007), 44–51.

44. Michael Knights, *Troubled Waters* (Washington, DC: Washington Institute for Near East Policy, 2006), 34.

45. "Saudis thwart oil refinery attack," CNN, February 24, 2006, http://edition.cnn.com/2006/WORLD/meast/02/24/saudi.refinery/.

46. Central Intelligence Agency, "Saudi Arabia," *The World Factbook 2007*, www.cia.gov/library/publications/the-world-factbook/geos/sa.html#Econ.

47. Bruce Hoffman, *Islam and the West: Searching for Common Ground: The Terrorist Threat and the Counter-Terrorism Effort* (Santa Monica, CA: RAND, 2006): 3, www.rand.org/pubs/testimonies/2006/RAND_CT263.pdf.

48. "NIE: Al-Qa'ida 'damaged,' becoming more scattered," CNN, September 26, 2006, www.cnn.com/2006/POLITICS/09/26/nie.iraq/index.html.

49. See John Gerard Ruggie, "Multilateralism: The Anatomy of an Institution," *International Organization* 46, no. 3 (Summer 1992): 561-598; Robert O. Keohane and Lisa L. Martin, "The Promise of Institutionalist Theory," *International Security* 20, no. 1 (Summer 1995): 39–51; and John Mearsheimer, "The False Promise of International Institutions," *International Security* 19, no. 3 (Winter 1994/1995): 5–49.

50. G. John Ikenberry, *After Victory: Institutions, Strategic Restraint, and the Rebuilding of Order After Major Wars* (Princeton, NJ: Princeton University Press, 2001), chap. 6; Stephen M. Walt, "Keeping the World 'Off-Balance': Self-Restraint and U.S. Foreign Policy," in *America Unrivaled: The Future of the Balance of Power*, ed. G. John Ikenberry (Ithaca, NY: Cornell University Press, 2002), chap. 4; Ethan B. Kapstein and Michael Mastanduno, eds., *Unipolar Politics: Realism and State Strategies After the Cold War* (New York: Columbia University Press, 1999).

51. George Bush and Brent Scowcroft, *A World Transformed* (New York: Alfred A. Knopf, 1998), 400.

52. The Korean conflict, four decades earlier, was the first U.S. chapter VII operation.

53. DOE, Energy Information Administration, World Crude Oil and Natural Gas Reserves, January 1, 2000.

54. *Frontline* interview with James Baker, www.pbs.org/wgbh/pages/frontline/gulf/oral/baker/1.html.

55. Ole R. Holsti, "American Public Opinion on Foreign Policy, Pre- and Post-September 11," in *Striking First: The Preventive War Doctrine and the Reshaping of U.S. Foreign Policy*, ed. Betty Glad and Chris J. Dolan (New York: Palgrave, 2004), 161.

56. Richard B. Cheney, *Annual Report to the President and Congress, Fiscal Year 2993* (Washington, DC: Department of Defense, January 1993).

57. H. Norman Schwarzkopf, *It Doesn't Take a Hero* (New York: Bantam Books, 1993), 593–594, 543–544.

58. Bush and Scowcroft, *A World Transformed*, 489, 491.

59. Jonathan Stevenson, "Hope Restored in Somalia?" *Foreign Policy* no. 91 (Summer 1993): 138.

60. John Mackinlay and Jarat Chopra, "Second Generation Multinational Operations," *Washington Quarterly* 15, no. 3 (Summer 1992): 113–131.

61. Deputy Assistant Secretary of Defense for African Affairs James L. Woods, "U.S. Government Decision-Making Processes During Humanitarian Operations in Somalia" (paper presented during the "Learning from Operation Restore Hope: Somalia Revisited" conference, Princeton University, April 1995) 16; Andrew S. Natsios, "Food Through Force: Humanitarian Intervention and U.S. Policy," *Washington Quarterly* 17, no. 1 (Winter 1994): 132–133; Alberto Coll, "For U.S. Hidden Risks in Somalia's Feudal Chaos," *Wall Street Journal*, 7 September 1993, A16; George Bush, "Humanitarian Mission to Somalia" (address to the nation, December 4, 1992); U.S. Department of State *Dispatch* (December 7, 1992), 865–866; Walter S. Clarke, "Testing the World's Resolve in Somalia," *Parameters* XXIII (Winter 1993/1994): 42–58.

62. Woods, "U.S. Government Decision-Making Processes During Humanitarian Operations in Somalia," 16.

63. Jennifer Sterling-Folker, "Between a Rock and a Hard Place: Assertive Multilateralism and Post–Cold War U.S. Foreign Policymaking," in *After the End: U.S. Foreign Policy in the Post–Cold War World*, ed. James M. Scott (Durham, NC: Duke University Press, 1998), 277–304.

64. "History of the Department of State During the Clinton Presidency," www.state.gov/r/pa/ho/pubs/c6059.htm.

65. Mark Bowden, *Black Hawk Down: A Story of Modern War* (New York: Atlantic Monthly Press, 1999).

66. Neil MacFarquhar, "Iraq Inspections Receive Approval from Arab League," *New York Times*, November 11, 2002, A1; Patrick E. Tyler, "NATO Leaders Say Iraq Must Disarm," *New York Times*, November 22, 2002, A1; Richard Bernstein, "Threats and Responses: Brussels Summit; European Union Says Iraq Must Disarm Quickly and Fully," *New York Times*, February 18, 2003, A1.

67. John Tagliabue, "Threats and Responses: Europe; France and Germany Draw a Line, Against Washington," *New York Times*, January 23, 2003, A10.

68. To be fair, while President Clinton signed the Kyoto Protocol in 1998, he never submitted this treaty for Senate ratification, because he knew that it would fail to gain sufficient support. In fact, in 1997, the Senate had voted 95 to 0 in opposition to the Kyoto restrictions for these same reasons, despite the common global interest in the problem of climate change.

69. Charles A. Stevenson, "Underlying Assumptions of the National Security Act of 1947," *Joint Forces Quarterly*, no. 48 (1st Quarter 2008): 129–133.

70. Title 10, section 118, U.S. Code, www.defenselink.mil/qdr/.

71. The best book on the 1997 QDR is by George Wilson, *This War Really Matters: Inside the Fight for Defense Dollars* (Washington, DC: CQ Press, 2000). Wilson quotes

Senator Lieberman describing the 1997 QDR as "largely a status quo product that cautiously make no changes" (29). After the 2006 QDR was published, similar criticisms were made. See Kori Schake, "Jurassic Pork," *New York Times*, February 9, 2006, A27; and Andrew Krepinevich, "Old Remedies for New Evils," *Wall Street Journal*, February 14, 2006, A3.

72. Michele A. Flournoy and Shawn W. Brimley, "Strategic Planning for U.S. National Security: A Project Solarium for the 21st Century," Princeton Project on National Security (Princeton, NJ: Princeton University, 2006).

73. "Project Solarium," www.eisenhowermemorial.org/stories/Project-Solarium.htm.

74. Clark A. Murdock, Michele A. Flournoy, Christopher A. Williams, and Kurt M. Campbell, *Beyond Goldwater-Nichols: Defense Reform for a New Strategic Era*, Phase I Report (Washington, DC: Center for Strategic and International Studies, March 2004).

75. Ibid., 9.

76. Ibid., 10

77. Ibid., 9.

78. Ibid.

79. Ibid., 10.

80. Ibid.

81. Robert B. Strassler, ed., *The Landmark Thucydides* (New York: Touchstone, 1996), 112–113.

82. Alexander Hamilton, "Federalist #8," *The Federalist Papers*, the Avalon Project at Yale Law School, www.yale.edu/lawweb/avalon/federal/fedo8.htm.

83. William H. Rehnquist, *All the Laws But One: Civil Liberties in Wartime* (New York: Vintage Books, 1998), 170–171.

84. Quote by Francis Biddle on Roosevelt's World War II internment program, Ibid., 223.

85. Ibid., 221.

86. Ibid., 224–225.

87. "War on Terrorism," *USA Today*/Gallup Poll, September 15–17, 2006, www.pollingreport.com/terror.htm.

88. The phrase "the Constitution is not a suicide pact" is often used in reference to President Lincoln suspending habeas corpus during the Civil War. Supreme Court Justice Robert Jackson used the term in his dissenting opinion in the 1949 case of *Terminiello v. Chicago*, in which the majority held that a breach of peace ordinance that restricted free speech that might stir the public to anger was unconstitutional. Jackson opined, "if the Court does not temper its doctrinaire logic with a little practical wisdom, it will convert the constitutional Bill of Rights into a suicide pact." See *Terminiello v. Chicago*, 337 U.S. 1 (1949).

89. Rehnquist, *All the Laws But One*, 223.

90. Alexis de Tocqueville, *Democracy in America*, trans. George Lawrence, ed. J. P. Mayer (New York: Perennial Classics, 2000), 649.

Index